Writing from Sources

FIFTH EDITION

Brenda Spatt

The City University of New York

BEDFORD/ST. MARTIN'S   Boston • New York

For Bedford/St. Martin's

Developmental Editor: Michael Gillespie
Project Management: Books By Design, Inc.
Production Supervisor: Scott Lavelle
Marketing Manager: Karen Melton
Cover Design: Lucy Krikorian
Cover Art: © 1995 Bill Westheimer
Composition: Thompson Type
Printing and Binding: Haddon Craftsmen, an R. R. Donnelley & Sons Company

President: Charles H. Christensen
Editorial Director: Joan E. Feinberg
Editor in Chief: Nancy Perry
Director of Editing, Design, and Production: Marcia Cohen
Manager, Publishing Services: Emily Berleth

Library of Congress Catalog Card Number: 98-84409

For information, write: Bedford/St. Martin's, 75 Arlington Street, Boston, MA 02116
(617-399-4000)

ISBN: 0-312-18323-2

Acknowledgments

Leach, William. Specified excerpt from pages 131–132 in *Land of Desire: Merchants, Power, and the Rise of a New American Culture.* Copyright © 1993 by William Leach. Reprinted by permission of Pantheon Books, a division of Random House, Inc.

Blank, Blanche D. "A Question of Degree." Excerpt from "Degrees: Who Needs Them?" by Blanche Blank. Autumn 1972, *AAUP Bulletin,* a publication of the American Association of University Professors. Reprinted by permission.

Paley, Grace. "Travelling" From *The New Yorker,* August 1997. Copyright © 1997 by Grace Paley. Reprinted by permission of Grace Paley. All rights reserved.

Acknowledgments and copyrights are continued at the back of the book on pages 544–546, which constitute an extension of the copyright page.

To the Instructor

Since I first began *Writing from Sources* two decades ago, many serious issues have confronted higher education: the controversy over standards and remediation, the movement towards greater inclusiveness, the challenge of new technology, the survival of the liberal arts. During the past twenty years, instructors of composition have been able to draw upon an ever-increasing array of pedagogical choices: traditional rhetoric, expressive writing, critical thinking, collaborative learning, cultural studies, interdisciplinary writing. In this period of flux and change, *Writing from Sources* has remained committed to providing students with the basic tools for successful academic writing in college and professional writing in the workplace.

Today, there is a renewed interest in writing based on sources. Instructors are eager to have their students read and write about current topical issues; to choose interesting, yet practical topics; and to develop strong, arguable thesis statements. They want to train students to analyze the information and ideas contained in sources, distinguishing between what's important for their topic and what's not. They expect students to organize their ideas coherently, clearly, and logically, using appropriate material from sources as support within their own essays. They are determined to teach students what plagiarism is and how to avoid it; they want to imbue students with respect for sources and for responsible documentation.

Unfortunately, now as twenty years ago, many students enter college inadequately prepared for academic work. They have particular difficulty working with the abstract ideas and disparate voices typical of assignments in their general education and major courses. They often don't know how to take good lecture notes, to pinpoint and paraphrase the key ideas of a chapter in a textbook, to evaluate a group of readings, or to undertake the extended synthesis necessary for presenting research. Unaccustomed to careful reading, analysis, and synthesis, these students feel impotent and frustrated when confronted by term paper assignments and essay examinations requiring the presentation of sources.

It was for these students that *Writing from Sources* pioneered a comprehensive, step-by-step approach to the research process, including strategies for the analysis, synthesis, presentation, citation, and documentation of sources. This practical method recognizes the fundamental importance of reading: analyzing the content, structure, tone, and diction of source materials. It also provides a corresponding progression of exercises and assignments leading up to the research essay.

Writing from Sources offers a great deal of information about the technical aspects of research. It shows students how to find sources from print and electronic materials, as well as obtaining interview and field research data. But today, with most libraries computerized, locating sources has become largely a mechanical task, unlikely in itself to teach students to think or write about what they have read. Knowing how to compile an impressive bibliography through the Internet or a CD-ROM will not enable students to select appropriate materials and write about them logically and coherently. But the information and practice provided by *Writing from Sources* empowers students to choose relevant, compatible sources and incorporate them into well-organized, readable essays.

Writing from Sources is skills-centered. Instead of starting with a description of the library, the text breaks down the research process into manageable segments of progressive difficulty, so that skills are readily assimilated yet cumulatively build upon each other. In this sequential approach, each academic writing skill—paraphrase or summary or synthesis—is first considered as an end in itself, to be explained, demonstrated, and practiced, like the skills necessary for mastering a sport. Students who understand how to incorporate passages from two authors into paragraphs of their own will be able to make the transition to organizing a stack of notes into an extended essay. To make each stage of the writing process more accessible, *Writing from Sources* uses explanations and readings that students can readily understand, including essays, opinions, interview data, lists, and notes.

In response to comments from instructors who have used previous editions, there are a number of changes in the fifth edition of *Writing from Sources* that enhance its usefulness as a text, a reader, an exercise book, and a research-essay guide.

- To accommodate instructors whose curriculum focuses on persuasive writing, there is a greater emphasis on argumentation. More arguments have been included among the readings, exercises, and textual examples, creating a better balance between persuasive and informative writing.

- New sections on argumentation have also been included throughout the book. In Chapter 1, for example, the basic presentation of argumentation is more detailed, including coverage of logical fallacies. New material in subsequent chapters includes information about developing an argumentative thesis, accommodating argument within paragraphs, and organizing a persuasive research essay.

- The chapter on library research has once again been greatly revised and expanded to reflect new opportunities for online research, especially on the Internet. Students are introduced to the use of Web sites and usenet groups, as well as options for browsers and search engines.

- The discussion of evaluating sources in Chapter 6 has been strengthened by the addition of a substantial section on assessing sources obtained from the Internet, including the issue of their potential unreliability. Student interest in the Internet makes these recommendations both timely and useful.

- Appendix B has been revised to reflect new MLA and APA guidelines for documenting electronic sources.

- More specific information about revision has been included in Chapter 3 as the final stage in the discussion of writing an essay based on a single source.

- Readings throughout the text have been strengthened by the selection of more full-length, free-standing essays than in previous editions. In addition, the new casebook of readings on "Racial Perceptions in America" contained in Appendix E can provide the basis for a complete research essay or, alternatively, can be supplemented by student research.

- Through four editions, *Writing from Sources* has been known for its myriad of exercises, offering instructors great flexibility in addressing the needs of their students. While offering the same comprehensive, skills-based approach to writing from sources, the fifth edition is more user-friendly than previous editions. To make the options less overwhelming, several peripheral exercises have been deleted, and some longer exercises now contain fewer choices. To accommodate the inclusion of longer essays as well as the new material on argumentation and technology, the text itself has been slightly scaled down.

The fifth edition of *Writing from Sources* includes enough reprinted articles and essays by authors such as Robert Bork, Grace Paley, and Shelby Steele to make supplements and handouts unnecessary. The readings, drawn from a variety of disciplines ranging from anthropology and ecology to political science and sociobiology, provide an assortment of topics that should interest both students and instructors. In addition to issues of race (the subject of the casebook), topics include boxing, romantic love, television news, pornography, the environment, first amendment rights, cults, immigration, open admissions, failing grades, social promotion, covenant marriage, school uniforms, American taste in ice cream, and John Wayne as an American icon.

In preparing the fifth edition of *Writing from Sources,* I remain grateful to the hundreds of my students who first taught me how to teach the research essay and to the thousands of students who used the first four editions and who, through their instructors, have expressed their approval of the book and suggested changes to make it more useful and effective. I would like to thank the following instructors who reviewed the text: Beverly Burch, Vincennes University; Gail Caylor, Phoenix College; Kathleen Costello-Sullivan, Bentley College; Patricia Coward, Frostburg State University; Kathleen Doherty, Framingham State College; Marleen Hein-Dunne, American University; Marcia M. Lavely, University of Tennessee at Martin; David G. Miller, Mississippi College; Lyle W. Morgan, Pittsburgh State University; Steven J. Rayshich, Westmoreland County Community College; and Susan Schmeling, Vincennes University. Emily Berleth, Donna Erickson, Michael Gillespie, and Nancy Perry of Bedford/St. Martin's have been extremely helpful throughout the preparation of this edition. In addition, I am obliged to Marianne Ahokas, who provided sections on deductive and inductive logic for the fourth edition; Eve Zarin, who prepared the basis for Appendix C for the fourth edition; and Kevin Wilson, who provided information about the technical aspects of the Internet for this edition. I owe my usual debt of gratitude and affection to Richard Barsam, who is responsible for introducing me to the Internet and who can take a matchmaker's credit if the acquaintance leads to a long-term relationship.

Brenda Spatt

To the Student

Every day, as you talk, write, and work, you use sources. Most of the knowledge and many of the ideas that you express to others originate outside yourself. You have learned from your formal schooling and from observing the world around you, from reading, from watching television and movies, from the Internet, and from a multitude of other experiences. Most of the time, you do not consciously think about where you got the information; you simply go about your activities, communicating with others and making decisions based on your acquired knowledge.

In college, however, using sources becomes more concentrated and deliberate. Each course bombards you with new facts and ideas. Your academic success depends on how well you can understand what you read and hear in your courses, distinguish the more important from the less important, relate new facts or ideas to what you already have learned, and, especially, communicate your findings to others.

Most college writing is both informative and interpretive; that is, it contains material that you take from sources and ideas that are your own. Depending on the individual course and assignment, a college paper may emphasize your own conclusions supported by knowledge you have gathered, or it may emphasize that knowledge, showing that you have mastered a certain body of information. In any case it will contain something of others and something of you. If twenty students in your class are all assigned the same topic, the other nineteen papers will all be somewhat different from yours.

The main purpose of college writing assignments is to help you consolidate what you have learned and to expand your capacity for constructive thinking and clear communication. These are not merely academic skills; there are few careers in which success does not depend on these abilities. You will listen to the opinions of your boss, your colleagues, and your customers; or read the case histories of your clients or patients; or study the marketing reports of your salespeople or the product specifications of your suppliers; or perhaps even analyze the papers of your students! Whatever your job, the decisions that you make and the actions that you take will depend on your ability to understand and evaluate what your sources are saying (whether orally or in writing), to recognize any important pattern or theme, and to form conclusions. As you build on other people's ideas, you certainly will be expected to remember which facts and opinions came from which source and to give appropriate credit. Chances are that you will also be expected to draft a memo, a letter, a report, or a case history that will summarize your information and present and support your conclusions.

To help you see the connection between college and professional writing, here are some typical essay topics for various college courses, each followed by a parallel writing assignment that you might have to do on the job. Notice that all of the pairs of assignments call for much the same skills: the writer must consult a variety of sources, present what he or she has learned from those sources, and interpret that knowledge in the light of experience.

ACADEMIC ASSIGNMENT	PROFESSIONAL ASSIGNMENT	SOURCES
For a *political science* course, you choose a law presently being debated in Congress or the state legislature, and argue for its passage.	As a *lobbyist, consumer advocate,* or *public relations expert,* you prepare a pamphlet to arouse public interest in your agency's program.	debates Congressional Record editorials periodical articles your opinions
For a *health sciences* course, you summarize present knowledge about the appropriate circumstances for prescribing tranquilizers and suggest some safeguards for their use.	As a *member of a medical research team,* you draft a report summarizing present knowledge about a specific medication and suggesting likely directions for your team's research.	books journals government and pharmaceutical industry reports online abstracts
For a *psychology* course, you analyze the positive and negative effects of peer group pressure.	As a *social worker* attached to a halfway house for adolescents, you write a case history of three boys, determining whether they are to be sent to separate homes or kept in the same facility.	textbooks journals case studies interviews Web sites personal experience
For a *business management* course, you decide which department or service of your college should be eliminated if the budget were cut by 3 percent next year; you defend your choice.	As an *assistant to a management consultant,* you draft a memo recommending measures to save a manufacturing company that is in severe financial trouble.	ledgers interviews newspapers journals financial reports Dow Jones news Dialog
For a *sociology* or *history* course, you compare reactions to unemployment in the 1990s with reactions in the 1930s.	As a *staff member in the social services agency* of a small city, you prepare a report on the social consequences that would result from closing of major factory.	newspapers magazines books interviews statistics

ACADEMIC ASSIGNMENT	PROFESSIONAL ASSIGNMENT	SOURCES
For a *physical education* course, you classify the ways in which a team can react to a losing streak and recommend some ways in which coaches can maintain team morale.	As a *member of a special committee of physical-education teachers,* you help plan an action paper that will improve your district's performance in interscholastic sports.	textbooks articles observation and personal experience
For an *anthropology* course, you contrast the system of punishment used by a tribe that you have studied with the penal code used in your home or college town.	As *assistant to the head of the local correction agency,* you prepare a report comparing the success of eight minimum-security prisons around the country.	textbooks lectures articles observation and personal experience
For a *physics* course, you write a definition of "black holes" and explain why theories about them were fully developed in the second half of the twentieth century—not earlier, not later.	As a *physicist* working for a university research team, you write a grant application based on an imminent breakthrough in your field.	books journals online abstracts E-mail
For a *nutrition* course, you explain why adolescents prefer junk food.	As a *dietician* at the cafeteria of a local high school, you write a memo that accounts for the increasing waste of food and recommends changes in the lunch menu.	textbooks articles interviews observation
For an *engineering* course, you describe changes and improvements in techniques of American coal mining over the last hundred years.	As a *mining engineer,* you write a report determining whether it is cost-effective for your company to take over the derelict mine that you were sent to survey.	books articles observation and experience E-mail

Writing from Sources will help you learn the basic procedures that are common to all kinds of academic and professional writing and will provide enough practice in these skills to enable you to write from sources confidently and successfully. Here are the basic skills.

1. *Choosing a topic:* deciding what you are actually writing about; interpreting the requests of your instructor, boss, or client, and determining the scope and limits of the assignment; making the project manageable.

2. *Finding sources and acquiring information:* deciding how much supporting information you are going to need (if any) and locating it; evaluating sources and determining which are most suitable and trustworthy for

your purpose; taking notes on your sources and on your own reactions; judging when you have sufficient information.

3. *Determining your main idea:* determining the purpose of what you are writing and your probable conclusions; redefining the scope and objective in the light of what you have learned from your sources.

4. *Taking notes:* presenting your sources through summary, outline, paraphrase, and quotation; learning when each skill is most appropriate.

5. *Organizing your material:* determining what must be included and what may be eliminated; arranging your evidence in the most efficient and convincing way, so that your reader will reach the same conclusions as you; calling attention to common patterns and ideas that will reinforce your thesis; making sure that your presentation has a beginning, middle, and end, and that the stages are in logical order.

6. *Writing your assignment:* breaking down the mass of information into easily understood units or paragraphs; constructing each paragraph so that the reader will receive a general idea that will advance your main idea, as well as providing supporting examples and details that will make it convincing.

7. *Giving credit to your sources:* ensuring that your reader knows who is responsible for which idea; distinguishing between the evidence of your sources and your own interpretation and evaluation; assessing the relative reliability and usefulness of each source so that the reader can appreciate your basis for judgment.

This list of skills may seem overwhelming right now. But remember: you will be learning these procedures *gradually.* In Part I, you will learn how to get the most out of what you read and how to use the skills of summary, quotation, and paraphrase to provide accurate accounts of your sources. In Part II, you will begin to apply these skills as you prepare an essay based on a single reading and then a synthesis essay drawing on a group of sources. Finally, in Part III, you will go to the library to locate your own sources and begin the complex process of research. The gradual increase in the number of sources will make each stage of the process more complex and demanding, but not essentially different.

The best way to gain confidence and facility in writing from sources is to master each skill so thoroughly that it becomes automatic, like riding a bicycle or driving a car. To help you break the task down into workable units, each procedure will first be illustrated with a variety of models and then followed by exercises to give you as much practice as you need before going on to the next step. As you go on to write essays for other courses, you can concentrate more and more on *what* you are writing and forget about *how* to write from sources, for these methods will have become natural and automatic.

Contents

2   *Presenting Sources to Others*   73

PART II
WRITING FROM SOURCES 123

3 *The Single-Source Essay* 127

6 *Evaluating Sources* 275

7 *Taking Notes* 319

Part I

MAKING YOUR SOURCES YOUR OWN

Academic writers continually study and use the ideas of others. However good and original their own ideas may be, academic writers must explore the work of authorities in their field, to estimate its value and its relevance to their own work, and then to place the ideas and the words of others side by side with their own. We call this process *research.*

To make use of another person's ideas in developing your own work, you need to appreciate (and even temporarily share) that person's point of view. Naturally, you need to read extensively and learn to understand what you read. In Chapter 1, you will learn to distinguish the main ideas of an essay and to grasp its strategy and development. You can measure your comprehension by your ability to sum up a group of related ideas briefly, yet completely. Chapter 1 ends with some practice in presenting a source through *summary.*

In order to use what you have learned from your reading and to write about your sources in essays, you must learn two other basic methods of presenting sources. Chapter 2 will show you how to use *quotation* and *paraphrase* to represent your sources fairly. You must make it clear to your reader whether a specific idea, sentence, or group of sentences is the product of your work or that of another.

- *Quotation* shows that someone else is responsible for the precise phrasing, as well as the ideas, in the quoted sentences.
- Through *paraphrase,* you express the ideas of others in your own words and so demonstrate your understanding of the source and your ability to integrate these ideas into your own work.

Using quotation or paraphrase and including the source's name helps you to avoid the dishonest "borrowings," called *plagiarism,* that occur when the reader cannot tell who wrote what and so gives you credit for work that you did not do. Finally, whether you paraphrase or quote, you must always acknowledge your source with a clear citation of the writer's name.

Although these methods of presentation are somewhat technical, requiring a high standard of accuracy, they are used throughout the academic and professional world. You will use them again and again, until they become automatic.

•1•

Reading for Understanding

Before class began, I happened to walk around the room and I glanced at some of the books lying open on the desks. Not one book had a mark in it! Not one underlining! Every page was absolutely clean! These twenty-five students all owned the book, and they'd all read it. They all knew that there'd be an exam at the end of the week; and yet not one of them had had the sense to make a marginal note!

Teacher of an English honors class

Why was this teacher so horrified? The students had fulfilled their part of the college contract by reading the book and coming to class. Why write anything down, they might argue, when the ideas are already printed on the page. All you have to do is read the assignment and, later on, review by skimming it again. Sometimes it pays to underline an important point, but only in very long chapters, so that you don't have to read every word all over again. Taking notes wastes a lot of time, and anyway, there's never enough space in the margins.

Effective reading—reading that is active, not passive—requires concentration. Reading is hard work.

Responding to what you are reading and participating in a mental dialogue between yourself and an author can be challenging but difficult. But only this kind of involvement can prevent your eyes from glazing over and your thoughts from wandering off to next weekend or next summer.

As with any job, active reading seems more rewarding if you have a product to show for your labors. *In active reading, this product is notes:* the result of contact (even friction) between your mind and the author's.

3

> ## Guidelines for Effective Reading
>
> - As you read and reread, notice which ideas make you react.
> - Pause frequently—not to take a break but to think about and respond to what you have read. If the reading has been difficult, these pauses will provide time for you to figure out what questions you need to ask yourself to gain full understanding.
> - As you read, have a pencil in your hand so that you can make lines, checks, and comments in and around what you are reading. You may even want to use several colored pens to help you distinguish between different ideas or themes as they recur. Of course, if you don't own the book, always take notes on separate paper. If you underline or write in a library book, you are committing an act of vandalism, like writing graffiti on a wall. Others will be using the book after you and will not benefit from your notes. If the material comes from a computer screen, you will often benefit from printing it out and working with a "hard" copy.

UNDERLINING

Underlining is used for selection and emphasis. *When you underline, you are distinguishing between what is important (and worth rereading) and what you can skip on later readings.* Underlining text on a first reading is usually hard, since you don't yet know what is crucial to the work's main ideas. Underlining, then, can be a sophisticated analytical skill.

On the other hand, underlining can also be the active sign of passive reading. You can underline while you are half asleep: the brain doesn't need to work in order to make the pencil move across the page. Too often, underlining merely represents so many minutes spent on an assignment: the pencil running over the page indicates that the eyes have run over the same lines. Many pages are underlined or colored with "hi-liter" so completely that there is hardly anything left over. *Everything* has been chosen for emphasis.

Underlining means selection. Some points are worth reviewing, and some are not. Try *underlining* and also *circling* and *bracketing* words and phrases that seem worth rereading and remembering. You probably would want to underline:

- *important generalizations* and *topic sentences*
- *examples* that have helped you understand a difficult idea
- *transitional points,* where the argument changes

Or try "underlining" by using *checks in the margin.* Either way, deciding *what* to mark is the important step.

ANNOTATING

Annotation refers to the comments you write in the margins when you interpret, evaluate, or question the author's meaning, define a word or phrase, or clarify a point. You are annotating when you jot down short explanations, summaries, or definitions in the margin. You are also annotating when you note down an idea of your own: a question or counterargument, perhaps, or a point for comparison. Annotation is different from taking notes on a separate page (a procedure that will be discussed in Chapter 7). *Not every reading deserves to be annotated.* Since the process takes time and concentration, save your marginal notes for material that is especially difficult or stimulating.

Here is an example of a passage that has been annotated on the second reading. Difficult words have been defined; a few ideas have been summarized; and some problems and questions have been raised.

from **LAND OF DESIRE**

William Leach

why quotes?

To make customers feel welcome, merchants trained workers to treat them as "special people" and as "guests." The numbers of <u>service workers</u>, including those

entrust: customers are precious possessions

(entrusted) with the care of customers, rose fivefold between 1870 and 1910, at two and a half times the rate of increase of <u>industrial workers</u>. Among them were the

service grew faster than industry (same in 1980s & 90s)

all European

restaurant and hotel employees hired to wait on tables in exchange for wages and "tips," nearly all recent immigrants, mostly poor <u>Germans</u> and <u>Austrians,</u> but also <u>Italians</u>, <u>Greeks</u>, and <u>Swiss</u>, who suffered nerve-wracking seven-day weeks, eleven-

Did they speak English? Who trained them?

True of all service workers?

hour days, low wages, and the sometimes terrible heat of the kitchens. <u>Neglected by major unions</u> until just before World War I, they endured (sweated) conditions equal in their misery only to those of the garment and textile workers of the day.

sweatshop = long hours / low wages

depends on luck, not good service

Tipping was supposed to encourage waiters and waitresses to (tolerate) these conditions in exchange for <u>possible windfalls</u> from customers. Tipping was an un-

barely endure

tastes and manners of the upper classes

usual practice in the United States before 1890 (although common in the luxurious and (aristocratic) European hotels), when the prevailing "<u>American Plan</u>" entailed serving meals at fixed times, no frills, no tipping, and little or no follow-up service.

"American Plan" based on middle-class culture

meals at any time; more choice in return for higher prices

After 1900 the <u>European system</u> of culinary service expanded very quickly in the United States, introduced first to the (fancy) establishments and then, year by year, to the more popularly priced places. By 1913 some European tourists were even

luxurious? expensive?

middle class attracted by upper class style

why extremely?

expressing "outrage" at the extent of tipping in the United States. Its effect on workers was (extremely) mixed. On the one hand, it helped keep wages low, increased the frenzy and tension of waiting, and <u>lengthened the hours.</u> "The tipping business is a great evil," wrote an old, retired waiter in the 1940s. "It gives the

Hours were longer because of tipping or because of greater service?

Waiter portrayed as victim

waiter an inferiority complex—<u>makes him feel he is at the mercy of the customers</u> all the time." On the other hand, some waiters were stirred by the "speculative excitement" of tipping, the risk and (chance) *chance = luck, not opportunity*

cliché
statement
of theme
expressed
in parag. 2

all these
quotation
marks are
distracting

all an
illusion

For customers, however, tipping was intended to have only one effect—to make   3
them feel at home and in the lap of luxury. On the backs of an ever-growing sweated
workforce, it aristocratized consumption, integrating upper-class patterns of comfort into the middle-class lifestyle. Tips rewarded waiters and waitresses for making   *tipping as*
the customer "feel like 'somebody,'" as one restaurant owner put it. Such a "feel-   *a marketing*
ing," he wrote, "depends" on the "service of the waiter," who ushers us to "our   *device*
table" and "anticipates our every want or whim." "Courteous service is a valuable   *it's the*
asset to the restaurateur. There is a curious little twist to most of us: We enjoy the   *customer*
luxurious feeling of affluence, of being 'somebody,' of having our wishes catered to."   *who has th*
                                                                                            inferiority
                                                                                            complex

As this annotated passage demonstrates, *annotation works best as an aid to memory*, reminding you of ideas that you have thought about and understood. Some
of these notes provide no more than a shorter version of the major ideas of the
passage. However, marginal notes can also remind you of places where you disagreed with the author, looked at the ideas in a new way, or thought of fresh evidence. Your marginal notes can even suggest the topic for an essay of your own.

Finally, when you write marginal notes, *try always to use your own words* instead of copying or abbreviating a phrase from the text. You will remember
the point more easily if you have made the effort to express it yourself.

EXERCISE 1: ANNOTATING A PASSAGE

Read the following passage carefully. Then reread it, underlining and circling
key ideas and inserting annotations in the margins.

from JOHN WAYNE'S AMERICA: THE POLITICS OF CELEBRITY

Garry Wills

who is American
Adam?

all explain John wayne
and American Adam

what genre?

seems out of place →

John Wayne is the most obvious recent embodiment of that American Adam—
untrammeled, unspoiled, free to roam, breathing a larger air than the cramped men
behind desks, the pygmy clerks and technicians. He is the avatar of the hero in that   *avatar —*
genre that best combines all these mythic ideas about American exceptionalism—
contact with nature, distrust of government, dignity achieved by performance, skep-
ticism toward the claims of experts. The yearning back toward such ideals of
freedom reemerges in the oddest places. When Jim Morrison of the rock group
The Doors sang of freedom, he asked, "What have they done to the Earth? . . .
Tied her in fences and dragged her down." In Westerns, the Easterner is a dude,   *western*
comically encumbered with useless knowledge, ignorant of the basics, too crippled   *movies wh*
with theory to act. In him, the instincts that lead to Wayne's easy responses have   *wayne ag*
been blunted, have atrophied in the stale air of commerce or technology, in the
conditioning to life on a smaller scale than the open range.   *where? who?*

westerns made proud Americans, restless Americans

The Western popularized the sophisticates' claims for American exceptionalism by putting them in vivid visual form—the frontier was a landscape with freely moving men and horses. The equality of opportunity was symbolized by "nature's noblemen." This ability to put so much of the American myth into such visual immediacy made the Western what Jean-Luc Godard [sic] called "the most cinematographic genre in cinema."

?

2

ASKING QUESTIONS

As you read actively and try to understand what you read, you will find yourself asking questions about your source. Sometimes you will want to write your answers down; sometimes answering your questions in your head is enough.

As the questions in the box below suggest, to understand what you read, your mind has to sweep back and forth between each sentence on the page and the larger context of the whole paragraph or essay. You can misunderstand the author's meaning if you interpret ideas *out of context,* ignoring the way in which they fit into the work as a whole.

Being a fast reader is not necessarily an advantage. Thorough comprehension takes time and careful reading. In fact, it is usually on the *second reading,* when you begin to understand the overall meaning and structure of the work, that questions begin to pop into your head and you begin to read more carefully.

Questions to Aid Understanding

- What is the *meaning* of this word?
- How should I *understand* that phrase?
- Where do I have *difficulty understanding the text?* Why? Which passages are *easy* for me? Why?
- What does this passage *remind me of?*
- What is the *topic sentence* of the paragraph?
- What is the *connection* between these two points?
- What is the *transitional* word telling me?
- This concept is difficult: how would I *express* it *in my own words?*
- Is this point a *digression* from the main idea, or does it fit in with what I've already read?
- Can the whole page be *summarized* briefly?
- Does the essay have a main idea—a *thesis?* Is the writer trying to make a particular point?

Annotating and Asking Questions: "A Question of Degree"

Read "A Question of Degree" once, and then go over it more slowly a second time. During your second reading, as you read each paragraph:

A. *Underline and annotate* the text, while asking yourself *comprehension questions* based on the list of questions on p. 7.

B. *Compare your annotations* with the annotated version of the first two paragraphs on p. 11.

C. *Compare your comprehension questions* with the list of sample questions starting on p. 12. (The paragraphs in the essay are numbered so that you can go back and forth from essay to list.) Think of your own response to each question, and then compare your answers with the ones that are provided in the right-hand column.

Some of the sample questions may seem very subtle to you, and you may wonder whether you would have thought of all of them yourself. But they are model questions, to show you what you *could* ask if you wanted to gain an especially thorough understanding of the essay.

A QUESTION OF DEGREE
Blanche D. Blank

everyone agrees

Perhaps we should rethink an idea fast becoming an undisputed premise of American life: that a college degree is a necessary (and perhaps even a sufficient) precondition for success. I do not wish to quarrel with the assumptions made about the benefits of orthodox education. I want only to expose its false god: the four-year, *false ideal* all-purpose, degree-granting college, aimed at the so-called college-age population and by now almost universally accepted as the stepping-stone to "meaningful" and "better" jobs.   1

referring to college as over emphasized

college = $

What is wrong with the current college/work cycle can be seen in the following anomalies: we are selling college to the youth of America as a take-off pad for the material good life. College is literally advertised and packaged as a means for getting more money through "better" jobs at the same time that Harvard graduates are taking jobs as taxi drivers. This situation is a perversion of the true spirit of a university, a perversion of a humane social ethic and, at bottom, a patent fraud. To take the last point first, the economy simply is not geared to guaranteeing these presumptive "better" jobs; the colleges are not geared to training for such jobs; and the ethical propriety of the entire enterprise is very questionable. We are by definition (rather than by analysis) establishing two kinds of work: work labeled "better" because it has a degree requirement tagged to it and nondegree work, which, through this logic, becomes automatically "low level."   2

practical is most important

This process is also destroying our universities. The "practical curriculum" must become paramount; the students must become prisoners; the colleges must be-   3

*universities &
students are stuck
practicality rather
than education*

come servants of big business and big government. Under these conditions the university can no longer be an independent source of scientific and philosophic truth-seeking and moral criticism.

Finally, and most important, we are destroying the spirit of youth by making college compulsory at adolescence, when it may be least congruent with emotional and physical needs; and we are denying college as an optional and continuing experience later in life, when it might be most congruent with intellectual and recreational needs.

important/true

*college later in
life may be more
benificial*

Let me propose an important step to reverse these trends and thus help restore freedom and dignity to both our colleges and our work-places. We should outlaw employment discrimination based on college degrees. This would simply be another facet of our "equal opportunity" policy and would add college degrees to sex, age, race, religion and ethnic group as inherently unfair bases for employment selection.

seems impossible?

People would, wherever possible, demonstrate their capacities on the job. Where that proved impractical, outside tests could still serve. The medical boards, bar exams, mechanical, mathematical and verbal aptitude tests might still be used by various enterprises. The burden of proof of their legitimacy, however, would remain with the using agencies. So too would the costs. Where the colleges were best equipped to impart a necessary skill they would do so, but only where it would be natural to the main thrust of a university endeavor.

*many skill
would still be
required for
jobs that are
not taught
before college!*

The need for this rethinking and for this type of legislation may best be illustrated by a case study. Joe V. is a typical liberal-arts graduate, fired by imaginative art and literature. He took a job with a large New York City bank, where he had the opportunity to enter the "assistant manager training program." The trainees rotated among different bank departments to gain technical know-how and experience and also received classroom instruction, including some sessions on "how to write a business letter." The program was virtually restricted to college graduates. At the end of the line, the trainees became assistant bank managers: a position consisting largely of giving simple advice to bank customers and a modest amount of supervision of employees. Joe searched for some connection between his job and the training program, on the one hand, and his college-whetted appetites and skills on the other. He found none.

In giving Joe preference for the training program, the bank had bypassed a few enthusiastic aspirants already dedicated to a banking career and daily demonstrating their competence in closely related jobs. After questioning his superiors about the system, Joe could only conclude that the "top brass" had some very diffuse and not-too-well-researched or even well-thought-out conceptions about college men. The executives admitted that a college degree did not of itself ensure the motivation or the verbal or social skills needed. Nor were they clear about what skills were most desirable for their increasingly diverse branches. Yet, they clung to the college prerequisite.

Business allows the colleges to act as recruiting, screening and training agencies for them because it saves money and time. Why colleges allow themselves to act as

*Reason for
business to allow
college degrees*

4

5

6

7

8

9

servicing agents may not be as apparent. One reason may be that colleges are increasingly becoming conventional bureaucracies. It is inevitable, therefore, that they should respond to the first and unchallenged law of bureaucracy: Expand! The more that colleges can persuade outside institutions to restrict employment in favor of their clientele, the stronger is the college's hold and attraction. This rationale becomes even clearer when we understand that the budgets of public universities hang on the number of students "serviced." Seen from this perspective, then, it is perhaps easier to understand why such matters as "university independence," or "the propriety" of using the public bankroll to support enterprises that are expected to make private profits, can be dismissed. Conflict of interest is difficult to discern when the interests involved are your own. . . .

What is equally questionable is whether a college degree, as such, is proper evidence that those new skills that are truly needed will be delivered. A friend who works for the Manpower Training Program feels that there is a clear divide between actual job needs and college-degree requirements. One of her chief frustrations is the knowledge that many persons with the ability to do paraprofessional mental-health work are lost to jobs they could hold with pleasure and profit because the training program also requires a two-year associate arts degree.

Obviously, society can and does manipulate job status. I hope that we can manipulate it in favor of the greatest number of people. More energy should be spent in trying to upgrade the dignity of all socially useful work and to eliminate the use of human beings for any work that proves to be truly destructive of the human spirit. Outlawing the use of degrees as prerequisites for virtually every job that our media portray as "better" should carry us a long step toward a healthier society. Among other things, there is far more evidence that work can make college meaningful than that college can make work meaningful.

My concern about this degree/work cycle might be far less acute, however, if everyone caught up in the system were having a good time. But we seem to be generating a college population that oscillates between apathy and hostility. One of the major reasons for this joylessness in our university life is that the students see themselves as prisoners of economic necessity. They have bought the media messages about better jobs, and so they do their time. But the promised land of "better" jobs is, on the one hand, not materializing; and on the other hand the student is by now socialized to find such "better" jobs distasteful even if they were to materialize.

One of the major improvements that could result from the proposed legislation against degree requirements for employment would be a new stocktaking on the part of all our educational agencies. Compulsory schools, for example, would understand that the basic skills for work and family life in our society would have to be compressed into those years of schooling.

Colleges and universities, on the other hand, might be encouraged to be as unrestricted, as continuous and as open as possible. They would be released from the pressures of ensuring economic survival through a practical curriculum. They might best be modeled after museums. Hours would be extensive, fees minimal, and ser-

vices available to anyone ready to comply with course-by-course demands. Col- *wouldn't it*
leges under these circumstances would have a clearly understood focus, which *be great*
might well be the traditional one of serving as a gathering place for those persons
who want to search for philosophic and scientific "truths."

All society
would have to
change! Big job!

This proposal should help our universities rid themselves of some strange and gra-   15
tuitous practices. For example, the university would no longer have to organize itself
into hierarchical levels: B.A., M.A., Ph.D. There would simply be courses of greater
and lesser complexity in each of the disciplines. In this way graduate education might
be more rationally understood and accepted for what it is—more education.

The new freedom might also relieve colleges of the growing practice of instituting   16
extensive "work programs," "internships" and "independent study" programs. The
very names of these enterprises are tacit admissions that the campus itself is not
necessary for many genuinely educational experiences. But, along with "external degree" programs, they seem to pronounce that whatever one has learned in life by
whatever diverse and interesting routes cannot be recognized as increasing one's
dignity, worth, usefulness or self-enjoyment until it is converted into degree credits.

The legislation I propose would offer a more rational order of priorities. It would   17
help recapture the genuine and variegated dignity of the workplace along with the
genuine and more specialized dignity of the university. It should help restore to
people of all ages and inclinations a sense of their own basic worth and offer them
as many roads as possible to reach Rome.

"A Question of Degree": Example of Annotations

everyone believes it

Perhaps we should rethink an idea fast becoming an undisputed premise of Amer-   1
ican life: that a college degree is a (necessary) (and perhaps even a (sufficient)) precon- *necessary*
vs.
everyone   dition for success. I do not wish to quarrel with the assumptions made about the   *sufficient?*
thinks is a
good   benefits of (orthodox) education. I want only to expose its (false god): the four-year, *=false idol*
education
all-purpose, degree-granting college, aimed at the (so-called) college-age population *18 yrs old*
and by now almost universally accepted as the stepping-stone to "meaningful" and
"better" jobs.   *college leads to work*   *B.B. doesn't agree*

inconsistencies   What is wrong with the current (college/work cycle) can be seen in the following   2
high salary   (anomalies): we are selling college to the youth of America as a take-off pad for the *presented*
+ expensive   (material) good life. College is literally (advertised and packaged) as a means for get- *to the*
possessions   *public*
therefore,   ting more money through "better" jobs at the same time that Harvard graduates
the premise   are taking jobs as taxi drivers. This situation is a (perversion) of the true spirit of a *=corruption*
is false
to reward   university, a perversion of a humane social ethic and, at bottom, a (patent) fraud. To *= obvious*
good work   take the last point first, the economy simply is not geared to guaranteeing these *colleges can't*
presumptive "better" jobs; the colleges are not geared to training for such jobs; *deliver what*
they promise
morality   and the (ethical propriety) of the entire enterprise is very questionable. We are by
definition=
by saying so   (definition) (rather than by (analysis)) establishing two kinds of work: work labeled
analysis =   "better" because it has a degree requirement tagged to it and nondegree work,
by observing   which, through this logic, becomes automatically "low level."   *2 levels exist because of*
what's right   *the convenience of these institutions. [But surely the "better" v.s. "low level"*
and true   *work existed long before colleges saw profit in the difference!]*

"A Question of Degree": Questions and Answers

Paragraph One

A. What does "false god" mean?

A. A false god is an idol that does not deserve to be worshiped.

B. In what context can a college degree be a false god?

B. Colleges are worshiped by students who believe that the degree will magically ensure a good career and a better life. Blank suggests that college degrees no longer have magic powers.

C. Why does Blank put "meaningful" and "better" in quotation marks?

C. Blank uses quotation marks around "meaningful" and "better" because she doesn't believe the adjectives are applicable; she is showing disagreement, disassociating herself through the quotation marks.

Paragraph Two

D. What is an anomaly?

D. An anomaly is anything that is inconsistent with ordinary rules and standards.

E. What conclusion can be drawn from the "Harvard graduates" sentence? (Note that the obvious conclusion is not stated.)

E. If Harvard graduates are driving taxis, a degree does not ensure a high-level job.

F. What does "perversion" mean? How many perversions does Blank mention? Can you distinguish between them?

F. Perversion means distortion or corruption of what is naturally good or normally done. If degrees are regarded as vocational qualifications, the university's proper purpose will be perverted, society's conception of proper qualifications for promotion and advancement will be perverted, and, by implication, young people's belief in the reliability of rewards promised by society will be perverted.

G. In the last two sentences, what are the two types of "fraud" that are described?

G. One kind of fraud is the deception practiced on young college students who won't get the good jobs that they expect. A second type of fraud is practiced on workers without degrees whose efforts and successes are under-valued because of the division into "better" and "worse" jobs.

Paragraph Three

H. What is the "practical curriculum"?

H. "Practical curriculum" refers to courses that will train college students for specific jobs; the term is probably being con-trasted with "liberal arts."

I. What is the danger to the univer-sities? (Use your own words.)

I. The emphasis on vocational training perverts the university's traditional pursuit of knowledge for its own sake, as it makes fi-nancing and curriculum very closely connected with the eco-nomic needs of the businesses and professions for which stu-dents will be trained.

J. What groups have suffered so far as a result of "compulsory" college?

J. Blank has so far referred to three groups: students in col-lege; workers who have never been to college; and members of universities, both staff and stu-dents, interested in a liberal-arts curriculum.

Paragraph Four

K. What new group, not mentioned before, does Blank introduce in this paragraph?

K. Blank introduces the needs of older people who might want to return to college after a working career.

Paragraph Five

L. Can you explain "'equal opportunity' policy" in your own words?

L. Equal-opportunity policy for employment means that the only prerequisite for hiring should be the applicant's ability to perform the job.

M. What is Blank's contribution to "our 'equal opportunity' policy"?

M. Blank suggests that a college de-gree does not indicate suitability for employment and therefore should be classed as discrimina-tory, along with sex, age, etc.

Paragraph Six

N. What does "legitimacy" mean in this context?

N. If certain professions choose to test the qualifications of aspirants, professional organizations should prove that examinations are necessary and that the results will measure the applicant's suitability for the job. These organizations should be responsible for the arrangements and the financing; at present, colleges serve as a "free" testing service.

Paragraphs Seven and Eight

O. What point(s) does the example of Joe help to prove?

O. Joe V.'s experience supports Blank's argument that college training is not often needed in order to perform most kinds of work. Joe V.'s expectations were also pitched too high, as Blank has suggested, while the experience of other bank employees whose place was taken by Joe exemplifies the plight of those workers without college degrees whose experience is not sufficiently valued.

Paragraph Nine

P. What are the colleges' reasons for cooperating with business? (Explain in your own words.)

P. Colleges are competing for students in order to increase their enrollment; they therefore want to be able to assure applicants that many companies prefer to hire their graduates. Having become overorganized, with many levels of authority, the bureaucratic universities regard enrollment as an end in itself.

Q. What is the conflict of interest mentioned in the last sentence, and why is it hard to discern?

Q. The interests of an institution funded by the public might be said to be in conflict with the interests of a private, profit-making company; but the conflict is not apparent now that colleges choose to strengthen their connections with business.

Paragraph Eleven

R. Can you restate the third sentence in your own words?

R. Instead of discriminating between kinds of workers and kinds of work, we should distinguish between work that benefits everyone and should therefore be considered admirable, and work that is degrading and should, if possible, not be performed by people.

S. Is Blank recommending that everyone go to work before attending college (last sentence)?

S. Although Blank is not insisting that working is preferable to or should have priority over a college education, she implies that most people gain more significant knowledge from the work than from college.

Paragraph Twelve

T. Can you explain the meaning of "prisoners of economic necessity"?

T. Young people who believe that a degree will get them better jobs have no choice but to spend a four-year term in college, whether or not they are intellectually and temperamentally suited to the experience.

Paragraph Thirteen

U. What are the "compulsory schools" and how would their role change if Blank's proposal were adopted?

U. Compulsory schools are grade and high schools, which students must attend up to a set age. If students were not automatically expected to go on to college, the lower schools would have to offer a more comprehensive and complete education than they do now.

Paragraph Fourteen

V. What role does Blank envisage for the university in a healthier society? (Try not to use "museum" in your answer.)

V. Blank sees the colleges in a role quite apart from the mainstream of life. Colleges would be storehouses of tradition, to which people could go for cultural refreshment in their spare time, rather than training centers.

Paragraph Fifteen

W. What are the "strange and gratuitous" practices of the universities? What purpose do they
serve?

W. The universities divide the process of education into a series of
clearly defined levels of attain-
ment. Blank finds these divisions
"gratuitous" or unnecessary,
perhaps because they are "hierarchical" and distinguish between those of greater or lesser
achievements and status.

Paragraph Seventeen

X. What, according to Blank, would
be a "rational order of priorities"? Does she see any connection at all between the work
experience and the educational
experience?

X. Blank's first priority is the self-
respect of the average member
of society who presently may be
disappointed and frustrated at
not being rewarded for his or
her work, whether at the job or
at college. Another priority is
restoration of the university to
its more purely intellectual role.

EXERCISE 2: UNDERSTANDING WHAT YOU READ

Read "Travelling" twice, and then answer the comprehension questions that
follow. You will notice that some of the "questions" resemble instructions, very
much like examination questions, directing you to explain, define, or in other
ways annotate the reading. *Answer in complete sentences,* and use your own
words as much as you can.

TRAVELLING

Grace Paley

My mother and sister were travelling South. The year was 1927. They had begun   1
their journey in New York. They were going to visit my brother, who was studying
at the Medical College of Virginia, in Richmond. Their bus was an express and had
stopped only in Philadelphia, Wilmington, and now Washington. Here the darker
people who had got on in Philadelphia or New York rose from their seats, put their
bags and boxes together, and moved to the back of the bus. People who boarded in
Washington knew where to seat themselves. My mother had heard that something
like this would happen. My sister had heard of it, too. They had not lived in it. This
reorganization of passengers by color happened in silence. My mother and sister
remained in their seats, which were about three-quarters of the way back.

When everyone was settled, the bus driver began to collect tickets. My sister   2
saw him coming. She pinched my mother—"Ma! Look!" Of course, my mother saw

him, too. What frightened my sister was the quietness. The white people in front, the black people in back—silent.

The driver sighed, said, "You can't sit here, ma'am. It's for them"—waving over his shoulder at the Negroes, among whom they were now sitting. "Move, please." 3

My mother said, "No." 4

He said, "You don't understand, ma'am. It's against the law. You have to move to the front." 5

My mother said, "No." 6

When I first tried to write this scene, I imagined my mother saying, "That's all right, mister. We're comfortable. I can't change my seat every minute." I read this invention to my sister. She said it was nothing like that. My mother did not try to be friendly or pretend innocence. While my sister trembled in the silence, my mother said for the third time—quietly—"No." 7

Somehow, finally, they were in Richmond. There was my brother, in school among so many American boys. After hugs and my mother's anxious looks at her young son, my sister said, "Vic, you know what Mama did?" 8

My brother remembers thinking, What? Oh! She wouldn't move? He had a class-mate, a Jewish boy like him, but from Virginia, who had had a public confrontation with a Negro man. He had punched that man hard, knocked him down. My brother couldn't believe it. He was stunned. He couldn't imagine a Jewish boy wanting to knock anyone down. He had never wanted to. But he thought, looking back, that he had been set down to work and study in a nearly foreign place, and had had to get used to it. Then he told me about the Second World War, when the disgrace of black soldiers forced to sit behind white German P.O.W.s shook him. Shamed him. 9

About fifteen years later, in 1943, in early summer, I rode the bus for about three days from New York to Miami Beach, where my husband and hundreds of other boys in sweaty fatigues were trudging up and down the streets and beaches to pre-pare themselves for war. 10

By late afternoon of the second long day, we were well into the South, beyond Richmond, maybe in South Carolina or Georgia. My excitement about travel in the wide world was damaged a little by a sudden fear that I might not recognize Jess, or he me. We hadn't seen each other for two months. I took a photograph out of my pocket; yes, I would know him. 11

I had been sleeping, waking, reading, writing, dozing, waking. So many hours, the movement of the passengers was like a tide that sometimes ebbed and now seemed to be noisily rising. I opened my eyes to the sound of people brushing past my aisle seat. And looked up to see a colored woman holding a large sleeping baby, who, with the heaviness of sleep, his arms tight around her neck, seemed to be pulling her head down. I looked around and noticed that I was in the last white row. The press of new travellers had made it impossible for her to move farther back. She seemed so tired, and I had been sitting and sitting for a day and a half at least. Not thinking, or maybe refusing to think, I offered her my seat. 12

She looked to the right and left as well as she could. Softly, she said, "Oh, no." I became fully awake. A white man was standing right beside her, but on the other 13 side of the invisible absolute racial border. Of course, she couldn't accept my seat. Her sleeping child hung mercilessly from her neck. She shifted a little to balance the burden. She whispered to herself, "Oh, I just don't know." So I said, "Well, at least give me the baby." First, she turned, barely looking at the man beside her. He made no move. Then, to my surprise, but obviously out of sheer exhaustion, she disengaged the child from her body and placed him on my lap. He was deep in child-sleep. He stirred, but not enough to bother himself or me. I liked holding him, aligning him along my twenty-year-old young woman's shape. I thought ahead to that holding, that breathing together that would happen in my life if this war would ever end. I was so comfortable under his nice weight. I closed my eyes for a couple of minutes but suddenly opened them to look up into the face of a white man talking. In a loud voice, he addressed me: "Lady, I wouldn't of touched that thing with a meat hook."

I thought, Oh, this world will end in ice. I could do nothing but look straight into   14
his eyes. I did not look away from him. Then I held that little boy a little tighter, kissed his curly head, pressed him even closer, so that he began to squirm. So sleepy, he reshaped himself inside my arms. His mother tried to narrow herself away from that dangerous border, too frightened at first to move at all. After a couple of minutes, she leaned forward a little, placed her hand on the baby's head, and held it there until the next stop. I couldn't look up into her mother face.

I write this remembrance more than fifty years later. I look back at that mother   15
and child. I see how young she is. Her hand on his head is quite small, though she tries by spreading her fingers wide to hide him from the white man. But the child I'm holding, his little face as he turns toward me, is the dark-brown face of my *own* grandson, my daughter's boy, the open mouth of the sleeper, the full lips, the thick little body of a child who runs wildly from one end of the yard to the other, leaps from dangerous heights with experienced caution, muscling his body, his mind, for coming realities.

Of course, when my mother and sister returned from Charlottesville the family   16
at home wanted to know: How was Vic doing in school among all those Gentiles? Was the long bus ride hard? Was the anti-Semitism really bad or just normal? What happened on the bus? I was probably present at that supper, the attentive listener and total forgetter of information that immediately started to form me.

Then, last year, my sister, casting the net of old age (through which recent expe-   17
rience easily slips), brought up that old story. First, I was angry. How come you never told me about your bus ride with Mama? I mean, really, so many years ago.

I don't know, she said. Anyway, you were only about four years old and, besides,   18
maybe I did.

I asked my brother why we'd never talked about that day. He said he thought   19
now that it had had a great effect on him; he had tried unravelling its meaning for years—then life, family, work happened. So I imagined him, a youngster, really, a kid from the Bronx in Virginia in 1927—why, he was a stranger there himself.

In the next couple of weeks, we continued to talk about our mother, the way   20
she was principled, adamant, and at the same time so shy. What else could we remember . . . Well, I said, I have a story about those buses, too. Then I told them:

how it happened on just such a journey, when I was still quite young, that I first knew my grandson, first held him close but could protect him for only about twenty minutes fifty years ago.

Paragraph One

A. Why does Paley begin with a series of facts, expressed in short sentences? *Paley starts with short sentences to set up the story.*

B. Why does Paley use the adjective "darker" (rather than "black" or—in the vocabulary of 1927—"Negro") to describe the people who move to the back of the bus? *Paley uses the word darker because her mother & sister are white and blar(?)*

C. What summarizes the paragraph? *The paragraph is about two women traveling on a segregated bus,*

D. Why does Paley include separate sentences for the mother's and sister's anticipation of what was happening? *seperate sentences are included to help understand who is thinking.*

Paragraph Two

E. In the first two paragraphs, is the reader supposed to understand that the mother and sister are white? *yes*

F. Why is the silence frightening? *The silence is frightening because it means people are uneasy*

Paragraphs Three through Six

G. Why does the driver sigh? What creates tension in the dialogue between the mother and the driver? Do we know why she refuses to move? *The driver signs because they are not obeying the law, the tension is from the mother not moving.*

Paragraph Seven

H. What is the effect of the intrusion of Grace Paley's voice and thoughts into the narrative? Why does she interrupt the story? *Interruption shows she is thinking reflecting on what happened*

I. Compare what did happen with Paley's "invention." *Paley's invention made her mom seem to make excuses.*

Paragraph Eight

J. Why does Paley omit the reaction to her mother's third "no"? Is "somehow" an adequate substitute? Do we need to know the driver's reaction? the reaction of the black travellers? the white? *we do not need to know.*

K. What is the significance of Vic's being "in school among so many American boys"? *Vic is Jewish.*

Paragraph Nine

L. There are four different points in time incorporated into this paragraph. Distinguish between the four, and suggest Paley's reasons for juxtaposing them in such a short space.

M. What do the two new examples of prejudice in this paragraph add to our understanding of the bus incident? *This family is Jewish, and blacks who fought against Germans were disgraced.*

Paragraph Ten

N. The description of the troops in Miami Beach is more detailed than any scene so far in the essay. Why does Paley use words like "sweaty" and "trudging"? *To show vividly*

Paragraph Eleven

O. What does Paley's description of her fears (about not recognizing her husband) add to our understanding of the story? She is married and has been seperated from her husband.

Paragraph Twelve

P. Contrast the image of the passengers as a "tide" with the "reorganization" in Paragraph One. Tide seems to mean just flow in.

Q. What is the difference between "not thinking" and "refusing to think"? Not thinking is not purposeful. Refusing to think is purposeful

R. Contrast the four situations described thus far.

Paragraphs Thirteen and Fourteen

S. Had a white man not been standing there, could the colored woman have accepted Paley's seat? I do not think so.

T. Consider the adjectives used to describe the baby and holding the baby. What do they tell us about the young Paley and the old Paley? The young paley was new to holding a child, but old paley understands.

U. Explain the difference between "if this war would ever end" and "this world will end in ice."

V. Why can Paley stare at the loud man, but not look at the baby's mother? I believe because Paley feels for the woman, but knows she isnt in the same place.

Paragraph Fifteen

W. What is Paley telling us when she merges the baby on the bus with her grandson? The images she uses to describe her grandson are different from the flat narrative of the essay. What is the effect of these more abstract phrases? These phrase show her maturity and reflection

Paragraph Sixteen

X. Why does Paley return to family reactions in 1927? In what way are the references to anti-Semitism a counter-theme? They both are anti discrimitory

Y. How does Paley's description of her youngest self—"the attentive listener and total forgetter of information that immediately started to form me"—serve as the key to the essay?

Paragraphs Seventeen to Nineteen

Z. Why is memory—and the frailty of memory—so important to this essay? This story is all out of memory.

Paragraph Nineteen

AA. How does the description of her brother apply to Paley herself in her experience on the bus? She is the same heritage. as her brother.

BB. Describe the interplay between public issues and private concerns in this essay. The essay interplays between public issues of segregation

Paragraph Twenty and human dignity.

CC. Explain the significance of the title. Could this story have been told in strict chronological order? What would be the difference in effect? I do not think chronological order would have been effective

LOGIC AND ARGUMENTATION

Drawing Inferences

When you are actively reading and annotating a text, you may sometimes find yourself projecting your own thoughts and assumptions into what you are reading. While you may intend to make a statement supported by information found in your source, your generalization may not accurately reflect the factual evidence. After a while, it becomes difficult to differentiate between your own ideas, inspired by what you have read, and the evidence found in the source. Should such confusion occur, *you can easily attribute to your source ideas that are not there at all.* When you generalize from specific facts—statistics, for example—you have to be especially careful to make sure that your statement is based on a correct interpretation of the information.

There are several different ways to describe how your source uses evidence and how you form conclusions from that evidence: *proving, stating, implying,* and *inferring.* These terms will be explained and illustrated with excerpts from an article about patterns of marriage in America during the early 1980s.

Quoting a Census Bureau report, this 1984 *New York Times* article begins by *stating* that:

> More and more young Americans are putting off marriage, possibly to begin careers. . . .

At this point in the article, the *Times* is offering no specific evidence to support this conclusion. You probably accept the statement as true because you know that the *Times* is a newspaper of record, and you assume that the Census Bureau has provided statistics that justify the claim. And, in fact, several paragraphs later, we find evidence to *prove* the statement:

> The trend toward postponed marriage has been growing steadily in recent years. The study found that 74.8 percent of men aged 20 to 24 had never married, compared with 68.8 percent in 1980 and 54.7 percent in 1970. Among women aged 20 to 24, 56.9 percent were single in this year's survey, as against 50.2 percent in 1980 and 35.8 percent in 1970.

Here is an example of a statement (in italics) that is immediately followed by proof:

> *Traditional married couples continue to make up the majority of family households in the United States, but the report documents the steady erosion of this group's dominance.* The 50.1 million traditional families constitute 58.6 percent of American households, compared with 60.8 percent in 1980 and 70.5 percent in 1970.

Since the article is about postponing marriage and also refers to the increasing number of unmarried couples living together, you might jump to the conclusion that most households in the United States consist of unmarried couples or single-parent families. As the previous paragraph clearly indicates, that would be a *false conclusion.*

So far, we have been examining only what the article *explicitly states* or what it *proves.* But, in addition, most sources inform you indirectly, by *implying* obvious conclusions that are not stated in so many words. The implications of a statement can be easily found within the statement itself; they just are not directly expressed. For example, according to the Census Bureau report,

> Three-quarters of American men and more than half of American women under 25 are still single.

Although it does not say so, it *implies*—and it would be perfectly safe to conclude—that *more men than women are waiting until they are over 25 to marry.* The following paragraph also contains implication as well as statement:

> "Many of these young adults may have postponed their entry into marriage in order to further their formal education, establish careers or pursue other goals that might conflict with assuming family responsibilities," said the bureau's study of households, families, marital status and living arrangements. The report also found that Americans are once again forming new households at high rates after a decline, apparently recession-induced, last year.

In addition to several *statements* about likely reasons for postponing marriage, the paragraph also provides you with an important *implication: Economic conditions seem to be a factor in predicting how many new households are formed in the United States.*

Finally, it is perfectly acceptable to draw a conclusion that is not implicit in the source, as long as you reach that conclusion through reasoning based on sound evidence. Unlike implication, *inference* requires the analysis of information—putting 2 and 2 together—for the hidden idea to be observed. The article implies; the reader infers.

In the following brief and factual statement from the article, little of interest is *implied,* but important conclusions can be *inferred:*

> A slight increase was noted in the number of unmarried couples living together; they totaled almost two million as of March and represent about 4 percent of the couples.

From this information, as well as previous evidence provided about postponement of marriage, it would be safe to *infer* that *one reason why people are marrying later may be that they are living together as unmarried couples first.*

It is perfectly correct to draw your own inferences from the sources that you are writing about, as long as you fulfill two conditions:

1. There must be a reasonable basis within the source for your inference.
2. The inferences should be clearly identified as yours, not the source's.

When in an essay you cite a specific work as the basis of an inference, your reader should be able to go to the source, locate the evidence there, and draw a similar inference.

What inferences can you draw from the following paragraph, when you put this information together with everything else that you have read in the article?

> Though the report said that most young people are expected to marry eventually, it noted that the longer marriage was delayed the greater the chance that it would not occur. "Consequently, the percentage of today's young adults that do not ever marry may turn out to be higher than the corresponding percentage of their predecessors," the report speculated.

First, notice that the connection between delaying marriage and never marrying at all is *stated*, not *proved*. Assuming that the statement is correct, and realizing that the years of fertility are limited, it would be reasonable to *infer* that *the trend to marry later in life may be a factor in the declining birth rate.*

Because inferences are not totally rooted in the information provided by your source, they tend to be expressed in tentative terms. Both inferences cited above, for example, use "may be" to convey an appropriate degree of uncertainty. The following inference hedges in a different way: *If the trend toward later marriages continues at a steady rate, eventually there will be no more married couples in this country.* Here, the sweeping and improbable generalization—no more married couples—is put into some perspective through the conditional: "*if* this trend continues at a steady rate. . . ." However, given the variety of unpredictable influences affecting the decision to marry, the negative trend is unlikely to continue at a steady rate. In fact, this inference is absurd.

EXERCISE 3: DRAWING INFERENCES

Read "Ice Cream: Giving in to Rich Temptation." Then decide which of the sentences that follow are *stated;* which are *implied* (or suggested by the essay); which can be *inferred* from the essay; and which are *false,* according to the information in the article.

ICE CREAM: GIVING IN TO RICH TEMPTATION
Fran McCullough

Sales of the richest ice creams—what the trade calls premium and super-premium—are up 28 percent in the first six months of 1997, while sales of low-fat ice creams have dropped 5 percent from last year. The dieter's old love, frozen yogurt, first showed signs of neglect in 1995; this year, sales are down 23 percent. | 1

Sales of frozen yogurt began to decline when new reduced-fat ice creams appeared in the market, said Martin Veeger, the group's director of market research. | 2

But, he added, the sharper recent decline also reflects a new desire among Americans to indulge the forbidden pleasures of the table.

If steak and french fries are back on the menu, then rich ice cream is dessert.   3

Ice cream has always been the favorite American dessert; Americans ate 1.5 billion gallons of it in 1996, or about 47 pints a person, 2 percent more than the year before. That's substantially more than in any other country in the world, with Finland's 38 pints a person and Denmark's 34 pints next in line. In the United States, Portland, Oregon, and Seattle lead in annual sales of ice cream at supermarkets, with 2.87 and 2.64 gallons a person respectively; New York is 50th, at 1.45 gallons. (Perhaps people who live with more inclement weather need ice cream to cheer them up.)   4

But it is taste that is driving the $11 billion ice cream business. Even Dr. Dean Ornish, the low-fat advocate, prefers to savor a nightly spoonful of full-fat Häagen-Dazs, rather than diving into a pint of what he calls "fake-fat frozen dessert."   5

And the dissatisfaction with taste is behind the drop in low-fat ice cream sales, said Lynda Utterback, the editor of the Chicago-based National Dipper, a newsletter for retail shops. "Low-fat ice cream? It's an oxymoron," she said. "Butterfat is what makes ice cream taste so good." Häagen-Dazs low-fat vanilla has 2.5 grams of fat a serving, compared with 18 grams of fat for its regular, super-premium vanilla.   6

"We've gone about as far as we can go with the nonfat ice creams," said Bob Howe, a consultant to ice cream companies who is based in Byron, California. "The replacements for the mouth feel, good body and texture of butterfat just aren't there, so it's going to be creative flavoring that takes up the slack. With low fat, the formulations are changing all the time, so it's getting better."   7

But creative flavoring almost inevitably means more sugars and mix-ins, like candy, that may be as much of a problem for dieters as fat.   8

"No one is saying these reduced-fat ice creams are low calorie," said Betty Campbell of the Food and Drug Administration's Office of Food Labeling. While the full-fat Java Chip at Starbucks has 250 calories a serving, its low-fat Mocha Mambo still has 170 calories.   9

Ice cream labeling can be confusing. Because ice cream is sold by volume—what is defined as a serving is a miserly half cup—and not by weight, it is impossible to figure out exactly how much of the product is air that has been pumped in, what the industry calls overrun. Some air needs to be added to packaged ice cream or it would be too hard to serve easily. But the overrun percentage varies widely. Super-premiums, which cost upward of $3 a pint, are usually from 10 to 20 percent air, while some economy ice creams, which are usually under $3 for a half gallon, are half air.   10

Consumers can get a rough idea of how much overrun different brands have by comparing the weight per serving of a plain variety like vanilla, which is listed on the label. Servings of Edy's and Turkey Hill, both premiums, weigh 65 and 66 grams, respectively; super-premium Häagen-Dazs and Ben & Jerry's weigh 106 and 108 grams a serving, respectively. Almost invariably, airy ice creams are less satisfying,   11 so people tend to compensate by having larger servings. That means that the amounts of fat and calories per serving listed on the labels are less relevant.

1. Dieters who used to eat frozen yogurt are now eating low-fat ice cream. Inferred
2. Full-fat ice cream has more than seven times the fat of low-fat ice cream. False
3. No other country eats as much ice cream as the United States. Implied
4. Eating low-fat ice cream isn't much help to dieters. Implied
5. Overrun enriches the flavor of ice cream. False
6. Heavy ice cream is good ice cream. Implied
7. Low-fat cake is likely to have lots of sugar in it. Inferred
8. Low-fat ice cream isn't as delicious as full-fat ice cream, so people eat smaller portions of it. False
9. Ice cream is a big seller in cold climates. Inferred

Logical Reasoning

When making an inference, you *generalize* or *draw a specific conclusion* from the available information, drawing on personal knowledge and experience to predict a likely conclusion or next step. For instance, if you look out a window and observe that the street and sidewalk are wet and the sky is overcast, you would most likely conclude that it had rained recently. You didn't directly observe the rain, but you can generalize from past experiences with the same evidence. Although this may seem like a simpleminded illustration, it is typical of the logical reasoning we all engage in every day.

There are two types of reasoning in formal logic—*deductive* reasoning and *inductive* reasoning, each a distinct process for arriving at defensible conclusions based on available evidence.

Deductive Reasoning

The classic format for deductive reasoning is the *syllogism,* which consists of a series of carefully limited statements, or premises, pursued to a circumscribed conclusion:

All reptiles are cold-blooded.	[premise]
Iguanas are reptiles.	[premise]
Therefore, iguanas are cold-blooded.	[conclusion]

This is a line of reasoning based on classification, that is, the creation of a generalized category based on shared traits. Members of the group we call "reptiles" have cold-bloodedness in common—in fact, cold-bloodedness is a defining trait of reptiles. Iguanas are members of the group reptiles, which means that they must also have that shared trait. Notice that the opening premise of a syllogism is a statement that the reader will be willing to grant as true without explicit proof. Deductive reasoning always begins with beliefs or knowledge that the writer and reader share, and the syllogism builds from that undisputed statement.

Deductive reasoning follows an almost mathematical rigor; provided the premises are true and the line of reasoning valid, the conclusion must necessarily be true.

Inductive Reasoning

In inductive reasoning, a conclusion or common principle is reached by generalizing from a body of evidence, as in the example of the wet street and overcast sky. The conclusions reached through inductive reasoning are always conditional to some extent—that is, there's always the possibility that some additional evidence may be introduced to suggest a different conclusion. Given the available evidence, you were perfectly justified in concluding that it had rained when you observed a wet street and overcast sky; but suppose you then turned on the radio and learned that a water main in the area had broken overnight. That overcast sky may be coincidental, and you should be prepared to revise your original conclusion based on the new information.

Inductive reasoning uses the available evidence to construct the most likely conclusion.

Logic in Argumentation

Most arguments contain elements of both inductive and deductive reasoning. In argumentation, the writer attempts to prove a claim by presenting evidence and reasoning so that the reader can recreate the writer's logic. The core of the argument is usually *deductive,* but rarely based on a classical syllogism; rather, it consists of a series of *premises* or *assumptions* that the reader shares—or can be persuaded to share—with the writer. These premises often depend on *common cultural values.* That is why arguments can lose their force over time as values change. One hundred years ago, writers could safely base arguments on the premise that heroism is defined by slaying the enemy in battle, or that engaging in sex before marriage warrants a girl's expulsion from polite society, or that whipping young children is an effective and acceptable punishment. Today, those arguments would not have wide credibility.

The point of argument is to convince your reader to view an issue as you do, to share your belief that a certain result is worth achieving, and to agree that the method you propose is the best way of achieving it. To do that, you must establish common ground between you and your reader. Don't assume that your underlying assumptions will automatically be shared. Spell them out; make them seem desirable, even inevitable.

For instance, few people would challenge you if you simply claimed that cruelty to animals is bad, but there is a wide range of opinion regarding exactly what constitutes cruelty, or whether certain specific activities (the use of animals in scientific research, for instance) are or are not cruel. Is inflicting pain, or even discomfort, "cruel" by definition? If inflicting pain serves some larger purpose, is it still cruel, or does "cruelty" refer only to *unnecessary* or *unjustifiable* pain? Before contesting the ethics of medical research practices, a persuasive argument about this issue would have to begin by establishing a premise—in this case, a definition of "cruelty"—that both the reader and the writer will find acceptable.

To be fully convincing, the argument that emerges from your premises must be *inductive* as well: it must be supported by a range of *evidence*, which you present, analyze, and interpret for your reader. Evidence usually consists of *facts*, which you verify and document by specifying the sources. If your evidence depends on *data* and *statistics*, the sources must be reliable, and the results based on an adequate and representative sample and an appropriate population. How many people took part in the survey? If percentages are cited, what was the base population? If you say that 60 percent of those surveyed want to raise the tax on cigarettes, do you mean fifty or five hundred or five thousand people? Were they smokers or nonsmokers? What was their age? their income? These and other factors have some bearing on the validity of such data as evidence.

- *Generalizing from a representative sample*
  Public opinion polls use limited evidence (the opinions of, say, 1,000 respondents) to predict the opinions of a much larger group—possibly the entire nation—by assuming that the opinions of the smaller group reflect proportionately the opinions of the larger. Here, for instance, is part of a survey on attitudes toward health care taken in 1989:

  The Harvard University School of Public Health and Louis Harris and Associates surveyed nearly 4,000 American, Canadian and British adults about their country's health care. . . . A full 89 percent of U.S. citizens feel our health-care system is fundamentally flawed. . . .

  You can readily see how the writer uses the responses of the 4,000 people surveyed to make larger claims about whole national groups ("A full 89 percent of U.S. citizens feel . . .").

- *Citing authority*
  Another source of evidence is *authority:* the testimony of experts whose reputation makes them credible. You need to cite the evidence of such authorities in reasonable detail and, if possible, convey the strength of their credentials. Your argument should not depend on nameless sources such as "1,000 doctors" or "authorities in the field."

- *Reasoning through analogies*
  One other basis for argument, loosely related to deduction, is *reasoning through analogies*. A writer may compare a disputed idea or situation to some other, less controversial idea in order to reveal an inconsistency or to advocate a particular course of action. For instance, some might claim that the wide availability of foreign-made consumer products is analogous to an infection that threatens to destroy the health of the nation's

economy. What similarities in the two situations is this writer exploiting? What parallels can be drawn between them?

nation	=	person
foreign-made consumer product • produced outside the nation • invades national economy	=	**infection** • originates outside the person • invades body of individual
harmful: threatens economic health of nation • workers laid off when American-made products aren't bought	=	**harmful:** threatens physical health of person • virus or infection destroys healthy cells, or otherwise weakens person
remedy: discourage imports	=	**remedy:** prevent invasive virus or infection; destroy existing virus or infection.

In both cases, some entity (in the first case a nation, and in the second a human being) is "invaded" by something potentially harmful (such as a Japanese-made VCR or German-built car in the case of the nation, and a virus or bacterial infection in the case of the person). Having suggested these similarities, the writer can extend the analogy: The undisputed remedy in the case of sickness—destroying or preventing the cause of the sickness—suggests the remedy for the economy's illness—discouraging the importation of foreign-made consumer products.

Analogies can provide vivid and persuasive images, but they are also easily distorted when pushed too far, and an alternative analogy may suggest itself to the reader. Foreign-made consumer products may have "invaded" the United States, but considering their popularity with U.S. consumers, they have also in some sense been "invited." To U.S. auto manufacturers or workers, foreign imports probably do seem very like opportunistic microbes, but consumers preparing to buy a new car are less likely to "destroy" them than to regard them as inexpensive generic medicines designed to heal ailing pocketbooks. Careful writers recognize the limits of their analogies.

Ineffective Arguments and Logical Fallacies

Not every argument convinces us to accept the writer's conclusion. What undermines the credibility or persuasiveness of an inductive or deductive argument?

- *An argument may be based on an initial premise that is unconvincing.*
- *The line of reasoning that connects premise to premise may be flawed.*
- *The evidence itself may be misrepresented in some way.*

It's easy to accept *initial premises* uncritically because they're generally expressed with confidence in the reader's agreement—remember, the writer assumes that the reader will grant the argument's opening premises without explicit proof. As you read, you should be careful to identify the assumptions a writer uses in constructing an argument. For example, look at the following opening premise, from the second paragraph of an unsigned editorial attacking the logic of a proposed ban on tobacco products. The editorial appeared in the magazine *National Review* in 1994.

> Even though nine-tenths of smokers don't die of lung cancer, there are clearly health dangers in cigarettes, dangers so constantly warned about that smokers are clearly aware that these dangers are the price they pay for the enjoyment and relaxation they get from smoking.

The writer claims here that because the health risks connected with smoking have been widely publicized, the decision to smoke is rational—that is, based on smokers' weighing their desire for "enjoyment and relaxation" against the potential health risks. You might grant the dangers of smoking have been well documented and publicized, but does it necessarily follow that knowing the risks involved ensures a rational decision? If, as has also been widely demonstrated, cigarettes are addictive, then the decision to smoke may *not* be entirely rational—that is, the decision to smoke may *not* be freely made after a careful consideration of the available data and the possible consequences.

The writer here is committing a common logical lapse known as *begging the question.* The assumption here is false; it assumes that a crucial point is self-evident and requires no further argument. The key word here is "clearly"—"smokers are clearly aware"—which may persuade the careless reader that the point has already been proven. When a writer is begging the question, you often find language that preempts the issue and discourages scrutiny: "obviously," "everyone knows," or "it goes without saying."

Sometimes, the process of begging the question is more subtle. Here, a writer arguing against euthanasia begins with a strong statement:

> Every human being has a natural inclination to continue living. Our reflexes and responses fit us to fight attackers, flee wild animals, and dodge out of the way of trucks. In our daily lives we exercise the caution and care necessary to protect ourselves. Our bodies are similarly structured for survival right down to the molecular level. . . . Euthanasia does violence to this natural goal of survival. It is literally acting against nature because all the processes of nature are bent towards the end of bodily survival.

By limiting his view of existence to purely bodily functions, J. Gay-Williams simplifies the complex issue of euthanasia. What he omits are the key functions of the mind, will, and emotions, which, some would say, can override the force of the instinct towards "bodily survival" and make the choice to die. The key here is the first sentence: "Every human being has a natural inclination to continue living." This broad assumption allows for no exceptions. It begs the question by telling only part of the story.

Even if the premises of an argument are valid, there may be *fallacies* in the reasoning that holds the premises together. Logical fallacies are breakdowns in the reasoning that connects the premises of an argument; they occur when the writer makes *unjustifiable* generalizations like the one above or draws *unjustifiable* conclusions from the available evidence. Cause-and-effect reasoning, for example, can slide into before-and-after fallacies (known as *post hoc propter ergo hoc*—after this, therefore, before this). This fallacy assumes that any event that precedes another must somehow *cause* the second event. It is often true that one event causes a second, later event, as in the case of rain causing the wet street you observe the next morning. But if you make that reasoning a universal rule, you might, for instance, conclude that because swimsuits habitually appear in your local clothing stores in May, and summer follows in June, swimsuits somehow *cause* summer. It may be perfectly true that swimsuits appear in stores in May and that summer usually begins in June, but this argument fails to consider *alternative explanations*—in this case, that the approach of summer actually causes manufacturers to ship and retailers to display swimsuits in May, rather than the other way around; the swimsuits *anticipate*, rather than *cause*, summer.

Most fallacies result from a tendency to oversimplify issues, to take shortcuts in dealing with complex and diverse ideas. An easy fallacy to slip into is the *false dilemma*. In effect, you limit the ground for argument by proceeding as if there were only two alternatives; everything else is ignored. Here is part of the argument presented by a writer who supports euthanasia:

> Reality dictates the necessity of such laws because, for some dying patients experiencing extreme suffering, a lethal prescription is the only way to end an extended and agonizing death. Consider the terrible dilemma created when so-called passive measures fail to bring about the hoped-for death. Are we to stand helplessly by while a patient whose suicide we legally agreed to assist continues to suffer and deteriorate—perhaps even more so than before? Or do we have a moral imperative, perhaps even a legal responsibility, to not only alleviate the further suffering we have brought about but to take action to fulfill our original agreement [to withdraw life support]?

Barbara Dority has reduced the situation to a simple choice: passive doctor and patient in agony versus active doctor who brings an end to suffering, who abides by morality, and who keeps her promise. There are many possibilities for intervention between these two extremes, but, at this point in her argument, the writer does not acknowledge them. Through her language, she also loads the dice: does one identify with the doctor "stand[ing] helplessly" by or the doctor with a "moral imperative" who knows how to "take action" to "alleviate . . . suffering"?

The tendency to oversimplify, to base our claims on insufficient evidence, can result in the *hasty generalization*. A convincing generalization will be supported by strong evidence. *Avoid generalizing on the basis of one or two examples.* And when you do cite examples, make sure that they are typical ones and that they clearly support your argument. Gertrude Himmelfarb, for example, builds her argument about the decline of morality in our society by criticizing an increasing tendency to be nonjudgmental. She offers the following generalization:

> Most of us are uncomfortable with the idea of making moral judgements even in our private lives, let alone with the "intrusion," as we say, of moral judgements into public affairs.

To support her generalization, she observes that public officials, such as the president's cabinet and the Surgeon General, tend to avoid using the word "immoral." In one of her two examples, the Secretary of Health and Human Services is quoted as saying:

> I don't like to put this in moral terms, but I do believe that having children out of wedlock is just wrong.

This last quotation, in itself, hardly strengthens Professor Himmelfarb's initial point since many would consider "wrong" a judgment equivalent to "immoral." Then, on the basis of these limited examples, she reiterates her original claim:

> It is not only our political and cultural leaders who are prone to this failure of moral nerve. Everyone has been infected by it, to one degree or another.

The argument has moved around in a circle, from one hasty generalization to another.

One unpleasant kind of logical fallacy is the *ad hominem* [about the man] argument. Here, the basis for argument is a personal attack: first you point out all the bad qualities of a prominent person who opposes your views; then, without considering whether those flaws are relevant to the issue, you conclude that they must taint that person's beliefs. As you have realized, the ad hominem argument is often used in political campaigns and in other well-publicized controversies. A discussion of euthanasia, for example, will sometimes get stuck in a consideration of Dr. Jack Kevorkian's conduct and motives.

Paul McHugh, for example, spends the first half of his argument against euthanasia demonstrating why he regards Dr. Kevorkian as "'certifiably' insane," comparing him with other zealots who would do anything to advance their cause, and finally citing "the potential for horror in an overvalued idea held by a person in high authority" such as Adolf Hitler. Certainly, the comparison is strained—Dr. Kevorkian is not "in high authority." Yet, even though Professor McHugh now moves to a completely different basis for argument, the opprobrium generated by the association between Kevorkian and Hitler reverberates throughout the rest of the essay.

Yet another logical fallacy derives from reasoning through analogies: in a *false analogy*, the two ideas or circumstances being compared are not actually comparable. Here is an example of a false analogy based on statistics that is being used in an argument against euthanasia:

> Gomez calculates that euthanasia accounts for about 7 percent of all deaths in the Netherlands. If the United States had a similar rate, there would be about 140,000 cases annually. If Fumento's 9 percent figure is correct, the United States number would be 180,000. And if it is correct that half of the Dutch euthanasias are unconsented, applying that proportion here would mean that the number of physician-inflicted unconsented deaths in this country would be between 70,000 and 90,000 annually.

Even though Robert Bork is not sure which of his sources is correct, he uses their statistics to develop an analogy between what has probably happened in the Netherlands (give or take a few percentage points) and what might happen in the United States. Are the two nations comparable in this regard? Professor Bork does not explore the national character, the nature of doctor-patient relationships, the availability of palliatives like medication or hospices. The only point of distinction that he raises is the higher cost of health care in the United States, which supports the conclusion encouraged by his analogy: if it were legalized in the United States, the incentive to bring down medical costs would turn euthanasia into "a license to kill."

For another example of false analogy, let's return to the editorial on the proposed tobacco ban from the *National Review.* Here's the entire paragraph.

> Even though nine-tenths of smokers don't die of lung cancer, there are clearly health dangers in cigarettes, dangers so constantly warned about that smokers are clearly aware that these dangers are the price they pay for the enjoyment and relaxation they get from smoking. As mortals we make all kinds of trade-offs between health and living. We drive automobiles knowing that forty thousand people die in them in the U.S. each year; we cross busy streets, tolerate potentially explosive gas in our homes, swim in fast-moving rivers, use electricity though it kills thousands, and eat meat and other foods that may clog our arteries and give us heart attacks and strokes. All the . . . demagoguery about the tobacco industry killing people could be applied with similar validity to the automobile industry, the electric utilities, aircraft manufacturers, the meat business, and more.

Here, the reader is asked to compare the health risks associated with smoking with those of parallel but comparatively uncontroversial activities, such as crossing a busy street. According to the writer, the situations are comparable because both involve voluntarily engaging in activities known to be health risks, and that similarity is used to suggest that laws *prohibiting* smoking would be logically inconsistent because we don't prohibit other risky activities. If potential health risks justify regulation or even prohibition, then any number of modern activities should, by analogy, be regulated. Yet, in spite of the risks in crossing busy streets, no one ever suggests preventing people from doing so for their own good; smoking, however, is singled out for regulation and possible prohibition. The reader can further *infer* from this line of reasoning that, since we daily engage in all kinds of risky activities, individuals in all cases should be allowed to decide without government interference which risks to take.

In arguments based on false analogies, the reasoning can be attacked merely by demonstrating that the differences in the two situations are more significant than the similarities. In this case, we need to consider:

- if the decision to smoke and the decision to cross a busy street are *genuinely* comparable; and
- if there may be sound reasons for regulating smoking, and equally sound reasons for *not* regulating crossing the street.

Most people could not live a normal life without crossing a busy street, but the same cannot be said of smoking. In addition, if a minimal amount of caution is exercised in crossing busy streets, most people will not be injured; when injuries do occur, they're the result of accidents or some other unexpected or unusual set of events. The same is true of the other "hazards" described in the editorial (driving automobiles, using gas appliances, and so on): injuries result from their *misuse*. By contrast, cigarettes pose a serious health threat when used exactly as intended by their manufacturers; no amount of caution will protect you from the risks associated with cigarettes.

You might also object to this argument on grounds that go beyond the logic of the reasoning to *the ways the evidence is presented*. The writer mentions, for instance, only that 9 in 10 smokers *don't die* of lung cancer, implying not only that a 10 percent death rate is insignificant but that death or lung cancer is the only potential health risk connected to smoking worth mentioning. The writer also states that "forty thousand people die" in automobiles each year in the United States, but because that number isn't presented as a percentage of all drivers on the road over the course of the year, it doesn't really address the *comparable* level of risk—those 40,000 may represent fewer than 1 percent of all drivers, which would make driving considerably less risky than smoking. Misrepresenting the evidence in this way prods the careful reader to question the writer's trustworthiness and credibility. (For another discussion of distortion in argumentation, see Chapter 8, pp. 353–355.)

Guidelines for Assessing Arguments

1. Examine the writer's initial premises. Are you willing to grant those statements without explicit proof?
2. How is the writer assembling the evidence? How is the reasoning structured, and is it sound? Can you see acceptable alternatives to the conclusion the writer has drawn?
3. Is the writer manipulating the facts and their presentation to suit the purposes of the argument?

OUTLINING

In addition to making marginal notes and asking yourself comprehension questions, you can better understand what you have read by *outlining the author's main ideas.*

When you outline, you are identifying the main points of a chapter or an essay, leaving them in roughly the same order as the original.

Outlines are built around the major points that the author uses to support the main idea, or *thesis.* In a short essay, the major points will probably all be parallel or of the same kind: the *reasons* why *x* is true, or the *ways* in which *y* happens, or the *differences* between *x* and *y*, or the chief *characteristics* of *z*, and so on. In a longer, more complex essay, the author may use several different sets of major points in shifting from one argument to another, or from the description of a problem to its solution.

These major points are given the most prominent place in the outline, usually in a numbered list at the left-hand margin. Secondary material—the ideas, information, or examples being used as supporting evidence—appears directly under each major point and slightly to the right. If there are different kinds of evidence presented, or several examples, or both, each should be listed on a separate line and assigned numbers or letters of the alphabet to keep them in order.

To demonstrate the standard format, here is an outline of some of the points that have been made so far in this chapter.

I.   Underlining
  A.   Important for active reading
    1.   select what's important
      a.   key generalizations and topic sentences
      b.   useful examples
      c.   transitional points
  B.   Works best on second reading
    1.   choose from alternative methods
      a.   underline
      b.   highlight
      c.   circle
      d.   bracket
      e.   marginal checks

II.   Annotation
  A.   Helps you to understand what you read
    1.   interpret, evaluate, or question meaning
    2.   define difficult words or phrases
    3.   clarify confusing points
    4.   introduce ideas of your own
  B.   Involves participatory process
    1.   read slowly
    2.   write notes in the margin
    3.   use your own words

For each of the two skills stated in the *first level* (I/II) this outline deals first with its purpose (in the *second level:* A) and then with ways of using the skill (in the *second level:* B). The *third level* (arabic numbers: 1/2/3) is reserved for examples, while the *fourth level* (small letters: a/b/c) contains more specific examples or explanations of points on the third level.

There is no fixed number of letters and numbers allocated for each section; whether you use only the four levels that you see in the preceding outline or include even more—the next two levels could be (1) and (a)—depends on the number and complexity of the supporting ideas that you find in your source.

The purpose of outlining is to show how the author has constructed the essay and to distinguish between main ideas and supporting material.

Multilevel numbering and lettering is not always necessary in an outline. It is possible to indicate the relationships between ideas simply by the way you place them on the page. However, the numbers and letters do provide an easy way of organizing and referring to a large number of points.

There are a few rules governing *the language used in outlining.* You may take the words of your outline directly from the original, or you may express the author's ideas in your own words. You may use complete sentences or fragmentary phrases, whichever is convenient. However, *consistency is important.* Try to make all points on the same level either fragments or complete sentences. For example, in the preceding outline, the points on the third level are consistently expressed as commands, while those on the second level are all sentence fragments.

Outlining Simple Essays

Outlining is the most effective way to record the main points of an essay whose structure is clear and straightforward. In "Must Doctors Serve Where They're Told?" for example, Harry Schwartz presents the arguments for both sides so clearly that underlining and numbering the key phrases in the essay would record its structure. (Each of the main points has been italicized in the essay.) However, since Schwartz moves back and forth from positive to negative reasons, it is helpful to outline the pairing of related arguments.

Read "Must Doctors Serve Where They're Told?" and then carefully examine the outline that follows.

MUST DOCTORS SERVE WHERE THEY'RE TOLD?
Harry Schwartz

Should young doctors be "drafted" and forced to serve some years in areas of physician shortage? Or, less dramatically, should a portion of the places in the nation's medical schools be reserved for young people who promise that in return for government financial aid they will agree to serve where the government wants them to? These and related issues have been debated in Congress . . . and are still unresolved.

Currently, it costs an estimated average of about $13,000 a year to train a medical student, but those students pay directly only about $1,000 to $6,000 in tuition. The remainder is paid by government funds, by return on endowments, by gifts and similar sources. Some lawmakers see a *compulsory service liability as a means of compensating the taxpayers for subsidizing the doctors' education.*

2

The specific proposals that have been debated in Congress have ranged from Senator Edward M. Kennedy's suggestion for a universal draft for all medical school graduates to milder schemes that would give young doctors a choice between repaying the Federal Government or serving for several years in designated areas. In New York there is already a medical training program whose students have agreed to serve two years in doctor-short areas after graduating from medical school. Those who fail to meet this "service commitment" will be required to reimburse the city and state for up to $25,000 for their free undergraduate education.

3

Some conservative economists have argued that *physician incomes, which average around $50,000, remove all excuse for government subsidy.* They would require medical students to pay the full costs, financing their way, if need be, by bank loans. Such an approach would remove the motive for any doctor draft, but many in Congress fear that this "solution" would close medical schools to children of the poor, the working class, and minorities.

4

Proponents of some service requirements for young doctors usually base their arguments on the *maldistribution of doctors in this country.* In 1973, for example, California had 265 doctors per 100,000 people, more than three times as many as South Dakota's 87 per 100,000. The actual disparities are even greater, because within each state physicians tend to congregate in metropolitan areas.

5

Opponents of forced service do not deny the existence of local shortages, but they question the wisdom of *sending new physicians into shortage areas where they will have little or no help* and consultation from older, more experienced doctors.

6

Opponents also ask *whether doctors serving in isolated areas against their will are likely to give satisfactory service.* And they ask why young doctors and dentists should be *singled out for coercion* when government helps finance the education of most professionals and there are great inequalities in the current distribution of lawyers, accountants, architects and engineers as well.

7

But more is involved in this debate than the allocation of physicians. The argument about young doctors is relevant to the broader national discussion about national economic planning and about the relative roles of government decision and market forces in directing the American economy.

8

On one side are those who emphasize the *obligation of government to use all its resources to reach desirable goals for all Americans.* If one assumes, as Mr. Kennedy and others do, that every American has a "right" to health care, then it seems reasonable for government to take whatever actions are needed to make sure that doctors and related personnel and facilities are available everywhere. If market forces do not produce the desired result, this school is prepared to use either government coercion or government financial persuasion. Moreover, this school of

9

thought wants to tailor the means to the end. Thus, instead of using government money just to expand the number of doctors in general, they want to assure that doctors are available wherever needed and available, moreover, in whatever distribution of specialities Congress or its servants decide is appropriate.

Opponents argue that such *regulation would be contrary to all American history and tradition,* except for times of war or emergency when the military draft has been in effect. The *American emphasis, these opponents hold, is primarily upon the freedom of the individual and affords no warrant for infringing one person's freedom in order to benefit someone else.* The whole structure of publicly financed education in this country, from kindergarten to M.D. and Ph.D., it is pointed out, has developed over the decades without any related service requirement or repayment of any kind whatsoever. If doctors are drafted, it will provide a precedent for drafting other categories of Americans.   10

The issue is not peculiarly American, of course, nor is the problem of physician maldistribution confined to the United States. *In the Soviet Union and its associated Communist states,* most graduates of higher educational institutions—not only physicians—are *assigned specific work locations* for the first few years after graduation.   11

Some non-Communist countries, like Mexico, have a requirement for compulsory service for a limited time by doctors before they can go into normal practice. In Israel there is a universal service obligation for all young adults. *But in most countries of Western Europe there is no draft of young doctors.*   12

Most of the other democratic countries of the world are relatively small, both in area and population . . . compared with the United States. So the advocates of a doctor draft in the United States argue that the absence of such compulsion in other countries is no conclusive argument against it here.   13

I. Obligations of young doctors: partial cost of education borne by public, which is entitled to compensation
    A. Debt to public can be repaid through service
        1. Kennedy plan
        2. New York two-year term of service
    B. Bank loan can be used for initial payment of medical school fees
        1. extremely high income will allow ultimate repayment
        2. possible difficulty in applying for initial loan

II. Needs of the public: not enough doctors to serve the country
    A. "Maldistribution" necessitates drafting: doctors tend to practice in certain populous states and cities
        1. California
        2. South Dakota
    B. Coercion would not ensure efficient service
        1. inexperienced doctors would be isolated from guidance
        2. unwilling doctors are inefficient

    III. Powers of the government vs. the rights of the individual

        A. The government is empowered to satisfy everyone's right to health care

        B. Public policy shouldn't encourage coercion of individuals to benefit others; to draft doctors would be an unfortunate precedent

            1. other professions aren't subject to a draft

            2. other beneficiaries of public education aren't forced to repay costs

    IV. Precedents in other countries

        A. Drafting doctors is routine in some countries

            1. Communist countries

            2. Mexico

            3. Israel

        B. Drafting doctors is not required in many countries with a democratic tradition similar to ours

            1. Western Europe

                a. these Western European countries are physically smaller than the United States and therefore have different requirements

Thesis: A decision to draft young doctors for service throughout the country will have to consider the obligations and rights of the doctors, as well as the responsibility of the government to serve the public.

This is a four-level outline, with the third and fourth levels (1,2,3/a) presenting either specific examples or more narrow statements than the broad ideas contained in the first and second levels. Notice how the language within each level remains relatively consistent: levels I through IV contain fragmentary phrases; levels A and B are written in complete sentences throughout; levels 1, 2, and 3 do vary, depending on whether the supporting material consists of examples (expressed as words or fragments) or narrow generalizations (complete sentences). The phrasing is parallel within each section; the clearest example is IV.A and IV.B, which use parallel participial constructions ("drafting doctors").

Outlining Complex Essays

Most essays are not as clearly organized as Harry Schwartz's. For example, the main ideas may not appear in the obvious place at the beginning of each paragraph. Some writers tend to put their topic sentences at the ends of paragraphs; others don't use topic sentences at all, or use them minimally.

Loosely organized essays are not bad essays or even badly constructed essays. They often deal with complex subjects, too complex to be easily contained in a tightly constructed sequence of paragraphs. Nevertheless, these essays do have a plan, a structure linking one idea with the next. And that plan means that these essays can be outlined.

Essays that deal with several main ideas simultaneously are especially difficult to outline, yet they usually require and repay careful, point-by-point outlining. Such an essay is Blanche Blank's "A Question of Degree" (see pp. 8–11).

Establishing a Thesis

The outline of Harry Schwartz's essay was followed by a statement of its *thesis*—the essay's central idea.

> *A thesis is usually a substantial generalization, written as a complete sentence, that can stand by itself as the basis of an essay's development.*

A thesis should be broad enough and arguable enough to be worth defending in a work of at least several pages. In the Schwartz essay, the thesis does no more than suggest the underlying issues, since Schwartz himself does not decisively support one side of the argument or the other.

In contrast, Blanche Blank, in "A Question of Degree," *is* attempting to convince her readers to accept a specific point of view. An adequate thesis, then, should convey some of her distaste for the excessive value placed on college degrees. But even if you fully understand Blank's position, you may still write an incomplete or an inadequate thesis. What is wrong with each of these examples?

1. According to Blanche Blank, universities need to change their outlook and curricula and return to a more traditional role.

2. Blanche Blank suggests that our present ideology about the purpose of college should be reconsidered and redefined.

3. I agree with Blanche Blank's belief that college degrees have too much importance.

4. Blanche Blank argues that employment discrimination arises from an emphasis on college degrees.

5. Blanche Blank believes that a college education isn't necessary at an early age.

Remember that *a good thesis would be a generalization broad enough to cover most of Blank's argument without being so vague as to be meaningless.* Consider the following criticisms of the five theses:

- Thesis 1 accurately presents only one—and not the chief one—of Blank's points.

- Thesis 2 is uninformative: what is "our present ideology" and what sort of redefinition is in order?
- Thesis 3 is also vague: Blank may have convinced one reader, but which of her arguments did the reader find effective?
- Thesis 4 is much too broad: Blank does not argue that degrees are the only cause of employment discrimination, nor does she suggest that employment is the only area adversely affected by the importance attached to degrees.
- Thesis 5 is inaccurate and incomplete: Blank is not urging all would-be freshmen to bypass college.

The following thesis is somewhat better than the first five: it conveys something of Blank's central idea, but it says nothing about work and the self-respect of the worker, which are ideas crucial to the essay.

> 6. In Blanche Blank's view, acquiring a college degree immediately after high
>   school should not be considered the best way to achieve a better life.

A satisfactory thesis would convey more precisely the dangers of overvaluing the college degree. Thesis 7 does so:

> 7. The possession of a college degree cannot automatically lead to a better life
>   and better earnings for a college graduate; the universal practice of regarding
>   the degree as an essential for getting a "good" job can only discourage a more
>   just and efficient system of employment.

Both parts of Thesis 7 deal with the consequences of overvaluing the college degree: the first part is concerned with the effect on the individual, whose expectations may not be fulfilled; the second is concerned with the effect on social institutions and organizations, which may value credentials at the expense of merit. It is not accidental that Thesis 7 is the longest of the group; complex ideas often require complex means of expression.

Constructing an Outline Based on Categories

Because the paragraphs of "A Question of Degree" are crowded with ideas, constructing an outline is difficult. For example, within the following single paragraph, Blank mentions most of her main points, some more than once, and in varying order. (The numbers here are keyed to the outline on pp. 41–42.)

What is wrong with the current college/work cycle can be seen in the following anomalies: we are selling college to the youth of America as a take-off pad for the material good life [I.A]. College is literally advertised and packaged as a means for getting more money through "better" jobs at the same time that Harvard graduates are taking jobs as taxi drivers [I.B]. This situation is a perversion of the true spirit of a university [III], a perversion of a humane social ethic [IV.A] and, at bottom, a patent fraud. To take the last point first, the economy simply is not geared to guaranteeing these presumptive "better" jobs [I.B]; the colleges are not geared to training for such jobs [III]; and the ethical propriety of the entire enterprise is very questionable [I and II]. We are by definition (rather than by analysis) establishing two kinds of work: work labeled "better" because it has a degree requirement tagged to it and nondegree work, which, through this logic, becomes automatically "low level" [IV.A].

When outlining a complex essay, you must look for organizing principles and categories of ideas as you read and reread it. *Experienced readers learn to watch for points that are repeated and emphasized to help them find a consistent way to organize and remember what they have read.* Earlier, you were asked about the different groups of people who are affected by the unfortunate worship of college degrees. The easiest way to break down the mass of assertions in Blanche Blank's essay is to *use those groups as a way to establish categories:*

A. Students who are in college unwillingly
B. College graduates who work at frustrating jobs
C. Workers who have not been to college and are undervalued
D. True scholars who resent the decline in the quality of university life

If you combine the first two groups (both with career expectations and both disappointed by college), you have the basis for an outline with three major entries, plus a conclusion that sums up Blanche Blank's central ideas.

Thesis: The possession of a college degree cannot automatically lead to a better life and better earnings for a college graduate; the universal practice of regarding the degree as an essential for getting a "good" job can only discourage a more just and efficient system of employment.

I. The frustration of students with vocational expectations
   A. Whether or not they are suited to college, students believe that they must spend four years getting a degree to get a good job.
   B. Rewarding jobs are not necessarily available, even to those with degrees.

II. The frustration of working people without college degrees but with hopes for advancement
   A. Workers with experience and good qualifications are bypassed for promotion and denied their rightful status.
   B. Since college is considered the province of the young, it is unlikely that an experienced older person will seek a college education.

III. The frustration of students and teachers with traditional views of college
   A. Instead of continuing to emphasize the traditional pursuit of knowledge for its own sake, universities are trying to function as a service industry, preparing students for careers.

IV. The deterioration of human values

  A. People are encouraged to make invidious comparisons between less and more desirable kinds of work.

  B. One form of educational experience is being elevated at the expense of the others.

There are a few important points to notice about the format of this outline.

First, in some ways, this is a traditional outline: *the main ideas are given Roman numerals and the secondary ideas are lettered.* As you have learned, this enables you to refer more easily to each of the items and, in the case of the lettered supporting arguments, to separate them clearly from one another. However, because the outline conforms to Blanche Blank's organization, the number of points included under each broad category varies. (For this reason, unlike some traditional outlines, it is permissible to have only one point [A] under III.)

Next, *the presentation need not be completely consistent, as long as it is consistent within each level.* In this outline, the main ideas are all written in sentence fragments and the supporting ideas are all complete sentences.

What is more important is that *all the entries are on roughly the same level of abstraction:* the main ideas are all very broad, while the secondary ideas suggest the more specific ways in which each paragraph in the essay will be developed. In contrast, here is an excerpt from an outline in which the main entries are both broad and specific:

  I. jobs aren't available

  II. Joe V. disappointed

  III. college students feel cheated

The example of Joe V. is used in the essay only to illustrate important ideas, not as an end in itself. Entry II is *evidence* in support of entries I and III, and therefore "Joe V." belongs in a more subordinate position:

  I. jobs aren't available

  II. college students feel cheated

    A. Joe V. disappointed

All the entries in the complete Blank outline are *rewordings* of ideas taken from the essay and are *self-contained and self-explanatory.* Outlines that retain the wording of the original sometimes don't make sense taken out of context. And, even if such fragmentary phrases serve as shorthand notes that you (and you alone) understand, they won't be very helpful if you want to communicate Blank's ideas to your reader in an essay of your own. Is this group of points easy to understand at a glance?

  I. Degree-granting colleges are like false gods.

  II. The college degree is regarded as a stepping-stone to "meaningful," "better" jobs.

III.   The ethical propriety of the entire system is in question.

IV.   Students see themselves as prisoners of economic necessity.

How these four points relate to each other or how they serve as arguments to support the essay's thesis is not immediately clear. Nor is it any more helpful to condense sentences into brief phrases.

I.   destruction of adolescents

II.   vocational schools instead of universities

III.   nondegree work menial

It would be impossible to understand and appreciate Blanche Blank's argument from reading an outline containing these entries.

EXERCISE 4: OUTLINING AN ESSAY

Read "What Our Education System Needs Is More F's," by Carl Singleton (pp. 135–137). Establish the essay's thesis and construct an outline of its main ideas.

WRITING A SUMMARY

When you underline and annotate a text, when you ask yourself questions about its contents, when you work out an outline of its structure, you are helping yourself to understand what you are reading. When you write a summary, you are *recording* your understanding for your own information; when you include the summary in an essay of your own, you are *reporting* your understanding to your reader.

A summary of a source is usually *a condensation of ideas or information.* It is neither necessary nor desirable to include every repetition and detail. Rather, you are to extract only those points that seem important—the main ideas, which in the original passage may have been interwoven with less important material. Thus, a summary of several pages can sometimes be as brief as one sentence.

In a brief summary, *you should add nothing new* to the material in the source, nor should you change the emphasis or provide any new interpretation or evaluation. For the sake of clarity and coherence, *you may rearrange the order of the ideas;* however, you should strive to remain in the background.

The brief summary is often used as part of a larger essay. You have probably summarized your own ideas in the topic sentence of a paragraph or in the conclusion of an essay. When you discuss another piece of writing, you generally summarize the contents briefly to establish for your reader the ideas that you intend to analyze. The writer of a research essay is especially dependent on the summary as a means of referring to source materials. Through summary, you can condense a broad range of information, and you can present and explain the relevance of a number of sources all dealing with the same subject.

Summarizing a Paragraph

Before you can begin to summarize a short reading—a paragraph, for example—you must, of course, read the passage carefully and understand the significance of each idea and the way it is linked to the other ideas. The summary should above all be *comprehensive,* conveying as much as possible the totality of thought within the passage. Sometimes, you will find a single comprehensive sentence in the text itself, to be taken out verbatim and used as a summary. But, as a rule, you will find your summary in the text only when the passage is short and contains a particularly strong and comprehensive topic sentence.

The following paragraph *can* be summarized adequately by one of its own sentences. Which one?

> It is often remarked that science has increasingly removed man from a position at the center of the universe. Once upon a time the earth was thought to be the center and the gods were thought to be in close touch with the daily actions of humans. It was not stupid to imagine the earth was at the center, because, one might think, if the earth were moving around the sun, and if you threw a ball vertically upward, it would seem the ball should come down a few feet away from you. Nevertheless, slowly, over many centuries, through the work of Copernicus, Galileo, and many others, we have mostly come to believe that we live on a typical planet orbiting a typical star in a typical galaxy, and indeed that no place in the universe is special.
>
> GORDON KANE, from "Are We the Center of the Universe?"

Both the first and last sentences are possibilities, but the first is a broader generalization and a more comprehensive summary.

Usually, even when you find a strong sentence that suggests the main idea of the paragraph, you will still need to tinker with that sentence, expanding its meaning by giving the language a more general focus. Here, for example, is a paragraph in which no one sentence is broad enough to sum up the main idea, but which contains a scattering of useful phrases:

> In a discussion [with] a class of teachers, I once said that I liked some of the kids in my class much more than others and that, without saying which ones I liked best, I had told them so. After all, this is something that children know, whatever we tell them; it is futile to lie about it. Naturally, these teachers were horrified. "What a terrible thing to say!" one said. "I love all the children in my class exactly the same." Nonsense; a teacher who says this is lying, to herself or to others, and probably doesn't like any of the children very much. Not that there is anything wrong with that; plenty of adults don't like children, and there is no reason why they should. But the trouble is that they feel they should, which makes them feel guilty, which makes them feel resentful, which in turn makes them try to work off their guilt with indulgence and their resentment with subtle cruelties—cruelties of a kind that can

be seen in many classrooms. Above all, it makes them put on the phony, syrupy, sickening voice and manner, and the fake smiles and forced, bright laughter that children see so much of in school, and rightly resent and hate.

JOHN HOLT, from How Children Fail

Here, you might begin by combining key phrases: "a teacher who says" that she "loves all the children" "is lying to herself, or to others," and makes herself (and probably the children) "feel guilty" and "resentful." However, this kind of summarizing sentence resembles a patchwork, with the *words and phrasing pulled straight out of the original.* Even if you acknowledged the borrowings, by using quotation marks, as above, you would still be left with a weak sentence that is neither yours nor the author's. It is far better to construct an entirely new sentence of your own, such as this one:

> In Holt's view, although it is only natural for teachers to prefer some students to others, many teachers cannot accept their failure to like all equally well and express their inadequacy and dissatisfaction in ways that are harmful to the children.

Finally, some diffuse paragraphs give you no starting point at all for the summary and force you to write an entirely new generalization. How would you summarize this paragraph?

> To parents who wish to lead a quiet life, I would say: Tell your children that they are very naughty—much naughtier than most children. Point to the young people of some acquaintances as models of perfection and impress your own children with a deep sense of their own inferiority. You carry so many more guns than they do that they cannot fight you. This is called moral influence, and it will enable you to bounce them as much as you please. They think you know and they will not have yet caught you lying often enough to suspect that you are not the unworldly and scrupulously truthful person which you represent yourself to be; nor yet will they know how great a coward you are, nor how soon you will run away, if they fight you with persistency and judgment. You keep the dice and throw them both for your children and yourself. Load them then, for you can easily manage to stop your children from examining them. Tell them how singularly indulgent you are; insist on the incalculable benefit you conferred on them, firstly in bringing them into the world at all, but more particularly in bringing them into it as your children rather than anyone else's. Say that you have their highest interests at stake whenever you are out of temper and wish to make yourself unpleasant by way of balm to your soul. Harp much upon these highest interests. Feed them spiritually upon such brimstone and treacle as the late Bishop of Winchester's Sunday stories. You hold all the trump cards, or if you do not you can filch them; if you play them with anything like judgment you will find yourselves heads of happy, united God-fearing families, even as did my old friend Mr. Pontifex. True, your children will probably find

out all about it some day, but not until too late to be of much service to them or inconvenience to yourself.

SAMUEL BUTLER, from *The Way of All Flesh*

Guidelines for Summarizing a Brief Passage

1. Find a summarizing sentence within the passage (and, if you are using it in your own essay, put it in quotation marks); *or*
2. Combine elements within the passage into a new summarizing sentence; *or*
3. Write your own summarizing sentence.

A summary of this paragraph would recommend that parents intimidate their children and thus put them in their place. However, although such a generalization sums up the series of examples contained in the paragraph, it does not convey the fact that, in his caricature of family life, Butler is exaggerating outrageously. *A comprehensive summary, then, would have to include not only the essence of Butler's recommendations, but also his implied point: that he does not expect anyone to follow his advice. Irony* is the term used to describe the conflict between Butler's real meaning—parents should not be monsters, but sometimes are— and the meaning apparently expressed by his words as he urges them to treat their children tyrannically. Here is one way to summarize the paragraph:

> When he ironically suggests that parents can gain tranquillity and domestic happiness by tyrannizing over their children and making them feel morally inferior, Butler seems to be urging parents to treat their children with respect and justice.

Notice that this summarizing sentence includes Butler's name. *Mentioning the author's name effectively emphasizes that what you are summarizing is not your own work.* By making it clear who is responsible for what, you are avoiding any possibility of *plagiarizing*—borrowing from your source without acknowledgment.

EXERCISE 5: SUMMARIZING A PARAGRAPH

Summarize each of the following paragraphs by doing *one* of three things:

A. Underline a sentence that will serve as a comprehensive summary; or
B. Combine existing phrases; then rewrite the sentence, based on these phrases, to create a comprehensive summary; or
C. Invent a new generalization to provide a comprehensive summary.

Be prepared to explain your summary in class discussion.

1. The neurotic individual may have had some special vulnerability as an infant. Perhaps he was ill a great deal and was given care that singled him out from other children. Perhaps he walked or talked much later—or earlier—than children were expected to, and this evoked unusual treatment. The child whose misshapen feet must be put in casts or the sickly little boy who never can play ball may get out of step with his age mates and with the expectations parents and other adults have about children. Or a child may be very unusually placed in his family. He may be the only boy with six sisters, or a tiny child born between two lusty sets of twins. Or the source of the child's difficulties may be a series of events that deeply affected his relations to people—the death of his mother at the birth of the next child or the prolonged illness or absence of his father. Or a series of coincidences—an accident to a parent, moving to a new town and a severe fright—taken together may alter the child's relationship to the world.

MARGARET MEAD, from *Some Personal Views*

2. The generic process of Blaming the Victim is applied to almost every American problem. The miserable health care of the poor is explained away on the grounds that the victim has poor motivation and lacks health information. The problems of slum housing are traced to the characteristics of tenants who are labeled as "Southern rural migrants" not yet "acculturated" to life in the big city. The "multiproblem" poor, it is claimed, suffer the psychological effects of impoverishment, the "culture of poverty," and the deviant value system of the lower classes; consequently, though unwittingly, they cause their own troubles. From such a viewpoint, the obvious fact that poverty is primarily an absence of money is easily overlooked or set aside.

WILLIAM RYAN, from *Blaming the Victim*

3. Americans are no closer than we were half a century ago to coming up with a sound scientific rationale for the myriad ways we regard race. Certainly, . . . different races exist—if only because we have decided that they do. We can theoretically create races at will. If Americans agreed, for instance, that people with red hair constitute a separate race, these people would be one. And if we proceeded to treat all people with red hair differently from everyone else, they would soon take on all the attributes we associate with "real" races. If, for instance, they were allowed only to do menial labor, refused an education, compelled to intermarry, forced to live in predominantly redhead communities, and told that their only real gifts were drinking and song, they would eventually develop a culture that embodied the new redhead stereotype. But all we would have proved is that human beings have the power to define (and thereby create) races—not that the classification has any value or makes any sense.

ELLIS COSE, from *Color-Blind*

4. The crippled have become the handicapped and now the differently abled. A wheelchair-bound person has become one who *uses* a wheelchair (that language is deemed to make him or her sound less passive). AIDS victims have become People with AIDS. In one of the most extreme versions, those born deaf have altered from being hearing-impaired to "having a birthright of silence." Every bit of plain speaking offends someone these days. When I metaphorically described the dancing in the ill-fated Broadway musical *Nick and Nora* as "clubfooted" in a review in *Time,* I predicted to the copy editor involved that we would get a letter from some organization for the clubfooted, objecting that this nomenclature implied a deformity—and I was right. My review of Stephen Sondheim's *Assassins* bore a headline that spoke of the killers and would-be killers of American presidents as "loony," which the vast majority of them irrefutably were. This prompted a two-page single-spaced letter from a spokeswoman for the insane, protesting that the reference to the mental state of these deranged shooters was unfair to the crazy. More recently I was struck by a lawsuit filed on behalf of a mentally retarded eighth-grader in Dayton, Ohio, whose guardian wanted the girl to be able to attend a prom limited to high school students. Noting that her daughter was the same age as others eligible to attend and asserting that the girl could exercise comparable judgment, Thelma Sell said, "Sherrie is handicapped. She's not stupid." If she is not stupid, then what exactly does mentally retarded mean?

WILLIAM A. HENRY III, from *In Defense of Elitism*

5. Executives in the communications industry exercise a power that is not merely concentrated but also propagandistic. They make far-reaching choices in a way that few others in our society can. They project their images of the world out into the world—"five hundred channels at a time!" being the latest industry boast; "five hundred channels of *Lucy* reruns" being the ubiquitous retort of a jaded viewing public. The media do not merely represent; they also recreate themselves and their vision of the world as desirable, salable. What they reproduce is chosen, not random, not neutral, not without consequence. To pretend (as we all do from time to time) that film or television, for example, is a neutral vessel, or contentless, mindless, or unpersuasive, is sheer denial. The media, for better and frequently for worse, constitute one of the major forces in the shaping of our national vision, a chief architect of the modern American sense of identity.

PATRICIA J. WILLIAMS, from "Unbirthing the Nation"

Summarizing an Article

When you want to summarize an essay in a few sentences, how do you judge which points are significant and which are not? Some essays, especially newspaper articles, have rambling structures and short paragraphs, so you don't even have fully developed paragraphs in which to search for summarizing topic sentences. Are there any standard procedures to help you decide which points to summarize?

Guidelines for Summarizing an Article

1. Read the entire article more than once.
2. Ask yourself why the article was written and published.
3. Look for repetitions of and variations on the same idea.

Read "Holdup Man Tells Detectives How to Do It" from the *New York Times*, and, on the second reading, observe your own method of pinpointing the key ideas.

HOLDUP MAN TELLS DETECTIVES HOW TO DO IT

Selwyn Raab

His face hidden by a shabby tan coat, the career holdup man peeked out at his audience of detectives and then proceeded to lecture them on how easy it was to succeed at his trade in New York. 1

"I don't think there's much any individual police officer can do," the guest lecturer told 50 detectives yesterday at an unusual crime seminar sponsored by the Police Department. "Once I knew what the police officer on the beat was up to I wasn't much concerned about the cops." 2

The holdup man, who identified himself only as "Nick," is serving a prison term of 6 to 13 years. He said his most serious arrest occurred after he was shot three times by a supermarket manager—not in any encounter with the police. 3

When asked by a detective taking a course in robbery investigations what the best deterrent would be against gunmen like himself, Nick replied crisply: "stiffer sentences." 4

After being seriously wounded in his last robbery attempt, Nick said he decided it was time to retire. 5

"I'm close to 40 and not getting any younger," he explained. "I just don't want to spend any more time in jail." 6

Nick also offered the detectives some tips on how robbers pick their targets and make their getaways in the city. 7

Except for wearing a hat, Nick said he affected no disguise. "I usually picked a store in a different neighborhood or in another borough where I was unknown." 8

Leads on places to hold up usually came from other criminals or from employees. There were no elaborate plannings or "casings," he said, adding: 9

"I liked supermarkets because there's always a lot of cash around. Uniformed guards didn't deter me because they're not armed, they usually just have sticks. It's 10

better to pick a busy area rather than the suburbs. The chances of someone noticing you are greater in residential or suburban areas."

The detectives, sitting at desks with notepaper in front of them, were rookies as   11
well as veterans. Besides city detectives, the audience included policemen from the
Transit Authority, the Housing Authority, the Yonkers Police Department and from
Seattle.

They listened carefully as Nick outlined how he or a confederate would inspect   12
the area for signs of uniformed or plainclothes police officers.

The retired robber said he had preferred supermarkets or stores with large win-   13
dow advertisements or displays because these materials prevented him from being
seen by passers-by on the street.

"I was always a little nervous or apprehensive before a job," he continued. "But   14
once you're inside and aware of the reaction of the people and you know the possibilities then your confidence comes back."

Nick said he always made his escape in a car and he preferred heavily trafficked   15
roads because it made the getaway vehicle less conspicuous than on little used side
streets.

In New York, cheap handguns were selling from $15 to $70, he told the detec-   16
tives. Such weapons as shotguns or automatic rifles, Nick said, could be rented for
about $100 an hour.

Nick said he had been a holdup man since the age of 20 and had committed about   17
30 "jobs," but was uncertain of the exact number. The biggest robbery he had participated in netted a total of $8,000, and overall he got about $30,000 in his criminal activities.

Asked why he went back to robbing after his first arrest, Nick said: "I wanted   18
whisky, women and big autos. Like most who rob I was not socially accepted. Big
money elevates you above the people you think are looking down on you."

Short prison sentences, for first arrests, Nick asserted, probably do little to dis-   19
courage holdup men. "I see them laying up in jail and it doesn't make any difference," he said. "They just go ahead planning the next one in a different way."

During his "on-and-off" criminal career, Nick said he had never fired any of the   20
guns he carried.

After his one-hour appearance as guest lecturer, Nick, his face still covered by his   21
coat, was escorted out of the classroom back to his cell at an undisclosed prison.

1. Read the entire article more than once.

This direction is not as simple as it sounds. Because you want to identify
main ideas, you may underline what you regard as the key sentences on first
reading, and, from then on, look only at the "boiled-down" parts. But *don't
eliminate minor facts and interesting details too soon.* They do have a function in
the article, supporting and illuminating the central ideas. For example, the fact
that Nick chose to hide his face during and after his "lecture" hardly seems

worth underlining and, in fact, would never by itself be regarded as crucial. But taken together with some of Nick's remarks, that minor fact helps you to recognize a key point of the article: The robber's reliance on *anonymity* enables him to commit a successful crime; Nick may at some point wish to resume his profession despite his "retirement." Although you should always underline your key points, remember to reread and consider every part of the article as you prepare your summary.

2. Ask yourself why the article was written and published.

What does the newspaper want its readers to learn? A news article's purpose is frequently twofold—to describe an event and to suggest the event's significance—and so it is easy for you to confuse the *facts* being recorded with the underlying *reasons* for recording them. Here are two one-sentence summaries of the article that are both off the mark because they concentrate too heavily on the event:

> Nick, a convicted retired criminal, was guest speaker at a police seminar and told detectives how robbers pick their targets and make their getaways in New York.

> Nick, after committing thirty robberies, suggested to detectives some possible methods of thwarting future robberies.

Both writers seem too concerned with Nick's colorful history and the peculiarity of his helping the police at all. They ignore the significance of what Nick was actually saying. The second summary—by emphasizing the phrase "thwarting future robberies"—is misleading and almost contradicts the point of the article; in fact, Nick is really suggesting that the police will continue to be ineffectual.

A news article can also mislead you into thinking that a headline is a summary: the headline "Holdup Man Tells Detectives How to Do It" does not summarize the material in the article, but, because it is broad and vague, it "sounds" good. What, for example, is meant by the "it" of the headline—robbery or detection? What does Nick tell the detectives?

3. Look for repetitions of and variations on the same idea.

There is one concrete point that Selwyn Raab and his readers and the police and Nick himself are all interested in: *ways of preventing criminals from committing crimes.* Not only are we told again and again about Nick's contempt for the police, but we are also given his flat statement that only fear of imprisonment ("stiffer sentences") will discourage a hardened criminal.

A brief summary of this article, then, would mention *tougher sentencing as a way of preventing crime.* But, in addition, the theme of *the criminal's need for anonymity* ought, if possible, to be incorporated into a complete summary. In

Nick's opinion, his career has been relatively successful because he has managed to appear normal and blend into the crowd. The primary and secondary ideas can be joined in a summary like this one:

> Observing with contempt that the police have rarely been able to penetrate his "anonymous" disguise, Nick, the successful robber, argues that the presence of police will not deter most experienced criminals and that only "stiffer sentences" will prevent crime.

EXERCISE 6: SUMMARIZING AN ARTICLE

Carefully read "School Uniforms Growing in Favor in California" from the *New York Times*. Determine the article's purpose and pick out the arguments that the author emphasizes; then write a comprehensive summary in two or three sentences.

SCHOOL UNIFORMS GROWING IN FAVOR IN CALIFORNIA

Surrounded by a sea of white shirts and navy blue shorts in a local department store's new section devoted to school uniforms, 7-year-old Sean Smith dangled his feet from a shopping cart and proudly puffed out his chest to display the Tasmanian devil emblazoned on his favorite T-shirt.   1

"I want to wear my own clothes," he said as his mother pulled a white shirt from the rows that lay before him. "These clothes look weird. They're ugly."   2

Sean is out of luck. His public school district here, fed up with baggy jeans, oversized T-shirts, bandanas and other trappings of gang attire, has become the nation's first urban system requiring students to wear uniforms. And the new Long Beach policy, which applies to the 57,000 children in the district's elementary and middle schools, has now led the state to enact a law that encourages the adoption of similar codes by school boards elsewhere.   3

Nationwide Influence

Further, the influence of the Long Beach model does not stop at the state line. Around the country, other urban districts are closely watching.   4

Baltimore is already experimenting with school uniform requirements, as are Los Angeles and San Diego, notes Dick Van Der Laan, spokesman for the Long Beach United School District, who adds that he has also received calls from interested principals and school boards in New York City, Miami, El Paso and Seattle.   5

"We are really the prototype for this kind of thing," Mr. Van Der Laan said. "Every large city in the U.S. has been concerned about the gangs. Their clothes really are an unofficial uniform of intimidation."   6

The movement requiring more conventional kinds of uniforms—black or navy trousers or skirts, white shirts or blouses—began here five years ago, when the   7

Long Beach district gave principals the option of adopting such requirements at individual schools. Those who did so, the district says, soon found that their students were making better grades, were better behaved and were less frequently absent than before.

So nine months ago the district decided to make uniforms mandatory, effective this fall. The requirement now applies only to the elementary and middle schools, where parents' demand for it was greatest and where the district hopes to influence its youngest students, nipping their fancy for gang attire in the bud. But if the program proves effective, it may be extended to the Long Beach high schools.

8

Action by the State

The district's initiative spurred action by the California Legislature, which in mid-August passed a measure, signed into law by Gov. Pete Wilson last week, that sets out a procedure for school boards elsewhere in the state to adopt their own codes.

9

The hope is that the new law's provisions will help immunize the boards against civil liberties challenges. One of those provisions requires a school district to consult with parents, teachers and principals before adopting a uniform code. A second requires that parents be given six months' notice before any such code takes effect. And yet another gives parents the opportunity to opt out by demonstrating to the board a good reason why their children should not be required to wear uniforms.

10

Here in Long Beach, the precise look of the uniform at any given school is left largely to the principal, although the district's code explicitly allows students of either sex to wear shorts and polo shirts (in the colors designated by the school) as an alternative to trousers and dress shirts, or skirts and blouses. The code does not generally extend to jackets or other outerwear.

11

Because some parents have told the district that they cannot afford the $30 or $40 cost of a uniform, the school system is now working with retailers and public interest groups to assist low-income families so that no child will be without one. The district is also looking into the possibility of starting up a uniform recycling center where the trousers, shirts, shorts, blouses and skirts would be passed down from older to younger students.

12

Although most parents seem enthusiastic, not everyone embraces the code. The American Civil Liberties Union says that as an effort to combat gang intimidation, the program is "meaningless." One local lawyer whose child is a student in the district has sued the school system on the ground that the code restricts freedom of expression. And a few people are even pulling their children out of the district's schools.

13

George Simmons, who works at a local gas station, said he was now sending his thirteen-year-old sister, Shamera, to a school in nearby Bellflower. "Uniforms aren't going to solve anything," he said. "The gangs are still going to be there; they'll just wear baggy uniforms."

14

And Susan Kelsey, buying a uniform for her 13-year-old daughter at the Target department store here the other day, said that if all students wore uniforms, then the well-behaved children might not be able to so easily spot the troublemakers.

15

"Is it necessarily good for a kid not to be able to know a gang member on her own campus?" Mrs. Kelsey said. "I don't think so."

But the prevalent view is that uniforms will only <u>improve the classroom atmosphere</u>. "Children will hate this, of course, because it takes away from their individuality," said another shopper, Melanie Valsvig, accompanied by her daughter. "But it's time that they learned that school is for schoolwork."   16

And Valentino Le Veauf, who was shopping with his two sons, said: "There are no sagging jeans in my house. And I think dress codes will also help keep the gang thing out of the schools."   17

There is some evidence, most of it anecdotal, <u>that violent acts have fallen and grades risen in schools where uniforms have already been tried</u>. For instance, after Newcomb Academy, an elementary and middle school in the Long Beach district, opted for uniforms last year, disciplinary problems declined, A's and B's rose by 17 percent, and F's dropped by 9 percent, said Joseph Palumbo, the school's co-director. And the school now has the highest attendance rate of any in the district.   18

A survey by the school this year found that all its teachers and 80 percent of parents supported standardized student dress.   19

Already, many parents are asking that Long Beach extend its program to the high schools.   20

"It is certainly being discussed," said Mr. Van Der Laan, the district spokesman. "We have found that the most chilling effect on a student's individuality is not in wearing a uniform; it's being surrounded by other children in gang attire. Whether it's saggy baggies or red bandannas, it's intimidating."   21

Alma Licon, a 16-year-old high school student, said she and most of her friends would not object to giving up their baggy jeans, double-sized T-shirts and high-top sneakers with the woolly laces. Pointing to her sister, Malena, who proudly wore her school uniform and was shopping for a newer model, Ms. Licon said the uniform had helped keep her sister out of trouble.   22

"I think it's good for her," Ms. Licon said, looking down at her own baggy Levis. "Sometimes people mistake me for being in a gang, and I get harassed. But that doesn't happen to her."   23

Summarizing a Complex Essay

When you are asked to summarize a reading containing a number of complex and abstract ideas, a reading that may be disorganized and therefore difficult to comprehend and condense, *the best way to prepare for your summary is to isolate each important point and note it down in a list.*

Here are some guidelines for summarizing a complex essay:

1. The summary must be comprehensive.
2. The summary must be concise.
3. The summary must be coherent.
4. The summary must be independent.

Here is an essay by Bertrand Russell, followed by a preliminary list of notes, a statement of Russell's thesis, and the final summary. (The numbers in the margin are keyed to the preliminary list of notes on pp. 57–58.) Russell's essay is difficult, so be sure to read it slowly, and more than once. If you get confused at any point, try referring to the list of notes that follows; but be sure to *go back to the essay* after you have identified and understood each numbered point.

THE SOCIAL RESPONSIBILITY OF SCIENTISTS
Bertrand Russell

Science, ever since it first existed, has had important effects in matters that lie outside the purview of pure science. Men of science have differed as to their responsibility for such effects. Some have said that the function of the scientist in society is to supply knowledge, and that he need not concern himself with the use to which this knowledge is put. I do not think that this view is tenable, especially in our age. The scientist is also a citizen; and citizens who have any special skill have a public duty to see, as far as they can, that their skill is utilized in accordance with the public interest. Historically, the functions of the scientist in public life have generally been recognized. The Royal Society was founded by Charles II as an antidote to "fanaticism" which had plunged England into a long period of civil strife. The scientists of that time did not hesitate to speak out on public issues, such as religious toleration and the folly of prosecutions for witchcraft. But although science has, in various ways at various times, favored what may be called a humanitarian outlook, it has from the first had an intimate and sinister connection with war. Archimedes sold his skill to the Tyrant of Syracuse for use against the Romans; Leonardo secured a salary from the Duke of Milan for his skill in the art of fortification; and Galileo got employment under the Grand Duke of Tuscany because he could calculate the trajectories of projectiles. In the French Revolution the scientists who were not guillotined were set to making new explosives, but Lavoisier was not spared, because he was only discovering hydrogen which, in those days, was not a weapon of war. There have been some honorable exceptions to the subservience of scientists to warmongers. During the Crimean War the British government consulted Faraday as to the feasibility of attack by poisonous gases. Faraday replied that it was entirely feasible, but that it was inhuman and he would have nothing to do with it.

Modern democracy and modern methods of publicity have made the problem of affecting public opinion quite different from what it used to be. The knowledge that the public possesses on any important issue is derived from vast and powerful organizations: the press, radio, and, above all, television. The knowledge that governments possess is more limited. They are too busy to search out the facts for themselves, and consequently they know only what their underlings think good for them unless there is such a powerful movement in a different sense that politicians cannot ignore it. Facts which ought to guide the decisions of statesmen—for

instance, as to the possible lethal qualities of fallout—do not acquire their due importance if they remain buried in scientific journals. They acquire their due importance only when they become known to so many voters that they affect the course of the elections. In general, there is an opposition to widespread publicity   7
for such facts. This opposition springs from various sources, some sinister, some comparatively respectable. At the bottom of the moral scale there is the financial interest of the various industries connected with armaments. Then there are various effects of a somewhat thoughtless patriotism, which believes in secrecy and in what is called "toughness." But perhaps more important than either of these is the   8
unpleasantness of the facts, which makes the general public turn aside to pleasanter topics such as divorces and murders. The consequence is that what ought to be known widely throughout the general public will not be known unless great efforts are made by disinterested persons to see that the information reaches the minds and hearts of vast numbers of people. I do not think this work can be successfully accomplished except by the help of men of science. They, alone, can speak with   9
the authority that is necessary to combat the misleading statements of those scientists who have permitted themselves to become merchants of death. If disinterested scientists do not speak out, the others will succeed in conveying a distorted impression, not only to the public but also to the politicians.

It must be admitted that there are obstacles to individual action in our age   10
which did not exist at earlier times. Galileo could make his own telescope. But once when I was talking with a very famous astronomer he explained that the telescope upon which his work depended owed its existence to the benefaction of enormously rich men, and, if he had not stood well with them, his astronomical discoveries would have been impossible. More frequently, a scientist only acquires access to enormously expensive equipment if he stands well with the government of his country. He knows that if he adopts a rebellious attitude he and his family are likely to perish along with the rest of civilized mankind. It is a tragic dilemma, and I do not think that one should censure a man whatever his decision; but I do think—and I think men of science should realize—that unless something rather drastic is done under the leadership or through the inspiration of some part of the scientific world, the human race, like the Gadarene swine, will rush down a steep place to destruction in blind ignorance of the fate that scientific skill has prepared for it.

It is impossible in the modern world for a man of science to say with any honesty, "My business is to provide knowledge, and what use is made of the knowledge is not my responsibility." The knowledge that a man of science provides may fall into the hands of men or institutions devoted to utterly unworthy objects. I do not suggest that a man of science, or even a large body of men of science, can altogether prevent this, but they can diminish the magnitude of the evil.

There is another direction in which men of science can attempt to provide leadership. They can suggest and urge in many ways the value of those branches of science of which the important and practical uses are beneficial and not harmful.   11

Consider what might be done if the money at present spent on armaments were spent on increasing and distributing the food supply of the world and diminishing the population pressure. In a few decades, poverty and malnutrition, which now afflict more than half the population of the globe, could be ended. But at present almost all the governments of great states consider that it is better to spend money on killing foreigners than on keeping their own subjects alive. Possibilities of a hopeful sort in whatever field can best be worked out and stated authoritatively by men of science; and, since they can do this work better than others, it is part of their duty to do it.

As the world becomes more technically unified, life in an ivory tower becomes increasingly impossible. Not only so; the man who stands out against the powerful organizations which control most of human activity is apt to find himself no longer in the ivory tower, with a wide outlook over a sunny landscape, but in the dark and subterranean dungeon upon which the ivory tower was erected. To risk such a habitation demands courage. It will not be necessary to inhabit the dungeon if there are many who are willing to risk it, for everybody knows that the modern world depends upon scientists, and, if they are insistent, they must be listened to. We have it in our power to make a good world; and, therefore, with whatever labor and risk, we must make it.

12

First Stage: List of Notes and Establishing a Thesis

1. Should scientists try to influence the way their discoveries are used?

2. One point of view: the scientist's role is to make the discovery; what happens afterward is not his concern.

3. Russell's point of view: scientists are like any other knowledgeable and public-spirited people; they must make sure that the products of their knowledge work for, not against, society.

4. In the past, some scientists have made public their views on controversial issues like freedom of religion; others have been servants of the war machine.

5. The power to inform and influence the public is now controlled by the news media.

6. Government officials are too busy to be well informed; subordinates feed them only enough information to get them reelected.

7. It is in the interests of various groups, ranging from weapons makers to patriots, to limit the amount of scientific information that the public receives.

8. The public is reluctant to listen to distasteful news.

9. Since the public deserves to hear the truth, scientists, who are respected for their knowledge and who belong to no party or faction, ought to do more to provide the public with information about the potentially lethal consequences of their discoveries. By doing so, they will correct the distortions of those scientists who have allied themselves with warmongers.

10. It is very difficult for scientists to speak out since they depend on government and business interests to finance their work.

11. While scientists cannot entirely stop others from using some of their discoveries for antisocial purposes, they can support other, more constructive kinds of research.

12. Speaking out is worth the risk of incurring the displeasure of powerful people; since the work of scientists is so vital, the risk isn't too great, especially if they act together.

Russell's Thesis: Contrary to the self-interested arguments of many scientists and other groups, scientists have a social responsibility to make sure that their work is used for, not against, the benefit of humanity.

Second Stage: Summary

Some scientists, as well as other groups, consider that they need not influence the way in which their discoveries are used. However, Bertrand Russell, in "The Social Responsibility of Scientists," believes that scientists have a responsibility to make sure that their work is used for, not against, the benefit of humanity. In modern times, he argues, it has been especially difficult for concerned scientists to speak out because many powerful groups prefer to limit and distort what the public is told, because government officials are too busy to be thoroughly informed, because scientists depend on the financial support of business and government, and because the public itself is reluctant to hear distasteful news. Nevertheless, Russell maintains that scientists have the knowledge and the prestige to command public attention, and their work is too vital for their voices to be suppressed. If they act together, they can warn us if their work is likely to be used for an antisocial purpose and, at least, they can propose less destructive alternatives.

This summary of Russell's essay is not a simple compilation of phrases taken from the text, nor a collection of topic sentences, one from each paragraph.

Rather, it is a clear, coherent, and unified summary of Russell's ideas, expressed in the writer's own voice and words.

A *framework* is immediately established in the first two sentences of the summary, which present *the two alternative views of the scientist's responsibility*. The next sentence, which describes the four obstacles to scientific freedom of speech, illustrates the rearrangement of ideas that is characteristic of summary. While reviewing the list of notes, the summarizer has noticed that points 6, 7, 8, and 10 each refers to a different way in which scientific truth is often suppressed; she has therefore brought them together and lined them up in a parallel construction based on the repeated word "because." Finally, the last two sentences contain *a restatement of Russell's thesis* and point out that the obstacles to action are not as formidable as they seem.

Notice that the Russell summary excludes points 1, 4, and 5 on the list of notes: point 1 is included in the presentation of points 2 and 3; point 4 is an example, one that is not essential to an understanding of the essay; and point 5 is not directly related to Russell's argument.

In summarizing Russell's essay, it would not be acceptable to include extraneous points, such as the dangers of making scientific secrets public, for that would be arguing with Russell. Such ideas should be reserved for a full-length

---

Guidelines for Summarizing a Complex Essay

1. *The summary must be comprehensive.* You should review all the notes on your list, and include in your summary all those ideas that are essential to the author's development of the thesis.

2. *The summary must be concise.* Eliminate repetitions in your list, even if the author restates the same points. Your summary should be considerably shorter than the source.

3. *The summary must be coherent.* It should make sense as a paragraph in its own right; it should not be taken directly from your list of notes and sound like a list of sentences that happen to be strung together in a paragraph format.

4. *The summary must be independent.* You are not being asked to imitate or identify yourself with the author about whom you are writing. On the contrary, you are expected to maintain your own voice throughout the summary. Even as you are jotting down your list of notes, you should try to use your own words. Nevertheless, while you want to make it clear that *you* are writing the summary, you should be careful not to create any misrepresentation or distortion by introducing comments or criticisms of your own. (Such distortion is most likely to occur when you strongly disagree with the material that you are summarizing.) You must make it clear to your reader when you are summarizing directly from the text and when you are commenting on, inferring from, or explaining what is being summarized.

essay whose purpose is to develop an argument of your own, not just to summarize Russell's. Within limits, however, it is acceptable to go beyond point-by-point summary, to *suggest the author's implied intention,* and, in a sense, to *interpret the work's meaning for your reader.* You might state, for example, that ours is an age that encourages interdependence and discourages independent action. *Such an interpretation would have to be supported by evidence from the reading.* While Russell does not say so specifically, in so many words, the assertion about interdependence is certainly substantiated by the material in the last two paragraphs.

ASSIGNMENT 1: SUMMARIZING AN ESSAY

Summarize one of the following two passages. Before you begin your summary (on your second reading), underline and annotate key ideas and arguments, and make a preliminary list of points.

THE CASE AGAINST NATURE
from *A Moment on Earth*
Gregg Easterbrook

In the year 1992 a graphite tube ruptured inside a Chernobyl-type reactor vessel at the Leningradskaya nuclear plant near Saint Petersburg, releasing some radioactive gas. The leak measured about 0.2 roentgens immediately downwind of the plant, according to the International Atomic Energy Agency. This is about one-fifth the radiation of a chest X-ray. The accident was banner headline news internationally. Four months later the heads of state of the G-7 nations pledged $700 million in emergency aid to former Eastern bloc countries to improve reactor safety.   1

Also in 1992 a tsunami struck the Pacific coast of Nicaragua, killing an estimated 2,500 people. When the wave reached the Nicaraguan shoreline it was about 65 feet tall and possessed of enough energy to move 1,000 yards inland, obliterating everything in its path. The deaths caused were sudden and horrible. Many peasants must have died trying desperately to cling to their children as waters strong enough to shatter concrete ripped apart all shelter. In addition to the loss of human life the ecology at the impact area was essentially wiped clean. The tsunami merited a blip box in the news-update sections of newspapers. Later that year another tsunami hit Indonesia, killing an estimated 1,000 people and causing extensive environmental destruction. This event also made no impression on the world's consciousness.   2

There are clear reasons to worry about nuclear power plants, especially those of the ill-designed Chernobyl class. Sixteen of these plumber's nightmares continue to make power in the former Eastern bloc: Investments in their safe operation represent money well spent. It is also sad but indubitable that reactors proximate to white Europeans are of greater concern to Western leaders and editors than any force imperiling the brown masses of the developing world. But the disparity in   3 reaction to these two categories of 1992 stories—an inconsequential artificial environmental event harming no one is widely viewed as a shocking horror, while natural environmental events killing thousands and leaving behind vast swaths of devastation are greeted with a collective ho-hum—reveals much about how human beings perceive the living world.

Today environmental problems caused by people are considered a maximum-priority concern, while environmental problems caused by nature are simply acts of God. This last is a curious phrase if ever there was one. It suggests that though God declines to intercede on Earth to prevent the sufferings and injustices of the world, the Maker does regularly act to hurl disasters at the innocent. Most people who use the figure of speech "act of God" do not, of course, believe that God wills the occurrence of tidal waves and similar calamities. They believe such things happen for no reason at all. In a limited sense, that will always be the best explanation. But somehow the popular understanding has come to hold that naturally occurring damage to the ecology does not count as an environmental problem: It's just something that happens. Only men and women cause environmental problems. Which events of the year 1992 were more likely to be troubling to nature, the gas leak at Saint Petersburg or the tsunamis at Nicaragua and Indonesia?

In order to highlight the transgressions of people, in contemporary environmental thought nature is depicted as a utopia. An occasional environmental slogan is "Back to Eden." This motto implies that if only humankind ceased its meddling the living world would revert to a previous condition of unlimited abundance and general bliss. Who's kidding who? The notion that nature absent man would be an Eden doubtless appeals to the fund-raising imperatives of environmental lobbies, and to modern humankind's inner need for self-opprobrium. But it is certain nature does not see itself as an Eden.

It is not inconsistent to assert that nature is learned and inspirational and also riven with faults. In a bureaucracy as monumental as the entire living world, failings are inevitable. People or institutions can be sublime at many levels yet flawed at others. Democracy is the best known form of government, but nobody pretends it does not have maddening faults. Wine is the most wonderful beverage; it's also full of calories and causes harm ranging from headaches to chronic degenerative illness. Shakespeare was a superb writer; he also penned plays and sonnets that fell to the ground with a loud clunk. And so on.

"Nature does not know best," said René Dubos, a pioneer of modern environmental thinking. Dubos, who died in 1982, was an advocate of wetlands conservation and originated the slogan "Think globally, act locally." He composed many works fiercely critical of human ecological abuses. But Dubos was also critical of nature. Dubos thought many natural systems wasteful or plagued by shortcomings. For example, he thought species such as deer that exhibit cycles of overpopulation and die-off demonstrate nature can be just as immoderate as humanity. Dubos felt veneration of nature a foolhardy distraction.

Because Dubos was critical of nature, today many in the environmental movement speak of him as having been some kind of double agent. A custom is developing in which saints of environmentalism are reclassified as demons if they criticize nature or fail to be adequately frenetic in condemnation of people. James Lovelock, once the leading science figure to environmentalists, became persona non grata when he began to say the biosphere was so resilient not even nuclear war could destroy it. The toxicologist Bruce Ames, a hero to environmentalists in the 1970s when he proved the fire retardant Tris carcinogenic, is now intensely detested because his last 20 years of research convinced him naturally occurring food-chain substances are more dangerous than additives or pesticide residues. Richard Doll, a British epidemiologist who established the link between cigarette smoking and lung cancer, was for a time an angelic figure to environmentalists. Now he's Lucifer incarnate, because his last two decades of research weigh against the notion that synthetic toxics in the environment are a leading cancer cause. Another former environmental hero whose name has been slipped down the memory hole is the oceanographer Roger Revelle, founder of modern greenhouse science. In his book *Earth in the Balance,* Vice President Al Gore cited Revelle as the great tutor who convinced him global warming was a threat of unspeakable urgency. But Revelle himself did not describe the greenhouse effect in the apocalyptic terms favored by Gore. Before his 1991 death, Revelle cautioned against greenhouse alarmism. Gore doesn't talk about Revelle any longer.

One ecological orthodoxy that has arisen in recent years is the notion that since human involvement with nature is invariably negative, the only constructive relationship people can establish regarding the biosphere is to leave it alone. There are times and places when people ought to leave nature alone: partly to preserve, partly to acknowledge our poor understanding of how the environment operates. A principle of wisdom holds: We don't know what we don't know. Not only is human understanding of the environment rudimentary but we don't yet know enough to guess where the worst gaps in our knowledge fall. Until such time as we do, people should interfere with the environment as little as possible.   9

But if people leave parts of the environment alone, we can be sure nature will not. Nature will keep changing, not in some pointless eternal vacillation but seeking refinement. Dubos believed that nature was engaged in a long-term undertaking of self-improvement and thought human beings might be able to assist nature. Before turning to the idea of people helping nature, let's review the case against the environment. It may be summarized in these words: People should not worry that they will destroy nature. It is more likely nature will destroy us.   10

Green sentiment currently holds that nature ought to be revered because natural arrangements are metaphysically superior to their artificial counterparts. There are many reasons to love nature. This is not one of them.   11

Physically the natural world is magnificent compared to most human concoctions. But metaphysically? It is easy for humans to impute sanctity to the natural scheme, since we sit at the pinnacle of the food chain. No species preys on us, no organisms save diseases challenge us. But to those of Earth's creatures that live to be chased and eaten, it is doubtful the natural scheme suggests Eden. What does   12 an antelope experience, dying in terror and agony as it is gored by a tiger—blissful oneness with the spheres? Nature may shrug at this, considering cruel death an inevitability of a biological system. Perhaps people should respect such an order. We should not offer it blind allegiance.

Nature may be a place of transcendence, but it is also a domain of danger. Danger may take the form of large-scale natural assaults such as asteroid strikes, ice ages, and eras of global volcanism. What might be called everyday natural badness can be as distressing. Consider a representative end of life under the natural scheme. Often in subarctic regions migrating caribou drown in large groups when they ford rivers that were safe to cross the year before but now are not, the water volumes and speed of wild rivers varying unpredictably. Should you think nature absent man is utopia, try to imagine drowning in a roaring subarctic river. You are seized with panic as icy water slops into your lungs. You flail helplessly, the world falling away under your feet. This is not some peaceful end to a gentle, contented cycle of birth and renewal. This is a horror. 13

As the animal expert Vicky Hearne has written, "The wild is not all that frolicsome a location." Hearne has noted that among wild lion cubs of Africa, 75 percent die before reaching their second year of life. This high level of mortality is what happens to the fiercest of predators—imagine what happens lower on the food chain. A statistic of significance to the debate on human population has been cited by the zoologist Ernest Mayr: In the wild on average only two of any mammal's offspring ever themselves reproduce. To people, this figure may suggest that population stability attained by replacement fertility rates would be in keeping with balancing mechanisms of nature. To animals that may bear dozens of offspring of which but two exist long enough to reproduce, this figure suggests the extreme cruelty of the natural world. Next time you coo over a litter of domesticated puppies whose secure lives are assured, reflect that if the litter were born in the cold and hungry wild, nearly all the pups would be dead in fairly short order. 14

Environmentalism has not come to terms with the inherent horribleness of many natural structures, considering recognition of this point to be poor public relations. For instance the Norwegian philosopher Arne Naess, inventor of the phrase "deep ecology," in his 1989 book *Ecology, Community and Lifestyle* danced around the fact that much of the natural order is based on violent death. "The ecological viewpoint presupposes acceptance of the fact that big fish eat small," Naess wrote. Deep ecologists are supposed to believe that in moral value human beings are the same as animals: no better or worse, just another creature. So if it's okay for animals to kill each other is it okay for people to kill each other? Naess waffles: "It is against my intuition of unity to say 'I can kill you because I am more valuable,' but not against that intuition to say 'I will kill you because I am hungry.'" Then would Naess object if a poor man who was hungry killed Naess to take his wallet? Because orthodox environmentalists feel they must pretend that there is nothing—not the slightest little thing—wrong with nature, they can easily be trapped, as Naess trapped himself, into declaring that it's okey-dokey to kill to eat. 15

Deep ecology can go even further than that, at its extreme asserting people are   16
no more valuable than rocks. For a time after its founding in the mid-1960s the
American wing of the deep ecology movement, led by Bill Sessions, a professor at
Humboldt State University in northern California, said it advocated "biocentrism,"
or the importance of life above technology. Believe it or not the term biocentrism
was attacked in politically correct ecological writing, as it dares imply that living
things are more important than inanimate objects. Today some deep ecologists say
they endorse "ecocentrism," which purports to grant rocks and plains the same
ethical significance as living things. "Let the river live!" is a phrase now found in
some deep ecology tracts.

So it's not only fine for a tiger to gore an antelope and a hungry robber to gun   17
down a passerby, it's fine for all these people and animals to drown in a river since
the river is only expressing its right to flow. If the question of whether it is bad
to be killed confounds environmental philosophers, small wonder they have such
trouble coming to grips with the practical flaws in nature.

Now let's expand the indictment against the environment. Nature makes pollu-   18
tants, poisons, and suffering on a scale so far unapproached by men and women except during periods of warfare.

For example, if the greenhouse gas carbon dioxide is considered a pollutant, as   19
environmentalists say it should be, then nature emits an estimated 200 billion tons
of this pollutant annually, versus a human-caused emission total of about seven billion tons per year. Nature makes huge quantities of the precursor chemicals for
acid rain. The 1991 eruption of Mount Pinatubo alone released an estimated 60
percent more sulfur dioxide, the primary cause of acid rain, than all United States
emissions that year. Lesser eruptions, and the many volcanos that release gases
without erupting, add to annual natural output of acid-rain chemicals. Natural
processes, mainly the photochemistry of tree leaves, place into the air volumes of
volatile organic chemicals, the same class of substances that evaporate from petro-
leum and help form smog. Though Ronald Reagan was wrong to say that trees cause
more air pollution than cars, his concept was not entirely fallacious. Pristine forest
areas often exhibit palls of natural smog caused by tree emissions interacting with
sunlight. Thomas Jefferson's beloved Blue Ridge Mountains are so named because
even in preindustrial times they often were shrouded in a bluish haze.

Nature generates toxins, venoms, carcinogens, and other objectionable sub-   20
stances in far larger quantities than do people, even considering the daunting output of man's petrochemical complexes. Current research is demonstrating that a
significant percentage of plants make dangerous compounds for defense against environmental competitors; and that since the living quantity of plants is substantially
greater than that of fauna, plants may be the principal toxin factories of the world.
Recently an important topic of public discourse has been the need to preserve
rainforests, in part so that drug companies can prospect for pharmaceuticals. Rain-
forest preservation is a good idea. But why do pharmaceutical companies find rain-
forest plants of such interest? Because they are rich in natural toxins that kill living
cells—what many medications, especially cancer drugs, are asked to do.

In recent years researchers have begun to understand that over eons of evolutionary time, plants have acquired sophisticated chemical defenses against being munched by animals and insects, including in some cases active "immune responses" that dispense toxins when competitors arrive. For instance researchers have found that when some pines are attacked by mountain pine beetles, the trees direct to the affected bark chemicals called terpenes that make pine beetles ill. Potatoes and tomatoes make toxins that interfere with the digestive systems of their perennial competitors, the caterpillar. When the coyote tobacco plant is nibbled on, its "immune system" directs an increase in nicotine, a powerful toxin, to the affected leaves. 21

The discovery that plants manufacture far more toxins than once assumed has led toxicologists such as Ames and Lois Gold, both of the University of California at Berkeley, to estimate that the typical American diet contains 10,000 times more naturally occurring carcinogens than those of the synthetic variety. Natural toxins comprise five to ten percent of most plants by dry weight, Ames and Gold think. Thus natural toxins are "by far the main source of toxic chemicals ingested by humans," Ames says. 22

People and animals must in turn have evolved resistance to natural carcinogens or their ancestors would have keeled over from consuming plants long ago. If people and animals carry some natural resistance to toxins, this hardly means consuming chemicals has no cost, any more than people who have natural resistance to certain diseases can be assured they will never get sick. But here the finger of badness points at nature more than people. For example, it may eventually be shown that natural chemicals are a leading cause of cancer. After all, if natural toxins outnumber the synthetic variety 10,000 to 1 in the typical diet, then nature is a more likely cancer cause than synthetics. In turn, if natural carcinogens in foodstuffs are an important cancer cause, the way to get rid of them would be through genetic engineering, a technology environmentalists oppose. 23

Next: Which would you say causes more deaths per year, industrial accidents or natural disasters? The answer is nature by a substantial margin. Theodore Glickman, Dominic Golding, and Emily Silverman, researchers at Resources for the Future, a Washington, D.C., think tank, compared significant natural disasters to significant industrial deaths for the postwar period. The study concentrated on immediate deaths, not long-term health degradation. The authors found that on average natural badness kills 55,786 people per year worldwide, while industrial accidents kill 356 people annually. Natural badness took forms such as these: 700,000 dead in a 1976 earthquake in China; perhaps 500,000 dead in a 1970 cyclone in Bangladesh; another 110,000 dead in a 1948 earthquake in the former Soviet Union; another 57,000 dead in a 1949 flood in China; at least 100,000 dead in a 1991 cyclone in Bangladesh. Industrial accidents through this same period often have been frightful, taking forms such as the death of about 4,100 innocents at Bhopal in 1984 or the loss of an estimated 2,700 lives in a 1982 fuel-truck explosion in a mountain tunnel in Afghanistan. All told, nature has consistently outdone man in generation of noncombat misfortune. 24

Environmental orthodoxy responds to figures like the ones above by saying that   25
if the human population were lower there would be fewer deaths in natural disasters; that far too many people live in dangerous places like the coastal plain of
Bangladesh, where the likelihood of natural badness from cyclones is high, or in the
fault zone of California, where the natural threat of earthquakes is high. Such points
contain measures of truth but are deceptive, skipping over the effects of natural
disasters on the nonhuman ecology—effects that would be awful whether people
existed or not. During cyclones and similar natural badness there is tremendous
loss of plant and animal life, plus destruction of the ecosphere generally. Environmentalists sometimes fudge this counterpoint by saying that the ecosphere usually
recovers rapidly from catastrophic "acts of God." Usually that is the case. But if the
environment routinely recovers from cyclones and tidal waves, events substantially
more destructive than human action, why is it that we are in panic mode regarding
human ecological impacts? And if there were fewer people, fewer would die in any
natural disaster. But if there were fewer snow leopards or sandhill cranes fewer of
them would die at nature's hand as well. Has anyone ever heard an environmental-
ist argue that therefore there are too many animals?

Meanwhile the occupation of dangerous areas such as the coastal plain of   26
Bangladesh usually occurs out of desperation on the part of the impoverished. That
genus *Homo* has built a society in which many millions of the impoverished have no
choice but to live in places vulnerable to disaster is an inculpation of human social
institutions, but is not out of accord with the behavior patterns of nature. Countless species populate ecological niches where exposure to natural badness is above
the norm. For instance, every plant and animal that lives near an active volcano is
crazy from a detached point of view. Nature, being flawed, puts creatures in such
places nonetheless.

WACO AND RELIGIOUS FREEDOM IN AMERICA
from *Why Waco?*

James D. Tabor and Eugene V. Gallagher

The intensity of commitment demanded by some religious groups, particularly   1
when it results in purportedly strange forms of behavior, disturbs many Americans.
We suspect that the common understanding of "cults" as dangerous to both individuals and society is indeed accurate but not for the reasons usually given. The
crucial issue is not the enormous power of a leader who exercises total control
over passive followers. Such groups are threatening because they offer, sometimes
with relentless aggressiveness, another way of seeing and being. Their very existence calls into question, as it is meant to do, what we hold most important and
what our society values above anything else. Serious belief in the imminent end of
the world, for example, challenges the prevailing secular view of time as stretching

into an indefinite future and drastically foreshortens the period in which we may forge an identity, make our place in the world, and shape our lives in conformity with a hoped-for future. Committed adoption of unconventional living arrangements similarly challenges our broad acceptance of the nuclear family as the most important and appropriate social institution for inculcating and preserving our central social values. Insistence that families are formed by affiliation and commitment, rather than by biology, introduces a disruptive and disturbing new set of connections and priorities that casts doubt on what many see as the eternal verities of the relationships between parents and children. Participation in unorthodox sexual relationships seriously tests our notions of intimacy, carnality, and passion. Accepting that a human prophet's communication represents an irresistible divine command supplants cherished notions of free will by a disturbing call to a higher obedience.

Cults are "dangerous" in American society, not merely for what they might do to an unfortunate few, but for what they actually do to an uneasy many. Cults offer alternatives, not on matters of superficial importance, but on what most intimately and ultimately concerns us. Cults explicitly endeavor to get us to examine what we care most about and to consider unsparingly whether we are satisfied with our own beliefs and commitments and with the state of the world. All the statistical evidence about membership in new and unconventional religious movements shows that they are rarely successful in inspiring many dramatic conversions. The widespread fear of cults and the diligent opposition to them, however, suggest that they are amazingly successful in raising fundamental questions about human life. Few want to confront directly any challenges to the status quo. It is easier to condemn the messenger than to take the implications of the message seriously, either on a personal or societal level. Thus the eagerness to condemn cults masks an unwillingness to confront ourselves and to question our society.

Opponents of "cults" spend much of their time keeping tabs on suspicious groups, answering queries from anxious relatives or friends, producing and disseminating literature in support of their position, and holding and attending meetings. But their efforts impinge most directly and intimately on the groups they oppose in the process of deprogramming. . . . That practice has long been passionately contested, and even when it is euphemistically labeled "exit counseling," the "cult" member is seen as under the control of external forces. According to its proponents, only intervention by skilled diagnosticians can return the victim to normality. Such attempts depend on a series of revealing assumptions that are crucial to the general anticult position. The fundamental premise is expressed most directly by David J. Bardin, the Washington counsel for both the American Family Foundation and CAN, in a pamphlet produced by the latter organization to mark the first anniversary of the fire at Mount Carmel and to answer critics of the anticult position. He voices an unshakable conviction that "mind control exists." Everything follows from that assertion. From that perspective, people are drawn into "cults" by mysterious powers that they cannot effectively resist. Their perceptions are manipulated and their actions controlled by an overwhelmingly powerful leader. They are,

2

3

in effect, programmed, just as a computer is, to perform certain tasks. The only way to get them out of the group is to erase the program. Only then, proponents of deprogramming claim, will former members be able to think and act for themselves. However, its advocates consistently refuse to follow the logic of their position to its conclusion and to acknowledge that former members of "cults" will need to be *reprogrammed* with a different and more acceptable program in order to function successfully after leaving their group. In the anticultists' view "cults" rigorously control the formation of their members' identities at the explicit direction of the leader. But outside the group, they imagine, former members are remarkably free to fashion themselves in any way they wish. Programming is limited to the activity of "cults," and the pressures to conform that typify life within the "cult" are apparently inoperative outside it. Clearly, this approach is naive and simplistic about the controls and pressures that exist outside the "cult." None of us is completely independent; no one is free from powerful forces of influence and persuasion, whether parental, conventionally religious, or political. . . .

In the end, cultbusters send confusing messages about the dimensions of the "cult" problem, the power of the "cult" leader, and the nature of the audience for "cults." The anticult position is founded on a logical contradiction. Either the attraction of "cults" is significantly weaker than their opponents would have the American public believe, or the willpower, commitment, and purpose of the general populace is significantly stronger. The opponents of "cults" bring to their discussion of the process of affiliation a short-circuited logic that signals something else is going on just out of sight. The hyperbole and exaggeration, which are the hallmarks of their argumentative styles, lend an edge of desperation to their pleadings. "Cults" come to represent fundamental challenges to their adversaries' view of the world and way of life, mirroring the cultbusters' anxieties about loss of control and acceptance.

4

Anticult activists see themselves as involved in a battle for the heart and soul of America. Ironically, the groups they oppose often see themselves in the same way though they are more likely to focus on a chosen few, such as the 144,000 whom [David] Koresh believed would be initially saved. The anticultists ruefully observe a society in which beliefs are quickly abandoned in favor of a new or exotic message presented with sufficient guile and flair. In that view, whatever success "cults" achieve testifies to the inherent weaknesses of contemporary American society, rather than to the personal situations of those who are attracted to such groups. On that point as well, cultbusters and cult members agree. Cults strive to provoke us to an unsparing examination of both self and society; they anticipate that we will find both wanting; and they claim to offer remedies for our individual and social problems. Cults offer a vision of an alternative society and a plan for implementing it. The anticult activists see a nation in which the necessary social support for traditional values no longer exists, and they see new and unconventional religions capitalizing on that weakness. In this view, "cults" appear a symptom, not a cause, a lamentable indication of the deterioration of a valued way of life.

5

Many new and unconventional religious movements offer a similar diagnosis of   6
life in America today. They see inattention to spiritual matters, moral laxity, a weak-
ening of communal ties, a failure to uphold biblical standards, and any number of
other problems, and they offer their own solutions. Their innovative remedies often derive from their perception that they enjoy the privilege of divine revelation;
and they typically demand a strong and uncompromising response.

Under the surface of the anticult position there is a pervasive dissatisfaction with   7
the prevailing ethos of contemporary American society, which has made the supposed proliferation of "cults" possible. The anticultists' vigorous defense of traditional religion, the nuclear family, personal autonomy, and other core values against
the challenge of the "cults" allows them to locate the vexing problems of Americans and American society outside themselves in a dangerous and alien "other."
Cults *are* alien in many ways. In some cases, they introduce foreign beliefs and practices into American society; but in others, such as the Branch Davidians, they give
distinctively different interpretations to common religious elements such as the
biblical book of Revelation. However, cultbusters see "cults" as alien whatever their
place of origin because they manifest psychological instability, moral evil, religious
error, or any combination of the three. By portraying "cults" as the "other," cultbusters absolve themselves of any complicity in the problems they discuss.

Since "cults" represent an invasive presence, rather than an acceptable variation   8
from the norm, anyone who rejects the cultbusters' values by participating in a
"cult" is asserted to have acted under external compulsion, rather than as a result
of a careful, rational choice. Such a view contrasts markedly to the democratic
ideal of our society as an arena for competing and conflicting ideas, thriving on debate, differences, and diversity. In such a society, persuasiveness is valued, and minority views are welcomed, often proving their enduring value to the majority. To
admit that one may join a new or unconventional religious group for "good" reasons leaves one's own choices and decisions open to evaluation and criticism. The
anticult polemicists fend off such critique by denying that anyone in his or her "right
mind" would join a "cult." Moreover, because affiliation is itself evidence of aber-
rant behavior, cultbusters can easily dismiss the diagnoses of American society that
such groups offer and the remedies that they propose. They act as if they have
nothing to learn and much to fear from the intruder. Their general response to
"cults" is exemplified by the unheeding responses that government officials made
to Koresh's religious pronouncements during the siege at Mount Carmel. When
Koresh spoke *his* truth, they heard only "Bible babble." Where the Branch Davidians saw a religious community prepared for the end of the world, the authorities
saw an armed compound full of "hostages."

The cultbusters' opposition to new and unconventional religious groups depends   9
not only on an image of a passive self but also on an image of a broadly *uniform society* whose values and ethical codes are commonly agreed upon. They see an American consensus and claim to speak for it. In their view, the uniformity of social values
guarantees the integrity of the family, harmonious interpersonal relations, and overall

social stability. Despite their emphasis on common values, however, cultbusters see their society as extremely fragile and besieged from without. Cult members also see the problems and weaknesses in contemporary American society, but they do not see the remedy in espousing a vaguely defined uniform set of core values without any secure links to a specific social group. Instead, they locate the remedy in the creation of an *ideal society,* a select voluntary association founded on intense commitment to explicit religious values. Their vision is often exclusive; it offers a path toward perfection for those willing to pursue it. That exclusivity, however, allows them to sharpen their critique of American society. Cults typically offer a closed system of internally consistent doctrine, such as Koresh's biblical interpretation, that is passionately espoused by the members of the elect and contributes to their distinctive individual and social identities. The exclusivity, passion, and sheer differentness that mark cult life have the potential to create considerable friction between members of the group and those outside. The Mount Carmel community maintained a sometimes uneasy, often bemused, and generally comfortable peace with its neighbors over the course of its sixty-year history. The introduction of actors who had neither personal nor doctrinal familiarity with the Branch Davidians was a scenario that presaged conflict.

Opposition to so-called cults enables many Americans to condemn much of what   10
they find wrong in their society by attributing it to the influence of an alien "other." That strategy allows opponents to draw clear and sharp lines between right and wrong, good and evil, and legitimate and illegitimate religion. It is based from the outset, however, on an unexamined reaction that presumes that one's own position is self-evidently true and unassailable. In that sense it represents a flight from self-examination, a refusal to think hard about one's own values and commitments, and an authoritarian willingness to impose one's views on others. It is a form of intellectual, spiritual, and social isolationism that denies the possibility of learning anything new or valuable from those significantly different from oneself. When such an attitude is adopted in defense of the fundamental values of American society, as it is by the cultbusters, it is out of tune with the demands of a democratic society, particularly one that is rapidly becoming more diverse. It provides constricting and oppressive answers to serious questions about how Americans should deal with any minority groups, however they are defined. At the same time, it raises the issue of whether those whose beliefs or way of life is unconventional should receive the same protection of the law that other minority groups enjoy. In sum, the cultbusters' appeal to a supposed consensus of values expresses a nostalgia for a homogeneous society that never existed, which can have pernicious effects.

Government action against new or unorthodox religious groups, advocated by   11
some anticult workers, bodes ill not only for such movements but also for everyone in our society. It arrogates to the state a power that all must oppose and depends on a very restricted reading of the constitutional guarantee of free exercise of religion. New and unconventional religions provide some of the most vivid examples of nay-saying in contemporary American society. To enlist the state in an effort to con-

trol or eradicate such groups is to deprive our common life of an invigorating diversity, as well as to sanction its immense power to enforce conformity. The anticult activists' claim to support the fundamental values of American democratic society is undermined by their willingness to suppress the exercise of religious freedom and, moreover, to engage the state in that campaign. If the purpose of the First Amendment is to protect religions from the state, rather than the state from religion, there is no constitutional basis for enlisting the power of the state in the campaign against so-called cults. That does not mean that the state is impotent to punish illegal acts done in the name of religion, but that the intervention must be carried out through normal legal channels. A wholesale government crusade against "destructive cults," such as that championed after Waco, is illegitimate and unconstitutional.

Much of the polemic against "cults" in America has taken an inappropriate form   12
based on a constricted view of human abilities of self-determination, an intolerant attitude toward differences in belief and practice, and an inflated expectation of the role of the government. Also, despite the anticultists' success in shaping the negative public attitude toward "cults," their efforts to deter individuals from pursuing their chosen religious path has been surprisingly ineffective. The efforts of cult-busters can be depreciated on the basis of their own testimony. For all the small "victories" that they can count, they admit that the enemy is far from conquered. The reasons are found both in the weakness of the anticult position and in the promise of personal and social transformation held out by new and unconventional religious groups. How often that promise has actually been fulfilled is another question.

The body counts alone at Jonestown and Mount Carmel should give anyone   13
pause. In addition, there are countless atrocity stories associated with so-called cults: tales of physical and psychological suffering, wasted opportunities and squandered fortunes, exploitation, and disillusionment. Even if the anticult forces have exaggerated the prevalence and misdiagnosed the cause of such experiences, they should not be ignored. There is no doubt that some people involved with new or unconventional religions suffer harm. Yet, so do many individuals who make personal choices outside the purview of the so-called cult. The important question is whether there is something *characteristic* about a given group that can *incontrovertibly* be shown to cause harm to its members or to others. Such a finding might provide justifiable cause for concern or even appropriate legal action against an entire group. The government prosecutor's assertion that Koresh preached a "theology of death" and his likening Koresh to Hitler and Stalin was an attempt to provide such a rationale for action against the Branch Davidians. But the question of the fundamental character of the whole religious group cannot be described by such facile comparisons.

In most instances, we believe, the damage attributed to "destructive cults" is not   14
only peripheral to their avowed purposes but is also almost totally subjective. Common living conditions at the Mount Carmel center were often substandard and never luxurious; meals were simple at best; some of the work was physically

draining, and the marathon Bible study sessions were undeniably arduous. Yet, those facts of Branch Davidian life were accepted and sometimes joyfully embraced by the faithful. Such conditions can be taken as evidence of damage done by Koresh only by ignoring his adult followers' professed commitment to their chosen way of life. Even where children are involved, our society allows a great measure of latitude and freedom to a family to follow its religious convictions, however strict or unconventional. In keeping with a proper concern over the issue of damage caused by cults, but in balance with our commitment to freedom of religion, a few simple principles of judgment are proposed.

Illegal actions should be evaluated according to the appropriate laws and pursued accordingly. The relevant criteria are explicit, public, and sanctioned by the force of the government and the will of the people it represents. The specific religious or ideological commitments of the perpetrators should be irrelevant to the process of assessing the legal status of their actions. With behavior that breaks religious or moral conventions, however, the waters become muddy. Despite cult-busters' claims to the contrary, their particular moral standards and religious convictions are not shared by the majority of the population, nor are they written into our laws. Our pluralistic society is intentionally designed to be hospitable to a wide range of moral persuasions and religious beliefs. Moral and religious judgments about cults are necessarily situated within specific subgroups of our society. Beyond the question of the legality of certain actions, where cult members must meet the same criteria as anyone else, the problem with so-called cults can only be articulated convincingly from a very specific standpoint in defense of very particular moral and religious values. By offering an alternative vision of individuals and society, cults deliberately provoke a conflict over values. Any opposition to such groups must itself offer a compelling alternative, not merely anxious alarms and exaggerated criticisms. Whatever the specific items at issue, the most effective critique of any cult would not only condemn its errors but also offer a path that the opponent would argue is closer to the truth. In other words, cults are most effectively encountered by committed representatives of the other religious communities that set forth a comprehensive view of the world and the proper place of human beings in it, which they attempt to make convincing. In that sense, cults make a signal contribution to American life by raising questions of ultimate value, by offering paradigms of commitment, and by making principled challenges to the status quo. Their presence in our society is undeniably disruptive and intentionally so. They may fade in and out of the public view, but they will not disappear as the history of religions, and particularly those in America, makes clear. Our democratic society serves, however imperfectly, as a free marketplace of ideas. Intolerant government policies, and particularly antidemocratic and military tactics like those used at Waco, have no place in such a society. Rather than conduct a war against so-called cults, we can more profitably and pointedly ask ourselves what we believe in, how we are practicing our beliefs, and what is our level of participation in the open and ongoing exchange of ideas that our society affords.

15

▪2▪

Presenting Sources to Others

I hate quotations. Tell me what you know.

Ralph Waldo Emerson (1849)

By necessity, by proclivity, and by delight, we all quote.

Ralph Waldo Emerson (1876)

These quotations appear to be contradictory, but they merely represent the development of one writer's understanding of his craft. Like Emerson in 1849, most writers hope to rely entirely on what they know and to express their knowledge in their own words. But, as Emerson realized later, one rarely writes about ideas that no one has ever explored. Someone has usually gone part of the way before, so it makes sense to build on that person's discoveries.

Because most of your writing in college will be based directly or indirectly on what you have read, you will need a working knowledge of two more methods of presenting other people's ideas to your readers: *quotation* and *paraphrase*.

REASONS FOR QUOTING

In academic writing, presenting the words of another writer through *quotation* is the most basic way to support your own ideas. Writers who know how to quote understand the need to give credit to their sources for both borrowed ideas and borrowed words.

- *Correct quotation* tells your reader that you respect your sources, that you know how to distinguish between your own work and theirs, and that you will not *plagiarize*—make unacknowledged use of another writer's words and ideas.

- *Appropriate quotation* tells your reader that you know when to quote and that you are not allowing your sources' words to dominate your writing.

Experienced writers hold quotation marks in reserve for those times when they think it essential to present the source's exact words.

Reasons to Use Quotation

1. For support
2. To preserve vivid or technical language
3. To comment on the quotation
4. To distance yourself from the quotation

---

1. Quoting for Support

You will most often refer to another writer's work as evidence in support of one of your own points. To ensure that the evidence retains its full meaning and impact, you retain the author's original language, instead of putting the sentences in your own words. Very often, quoted material appears in an essay as an *appeal to authority;* the source being quoted is important enough or familiar enough with the subject (as in an eyewitness account) to make the original words worth quoting. For example, the only quotation in a *New York Times* article describing political and economic chaos in Bolivia presents the opinion of a government official:

> Even the Government acknowledges its shaky position. "The polity is unstable, capricious and chaotic," Adolfo Linares Arraya, Minister of Planning and Coordination, said. "The predominance of crisis situations has made the future unforeseeable."

The minister's words in themselves seem vague and glib, and therefore not especially quotable. (Indeed, they may not even be true.) But his position as representative of the government makes the minister's exact words necessary evidence for the reporter's presentation of the Bolivian crisis.

2. Quoting Vivid or Technical Language

The wording of the source material may be so ingenious that the point will be lost if you express it in your own words. *You will want to quote a sentence that is very compact or that relies on a striking image to make its point.* For example, here is a paragraph from a review of a book about Vietnamese history:

> Not many nations have had such a history of scrapping: against Mongols and Chinese seeking to dominate them from the north, and to the south against weaker and more innocent peoples who stood in the way of the Vietnamese march to the rich Mekong Delta and the underpopulated land of Cambodia. Mr. Hodgkin [the author] quotes from a poem by a medieval Vietnamese hero: "By its tradition of defending the country / the army is so powerful it can swallow the evening star."

The quotation adds authentic evidence to the reviewer's discussion and provides a memorable image for the reader.

It is also important to retain the precise terminology of a *technical or legal document.* Changing one word of the text can significantly change its meaning. Here is a sentence from the final paragraph of a Supreme Court decision upholding the civil rights of three tenth-graders who had been suspended by school officials for "spiking" the punch at a meeting of an extracurricular club:

> We hold that a school board member is not immune from liability for damages if he knew or reasonably should have known that the action he took within his sphere of official responsibility would violate the constitutional rights of the student affected, or if he took the action with the malicious intention to cause a deprivation of constitutional rights or other injury to the student.

Virtually every word of the sentence has potential impact on the way this decision will be interpreted in subsequent legal suits. Note, for example, the distinction between "knew" and "reasonably should have known" and the way in which "intention" is qualified by "malicious."

3. Quoting Another Writer to Comment on the Quotation

In your essay, you may want to analyze or comment on a statement made by another writer. Your readers should have that writer's exact words in front of them if they are to get the full benefit of your commentary; *you have to quote it in order to talk about it.* Thus, when a writer reviewing Philip Norman's biography of the Beatles wants to criticize the biographer's style, he must supply a sample quotation so that his readers can make up their own minds.

> Worst of all is the overwritten prologue, about John Lennon's death and its impact in Liverpool: "The ruined imperial city, its abandoned river, its tormented suburban plain, knew an anguish greater than the recession and unemployment which have laid Merseyside waste under bombardments more deadly than Hitler's blitz." A moment's thought should have made Norman and his publishers realize that this sort of thing, dashed off in the heat of the moment, would quickly come to seem very embarrassing indeed.

4. Gaining Distance through Quotation

Writers generally use quotation to distinguish between the writer of the essay and the writer being cited in the essay. Sometimes, however, you want to distance yourself from your own choice of language. For example, you may use quotation marks to indicate that a word or phrase is not in common or standard use. A phrase may be *obsolete,* no longer in current usage:

Many "flower children" gathered at the rock festivals of the late 1960s.

Or a phrase may be *slang,* not yet having been absorbed into standard English:

She tried to "cop out" of doing her share of the work.

In effect, you want to use the phrase and at the same time "cover" yourself by signaling your awareness that the phrase is not quite right: you are distancing yourself from your own vocabulary. *It is usually better to take full responsibility for your choice of words and to avoid using slang or obsolete vocabulary, with or without quotation marks.* But if the context requires such phrasing, you may use quotation marks to gain the necessary distance.

You can achieve a different kind of distance when you use quotation marks to suggest *irony:*

The actor was joined by his "constant companion."

The quoted phrase is a familiar *euphemism,* a bland expression substituted for a more blunt term. Again, by placing it in quotation marks, the author is both *calling attention to* and *distancing him- or herself from* the euphemism.

Quotation marks also serve as a means of *disassociation* for journalists who wish to avoid taking sides on an issue or making editorial comments.

A fire that roared through a 120-year-old hotel and took at least 11 lives was the work of a "sick arsonist," the county coroner said today. Robert Jennings, the Wayne County coroner, said that he had told county officials that the building was a "fire trap."

The author of this article did not want the responsibility of attributing the fire to a "sick arsonist" or labeling the building a "fire trap"—at any rate, not until the findings of an investigation or a trial make the terminology unquestionably true. Thus, he is careful not only to use quotation marks around certain phrases, but also to cite the precise source of the statement.

USING QUOTATIONS

The apparatus for quotation is twofold:

1. By *inserting quotation marks,* you indicate that you are borrowing certain words, as well as certain ideas, that appear in your writing.
2. By *inserting a citation* containing the source's name, you give credit for both ideas and words to the author.

Citation	Quotation
Theodore Roosevelt said,	"Speak softly and carry a big stick; you will go far."

Direct Quotation: Separating Quotations from Your Own Writing

The simplest way to quote is to combine the citation (written by you) with the words you are quoting (*exactly as they were said or written by your source*). This method of quotation joins together two separate statements, with punctuation—comma or colon—bridging the gap and a capital letter beginning the quoted phrase.

Pause

St. Paul declared, "It is better to marry than to burn."

used after long introduction

In his first epistle to the Corinthians, St. Paul commented on lust: "It is better to marry than to burn."

In both these forms of direct quotation, the quoted words are *not* fully integrated into the grammatical structure of your sentence. The *comma or colon* and the *capital letter* at the beginning of the quoted sentence separate the two parts, making it clear that *two voices appear in the sentence: yours and your source's.* In general, you should choose this kind of direct quotation when you want to differentiate between yourself and the quoted words. There are many reasons for wanting to emphasize this difference; an obvious example would be your own disagreement with the quotation.

The *colon* is used less frequently than the comma. It usually follows a clause that can stand alone as a complete sentence. As such, the colon separates a complete idea of your own from a complementary or supporting idea taken from your source.

Direct Quotation: Integrating Quotations into Your Sentences

In an alternative kind of direct quotation, *only the quotation marks indicate that you are using someone else's words.*

Key word for integrating

St. Paul declared that "it is better to marry than to burn."

Alvin Toffler defined future shock as "the shattering stress and disorientation that we induce in individuals by subjecting them to too much change in too short a time."

There is no signal for the reader that separates citation from quotation—no comma or colon, no capital letter. The first word of the quoted material, in this second type of direct quotation, is *not* capitalized, even if it was capitalized in the source.

Original

Beware of all enterprises that require new clothes.

HENRY DAVID THOREAU

Quotation

Thoreau warned his readers to "beware of all enterprises that require new clothes."

The effect is very smooth, and the reader's attention is not distracted from the flow of sentences.

The Two Kinds of Direct Quotation

Separated

- Comma or colon and quotation marks separate citation and quotation.
- The first letter of the quotation is capitalized.
- You are distinguishing between your ideas and those of your source.

Integrated

- No punctuation (but quotation marks) separates citation and quotation.
- The first letter of the quotation is not capitalized.
- You are integrating your ideas with those of your source.

Because integrating the quotation tends to blur the distinction between writer and source, you must be careful to avoid confusion. Look, for example, at the various ways of quoting this first-person sentence, which was originally spoken by a motorist: "I hate all pedestrians."

Separated Quotation

The motorist said, "I hate all pedestrians."

Integrated Quotation

The motorist said that "I hate all pedestrians."

The first method, quoting with separation by punctuation, requires no alteration in the original sentence. But in the second version, quoting with integration, the original wording does not quite fit.

- The first-person "I" conflicts with the third-person "motorist" (the reader may wonder who "I" is—the motorist or the writer!).
- The present-tense "hate" conflicts with the past-tense "said," so "hate" must be turned into "hated."

But once the person [I] and the tense [hate] of the original statement have been altered for clarity and consistency, only two words—"all pedestrians"—are actually being quoted:

Direct Quotation

The motorist said that she hated "all pedestrians."

You may even prefer not to put quotations around the remaining two words taken from the original source. If so, you are not quoting anything directly; you are using indirect quotation. *In indirect quotation, you report rather than quote what has been said.*

Indirect Quotation

The motorist said that she hated all pedestrians.

However, the absence of quotation marks in the indirect quotation could be confusing. If you were collecting evidence for a legal suit, quotation marks would indicate that the motorist was responsible for the precise wording. Therefore, direct quotation, separated by punctuation, is probably the most appropriate method of presenting the motorist's opinion of pedestrians.

As a rule, the writer has the obligation to insert quotation marks when using a source's exact words, whether written or oral.

Direct Quotation

Robert Ingersoll condemned those who deny others their civil liberties: "I am the inferior of any man whose rights I trample underfoot."

Indirect Quotation

Robert Ingersoll proclaimed that he was the inferior of any man whose rights he trampled underfoot.

The indirect quotation does not indicate exactly who wrote this sentence. Even if you changed "I" to "he" and the present to the past tense, *you are still not using your own words;* the basic phrasing of the sentence remains Ingersoll's. *To imply, as this indirect quotation could, that the wording is yours, not Ingersoll's, would be plagiarism.*

For this reason, *writers should use indirect quotation with great care.* If one of the two forms of direct quotation does not seem appropriate, you should invent your own phrasing—called *paraphrase*—to express the source's original statement.

The Historical Present Tense

Certain ideas and statements remain true long after their creators have died. By convention, or general agreement, writers often refer to these statements in the present tense.

Shakespeare states, "This above all: to thine own self be true."

When you are devoting part of your own essay to a "discussion" with another writer, you may prefer to conduct the discussion on a common ground of time and use the present tense, called the *historical present*. The historical present is also useful to *place a variety of different sources on equal terms, especially when they are from different eras*. In the following example, the introductory verbs, all in the present tense, are underlined:

> While Shelley <u>acknowledges</u> that poets are creators of language and music and art, he also <u>asserts</u> that they have a civic role: "They are the institutors of laws, and the founders of civil society, and the inventors of the arts of life." Writing one hundred years later, Benedetto Croce <u>affirms</u> Shelley's insistence upon the social and spiritual responsibilities of the poet. According to Croce, Shelley <u>sees</u> poetry "as the eternal source of all intellectual, moral, and civil vitality."

Finally, the historical present is almost always used when you refer to *important documents* (often written by a group of people, rather than a single author) that remain in force long after they were created. Obvious examples include the Constitution, the Declaration of Independence, the laws of Congress, Supreme Court decisions, the charter of your state government, and the bylaws governing your college or university.

> The Constitution guarantees that women—and, indeed, all citizens—shall have the vote in elections; Amendment XIX states that the right to vote "shall not be denied or abridged by the United States or by any State on account of sex."

Punctuating Direct Quotations

You have already learned about punctuating *the beginning of the quotation:*

1. In a separated direct quotation, the citation is followed by a comma or a colon.
2. In an integrated direct quotation, the citation is followed by no punctuation at all.

Some writers tend to forget this second point and include an unnecessary comma:

Incorrect Quotation

Ernest Hemingway believed that, "what is moral is what you feel good after and what is immoral is what you feel bad after."

Remember that *an integrated quotation should have no barriers between citation and quotation:*

Correct Quotation

Ernest Hemingway believed that "what is moral is what you feel good after and what is immoral is what you feel bad after."

In the integrated direct quotation, note that the first letter of the quotation is not capitalized.

There is no easy way of remembering the proper sequence of punctuation for *closing a quotation*. The procedure has been determined by conventional and arbitrary agreement, originally for the convenience of printers. Although other countries abide by different conventions, in the United States the following rules apply—and *there are no exceptions.*

1. All periods and commas are placed inside the terminal quotation marks.

It does not matter whether the period belongs to your sentence or to the quoted sentence: it goes *inside* the marks. This is the most important rule and the one most often ignored. Don't resort to ambiguous devices such as placing the quotes directly over the period (".).

> P. T. Barnum is reputed to have said that "there's a sucker born every minute."

> P. T. Barnum is reputed to have said that "there's a sucker born every minute," and Barnum's circuses undertook to entertain each and every one.

Notice that, in the second example, the comma at the end of the quotation really belongs to the framework sentence, not to the quotation itself; nevertheless, it goes *inside* the marks.

2. All semicolons, colons, and dashes are placed outside the terminal quotation marks.

They should be regarded as the punctuation for *your* sentence, and not for the quotation.

> George Santayana wrote that "those who cannot remember the past are condemned to repeat it"; today, we are in danger of forgetting the lessons of history.

Occasionally, when a semicolon, colon, or (most likely) a dash appears at the end of the material to be quoted, you will decide to include the punctuation in the quotation; in that case, the punctuation should be placed inside the marks. In the following example, the dash appears in Lucretia Mott's original statement, so it is placed inside the quotation marks.

> Lucretia Mott argued urgently for women's rights: "Let woman then go on—not asking favors, but claiming as a right the removal of all hindrances to her elevation in the scale of being—" so that, as a result, she might "enter profitably into the active business of man."

3. Question marks and exclamation points are sometimes placed inside the quotation marks and sometimes placed outside.

- If the quotation is itself a question or an exclamation, the mark or point goes *inside* the quotation marks.
- If your own sentence is a question or an exclamation, the mark or point goes *outside* a quotation placed at the *very end* of your sentence.

In 1864, General Sherman signaled the arrival of his reinforcements: "Hold the fort! I am coming!"

The exclamation is General Sherman's; the exclamation point goes inside the quotation.

Can anyone in the 1980s agree with Dumas that "woman inspires us to great things and prevents us from achieving them"?

Dumas was *not* asking a question; the question mark goes at the very end of the sentence, after the quotation marks.

Sigmund Freud's writings occasionally reveal a remarkable lack of insight: "The great question that has never been answered, and which I have not yet been able to answer despite my thirty years of research into the feminine soul, is: What does a woman want?"

Freud himself asked this famous question; the question mark goes inside the quotation.

Freud was demonstrating remarkably little insight when he wrote, "What does a woman want?" citing his "thirty years of research into the feminine soul"!

The exclamation is the writer's, not Freud's; the exclamation point goes outside the quotation marks.

It is possible to construct a sentence that ends logically in two question marks (or exclamation points): one for the quotation and one for your own sentence. In such cases, you need include only one—and, by convention, it should be placed *inside* the quotation marks:

What did Freud mean when he asked, "What does a woman want?"

These rules apply only to the quotation of complete sentences or reasonably long phrases. *Whether it is a quotation or an obsolete, slang, or ironic reference, a single word or a brief phrase should be fully integrated into your sentence, without being preceded or followed by commas.*

Winston Churchill's reference to "blood, sweat and tears" rallied the English to prepare for war.

Be careful not to quote words or phrases excessively. Even though the quotation marks make it clear that you are borrowing the words, using more than one quotation, however brief, in a sentence or quoting sentence after sentence creates the impression that you cannot express your thoughts in your own words.

Interrupting Quotations

Sometimes it is desirable to break up a long quotation or to vary the way you quote your sources by interrupting a quotation *and placing the citation in the middle.*

"I do not mind lying," wrote Samuel Butler, "but I hate inaccuracy."

Butler's statement is divided into two separate parts, and therefore you need to use *four* sets of quotation marks: two introductory and two terminal. The citation is joined to the quotation by a comma on either side. There are two danger points:

- If you forget to use the marks at the beginning of the second half of the quotation, you are failing to distinguish your words from Butler's.
- You must also put the first comma *inside* the terminal quotation marks (because terminal commas *always* go inside the quotation marks) and put the comma that concludes the citation *before* the quotation marks (because it is *your* comma, not Butler's).

Quoting inside a Quotation

Sometimes a statement that you want to quote already contains a quotation. In that case, you must use *two sets of quotation marks, double and single,* to help your reader to distinguish between the two separate sources.

- *Single quotation* marks are used for the words already quoted by your source (and this is the *only* time when it is appropriate to use single quotation marks).
- *Double quotation* marks are used around the words that you are quoting.

Goethe at times expressed a notable lack of self-confidence: "'Know thyself?' If I knew myself, I'd run away."

At the beginning of World War I, Winston Churchill observed that "the maxim of the British people is 'Business as usual.'"

The same single/double procedure is used even when there is no author's name to be cited.

A Yiddish proverb states that "'for example' is not proof."

Very occasionally, you may need to use triple quotation marks, usually to quote a source who is quoting another source who is using a quoted word or phrase. An article about the author Muriel Spark included the following statement by that novelist:

I draw the line at "forever."

Victoria Glendinning, the author of the article, quoted Spark's statement using single and double quotation marks.

Eternally inquiring and curious about places and people, "I draw the line at 'forever.'"

To quote that sentence in your essay, you would need to distinguish yourself from Victoria Glendinning and Muriel Spark.

In her recent profile, Victoria Glendinning emphasizes Muriel Spark's search for variety: "Eternally inquiring and curious about places and people, 'I draw the line at "forever."'"

Notice that you would deliberately plan the quotation marks so that the double marks are used for the framework quotation.

EXERCISE 7: QUOTING CORRECTLY

A. Correct the errors in the following sentences:

1. The *Chicago Times* asserted in 1861 that, "It is a newspaper's duty to print the news and raise hell."
2. Baron de Montesquieu, a philosopher of the eighteenth-century Enlightenment, sympathized with the needs of the masses; "The real wants of the people," he wrote, "ought never to give way to the imaginary wants of the state".
3. In Proust's view, "Everybody calls "clear" those ideas which have the same degree of confusion as his own".
4. Thoreau warned his readers to, "Beware of all enterprises that require new clothes."
5. Robert F. Wagner, former mayor of New York, believed in keeping a low profile and offered this advice—"When in danger, ponder; when in trouble, delegate; when in doubt, mumble."
6. "Beggars should be abolished," said Friedrich Nietzsche. "it annoys one to give to them and it annoys one not to give to them".
7. "Have you anything to declare?" said the customs official. "No", replied Oscar Wilde, "I have nothing to declare", he paused, "except my genius."

8. Before the Revolutionary War, Patrick Henry made a passionate speech "is life so dear or peace so sweet, as to be purchased at the price of chains and slavery? Forbid it, Almighty God I know not what course others may take, but as for me, give me liberty or give me death

B. Use quotations from the following group as directed:

■ Choose one quotation and write a sentence that introduces a direct quotation with separation.

■ Choose a second quotation and write a sentence that introduces a direct quotation with integration.

■ Choose a third quotation and write a sentence that interrupts a quotation with a citation in the middle.

1. Early in life I had to choose between honest arrogance and hypocritical humility. I chose honest arrogance and have seen no occasion to change. (Frank Lloyd Wright)

2. I must say acting was good training for the political life which lay ahead for us. (Nancy Reagan)

3. My folks didn't come over on the *Mayflower*, but they were there to meet the boat. (Will Rogers)

4. The reason so many people showed up at his funeral was because they wanted to make sure he was dead. (Samuel Goldwyn on L. B. Mayer)

5. I hear much of people's call out to punish the guilty, but very few are concerned to clear the innocent. (Daniel Defoe)

6. This has always been a man's world, and none of the reasons hitherto brought forward in explanation of this fact has seemed adequate. (Simone de Beauvoir)

7. I have now come to the conclusion never again to think of marrying, and for this reason: I can never be satisfied with anyone who would be blockhead enough to have me. (Abraham Lincoln)

Quoting Accurately

Quoting is not a collaboration in which you try to improve on your source's writing. If you value a writer's words enough to want to quote them, you should respect the integrity of the sentence.

Unless you are applying the conventional methods of presenting quotations, don't make minor changes or carelessly leave words out, but faithfully transcribe the exact words, the exact spelling, and the exact punctuation that you find in the original.

Original

Those who corrupt the public mind are just as evil as those who steal from the public purse.

ADLAI STEVENSON

Inexact Quotation

Adlai Stevenson believed that "those who act against the public interest are just as evil as those who steal from the public purse."

Exact Quotation

Adlai Stevenson believed that "those who corrupt the public mind are just as evil as those who steal from the public purse."

Even if you notice an error (or what you regard as an error), you still must copy the original wording. For example, old-fashioned spelling should be retained, as well as regional or national dialect and spelling conventions:

One of Heywood's <u>Proverbes</u> tells us that "a new brome swepeth clean."

In one of his humorous stories, Colonel Davy Crockett predicted the reactions to his own death: "It war a great loss to the country and the world, and to ole Kaintuck in particklar. Thar were never known such a member of Congress as Crockett, and never will be agin. The painters and bears will miss him, for he never missed them."

You do not have to assume the blame if the material that you are quoting contains errors of syntax, punctuation, or spelling. You can use a conventional way to point out such errors and inform the reader that the mistake was made, not by you, but by the author whom you are quoting. *The Latin word sic (meaning "thus") is placed in square brackets and inserted immediately after the error.* The [sic] signals that the quotation was "thus" and that you, the writer, were aware of the error, which was not the result of your own carelessness in transcribing the quotation.

In the following example, [sic] calls attention to an error in subject-verb agreement:

Richard Farson points out that "increased understanding and concern has [sic] not been coupled with increased rights."

You may also want to use [sic] to indicate that the source used archaic spelling:

In describing Elizabeth Billington, an early nineteenth-century singer, W. Clark Russell observed that "her voice was powerful, and resembled the tone of a clarionet [sic]."

It would be tedious, however, to use [sic] to indicate each misspelling in the Davy Crockett quotation; in your essay about Crockett, you could, instead, explain his use of dialect as you discuss his life and writing.

TAILORING QUOTATIONS TO FIT YOUR WRITING

There are several ways to change quotations to fit the quoted material naturally into your own sentences. Like [sic], these devices are *conventions*, established by generally accepted agreement: *you cannot improvise; you must follow these rules.* Usually, the conventional rules require you to inform your reader that a change is being made; in other words, they make clear the distinction between your wording and the author's.

Changing Capital and Small Letters

The first way of altering quotations depends entirely on how and where the quotation fits into your sentence.

- When a quotation is *integrated* completely into your sentence (usually when your citation ends in "that"), the first letter of the quotation will be small, whether or not it is a capital in the original. (Two exceptions are the pronoun "I" and proper nouns, which are always capitalized.)
- When a quotation is *separated* from your sentence, and your citation ends in a comma or a colon, the first letter of the quotation will be a capital, whether or not it is a capital in the original.

Integrated Quotation

The poet Frost wrote that "good fences make good neighbors."

Separated Quotation

The poet Frost wrote, "Good fences make good neighbors."

As a rule, it is not necessary to indicate to your readers that you have altered the first letter of your quotation from small to capital or from capital to small.

Using Ellipses to Delete Words

It is permissible to *delete* words from a quotation, provided that you indicate to the reader that something has been omitted. Your condensed version is as accurate as the original; it is just shorter. But you must remember to insert the conventional symbol for deletion, *three spaced dots*, called an *ellipsis*. Once made aware by the three dots that your version omits part of the original, any reader who wants to see the omitted portion can consult the original source.

Original

It is not true that suffering ennobles the character; happiness does that sometimes, but suffering, for the most part, makes men petty and vindictive.

W. SOMERSET MAUGHAM

Quotation with Ellipsis

Maugham does not believe that "suffering ennobles the character; . . . suffering, for the most part, makes men petty and vindictive."

Notice that:

- The three dots are spaced equally.
- The dots *must* be three—not two or a dozen.
- The semicolon is retained, to provide terminal punctuation for the first part of the quotation.

If you wish to delete the end of a quotation, and the ellipsis coincides with the end of your sentence, you must use the three dots, plus a fourth to signify the sentence's end.

Quotation with Terminal Ellipsis

Maugham does not believe that "suffering ennobles the character; happiness does that sometimes. . . . "

Here, you'll note:

- There are four dots, three to indicate a deletion and a fourth to indicate the period at the end of the sentence.
- The first dot is placed immediately after the last letter.
- The sentence ends with quotation marks, as usual, with the marks placed *after* the dots, not before.

You can also use the three dots to link two separate quotations from the same paragraph in your source; the ellipsis will indicate the deletion of one or more sentences, but *only* if the two sentences that you are quoting are fairly near each other in the original. *An ellipsis cannot cover a gap of more than a few sentences.* When you use an ellipsis to bridge one or more sentences, use only *one* set of quotation marks. Your full quotation, with an ellipsis in the middle, is still continuous—a single quotation—even though there is a gap.

When an ellipsis is used following a quoted complete sentence, the period of the quoted sentence is retained so that a total of four dots is used, as in the following example.

Original

In one sense there is no death. The life of a soul on earth lasts beyond his departure. You will always feel that life touching yours, that voice speaking to you, that spirit looking out of other eyes, talking to you in the familiar things he touched, worked with, loved as familiar friends. He lives on in your life and in the lives of all others that knew him.

ANGELO PATRI

Quotation with Ellipsis

Patri states that "in one sense there is no death. The life of a soul on earth lasts beyond his departure. . . . He lives on in your life and in the lives of all others that knew him."

An ellipsis should be used to make a quotation fit more smoothly into your own sentence. It is especially convenient when you are working with a long passage that contains several separate points that you wish to quote. But ellipses should *not* be used to condense long, tedious quotations or to replace summary and paraphrase. If you only want to quote a brief extract from a lengthy passage, then simply quote that portion and ignore the surrounding material. An ellipsis is poorly used when it is used too often. Reading a paragraph full of dots can be very distracting.

The meaning of the original quotation must always be exactly preserved, despite the deletion represented by the ellipsis.

Original

As long as there are sovereign nations possessing great power, war is inevitable.

ALBERT EINSTEIN

Inexact Quotation

Einstein believes that " . . . war is inevitable."

It would not be accurate to suggest that Einstein believed in the inevitability of war, under all circumstances, without qualifications. *To extract only a portion of this statement with ellipsis is to oversimplify and thus to falsify the evidence.*

Using Brackets to Insert Words

Brackets have an opposite function: ellipsis signifies deletion; *brackets signify addition or alteration.* Brackets are not the same as parentheses. Parentheses would be confusing for this purpose, for the quotation might itself include a parenthetical statement, and the reader could not be sure whether the parentheses contained the author's insertion or yours. Instead, brackets, a relatively unusual form of punctuation, are used as a conventional way of informing the reader that material has been inserted. (You have already seen how to use brackets with [sic], which enables you to comment on the material that you are quoting.) You simply insert the information *inside* the quotation, placing it in square brackets.

> ## *Reasons to Use Brackets*
>
> - To explain a vague word
> - To replace a confusing phrase
> - To suggest an antecedent
> - To correct an error in a quotation
> - To adjust a quotation to fit your own writing

The most common reason for using brackets is to clarify a vague word. You may, for example, choose to quote only the last portion of a passage, omitting an important antecedent:

Original

Man lives *by* habits, indeed, but what he lives *for* is thrills and excitement.

WILLIAM JAMES

Quotation with Brackets

William James argues that "what he [man] lives <u>for</u> is thrills and excitement."

William James argues that "what [man] lives <u>for</u> is thrills and excitement."

In the second example, the vague word "he" has been deleted entirely; the brackets themselves indicate that there has been a substitution, but the reader doesn't know what was originally there. For that reason, unless the presentation of both wordings seems very awkward, *it is better to follow the first example: quote the original and also provide the clarification in brackets.* This way, you will leave your reader in no doubt about your source's words.

Brackets can also be used to complete a thought that has been obscured by the omission (often through ellipsis) of an earlier sentence:

Original

A well-trained sensible family doctor is one of the most valuable assets in a community. . . . Few men live lives of more devoted self-sacrifice.

SIR WILLIAM OSLER

Quotation with Brackets

The great surgeon Sir William Osler had enormous respect for his less famous colleagues: "Few men live lives of more devoted self-sacrifice [than good family doctors]."

Here, the quotation marks are placed *after* the brackets, even though the quoted material ends after the word "self-sacrifice." The explanatory material inside the brackets is considered part of the quotation, even though it is not in the source's own words.

Your own explanatory comments in brackets should be very brief and to the point. You might, for example, want to include an important *date* or *name* as essential background information. But whatever is inside the brackets should fit smoothly into the syntax of the quotation and should not distract the reader. For example, do not use brackets to argue with the author you are quoting. The following running dialogue with the entertainer Sophie Tucker is poorly conveyed through the use of brackets.

Confusing Use of Brackets

Sophie Tucker suggests that up to the age of eighteen "a girl needs good parents. [This is true for men, too.] From eighteen to thirty-five, she needs good looks. [Good looks aren't that essential anymore.] From thirty-five to fifty-five, she needs a good personality. [I disagree because personality is important at any age.] From fifty-five on, she needs good cash."

EXERCISE 8: USING ELLIPSES AND BRACKETS IN QUOTATIONS

A. Choose one of the following quotations. By using *ellipses*, incorporate a portion of the quotation into a sentence of your own; remember to include the author's name in the citation.

B. Choose a second quotation. Incorporate a portion of the quotation into another sentence of your own; insert words in *brackets* to clarify one or more of the quoted words.

1. Man, biologically considered, and whatever else he may be in the bargain, is simply the most formidable of all the beasts of prey, and, indeed, the only one that preys systematically on its own species. (William James)

2. I have never taken any exercise, except sleeping and resting, and I never intend to take any. Exercise is loathsome. And it cannot be any benefit when you are tired, and I am always tired. (Mark Twain)

3. I love America more than any other country in the world, and, exactly for this reason, I insist on the right to criticize her perpetually. (James Baldwin)

4. I do not believe that civilization will be wiped out in a war fought with the atomic bomb. Perhaps two-thirds of the people of the earth might be killed, but enough men capable of thinking, and enough books, would be left to start again, and civilization would be restored. (Albert Einstein)

5. Unconditional war can no longer lead to unconditional victory. It can no longer serve to settle disputes. It can no longer be of concern to great powers alone. For a nuclear disaster, spread by winds and waters and fear, could well engulf the great and the small, the rich and the poor, the committed and the uncommitted alike. (John F. Kennedy)

6. I never listen to debates. They are dreadful things indeed. The plain truth is that I am not a fair man, and don't want to hear both sides. On

all known subjects, ranging from aviation to xylophone-playing, I have fixed and invariable ideas. They have not changed since I was four or five. (H. L. Mencken)

WRITING CITATIONS

Citing the Author's Name

The first time that you refer to a source, use the author's full name—without Mr. or Miss, Mrs., or Ms.

First Reference

John Stuart Mill writes, "The opinion which it is attempted to suppress by authority may possibly be true."

After that, should you need to cite the author again, use the *last name only.* Conventional usage discourages casual and distracting references such as "John thinks," "JSM thinks," or "Mr. Mill thinks."

Second Reference

Mill continues to point out that "all silencing of discussion is an assumption of infallibility."

When you cite the author's name:

- At first reference, you may (and usually should) include the *title* of the work from which the quotation is taken:

  In *On Liberty,* John Stuart Mill writes . . .

- If there is a long break between references to the same author, or if the names of several other authors intervene, you may wish to repeat the full name and remind your reader of the earlier citation.

  In addition to his warnings about the dangers of majority rule, which were cited earlier in the discussion of public opinion, John Stuart Mill also expresses concern about "the functions of police; how far liberty may legitimately be invaded for the prevention of crime, or of accident."

- Avoid referring to the author twice in the same citation, once by name and once by pronoun. In the following citation, we really can't be sure who "he" is:

  In John Stuart Mill's *On Liberty,* he writes . . .

- Finally, unless you genuinely do not know the author's name, use it! There is no point in being coy, even for the sake of variety:

A famous man once made an ironic observation about child-rearing: "If you strike a child, take care that you strike it in anger. . . . A blow in cold blood neither can nor should be forgiven."

Your guessing game will only irritate readers who are not aware that this famous man was George Bernard Shaw.

Choosing the Introductory Verb

The citation provides an important link between your thoughts and those of your source. The introductory verb can tell your reader something about your reasons for presenting the quotation and its context in the work that you are quoting. Will you choose "J. S. Mill says," or "J. S. Mill writes," or "J. S. Mill thinks," or "J. S. Mill feels"? Those are the most common introductory verbs—so common that they have become boring! Whenever appropriate, select less stereotyped verbs. As the senses are not directly involved in writing, avoid "feels" entirely. And, unless you are quoting someone's spoken words, substitute a more accurate verb for "says."

Here are some introductory verbs:

argues	adds	concludes
establishes	explains	agrees
emphasizes	believes	insists
finds	continues	maintains
points out	declares	disagrees
notes	observes	states
suggests	proposes	compares

Of course, once you stop using the all-purpose "says" or "writes," you have to remember that verbs are not interchangeable and that you should choose the verb that best suits your purpose.

The citation should suggest the relationship between your own ideas (in the previous sentence) and the statement that you are about to quote.

You should examine the quotation before writing the citation to define the way in which the author makes a point:

- Is it being asserted forcefully?
  Use "argues" or "declares" or "insists."
- Is the statement being offered only as a possibility?
  Use "suggests" or "proposes" or "finds."
- Does the statement immediately follow a previous reference?
  Use "continues" or "adds."

For clarity, the introductory verb may be expanded:

X is aware that . . .
X stresses the opposite view

X provides one answer to the question
X makes the same point as Y
X erroneously assumes . . .

But make sure that the antecedent for the "view" or the "question" or the "point" can be found in the previous sentences of your essay. Finally, all the examples of introductory verbs are given in the *present tense*, which is the conventional way of introducing most quotations.

Varying Your Sentence Patterns

Even if you choose a different verb for each quotation, the combination of the author's name, introductory verb, and quotation can become repetitious and tiresome. One way to vary the citations is occasionally to place the name of the source in a less prominent position, tucked into the quotation instead of calling attention to itself at the beginning.

1. You can interrupt the quotation by placing the citation in the middle.

"I made my mistakes," acknowledged Richard Nixon, "but in all my years of public service, I have never profited from public service. I have earned every cent."

The verb and the name may be placed in reverse order (instead of "Richard Nixon acknowledged") when the citation appears in the middle of the quotation. Remember to include two commas: one at the end of the first portion of the quotation (*inside* the quotation marks), one at the end of the citation.

One citation is quite enough. There is no need to inform your reader back to back, as in this repetitive example:

"The only prize much cared for by the powerful is power," states Oliver Wendell Holmes. He concludes, "The prize of the general . . . is command."

2. You can avoid the monotonous "X says that . . ." pattern by phrasing the citation as a subordinate clause or phrase.

In Henry Kissinger's opinion, "Power is 'the great aphrodisiac.'"

As John F. Kennedy declares, "Mankind must put an end to war or war will put an end to mankind."

3. In your quest for variety, avoid placing the citation after the quotation.

The author's name at the end may weaken the statement, especially if the citation is pretentiously or awkwardly phrased:

Awkward Citation

"I am the inferior of any man whose rights I trample underfoot," as quoted from the writings of Robert Ingersoll.

Clear Citation

A champion of civil liberties, Robert Ingersoll insisted, "I am the inferior of any man whose rights I trample underfoot."

Two rules should govern your choice of citation:

1. Don't be too fancy.
2. Be both precise and varied in your phrasing.

Presenting an Extended Quotation

Occasionally, you may have reason to present *an extended quotation,* a single extract from the same source that runs *more than four printed or typewritten lines.* For extended quotations, you must, by conventional rule, set off the quoted passage by *indenting the entire quotation on the left.*

- Introduce an extended quotation with a colon.
- Start each line of the quotation *10* spaces from the left-hand margin; stop each line at your normal right-hand margin.
- Some instructors prefer single-spacing within extended quotations; some prefer double-spacing. If possible, consult your instructor about the style appropriate for your course or discipline. If you are given no guidelines, use double-spacing.
- Omit quotation marks at the beginning and end of the quoted passage; the indented margin (and the introductory citation) will tell your readers that you are quoting.

Here is an example of an extended quotation:

Although he worked "hard as hell" all winter, Fitzgerald had difficulty finishing The Great Gatsby. On April 10, 1924, he wrote to Maxwell Perkins, his editor at Scribner's:

> While I have every hope & plan of finishing my novel in June . . . even [if] it takes me 10 times that long I cannot let it go unless it has the very best I'm capable of in it or even as I feel sometimes better than I'm capable of. It is only in the last four months that I've realized how much I've—well, almost deteriorated. . . . What I'm trying to say is just that . . . at last, or at least for the first time in years, I'm doing the best I can.

INTEGRATING QUOTATIONS INTO YOUR PARAGRAPHS

You have learned how to present the words of others with accuracy and appropriate acknowledgment; now, you must learn to make the quotation serve the larger purpose of your paragraph or essay. Here are some suggestions for integrating quotations into your writing:

1. **Use quotation sparingly.**

   If quotation seems to be your primary purpose in writing, your reader will assume that you have nothing of your own to say. *Quote only when you have a clear reason for doing so:* when you are intending to analyze a quotation, when you are sure that the wording of the quotation is essential to your argument, or when you simply cannot say it in your own words.

2. **Quotations generally belong in the body of your paragraph, not at the very beginning as a replacement for the topic sentence.**

   The topic sentence should establish—in your own words—what you are about to explain or prove. The quotation should appear later in the paragraph, as supporting evidence.

3. **Let the quotation make its point; your job is to explain or interpret its meaning, not to translate it word for word.**

   Once you have presented a quotation, it is usually not necessary to provide an exact repetition of the same idea in your own words, making the same point twice. Instead, follow up a quotation with an *explanation* of its relevance to your paragraph or an *interpretation* of its meaning; but make sure that your commentary does more than echo the quotation.

In the following student example, the quotation used in the development of the paragraph is no more or less important than any of the other supporting sentences. The quotation adds interest to the paragraph because of the shift in tone and the shift to a sharper, narrower focus.

Some parents insist on allowing their children to learn through experience. Once a child has actually performed a dangerous action and realized its consequences, he will always remember the circumstances and the possible ill effects. Yvonne Realle illustrates the adage that experience is the best teacher by describing a boy who was slapped just as he reached for a hot iron. The child, not realizing that he might have been burned, had no idea why he had been slapped. An observer noted that "if he had learned by experience, if he'd suffered some discomfort in the process, then he'd know enough to avoid the iron next time." In the view of parents like Yvonne Realle, letting a child experiment with his environment will result in a stronger lesson than slapping or scolding the child for trying to explore his surroundings.

EXERCISE 9: INTEGRATING QUOTATIONS INTO A PARAGRAPH

1. The following student paragraph is taken from an essay, "The Compulsive Gambler." The second passage comes from *The Psychology of Gambling* by Edmund Bergler.

    Choose one appropriate supporting quotation from the Bergler passage, decide where to place it in the student paragraph, and insert the quotation correctly and smoothly into the paragraph. Remember to lead into the quotation by citing the source.

Student Paragraph

One obvious reason for gambling is to make money. Because some gamblers are lucky when they play, they never want to stop. Even when quite a lot of money has been lost, they go on, assuming that they can get rich through gambling. Once a fortune is made, they will feel really powerful, free of all dependency and responsibilities. Instead, in most cases, gambling becomes a daily routine. There is no freedom, no escape.

Source

Every gambler gives the impression of a man who has signed a contract with Fate, stipulating that persistence must be rewarded. With that imaginary contract in his pocket, he is beyond the reach of all logical objection and argument.

The result of this pathologic optimism is that the true gambler never stops when he is winning, for he is convinced that he must win more and more. Inevitably, he loses. He does not consider his winnings the result of chance; to him they are a down payment on that contract he has with Fate which guarantees that he will be a permanent winner. This inability to stop while fortune is still smiling is one of the strongest arguments against the earnest assumption, common to all gamblers, that one can get rich through gambling.

ASSIGNMENT 2: WRITING A PARAGRAPH THAT INCLUDES A QUOTATION

1. Choose one of the following topics. Each is a specific question that can be answered adequately in a single paragraph.
    A. Question: Should children be spanked?
    B. Question: Should single-sex high schools receive public funding?
    C. Question: What is the best way to deal with sibling rivalry?

2. Ask someone you know to comment briefly on the question you have chosen, offering a suggestion or an example. Write down any part of the comment that you think might be worth quoting, transcribe the words accurately, and show the statement to your source to confirm its accuracy. Make sure

that you have the name properly spelled. If the first person you ask does not provide you with a suitable quotation, try someone else.

3. Answer your own question in a single paragraph of four to eight sentences, limiting the paragraph to ideas that can be clearly developed in such a brief space. The paragraph as a whole should express *your* views, not those of your source. Choose a *single* quotation from your source and integrate it into the development of your paragraph, using proper punctuation, citation, and (if necessary) ellipses and brackets. If your source agrees with you, use the quotation as support. If your source disagrees, answer the objection in your own way. Try not to quote in the first or second sentence of your paragraph. Hand in both your paragraph and the sheet on which you originally wrote down the quotation.

AVOIDING PLAGIARISM

Quoting without quotation marks is called plagiarism. Even if you cite the source's name somewhere on your page, a word-for-word quotation without marks would still be considered a plagiarism.

Plagiarism is the unacknowledged use of another writer's words or ideas. The only way to acknowledge that you are using someone else's actual words is through citation and quotation marks.

Chapter 9 discusses plagiarism in detail. At this point, you should understand that:

- If you plagiarize, you will never learn to write.
- Literate people consider plagiarism to be equivalent to theft.
- Plagiarists eventually get caught!

It is easy for an experienced reader to detect plagiarism. Every writer, professional or amateur, has a characteristic style or voice that readers quickly learn to recognize. In a few paragraphs or pages, the writer's voice becomes familiar enough for the reader to notice that the style has changed and that, suddenly, there is a new, unfamiliar voice. When there are frequent acknowledged quotations, the reader simply adjusts to a series of new voices. *When there are unacknowledged quotations, the absence of quotation marks and the change of voices usually suggest to an experienced reader that the work is poorly integrated and probably plagiarized.* Plagiarized essays are often identified in this way.

Instructors are well aware of style and are trained to recognize inconsistencies and awkward transitions. A revealing clue is the patched-together, mosaic effect. The next exercise will improve your own perception of shifting voices and encourage you to rely on your own characteristic style as the dominant voice in everything that you write.

EXERCISE 10: IDENTIFYING PLAGIARISM

The following paragraphs contain several plagiarized sentences. Examine the language and tone of each sentence, as well as the continuity of the entire paragraph. Then underline the plagiarized sentences.

A.   The Beatles' music in the early years was just plain melodic. It had a nice beat to it. The Beatles were simple lads, writing simple songs simply to play to screaming fans on one-night stands. There was no deep, inner meaning to the lyrics. Their songs included many words like I, and me, and you. As the years went by, the Beatles' music became more poetic. Sergeant Pepper is a stupefying collage of music, words, background noises, cryptic utterances, orchestral effects, hallucinogenic bells, farmyard sounds, dream sequences, social observations, and apocalyptic vision, all masterfully blended together on a four-track tape machine over nine agonizing and expensive months. Their music was beginning to be more philosophical, with a deep, inner, more secret meaning. After it was known that they took drugs, references to drugs were seen in many songs. The "help" in Ringo's "A Little Help From My Friends" was said to have meant pot. The songs were poetic, mystical; they emerged from a self-contained world of bizarre carnival colors; they spoke in a language and a musical idiom all their own.

B.   Before the Civil War, minstrelsy spread quickly across America. Americans all over the country enjoyed minstrelsy because it reflected something of their own point of view. For instance, Negro plantation hands, played usually by white actors in blackface, were portrayed as devil-may-care outcasts and minstrelmen played them with an air of comic triumph, irreverent wisdom, and an underlying note of rebellion, which had a special appeal to citizens of a young country. Minstrelsy was ironically the beginning of black involvement in the American theater. The American people learned to identify with certain aspects of the black people. The Negro became a sympathetic symbol for a pioneer people who required resilience as a prime trait.

PARAPHRASING

Some passages are worth quoting for the sake of their precise or elegant style or their distinguished author. But many sources that you will use in your college essays are written in more ordinary language. Indeed, some of your sources may be written in the jargon of an academic discipline or the bureau-cratic prose of a government agency. (There are few examples of jargon in this book; however, look at Excerpt 3 on p. 114 to sample the kind of prose you probably would not want to quote.) You will gain nothing by quoting such material; rather, you have a positive duty to help your readers by providing them with a clear paraphrase.

> *Paraphrase is the point-by-point recapitulation of another person's ideas, expressed in your own words.*

Through paraphrase, you are both informing your reader and proving that you understand what you are writing about. When you paraphrase, you retain everything about the original writing but the words. The primary differences between *paraphrase* and *summary* are length and emphasis. See the box on p. 105 for a comparison of paraphrase and summary.

Using Paraphrase in Your Essays

Your paraphrased explanations help your readers to gain a detailed understanding of sources that they may never have read and, indirectly, to accept your own thesis as valid. There are two major reasons for using paraphrase in your essays.

1. Use paraphrase to present ideas or evidence whenever there is no special reason for using a direct quotation.

Many of your sources will not have sufficient authority or a distinctive enough style to justify your quoting their words. The following illustration, taken from a *New York Times* article, paraphrases a report written by an anonymous group of "municipal auditors" whose writing merits only paraphrase, not quotation:

A city warehouse in Middle Village, Queens, stocked with such things as snow shovels, light bulbs, sponges, waxed paper, laundry soap and tinned herring, has been found to be vastly overstocked with some items and lacking in others. Municipal auditors, in a report issued yesterday, said that security was fine and that the warehouse was quicker in delivering goods to city agencies than it was when the auditors made their last check, in August, 1976. But in one corner of the warehouse, they said, nearly 59,000 paper binders, the 8½-by-11 size, are gathering dust, enough to meet the city's needs for nearly seven years. Nearby, there is a 10½-year supply of cotton coveralls.

Both the overstock and shortages cost the city money, the auditors said. They estimated that by reducing warehouse inventories, the city could save $1.4 million, plus $112,000 in interest. . . .

2. Use paraphrase to give your readers an accurate and comprehensive account of ideas taken from a source—ideas that you intend to explain, interpret, or disagree with in your essay.

The first illustration comes from a *Times* article about the data and photographs provided by *Voyager 2* as it explored the farthest reaches of the solar system. In summarizing a press conference, the article paraphrases various scientists' descriptions of what *Voyager* had achieved during its journey near Triton, one of the moons of the planet Neptune. Note the limited use of carefully selected quotations within the paraphrase.

> Out of the fissures [on Triton], roughly analogous to faults in the Earth's crust, flowed mushy ice. There was no eruption in the sense of the usual terrestrial volcanism or the geyser-like activity discovered on Io, one of Jupiter's moons. It was more of an extrusion through cracks in the surface ice.
>
> Although scientists classify such a process as volcanism, Dr. Miner said it could better be described as a "slow-flow volcanic activity." A somewhat comparable process, he said, seemed to have shaped some of the surface features of Ariel, one of the moons of Uranus.
>
> Dr. Soderblom said Triton's surface appeared to be geologically young or "millions to hundreds of millions of years old." The absence of many impact craters was the main evidence for the relatively recent resurfacing of the terrain with new ice.

The next example shows how paraphrase can be used more briefly, to present another writer's point of view as the basis for discussion. Again, the writer of this description of a conference on nuclear deterrence has reserved quotation to express the precise point of potential dispute:

> Scientists engaged in research on the effects of nuclear war may be "wasting their time" studying a phenomenon that is far less dangerous than the natural explosions that have periodically produced widespread extinctions of plant and animal life in the past, a University of Chicago scientist said last week. Joseph V. Smith, a professor of geophysical sciences, told a conference on nuclear deterrence here that such natural catastrophes as exploding volcanoes, violent earthquakes, and collisions with comets or asteroids could produce more immediate and destructive explosions than any nuclear war.

Using Paraphrase as Preparation for Reading and Writing Essays

Paraphrase is sometimes undertaken as *an end in itself.* Paraphrasing difficult passages can help you to improve your understanding of a complex essay or chapter. When you grasp an essay at first reading, when its ideas are clearly stated in familiar terms, then you can be satisfied with annotating it or writing a brief outline or summary. But when you find an essay hard to understand, writing down each sentence in your own words forces you to stop and make sense of what you have read, so that you can succeed in working out ideas that at first seem beyond your comprehension.

Paraphrase can also be *a means to an end,* a preparation for writing an essay of your own. Assume that you are taking notes for an essay based on one or more sources. If you write down nothing but exact quotations, you will not only be doing a good deal of unnecessary transcription, but you may also be tempted to quote excessively in your essay.

When you take notes, paraphrase; quote only when recording phrases or sentences that, in your opinion, merit quotation.

All academic writers are expected to be scrupulously accurate in their presentation of material taken from their sources. All quotable phrases and sentences should be transcribed accurately in your notes, with quotation marks clearly separating the paraphrase from the quotation.

Comparing Paraphrase and Outline

Paraphrase

- Presents ideas in the same order as the original

- Doesn't emphasize any one point more than another (unless the original writer does so)

- Suggests the scope and reasoning of the original passage, and specifies the main ideas

- Can be as long as necessary—as long as the original text or even longer if there are complex ideas to be explained; *it is a full presentation of the text.*

Outline

- Presents ideas in the same order as the original

- Doesn't emphasize any one point more than another (unless the original writer does so)

- Lists the main ideas, but doesn't attempt to present all the reasoning leading up to them

- Can be as short and condensed as you wish, provided that you include all the main ideas; *it is a memorandum for future reference.*

Writing a Good Paraphrase

In a good paraphrase, the sentences and the vocabulary do not duplicate those of the original. *You cannot merely substitute synonyms for key words and leave the sentences otherwise unchanged; that is plagiarism in spirit, if not in fact;* nor does word-for-word substitution really demonstrate that you have understood the ideas.

The level of abstraction within your paraphrase should resemble that of the original: It should be neither more general nor more specific. If you do not understand a sentence, do not try to guess or cover it up with a vague phrase that slides over the idea. Instead:

- Look up difficult words.
- Think of what they mean and how they are used together.
- Consider how the sentences are formed and how they fit into the context of the entire paragraph.
- Then, to test your understanding, write it all out.

Remember that a good paraphrase makes sense by itself; it is coherent and readable, without requiring reference to the original essay.

Guidelines for a Successful Paraphrase

- A paraphrase must be accurate.
- A paraphrase must be complete.
- A paraphrase must be written in your own voice.
- A paraphrase must make sense by itself.

Free Paraphrase

When a paraphrase moves completely away from the words and sentence structure of the original text and presents ideas in the paraphraser's own style and idiom, then it is said to be "free." A free paraphrase is not only challenging to write but can be as interesting to read as the original—provided that the substance of the source has not been altered, disguised, or substantially condensed. Because a free paraphrase can summarize repetitious parts of the original text, it may be somewhat briefer than the original, but it will present ideas in much the same order.

Here, side by side with the original, is a free paraphrase of an excerpt from Machiavelli's *The Prince.* This passage exemplifies the kind of text—very famous, very difficult—that really benefits from a comprehensive paraphrase. *The Prince* was written in 1513. Even though the translation from the Italian used here was revised in this century, the paraphraser has to bridge a tremendous gap in time and in style to present Machiavelli in an idiom suitable for modern readers.

Original Version	*Paraphrase*
It is not, therefore, necessary for a prince to have [good faith and integrity], but it is very necessary to seem to have them. I would even be bold to say that to possess them and always to observe them is dangerous, but to appear to possess them is useful. Thus it is well to seem merciful,	It is more important for a ruler to give the impression of goodness than to be good. In fact, real goodness can be a liability, but the pretense is always very effective. It is all very well to be virtuous, but it is vital to be able to shift in the other

(continued)

Original Version (continued)

faithful, humane, sincere, religious, and also to be so; but you must have the mind so disposed that when it is needful to be otherwise you may be able to change to the opposite qualities. And it must be understood that a prince, and especially a new prince, cannot observe all those things which are considered good in men, being often obliged, in order to maintain the state, to act against faith, against charity, against humanity, and against religion. And therefore, he must have a mind disposed to adapt itself according to the wind, and as the variations of fortune dictate, and . . . not deviate from what is good, if possible, but be able to do evil if constrained.

A prince must take great care that nothing goes out of his mouth which is not full of the above-mentioned five qualities, and to see and hear him, he should seem to be all mercy, faith, integrity, humanity, and religion. . . . Everyone sees what you appear to be, few feel what you are, and those few will not dare to oppose themselves to the many, who have the majesty of the state to defend them; and in the actions of men, and especially of princes, from which there is no appeal, the end justifies the means. Let a prince therefore aim at conquering and maintaining the state, and the means will always be judged honorable and praised by every one, for the vulgar are always taken by appearances and the issue of the event; and the world consists only of the vulgar, and the few who are not vulgar are isolated when the many have a rallying point in the prince.

Paraphrase (continued)

direction whenever circumstances require it. After all, rulers, especially recently elevated ones, have a duty to perform which may absolutely require them to act against the dictates of faith and compassion and kindness. One must act as circumstances require and, while it's good to be virtuous if you can, it's better to be bad if you must.

In public, however, the ruler should appear to be entirely virtuous, and if his pretense is successful with the majority of people, then those who do see through the act will be outnumbered and impotent, especially since the ruler has the authority of government on his side. In the case of rulers, even more than for most men, "the end justifies the means." If the ruler is able to assume power and administer it successfully, his methods will always be judged proper and satisfactory; for the common people will accept the pretense of virtue and the reality of success, and the astute will find no one is listening to their warnings.

Paraphrase and Summary

To clarify the difference between paraphrase and summary, here is a paragraph that *summarizes* the excerpt from *The Prince*.

> According to Machiavelli, perpetuating power is a more important goal for a ruler than achieving personal goodness or integrity. Although he should act virtuously if he can, and always appear to do so, it is more important for him to adapt quickly to changing circumstances. The masses will be so swayed by his pretended virtue and by his success that any opposition will be ineffective. The wise ruler's maxim is that "the end justifies the means."

To make the distinction between summary and paraphrase entirely clear, here is a recapitulation of the guidelines for writing a brief summary:

1. *A summary is comprehensive.* Like the paraphrase, the summary of *The Prince* says more than "the end justifies the means." While that is probably the most important idea in the passage, it does not by itself convey Machiavelli's full meaning. For one thing, it contains no reference at all to princes and how they should rule—and that, after all, is Machiavelli's subject.

2. *A summary is concise.* It should say exactly as much as you need—and no more. The summary of *The Prince* is considerably shorter than the paraphrase.

3. *A summary is coherent.* The ideas are not presented in the same sequence as that of the original passage, as they are in the paraphrase; nor are the language and tone at all reminiscent of the original. Rather, the summary includes only the passage's most important points, linking them together in a unified paragraph.

Comparing Paraphrase and Summary

Paraphrase	*Summary*
■ Reports your understanding to your reader	■ Reports your understanding to your reader
■ Records a relatively short passage	■ Records a passage of any length
■ Records every point in the passage	■ Selects and condenses, recording only the main ideas
■ Records these points consecutively	■ Changes the order of ideas when necessary
■ Includes no interpretation	■ Explains and (if the writer wishes) interprets

4. *A summary is independent.* What is most striking about the summary, compared with the paraphrase, is the writer's attitude toward the original text. While the paraphraser has to follow closely Machiavelli's ideas and point of view, the summarizer does not. Characteristically, Machiavelli's name is cited in the summary, calling attention to the fact that it is based on another person's ideas.

Either summary or paraphrase should enable you to refer to this passage quite easily in an essay. Which you would choose to use depends on your topic, on the way you are developing your essay, and on the extent to which you wish to discuss Machiavelli.

- In an essay citing Machiavelli as only one among many political theorists, you might use the brief four-sentence summary; then you might briefly comment on Machiavelli's ideas before going on to summarize (and perhaps compare them with) another writer's theories.

- In an essay about a contemporary politician, you might analyze the way in which your subject does or does not carry out Machiavelli's strategies; then you probably would want to familiarize your readers with *The Prince* in some detail through paraphrase. You might include the full paraphrase, interspersed, perhaps, with an analysis of your present-day "prince."

Writing an Accurate Paraphrase

The basic purpose of paraphrase is to present the main ideas contained in the original text. When paraphrase fails to convey the substance of the source, there are three possible explanations:

1. *Misreading:* The writer genuinely misunderstood the text.
2. *Projecting:* The writer insisted on reading his or her own ideas into the text.
3. *Guessing:* The writer had a spark of understanding and constructed a paraphrase centered around that spark, but ignored too much of the original text.

Read Christopher Lasch's analysis of the changing role of the child in family life. Then examine each of the three paraphrases that follow, deciding whether it conveys Lasch's principal ideas and, if not, why it has gone astray. Compare your reactions with the analysis that follows each paraphrase.

Original

The family by its very nature is a means of raising children, but this fact should not blind us to the important change that occurred when child-rearing ceased to be simply one of many activities and became the central concern—one is tempted to say the central obsession—of family life. This development had to wait for the recognition of the child as a distinctive kind of person, more impressionable and hence more vulnerable than adults, to be treated in a special manner befitting his peculiar requirements. Again, we take these things for granted and find it hard to imagine anything else. Earlier, children had been clothed, fed, spoken to, and educated as little adults; more specifically, as servants, the difference between childhood and servitude having been remarkably obscure throughout much of Western history. . . . It was only in the seventeenth century in certain classes that childhood came to be seen as a special category of experience. When that happened, people recognized the enormous formative influence of family life, and the family became above all an agency for building character, for consciously and deliberately forming the child from birth to adulthood.

"Divorce and the Family in America," *Atlantic Monthly*

Paraphrase A

The average family wants to raise children with a good education and to encourage, for example, the ability to read and write well. They must be taught to practice and learn on their own. Children can be treated well without being pampered. They must be treated as adults as they get older and experience more of life. A parent must build character and the feeling of independence in a child. No longer should children be treated as kids or servants, for that can cause conflict in a family relationship.

This paraphrase has very little in common with the original passage. True, it is about child-rearing, but the writer chooses to give advice to parents, rather than present the contrast between early and modern attitudes toward children, as Lasch does. Since the only clear connection between Lasch and this paragraph is the reference to servants, the writer was probably confused by the passage, and (instead of slowing down the process and paraphrasing it sentence by sentence) guessed—mistakenly—at its meaning. There is also some projection of the writer's ideas about family life. Notice how assertive the tone is; the writer seems to be admonishing parents rather than presenting Lasch's detached analysis.

Paraphrase B

When two people get married, they usually produce a child. They get married because they want a family. Raising a family is now different from the way it used to be. The child is looked upon as a human being, with feelings and thoughts of his own. Centuries ago, children were treated like robots, little more than hired help. Now, children are seen as people who need a strong, dependable family background to grow into persons of good character. Parents are needed to get children ready to be the adults of tomorrow.

This paragraph also seems to combine guessing (beginning) and projection (end). The middle sentences do present Lasch's basic point, but the beginning and the end move so far away from the main ideas that the paraphrase as a whole does not bear much resemblance to the original text. It also includes an exaggeration: are servants "robots"?

Paraphrase C

> Though the family has always been an important institution, its child-rearing function has only in recent centuries become its most important activity. This change has resulted from the relatively new idea that children have a special, unique personality. In the past, there was little difference seen between childhood and adulthood. But today people realize the importance of family life, especially the family unit as a means of molding the personalities of children from childhood to adulthood.

Although this paraphrase is certainly the most accurate of the three, it is too brief to be a complete paraphrase. In fact, the writer seems to be summarizing, not paraphrasing. Lasch's main idea is there, but the following points are missing:

1. There is a tremendous difference between pre-seventeenth-century and twentieth-century perceptions of childhood.
2. Before the seventeenth century, it was difficult to distinguish between the status and treatment of children and that of servants.
3. Child-rearing has now become of overriding ("obsessive") importance to the family.
4. Children are different from adults in that they are less hardened and less experienced.

The author of Paraphrase C has done a thorough job of the beginning and the end of Lasch's passage, and evidently left the middle to take care of itself. But a paraphrase cannot be considered a reliable "translation" of the original text unless all the supporting ideas are given appropriate emphasis. The omission of Point 2 is particularly important.

Here is a more comprehensive paraphrase of the passage:

> Though the family has always been the institution responsible for bringing up children, only in recent times has its child-raising function become the family's overriding purpose and its reason for being. This striking shift to the child-centered family has resulted from the gradual realization that children have a special, unique personality, easy to influence and easy to hurt, and that they must be treated accordingly. Special treatment for children is the norm in our time; but hundreds of years ago, people saw little or no difference between childhood and adulthood, and, in fact, the child's role in the family resembled that of a servant. It was not until the seventeenth century that people began to regard childhood as a distinctive stage of growth. That recognition led them to understand what a powerful influence the family environment must have on the child and to define "family" as the chief instrument for molding the child's personality and moral attitudes.

EXERCISE 11: IDENTIFYING A GOOD PARAPHRASE

The next passage is followed by a group of paraphrases. Examine each one and identify those that conform to the guidelines for paraphrasing. Ask yourself whether the paraphrase contains any point that is not in the original passage and whether the key points of the original are *all* clearly presented in the paraphrase.

from MULTICULTURALISM'S SILENT PARTNER
David Rieff

One of the central tenets [of multiculturalism] is to undermine the idea of the masterpiece—of the criterion of quality—as anti-democratic. For the multiculturalist, notions such as "quality" are tainted; their real purpose is to preserve the privileges of a dominant group: in the American context, dead white males. And the multiculturalists are in command—sort of—of a couple of truths: Western culture has excluded many things; art in the traditional sense is anti-egalitarian, in that it demands that people judge a given work not only subjectively but objectively superior to another. It is the innately hierarchical nature of art, or even, as they used to say, art appreciation, that sets the multiculturalists' teeth on edge—they are suspicious of hierarchy. For, as they rightly surmise, if there is hierarchy how can there be liberation?

So far, so good, radically speaking. The mistake the multiculturalists make is in imagining that their efforts are in some crucial way bound to undermine the fundamental interests of capitalism. The contrary is surely closer to the truth: the multiculturalist mode is what any smart businessman would prefer. For if all art is deemed as good as all other art, and, for that matter, if the point of art is not greatness but the production of works of art that reflect the culture and aspirations of various ethnic, sexual, or racial subgroups within a society, then one is in a position to increase supply almost at will in order to meet increases in demand. Instead of being a rare and costly thing, culture becomes simultaneously a product, like a car—something that can be made new every few years—and an abundant resource, like, well, people. The result is that the consumption of culture can increasingly come to resemble the consumption of goods.

1. Multiculturalism is opposed to the creation of great works of art because they are usually created by the kind of people, like dead white males, who dominate society. In some ways, the multiculturalists are right. The old-fashioned view of art means that some works are better than others, which multiculturalists don't like since that leads to cultural oppression.

   The multicultural view of art is good for business. If one work of art is as good as the next, then they're interchangeable, and you can sell more of them. That way, we can buy and sell culture, just like anything else we buy and sell.

2. Multiculturalists have very democratic ideas about art, and they don't like the idea of high quality art, which is too exclusive for them. It is better that people look at art objectively, not subjectively, and it is better to lower standards and not rank one picture against another. Dividing culture into better or worse art isn't liberating.

The multiculturalist point of view is opposed to capitalism, but they're wrong. A good businessman can make use of multicultural ideas. Art is all alike, whatever you produce, especially if it reflects racial or sexual segments of society. The more you make, the more you sell. So, culture becomes like anything else that's for sale.

3. Because multiculturalists believe strongly in equality and reject the authority of any single powerful group, they are opposed to applying fixed standards to judging works of art. In America, what's called a great work of art conforms to and perpetuates the standards of the ruling group of white males, not the feelings of those who look at the picture. That cultural system is based on status, with those at the top as oppressors, determining what everyone else thinks.

In their enthusiasm, multiculturalists mistakenly conclude that cultural equality would chip away at this country's business ethic. In actuality, doing away with a single standard for distinguishing between good art and bad art and substituting art that satisfies the needs of society's various subcultures makes it possible for businesses to order pictures by the yard and to adjust inventory based on market research. Without the idea of quality, art becomes a consumable commodity like anything else.

Paraphrasing a Difficult Text

Since translating another writer's idiom into your own can be difficult, a paraphrase is often written in two stages.

- In your first version, you work out a *word-for-word substitution,* staying close to the sentence structure of the original, as if, indeed, you are writing a translation. This is the *literal paraphrase.*

- In your second version, you work from your own literal paraphrase, turning it into a *free paraphrase* by reconstructing and rephrasing the sentences to make them more natural and more characteristic of *your own writing style.*

Writing a Literal Paraphrase

To write a paraphrase that is faithful to the original text is impossible if you are uncertain of the meaning of any of the words. To write a literal paraphrase of a difficult passage:

- Use a dictionary, especially if the passage contains obsolete or archaic language.

- Write down a few possible synonyms for each difficult word, making sure that you understand the connotations of each synonym.

- Choose the substitute that best fits the context of your literal paraphrase.

Too often, the writer of a paraphrase forgets that there *is* a choice and quickly substitutes the first synonym in the dictionary. Even when appropriate synonyms have been carefully chosen, the literal paraphrase can look peculiar and sound dreadful. While the old sentence structure has been retained, the key words have been yanked out and new ones plugged in.

To illustrate the pitfalls of this process, here is a short excerpt from Francis Bacon's essay "Of Marriage and Single Life," written around 1600. Some of the phrasing and word combinations are archaic and may sound unnatural, but nothing in the passage is too difficult for modern understanding *if* the sentences are read slowly and carefully.

> He that hath wife and children hath given hostages to fortune; for they are impediments to great enterprises, either of virtue or mischief. Certainly, the best works and of greatest merit for the public have proceeded from the unmarried or childless men: which both in affection and means have endowed the public.

The passage's main idea is not too difficult to establish: *Unmarried men, without the burden of a family, can afford to contribute to the public good.* But by now you must realize that such a brief summary is not the same as a paraphrase, for it does not fully present Bacon's reasoning.

Paraphrase A

He who has a wife and children has <u>bestowed</u> <u>prisoners</u> to <u>riches</u>; for they are <u>defects</u> in huge <u>business</u> <u>organizations</u> either for <u>morality</u> or <u>damage</u>.

Paraphrase B

He who has a wife and children has <u>given</u> a <u>pledge</u> to <u>destiny</u>; for they are <u>hindrances</u> to large <u>endeavor</u>, either for <u>good</u> or for <u>ill</u>.

Neither sentence sounds very normal or very clear; but the second has potential, while the first makes no sense. Yet, in *both* cases, the inserted words *are* synonyms for the original vocabulary. In Paraphrase A the words do not fit Bacon's context; in Paraphrase B they do. For example, it is misleading to choose "business organizations" as a synonym for "enterprises," since the passage doesn't actually concern business, but refers to any sort of undertaking requiring freedom from responsibility. "Impediment" can mean either "defect" (as in speech impediment) or "hindrance" (as in impediment to learning); but—again, given the context—it is the latter meaning that Bacon has in mind. You will choose the correct connotation or nuance only if you think carefully about the synonyms and use your judgment: the process cannot be hurried.

A phrase like "hostage to fortune" offers special difficulty, since it is a powerful image expressing a highly abstract idea. No paraphraser can improve on the original wording or even find an equivalent phrase. However, expressing the idea is useful: a bargain made with life—the renunciation of future independent action in exchange for a family. Wife and children become a kind of bond ("hostage") to ensure one's future social conformity. The aptness and singularity of Bacon's original phrase are measured by the difficulty of paraphrasing three words in less than two sentences!

Writing a Free Version of the Literal Paraphrase

Correct though the synonyms may be, the passage from Bacon cannot be left as it is in Paraphrase B, for no reader could readily understand this stilted, artificial sentence. It is necessary to rephrase the paraphrase, ensuring that the meaning of the words is retained, but making the sentence sound more natural. The first attempt at "freeing up" the paraphrase stays as close as possible to the literal version, leaving everything in the same sequence, but using a more modern idiom:

Paraphrase C

Married men with children are hindered from embarking on any important undertaking, good or bad. Indeed, unmarried and childless men are the ones who have done the most for society and have dedicated their love and their money to the public good.

The second sentence (which is simpler to paraphrase than the first) has been inverted here, but the paraphrase is still a point-by-point recapitulation of Bacon. Paraphrase C is acceptable, but can be improved, both to clarify Bacon's meaning and to introduce a more personal voice. What exactly *are* these unmarried men dedicating to the public good? "Affection and means." And what is the modern equivalent of means? Money? Effort? Time? Energy?

Paraphrase D

A man with a family has obligations that prevent him from devoting himself to any activity that pleases him. On the other hand, a single man or a man without children has a greater opportunity to be a philanthropist. That's why most great contributions of energy and resources to the good of society are made by single men.

The writer of Paraphrase D has not supplied a synonym for "affection," assuming perhaps that the expenditure of energy and resources result from interest and concern; affection is almost too weak a motivation for the philanthropist as he is described here.

Paraphrase E

The responsibility of a wife and children prevents a man from taking risks with his money, time, and energy. The greatest social benefactors have been men who have adopted the public as their family.

The second sentence here is the only one of the five versions that approaches Bacon's economy of style. "Adopted the public" is not quite the same as "endowed the public" with one's "affection and means"; but nevertheless, this paraphrase is successful because it speaks for itself. It has a life and an importance of its own, independent of Bacon's original passage, yet it makes the same point that Bacon does.

Guidelines for Paraphrasing a Difficult Passage

1. Look up in a dictionary the meanings of all the words of which you are uncertain. Pay special attention to the difficult words, considering the context of the whole passage.
2. Write a literal paraphrase of each passage by substituting appropriate synonyms within the original sentence structure.
3. Revise your literal paraphrase, keeping roughly to the same length and number of sentences as the original, but using your own sentence style and phrasing throughout. You may prefer to put the original passage aside at this point, and work entirely from your own version.
4. Read your free paraphrase aloud to make sure that it makes sense.

ASSIGNMENT 3: PARAPHRASING A DIFFICULT PASSAGE

Paraphrase one of the following passages, using the guidelines in the box above. (Your instructor may assign a specific paragraph for the entire class to paraphrase; you may be asked to work together with one or more of your classmates.)

1. The death of the cowboy as a viable persona for Hollywood's A-list actors means there is no archetype left that allows latter-day Coopers, Waynes and Fondas to act with exemplary courage and yet remain regular guys. Of late, any actor wanting to be a hero has, more often than not, found himself playing second fiddle to a piece of technology in a distant precinct of space or the future. Acts of great bravery have become more and more divorced from common experience. Everyday valor, in which an average Joe armed with little more than his guts and wits does battle with an intractable foe, is in danger of becoming a thing of the past.

   STEPHEN AMIDON, from "Back to the Front"

2. There used to be a social modification which, excused by the erroneous belief that men were naturally more polygamous than women, gave the sort of glancing blow that is really an approving pat to men who broke out of monogamy but seriously and cruelly disapproved of women who did. The injustice of this "double standard" is now pretty clear to everyone, and in its place we have introduced a legal modification of monogamy. Divorce is a device which makes polygamy permissible, but only nonsimultaneous polygamy. In practice, even this is modified. The law sometimes insists that a divorcée remain a man's wife economically even though she is no longer so in name or in bed. The result is, just as in Moslem countries where the number of wives a man may legally have simultaneously is often whittled down in practice to the number he can support, so in Europe and the United States, under our modified monogamy, the number of ex-wives a man may legally have simultaneously is often limited to the number of those he can support.

   BRIGID BROPHY, from "Monogamy"

3. It is somewhat ironic to note that grading *systems* evolved in part because of [problems in evaluating performance]. In situations where reward and recognition often depended more on who you knew than on what you knew, and lineage was more important than ability, the cause of justice seemed to demand a method whereby the individual could demonstrate specific abilities on the basis of objective criteria. This led to the establishment of specific standards and public criteria as ways of reducing prejudicial treatment and, in cases where appropriate standards could not be specified in advance, to the normal curve system of establishing levels on the basis of group performance. The imperfect achievement of the goals of such systems in no way negates the importance of the underlying purposes.

   WAYNE MOELLENBERG, from "To Grade or
   Not to Grade—Is That the Question?"

4. Work is not simply a way to make a living and support one's family. It also constitutes a framework for daily behavior and patterns of interaction because it imposes disciplines and regularities. Thus, in the absence of regular employment,

a person lacks not only a place in which to work and the receipt of regular income but also a coherent organization of the present—that is, a system of concrete expectations and goals. Regular employment provides the anchor for the spatial and temporal aspects of daily life. It determines where you are going to be and when you are going to be there. In the absence of regular employment, life, including family life, becomes less coherent. Persistent unemployment and irregular employment hinder rational planning in daily life, the necessary condition of adaptation to an industrial economy.

WILLIAM JULIUS WILSON, from *When Work Disappears*

INCORPORATING PARAPHRASE INTO YOUR ESSAY

The paraphrased ideas of other writers should never take control of your essay, but should always be subordinate to *your* ideas. When you insert a paraphrased sentence or a brief paraphrased passage (rather than a quotation) into one of your paragraphs, you minimize the risk that the source material will dominate your writing.

Most academic writers rely on a combination of quotation, paraphrase, and summary to present their sources.

To illustrate the way in which these three techniques of presentation can be successfully combined, here is an extract from an article by Conor Cruise O'Brien that depends on a careful mixture of paraphrase, summary, and quotation. In "Violence—And Two Schools of Thought," O'Brien gives an account of a medical conference concerned with the origins of violence. Specifically, he undertakes to present and (at the end) comment on the ideas of two speakers at the conference.

VIOLENCE—AND TWO SCHOOLS OF THOUGHT*
Conor Cruise O'Brien

Summary   The opening speakers were fairly representative of the main schools of thought which almost always declare themselves when violence is discussed. The first school sees a propensity to aggression as biological but capable of being socially conditioned into patterns of acceptable behavior. The second sees it as essentially created by social conditions and therefore capable of being removed by benign social change.

*In its original format in *The Observer,* the article's paragraphing, in accordance with usual journalistic practice, occurs with distracting frequency; the number of paragraphs has been reduced here, without any alteration of the text.

Quotation   The first speaker held that violence was "a bio-social phenome-   2
non." He rejected the notion that human beings were blank paper
"on which the environment can write whatever it likes." He de-
Paraphrase   scribed how a puppy could be conditioned to choose a dog food it
did not like and to reject one it did like. This was the creation of
conscience in the puppy. It was done by mild punishment. If human
beings were acting more aggressively and anti-socially, despite the
advent of better social conditions and better housing, this might be
because permissiveness, in school and home, had checked the process of social conditioning, and therefore of conscience-building. He
favored the reinstatement of conscience-building, through the use
Quotation   of mild punishment and token rewards. "We cannot eliminate violence," he said, "but we can do a great deal to reduce it."

Summary   The second speaker thought that violence was the result of stress;   3
in almost all the examples he cited it was stress from overcrowding.
The behavior of apes and monkeys in zoos was "totally different" from
the way they behaved in "the completely relaxed conditions in the
Paraphase/   wild." In crowded zoos the most aggressive males became leaders
Quotation   and a general reign of terror set in; in the relaxed wild, on the other
hand, the least aggressive males ruled benevolently. Space was all: "If
Paraphase/   we could eliminate population pressures, violence would vanish."
Quotation

Summary   The student [reacting to the argument of the two speakers] pre-   4
ferred the second speaker. He [the second speaker] spoke with ebullient confidence, fast but clear, and at one point ran across the vast
platform, in a lively imitation of the behavior of a charging ape. Also,
his message was simple and hopeful. Speaker one, in contrast, looked
sad, and his message sounded faintly sinister. Such impressions,
Author's   rather than the weight of argument, determine the reception of pa-
Comment   pers read in such circumstances.

Summary/   Nonetheless, a student queried speaker two's "relaxed wild." He   5
Paraphase   seemed to recall a case in which a troop of chimpanzees had completely wiped out another troop. The speaker was glad the student
had raised that question because it proved the point. You see, where
that had occurred, there had been an overcrowding in the jungle,
just as happens in zoos, and this was a response to overcrowding.
Conditions in the wild, it seems, are not always "completely re-
Author's   laxed." And when they attain that attributed condition—through
Comment   the absence of overcrowding—this surely has to be due to the "natural controls," including the predators, whose attentions can hardly
be all that relaxing, or, indeed, all that demonstrative of the validity
of the proposition that violence is not a part of nature. Speaker two
did not allude to predators. Nonetheless, they are still around, on
two legs as well as on four.

Selecting Quotations When You Paraphrase

Although we do not have the texts of the original papers given at the conference to compare with O'Brien's description, this article seems to present a clear and comprehensive account of a complex discussion. In the first paragraph, O'Brien uses brief summaries to help us distinguish between the two speakers; next, he provides us with two separate, noncommittal descriptions of the two main points of view.

The ratio of quotation to paraphrase to summary works very effectively. O'Brien quotes for two reasons: *aptness of expression* and *the desire to distance himself from the statement.* For example, he chooses to quote the vivid image of the blank paper "on which the environment can write whatever it likes." And he also selects points for quotation that he regards as open to dispute—"totally different"; "completely relaxed"; "violence would vanish." Such strong or sweeping statements are often quoted so that writers can disassociate themselves from the implications of their source material; this way, they cannot be accused of either toning down or exaggerating the meaning in their paraphrases.

Reasons to Use Quotation

- You can find no words to convey the economy and aptness of phrasing of the original text.
- A paraphrase might alter the statement's meaning.
- A paraphrase would not clearly distinguish between your views and the author's.

Avoiding Plagiarism: Citing Your Paraphrased Sources

The one possible source of confusion in O'Brien's article occurs when he begins his own commentary. In the last two paragraphs, it is not always easy to determine where O'Brien's paraphrase of the speakers' ideas ends and his own opinions begin. In Paragraph 4, his description of the student's reactions to the two speakers appears objective. At the end of the paragraph, however, we learn that O'Brien is scornful of the criteria that the student is using to evaluate these ideas. But at first we cannot be sure whether O'Brien is describing the *student's observation* or giving *his own account* of the speaker's platform maneuvers. It would be clearer to us if the sentence began: "According to the responding student, the second speaker spoke with ebullient confidence. . . . " Similarly, the last sentence of Paragraph 4 is undoubtedly O'Brien's opinion, yet there is nothing to indicate the transition from the student to O'Brien as the source of commentary.

This *confusion of point of view* is especially deceptive in Paragraph 5 as O'Brien moves from his paraphrased and neutral account of the dialogue between student and speaker to his own opinion that certain predators influence behavior in civilization as well as in the wild. It takes two readings to notice the point at which O'Brien is no longer paraphrasing but beginning to speak in his own voice. Such confusions could have been clarified by inserting citations—the name of the source or an appropriate pronoun—in the appropriate places.

In academic writing the clear acknowledgment of the source is not merely a matter of courtesy or clarity; it is an assurance of the writer's honesty.

When you paraphrase another person's ideas, you must cite the author's name, as you do when you quote, or else risk being charged with plagiarism. Borrowing ideas is just as much theft as borrowing words.

You omit the quotation marks when you paraphrase, but you must not omit the citation. Of course, the citation of the name should be smoothly integrated into your sentence, following the guidelines used for citation of quotations. The source's name need not appear at the beginning of the sentence, but it should signal the beginning of the paraphrase:

Not everyone enjoys working, but most people would agree with Jones's belief that work is an essential experience of life.

The writer of the essay is responsible for the declaration that "not everyone enjoys working" and that most people would agree with Jones's views; but the belief that "work is an essential experience of life" is attributed to Jones. Here, the citation is well and unobtrusively placed; there are no quotation marks, so presumably Jones used a different wording.

Here, then, are additional guidelines for the proper citation of sources:

- When you *quote,* there can never be any doubt about where the borrowed material begins and where it ends: the quotation marks provide a clear indication of the boundaries.

- When you *paraphrase,* although the citation may signal the *beginning* of the source material, your reader may not be sure exactly where the paraphrase *ends.*

There is no easy method of indicating the termination of paraphrased material. (As you will see in Chapter 9, the author's name in parentheses works well if you are using that method of documentation.) It is possible to signal the end of a paraphrase simply by starting a new paragraph. However, you may need to incorporate more than one person's ideas into a single paragraph. *When you present several points of view in succession, be careful to acknowledge the change of source by citing names.*

In some kinds of essays, it may be appropriate to signal the shift from paraphrased material to your own opinions by using the first person. Instructors' attitudes toward the first person vary, but some find it acceptable to use "I" in certain kinds of writing as long as it is not inserted excessively or monotonously. A carefully placed "I" can leave your reader in no doubt as to whose voice is being heard. Make sure, however, that using "I" is consistent with the tone and point of view of your essay. If you are presenting sources through a narrative in which you otherwise remain in the background, the sudden appearance of "I" would mean a sharp break in the overall tone and would therefore be inappropriate.

EXERCISE 12: DISTINGUISHING BETWEEN QUOTATION, PARAPHRASE, SUMMARY, AND COMMENTARY

1. Read "A Prominent Scholar's Plan for the Inner Cities Draws Fire," by Chris Shea.
2. In the margin, indicate where the author uses quotation (Q), paraphrase (P), summary (S), and commentary (C).
3. In class discussion, be prepared to evaluate the use of quotation, paraphrase, and summary, and to indicate those places in the article where, in your opinion, one of the techniques is inappropriately or unnecessarily used, or where the transition from one technique to the other is not clearly identified.

A PROMINENT SCHOLAR'S PLAN FOR THE INNER CITIES DRAWS FIRE

Chris Shea

William Julius Wilson, one of the country's most prominent experts on the problems of America's inner cities, came in for some tough criticism at the annual meeting of the American Sociological Association here last month.   1

His latest book, *When Work Disappears: The World of the New Urban Poor*, published last fall by Alfred A. Knopf, has been widely and respectfully reviewed. It is the broadest statement yet on America's social ills by the sociologist, who spent most of his career at the University of Chicago before moving to Harvard University last year.   2

But in a debate that drew a large crowd—about 400 people in a room intended for two-thirds that number—Dr. Wilson's proposals for helping cities were blasted by Douglas S. Massey, chairman of the University of Pennsylvania's sociology department.   3

Dr. Massey did not contest Dr. Wilson's observations about rising unemployment and poverty rates in Chicago ghettos. In some of the neighborhoods he describes in his book, only one in three people over the age of 16 has a job.   4

Instead, Dr. Massey took aim at Dr. Wilson's policy proposals, which emphasize strategies to help unskilled workers of all races rather than singling out black workers.   5

For example, he has proposed a program modeled on the New Deal's Works Progress Administration, which would give unemployed people such jobs as sweeping streets and picking up garbage.   6

Dr. Wilson argues that massive interventions to desegregate cities and expand affirmative action are impractical, given Americans' resistance to race-specific policies. At   7 the meeting, he said he hoped to galvanize "progressives" across racial lines with a race-blind vision of social justice.

But Dr. Massey said Dr. Wilson was using a double standard in evaluating the feasibility of race-based and class-based solutions.   8

"In essence, Wilson argues that race-based remedies are a political loser," he said.   9
But a W. P. A.–style program is no less pie-in-the-sky, Dr. Massey said, given today's conservative climate.

And Dr. Wilson is dead wrong, he added, to think he can do an end-run around the   10
charged issue of race. "It will not be possible to deal with class-based divisions without addressing race-based issues with equal verve," he said. "Putting race on the back burner would leave the field open to those who would undermine the class-based strategies we all think we need, by manipulating racial attitudes that are still there."

Welfare is a race-neutral program, he pointed out. But editorials about black "wel-   11
fare queens," who were said to live largely off the dole, helped turn public sentiment against it.

Cynical conservative operatives could just as easily "racialize" a W. P. A.–style pro-   12
gram by caricaturing its beneficiaries as lazy black shirkers in do-nothing jobs, he said.

No solution to the problem of urban poverty, Dr. Massey said, can escape the need   13
for a dismantling of what he called "the system of *de facto* apartheid" in many cities.

In his response, Dr. Wilson shed his usual courtly demeanor. "Massey argues that I   14
have moved away from racial-specific policies," he said, his voice rising to a near shout.
"*I do not.* I want to say that categorically: *I do not.*"

He said his proposals should be paired with affirmative-action policies that take   15
both class and race into account. And he said he had called for better enforcement of federal housing-discrimination laws. In a pointed allusion to his own political influence, he also noted that the Urban League, a national black civil-rights group, had embraced many of his race-neutral policies. "Now, more than ever, we need broader solutions than we have had in the past," he said.

In the current issue of *Contemporary Sociology,* Dr. Massey offers some criticisms of   16
Dr. Wilson's research that did not come up in the debate.

He calls Dr. Wilson's massive research on Chicago ghettos, known as the "Urban   17
Poverty and Family Life Study," "rather a disappointment," arguing that "despite the investment of hundreds of thousands of research dollars," few resulting articles have appeared in refereed social-science journals. "The U. P. F. L. has simply not affected social science in a manner commensurate with its size and scope," he writes.

In a telephone interview, Dr. Wilson said that aside from his own book, which uses   18
the data, some 20 refereed journal articles and book chapters had emerged from the project, and more books—including one from Marta Tienda, a University of Chicago sociologist—are due soon.

After the debate, Dr. Massey said, "I keep pushing Wilson on the issue of race, and he   19
keeps moving slowly and grudgingly toward accepting it, but more in person than in print."

The audience seemed to agree that frontal attacks on both racial and class issues   20
are necessary, yet pessimism was the dominant mood at the meeting.

"This is rather depressing," one graduate student told the two professors. "It sounds like you are saying we need a sea change in public attitudes for anything to happen." Neither scholar disagreed.

21

PRESENTING SOURCES: A SUMMARY OF PRELIMINARY WRITING SKILLS

1. **Annotation: underlining the text and inserting marginal comments on the page.**

   The notes can explain points that are unclear, define difficult words, emphasize key ideas, point out connections to previous or subsequent paragraphs, or suggest the reader's own reactions to what is being discussed.

2. **Outlining: constructing a systematic list of ideas that reflects the basic structure of an essay or book, with major and minor points distributed on different levels.**

   Outlining is a reductive skill that presents the bones of a work, but little of its flesh or outward appearance. Outlining is especially useful for covering a long sequence of material containing ideas whose relationship is easy to grasp. Densely written passages that rely on frequent and subtle distinctions and dexterous use of language are not easily condensed into an outline.

3. **Paraphrasing: recapitulating, point by point, using your own words.**

   A paraphrase is a faithful and complete rendition of the original, following much the same order of ideas. Although full-length paraphrase is practical only with relatively brief passages, it is the most reliable way to make sense out of a difficult text. Paraphrasing a sentence or two, together with a citation of the author's name, is the best method of presenting another person's ideas within your own essay.

4. **Quotation: including another person's exact words within your own writing.**

   Although quotation requires the least amount of invention, it is the most technical of all these skills, demanding an understanding of conventional and complex punctuation. In your notes and in your essays, quotation should be a last resort. If the phrasing is unique, if the presentation is subtle, if the point at issue is easily misunderstood or hotly debated, quotation may be appropriate. When in doubt, paraphrase.

5. **Summary: condensing a paragraph or an essay or a chapter into a relatively brief presentation of the main ideas.**

   Unlike annotation, a summary should make sense as an independent, coherent piece of writing. Unlike paraphrase, a summary includes only main ideas. However, the summary should be complete in the sense that it provides a fair representation of the work and its parts. Summary is the all-purpose skill; it is neither crude nor overly detailed.

Part II

WRITING
FROM
SOURCES

The previous two chapters have described some basic ways to understand another writer's ideas and present them accurately and naturally, as part of your own writing. Until now, however, you have been working with forms of writing that are brief and limited—the sentence and the paragraph. Now you can use the skills that you practiced in Part I to develop your own ideas in a full-length essay based on sources.

When you write at length from sources, you must work with *two points of view—your own* and *those of the authors you're writing about.* You therefore have a dual responsibility: You must do justice to yourself by developing your own ideas, and you must do justice to each source by fairly representing its author's ideas. But blending the ideas of two or more people within the same essay can create confusion: Who should dominate? How much of yourself should you include? How much of your source? Moreover, in academic and professional writing you may have to consider a third voice—that of your teacher or supervisor, who may assign a topic or otherwise set limits and goals for your work.

Chapter 3 discusses two approaches to writing based on a single source. Each demonstrates a way to reconcile the competing influences on your writing and blend the voices that your reader ought to hear:

- You can distinguish between your source and yourself by writing about the two separately, first the source and then yourself, and, in the process, developing an argument that supports or refutes your source's thesis.
- You can use your source as the basis for the development of your own ideas by writing an essay on a similar or related topic.

In the end, *your voice should dominate.* It is you who will choose the thesis and control the essay's structure and direction; it is your understanding and judgment that will interpret the source materials for your reader. When you and your classmates are asked to write about the same reading, your teacher hopes to receive, not an identical set of essays, but rather a series of individual interpretations with a common starting point in the same source.

Combining your own ideas with those of others inevitably becomes more difficult when you begin to work with *a group of sources* and must represent several authors. This is the subject of Chapter 4. It is more than ever vital that your own voice dominate your essay and that you do not simply summarize first one source and then the next, without any perspective of your own.

Blending together a variety of sources is usually called *synthesis*. You try to look beyond each separate assertion and, instead, develop a broad generalization that will encompass your source material. Your own generalized conclusions become the basis for your essay's thesis and organization, while the ideas of your sources serve as the evidence that supports those conclusions.

Chapter 4 emphasizes the standard methods of presenting multiple sources:

- The analysis of each source in a search for common themes.
- The establishment of common denominators or categories that cut across the separate sources and provide the structure for your essay.
- The evaluation of each source's relative significance as you decide which to emphasize.
- The citation of references from several different sources in support of a single point.

These skills are closely related to some of the most common and useful strategies for constructing an essay: *definition, classification,* and *comparison.*

▪ 3 ▪
The Single-Source Essay

When you write from a source, you must understand another writer's ideas as thoroughly as you understand your own. The first step in carrying out the strategies described in this chapter is to *read carefully through the source essay*, using the skills for comprehension that you learned about in Chapters 1 and 2: annotation, outlining, paraphrase, and summary. Once you are able to explain to your reader what the source is all about, you can begin to plan your analysis and rebuttal of the author's ideas; or you can write your own essay on a similar topic.

STRATEGY ONE:
ARGUING AGAINST YOUR SOURCE

The simplest way to argue against someone else's ideas is *complete separation between your source and yourself.* The structure of your essay breaks into two parts, with the source's views presented first, and your own reactions given equal (or greater) space immediately afterward. Instead of treating the reading as evidence in support of your point of view and blending it with your own ideas, you write an essay that *first analyzes and then refutes your source's basic themes.* Look, for example, at Roger Sipher's "So That Nobody Has to Go to School If They Don't Want To."

SO THAT NOBODY HAS TO GO TO SCHOOL
IF THEY DON'T WANT TO
Roger Sipher

A decline in standardized test scores is but the most recent indicator that American education is in trouble.   1

One reason for the crisis is that present mandatory-attendance laws force many to attend school who have no wish to be there. Such children have little desire to learn and are so antagonistic to school that neither they nor more highly motivated students receive the quality education that is the birthright of every American.   2

The solution to this problem is simple: Abolish compulsory-attendance laws and allow only those who are committed to getting an education to attend.   3

This will not end public education. Contrary to conventional belief, legislators enacted compulsory-attendance laws to legalize what already existed. William Landes and Lewis Solomon, economists, found little evidence that mandatory-attendance laws increased the number of children in school. They found, too, that school systems have never effectively enforced such laws, usually because of the expense involved.   4

There is no contradiction between the assertion that compulsory attendance has had little effect on the number of children attending school and the argument that repeal would be a positive step toward improving education. Most parents want a high school education for their children. Unfortunately, compulsory attendance hampers the ability of public school officials to enforce legitimate educational and disciplinary policies and thereby make the education a good one.   5

Private schools have no such problem. They can fail or dismiss students, knowing such students can attend public school. Without compulsory attendance, public schools would be freer to oust students whose academic or personal behavior undermines the educational mission of the institution.   6

Has not the noble experiment of a formal education for everyone failed? While we pay homage to the homily, "You can lead a horse to water but you can't make him drink," we have pretended it is not true in education.   7

Ask high school teachers if recalcitrant students learn anything of value. Ask teachers if these students do any homework. Quite the contrary, these students know they will be passed from grade to grade until they are old enough to quit or until, as is more likely, they receive a high school diploma. At the point when students could legally quit, most choose to remain since they know they are likely to be allowed to graduate whether they do acceptable work or not.   8

Abolition of archaic attendance laws would produce enormous dividends.   9

First, it would alert everyone that school is a serious place where one goes to learn. Schools are neither day-care centers nor indoor street corners. Young people who resist learning should stay away; indeed, an end to compulsory schooling would require them to stay away.   10

Second, students opposed to learning would not be able to pollute the educational atmosphere for those who want to learn. Teachers could stop policing recalcitrant students and start educating.   11

Third, grades would show what they are supposed to: how well a student is learn- 12
ing. Parents could again read report cards and know if their children were making
progress.

Fourth, public esteem for schools would increase. People would stop regarding 13
them as way stations for adolescents and start thinking of them as institutions for
educating America's youth.

Fifth, elementary schools would change because students would find out early 14
that they had better learn something or risk flunking out later. Elementary teachers
would no longer have to pass their failures on to junior high and high school.

Sixth, the cost of enforcing compulsory education would be eliminated. Despite 15
enforcement efforts, nearly 15 percent of the school-age children in our largest
cities are almost permanently absent from school.

Communities could use these savings to support institutions to deal with young 16
people not in school. If, in the long run, these institutions prove more costly, at
least we would not confuse their mission with that of schools.

Schools should be for education. At present, they are only tangentially so. They 17
have attempted to serve an all-encompassing social function, trying to be all things
to all people. In the process they have failed miserably at what they were originally
formed to accomplish. •

Presenting Your Source's Point of View

Sipher opposes compulsory attendance laws. On the other hand, suppose
that you can see advantages in imposing a very strict rule for attendance. In
order to challenge Sipher convincingly, you incorporate both his point of view
and yours within a single essay.

Since your objective is to *respond* to Sipher, you begin by *acknowledging his
ideas and presenting them to your readers.* State them as fairly as you can, without
pausing to argue with him or to offer your own point of view about mandatory attendance.

At first it may seem easiest to follow Sipher's sequence of ideas (especially
since his points are so clearly numbered). But Sipher is more likely to dominate
if you follow the structure of his essay, presenting and answering each of his
points one by one; for you will be arguing on *his* terms, according to *his* conception of the issue rather than yours. Instead, make sure that your reader understands what Sipher is actually saying, see if you can find any common
ground between your points of view, and then begin your rebuttal.

1. Briefly summarize the issue and the reasons that prompted the author to write the essay.

You do this by writing a brief summary, as explained in Chapter 1. Here is a
summary of Sipher's article:

Roger Sipher argues that the presence in the classroom of unwilling
students who are indifferent to learning can explain why public school students

as a whole are learning less and less. Sipher therefore recommends that public schools discontinue the policy of mandatory attendance. Instead, students would be allowed to drop out if they wished, and faculty would be able to expel students whose behavior made it difficult for serious students to do their work. Once unwilling students were no longer forced to attend, schools would once again be able to maintain high standards of achievement; they could devote money and energy to education, rather than custodial care.

You can make such a summary more detailed by paraphrasing some of the author's arguments and, if you wish, quoting once or twice.

2. Analyze and present some of the basic principles that underlie the author's position on this issue.

In debating the issue with the author, you will need to do more than just contradict his main ideas: Sipher says mandatory attendance is bad, and you say it is good; Sipher says difficult students don't learn anything, and you say all students learn something useful; and so on. This point-by-point rebuttal shows that you disagree, but it provides no common context so that readers can decide who is right and who is wrong. You have no starting point for your counterarguments and no choice but to sound arbitrary.

Instead, *ask yourself why the author has taken this position*, one that you find so easy to reject.

- What are the foundations of his arguments?
- What larger principles do they suggest?
- What policies is he objecting to? Why?
- What values is he determined to defend?
- Can these values or principles be applied to issues other than attendance?

You are now examining Sipher's specific responses to the practical problem of attendance in order to *analyze his premises* and *infer some broad generalizations* about his philosophy of education.

Although Sipher does not specifically state such generalizations in this article, you would be safe in concluding that Sipher's views on attendance derive from a *conflict of two principles:*

1. The belief that education is a right that may not be denied under any circumstances, and

2. The belief that education is a privilege to be earned.

Sipher advocates the second position. Thus, after your summary of the article, you should analyze Sipher's implicit position in a separate paragraph.

Sipher's argument implies that there is no such thing as the right to an education. A successful education can only depend on the student's willing presence and active participation. Passive or rebellious students cannot be educated and should not be forced to stay in school. Although everyone has the right to an opportunity for education, its acquisition is actually the privilege of those who choose to work for it.

Through this analysis of Sipher's position, you have not only found out more about the issue being argued, but you have also established a common context—*eligibility for education*—within which you and he disagree. Nor is there much room for compromise here; it is hard to reconcile the belief that education should be a privilege with the concept of education as an entitlement. Provided with a clear understanding of the differences between you, your reader now has a real basis for choosing between your opposing views. At the same time, your reader is being assured that this point and no other is the essential point for debate; thus, you will be fighting on ground that *you* have chosen.

You might also note that Sipher's argument is largely *deductive*: a series of premises that derive their power from an appeal to parents' concerns that their children (who faithfully attend) will have their education compromised by the recalcitrant students (who don't). His *supporting evidence* consists of one allusion to the testimony of two economists and one statistic. Both pieces of evidence confirm the subsidiary idea that attendance laws haven't succeeded in improving attendance. His third source of support—the adage about leading a horse to water—does deal more directly with the problem of learning; but can it be regarded as serious evidence?

Presenting Your Point of View

3. *Present your reasons for disagreeing with your source.*

Once you have established your opponent's position, you may then plan your own counterarguments by writing down your reactions and pinpointing the exact reasons for your disagreement. (All the statements analyzed in this section are taken from such preliminary responses; they are *not* excerpts from finished essays.) Your reasons for disagreeing with Sipher might fit into one of three categories:

- You believe that his basic principle is not valid (Student B).
- You decide that his principle, although valid, cannot be strictly applied to the practical situation under discussion (Student C).
- You accept Sipher's principle, but you are aware of other, stronger influences that diminish its importance (Student E).

Whichever line of argument you follow, it is impossible to present your case successfully if you *wholly ignore Sipher's basic principle*, as Student A does:

Student A

Sipher's isn't a constructive solution. Without strict attendance laws, many students wouldn't come to school at all.

Nonattendance is exactly what Sipher wants: he argues that indifferent students should be permitted to stay away, that their absence would benefit everyone. Student A makes no effort to refute Sipher's point; he is, in effect, saying to his source, "You're wrong!" without explaining why.

Student B, however, tries to *establish a basis for disagreement*:

Student B

If mandatory attendance were to be abolished, how would children acquire the skills to survive in an educated society such as ours?

According to Student B, the practical uses of education have become so important that a student's very survival may one day depend on having been well educated. *Implied here is the principle, in opposition to Sipher's, that receiving an education cannot be a matter of choice or a privilege to be earned.* What children learn in school is so important to their future lives that they should be forced to attend classes, even against their will, for their own good.

But this response is still superficial. Student B is confusing the desired object—*getting an education*—with one of the means of achieving that object—*being present in the classroom*; attendance, the means, has become an end in itself. Since students who attend but do not participate will not learn, mandatory attendance cannot by itself create an educated population.

On the other hand, although attendance may not be the *only* condition for getting an education, the student's physical presence in the classroom is certainly important. In that case, should the decision about attendance, a decision likely to affect much of their future lives, be placed in the hands of those too young to understand the consequences?

Student C

The absence of attendance laws would be too tempting for students and might create a generation of semi-illiterates. Consider the marginal student who, despite general indifference and occasional bad behavior, shows some promise and capacity for learning. Without a policy of mandatory attendance, he might choose the easy way out instead of trying to develop his abilities. As a society, we owe these students, at whatever cost, a chance at a good and sound education.

Notice that Student C specifies a "chance" at education. Here is a basic accommodation between Student C's views and Sipher's. *Both agree in principle that society can provide the opportunity, but not the certainty, of being educated.* The distinction here lies in the way in which the principle is applied. With his argument based on a sweeping generalization, Sipher makes no allowances or exceptions: there are limits to the opportunities that society is obliged to provide. Student C, however, believes that society must act in the best interests of those too young to make such decisions; for their sake, the principle of education as a privilege should be less rigorously applied. Students should be exposed to the conditions for (if not the fact of) education, whether they like it or not, until they become adults, capable of choice.

Student D goes even further, suggesting that not only is society obliged to provide the student with educational opportunities, but schools are responsible for making the experience as attractive as possible.

Student D

Maybe the reason for a decrease in attendance and an unwillingness to learn is not that students do not want an education, but that the whole system of discipline and learning is ineffective. If schools concentrated on making classes more appealing, the result would be better attendance, and students would learn more.

In Student D's analysis, passive students are like consumers who need to be encouraged to take advantage of an excellent product that is not selling well. To encourage good attendance, the schools ought to consider using more attractive marketing methods. *Implicit in this view is a transferral of blame from the student to the school.* Other arguments of this sort might blame the parents, rather than the schools, for not teaching their children to understand that it is in their own best interests to get an education.

Finally, Student E accepts the validity of Sipher's view of education, but finds that the whole issue has become subordinate to a more important problem.

Student E

We already have a problem with youths roaming the street, getting into serious trouble. Just multiply the current number of unruly kids by five or ten, and you will come up with the number of potential delinquents that will be hanging around the streets if we do away with the attendance laws that keep them in school. Sipher may be right when he argues that the quality of education would improve if unwilling students were permitted to drop out, but he would be wise to remember that those remaining inside school will have to deal with those on the outside sooner or later.

In this perspective, *security becomes more important than education.* Student E implicitly accepts and gives some social value to the image (rejected by Sipher) of school as a prison, with students sentenced to mandatory confinement.

Student E also ignores Sipher's tentative suggestion (in paragraph 16) that society provide these students with their own "institution," which he describes only in terms of its potential costs. What would its curriculum be? Would they be "special schools" or junior prisons? And when these students "graduate," how will they take their place in society?

A reasonably full response, like those of Students C and E, can provide the material for a series of paragraphs that argue against Sipher's position. Here, for example, is Student E's statement analyzed into the basic topics for a four-paragraph rebuttal within the essay. (The topics are on the left.)

Student E

danger from dropouts if Sipher's plan is adopted (3)

custodial function of school (2)

concession that Sipher is right about education (1)

interests of law and order outweigh interests of education (4)

We already have a problem with youths roaming the street, getting into serious trouble. Just multiply the current number of unruly kids by five or ten, and you will come up with the number of potential delinquents that will be hanging around the streets if we do away with the attendance laws that keep them in school. Sipher may be right when he argues that the quality of education would improve if unwilling students were permitted to drop out, but he would be wise to remember that those remaining inside school will have to deal with those on the outside sooner or later.

Here are Student E's four topics, with the sequence reordered, in outline format. The student's basic agreement with Sipher has become the starting point.

I. Sipher is right about education.
    A. It is possible that the quality of education would improve if unwilling students were allowed to drop out.
II. School, however, has taken on a custodial function.
    A. It is attendance laws that keep students in school.
III. If Sipher's plan is adopted, dropouts might be a problem.
    A. Youths are already roaming the streets getting into trouble.
    B. An increase in the number of unruly kids hanging out in the streets means even greater possibility of disorder.
IV. The interests of law and order outweigh the interests of education.
    A. Educators will not be able to remain aloof from the problems that will develop outside the schools if students are permitted to drop out at will.

Student E can now write a brief essay, with a summary and analysis of Sipher's argument, followed by four full-length paragraphs explaining each point. If a longer essay is assigned, Student E should go to the library to find supporting evidence—statistics and authoritative testimony—to develop these paragraphs. A starting point might be the issue that Sipher omits: how do these nonattenders fare later on when they look for work? What methods have been successful in persuading such students to stay in school?

Guidelines for Writing a One-Source Argument

- Present your source's point of view.
  1. Briefly summarize the issue and the reasons that prompted the author to write the essay.
  2. Analyze and present some of the basic principles that underlie the author's position on this issue.
- Present your point of view.
  3. Present your reasons for disagreeing with (or, if you prefer, supporting) your source.

ASSIGNMENT 4: WRITING AN ARGUMENT BASED ON A SINGLE SOURCE

Read "What Our Education System Needs Is More F's," "The Case for Censorship," "The Museum of Clear Ideas," and "'Sex' Is Also a Dirty Word." As the starting point for an essay, select one source with which you disagree. (Or, with your instructor's permission, bring in an essay that you are certain that you disagree with, and have your instructor approve your choice.)

1. Write a two-part summary of the essay, the first part describing the author's position and explicitly stated arguments, the second analyzing the principles underlying that position.
2. Then present your own rebuttal of the author's point of view.

The length of your essay will depend on the number and complexity of the ideas that you find in the source and the number of counterarguments that you can assemble. The minimum acceptable length for the entire assignment is two printed pages (approximately 500–600 words).

WHAT OUR EDUCATION SYSTEM NEEDS IS MORE F'S

Carl Singleton

I suggest that instituting merit raises, getting back to basics, marrying the university to industry, and . . . other recommendations will not achieve measurable success [in restoring quality to American education] until something even more basic is returned to practice. The immediate need for our educational system from pre-kindergarten through post-Ph.D. is not more money or better teaching but simply a widespread giving of F's.

Before hastily dismissing the idea as banal and simplistic, think for a moment about the implications of a massive dispensing of failing grades. It would dramatically, emphatically, and immediately force into the open every major issue related to the inadequacies of American education.

Let me make it clear that I recommend giving those F's—by the dozens, hun-   3
dreds, thousands, even millions—only to students who haven't learned the required material. The basic problem of our educational system is the common
practice of giving credit where none has been earned, a practice that has resulted
in the sundry faults delineated by all the reports and studies over recent years. Il-
literacy among high-school graduates is growing because those students have been
passed rather than flunked; we have low-quality teaching because of low-quality
teachers who never should have been certified in the first place; college students
have to take basic reading, writing, and mathematics courses because they never
learned those skills in classrooms from which they never should have been granted
egress.

School systems have contributed to massive ignorance by issuing unearned pass-   4
ing grades over a period of some 20 years. At first there was a tolerance of students who did not fully measure up (giving D's to students who should have
received firm F's); then our grading system continued to deteriorate (D's became
C's, and B became the average grade); finally we arrived at total accommodation
(come to class and get your C's, laugh at my jokes and take home B's).

Higher salaries, more stringent certification procedures, getting back to basics   5
will have little or no effect on the problem of quality education unless and until we
insist, as a profession, on giving F's whenever students fail to master the material.

Sending students home with final grades of F would force most parents to deal   6
with the realities of their children's failure while it is happening and when it is yet
possible to do something about it (less time on TV, and more time on homework,
perhaps?). As long as it is the practice of teachers to pass students who should not
be passed, the responsibility will not go home to the parents, where, I hope, it belongs. (I am tempted to make an analogy to then Gov. Lester Maddox's statement
some years ago about prison conditions in Georgia—"We'll get a better grade of
prisons when we get a better grade of prisoners"—but I shall refrain.)

Giving an F where it is deserved would force concerned parents to get them-   7
selves away from the TV set, too, and take an active part in their children's education. I realize, of course, that some parents would not help; some cannot help.
However, Johnny does not deserve to pass just because Daddy doesn't care or is
ignorant. Johnny should pass only when and if he knows the required material.

Giving an F whenever and wherever it is the only appropriate grade would force   8
principals, school boards, and voters to come to terms with cost as a factor in improving our educational system. As the numbers of students at various levels were
increased by those not being passed, more money would have to be spent to accommodate them. We could not be accommodating them in the old sense of passing them on, but by keeping them at one level until they did in time, one way or
another, learn the material.

Insisting on respecting the line between passing and failing would also require us   9
to demand as much of ourselves as of our students. As every teacher knows, a
failed student can be the product of a failed teacher.

Teaching methods, classroom presentations, and testing procedures would have 10
to be of a very high standard—we could not, after all, consciably give F's if we
have to go home at night thinking it might somehow be our own fault.

The results of giving an F where it is deserved would be immediately evident. 11
There would be no illiterate college graduates next spring—none. The same would
be true of high-school graduates, and consequently next year's college freshmen—
all of them—would be able to read.

I don't claim that giving F's will solve all of the problems, but I do argue that un- 12
less and until we start failing those students who should be failed, other suggested
solutions will make little progress toward improving education. Students in our
schools and colleges should be permitted to pass only after they have fully met established standards; borderline cases should be retained.

The single most important requirement for solving the problems of education in 13
America today is the big fat F, written decisively in red ink millions of times in
schools and colleges across the country.

THE CASE FOR CENSORSHIP
from *Slouching Towards Gomorrah*
Robert H. Bork

. . . Sooner or later censorship is going to have to be considered as popular 1
culture continues plunging to ever more sickening lows. The alternative to censorship, legal and moral, will be a brutalized and chaotic culture, with all that that
entails for our society, economy, politics, and physical safety. It is important to be
clear about the topic. I am *not* suggesting that censorship should, or constitutionally could, be employed to counter the liberal political and cultural propagandiz-
ing of movies, television, network news, and music. They are protected, and
properly so, by the First Amendment's guarantees of freedom of speech and of
the press. I *am* suggesting that censorship be considered for the most violent and
sexually explicit material now on offer, starting with the obscene prose and pictures available on the Internet, motion pictures that are mere rhapsodies to violence, and the more degenerate lyrics of rap music. . . .

Is censorship really as unthinkable as we all seem to assume? That it is unthink- 2
able is a very recent conceit. From the earliest colonies on this continent over
300 hundred [sic] years ago, and for about 175 years of our existence as a nation, we endorsed and lived with censorship. We do not have to imagine what
censorship might be like; we know from experience. Some of it was formal, written in statutes or city ordinances; some of it was informal, as in the movie producers' agreement to abide by the rulings of the Hayes office. Some of it was
inevitably silly—the rule that the movies could not show even a husband and wife
fully dressed on a bed unless each had one foot on the floor—and some of it was

no doubt pernicious. The period of Hayes office censorship was also, perhaps not coincidentally, the golden age of the movies.

The questions to be considered are whether such material has harmful effects, whether it is constitutionally possible to censor it, and whether technology may put some of it beyond society's capacity to control it.

3

It is possible to argue for censorship, as Stanley Brubaker, a professor of political science, does, on the ground that in a republican form of government where the people rule, it is crucial that the character of the citizenry not be debased. By now we should have gotten over the liberal notion that its citizens' characters are none of the business of government. The government ought not try to impose virtue, but it can deter incitements to vice. "Liberals have always taken the position," the late Christopher Lasch wrote, "that democracy can dispense with civic virtue. According to this way of thinking, it is liberal institutions, not the character of citizens, that make democracy work." He cited India and Latin America as proof that formally democratic institutions are not enough for a workable social order, a proof that is disheartening as the conditions in parts of large American cities approach those of the Third World.

4

Lasch stressed "the degree to which liberal democracy has lived off the borrowed capital of moral and religious traditions antedating the rise of liberalism." Certainly, the great religions of the West—Christianity and Judaism—taught moral truths about respect for others, honesty, sexual fidelity, truth-speaking, the value of work, respect for the property of others, and self-restraint. With the decline of religious influence, the moral lessons attenuate as well. Morality is an essential soil for free and democratic governments. A people addicted to instant gratification through the vicarious (and sometimes not so vicarious) enjoyment of mindless violence and brutal sex is unlikely to provide such a soil. A population whose mental faculties are coarsened and blunted, whose emotions are few and simple, is unlikely to be able to make the distinctions and engage in the discourse that democratic government requires.

5

I find Brubaker and Lasch persuasive. We tend to think of virtue as a personal matter, each of us to choose which virtues to practice or not practice—the privatization of morality, or, if you will, the "pursuit of happiness," as each of us defines happiness. But only a public morality, in which trust, truth-telling, and self-control are prominent features, can long sustain a decent social order and hence a stable and just democratic order. If the social order continues to unravel, we may respond with a more authoritarian government that is capable of providing at least personal safety.

6

There is, of course, more to the case for censorship than the need to preserve a viable democracy. We need also to avoid the social devastation wrought by pornography and endless incitements to murder and mayhem. Whatever the effects upon our capacity to govern ourselves, living in a culture that saturates us with pictures of sex and violence is aesthetically ugly, emotionally flattening, and physically dangerous.

7

There are, no doubt, complex causes for illegitimacy and violence in today's society, but it seems impossible to deny that one cause is the messages popular

8

culture insistently presses on us. Asked about how to diminish illegitimacy, a woman who worked with unmarried teenage mothers replied tersely: "Shoot Madonna." That may be carrying censorship a bit far, but one sees her point. Madonna's forte is sexual incitement. We live in a sex-drenched culture. The forms of sexual entertainment rampant in our time are overwhelming to the young, who would, even without such stimulations, have difficulty enough resisting the song their hormones sing. There was a time, coinciding with the era of censorship, when most did resist.

Young males, who are more prone to violence than females or older males, witness so many gory depictions of killing that they are bound to become desensitized to it. We now have teenagers and even subteenagers who shoot if they feel they have been "dissed" (shown disrespect). Indeed, the newspapers bring us stories of murders done for simple pleasure, the killing of a stranger simply because the youth felt like killing someone, anyone. That is why, for the first time in American history, you are more likely to be murdered by a complete stranger than by someone you know. That is why our prisons contain convicted killers who show absolutely no remorse and frequently cannot even remember the names of the persons they killed.   9

One response of the entertainment industry to criticisms has been that Hollywood and the music business did not create violence or sexual chaos in America. Of course not. But they contribute to it. They are one of the "root causes" they want us to seek elsewhere and leave them alone. The denial that what the young see and hear has any effect on their behavior is the last line of the modern liberal defense of decadence, and it is willfully specious. Accusing Senator Dole of "pandering to the right" in his speech deploring obscene and violent entertainment, the *New York Times* argued: "There is much in the movies and in hard-core rap music that is disturbing and demeaning to many Americans. Rap music, which often reaches the top of the charts, is also the music in which women are degraded and men seem to murder each other for sport. But no one has ever dropped dead from viewing 'Natural Born Killers,' or listening to gangster rap records." To which George Will replied: "No one ever dropped dead reading 'Der Sturmer,' the Nazi anti-Semitic newspaper, but the culture it served caused six million Jews to drop dead."   10

Those who oppose any form of restraint, including self-restraint, on what is produced insist that there is no connection between what people watch and hear and their behavior. It is clear why people who sell gangsta rap make that claim, but it is less clear why anyone should believe them. Studies show that the evidence of the causal connection between popular culture's violence and violent behavior is overwhelming. A recent study, *Sex and the Mass Media,* asked: "Does the talk about the images of love, sex and relationships promote irresponsible sexual behavior? Do they encourage unplanned and unwanted pregnancy? Are the media responsible for teenagers having sex earlier, more frequently and outside of marriage?" The researchers concluded: "The answer to all these questions is a qualified 'yes'." The answer was qualified because not enough research has as   11 yet been done on the effects of sexual images. The authors relied in part on the analogous question of media depictions of violence and their effect on aggressive behavior, which would appear to be a parallel situation. Some of the studies found positive but relatively small effects, between 5 and 15 percent. "One of the most compelling of the naturalistic studies . . . found that the homicide rates in three countries (U.S., Canada, and South Africa) increased dramatically 10–15 years after the introduction of television." That study "estimated that exposure to television violence is a causal factor in about half of the 21,000 homicides per year in the United States and perhaps half of all rapes and assaults."

The studies confirm what seems obvious. Common sense and experience are sufficient to reach the same conclusions. Music, for example, is used everywhere to create attitudes—armies use martial music, couples listen to romantic music, churches use organs, choirs, and hymns. How can anyone suppose that music (plus the images of television, movies, and advertisements) about sex and violence has no effect? 12

Indeed, Hollywood's writers, producers, and executives think popular entertainment affects behavior. It is not merely that they sell billions of dollars of advertising on television on the premise that they can influence behavior; they also think that the content of their programs can reform society in a liberal direction. They understand that no single program will change attitudes much, but they rely upon the cumulative impact of years of television indoctrination. Why should we listen to the same people saying that their programs and music have no effect on behavior? That argument is over. The depravity sold by Hollywood and the record companies is feeding the depravity we see around us. 13

The television industry, under considerable political pressure, has agreed to a ratings system for its programs. Since assigning ratings to every program—including every episode in a series—will be much more difficult than assigning ratings to motion pictures, it is doubtful that the television rating system will add much except confusion and rancor. The movie ratings have not prevented underage children from freely seeing movies they were not meant to see. No doubt the same will be true of television ratings. The vaunted V chip will prove no solution. Aside from the fact that many parents simply will not bother with it, the V chip will likely lead to even more degrading programming by providing producers with the excuse that the chip adequately safeguards children, though it does not. And the chip certainly does nothing to prevent adults from enjoying the increasingly salacious and even perverted material that is on the way. 14

The debate about censorship, insofar as there can be said to be a debate, usually centers on the issue of keeping children away from pornography. There is, of course, a good deal of merit to that, but it makes the issue sound like one of child rearing, which most people would like the government to butt out of. Opponents say parents can protect their children by using control features offered by many services. Both sides are missing a major point. Aside from the fact that many parents will not use control features, censorship is also crucial to protect children—and the rest of us—from men encouraged to act by a steady diet of 15 computerized pedophilia, murder, rape, and sado-masochism. No one supposes that every addict of such material will act out his fantasies, but it is willfully blind to think that none will. The pleasures the viewers of such material get from watching a thousand rape scenes or child kidnappings is not worth one actual rape or kidnapping.

There are those who say that the only solution is to rebuild a stable public culture. How one does that when the institutions we have long relied on to maintain and transmit such a culture—the two-parent family, schools, churches, and popular entertainment itself—are all themselves in decline it is not easy to say. Nevertheless, there is something to the point. Determined individuals and groups may be able to revitalize some of those institutions. For much that afflicts us, that is the only acceptable course. Law cannot be the answer in all or even most areas. And there are signs not just of resistance but of positive action against the forces of decadence. For the very worst manifestations of the culture, however, more directly coercive responses may be required. Whether as a society we any longer have the will to make such responses is very much in question.

Arguments that society may properly set limits to what may be shown, said, and sung run directly counter to the mood of our cultural elites in general, and in particular the attitude (it is hardly more than that) of our judges, many of whom, most unfortunately, are members in good standing of that elite. As constitutional law now stands, censorship would be extremely difficult, if not impossible. In *Miller* v. *California,* the Supreme Court laid down a three-part test that must be met if sexually explicit material is to be banned. It must be shown that: (1) the average person, applying contemporary community standards, would find that the work, taken as a whole, appeals to the prurient interest; (2) the work depicts or describes, in a patently offensive way, sexual conduct specifically defined by the applicable state law; and (3) the work, taken as a whole, lacks serious literary, artistic, political, or scientific value.

The first two prongs of the test become increasingly difficult to satisfy as contemporary community standards decline and as fewer and fewer descriptions of sexual conduct are regarded as patently offensive. But it is the third part that poses the most difficulty. There is apparently nothing that a flummery of professors will not testify has "serious value." When Cincinnati prosecuted the museum that displayed Mapplethorpe's photographs, the jury deferred to defense witnesses who said the pictures were art and hence could not be obscene. Cincinnati was widely ridiculed and portrayed as benighted for even attempting to punish obscenity. One typical cartoon showed a furtive figure stepping out of an alley in the city to offer "feelthy pictures" to a surprised passerby. The picture was a reproduction of a Michelangelo. It is typical of our collapse of standards that Mapplethorpe's grotesqueries can be compared even in a cartoon to Michelangelo's art.

It is difficult to see merit in the serious value test. Serious literary, artistic, political, or scientific value can certainly be achieved without including descriptions of "patently offensive" sexual conduct. This third criterion serves merely as an

16

17

18

19

escape hatch for pornographers whose "experts" can overbear juries. No doubt professors of literature can be found to testify to the serious literary value of the prose found in alt.sex.stories. Some of them are said to be very well written.

Without censorship, it has proved impossible to maintain any standards of de-   20
cency. "[O]nly a deeply confused society," George Will wrote, "is more concerned about protecting lungs than minds, trout than black women. We legislate
against smoking in restaurants; singing 'Me So Horny' is a constitutional right.
Secondary smoke is carcinogenic; celebration of torn vaginas is 'mere words.'"
The massive confusion Will describes is in large measure a confusion that first
enveloped the courts, which they then imposed on us.

It will be said that to propose banning anything that can be called "expression"   21
is an attempt to "take away our constitutional rights." A radio talk show host said
that the proposal to censor obscenities on the Internet was a denial of the First
Amendment rights of teenagers. Such reactions reveal a profound ignorance of
the history of the First Amendment. Until quite recently, nobody even raised the
question of that amendment in prosecutions of pornographers; it was not thought
relevant even by the pornographers. As late as 1942, in the *Chaplinsky* decision, a
unanimous Supreme Court could agree:

> There are certain well-defined and narrowly limited classes of speech, the preven-
> tion and punishment of which have never been thought to raise any Constitu-
> tional problem. These include the lewd and obscene, the profane, the libelous,
> and the insulting or "fighting" words—those which by their very utterance inflict
> injury or tend to incite an immediate breach of the peace. It has been well ob-
> served that such utterances are no essential part of any exposition of ideas, and
> are of such slight social value as a step to truth that any benefit that may be de-
> rived from them is clearly outweighed by the social interest in order and morality.

Under today's constitutional doctrine, it would be difficult to impossible to pro-   22
hibit or punish the lewd and obscene, or the profane. First Amendment jurisprudence has shifted from the protection of the exposition of ideas towards the
protection of self-expression—however lewd, obscene, or profane. Time Warner,
citing the authority of a 1992 statute, proposed to scramble sexually explicit programs on a New York cable channel. . . . Those who wanted the shows with strip-
pers, excerpts from pornographic movies, and advertisements for phone sex and
"escort" services would have to send in cards to the cable operator. A federal district judge in New York, disagreeing with the federal court of appeals in Washington,
D.C., granted a preliminary injunction against Time Warner, saying that the statute
probably violated the First Amendment. The plaintiffs who produce these shows said
the scrambling would hurt their ability to reach their audience and stigmatize viewers
who tune in to the shows. Both are results that would have been considered laudable
rather than forbidden under the First Amendment not many years ago.

Yet it is clear that if there is something special about speech, something that   23
warrants a constitutional guarantee, it is the capacity of speech to communicate
ideas. There is no other distinction between speech and other human activities

that go unprotected by the Constitution. That is the point the *Chaplinsky* Court grasped. Non-speech activities can give as much pleasure as speech, develop as many human faculties, and contribute to personal and social well-being. The only difference between speech and other behavior is speech's capacity to communicate ideas in the effort to reach varieties of truth. Celebration in song of the ripping of vaginas or forced oral sex or stories depicting the kidnapping, mutilation, raping, and murder of children do not, to anyone with a degree of common sense, qualify as ideas. And when something worthy of being called an idea is involved, there is no reason to protect its expression in lewd, obscene, or profane language. Such language adds nothing to the idea but, instead, detracts from it.

Today's Court majority would have difficulty understanding *Chaplinsky*'s state-   24
ment that an utterance could inflict an injury to morality. Morality itself has be-come relativized in our constitutional jurisprudence, so that the Court no longer has the vocabulary to say that something is immoral and, for that reason, may be banned by the legislature. As Walter Berns wrote:

> The Court decontrolled the arts, so to speak, and the impact of that has been profound. It not only permitted the publication of sex but it *caused* the publica-tion of sex—or, to coin a word, the "publification" of sex. . . . The immediate and obvious consequence of [the end of censorship] is that sex is now being made into the measure of existence, and such uniquely human qualities as mod-esty, fidelity, abstinence, chastity, delicacy, and shame, qualities that formerly pro-vided the constraints on sexual activity and the setting within which the erotic passion was enjoyed, discussed, and evaluated, are today ridiculed as merely ar-bitrary interferences "with the health of the sexual parts."

Berns wrote that in 1976, when he could have had no idea just how far the publi-   25
fication of sex would be carried. We may not know that even now. Our experience after the end of censorship suggests that there are few or no limits to depravity.

It may be too much to ask that the Supreme Court, as presently constituted, re-   26
visit and revise its First Amendment jurisprudence. Most people think of the Court as a legal institution because its pronouncements have the force of law. But the per-ception is flawed. The Court is also a cultural institution, one whose pronounce-ments are significantly guided not by the historical meaning of the Constitution but by the values of the class that is dominant in our culture. In our day, that means the cultural elite: academics, clergy, journalists, entertainers, foundation staffs, "public interest" groups, and the like. The First Amendment is central to the concerns of such folk because they are chatterers by profession, and their attitudes are relativis-tic and permissive. The mention of censorship, even of the most worthless and harmful materials, causes apoplexy in the members of that class.

The truth is that the judiciary's view of pornographic sex and pornographic vio-   27
lence will not change until the culture to which the Court responds changes. There is no sign that that will occur any time soon. The public debate in the area of the "arts" is not encouraging. Mapplethorpe's homoerotic photos and Serrano's "Piss Christ" were displayed with grants from the National Endowment for the Arts. So

intimidating has the culture of modern liberalism become that cultural conservatives were reduced to complaining that works like these should not be subsidized with "taxpayers' dollars," as if taxpayers should never be required to subsidize things they don't like. If that were the case, government would have to close down altogether. Both spending and taxation would be at zero. To complain about the source of the dollars involved is to cheapen a moral position. The photographs would be just as offensive if their display were financed by a scatter-brained billionaire. We seem too timid to state that Mapplethorpe's and Serrano's pictures should not be shown in public, whoever pays for them. We are going to have to overcome that timidity if our culture is not to decline still further.

Libertarians join forces with modern liberals in opposing censorship, though libertarians are far from being modern liberals in other respects. For one thing, libertarians do not like the coercion that necessarily accompanies radical egalitarianism. But because both libertarians and modern liberals are oblivious to social reality, both demand radical personal autonomy in expression. That is one reason libertarians are not to be confused, as they often are, with conservatives. They are quasi- or semiconservatives. Nor are they to be confused with classical liberals, who considered restraints on individual autonomy to be essential.   28

The nature of the liberal and libertarian errors is easily seen in discussions of pornography. The leader of the explosion of pornographic videos, described admiringly by a competitor as the Ted Turner of the business, offers the usual defenses of decadence: "Adults have a right to see [pornography] if they want to. If it offends you, don't buy it." Those statements neatly sum up both the errors and the (unintended) perniciousness of the alliance between libertarians and modern liberals with respect to popular culture.   29

Modern liberals employ the rhetoric of "rights" incessantly, not only to delegitimate the idea of restraints on individuals by communities but to prevent discussion of the topic. Once something is announced, usually flatly and stridently, to be a right—whether pornography or abortion or what have you—discussion becomes difficult to impossible. Rights inhere in the person, are claimed to be absolute, and cannot be diminished or taken away by reason; in fact, reason that suggests the nonexistence of an asserted right is viewed as a moral evil by the claimant. If there is to be anything that can be called a community, rather than an agglomeration of hedonists, the case for previously unrecognized individual freedoms (as well as some that have been previously recognized) must be thought through and argued, and "rights" cannot win every time. Why there is a right for adults to enjoy pornography remains unexplained and unexplainable.   30

The second bit of advice—"If it offends you, don't buy it"—is both lulling and destructive. Whether you buy it or not, you will be greatly affected by those who do. The aesthetic and moral environment in which you and your family live will be coarsened and degraded. Economists call the effects an activity has on others "externalities"; why so many of them do not understand the externalities here is a mystery. They understand quite well that a person who decides not to run a smelter will nevertheless be seriously affected if someone else runs one nearby.   31

Free market economists are particularly vulnerable to the libertarian virus. They know that free economic exchanges usually benefit both parties to them. But they mistake that general rule for a universal rule. Benefits do not invariably result from free market exchanges. When it comes to pornography or addictive drugs, libertarians all too often confuse the idea that markets should be free with the idea that everything should be available on the market. The first of those ideas rests on the efficiency of the free market in satisfying wants. The second ignores the question of which wants it is moral to satisfy. That is a question of an entirely different nature. I have heard economists say that, as economists, they do not deal with questions of morality. Quite right. But nobody is just an economist. Economists are also fathers or mothers, husbands or wives, voters, citizens, members of communities. In these latter roles, they cannot avoid questions of morality.

The externalities of depictions of violence and pornography are clear. To complaints about those products being on the market, libertarians respond with something like "Just hit the remote control and change channels on your TV set." But, like the person who chooses not to run a smelter while others do, you, your family, and your neighbors will be affected by the people who do not change the channel, who do rent the pornographic videos, who do read alt.sex.stories. As film critic Michael Medved put it: "To say that if you don't like the popular culture, then turn it off, is like saying if you don't like the smog, stop breathing. . . . There are Amish kids in Pennsylvania who know about Madonna." And their parents can do nothing about it.

Can there be any doubt that as pornography and depictions of violence become increasingly popular and increasingly accessible, attitudes about marriage, fidelity, divorce, obligations to children, the use of force, and permissible public behavior and language will change? Or that with the changes in attitudes will come changes in conduct, both public and private? We have seen those changes already and they are continuing. Advocates of liberal arts education assure us that those studies improve character. Can it be that only uplifting reading affects character and the most degrading reading has no effects whatever? "Don't buy it" and "Change the channel," however intended, are effectively advice to accept a degenerating culture and its consequences.

The obstacles to censorship of pornographic and violence-filled materials are, of course, enormous. Radical individualism in such matters is now pervasive even among sedate, upper middle-class people. At a dinner I sat next to a retired Army general who was now a senior corporate executive. The subject of Robert Mapplethorpe's photographs came up. This most conventional of dinner companions said casually that people ought to be allowed to see whatever they wanted to see. It would seem to follow that others ought to be allowed to do whatever some want to see.

The entertainment industry will battle ferociously against restraints, one segment of it because its economic interests would be directly threatened, the rest because, to avoid thinking, they have become absolutists about First Amendment freedoms. Then there are the First Amendment voluptuaries. The ACLU is to the First Amendment what the National Rifle Association is to the Second Amendment and the right to bear arms. The head of the ACLU announced in a panel discussion that the Supreme Court's failure to throw protection around nude dancing in night clubs was a terrible blow to our freedom of speech. Some years back, when I suggested to a law school audience that the courts had gone too far in preventing communities from prohibiting pornography, the then president of the organization compared me to Salazar of Portugal and the Greek colonels. Afterward he said he had called me a fascist. It is fascinating that when one calls for greater democratic control and less governance by a judicial oligarchy, one is immediately called a fascist. The ACLU seems to think democracy is tyranny and government by judges is freedom. That is a proposition that in the last half of this century our judiciary has all too readily accepted. Any serious attempt to root out the worst in our popular culture may be doomed unless the judiciary comes to understand that the First Amendment was adopted for good reasons, and those reasons did not include the furtherance of radical personal autonomy.

It is not clear how effective censorship of the Internet or of digital films on home computers can be. Perhaps it is true, as has been said, that technology is on the side of anarchy. Violence and pornography can be supplied from all over the world, and it can be wireless, further complicating the problem of barring it. We may soon be at the mercy of a combination of technology and perversion. It's enough to make one a Luddite. But there are methods of presentation that can be censored. Lyrics, motion pictures, television, and printed material are candidates.   37

What we see in popular culture, from "Big Man with a Gun" to alt.sex.stories, is the product, though not, it is to be feared, the final product, of liberalism's constant thrust. Doing anything to curb the spreading rot would violate liberalism's central tenet, John Stuart Mill's "one very simple principle." Mill himself would be horrified at what we have become; he never intended this; but he bequeathed us the principle that modern liberals embrace and that makes it possible. We have learned that the founders of liberalism were wrong. Unconstrained human nature will seek degeneracy often enough to create a disorderly, hedonistic, and dangerous society. Modern liberalism and popular culture are creating that society.   38

THE MUSEUM OF CLEAR IDEAS
from *In Defense of Elitism*
William A. Henry III

Why do people go to college? In an idealistic world, they might go to develop a capacity for critical thinking, enhance an already grounded knowledge of the sciences and world culture, learn further how to deal with other people's diversity of opinion and background, and in general become better citizens. They might go for fun, for friendship, for a network of contacts. They might go for spiritual enrichment or for pragmatic honing of skills.   1

In the real world, though, mostly they go to college to make money.   2

This reality is acknowledged in the mass media, which are forever running stories and charts showing how much a college degree contributes to lifetime income (with the more sophisticated publications very occasionally noting the counterweight costs of tuition paid and income foregone during the years of full-time study). These stories are no surprise to parents, who certainly wouldn't shell out the same money for travel or other exercises in fulfillment that do not result in a marketable credential. The income statistics are, similarly, no surprise to banks, which avidly market student loans and have been known to shower new graduates or even undergraduates with credit cards. And of course the stories are no surprise to students, who avidly follow news of where the jobs are and what starting salaries they command.

But the equation between college and wealth is not so simple. College graduates unquestionably do better on average economically than those who don't go at all. At the extremes, those with five or more years of college earn about triple the income of those with eight or fewer years of total schooling. Taking more typical examples, one finds that those who stop their educations after earning a four-year degree earn about one and a half times as much as those who stop at the end of high school. These outcomes, however, reflect other things besides the impact of the degree itself. College graduates are winners in part because colleges attract people who are already winners—people with enough brains and drive that they would do well in almost any generation and under almost any circumstances, with or without formal credentialing. The harder and more meaningful question is whether the mediocrities who have also flooded into colleges in the past couple of generations do better than they otherwise would have. And if they do, is it because college actually made them better employees or because it simply gave them the requisite credential to get interviewed and hired? Does having gone to college truly make one a better salesman of stocks or real estate or insurance? Does it enhance the work of a secretary or nanny or hairdresser? Does it make one more adept at running a car dealership or a catering company? Or being a messenger boy? All these occupations are being pursued, on more than an interim basis, by college graduates of my acquaintance. Most readers can probably think of parallel or equivalent examples. It need hardly be added that these occupations are also pursued, often with equal success, by people who didn't go to college at all, and in generations past were pursued primarily by people who hadn't stepped onto a campus. Indeed, the United States Labor Department's Bureau of Labor Statistics reported in 1994 that about twenty percent of all college graduates toil in fields not requiring a degree, and this total is projected to exceed thirty percent by the year 2005. For the individual, college may well be a credential without being a qualification, required without being requisite.

For American society, the big lie underlying higher education is akin to the . . . big lie about childrearing in Garrison Keillor's Lake Wobegon: that everyone can be above average. In the unexamined American Dream rhetoric promoting mass higher education in the nation of my youth, the implicit vision was that one day everyone, or at least practically everyone, would be a manager or a professional. We would use the most elitist of all means, scholarship, toward the most egalitarian of ends. We would all become chiefs; hardly anyone would be left a mere Indian. On the surface this New Jerusalem appears to have arrived. Where half a century ago the bulk of jobs were blue collar, now a majority are white or pink collar. They are performed in an office instead of on a factory floor. If they still tend to involve repetition and drudgery, at least they do not require heavy lifting.

But the wages for them are going down virtually as often as up. It has become an axiom of union lobbying that replacing a manufacturing economy with a service economy has meant exporting once-lucrative jobs to places where they can be done more cheaply. And as a great many disappointed office workers have discovered, being better educated and better dressed at the workplace does not transform one's place in the pecking order. There are still plenty more Indians than chiefs. Lately, indeed, the chiefs are becoming even fewer. If, for a generation or so, corporate America bought into the daydream of making everyone a boss, the wakeup call has come. The major focus of the "downsizing" of recent years has been eliminating layers of middle management—much of it drawn from the ranks of those lured to college a generation or two ago by the idea that a degree would transform them from mediocre to magisterial.

Yet our colleges blithely go on "educating" many more prospective managers and professionals than we are likely to need. In my own field, there are typically more students majoring in journalism at any given moment than there are journalists employed at all the daily newspapers in the United States. A few years ago there were more students enrolled in law school than there were partners in all law firms. As trends shift, there have been periodic oversupplies of M.B.A.-wielding financial analysts, of grade school and high school teachers, of computer programmers, even of engineers. Inevitably many students of limited talent spend huge amounts of time and money pursuing some brass ring occupation, only to see their dreams denied. As a society we consider it cruel not to give them every chance at success. It may be more cruel to let them go on fooling themselves.

Just when it should seem clear that we are probably already doing too much to entice people into college, Bill Clinton is suggesting we do even more. In February 1994, for example, the President asserted that America needs a greater fusion between academic and vocational training—not because too many mediocre people misplaced on the college track are failing to acquire marketable vocational and technical skills, but because too many people on the vocational track are being denied courses that will secure them admission to college. Surely what we Americans need is not a fusion of the two tracks but a sharper division between them, coupled with a forceful program for diverting intellectual also-rans out of the academic track and into the vocational one. That is where most of them are heading in life anyway. Why should they wait until they are older and must enroll in high-priced proprietary vocational programs of often dubious efficacy—frequently throwing away not only their own funds but federal loans in the process—because they

6

7

8

emerged from high school heading nowhere and knowing nothing that is useful in the marketplace?

If the massive numbers of college students reflected a national boom in love of learning and a prevalent yen for self-improvement, America's investment in the classroom might make sense. There are introspective qualities that can enrich any society in ways beyond the material. But one need look no further than the curricular wars to understand that most students are not looking to broaden their spiritual or intellectual horizons. They see themselves as consumers buying a product, and insist on applying egalitarian rules of the marketplace to what used to be an unchallenged elitism of the intellect.

Consider three basic trends, all of them implicit rejections of intellectual adventure, all based on seeing college in transactional terms. First, students are demanding courses that reflect and affirm their own identities in the most literal way. Rather than read a Greek dramatist of two thousand years ago and thrill to the discovery that some ideas and emotions are universal, many insist on reading writers of their own gender or ethnicity or sexual preference, ideally writers of the present or the recent past. They proclaim that they cannot (meaning, of course, *will* not) relate to heritages other than their own. Furthermore, they repudiate the idea that anyone can transcend his heritage—apparently because few if any people of their own heritage are judged to have done so, and they see the very idea of "universal values" in terms of some sort of competition that their group cannot win. This is parallel to the appalling trend in history, scathingly described in several recent essays by that brilliant traditionalist Gertrude Himmelfarb, in which all fact and analysis are dismissed as "relative" and theoretical opinion is enshrined as a liberating and morally superior form of scholarship. Historians have always known, she writes in *On Looking into the Abyss,* "what postmodernism professes to have just discovered"—that historical writing "is necessarily imperfect, tentative and partial." But previous generations did not embrace the drive to be "imaginative," "inventive," and "creative" rather than as truthful as circumstances permit.

Professors who pander to these students often talk in terms of liberation but they reject the most liberating of all intellectual undertakings, the journey beyond one's own place and time. For their part, many students do not want college to liberate or change them. They want it merely to reinforce them as they are, and they are in their way as unimaginative and smug as the white-bread fraternity dolts Sinclair Lewis so deftly sketched in *Elmer Gantry* and *Babbitt.* Often this self-absorption and lack of intellectual humility leads them to demand a curriculum that fails to serve even their base interests. At my own alma mater, Yale, undergraduates have been able to study Yoruba and other African tribal languages of extremely limited economic utility because these pursuits had sentimental or political appeal. But because there wasn't similar pressure for teaching Korean, they were denied the opportunity to enroll in a tongue that might actually have enabled them to get a job. San Francisco State has been offering a minor in gay studies for years, and organizations of professorial ideologues are pushing nationally for majors and even graduate degrees in the field. This may lead to a self-perpetuating career stream in academe. But what happens to an unsuspecting adolescent who minors in gay studies and then has to tell a job interviewer at, say, an insurance company that during the years when he might have been acquiring economically useful knowledge he was instead enrolled in such actual courses as Gay Male Relationships and Gays in Film? I'm not just worrying about the chilling effect of homophobia here. The same caveat applies to all ideologically based and impractical studies, like the feminist dialectics in the humanities that one female Columbia professor of my acquaintance dismisses as "clit lit," or Stanford's Black Hair as Culture and History. This sort of feel-good learning epitomizes the endemic confusion of the roles of the curriculum with those of the counseling service.

The second trend, implicit in the first, is that the curriculum has shifted from being what professors desire to teach to being what students desire to learn. In the heydey of faculty authority, professors devised set courses based on their view of the general basis for a liberal education, the essentials in each particular field, and, frequently, their personal intellectual interests. This system clearly served the professors (and nothing wrong with that), but it also served students by giving them teachers who were motivated, even excited, by the topics under discussion. My own college education took place during the Vietnam era, a time of abundance at most colleges because of government subsidy coupled with burgeoning enrollments due to the baby boom and draft avoidance. Professors could indulge their eccentricities; my freshman calculus teacher spent the entire fall term talking about his true love, Babylonian number theory, and I am probably the better for it, if only for a sense of the eons of continuity underlying all the great branches of scholarship. 12

Nowadays colleges have to hustle for students by truckling trendily. If the students want media studies programs so they can all fantasize about becoming TV news anchors, then media studies will abound, even though most real journalists have studied something substantive in college and that subset of TV news people who are mere personalities get by, of course, on charm and cheekbones rather than anything learned in a classroom. There are in any given year some three hundred thousand students enrolled in undergraduate communications courses. I know this because I was romanced heavily by a publishing house to write a textbook for this field. My interest dwindled when I learned that I should not expect to sustain any passage on a particular topic for even as much as a thousand words because these "future communicators" had short attention spans and didn't like to read. The idea of basing a text on what and how students *ought* to learn rather than on what and how they *wish* to learn apparently never enters the discussion. The market makes the rules, and control of the market has slipped from deservedly imperious professors to baselessly arrogant students. It is one thing to question authority, as the lapel buttons of my youth urged. It is quite another to ignore it altogether, as students often do today. 13

This shift of curricular power from teachers to students plainly affects what goes on in the classroom. I suspect it also affects scholarship for the worse. While one hopes that professors would use scholarly writing as an avenue for highbrow concerns that they find increasingly difficult to pursue within their courses, anecdotal 14 evidence strongly suggests they don't. In reporting several stories for *Time* on the general topics of political correctness and multiculturalism, I discovered again and again that professors were instead writing to position themselves favorably on the ideological battlefield—or at least to exploit the marketplace for fulmination created by the culture wars.

Of even greater significance than the solipsism of students and the pusillanimity of teachers is the third trend, the sheer decline in the amount and quality of work expected in class. In an egalitarian environment the influx of mediocrities relentlessly lowers the general standard at colleges to the level the weak ones can meet. When my mother went to Trinity College in Washington in the early 1940s, at a time when it was regarded more as a finishing school for nice Catholic girls from the Northeast than as a temple of discipline, an English major there was expected to be conversant not only in English and Latin but also in Anglo-Saxon and medieval French. A course labeled "Carlisle, Ruskin, and Newman" meant, as my mother wearily recalled, "everything ever written by Carlisle, Ruskin, or Newman and also, it seemed, everything ever written *about* Carlisle, Ruskin, or Newman." A course in Shakespeare meant reading the plays, all thirty-seven of them. By the time I went to college, it was possible to get out of Yale as an honors English major without ever having read Chaucer or Spenser; I know, because I did. In today's indulgent climate, a professor friend at a fancy college told me as I was writing this chapter, taking a half semester of Shakespeare compels students to read exactly four plays. "Anything more than one a week," he explained, "is considered too heavy a load."

This probably should not be thought surprising in an era when most colleges, even prestigious ones, run some sort of remedial program for freshmen to learn the reading and writing skills they ought to have developed in junior high school—not to mention an era when many students vociferously object to being marked down for spelling or grammar. Indeed, all the media attention paid to curriculum battles at Stanford, Dartmouth, and the like obscures the even bleaker reality of American higher education. Or so argues Russell Jacoby, a sometime professor of history at various American and Canadian universities, in his compellingly cranky *Dogmatic Wisdom.* Most students, he notes, are enrolled at vastly less demanding institutions, where any substantial reading list, of whatever ethnicity, would be an improvement. Jacoby admiringly cites Clifford Adelman's *Tourists in Our Land,* based on a survey of the schooling of some twenty thousand high school students, most of them not elite. "When one looks at the archive left by an entire generation," he quotes Adelman as saying, "it should be rather obvious that Stanford is not where America goes to college. Whether Stanford freshmen read Cicero or Frantz Fanon is a matter worthy of a raree show." Well, not quite. For all its intermittent palaver about the individual, the academy is one of the national centers of copycat behavior and groupthink. If a Stanford professor makes a curricular choice, dozens if not hundreds of his would-be peers elsewhere will imitate that choice. Some of them daydream that by doing so they will one day actually teach at Stanford. Most of the rest fantasize that by aping Stanford and its ilk they make their vastly lesser institutions somehow part of the same echelon.

Perhaps it seems pettish to include community colleges and erstwhile state   17
teachers' colleges when talking about the shortcomings of higher education. Most
readers who went to more prestigious institutions think of "college" as meaning
only their alma maters and the equivalents in cachet, and many expect (perhaps secretly even welcome) deficiencies at lesser places, because those failings reaffirm
the hierarchy. But in terms of public expenditure, community colleges are probably
much more expensive per capita for the taxpayer than any serious centers of learning, precisely because they tend to be relatively cheap for the student—and unlike
private colleges, they rarely have significant endowments or other resources to offset the gap between the subsidized price and the true cost. Moreover, so long as
these schools go on labeling themselves "colleges"—the word "junior" was widely
dropped because it was demeaning, a perfect example of both euphemism and
grade inflation—and so long as their students think of themselves as having "gone
to college," their academic standards will color the public understanding of what
college is.

When Vance Packard wrote *The Status Seekers* in the 1950s, he described the   18
role of the better prep schools and colleges as grooming the next generation of
the traditional ruling class while credentialing the ablest of those not quite to the
manor born. The America he described was unprepared for the radicalism of college students in the 1960s. That political aggression was bred in part by Vietnam
and the civil rights movement, but at least as much by social class anxieties among
the burgeoning numbers of students whose parents had not gone to college and
whose toehold on privilege was either shaky or nonexistent. The current college
generation is similarly radical and dismissive of tradition for much the same reasons.

Those whose parents didn't go to college come disproportionately from ethnic   19
minorities who are demanding a rewriting of the curriculum. This, not incidentally, is
an effective means of leveling the playing field to their competitive advantage. If your
classroom competitor possesses knowledge you don't, you better your prospects if
you can get that knowledge declared irrelevant—and even more if you can get your
homeboy hairstyle studied as culture and history.

Those whose parents did go to college are not necessarily any more confident.   20
They have witnessed the economic erosion of the past couple of decades, in which
it now takes two incomes for a family to live as well as it used to on one.

Both groups are understandably insistent on keeping the number of places in   21
college as large as possible, for fear of having to drop their dreams. This form of
middle-class welfare (even college students not raised in the middle class are by definition seeking to enter it) is shamelessly indulged by state legislators who recognize it as a necessity for reelection.

Other constituencies join in pushing for the maintenance and expansion of pub-   22
lic higher education. Faculty and administrators seek to protect their jobs. Merchants and civic boosters serve their interests, both economic and sentimental, by
bolstering institutions that bear the name of their town or state. Alumni often
combine a nostalgic loyalty with a pragmatic one. They think, with some justice,

that burnishing the luster of their alma mater adds to the sheen of their own education, even though it was acquired years or decades ago and has nothing to do with the merits or deficiencies of the institution of today.

But none of these social pressures justifies spending one hundred fifty billion dollars a year overeducating a populace that is neither consistently eager for intellectual expansion of horizons nor consistently likely to gain the economic and professional status for which the education is undertaken. Nor can one justify such expenditures by citing the racial and ethnic pressures from those who argue that only a wide-open system of higher education will give minorities a sufficient chance. Whatever the legacy of discrimination or the inadequacies of big-city high schools, a C student is a C student and turning colleges into remedial institutions for C students (or worse) only debases the value of the degrees the schools confer.   23

Beyond the material cost of college, there are other social costs implicit in our system of mass higher education. If college is not difficult to get into, students are not as likely to be motivated in high school. If the authority of a teacher's grade or recommendation is not vital because there will always be a place open at some college somewhere, students have yet another reason for disrespecting authority and learning less efficiently. Paying for their children's college education often imposes a massive financial drain on parents during the years when they should be most intent on preparing for retirement, and leaves many of them too dependent on Social Security and other welfare programs. . . . This expenditure may make sense when the education has real value for the child being supported. But some parents are wasting their money.   24

For many adolescents who finish high school without a clear sense of direction, college is simply a holding pattern until they get on with their lives. It is understandable that they should want to extend their youth and ponder their identities (or navels) for a bit; what is rather less clear is why they should do so at public as well as parental expense. At minimum, that opportunity ought to be limited to students who have shown some predisposition to absorb a bit of learning while they are waiting to discover their identities.   25

My modest proposal is this. Let us reduce, over perhaps a five-year span, the number of high school graduates who go on to college from nearly sixty percent to a still generous thirty-three percent. This will mean closing a lot of institutions. Most of them, in my view, should be community colleges, current or former state teachers' colleges, and the like. These schools serve the academically marginal and would be better replaced by vocational training in high school and on-the-job training at work. Two standards should apply in judging which schools to shut down. First, what is the general academic level attained by the student body? That might be assessed in a rough and ready way by requiring any institution wishing to survive to give a standardized test—say, the Graduate Record Examination—to all its seniors. Those schools whose students perform below the state norm would face cutbacks or closing. Second, what community is being served? A school that serves a high percentage of disadvantaged students (this ought to be measured by family   26 finances rather than just race or ethnicity) can make a better case for receiving tax dollars than one that subsidizes the children of the prosperous, who have private alternatives. Even ardent egalitarians should recognize the injustice of taxing people who wash dishes or mop floors for a living to pay for the below-cost public higher education of the children of lawyers, so that they can go on to become lawyers too.

This reduction would have several salutary effects. The public cost of education 27 would be sharply reduced. Competitive pressures would probably make high school students and their schools perform better. Businesses, which now depend on colleges to make their prospective employees at least minimally functional, would foot some of the bills—and doubtless would start demanding that high schools fulfill their duty of turning out literate, competent graduates. And, of course, those who devise college curricula might get the message that skills and analytical thinking are the foremost objects of learning—not sociopolitical self-fulfillment and ideological attitudinizing.

I would like to preserve, however, one of the few indisputably healthy trends in 28 higher education, the opening up of the system to so-called mature students (meaning, in practice, mostly housewives). Here is where open admission makes sense. Anyone who has been out of high school for, say, seven or perhaps ten years ought to be allowed to enroll and perhaps even be offered the chance to purchase a semester of not-for-credit refresher courses. If people of that age are prepared to make the sacrifices and undertake the disciplines of being students again, they are likely to succeed—indeed, at most schools that actively solicit mature students, the older enrollees outperform the younger ones.

Massive cuts in total college enrollment would, of course, necessitate massive 29 layoffs of faculty. In my educational utopia, that would be the moment to eliminate tenure and replace it with contracts of no more than five years, after which renewal should be possible but not presumed. This would allow universities to do some of the same weeding out of underproductive managers and professionals that has made American business more efficient, and would compel crackpot ideologues of whatever stripe to justify their scholarship, at least to their peers and conceivably to the broader public. The justification normally offered for tenure—the potential for a revival of McCarthyism—is so remote from present-day academic reality as not to be worthy of discussion. And just what is wrong with having to defend one's opinion anyway? A college teaching position is an opportunity to think and serve, not a professor's personal capital asset. Apart from the self-interest of professors, it is hard to concoct any other rationale for affording college teachers a tenure protection enjoyed by few other managers and professionals, save civil servants who operate under much closer supervision and scrutiny. Competing for one's job on an ongoing basis could introduce a little more healthy elitism into the professorial lifestyle. Teachers might strive to meet standards more widely held than their own ideology. The risk is that the loss of tenure could make professors even more apt to kowtow to the consumerist demands of students, so as to remain popular and employed. But that is happening anyway.

In truth, I don't expect any suggestion as sweeping as mine to be enacted. America is in the grip of an egalitarianism so pervasive that low grades are automatically assumed to be the failure of the school and the teacher and perhaps the community at large—anyone but the student himself. We insist on saying that pretty much everyone can learn, that it's only a matter of tapping untouched potential. While we are ready to call someone handicapped "differently abled," we are not ready to label the dull-witted as "differently smart." Even more than in my youth, we cling to the dream of a world in which everyone will be educated, affluent, technically adept, his or her own boss. There is nothing wrong with discontent at having a modest place in the scheme of things. That very discontent produced the ambition that built the culture of yesterday and today. But the discontent of those times was accompanied by discipline, willingness to work hard, and ready acceptance of a competitive society.

Some readers may find it paradoxical that a[n argument] for greater literacy and intellectual discipline should lead to a call for less rather than more education. Even if college students do not learn all they should, the readers' counterargument would go, surely they learn something, and that is better than their learning nothing. Maybe it is. But at what price? One hundred fifty billion dollars is awfully high for deferring the day when the idle or ungifted take individual responsibility and face up to their fate. And the price is even steeper when the egalitarian urge has turned our universities, once museums of clear ideas, into soapboxes for hazy and tribalist ones. Ultimately it is the yearning to believe that anyone can be brought up to college level that has brought colleges down to everyone's level.

"SEX" IS ALSO A DIRTY WORD
from *Defending Pornography*
Nadine Strossen

This culture always treats sex with suspicion. . . . Sex is presumed guilty until proven innocent.   Gayle Rubin, *anthropologist*

Although [those who] campaign against sexual speech . . . employ some differing rhetoric in their unified call for censoring sexually oriented expression, they sound many common chords, notably that sex and materials that depict or describe it inevitably degrade and endanger women. In short, the war on sexual expression is, at bottom, a war on sex itself, at least as far as women are concerned. Because the philosophy of leading antipornography, procensorship feminists reflects a deep distrust of sex for women, such feminists are, in my view and in the view of others, aptly labeled "antisex."

Taken together, the traditional and feminist antipornography, antisex crusaders appeal to a broad gamut of the ideological spectrum in both the government and the public. They pose an unprecedented danger to sexual expression, which has always been uniquely vulnerable in the United States, as well as to the concept that the First Amendment protects such expression. Moreover, their attacks have been alarmingly successful.

We are in the midst of a full-fledged "sex panic," in which seemingly all descriptions and depictions of human sexuality are becoming embattled. Right-wing senators have attacked National Endowment for the Arts grants for art whose sexual themes—such as homoeroticism or feminism—are allegedly inconsistent with "traditional family values." At the opposite end of the political spectrum, students and faculty have attacked myriad words and images on campus as purportedly constituting sexual harassment. Any expression about sex is now seen as especially dangerous, and hence is especially endangered. The pornophobic feminists have played a very significant role in fomenting this sex panic, especially among liberals and on campuses across the county.   3

The fear of sexual expression has become so high-pitched lately that it even has deterred an AIDS clinic from giving out information about combating the deadly spread of the virus. In Oklahoma City, the American Civil Liberties Union (ACLU) represented a doctor who was prosecuted for displaying a safe-sex poster on the windows of his AIDS clinic, which was located in an area frequented by gay men. Yet public health experts maintain that the allegedly illegal and offensive image in the poster—a man wearing a condom—is an important instrument in the life-or-death campaign to halt the spread of HIV. Although the charges were dismissed, the city has threatened further prosecutions, thus deterring the clinic from mounting similarly explicit educational displays in the future.   4

Society's wariness toward sex is highlighted by contrasting it with the greater societal tolerance toward violence. This dichotomy is especially vivid in the media and mass culture, where violent depictions are far more accepted than sexual ones. The contrast was aptly capsulized by Martin Shafer, a top executive at a film production company, when he noted, "If a man touches a woman's breast in a movie, it's an R rating, but if he cuts off a limb with a chain saw, it's a PG-13."   5

Because the domain of sexual expression, always a difficult terrain, has lately been laced with land mines placed by diverse enemies, it has become more treacherous than ever. Not surprisingly, artists, academics, and others are increasingly deterred from entering and exploring this potentially explosive—but also rich, wonderful, and important—territory.   6

All over the country, artists say that they dare not pursue sexual themes for fear that their work will be perceived as too controversial to be funded or displayed. Indeed, outraged officials and citizens alike have indignantly demanded the defunding and deposing from display of art with a wide range of sexual themes; lately it seems that even a mere sexual connotation, no matter how subtle, is vulnerable.   7

In our current epidemic of erotophobia, even images of nude or seminude bodies in wholly nonsexual contexts have been attacked. For example, in 1993, Vermont officials hung bedsheets over a mural that artist Sam Kerson had painted in a   8 state building's conference room. One press account described the mural, which was commissioned to mark the five-hundredth anniversary of Christopher Columbus's voyage, as "a politically correct rendition of Columbus and his men arriving in the New World, battle-axes and crucifix raised, ready to oppress the natives." But the painting was not politically correct enough for a number of female employees, who complained that its depictions of bare-breasted native women constituted sexual harassment. Because the mural could not be removed without destroying it, the state resorted to the bedsheet "solution."

In 1992, a painting of the classical seminude statue the Venus de Milo was removed from a store in a Springfield, Missouri, shopping mall because mall managers considered the topless masterpiece "too shocking." The painting of the ancient Greek sculpture, which was carved about 150 B.C., and which stands in a place of honor in Paris's Louvre museum, was replaced by a painting of a woman wearing a long, frilly dress.   9

Another example of a famous artistic masterpiece that has been suppressed in the current sex panic is *The Nude Maja,* or *Maja Desnuda,* by the celebrated Spanish painter Francisco de Goya. In 1992, Pennsylvania State University officials removed a reproduction of this acclaimed work from the front wall of a classroom following a complaint by English professor Nancy Stumhofer that it embarrassed her and made her female students "uncomfortable."   10

No matter that the reproduction hung, along with reproductions of other masterpieces, in a room used for art history classes. No matter that university officials offered to move the painting to a less prominent position in the classroom, such as the back wall. No matter that they also offered to remove the Goya from the classroom altogether whenever Professor Stumhofer taught there, or even to relocate her classes to another classroom. No. Apparently, nothing short of extirpating the work from all campus classrooms would purge its taint, from her perspective. And the university capitulated. As writer Nat Hentoff commented, at that Penn State campus the administration defines sexual harassment as "anything that makes people uncomfortable about sexual issues."   11

Moving even beyond nudity or partial nudity, the sex panic has engulfed certain forms of clothing that some observers might deem provocative. In a 1994 *Ms.* magazine discussion on pornography, writer Ntozake Shange described one such situation that she said was "very heavy on my heart":   12

> I was on the cover of *Poets & Writers* and I wore a pretty lace top. In the next two issues, there were letters asking if *Poets & Writers* is now a flesh magazine— why was I appearing in my underwear? Bare shoulders are exploitation now?

In response, Andrea Dworkin, another participant in the *Ms.* discussion, confirmed that she would indeed see Shange's photograph as exploitation: "It's very hard to look at a picture of a woman's body and not see it with the perception that her body is being exploited."

Whether the stigmatizing epithet of choice for particular protesters happens to be "pornography" or "sexual harassment," the result is the same: the conclusory   13 label intimidates campus officials and others who should defend artistic expression, so they instead suppress it. Objecting to another such suppressive incident, which occurred at Vanderbilt University in 1993 . . . Vanderbilt art professor Marilyn Murphy said, "Human sexuality has been a recurring theme in art since antiquity. Visual arts is the most misunderstood discipline on this campus and on college campuses everywhere."

Liza Mundy, a writer who has chronicled campus attacks on art with sexual themes, has concluded that "MacKinnonite ideas underlie many" such attacks, noting the irony that many of these battles "pit feminist students against feminist artists." At the University of Arizona in Tucson, students physically attacked a group of photographic self-portraits by graduate student Laurie Blakeslee, which were displayed in the student union. The alleged offense? Blakeslee had photographed herself in her underwear. In Mundy's words, "Young women and men influenced by crusading law professor Catharine MacKinnon—and these are in the ascendance on many campuses—believe that . . . sexually explicit imagery create[s] an atmosphere in which rape is tolerated and even encouraged." 14

An essential aspect of women's right to equal opportunity in employment and education is the right to be free from sexual harassment. What is troubling, though, is the spreading sense—perpetuated by the feminist antipornography movement—that *any* sexual expression about a woman, or in her presence, *necessarily* constitutes such harassment. This presumption is stated expressly as the basis for the sweeping sexual harassment codes that are becoming increasingly common on campuses. 15

Syracuse University, for example, adopted a sexual harassment code in 1993 that prohibits not only "requests for sexual relations combined with threats of adverse consequences" if refused, and assaultive acts such as "pinching or fondling," but also nonassaultive, vaguely described acts such as "leering, ogling and physical gestures conveying a sexual meaning," and loosely described expressions including "sexual innuendoes, suggestive remarks, [and] sexually derogatory jokes." What all of these seemingly disparate behaviors have in common, the code informs us, "is that they focus on men and women's sexuality, rather than on their contributions as students or employees in the University." 16

But this should not be an either-or choice, should it? Are women not—along with men—sexual beings, as well as students or employees? Is women's sexuality really incompatible with their professional roles? Is it really increasing women's autonomy, options, and full-fledged societal participation to posit such an incompatibility? Have we not learned from history, and from other cultures, that the suppression of women's sexuality tends to coincide with the suppression of women's equality? And that when women's sexuality has been banished from the public sphere, women themselves are also banished from key roles in that sphere? 17

Far from advancing women's equality, this growing tendency to equate any sexual expression with gender discrimination undermines women's equality. Women are, in effect, told that we have to choose between sexuality and equality, between sexual liberation and other aspects of "women's liberation," between sexual freedom 18 and economic, social, and political freedom. This dangerous equation of sexual expression with gender discrimination, which is at the heart of the feminist antipornography movement, is a central reason that movement is so threatening to the women's rights cause.

The misguided zeal to strip all sexual expression from workplaces and campuses, in an alleged effort to strip those places of gender-based discrimination, now has reached even to subtle interpersonal expressions, prone to subjective perceptions and interpretations, such as looks and glances. A growing number of campus policies, including the one at Syracuse University already quoted, extend the concept of harassment to "sexually suggestive looks." Likewise, a survey about the sexual harassment of female doctors by their patients, published in the prestigious *New England Journal of Medicine* in December 1993, included "suggestive looks" among the "offenses" reported. In fact, though newspaper headlines trumpeted the dramatic conclusion that 75 percent of the female doctors surveyed said that they had been sexually harassed by patients, further reading revealed that "most of the offenses involved suggestive looks and sexual remarks." 19

Are women doctors, faculty, and students to be relegated to a figurative equivalent of the purdah of traditional Hindus and Muslims, or the clothing and segregation requirements of orthodox Jews—designed to prevent men from looking at women, and to "protect" women from men's looks? While these traditional religious practices shield women from the eyes of anyone outside their domestic circles, they also imprison women within those domestic circles. The outside world cannot see women, and women cannot see the outside world. 20

To be sure, "sexual looks," as well as the other nonassaultive conduct proscribed in the Syracuse code, could constitute sexual harassment if they were sufficiently severe or pervasive—for example, if a professor repeatedly subjected a young student to such behavior. In contrast, isolated incidents where the behavior is not targeted at someone who has less authority or status should not be deemed harassment. 21

STRATEGY TWO: DEVELOPING AN ESSAY BASED ON A SOURCE

This strategy gives you the freedom to develop your own ideas and present your own point of view in an essay that is only loosely linked to the source. Reading an assigned essay helps you to generate ideas and topics and provides you with evidence or information to cite in your own essay; but *the thesis, scope, and organization of your essay are entirely your own.*

1. Finding and Narrowing a Topic

As always, you begin by studying the assigned essay carefully, establishing its thesis and main ideas. As you read, start *brainstorming: noting ideas of your own* that might be worth developing. You need not cover exactly the same material as the source essay. What you want is a *spin-off* from the original reading, not a summary.

Here is one student's preliminary list of topics for an essay based on Blanche Blank's "A Question of Degree." (Blank's essay can be found on pp. 8–11.) Notice that, initially, this student's ideas are mostly personal.

- "selling college": how do colleges recruit students? how did I choose this college? has my college experience met my expectations?
- "practical curriculum": what are my courses preparing me for? what is the connection between my courses and my future career? Why am I here?
- "college compulsory at adolescence": what were my parental expectations? teachers' expectations? did we have any choices?
- "employment discrimination based on college degrees": what kinds of jobs now require a B.A.? was it always like that? what other kinds of training are possible—for clerks? for civil servants? for teacher's aides?
- financing college: how much is tuition? are we getting what we pay for? is education something to be purchased, like a winter coat?
- "dignity of work": job experience/work environment
- "joylessness in university life": describe students' attitudes—is the experience mechanical? is the environment bureaucratic?
- "hierarchical levels": what do the different college degrees mean? should they take as long as they do? should a BA take four years?

If you read the essay a few times without thinking of a topic or if you can't see how your ideas can be developed into an essay, *test some standard strategies,* applying them to the source essay in ways that might not have occurred to the original author. Here, for example, are some strategies that generate topics for an essay based on "A Question of Degree."

Process

You might examine in detail one of the processes that Blank describes only generally. For example, you could write about your own experience to explain the ways in which teenagers are encouraged to believe that a college degree is essential, citing high school counseling and college catalogues and analyzing the unrealistic expectations that young students are encouraged to have. Or, if you have sufficient knowledge, you might describe the unjust manipulation of hiring procedures that favor college graduates or the process by which a college's liberal arts curriculum gradually becomes "practical."

Illustration

If you focused on a single discouraged employee, showing in what ways ambition for increased status and salary have been frustrated, or a single disillusioned college graduate, showing how career prospects have failed to measure up to training and expectations, your strategy would be an illustration proving one of Blank's themes.

Definition

Definition often emerges from a discussion of the background of an issue. What should the work experience be like? What is the function of a university? What is a good education? By attempting to define one of the components of Blank's theme in terms of the ideal, you are helping your reader to understand her arguments and evaluate her conclusions more rationally.

Cause and Effect

You can examine one or more of the reasons why a college degree has become a necessary credential for employment. You can also suggest a wider context for discussing Blank's views by describing the kind of society that encourages this set of values. In either case, you will be accounting for, but not necessarily justifying, the nation's obsession with degrees. Or you can predict the consequences, good or bad, that might result if Blank's suggested legislation were passed. Or you might explore some hypothetical possibilities and focus on the circumstances and causes of a situation different from the one that Blank describes. What if everyone in the United States earned a college degree? What if education after the eighth grade were abolished? By taking this approach, you are radically changing the circumstances that Blank depicts, but still sharing her concerns and exploring the principles discussed in her essay.

Problem and Solution

If Cause and Effect asks "why," then Problem and Solution explains "how." Blank raises several problems that, in her view, have harmful social consequences. What are some solutions? What changes are possible? How can we effect them? How, for example, can we change students' expectations of education and make them both more realistic and more idealistic? Note that exploring such solutions means that you are basically in agreement with Blank's thesis.

Comparison

You can alter the reader's perspective by moving the theme of Blank's essay to another time or place. Did our present obsession with education exist a hundred years ago? Is it a problem outside the United States at this moment? Will it probably continue into the twenty-first century? Or, focusing on late-twentieth-century America, how do contemporary trends in education and employment compare with trends in other areas of life—housing, finance, recreation, child-rearing, or communications? With all these approaches, you begin with a description of Blank's issue and contrast it with another set of circumstances, past or present, real or hypothetical.

Before choosing any of these speculative topics, you must first decide:

- What is practical in a brief essay
- Whether it requires research
- Whether, when fully developed, it will retain some connection with the source essay

For example, there may be some value in comparing the current emphasis on higher education with monastic education in the Middle Ages. Can you write such an essay? How much research will it require? Will a discussion of monastic education help your reader better to understand Blank's ideas? Or will you immediately move away from your starting point—and find no opportunity to return to it? Do you have a serious objective, or are you simply making the comparison "because it's there"?

2. Taking Notes and Writing a Thesis

Consider how you might develop an essay based on one of the topics suggested in the previous section. Notice that the chosen topic is expressed as a question.

Topic: What is the function of a university in the 1990s?

- After thinking about your topic, start your list of notes *before* you reread the essay, to make sure that you are not overly influenced by the author's point of view and to enable you to include some ideas of your own in your notes.
- Next, review the essay and add any relevant ideas to your list, *remembering to indicate when an idea originated with the source and not with you.*

Here is a complete list of notes for an essay defining the function of a university in the 1990s. The paragraph references, added later, indicate which points were made by Blank and where in her essay they can be found. The thesis, which follows the notes, was written after the list was complete.

WHAT THE UNIVERSITY SHOULD DO

1. to increase students' understanding of the world around them

    e.g., to become more observant and aware of natural phenomena (weather, for example) and social systems (like family relationships)

2. to help students to live more fulfilling lives

    to enable them to test their powers and know more and become more versatile; to speak with authority on topics that they didn't understand before

3. to help students live more productive lives

    to increase their working credentials and qualify for more interesting and well-paying jobs (B.B., Paragraphs 3–9)

4. to serve society by creating better informed, more rational citizens not only through college courses (like political science) but through the increased ability to observe and analyze and argue (B.B., Paragraphs 3, 14)

5. to contribute to research that will help to solve scientific and social problems (not a teaching function) (B.B., Paragraphs 3, 14)

6. to serve as a center for debate to clarify the issues of the day

    people should regard the university as a source of unbiased information and counsel; notable people should come to lecture (B.B., Paragraphs 3, 14)

7. to serve as a gathering place for great teachers

    students should be able to regard their teachers as worth emulating

8. to allow students to examine the opportunities for personal change and growth

    this includes vocational goals, e.g., career changes (B.B., Paragraph 4)

WHAT THE UNIVERSITY SHOULD NOT DO

9. it should not divide the haves from the have-nots

    college should not be considered essential; it should be possible to be successful without a college degree (B.B., Paragraphs 8, 10)

10. it should not use marketing techniques to appeal to the greatest number

    what the university teaches should be determined primarily by the faculty and to a lesser extent by the students; standards of achievement should not be determined by students who haven't learned anything yet

11. it should not ignore the needs of its students and its community by clinging to outdated courses and programs

12. it should not cooperate with business and government to the extent that it loses its autonomy (B.B., Paragraphs 6, 9)

13. it should not be an employment agency and vocational center to the exclusion of its more important functions (B.B., Paragraphs 6, 9, 16)

Thesis: As Blanche Blank points out, a university education is not a commodity to be marketed and sold; a university should be a resource center for those who want the opportunity to develop their intellectual powers and lead more productive, useful, and fulfilling lives.

3. Deciding on a Strategy

As a rule, you would consider strategies for your essay as soon as you have established your thesis. In this case, however, the choice of strategy—definition—was made earlier when you chose your topic and considered several possible strategies. *The notes, divided into what a university should and should not do, already follow a definition strategy, with its emphasis on differentiation.*

4. Constructing an Outline

Having made all the preliminary decisions, you are ready to plan the structure of your essay.

- Mark those portions of the reading that you will need to use in support of your thesis. Your essay will be based on both your own ideas and the ideas of your source.
- Check whether your notes accurately paraphrase the source, and decide how many source references you intend to make so that you can write a balanced outline.
- Double-check to make sure that you are giving the source credit for all paraphrased ideas.
- If appropriate, include some examples from your own experience.
- Organize your notes in groups or categories, each of which will be developed as a separate paragraph or sequence of related paragraphs.
- Decide the order of your categories (or paragraphs).
- Incorporate in your outline some of the points from Blanche Blank's essay that you intend to include. Cite the paragraph number of the relevant material with your outline entry. If the source paragraph contains several references that you expect to place in different parts of your outline, use a sentence number or a set of symbols or a brief quotation for differentiation.

Here is one section of the completed outline for an essay on "Defining a University for the 1990s." This outline incorporates notes 3, 13, 9, and 8 from the list on pp. 162–163.

I. The university should help students to live more productive lives, to increase their working credentials, and to qualify for more interesting and well-paying jobs. (Paragraph 6—last sentence)

    A. But it should not be an employment agency and vocational center to the exclusion of its more important functions. (Paragraph 9—"servicing agents"; Paragraph 12—"joylessness in our university life"; Paragraph 16)

    B. It should not divide the haves from the have-nots; success without a college degree should be possible. (Paragraph 2—"two kinds of work"; Paragraph 17)

II. The university should allow students to examine the opportunities for personal growth and change; this includes vocational goals, e.g., career changes. (Paragraph 4—"an optional and continuing experience later in life")

5. Writing the Essay

When you write from sources, you are engaged in a kind of partnership. *You strive for an appropriate balance between your own ideas and those of your source.* By reading your source carefully and using annotation, outlining, and paraphrase, you familiarize yourself with the source's main ideas and reasoning and prepare to put those ideas in your essay. But *it is your voice that should dominate the essay.* You, after all, are writing it; you are responsible for its contents and its effect on the reader. For this reason, *all the important "positions" in the structure of your essay should be filled by you.* The topic sentences, as well as the introduction, should be written in your own words and should stress your views, not those of your author. On the other hand, your reader should not be allowed to lose sight of the source essay; it should be treated as a form of evidence and cited whenever it is relevant, but always as a context in which to develop your own strategy and assert your own thesis.

Here is the completed paragraph based on Points I and IA in the outline:

To achieve certain goals, all of us have agreed to take four years out of our lives, at great expense, for higher education. What I learn here will, I hope, give me the communication skills, the range of knowledge, and the discipline to succeed in a career as a journalist. But, as Blanche Blank points out, a college education may not be the best way to prepare for every kind of job. Is it necessary to spend four years at this college to become a supermarket manager? a computer programmer? a clerk in the social security office? If colleges become no more than high-level job training or employment centers, or, in Blank's words, "servicing agents" to screen workers for business, then they lose their original purpose as centers of a higher form of learning. Blank is rightly concerned that, if a college degree becomes a mandatory credential, I and my contemporaries will regard ourselves "as prisoners of economic necessity," alienated from the rich possibilities of education by the "joylessness in our university life."

6. Revising the Essay

Your work isn't finished until you have reviewed your essay carefully to ensure that the organization is logical, the paragraphs coherent, and the sentences complete. To gain some distance and objectivity, most people put their work aside for a while before starting to revise it. You can also ask someone else to read and comment on your essay, but make sure that you have reason to trust that person's judgment and commitment to the task. It isn't helpful to be told only that "paragraph three doesn't work" or "I don't get that sentence"; your reader should be willing to spend some time and trouble to pinpoint what's wrong so that you can go back to your manuscript and make revisions. Problems usually arise in these three areas.

Overall Structure

If you follow your outline or your revised list of notes, your paragraphs should follow each other fairly well. But extraneous ideas—some of them good ones—tend to creep in as you write, and sometimes you need to make adjustments to accommodate them. As you look carefully at the sequence of paragraphs, make sure that they lead into each other. Are parallel points presented in a series or are they scattered throughout the essay? Sometimes, two paragraphs need to be reversed, or two paragraphs belong together and need to be merged. In addition, your reader should be guided through the sequence of paragraphs by the "traffic signals" provided by transitional phrases, such as "in addition" or "nevertheless" or "in fact." The transitions need not be elaborate: words like "also," "so," and "too" keep the reader on track.

Paragraph Development

The paragraphs should be of roughly comparable length, each containing a topic sentence (not necessarily placed at the beginning), explanatory sentences, details or examples provided by your source or yourself, and (possibly) quotations from your source. It's important to have this mix of general material and detail to keep your essay from being too abstract or too specific. Make sure that every sentence contributes to the point of the paragraph. Look for sentences without content, or sentences that make the same point over again. If, after such deletions, a paragraph seems overly brief or stark, consider what illustrations or details might be added to support and add interest to the topic. Check back to the source to see if there are still some points worth paraphrasing or quoting.

Sentence Style

Your writing should meet a basic acceptable standard. Are the sentences complete? Eliminate fragments or run-ons. Is the sentence style monotonous, with the same pattern repeated again and again? Look for repetitions, and consider ways to vary the style, such as starting some sentences with a phrase or

Guidelines for Writing a Single-Source Essay

1. Identify the source essay's thesis; analyze its underlying themes, if any, and its strategy; and construct a rough outline of its main ideas.

2. Decide on two or three possible essay topics based on your work in Step 1, and narrow down one of them. (Be prepared to submit your topics for your teacher's approval and, in conference, to choose the most suitable one.)

3. Write down a list of notes about your own ideas on the topic, being careful to distinguish between points that are yours and points that are derived from the source.

4. Write a thesis of your own that fairly represents your list of ideas. Mention the source in your thesis if appropriate.

5. If you have not done so already, choose a strategy that will best carry out your thesis; it need not be the same strategy as that of the source essay.

6. Mark (by brackets or underlining) those paragraphs or sentences in the source that will help to develop your topic.

7. Draw up an outline for your essay. Combine repetitious points; bring together similar and related points. Decide on the best sequence for your paragraphs.

8. Decide which parts of the reading should be cited as evidence or refuted; place paragraph or page references to the source in the appropriate sections of your outline. Then decide which sentences of the reading to quote and which to paraphrase.

9. Write the rough draft, making sure that, whenever possible, your topic sentences express your views, introduce the material that you intend to present in that paragraph, and are written in your voice. Later in the paragraph, incorporate references to the source, and link your paragraphs together with transitions. Do not be concerned about a bibliography for this single-source essay. Cite the author's full name and the exact title of the work early in your essay. (See pp. 92–95 for a review of citations.)

10. Write an introduction that contains a clear statement of your thesis, as well as a reference to the source essay and its role in the development of your ideas. You may also decide to draft a conclusion.

11. Review your first draft to note problems with organization, transitions, or language. Proofread your first draft very carefully to correct errors of grammar, style, reference, and spelling.

12. Using standard-size paper and leaving adequate margins and spacing, prepare the final draft. Proofread once again to catch careless errors in copying.

subordinate clause. Are you using the same vocabulary again and again? Are too many of your sentences built around "is" or "are"? Search for stronger verbs, and vary your choice of words, perhaps consulting the thesaurus. (But think twice about using words that are totally new to you, or you'll risk sounding awkward. Use the thesaurus to remind yourself of possible choices, not to increase your vocabulary.) Finally, consider basic grammar. Check for apostrophes, for subject-verb agreement, for quotation marks. Don't let careless errors detract from your hard work in preparing and writing this essay.

ASSIGNMENT 5: WRITING AN ESSAY BASED ON A SINGLE SOURCE

A. Read "The Other Side of Suicide," "Love as an Experience of Transcendence," and "Getting Them into the Electronic Tent." One of these three essays will serve as the starting point for an essay of your own. Assume that the essay you are planning will be approximately three pages long, or 600–900 words. Using steps 1 and 2, think of *three* possible topics for an essay of that length, and submit the most promising (or, if your teacher suggests it, all three) for approval.

B. Plan your essay by working from notes to an outline. Be prepared to submit your thesis and outline of paragraphs (with indications of relevant references to the source) to your teacher for approval.

C. Write a rough draft after deciding which parts of the essay should be cited as evidence, distributing references to the source among appropriate sections of your outline, and determining which parts of the reading should be quoted and which should be paraphrased.

D. Write a final draft of your essay.

THE OTHER SIDE OF SUICIDE
from *The Beauty of the Beastly*
Natalie Angier

Considered on its face, suicide flouts the laws of nature, slashing through the sturdy instinct that wills all beings to fight for their lives until they can fight no longer.   1

Yet by a coolheaded evolutionary accounting, suicide cannot be entirely explained as a violent aberration or a human pathology lying outside the ebbs and pulls of natural selection and adaptation. Suicide, for all its private, tangled sorrows, is surprisingly common in most countries, accounting on average for about 1 percent of all deaths. And when the number of unsuccessful suicide attempts is taken into account, the prevalence of the behavior jumps considerably. The incidence, some evolutionary geneticists say, is too great to be accounted for by standard explanations like social malaise or random cases of psychiatric disease.   2

Instead, the persistence of suicide at a high rate across most cultures of the world suggests an underlying evolutionary component, a possible Darwinian rationale for an act that too often appears starkly irrational. The inclination toward suicide could be a concomitant of a trait or group of traits that at some point in evolutionary history conferred benefits on those who bore it.

Further bolstering the case for a genetic basis to suicide is its tendency to run in families. Although suicide occurs in nearly all countries, it is far more common among some ethnic groups than others. The Hungarians and Finns, for example, suffer from suicide rates two to three times those in the United States and most of Europe. Significantly, the Hungarians and Finns are thought to share genetic roots in the distant past (as well as the linguistic roots that bind the Hungarian and Finnish tongues and set them apart from Indo-European languages). In addition, the elevated incidence of suicide holds true not only in those nations, where socioeconomic conditions could be responsible, but also for Finns and Hungarians who have emigrated to other countries, again hinting at a biological substrate.

Nobody argues that there is a single gene for suicide, or that suicide or mental illness should be thought of as good. The lure of suicide too often beckons to the young, who clothe it in the romantic chiffon of nobility and poetry and see it as a reasonable option should the transition to adulthood prove too traumatic, a way of thinking that no sane adult would condone.

Nevertheless, there may be plausible evolutionary explanations for at least some self-destructive acts. A number of theorists propose that the impulse to kill oneself may be an expression of an instinct toward self-sacrifice for the good of surviving relatives, either because those relatives will be rescued from their own death, or because they will benefit richly from the resources that will now accrue to them. The surviving relatives will in turn pass on the sacrificial victim's genes. To take a short and admittedly simplistic example, a hominid in the jungle may have enhanced his genetic survival by sacrificing himself to a leopard that would otherwise have slain six of his brothers or sisters. However, because we live in complex social groups, such an impulse toward martyrdom might on occasion show itself in complex, distorted forms, tugging miserably at the psyches of even those who have no families to benefit from their deaths or to ensure that their genetic legacies survive.

In another scenario, suicide is viewed not as heritable but as the most tragic outcome of another trait that may derive from natural selection—the tendency toward depression. Some Darwinian thinkers say that extremely bleak moods are themselves too common to be the result of pathology alone. They propose that bouts of depression may be useful, forcing people into a kind of emotional hibernation and giving them time to reflect on their mistakes. But such a strategy, if sustained too long or repeated too often, becomes maladaptive and even fatal, showing itself as the harrowing disease called major depression.

Reasoning that human beings invent few traits but instead display intricate versions of behaviors seen elsewhere in the animal kingdom, some biologists have looked to other species for clues to the genesis of suicide and depression. The exercise is fraught with perils. Nonhuman animals obviously do not leave behind anything as clear as a note, nor are they likely to have sufficient awareness to do something as deliberate as jump off a cliff. Still, there are numerous examples of creatures that sacrifice themselves for their kin, including termites that explode their guts, releasing the slimy, foul contents over enemies that threaten their nest, and rodents that deliberately starve themselves to death rather than risk spreading an infection to others in their burrow. What is more compelling, many species of nonhuman primates will suffer serious depression when stressed; on falling into an episode of melancholy, the monkeys may engage in all sorts of life-threatening activities— refusing food until they die of malnutrition, or swinging from dangerous tree limbs that no normal monkey would go near. So similar is monkey depression to our own that the symptoms of the mood disorder dissipate when the primates are given an antidepressant like Prozac.

Admittedly, one must approach this theoretical terrain with enormous trepidation, for it's all too easy to sound insensitive or glib in ascribing suicide and depression to the handiwork of natural selection. Psychiatrists have struggled long and hard to get the public to view mental illness as an organic disorder rather than a self-indulgence or character flaw, and most are reluctant to describe something like depression in anything other than the most strictly disease-oriented and condemnatory terms—as the mind's version of diabetes or cancer. Researchers know too well how easily a Darwinian explanation for complex behaviors can be overdone and oversimplified.   9

Certainly the affairs of animals much simpler than people have been misinterpreted in the past. For example, the mention of suicide in nonhuman species invariably raises the famed case of lemmings, rodents that were long thought to kill themselves en masse by running into the sea, as though alerted by a group alarm clock that today is a good day to die. As recent research has revealed, however, the tale of the suicidal lemming is false. The tawny, thickset rodents will die by the group, but that is a result of an error in judgment. Lemmings are the locusts of mammals, and they will strip a habitat bare. They then begin migrating to find new feeding grounds, swarming over boulders, around trees, whatever stands in their way. If they run into a body of water, they try to swim across, a routine that works fine for streams and ponds. If they happen to hit a lake or an ocean, they discover too late into their paddling that they can't make it.   10

Often it is not clear whether a death in the wilderness is deliberate or accidental. Some animal behaviorists have developed models predicting that, under certain circumstances, a hatchling bird in a multichick brood does better from the perspective of its genetic legacy to let itself be killed by its siblings than to fight back. Among crested penguins, for instance, a mother always lays two eggs a season, one large, one small. Given the harshness of her arctic surroundings, she can rear only one bird to independence, and usually that lucky penguin will come from the large egg. Still, she lays the double dose as an insurance policy, in case the big egg is preyed on. Should the big and little eggs both end up hatching, the smaller offspring   11 in theory would do best to permit the bigger sibling to kill it off without putting up a fuss—essentially, to throw itself on its sibling's sword. After all, both birds can't possibly survive, so why divert resources from the relative with the greater chance of success?

The theory has some observational data to back it up: in encounters between sibling penguins, the little ones do appear to die off without ruffling anybody's feathers. However, critics of the scenario do not buy that the smaller contender is going gently into that good night. They point out that if your ordinary Joe were stuck in a lifeboat with Mike Tyson and a very limited quantity of food, the nonboxer would be foolish to challenge Tyson to a fight; instead, the little fellow is likely to lie low and look for a chance to push him overboard, or simply pray that Tyson gets struck by lightning.

12

In general, scientists will call a death a suicide only when the animal has much to gain and little to lose, reproductively speaking, from the act. Among this group some put cryptically colored butterflies that escape being eaten by blending into their surroundings. Once an adult is past its reproductive time, it becomes a risk to its surviving offspring, for if the elder insect is discovered by a bird, the predators will gain clues from the butterfly's pattern to discriminate prey from background; thereafter, the younger butterflies will also be in danger. As it happens, the postfertile adults are known to drop to the groundcover and begin beating their wings rapidly until they die of exhaustion. They obliterate themselves and their secrets before they get caught.

13

Other exemplars of self-sacrifice abound. In some gall midges—tiny gnatlike insects—a mother offers up her body as a meal to offspring, and they happily consume every last segmented bit of her. Among naked mole rats, hairless and blind rodents that live underground and are almost as closely related to one another as are bees in a hive, an animal that is infested with parasites knows what it must do: go off to the communal toilet area of the burrow and remain there until it dies. Once its decision is made, it won't move, and it can't be force-fed, even under laboratory conditions; the sickly mole rat will not risk infecting the whole colony.

14

In applying to human beings the idea of self-sacrifice for the good of one's kith and kin, scientists cite obvious examples: mothers who gladly die to save their children, war heroes who go down in flames for their buddies, or even the recent spate of so-called rational suicides, in which elderly or terminally ill patients request that they be allowed to die quickly to avoid being a drain on their families. Researchers are much more reluctant to use such reasoning to justify the behavior of suicidal patients who very often are mentally ill, lonely, and alienated from those who care about them. Yet psychiatrists observe that people who are contemplating suicide frequently think of it in extravagantly selfless terms, as the option that would be best for the suicide's family and friends. Those who have talked to people immediately after they made a serious suicide attempt report that the patients often have an altruistic explanation for what they did, believing the action to be the wise, clever, and thoughtful thing to do. In that sense, our own version of suicide sounds

15

remarkably similar to the response of a parasitized naked mole rat. Those who consider killing themselves feel grotesque, polluted, infected, and they may think it best to destroy the source of disease before it contaminates their loved ones.

Of course, it's true that the majority of those who attempt suicide are afflicted by a disease—a mood disorder, in most cases depression or manic-depression. Such conditions are characterized by a dramatic drop in neurotransmitters like norepinephrine or serotonin, the molecules that allow nerve cells to communicate and that help modulate emotions and aggression.   16

Studying nonhuman primates, scientists say they have witnessed many of the symptoms of serious depression in their subjects, including a disregard for self-preservation. Jane Goodall, the renowned chimpanzee champion, once observed a seven-and-a-half-year-old male chimp experience such profound despair after the death of his mother that he refused to leave her corpse even to eat. The monkey slowly withered away, lay down, and died—of a broken heart, Ms. Goodall said.   17

Monkey depression resembles our own not only behaviorally but biochemically. Working with a free-ranging colony of rhesus monkeys, behavioral scientists have learned that about 20 percent of the primates are predisposed to serious depression, roughly the same as our own lifetime risk of the disorder. The monkeys fall into their slump when they lose a relative or close partner, or suffer a drop in social status, events that likewise set off human depression. In addition, the depressed monkeys show some of the same changes in brain chemistry that have been observed in human patients, including a drop in cerebrospinal levels of norepinephrine.   18

Depression, then, is evolutionarily ancient, preceding the appearance of hominids. Its purpose could be protective, allowing people and other animals with advanced cognitive skills to assess their situations, consider how their tactics may have backfired, and figure out a way to avoid repetitions of the costly error. Alternatively, depression could be the inevitable downside of a personality that offers great payoffs when times are good. In the case of the rhesus monkey, the same animals that are susceptible to depression often rise to the top of the social hierarchy because of their heightened sensory and emotional sensitivity. They're more aware than their peers of critical changes in the environment—the sound of an approaching predator, the tentative gestures of a possible new ally. They see and hear and smell everything. They are like taut strings on a beautiful violin. If bowed too hard, the strings will snap.   19

LOVE AS AN EXPERIENCE OF TRANSCENDENCE
Charles Lindholm

George Simenon, the prolific French author who was equally active as a Don Juan, was once asked to describe the difference between sexual passion and romantic love. "Passion," Simenon said, "is a malady. It's possession, something dark. You are jealous of everything. There's no lightness, no harmony. Love, that's com-   1 pletely different. It is beautiful. Love is being two in one. It is being so close that when one opens his mouth to speak, the other says exactly what you meant to say. Love is a quiet understanding and a fusion."

The erotically experienced Simenon here disengages the imperative demands of sexual desire from romantic love, which he describes as engendering a powerful and expansive sense of self-loss through merger with the beloved other. This experience of self-transcendence, I will argue in the following pages, is the essence of romantic love; it is above all a creative act of human imagination, arising as a cultural expression of deep existential longings for an escape from the prison of the self. I shall contrast this view of love with another, more prevalent view, which understands love as contingent upon sexual desire.

2

In making my case about the nature of falling in love, I am hardly being original. Rather, the question of the nature of love has divided and puzzled Western philosophers at least from the time of the Greeks. Irving Singer, in his exhaustive study of the philosophical and literary roots of the concept of romantic love, has outlined this debate, showing that the way love has been conceptualized throughout Western history can be divided into two opposing, but necessarily intertwined, perspectives. In the first, love is based on appraisal, and those who are beloved are thought capable of satisfying our deepest appetites. In other words, we assess the other to discover if they have the attributes we long for; if they do, we love them. Broadly defined, love is a matter of calculated self-interest.

3

Self-interest, however, can take on a transcendental hue. The beloved can appeal to us as an avenue to a higher level of being. There are many versions of this way of understanding love. For instance, Plato portrays love of persons as a plateau in the soul's impassioned pursuit of the ideal good. The beloved is adulated as an earthly and imperfect expression of divine harmony and beauty. But the wise man realizes that the love of persons is shallow compared to the spiritual rewards of pure reason, and progresses through enjoyment of the flawed body of the other to meditation on the abstract realm of the ideal, where beauty is absolute and eternal. Love for a person then is a means to a higher end, much like the contemplation of a work of art.

4

A more down-to-earth stance is taken by Ovid, for whom the Platonic search for a higher love in the realm of the absolute through the body of the lover is a ludicrous subterfuge. Ovid says that what the lover wants is clear enough: sexual enjoyment. His emphasis is on the game of love, and he teaches his readers, both male and female, how the idealizing imagery of romantic passion can be used with style and grace by intelligent seducers to help them gain sexual access to those whom they desire while avoiding the attentions of others whom they find unattractive. Professions of love serve to conceal a seducer's deliberate machinations and thereby render lust more attractive.

5

Ovid's appetitive perspective on love has been a dominant view for scientific minds ever since Plato's notion of the spiritual progress of the soul lost its persuasiveness. But while Ovid's portrayal of sexual desire as the underlying source of

6

love was retained, his playful attitude toward sexuality was repudiated as morally suspect by more puritanical writers such as Jonathan Swift, who wrote that love is "a ridiculous passion which hath no being but in play-books and romances."

Anthropologists, in the little they have to say about romantic love . . . have tended   7
to fall generally within the Swiftian paradigm. Most famous and representative is Ralph Linton's statement:

> The hero of the modern American movie is always a romantic lover, just as the hero of an old Arab epic is always an epileptic. A cynic may suspect that in any ordinary population the percentage of individuals with capacity for romantic love of the Hollywood type was about as large as that of persons able to throw genuine epileptic fits. However, given a little social encouragement, either one can be adequately imitated without the performer admitting even to himself that the performance is not genuine.

Similarly, Robert Lowie argues that in all cultures "passion, of course is taken for   8
granted; affection, which many travellers vouch for, might be conceded; but Love? Well, the romantic sentiment occurs in simpler conditions, as with us—in fiction."

Romantic love, from this point of view, is nothing but a self-delusion, derived   9
from the arts, used to persuade lovers that their sexual desires are actually ethereal and transcendent. Where Ovid saw the idealizing content of romantic love as an attractive and necessary convention, it now becomes a hypocritical lie. Jean-Paul Sartre has immortalized this modern perspective in a famous section in *Being and Nothingness* (1956), where he scathingly imagines the bad faith of a young girl absently permitting her hand to be stroked by a suitor while she simultaneously imagines herself admired solely as a creature of purity and abstract intellect.

This approach has the virtue of simplicity and coherence; falling in love is always   10
a fraud, and men and women who claim to be in love are invariably hypocrites or, at best, seducers. But it does little justice to the actual self-reports of lovers, who clearly do not always fit into the categories of self-deceivers and sexual predators. A more sympathetic modern version of the "eros tradition" (as Singer has called it) is to be found in sociobiology, which takes a somewhat different tack toward understanding romantic love. The aim is to give more credit to the lovers' own inner experience while still retaining the materialistic view of romantic love as essentially an expression of sexuality.

The twist is that rather than debunking romantic sentiment as self-delusion,   11
these writers understand love as a compulsive drive toward sexual contact with a specific beloved other. This compulsion is connected to evolutionary biology by utilizing contemporary theories of genetic success. Instead of consciously manipulating one another, as enjoined by Ovid, the lovers now are themselves unconscious puppets of the deep evolutionary forces that are propelling their behaviors.

This argument was first proposed by Schopenhauer, who asserted that romantic   12
love is a trick played by the Will in order to compel human beings to reproduce and carry on the movement of the *Geist* toward the future. Thus he writes that

lovers desire a "fusion into a single being, in order then to go on living only as this being; and this longing receives its fulfillment in the child they produce"; or, put more prosaically: "If Petrarch's passion had been satisfied, his song would have been silenced from that moment, just as is that of the bird, as soon as the eggs are laid."

As reworked in modern rhetoric Schopenhauer's argument is used by socio-biologists to assert that romantic love is a genetically innate mechanism serving to offset the male's natural tendency to maximize his gene pool through promiscuity. It does this by tying him to a particular female via the emotionally charged sexual contact that is understood to be the heart of romance. The enhanced pairbonding that results serves the evolutionary purpose of increasing the overall rate of survival for human children.

13

From this perspective falling in love is therefore a very real experience, probably a consequence of the manufacture of powerful chemicals in the brain that incite the potent feelings of merger and ecstasy lovers report; but love is not sufficient onto itself, rather it is a means to an end—perpetuation of the species. Thus socio-biology shares with the Platonic perspective a concern with teleology. But where Plato saw love as a step in the pursuit of the ideal, now the goal of romantic love is disconcertingly mundane: evolutionary success.

14

Some of the cultural background that informs this argument can be illustrated in a balance sheet made up by the twenty-nine-year-old Charles Darwin, who was weighing the good points and bad points of marriage. The main good point was companionship ("a nice soft wife on a sofa" . . . "better than a dog anyhow"); children were also mentioned, as Darwin expresses his fear of being a "neuter bee." The bad points were more numerous, and included the considerable financial burden a wife and children would impose on him, the inevitable constraints a family would place on his freedom of action, the "loss of time," the "anxiety and responsibility" and the fear that marriage might end as "banishment and degradation with (an) indolent, idle fool."

15

In reading Darwin's lists, it seems clear that the disadvantages of marriage, which are many and concrete, appear to far outweigh the advantages, which are few and abstract. As Alan MacFarlane writes, speaking from a strictly rational perspective, marriage in England "was not sane behavior, for almost all the advantages of marriage could be bought in the market—from sex to housekeeping and friendship." But Darwin married nonetheless, persuading himself that "there is many a happy slave." Why did he act so irrationally?

16

MacFarlane argues that in Western history, and especially in the history of England, romantic love has been precisely the factor that has been invoked as the source of the marriage tie. In a society where arranged marriage was never pervasive, where lineages were more or less nonexistent, and where personal autonomy prevailed, love acts as a deus ex machina, overcoming the reasonable reluctance of rational self-seeking individuals to commit themselves to marriage bonds they would otherwise avoid. Furthermore, love also focuses sexuality in the open market of potential partners, "some external force of desire is needed to help the individual to

17

make a choice. Hence passionate 'love' overwhelms and justifies and provides compulsive authority."

Although MacFarlane does not carry his argument through to claim a biological source for romance, it is perfectly plausible to reconcile his position with a concept of falling in love as an expression of a biological pressure that compels individuals toward erotic encounters with a specific other. The historian Laurence Stone states this point of view most candidly when he describes falling in love as "an urgent desire for sexual intercourse with a particular individual"; a sexual encounter that, from the sociobiological standpoint, can induce the commitment and reciprocal caring necessary for maintaining a human family unit.

Following the logic of the argument further, if romantic love is simply a strong, biologically generated, hormonally induced sexual urge for a unique other, culture becomes a variable that may have an enhancing or suppressing effect on the erotic romantic impulse, and it would make sense to argue that societies valuing choice and individualism would be most conducive to romantic love, while those valuing obligation and communalism would work to control romantic desire by cultural mechanisms, such as arranged marriage, chaperoning of youth, child betrothal, and so on. On the other hand, Western culture, which favors personal autonomy and free choice, is the location where love can take its "natural," biologically induced, course, permitting romance to replace formal bonds of kinship and alliance as the motivation for marriage.

To restate: from the standpoint of the contemporary sociobiological version of the eros tradition, falling in love is understood as a biological drive, probably deriving from hormonal secretions, that intensifies sexual desire and thereby leads to strong pairbonding. It is favorable to the reproduction and care of human children, and its transcendental consummation is the successful maximization of genetic potential. It can be assumed that some cultures will favor this compulsion while others will attempt to suppress it; nonetheless it will remain as a universal and ineradicable desire for mating with a particular other person—a desire interpreted as romantic love.

But there are problems with this perspective, and they have to do with the place romantic love fills in different cultural contexts. Although giving some reluctant credit to cultural processes, sociobiology generally assumes that millions of years of evolution outweigh a few millennia of culture. Therefore, human beings, like their simian ancestors, are portrayed as basically governed by instinct, though the instincts may have been distorted, channeled, and partially curbed by cultural conditioning. However, postulating a primary cause requires a demonstration of at least some discernible secondary effect; and if culture can completely rewrite, overturn, or cancel the supposed biological matrix of romantic love, sexuality, and reproduction, then the logic of the sociobiological argument is seriously challenged.

This challenge is most evident in the aspect of culture that has most to do with evolutionary biology; that is, the institution of marriage. In all human societies marriage serves as a ritualized way of formalizing and legitimizing the sexual relation-

18

19

20

21

22

ship between couples. Furthermore, in almost every known culture married couples produce and raise the vast majority of children. Given this basic fact, one would expect that if romantic love is linked to reproduction, then marriage should be correlated with romantic love.

In the modern West, of course, this works well enough, since romantic love, marriage, and children indeed usually *do* go together and, as we shall see, have gone together for some centuries. However, in most human cultures this is not the case, nor was it necessarily the case everywhere in Western culture in the past. For example, in the courtly society of Louis XIV in France, marriage and love were decidedly opposed, since marriage was arranged for political advantage, not for romantic attraction. In this culture courtesans were the objects of romantic attraction, not wives. Interestingly, these courtesans, who stood outside of the political structure of the society because of their base birth, were prized not so much for their sexuality as for their charm and wit. Of course, having children was something these women avoided at all costs.

Similarly, in Rome of the Imperial Age conjugal love between husband and wife was considered ridiculous and impossible, so much so that Seneca writes, "to love one's wife with an ardent passion is to commit adultery." Rather, noble lineages were tied together through marriage bonds based on Roman virtues of austerity and piety; virtues that were sorely tested with the vast expansion of Roman conquests and the importation of huge numbers of slaves who could serve as concubines. In these circumstances marriage came to be regarded, as Plautus notes, as "an unavoidable calamity," while love was to be found with slave prostitutes of both sexes who were outside the power struggle that pitted husband against wife.

As in France, the romantic relationship with the courtesan had nothing to do with children: reproduction was reserved for the far more mundane and pragmatic relationship of marriage. Eventually, elite evasion of the constraints of marriage in favor of romantic (but sterile) involvement with prostitutes became so prevalent that the birthrate of the nobility dropped precipitously, obliging Augustus to offer special privileges to men producing children in aristocratic marriages.

Nor is this a configuration found only in complex state societies, though many more examples from such societies could easily be cited. A similar pattern occurs in Northern Pakistan, where the patrilineal Pukhtun organized marriages to cement alliances between clans, while individual men pursued romances clandestinely. Prostitutes and adolescent boys were most often the objects of their romantic desires, and neither of these ever produced children.

Furthermore, if romantic love is assumed to correlate with reproductive success, one would expect that societies most favoring the cultural expression of love would have the highest birth rate. However, the converse is the case. Cultures where marriages are between strangers and are arranged for political and economic benefit by parents have generally had far higher birthrates than the West.

For instance, if we look at English and Germanic society prior to the advances of medical knowledge, we can see the birthrates there have long been low, and population growth slow, largely because of late marriage and a cautious attitude toward having children. This pattern has persisted from at least the early middle ages, and possibly much earlier. It is associated with an Anglo-Saxon cultural milieu in which personal autonomy and maximization of individual benefits outside of the extended family circle prevailed. In this context children have been (quite realistically) viewed as a cost, whose major value is as pets or as monuments to their parents. Thus Britain and Northern Europe generally have never been home to cults of fertility, nor have bachelorhood, spinsterhood, or barrenness ever been sanctioned against.

All this is in obvious contrast to cultures where the extended family is the unit   29
of production and of political power, where more children mean more labor, wealth, and physical strength invested in the extended family, and where fertility is consequently highly valued. Given these circumstances, it is difficult to see how the sociobiological paradigm could explain the fact that the Northern European constellation of low birthrate, late marriage, nuclear families, and individual autonomy *correlates* with the most highly evolved tradition of romantic love in the world!

The premise of a "deep structure" of genetic predisposition for romantic love is   30
further undercut when we consider the relationship between romantic love and sexual desire. It is taken for granted in the eros tradition that romantic love is intertwined with sexuality and is, in fact, a consequence of the erotic impulse. Thus any disavowal of sexual desire in a romantic relationship is assumed, a priori, to be self-delusive. However, this assumption requires us to dismiss ethnographic and historical examples that point in precisely the opposite direction.

For example, consider the Southern European expressions of courtly love in the   31
Medieval period. Here, in a transformation of the cult of the virgin Mary, the courtier explicitly denied any carnal feelings for his beloved, who was worshiped as an angel above the realm of earthly lust, not to be sullied in thought or deed. These courtiers singing of *fin amor* were often married men with active sex lives and children, and the lady herself was always a married woman, with husband and children of her own. However, romantic love was not to be found in these legitimized sexual relations, but only in adulation of the lady. To assume this chaste and idealizing ideology was simply a mask disguising sexual desire is taking for granted what one wishes to prove; rather, we should take at face value the truth of the courtier's song; that is, that the lady was, *for the poet,* beloved as a creature of sanctified innocence and virtue.

Such behavior patterns and idealizations are hardly unusual, though the structure   32
of the relationship may vary considerably. For example, the Marri Baluch, another patrilineal Middle Eastern people much like the Pukhtun, have a highly elaborated romantic love complex. Men and women, married for political and economic purposes, long to participate in secret and highly dangerous illicit love affairs. These passionate relationships are hugely valued in Marri culture and are the subject of innumerable poems and songs.

According to the Marri, when lovers meet they exchange tokens of mutual affec-   33
tion and talk heart to heart, without dissimulation. In marked contrast to the ele-

vation of the lady in courtly love, and in marked contrast as well to the reality of male domination in Marri society, Marri lovers regard one another as equals. For this reason the lovers should be chaste: sexuality, culturally understood as an expression of male power, imposes an element of oppression and subordination that the cultural ideal of mutuality and respect between lovers cannot permit. How many of these relationships are indeed sexless is impossible to say, but chastity is what the Marri believe to be characteristic of the deepest forms of love between men and women; once again, to suppose that this belief is a falsehood is to do them and their culture an injustice by assuming that we know the truth behind their ideals.

The separation between sexual desire and romantic love may be especially common in societies such as the Marri, where sexual intercourse is regarded as an act of violence and domination, or in Melanesia, where sexuality is associated with pollution and spiritual danger. An example of the latter is found in Manus, described by Margaret Mead, where sex is a perilous act, and marriage itself is a distasteful and shameful business. As among the Marri, Manus men and women are drawn into extramarital liaisons, but, Mead writes: "Illicit love affairs, affairs of choice, are, significantly enough, described as situations in which people need not have sex if they do not wish to, but can simply sit and talk and laugh together. . . . The wonderful thing about lovers is that your [sic] don't have to sleep with them." 34

If these examples are too exotic, we need look no further than our own Victorian forbears. The familiar split between whore and virgin was a reality for the Victorians, and sexual desire was, as much as possible, divorced from middle-class marriage, since women of culture were assumed to be without demeaning sexual impulses. Men demanded virginal purity in the women they married, while wives appear, from their own accounts, to have often managed actually to live up to the ideal. Thus sexual contact between a husband and his beloved wife was regarded as an unfortunate necessity of marriage, to be engaged in as a duty; men overcome by sexual passion were expected to spend themselves in the company of prostitutes, whom they certainly did not love. This characteristic Victorian division between love and sexuality is a mode of feeling that must be taken on its own terms. 35

It seems, then, that the correlation between falling in love, sexual desire, and reproduction has to be reconsidered. It appears that the eros tradition in its modern guise renders biological, and therefore primary and irresistible, a peculiarly modern and Western form of relationship that does indeed unite romantic love, sexual intimacy, and reproduction—elements that may certainly have a powerful affinity, but that also may be separated, both in logic and in cultural reality. The postulated biological matrix thus does not have any provable effect. 36

However, there is another standard Western way of looking at love that I wish to put forward here as an alternative to the eros paradigm in all its guises. From this alternative perspective love is not motivated by the desire to reproduce, or lust, or the ideal of beauty; rather, the beloved other is adulated *in himself or herself* as the fountainhead of all that is beautiful, good, and desirable. As Francesco Alberoni puts it, when we fall in love "the possible opens before us and the pure 37 object of eros appears, the unambivalent object, in which duty and pleasure coincide, in which all alienation is extinguished."

However, it is crucial to note that this adulation is offered in spite of the beloved's *actual* characteristics; in other words, falling in love is an act of imagination in which the other is invested with absolute value; the beloved can even be loved for his very faults. Singer calls this idealistic form of love the "bestowal tradition" to stress the lover's creativity in manufacturing the perfection of the beloved.   38

From within this framework any overt or covert calculated appraisal of the other as a good provider, a useful ally, or even as an avenue to God is felt to be a sin against the very nature of romantic love, which is defined and experienced as spontaneous, total, and boundless in its devotion to the actual person of the other. Thus, to love "for a reason" is not to love at all. We love because we love, and not because of any advantage that the beloved other has to offer us.   39

This alternative notion of unqualified love has deep intellectual and spiritual roots in the West: its heritage includes the Jewish concept of *nomos* transformed into Christian notions of God's unconditional, unreserved, and undeserved love for humanity (agape), as expressed in the sacrifice of Jesus. This notion of God's boundless love of humanity made love itself a value in Western culture while simultaneously devaluing sexuality. Love was further humanized in the cult of Mary, and, as we have seen, afterward was secularized in the courtly love that bound the courtier to his lady. As Singer writes, "Henceforth the Christian could hold not only that God is Love but also that Love is God."   40

In this context, and over time, "the idea that love is the unmerited sanctification of the sinner degenerated into the notion that sinners become sanctified through *any* love whatsoever. God disappeared, but there remained the holiness of indiscriminate love binding one worthless person to another." Love became reciprocal and individualized, as it was secularized and institutionalized into the romantic experience that is the expected prelude to marriage in contemporary culture in the West and, increasingly, everywhere in the world.   41

It is this secularized form of romantic love that is rhapsodically portrayed in songs, poems, novels, and films as an ultimate value in itself: compelling, overwhelming, ecstatic, uniquely blissful—indeed, the most powerful emotional event of one's life. This is the love in which, as the young Hegel writes, "consciousness of a separate self disappears, and all distinction between the lovers is annulled"; it is the love apostrophized by the philosopher Roberto Unger as "the most influential mode of moral vision in our culture."   42

Is this experience of falling in love as a way of imagining and experiencing transcendence through a relationship of communion in selfless and fervent merger with an idealized other a peculiarly Western one, as Singer's philosophical approach would seem to indicate? I would say not, but it is also not universal.   43

Rather, falling in love can usefully be conceived as one possible response to the human existential condition of contingency and self-consciousness. As Andre Bataille writes, "We are discontinuous beings, individuals who perish in isolation in   44 the midst of an incomprehensible adventure, but we yearn for our lost continuity." In response to this unbearable but inescapable dilemma, human beings search for ways to escape the burden of loneliness while avoiding confrontation with a cold and indifferent cosmos. One of the ways this escape can be attained is in the experience of falling in love. To quote Bataille once more, "Only the beloved can in this world bring about what our human limitations deny, a total blending of two beings, a continuity between two discontinuous creatures." Thus, instead of resembling a biological drive, falling in love is more akin to religious revelation, but with a particular real person as the focus of devotion.

I was led to this view of romantic love because in the last few years I have been   45
involved in cross-cultural research on charismatic movements and idealization. My studies indicated that charisma, which is experienced as a compulsive and overwhelming attraction of a follower to a leader, is in almost all respects parallel to the experience of romantic love. For example, in both instances there is an intense idealization of one particular other person; in both there is a fervent subjective perception of merger with the beloved—a merger experienced as "exaltation, ecstasy and exaggeration of the ego."

Furthermore, in love, as in charisma, participants feel they are capable of obliter-   46
ating boundaries of convention in their quest for a state of absolute communion. Both states also are characterized by a fear of loss of the idealized other—and suicidal despair if that loss occurs—and both have a strong tendency toward rationalization (charismatic groups become bureaucracies; romantic lovers become companionate couples). In both rationalization can be offset if mystery and danger are maintained by distance and obstacles that separate follower and leader, lover and beloved (the Romeo and Juliet effect).

Charisma and romance also appeared to be mutually exclusive—a person in-   47
volved in a charismatic group generally could not be immersed in a romantic relation, and vice versa. As Kernberg writes, following Freud, "the opposition between the couple and the group is an essential characteristic of human love life"; an insight borne out in ethnographic data. People who leave charismatic organizations often do so because they have fallen in love; conversely, people who become devotees have often been disappointed in love. This fact also indicates that both arise from the same psychological matrix. The main differences are a result of the influence of the group dynamic in the charismatic relation, which renders it less susceptible to rationalization, while making real reciprocity between the leader and the disciples impossible.

Given these parallels, Alberoni can reasonably write that "the experience of   48
falling in love is the simplest form of collective movement," and Miller can argue that there is an "equivalence between leaders and lovers that brings about the same kind of elevation, idealization and incorporation that endows the leader and lover with special status and powers." Falling in love and charisma thus can be plausibly conceptualized as variations on a very deep and basic human existential search— the quest for transcendence.

If we accept the proposition that charisma and love are parallel attempts to escape from contingency and solipsism, this means downplaying some of the elements that have generally been seen as diagnostic of falling in love. For instance, romantic love does not occur only among adolescents, nor does it *necessarily* imply equality between the lovers, or the transformation of love into marriage, or even powerful sexual desire.

49

If this perspective is accepted, then further research should be oriented toward understanding what sorts of social formations and historical conditions favor various characteristic expressions of the human impulse toward self-loss in ecstatic states of union with an idealized other. We should also compare and contrast romantic love and charisma with other apparently similar experiences such as mystical and religious communion, possession trance, reverie, artistic inspiration, and so on. By taking this pathway, we can avoid reducing romantic love to an instrumentality and recognize instead that it stands on its own as a specific state of transcendence—the one most characteristic of the modern world.

50

GETTING THEM INTO THE ELECTRONIC TENT
from *How to Watch TV News*
Neil Postman and Steve Powers

At carnival sideshows, the barkers used to shout intriguing things to attract an audience. "Step right up. For one thin dime, see what men have died for and others lusted after. The Dance of the Veils as only Tanya can do it." The crowd would gather as lovely Tanya, wrapped in diaphanous garb, would wiggle a bit, and entice grown men who should have known better to part with their money for a ticket. Instead of seeing Tanya shed her clothes, her customers shed their money.

1

In television news there is no Tanya we know of but there are plenty of Sonyas, Marias, Ricks, and Brads who have the job of getting you into the electronic tent. They come on the air and try to intrigue you with come-ons to get you to watch their show. "Step right up" becomes "Coming up at eleven o'clock." And, instead of veils, you get a glimpse of some videotape which may intrigue you enough to part with your time instead of a dime. It is no accident that in the television news industry, the short blurb aimed at getting you to watch a program is called a "tease." Sometimes it delivers what it advertises but often hooks us into the electronic tent and keeps us there long enough that we don't remember why we were there in the first place.

2

The tease is designed to be very effective, very quickly. By definition, a tease lasts about ten seconds or less and the information it contains works like a headline. Its purpose is to grab your attention and keep you watching. In the blink of a tease you are enticed to stay tuned with promises of exclusive stories and tape, good-looking anchors, helicopters, team coverage, hidden cameras, uniform blazers, and even, yes, better journalism. It is all designed to stop you from using the

3

remote-control button to switch channels. But the teasing doesn't stop there. During each news program, just before each commercial, you will see what are known as "bumpers"—teases that are aimed at keeping you in the tent, keeping you from straying to another channel where other wonders are being touted. And the electronic temptations do not even cease with the end of the program. When the news show is over, you are still being pleaded with "not to turn that dial" so that you can tune in the next day for an early-morning newscast, which in turn will suggest you watch the next news program and so on. If news programmers had it their way, you would watch a steady diet of news programs, one hooking you into the next with only slight moments of relief during station breaks.

If you think you can beat the system by not watching teases, you'll need to think again. We are dealing here with serious professional hucksters. The game plan, aimed at getting you to watch the news, starts even before you have seen the first tease. It starts while you're watching the entertainment shows *before* the news. Whether you know it or not, we are programmed to watch the news, by programmers. They know that most of us tend to be lazy. Even with remote controls at our fingertips, we are likely to stay tuned to the channel we have been watching. So the United Couch Potatoes of America sit and sit, and sit, and before they know it, Marsha and Rick have hooked us into their news program, promising "team coverage," no less, of today's latest disaster. In the textbook vernacular: the lead-in programs must leave a residual audience for the news shows which follow. To put it plainly, a station with a strong lineup of entertainment programs can attract a large audience to the news tent. High-rated shows such as "Oprah Winfrey," programmed just before the news, bring in a big audience and premium prices at the broadcast marketplace. This is why the best news program may not have ratings as high as a news program with a strong lead-in. It may not be fair but it is television.   4

Now, let us say all things are equal. Station A and station B both have excellent lead-ins. What news program will you watch? Most people will say something like "I want the latest news, the best reporting with state-of-the-art technology presented by people I can trust and respect."   5

But while people might say they like the most experienced journalists presenting the news, many news consultants claim that no matter what they *say*, the audience prefers to watch good-looking, likable people it can relate to (perhaps of the same age group, race, etc.). News organizations spend a lot of time and money building up the reputations of their anchors, sending them to high-visibility stories that they hope will convince viewers that they are watching top-level journalists. Unfortunately, in some markets the top anchors are sometimes "hat racks" who read beautifully but who can barely type a sentence or two without the aid of a producer and writer. They may know how to anchor but many are strictly lightweights. In television, looking the part is better than being the real item, a situation you would rightly reject in other contexts. Imagine going to a doctor who hadn't studied medicine, but rather looks like a doctor—authoritative, kindly, understanding, and surrounded by formidable machinery. We assume you would reject such a professional fraud   6 especially if he or she had majored in theater arts in college. But this kind of play-acting is perfectly acceptable in the world of television news and entertainment where actors who have played lawyers on a TV series frequently are called on to give speeches at lawyers' conventions and men who have played doctors are invited to speak at gatherings of medical professionals. If you can read news convincingly on television, you can have a successful career as an anchor, no journalism experience required. This is not to say there aren't bright men and women who are knowledge-able journalists and who can and do serve as anchors. But the problem is that it is almost impossible for the viewer to figure out which anchor knows his stuff and who's faking it. A good anchor is a good actor and with the lift of an eyebrow or with studied seriousness of visage, he or she can convince you that you are seeing the real thing, that is, a concerned, solid journalist.

You may wonder at this point, what difference does it make? Even if one cannot   7
distinguish an experienced journalist from a good actor playing the part of an expe-rienced journalist, wouldn't the news be the same? Not quite. An experienced jour-nalist is likely to have a sense of what is particularly relevant about a story and insist on including certain facts and a perspective that the actor-anchor would have no knowledge of. Of course, it is true that often an experienced journalist, work-ing behind the cameras, has prepared the script for the actor-anchor. But when the anchor is himself or herself a journalist, the story is likely to be given additional di-mensions, especially if the journalist-anchor does his or her own script writing.

And there is one more point: even if there were no differences between the sto-   8
ries presented by actor-anchors and journalist-anchors, the fact that the audience is being deluded into thinking that an actor-anchor is a journalist contributes a note of fakery to the enterprise. It encourages producers and news directors to think about what they are doing as artifice, as a show in which truth-telling is less impor-tant than the appearance of truth-telling. One can hardly blame them. They know that everything depends on their winning the audience's favor, and the anchor is the key weapon in their arsenal.

If you are skeptical about the importance of the anchor in attracting the audience   9
to the electronic tent, you must ask yourself why they are paid so much. Network anchors earn over a million dollars a year. Over two million dollars a year. Do we hear three? Yes, more than three million dollars a year in the case of Dan Rather at CBS. Is he worth it? From a financial point of view, certainly. He brings people into the tent because they perceive him to be an experienced, solid reporter, who has paid his dues and knows what's going on. And an experienced newsman such as Rather starts to look like a bargain when you think of local anchors being paid as much as 750,000 to a million dollars without serious journalistic credentials. An-chors who work for network-affiliated stations in the top ten markets make an av-erage of $139,447 a year. Nationwide, the average anchor, as of this writing, makes $52,284 a year, according to the National Association of Broadcasters.

So there you are ready to watch the news presented by a high-priced anchor and   10
on comes the show, complete with a fancy opening, and music sounding as though it

was composed for a Hollywood epic. The host appears—an anchor god or goddess sculpted on Mount Arbitron, at least the best of them. But even the worst looks authoritative. Of course, the anchor has had plenty of help from plenty of crafts people in creating the illusion of calm omniscience. After all, it's not all hair spray. That glittering, well-coiffed, Commanding Presence has been placed in a setting that has been designed, built, and painted to make him or her look as wonderful as possible. Consultants have been used to make sure the lights are fine-tuned to highlight the hair and to fill in wrinkles. Color experts have complemented the star's complexion with favorable background hues. Short anchors have their seats raised to look taller, with makeup applied to create just the right look, accenting cheekbones, covering baldness, enlarging small eyes, hiding blemishes, perhaps obscuring a double chin.

And of course there is camera magic. A low camera angle can make a slight anchor look imposing. Long and medium shots, rather than close-ups, can hide bags under the eyes. The anchor-star has probably had the benefit of a clothing allowance and the best hairdressers and consultants. It is cosmetic television at its finest. 11

The music fades and the parade of stories and the people reporting them begins. Whom you see depends sometimes on professional competence and journalistic ability. But it may also depend on the results of "focus groups," where ordinary viewers are shown videotapes and are then asked which anchors and reporters they prefer to watch and why. The group gives its opinion without the benefit of observing a performer over a period of time or knowledge of the reporter's background and experience. What is wanted is an immediate, largely emotional reaction. Performers are also evaluated by a service called "TV Q," which claims to rate television performers on the basis of who the public recognizes. The company, called Marketing Evaluations/TV Q, polls about six thousand Americans by mail, then sells the results to networks, advertising agencies, and anyone else willing to spend about a thousand dollars to find out someone's Q score. 12

Some news show consultants believe in forming a television news pseudo-family to attract audiences. After the "Today" show started to slide in the ratings, NBC brought back sportscaster Joe Garagiola to try to pep up the ratings. Garagiola had been on the program from 1969 to 1973. NBC had alienated its viewers by replacing popular coanchor Jane Pauley with Deborah Norville, who was supposed to be a hot ratings-getter. She wasn't. The show nosedived. Executives realized they needed something or somebody with pizzazz. They reached for a person who, they hoped, could make the "Today" show cast a family again. Warm, affable Joe Garagiola. The return of the Prodigal Son. Exit Norville, now cast as the "other woman." 13

The "family" concept is at work at many local stations. The anchors probably will be a couple, male and female, both good-looking and in the same relative age category as husband-wife (although in our modern society with second marriages common, the male anchor may be twenty years older than his female counterpart). The other "family" members may be like Archie and Veronica to appeal to the younger set: Archie the sportscaster, who never tires of watching videotapes of highlights and bloopers, and Veronica the weather person. There is also Mr. or Ms. Breathless 14

Showbiz who always feigns being thrilled to see the heartthrob or hottest rock group of the moment.

Whatever kind of television family is presented, it always has one thing in com-   15
mon. It is a happy family, where everybody gets along with everyone else (at least for thirty minutes) and knows his or her place. The viewer usually gets to see the whole "family" at the "top," or beginning, of the show. They will either be featured in a taped introduction or be sitting on the set, en masse, to create a sense of co-hesion and stability. Throughout the program, members of the family will come on the set and do their turn, depending on their specialty. No newscast is complete without Archie the Sportscaster rattling off a list of clichés that he believes bond him to his fans. "Yes!" "In your face!" "Let's go to the videotape!" "Swish!"

Theoretically, sportscasters are supposed to be reporters, not fans. But depend-   16
ing on what they believe to be the roots of their popularity they might decide to bask in the glorious light of sports heroes and become cheerleaders. It is, in any event, the sportscaster's job to keep the audience excited, complete with taped highlights and interviews with the top players who often have nothing more to con-tribute than standard-brand sports-hero remarks: "It's not important how I played, as long as I can contribute to the team" or "I might have scored a few more touch-downs, but the real credit has to go to the front line who made it all possible." Pic-ture and cliché blend to fill the eye with a sense of action and the nose with the macho smell of the locker room.

No newscast would be complete without a weather report that usually starts   17
with a review of what already happened that day. The report is supposedly made interesting by moving H's and L's and by making clouds and isobars stalk across a map. Whatever the weather, the one thing you can always count on is a commer-cial break *before* tomorrow's weather forecast. You can also count on the peculiar tendency of anchors to endow the weather person with God-like meteorological power as in, "Well, Veronica, I hope you'll bring us some relief from this rain." To which the reply is something like "Oh, Chuck, I'm afraid we've got some more rain coming tomorrow, but wait till you see what I've got for you this weekend."

If you have ever wondered why all this fuss is made about the weather, the an-   18
swer is that, for reasons no one knows, weather information is of almost universal interest. This means that it usually attracts an attentive audience, which in turn means it provides a good environment for commercials. The executive producer of the "CBS This Morning" show, Eric Sorensen, has remarked that research shows weather news is the most important reason why people watch TV in the morning. The weather segments also give the anchors a chance to banter with the weather people and lighten the proceedings. A pleasing personality is almost certainly more important to a weathercaster than a degree in meteorology. How significant per-sonality is can be gauged by what these people earn. Weather people in small mar-kets earn an average of $21,980 a year, according to the National Association of Broadcasters. Weathercasters make an average of $86,589 in the top ten markets, with some earning half a million dollars or more. Nonetheless, it should not sur-

prise you to know that these people rarely prepare weather forecasts. There are staff meteorologists for that. The on-air weather person is expected to draw audiences, not weather maps.

Feature reporters usually ply their craft near the "back of the book," close by the weather. They keep the mood light, and try to leave the viewer with a smile. The subject matter of some feature vignettes is called "evergreen" because it is not supposed to wilt with the passage of time. It can be stored until needed. (Two of the best practitioners of "evergreen art" are Charles Kuralt and Andy Rooney.) Locally, you usually see "evergreen" reports on slow news days, when the editor has trouble filling the news budget (the newsworthy events of the day). But as entertaining news becomes more of a commodity, feature reports are being used more and more to attract and hold audiences through the news program. 19

No news "family" would be complete without a science reporter, a Doctor Wizard, who usually wears glasses, may have an advanced degree, and is certainly gray around the temples. These experts bring to the audience the latest in everything from cancer research to the designer disease of the year. 20

Once the family has gathered, everyone in place, each with a specific role, the show is ready to begin. The anchor reads the lead story. If you are expecting to hear the most important news to you, on any given day, you will often be disappointed. Never forget that the producer of the program is trying to grab you before you zap away to another news show. Therefore, chances are you will hear a story such as Zsa Zsa's run-in with the law, Rob Lowe's home videos, Royal Family happenings, or news of a Michael Jackson tour. Those stories have glitter and glamour in today's journalism. And if glitter and glamour won't do the job, gore will. Body bags have become an important currency of TV news and a four-bagger is a grand slam. 21

If viewers have stayed through the lead story, they probably will be hooked for a while because the newscast is designed to keep their attention through the commercial breaks into the next "section," when the process starts again. Taped stories from reporters are peppered throughout the show to keep interest from flagging as anchors keep the show on track "eyeballing," or reading, stories on camera. When the news stories thin out, there are sports, features, and weather to fill up the time. 22

All this is presented with slick lighting and production values, moving along at a crisp pace. The tempo is usually fast since some programmers believe that fast-paced news programs attract younger audiences. Older audiences, they believe, are attracted to a slower-paced, quieter presentation. No matter how fast or slow the pace of the show, there is not much time to present anything but truncated information. After we have subtracted commercial time, about twenty-two minutes of editorial time are available in a half-hour broadcast. If we subtract, further, the time used for introductions, closings, sports, and the weather, we are left with about fifteen minutes. If there are five taped stories of two minutes each, that leaves five or six minutes to cover the rest of the world's events. And if more time is 23 subtracted for "happy talk," chalk up another minute or so just for "schmoozing" on the set.

Given the limited time and objectives of a television newscast, a viewer has to realize that he or she is not getting a full meal but rather a snack. And depending on the organization presenting the news, the meal may contain plenty of empty calories.

24

▪ 4 ▪

The Multiple-Source Essay

Until now, most of your writing assignments have been based on information derived from a *single* source. You have learned to paraphrase, summarize, rearrange, and unify your evidence without sacrificing accuracy or completeness.

Now, as you begin to work with *many* different sources, you will need to understand and organize a wider range of materials. You will want to present the ideas of your sources in all their variety while at the same time maintaining your own perspective, encompassing all the shades of opinion.

- How can you describe each author's ideas without taking up too much space for each one?
- How can you fit all your sources smoothly into your essay without allowing one to dominate?
- How can you transform a group of disparate sources into an essay that is yours?

Some of the informal sources that you will work with in this chapter have their equivalents in professional writing. Lawyers, doctors, engineers, social workers, and other professionals often work from notes taken at interviews to prepare case notes, case studies, legal testimony, reports, and market research.

SELECTING INFORMATION FOR A MULTIPLE-SOURCE ESSAY

In academic writing, you do not usually find the materials for an essay in a neatly assembled package. On the contrary, before beginning an essay, you must find and select your materials. The first stage of a research project is traditionally working in the library or on the computer with a topic to explore and questions to ask, a search for information that will later be interpreted, sifted, and synthesized into a finished essay.

To demonstrate this process, assume that you have been assigned the following project, which calls for a *narrow range of research:*

> Read an entire newspaper or news magazine published on a day of your choice during this century (such as your birthday), and write a summary describing what life was like on that day. Your sources are the articles and advertisements in that day's paper.

Given the amount and variety of information contained in the average newspaper, you must first narrow the topic by deciding what and how much to include. You would look for two kinds of evidence—major events that might have altered the fabric of most people's lives, and more ordinary happenings that might suggest how people typically spent their days. While these events may have taken place before your birth, your not having been there may give you the advantage of perspective: as an outsider, you can more easily distinguish between stories of lasting historic importance and those that simply reflect their era.

To begin this project, follow these steps:

1. Read rapidly through the entire newspaper. Then read the same issue again more slowly, jotting down your impressions of important *kinds* of events or *characteristics* of daily life. Search for a pattern, a thesis that sums up what you have read.

2. Review your notes, and isolate a few main ideas that seem worth developing. Then read the issue a third time, making sure that there really is sufficient evidence for the points that you wish to make. Note any additional information that you expect to use, and write down the page number next to each reference in your notes. Remember that you are not trying to "use up" all the available information.

3. Plan a series of paragraphs, each focusing on a somewhat different theme that is either significant in itself or typical of the day that you are describing. Spend some time choosing a strategy for a sequence of paragraphs that will not only introduce your reader to the world that you are describing, but also make apparent the pattern of events—the thesis—that seems to characterize that day.

Drawing Conclusions from Your Information

Through your essay, you should help your readers to form conclusions about the significance of the information it contains. *The evidence should not be expected to speak for itself.* Consider the following paragraph:

Some popular books in the first week of 1945 were Brave Men by Ernie Pyle, Forever Amber by Kathleen Winsor, and The Time for Decision by Sumner Welles. The average price of these new, hardcover books was about three dollars each. The price of the daily Times was three cents, and Life magazine was ten cents.

What is probably most interesting to your reader is how little the reading material cost. This evidence would be very informative in a paragraph devoted to the cost of living or the accessibility of information through the media. Here, however, the emphasis is on the books. Can you tell why they were popular? Do they seem typical of 1945's bestseller list? If you don't have sufficient knowledge to answer questions like these, you will do better to focus on some other aspect of daily life that the paper describes in greater detail. *Unexplained information is of no value to your reader,* who cannot be assumed to know more than—or even as much as—you do.

In contrast, another student, writing about a day shortly after the end of World War II, built a paragraph around a casualty list in the *New York Times.* What seemed significant about the list was the fact that, by the end of the war, casualties had become so routine that they assumed a relatively minor place in daily life. Notice that the paragraph begins with a topic sentence that establishes the context and draws its conclusion at the end.

For much of the civilian population, the worst part of the war had been the separation from their loved ones, who had gone off to fight in Europe, Africa, and the Pacific. Even after the end of the war, they still had to wait for the safe arrival home of the troops. In order to inform the public, the New York Times ran a daily list of troop arrivals. However, not everyone was destined to return, and the Times also ran a list of casualties. On September 4, that list appeared at the very bottom of page 2, a place where it would be easily overlooked except by those interested in finding a particular name.

Another paragraph about May 6, 1946, informs the reader that the postwar mid-forties were a transitional period.

The process of switching over from a wartime to a peacetime economy was not without its pains. Then, as now, there was a high rate of unemployment. The Times featured a story about the million women production workers who had recently lost their jobs in war industries. Returning male and female veterans were also flooding the job market. Some working wives were waiting to see how their husbands readjusted to postwar jobs. If their ex-GI husbands could bring home enough money to support the family, they could return to their roles as housewives. If their husbands chose to continue their education or vocational training under the GI Bill, they would expect to stay on the job as long as they could.

This paragraph appears to be a straightforward account of the transition from a wartime economy, as expressed in the topic sentence; but the writer is, in fact, summarizing information taken from *several* articles in that day's newspaper. (Notice that, while the source of the information—the *Times*—is cited, the names of the reporters are not considered significant in this very general summary.) The suggestion of a personal comment—unemployment, one gathers, is a recurring problem—adds immediacy and significance to a topic that might otherwise be remote to today's readers.

Finally, it is not always necessary to present your conclusion in a topic sentence at the *beginning* of your paragraph. Here is one in which the evidence is presented first:

> The July 30, 1945, issue of Newsweek lists three bills that were going before Congress. The first, the Burton-Ball-Hatch Bill, proposed that all industries institute a labor management mediation system. The second, the Kilgore Bill, proposed providing $25 a week in unemployment for a period of 26 weeks. And the third, the Mead Bill, proposed raising the minimum wage from 40 cents to 65 cents. It is obvious from these three bills that a great deal of attention was being focused on employment, or the lack of it. Here we have another clue about the lifestyle of 1945. The majority of the working class must have been greatly dissatisfied with economic conditions for their congressmen to have proposed these improvements. These bills were also in keeping with the late President Roosevelt's New Deal policy, which was primarily directed toward the improvement of economic conditions. From these bills, it is safe to assume that the cost of living may have been rising, that unemployment was still something of a problem, and that strikes by workers were becoming so prevalent that a mediation system seemed necessary.

This paragraph explicitly links together three related points, suggests their possible significance, and provides a historical context (the New Deal) in which to understand them.

EXERCISE 13: SELECTING AND PRESENTING INFORMATION

Read the following student essay, a description of life taken from the *New York Times* of September 21, 1967. Analyze each paragraph and be prepared to discuss the following questions:

1. What are the writer's reasons for building a paragraph around that piece of information? (Use your own knowledge of the contents of the average newspaper today to estimate the range of choices that the writer might have had.)

2. How clear is the presentation of the information?
3. Do the topic sentences interpret the information and suggest its significance for the reader?
4. How is the essay organized: the relationship between paragraphs; the sequence of paragraphs; the unity within each paragraph; the transitions between paragraphs?
5. What is the thesis and how well does the author characterize September 21, 1967, as typical of its era and as a contrast to her own era?

According to the New York Times, on September 21, 1967, there was considerable violence and unrest in the United States, much of it in response to the United States' involvement in the Vietnam War. The United States had increased its bombing of Vietnam in an attempt to cut off the port of Haiphong from contact with the rest of the world. As a result, a group opposed to President Johnson's Vietnam policy began an "anti-Johnson" campaign. They were a coalition of Democrats who hoped to block his reelection. Meanwhile, seventy female antiwar demonstrators were arrested outside the White House. Later, to protest their arrest, 500 members of Women Strike for Peace marched to the White House and clashed with police.

There was not only civil unrest on this day, but also a conflict between President Johnson and the House Ways and Means Committee over the president's proposed tax increase. The committee would not approve the increase without a 5 billion dollar cut in spending. The Senate proposed the following cuts: a 2 billion dollar decrease in defense spending; a 1 billion dollar decrease in "long-range research"; and a 2 billion dollar decrease in other civilian services. However, aid to the poor and to cities was not to be cut. In defense of the president's request, Secretary of Commerce Trowbridge said that a tax increase would be necessary because of inflation.

Throughout the rest of the country, there was much racial tension and violence. There had been days of fighting in Dayton, Ohio's West Side, which had a large black population. A rally took place there to protest the killing of a black Social Security Administration field-worker. There was also a supermarket fire in Dayton, which resulted in $20,000 of damage. In the end, twenty teenagers were arrested. In the Casa Central Outpost, a Puerto Rican neighborhood in Chicago, Governor Romney of Michigan, a would-be presidential candidate, was given a hostile welcome. His visit to the Outpost was blocked by its director, Luis Cuza, who handed him a two-page press release claiming that the Governor was only touring these poor neighborhoods for political gain. Governor Romney expressed outrage at the accusation and the fact that the Outpost had not informed him earlier that he would not be welcome. In the meantime, the streets of Hartford, Connecticut's North End were quiet after three days of racial violence. Civil rights demonstrators were marching against housing discrimination in the South End, a predominantly middle-class Italian neighborhood. There were 66 arrests, mainly of young blacks. To control the violence, five to ten policemen were posted at every intersection, and the mayor asked for a voluntary curfew.

On the local level, a protest against traffic conditions took place in the Bronx, at 149th Street and Courtlandt Avenue. The protesters, four clergymen and dozens of neighbors, wanted Courtlandt Avenue to be one way. Two men refused to leave after police tried to disperse the crowd.

4

There was not only racial unrest in the country on this day, but also many labor disputes and strikes. Seventeen thousand Prudential Insurance Company of America agents threatened to strike if no contract was agreed on in four days. They could not accept any of the proposals previously given to them. Also, the steelhaulers' strike in Chicago was spreading east, and had already resulted in a violent confrontation in Pittsburgh. Finally, on strike were the 59,500 New York public school teachers, whose refusal to enter the classrooms had kept more than a million students out of school for eight days. The teachers' slogan was "no contract, no work."

5

Even the weather was in turmoil. Hurricane Beulah, in Texas, had winds estimated at 80 miles per hour at the center of the storm and 120–150 miles per hour at its peak. Eighty-five percent of Port Isabel, a town at the southern tip of Texas, was destroyed, and four people were killed by the record number of twenty-seven tornadoes spawned by Beulah. All the Gulf states experienced heavy rain in Beulah's aftermath. Meanwhile, rain and thunderstorms also battered the east coast.

6

ASSIGNMENT 6: WRITING AN ESSAY FROM FACTUAL INFORMATION

Choose *one* of the following:

1. At the library, examine the issue of the *New York Times* that was published on the day that your mother or father was born. Most libraries keep complete microfilms of the *New York Times*. Ask your librarian how to locate and use these microfilms. (Alternatively, locate an issue of a news magazine that covers that week.) Select the articles that seem most interesting and typical of the period, and use them as evidence for an account of what it was like to live on that day. *This essay should not merely be a collection of facts; you should suggest the overall significance of the information that you include.* Remember

that your reader was almost certainly not born on that date, and that your job is to arouse that reader's interest. If you like, draw some parallels with the present time, but don't strain the comparison. The essay should not run much more than 1,000 words: select carefully and refer briefly to the evidence.

2. Use a newspaper or magazine published this week and try to construct a partial portrait of what it is like to live in America (or in your city or town) right now. Don't rely entirely on news stories, but, instead, draw your evidence as much as possible from advertisements and features (like TV listings, classifieds, announcements of all sorts). Try, if you can, to disregard personal knowledge; pretend you are a Martian if that will enable you to become detached from your familiar environment. Don't offer conclusions that the evidence does not substantiate, and don't try to say *everything* that could possibly be said. The essay should not run much more than 1,000 words: select carefully and refer briefly to the evidence.

GENERALIZING FROM EXAMPLES

Summarizing the contents of a newspaper can be difficult because newspaper stories often have little in common except that they all happened on the same day. By contrast, in academic writing *a common theme often links apparently dissimilar ideas or facts.* The writer has to find that common theme and make it clear to the reader through generalizations that cover several items in the sources.

Assume that you have been asked to consider and react to *seven different but related situations*, and then formulate *two generalizations.*

A. In a sentence or two, write down your probable reaction if you found yourself in each of the following situations.* Write quickly; this exercise calls for immediate, instinctive responses.

1. You are walking behind someone. You see him take out a cigarette pack, pull out the last cigarette, put the cigarette in his mouth, crumple the package, and nonchalantly toss it over his shoulder onto the sidewalk. What would you do?

2. You are sitting on a train and you notice a person (same age, sex, and type as yourself) lighting up a cigarette, despite the no smoking sign. No one in authority is around. What would you do?

3. You are pushing a shopping cart in a supermarket and you hear the thunderous crash of cans. As you round the corner, you see a two-year-old child being beaten, quite severely, by his mother, apparently for pulling out the bottom can of the pile. What would you do?

4. You see a teenager that you recognize shoplifting at the local discount store. You're concerned that she'll get into serious trouble if the store detective catches her. What would you do?

*Adapted from "Strategy 24" in Sidney B. Simon et al., *Values Clarification* (New York: Hart, 1972).

5. You're driving on a two-lane road behind another car. You notice that one of its wheels is wobbling more and more. It looks as if the lugs are coming off one by one. There's no way to pass, because cars are coming from the other direction in a steady stream. What would you do?

6. You've been waiting in line (at a supermarket or gas station) for longer than you expected and you're irritated at the delay. Suddenly, you notice that someone very much like yourself has sneaked in ahead of you in the line. There are a couple of people before you. What would you do?

7. You've raised your son not to play with guns. Your rich uncle comes for a long-awaited visit and he brings your son a .22 rifle with lots of ammunition. What would you do?

B. Read over your responses to the seven situations and try to form two general statements (in one or two sentences each), one about *the circumstances in which you would take action* and a second about *the circumstances in which you would choose to do nothing*. Do *not* simply list the incidents, one after the other, divided in two groups.

You form your generalizations by examining the group of situations in which you *do* choose to take action and determining *what they have in common*. (It is also important to examine the "leftovers," and to understand why these incidents did *not* warrant your interference.) As a first step, you might try looking at each situation in terms of either its *causes* or its *consequences*. For example, in each case there is someone to blame, someone who is responsible for creating the problem—except for number five, where fate (or poor auto maintenance) threatens to cause an accident.

As for consequences, in some of the situations (littering, for example), there is *little potential danger*, either to you or to the public. Do these circumstances discourage action? In others, however, the possible victim is oneself or a member of one's family. Does self-interest alone drive one to act? Do adults tend to intervene in defense of children—even someone else's child—since they cannot stand up for themselves? Or, instead of calculating the consequences of *not* intervening, perhaps you should imagine *the possible consequences of interference*. In which situations can you expect to receive abuse for failing to mind your own business? Would this prevent you from intervening? As always, *only by examining the evidence can you discover the basis for a generalization*.

The list of examples has two characteristics worth noting:

1. Each item is intended to illustrate a specific and very different situation. Thus, although it does not include every possible example, the list as a whole constitutes a *set* of public occasions for interfering with a stranger's conduct.

2. Since you probably would not choose to act in every situation, you cannot use the entire list as the basis for your generalization. Rather, you must *establish a boundary line*, dividing those occasions when you would intervene from those times when you would decide not to act. The ex-

act boundary between intervention and nonintervention will probably differ from person to person, as will the exact composition of the list of occasions justifying intervention. Thus, there is no one correct generalization.

This exercise results in a set of guidelines for justifiably minding other people's business. *You formulate the guidelines by applying your own standards to a sampling of possible examples.*

Broad concepts offer a great deal of room for disagreement and ambiguity and therefore allow a great many interpretations. You can clarify your ideas and opinions about any important abstract issue by inventing a set of illustrations, marking off a subgroup, and then constructing a generalization that describes what is *inside* the boundary: the common characteristics of the contents of the subgroup. Thus, in the previous problem, one person might consider the set of seven examples and then decide to intervene only in Situations 3 (the child beaten in a supermarket), 5 (the wobbly wheel), and 7 (the gift of a gun). What makes these three cases different from the others? They and they alone involve protecting some person from physical harm.

This process of *differentiation*, followed by *generalized description,* is usually called "definition"; it can serve as an essay strategy in its own right or form the basis for a comparison, classification, argumentation, or evaluation essay.

ANALYZING MULTIPLE SOURCES

When you write from sources, your object is not to establish a single "right" conclusion but rather to present a thesis statement of your own that is based on your examination of a variety of views. Some of these views may conflict with your own and with each other. Because of this diversity, organizing multiple sources is more difficult than working with a series of examples, with the contents of a newspaper, or with even a highly complex single essay.

The writing process for multiple sources begins with the *analysis of ideas.*

Analysis is first breaking down a mass of information into individual pieces and then examining the pieces.

As you underline and annotate your sources, you look for similarities and distinctions in meaning, as well as the basic principles underlying what you read. Only when you have taken apart the evidence of each source to see how it works can you begin to find ways of putting everything back together again in your own essay.

To illustrate the analysis of sources, assume that you have asked five people what the word *foreign* means. You want to provide a reasonably complete definition of the word by exploring all the shades of meaning (or connotations) that the five sources suggest. If each one of the five gives you a completely different answer, then you will not have much choice in the organization of your definition. In that case, you would probably present each separate definition of *foreign* in a separate paragraph, citing a different person as the source for each one. But *responses from multiple sources almost always overlap,* as these do. Notice the common meanings in this condensed list of the five sources' responses:

John Brown: "Foreign" means unfamiliar and exotic.

Lynne Williams: "Foreign" means strange and unusual.

Bill White: "Foreign" means strange and alien (as in "foreign body").

Mary Green: "Foreign" means exciting and exotic.

Bob Friedman: "Foreign" means difficult and incomprehensible (as in "foreign language").

Planning your essay depends on finding common meanings, not writing down the names of the five sources. That is why the one-source-per-paragraph method should hardly ever be used (except on those rare occasions when all the sources completely disagree).

When you organize ideas taken from multiple sources, you should reject the idea of devoting one paragraph to each page of your notes, simply because all the ideas on that page happen to have come from the same source.

If you did so, each paragraph would have a topic sentence that might read, "Then I asked John Brown for his definition," as if John Brown were the topic for discussion, instead of his views on "foreign." And if John Brown and Mary Green each get a separate paragraph, there will be some repetition because both think that one of the meanings of "foreign" is "exotic." "Exotic" should be the topic of one of your paragraphs, not the person (or people) who suggested that meaning.

Analyzing Shades of Meaning

Here is a set of notes, summarizing the ideas of four different people about the meaning of the word *individualist.* How would you analyze these notes?

Richard Becker: an "individualist" is a person who is unique and does not "fall into the common mode of doing things"; would not follow a pattern set by society. "A youngster who is not involved in the drug scene just because his friends are." A good word; it would be insulting only if it referred to a troublemaker.

Simon Jackson: doing things on your own, by yourself. "She's such an individualist that she insisted on answering the question in her own way." Sometimes the word is good, but mostly it has a bad connotation: someone who rebels against society or authority.

Lois Asher: one who doesn't "follow the flock." The word refers to someone who is very independent. "I respect Jane because she is an individualist and her own person." Usually very complimentary.

Vera Lewis: an extremely independent person. "An individualist is a person who does not want to contribute to society." Bad meaning: usually antisocial. She first heard the word in psych class, describing the characteristics of the individualist and "how he reacts to society."

At first glance, all the sources seem to say much the same thing: the individualist is different and "independent." However, it is worthwhile to examine the context in which the four sources are defining this word. First, *all the responses define the individualist in terms of other people,* either the "group," or the "flock," or "society." Oddly enough, it is not easy to describe the individualist as an individual, even though it is that person's isolation that each source is emphasizing. Whatever is "unique" about the individualist—what is described as "independent"—is defined by *the gap between that person and everyone else.* (Notice that both "unique" and "independent" are words that also suggest a larger group in the background; after all, one has to be independent *of* something!)

Having found a meaning that is common to all four sources ("independence") and, just as important, having established the context for a definition ("from the group"), you must now look for differences. Obviously, Lois Asher thinks that to be an individualist is a good thing; Vera Lewis believes that individualism is bad; and the other two suggest that both connotations are possible. But simply describing the reactions of the four sources stops short of defining the word according to those reactions.

Richard Becker and Lois Asher, two people who suggest a favorable meaning, describe the group from which the individual is set apart in similar and somewhat disapproving terms: "common"; "pattern set by society"; "follow the flock." Becker and Asher both seem to suggest *a degree of conformity or sameness which the individualist is right to reject,* as Becker's youngster rejects his friends' drugs. But Vera Lewis, who thinks that the word's connotation is bad, sees the individualist in a more benign society, with which the individual ought to identify himself and to which he ought to contribute. To be antisocial is to be an undesirable person—from the point of view of Lewis and society. Simon Jackson (who is ambivalent about the word) uses the phrases "by yourself" and "on your own," which suggest the isolation and the lack of support, as well as the admirable independence, of the individualist. In Jackson's view, the individualist's self-assertion becomes threatening to all of us in society ("antisocial") only when the person begins to rebel against authority. Probably for Jackson, and certainly for Vera Lewis, the ultimate authority should rest with society as a whole, not with the individualist. Even Richard Becker, who admires independence, draws the line at allowing the individualist complete autonomy: when reliance on one's own authority leads to "troublemaking," the term becomes an insult.

EXERCISE 14: ANALYZING SHADES OF MEANING IN MULTIPLE SOURCES

Analyze the following set of notes for a definition of the word *clever*. Then explore some ways to organize these notes by following these steps:

A. Find the important terms or concepts that can lead to a context for defining *clever*.

B. Write two generalizations that might serve as topic sentences for a two-paragraph essay. (Do not use "favorable" and "unfavorable" as your two topics.)

Harry Barton: smart, successful, able to get what you want. A "clever" person sees how to get around obstacles. It's an inborn asset, like being handsome. "If you can't be rich, be clever."

Fred Durkin: smart to the point of being slick; likely to pull a fast one; not always reliable; looking for new ways of doing things; can get you into trouble. "She's too clever by half" or "He's a clever devil."

Anna Mercurio: a problem-solving skill; mostly used for intellectual and professional work; attracts admiration and possibly envy, but not affection. "She's always been clever at taking tests; that's why she did so well at school."

Paul Perkins: different from "intelligent"; not the same as "smart"; implies a certain speed in calculating, in sizing up a situation and thinking of a good response; not worth much unless you can use it in a situation. "He figured out a clever way to impress the client and clinch the contract."

Amy Samuels: good at finding solutions, but likely to cut corners and defeat his own purpose; calculates the odds very quickly; tends to make people around him look slow and stupid. "He may be clever at what he does, but he's not a team player."

ASSIGNMENT 7: WRITING A DEFINITION ESSAY FROM MULTIPLE SOURCES

All the words in the following list are in common use and have either more than one usual meaning or a meaning that can be interpreted both favorably and unfavorably. Choose one word from the list as the topic for a definition essay. (Or, if your teacher asks you to do so, select a word from the dictionary or the thesaurus.)

shrewd	justice	self-interest
curiosity	ordinary	respectable
capitalism	power	conservative
bias	flamboyant	polite

progress	eccentric	obedience
habit	politician	ambition
credit	genius	duty
ladylike	failure	poverty
royalty	competition	sophisticated
masculine	peace	humility
cautious	welfare	solitude
bias	immature	spiritual
dominance	culture	sentimental
revolution	aggression	glamorous
passive	failure	self-confidence
influential	feminine	passionate
criticism	imagination	impetuous
jealousy	romantic	successful
small	workman	smooth
cheap	privilege	intrigue
fashion	enthusiast	smart
pompous	mercenary	criticize
obligation	shame	freedom
control	idealistic	artificial
ambition	ethical	perfection

1. Clarify your own definition of the word by writing down your ideas about its meaning.

2. Interview five or six people, or as many as you need, to get a variety of re-actions. Your purpose is to become aware of several ways of using your word. Take careful and complete notes of each reaction that you receive.

3. Each person should be asked the following questions:

   ■ What do you think *X* means? Has it any other meanings that you know of?

   ■ How would you use this word in a sentence? (Pay special attention to the way in which the word is used, and note down the differences. Two people might say that a word means the same thing and yet use it differently.)

   ■ Is this a positive word or a negative word? In what situation could it possibly have a favorable or unfavorable connotation?

   In listening to the answers to these questions, do not hesitate to ask, "What do you mean?" It may be necessary to make people think hard about a word that they use casually.

4. As you note reactions, consider how the meaning of the word changes and try to identify the different circumstances and usages that cause these vari-ations. Be alert, for example, for a difference between the *ideal* meaning of the word and its *practical* application in daily life.

5. If one person's reaction is merely an echo of something that you already have in your notes, you may summarize the second response more briefly, but keep an accurate record of who (and how many) said what.

6. Although your notes for each source may run only a few sentences, plan to use a separate sheet for each person.

7. Your notes should include not only a summary of each reaction, but also, if possible, a few quotations. If someone suggests a good definition or uses the word in an interesting way, try to record the exact words; read the quotation back to the speaker to make sure that what you have quoted is accurate; put quotation marks around the direct quotation.

8. Make sure that the names of all your sources are accurately spelled.

9. Analyze your notes and make an outline of possible meanings and contexts.

10. Write a series of paragraphs, first explaining *the most common meaning attributed to the word,* according to your sources. Be sure to cite different examples of this common usage. Then, in successive paragraphs, review the other connotations, favorable and unfavorable, always trying to trace the relationships and common contexts among the different meanings. With your overview of all the variations of meaning, you are in an excellent position to observe and explain what the worst and the best connotations of the word have in common.

There is no set length for this essay. Contents and organization are governed entirely by the kind and extent of the material in your notes. *Your notes should be handed in with your completed essay.*

SYNTHESIZING MULTIPLE SOURCES

Once you have analyzed each of your sources and discovered their similarities and differences, you then reassemble these parts into a more coherent whole. This process is called *synthesis.* Although at first you may regard analysis and synthesis as contradictory operations, *they are actually overlapping stages of a single, larger process.*

To illustrate the way in which analysis and synthesis work together, let us examine a set of answers to the question: "Would you buy a lottery ticket? Why?" First, read through these summaries of all seven responses.

Mary Smith: She thinks that lottery tickets were made for people to enjoy and win. It's fun to try your luck. She looks forward to buying her ticket, because she feels that, for one dollar, you have a chance to win a lot more. It's also fun scratching off the numbers to see what you've won. Some people don't buy tickets because they think the lottery is a big rip-off; but "a dollar can't buy that much today, so why not spend it and have a good time?"

John Jones: He would buy a lottery ticket for three reasons. The first reason is that he would love to win. The odds are like a challenge, and he likes to take a chance. The second reason is just for fun. When he has two matching tickets, he really feels happy, especially when he thinks that dollars can be multiplied into hundreds or thousands. "It's like Russian roulette." The third reason is that part of the money from the lottery goes toward his education. The only problem, he says, is that they are always sold out!

Michael Green: He has never bought a lottery ticket in his life because he doesn't want to lose money. He wants to be sure of winning. Also, he says that he isn't patient enough. The buyer of a lottery ticket has to be very patient to wait for his chance to win. He thinks that people who buy tickets all the time must enjoy "living dangerously."

Anne White: Buying a lottery ticket gives her a sense of excitement. She regards herself as a gambler. "When you win two dollars or five dollars you get a thrill of victory, and when you see that you haven't, you feel the agony of defeat." She thinks that people who don't buy tickets must be very cautious and noncompetitive, since the lottery brings "a sense of competition with you against millions of other people." She also knows that the money she spends on tickets goes toward education.

Margaret Brown: She feels that people who buy tickets are wasting their money. The dollars spent on the lottery could be in the bank, getting interest. Those people who buy tickets should expect to have thrown out their money, and should take their losses philosophically, instead of jumping up and down and screaming about their disappointment. Finally, even if she could afford the risk, the laws of her religion forbid her to participate in "any sort of game that is a form of gambling."

William Black: He would buy a lottery ticket, because he thinks it can be fun, but he wouldn't buy too many, because he thinks it's easy for people to get carried away and obsessed by the lottery. He enjoys the anticipation of wanting to win and maybe winning. "I think that you should participate, but in proportion to your budget; after all, one day you might just be a winner."

Elizabeth Watson: She wouldn't buy a lottery ticket because she considers them a rip-off. The odds are too much against you, 240,000 to 1. Also, it is much too expensive, "and I don't have the money to be throwing away on such foolishness." She thinks that people who indulge themselves with lottery tickets become gamblers, and she's against all kinds of gambling. Such people have no sense or self-control. Finally, "I'm a sore loser, so buying lottery tickets just isn't for me."

Making a Chart of Common Ideas

Since you are working with seven sources with varying opinions, you need a way to record the process of analysis. One effective way is to make a *chart of commonly held views*. To do so, follow these two steps, which should be carried out *simultaneously:*

1. Read each statement carefully, and identify each separate reason that is being cited for and against playing the lottery by writing a number above

or next to the relevant comment. When a similar comment is made by another person, use *the same number* to provide a key to the final list of common reasons. In this step, you are analyzing your sources. Here is what the first two sets of notes might look like once the topic numbers have been inserted:

Mary Smith: She thinks that lottery tickets were made for people to enjoy and win. ① ② It's fun to try your luck. She looks forward to buying her ticket, because she feels that, for one dollar, you have a chance to win a lot more. ② It's also fun ① scratching off the numbers to see what you've won. Some people don't buy tickets because they think the lottery is a big rip-off; ③ but "a dollar can't buy that much today, so why not spend it and have ① a good time?"

John Jones: He would buy a lottery ticket for three reasons. The first reason is that he would love to win. The odds are like a challenge, and he likes ② to take a chance. The second reason is just for ① fun. When he has two matching tickets, he really feels happy, especially when he thinks that dollars can be multiplied into hundreds or thousands. ② "It's like Russian roulette." The third reason is that part of the money from the lottery goes ④ toward his education. The only problem, he says, is that they are always sold out!

2. At the same time as you number each of your reasons, also write a list or chart of reasons on a separate sheet of paper. Each reason should be assigned *the same number* you wrote next to it in the original statement. Don't make a new entry when the same reason is repeated by a second source. Next to each entry on your chart, put the names of the people who have mentioned that reason. You are now beginning to synthesize your sources.

Here's what your completed list of reasons might look like:

Reason	Sources
1. People play the lottery because it's fun.	Smith; Jones
2. People play the lottery because they like the excitement of taking a chance and winning.	Smith; Jones; Green; White; Black
3. People don't play the lottery because they think it's a rip-off.	Smith; Watson

4. People play the lottery because they are contributing to education. — Jones; White

5. People don't play the lottery because they have better things to do with their money. — Green; Brown; Watson

6. People play the lottery because they like to gamble. — White; Brown; Watson

7. People who play the lottery and those who refuse to play worry about the emotional reactions of the players. — Green; White; Brown; Black; Watson

The process of synthesis starts as soon as you start to make your list. The list of common reasons represents the reworking of seven separate sources into a single new pattern that can serve as the basis for a new essay.

Distinguishing between Reasons

One of the biggest problems in synthesis is deciding, in cases of overlapping, whether you actually have one reason or two. Since overlapping reasons were deliberately not combined, the preceding list may be unnecessarily long.

For example, Reasons 1 and 2 reflect *the difference between the experiences of having fun and feeling the thrill of excitement*—a difference in sensation that most people would understand. You might ask yourself, "Would someone play the lottery just for fun without the anticipation of winning? Or would someone experience a thrill of excitement without any sense of fun at all?" If one sensation can exist without the other, you have sufficient reason for putting both items on your chart. Later on, the similarities, not the differences, might make you want to combine the two; but, *at the beginning, it is important to note down exactly what ideas and information are available to you.*

The distinction between the thrill of excitement (2) and the pleasure of gambling (6) is more difficult to perceive. The former is, perhaps, more innocent than the latter and does not carry with it any of the obsessive overtones of gambling.

Resenting the lottery because it is a rip-off (3) and resenting the lottery because the players are wasting their money (5) appear at first glance to be similar reactions. However, references to the rip-off tend to emphasize the "injured victim" whose money is being whisked away by a public agency. In other words, Reason 3 emphasizes *self-protection from robbery;* Reason 5 emphasizes *the personal virtue of thrift.*

Reason 7 is not really a reason at all. Some comments in the notes do not fit into a tidy list of reasons for playing, yet they provide a valuable insight into human motivation and behavior as expressed in lottery-playing. An exploration of the emotions that characterize the player and the nonplayer (always allowing for the lottery preference of the source) might be an interesting way to conclude an essay.

Deciding on a Sequence of Topics

The topics in your chart appear in the same random order as your notes. Once the chart is completed, you should decide on a more logical sequence of topics by ordering the entries in the list. You can make an indirect impact on your reader by choosing a logical sequence that supports the pattern that you discovered in analyzing your sources.

Here are two possible ways to arrange the "lottery" reasons. Which sequence do you prefer? Why?

1. fun	1. fun
2. excitement	2. rip-off
3. gambling	3. excitement and gambling
4. education	4. misuse of money
5. rip-off	5. education
6. misuse of money	6. personality of the gambler
7. personality of the gambler	

The right-hand sequence *contrasts the advantages and disadvantages* of playing the lottery. Moving back and forth between paired reasons calls attention to the relation between opposites and, through constant contrast, makes the material interesting for the reader. The left-hand sequence places all the advantages and disadvantages together, providing an opportunity to *explore positive and negative reactions to the lottery separately* without interruption, therefore encouraging more complex development. Both sequences are acceptable.

EXERCISE 15: IDENTIFYING COMMON IDEAS

This exercise is based on a set of interview notes, answering the question "Would you give money to a beggar?"

A. Read through the notes. (1) Identify distinct and different reasons by placing numbers next to the relevant sentences. (2) As you number each new reason, add an entry to the chart. (The first reason is already filled in.)

Reason	Sources
1. I can afford to give to beggars.	
2.	
3.	
4.	
5.	
6.	
7.	
8.	
9.	
10.	

B. Arrange the numbered reasons in a logical sequence. If it makes sense to you, combine those reasons that belong together. Be prepared to explain the logic behind your sequence of points. If you can find two possible sequences, include both, explaining the advantages of each.

⅄ Would You Give Money to a Beggar?

Jonathan Cohen: When asked for money on the street, I often apply a maxim of a friend of mine. He takes the question, "Have you got any spare change?" literally: if he has any loose change, he hands it over, without regard for his impression of what the money's for, since he doesn't think ulterior motives are any of his business. Since I can always afford the kind of contribution that's usually asked for—fifty cents or a dollar—or am at least less likely to miss it than the person asking me for it, I usually take the request as the only qualification of "need." I'm more likely to give out money if I don't have to go into my billfold for it, however, and would rather give out transit tokens or food, if I have them. But I want to be sympathetic; I often think, "There but for the grace of God go I."

Jennifer Sharone: I hate to think about what people who beg have to undergo; it makes me feel so fortunate to be well dressed and to have good food to eat and a home and a job. Begging seems kind of horrifying to me—that in this country there are people actually relying on the moods of strangers just to stay alive. I give to people who seem to have fallen on hard times, who aren't too brazen, who seem embarrassed to be asking me for money. I guess I do identify with them a lot.

Michael Aldrich: If a person meets my eye and asks plainly and forthrightly (and isn't falling-down drunk), I try to empty my pocket, or at least come up with a quarter or two. If the person has an unusually witty spiel—even if it's outlandish—I give more freely. I don't mind giving small change; it's quick and easy. I try not to think about whether or not the person really "needs" the money—how could you ever know? On some level, I think that if someone's begging, they need the money. Period. There's an old guy who stands on my corner—he's been there for years. I always give him money, if I have the change. If I don't have it, he says a smile will do. I would hate to think of him going without a meal for a long time or having to sleep out in the rain. He reminds me of my father and my uncle.

Marianne Lauro: I used to give people money, but frankly, I'm too embarrassed by the whole process. It seems to me that folks who really couldn't be all that grateful for somebody's pocket change still make an effort to appear grateful, and then I'm supposed to get to feel magnanimous when I really feel ridiculous telling them they're welcome to a couple of coins that don't even amount to carfare. So the whole transaction seems vaguely humiliating for everyone concerned. Really, the city or the state or the federal government should be doing something about this—not expecting ordinary people, going home from work, or whatever, to support people who have mental or physical impairments or addictions, especially when you're never sure what their money will be used for. But maybe I'm just rationalizing now—maybe the most "humane" thing about these kinds of transactions is the mutual embarrassment.

Donald Garder: I try, when possible, to respond to the person approaching me, by looking at them, perhaps even making eye contact, which frequently lends some dignity to the moment. But then I don't always reach into my pocket. I often give to people with visible physical handicaps, but rarely to someone who's "young and able-bodied." Sometimes I feel guilty, but I'm never sure if the person is for real or not—I've known people who swindled people out of money by pretending to be homeless, so I have a nagging doubt about whether or not a beggar is legitimate.

Darrin Johnson: I never give on the subway—I hate the feeling of entrapment, of being held hostage. The "O.K., so I have you until the next stop so I'm going to wear you down with guilt until I get the money out of you." I really resent that. I flatly refuse to give under those circumstances because it just pisses me off. I might give to somebody just sitting on the street, with a sign and a cup or something—someone who isn't making a big scene, who leaves it up to me whether I give or not. But I hate feeling coerced.

Jenny Nagel: I never give to people on the streets anymore—there are places where people who are really in need can go if they're really starving or need drug treatment or something. Someone once told me, after I'd given money to some derelict looking guy, that he'd probably buy rubbing alcohol or boot polish and melt it down for the alcohol content—that my money was just helping him kill himself. After that I never gave to anyone on the street. I'd rather make a contribution to a social agency.

Paul O'Rourke: I used to give money or if asked I'd give a cigarette. But one day a beggar let loose with a stream of obscenities after I gave him some money. A lot of these people are really messed up—the government should be looking after them, doing more to help them; if they keep getting money from people off the street, they'll just keep on begging. So now I volunteer once a month at a food shelf, and give to charitable organizations, rather than hand out money on the street.

ASSIGNMENT 8: WRITING ABOUT AN ISSUE FROM MULTIPLE SOURCES

Choose a topic from the following list; or think of a question that might stimulate a wide range of responses, and submit the question for your teacher's approval. Try to avoid political issues and very controversial subjects that may make it difficult for you to control the interview and prevent you from getting a well-balanced set of notes. You want a topic in which everyone you interview can take an interest, without becoming intensely partisan.

Suggestions for Topics

Should wives get paid for housework?

Is jealousy a healthy sign in a relationship, or is it always destructive?

Should boys play with dolls?

Is "traditional" dating still desirable today?

Is it a good idea for couples to live together before marriage?

Does it matter whether an elementary-school child has a male or female teacher?

Is there a right age to get married?

What are the ingredients for a lasting marriage?

Should children be given the same first names as their parents?

Is it better to keep a friend by not speaking your mind or risk losing a friend by honesty?

Should community service become a compulsory part of the high school curriculum?

Should English be made the official language of the United States?

Are laws requiring the wearing of seat belts an infringement of individual rights?

Is graffiti vandalism?

Should animals be used in laboratory research?

Should colleges ban drinking alcohol on campus and in fraternity houses?

How should ethics be taught in the schools?

How should the commandment "honor thy parents" be put into practice today?

What, if anything, is wrong with the nuclear family?

Are students forced to specialize too soon in their college experience?

Should schools stay in session all year round?

Should citizens have to pay a fine for not voting?

Should movies have a rating system?

Should elementary-school students be left back?

Should children's TV time be rationed?

Should parents be held legally or financially responsible for damage done by their children?

At what age is it acceptable for children to work (outside the family)?

Should high school students be tested for drug use?

Should hosts who serve alcohol be held responsible if their guests later are involved in auto accidents?

Should students have to maintain passing grades in order to participate in school athletics?

How should society deal with homeless people?

When should parents cease to be financially responsible for their children?

1. Once your topic is decided (and, if necessary, approved), interview at least six people, or as many as you need to get a variety of reactions. (Some of your sources should be students in your class.) Your purpose is to learn about several ways of looking at the topic, not to argue, but to exchange views. If you wish, use the following format for conducting each interview:

   Name: (first and last: check the spelling!)

   Do you think . . . .?

   Why do you think so? What are some of your reasons? (later) Are there any other reasons?

   Why do you think people who take the opposite view would do so?

   Do any examples come to your mind to illustrate your point?

   Quotation:

2. Take careful and complete notes of the comments that you receive. (*You will be expected to hand in all your notes, in their original form, with your completed essay.*) Keep a separate sheet for each person. If one of your sources says something worth quoting, write down the exact words; read them back to make sure that what you have quoted is what the speaker meant to say; then put quotation marks around the direct quotation. Otherwise, use summary or paraphrase. Do not hesitate to ask, "What do you mean?" or "Is this what I heard you say?" or "How does that fit in with what you said just before?"

3. List the ideas from your notes and arrange the points in a sequence of your choice.

4. Write an essay that presents the full range of opinion, paraphrasing and (occasionally) quoting from representative sources. After analyzing the arguments of your sources, conclude your essay with one or two paragraphs explaining which point of view, in your opinion, has the most validity, and why.

ORGANIZING MULTIPLE SOURCES

Playing the lottery is not a subject that lends itself to lengthy or abstract discussion; therefore, charting reasons for and against playing the lottery is not difficult. The article that follows defines a social, political, and humanitarian problem and suggests two methods of dealing with it, without favoring either "solution" or the values on which each is based. The reporter's sources, quoted in the article, simply cite aspects of the problem and the hope that the courts will deal with it.

Fifteen students were asked to read the article and to offer their opinions; these are presented following the article. As you read the article and the student opinions, assume that you plan to address the issue and synthesize the opinions in an essay of your own.

CITY LAYOFFS HURT MINORITIES MOST
Francis X. Clines

City officials reported yesterday that layoffs resulting from the fiscal crisis were having "devastating" effects on minority employment in government.

In the last 18 months, they disclosed, the city lost half of its Spanish-speaking workers, 40 percent of the black males on the payroll and almost a third of its female workers.

"You are close to wiping out the minority work force in the City of New York," said Eleanor Holmes Norton, the chairman of the Commission on Human Rights, after releasing the data in response to a request.

The dwindling employment, in turn, has put the city in "serious jeopardy" of losing various kinds of Federal aid, according to Deputy Mayor Paul Gibson, Jr.

The city's fiscal failure and the resultant layoffs have worsened the situation in such predominantly male, white agencies as the Police Department, where, after some limited gains in recent years, the ranks of women police officers have been reduced by 55 percent because of the budget crisis, according to the city's latest data.

Meanwhile, a Federal appeals court declared that Civil Service seniority was not immune from legal challenge by women police officers who were dismissed because of the city's fiscal crisis.

Scores of complaints alleging discrimination have been filed by laid-off workers, both as class members and individuals, squeezing the city between the pressures of the traditional primacy of union seniority protections and Federal equal-employment requirements.

Federal officials said yesterday they were processing the complaints, which could result in a cut-off of funds. They added that they were hoping for guidance from the United States Supreme Court this year on the clash between the seniority principle, which tends to protect male white workers, and the Federal minority employment guidelines of Federal law.

The data on dismissals, which had been quietly compiled by city officials in recent weeks, were a further indication of the price the city is paying in the campaign to balance the budget and come to grips with its huge legacy of excessive debt.

Inevitably, the requirements of the austerity drive interfere, too, with attempts to soften the layoff effects on minority-group workers and women.

For example, Commissioner Norton emphasized that the levying of budget cuts on an even percentage basis in city agencies was the best way to protect equal opportunity. But various fiscal experts intent on improving the city's management say across-the-board cutting is the worst way of economizing because it ignores the relative quality of programs.

"We had begun to make an effort," Commissioner Norton said, "But one recession takes it all out in an instant."

Since the budget crisis surfaced in the summer of 1974, the city payroll has been reduced by 40,000 jobs—two-thirds of them reported as layoffs. This was a total cut of 13 percent to the current level of about 255,000 workers, according to city records.

A maxim of the seniority system that the last hired should be the first dismissed is the chief factor preventing an even 13 percent sharing of the layoff burden without regard to race or sex, city officials say.   14

The austerity drive, in which the city must try to cut its spending by $1 billion in less than three years, is forcing the conflict between what Commissioner Norton describes as "two competing and legitimate interests"—seniority and equal opportunity.   15

Federal and city civil rights officials were reluctant to discuss the scope of the complaints that have been filed. Werner H. Kramarsky, the state's Commissioner of Human Rights, described the issues raised as "very thorny" and extending to such questions as whether provisional, or temporary, employees should be credited with time on the job in determining relative seniority.   16

The available public records indicate that the state commission is handling at least 35 cases, some of them class complaints, and has sent 98 cases involving former city welfare workers to Federal officials of the Equal Employment Opportunity Commission, which already has received about 160 complaints from welfare workers alone.   17

The complaints are being pressed not only by women and minority group members, but also by a group of a half dozen disabled persons who contend that they were unfairly victimized in the layoff drive, according to state records.   18

There have been various court challenges in recent years of the seniority protections, which generally have been unsuccessful. One recent ruling threw out a racial quota program for city school principals. Federal civil rights officials emphasize that the Supreme Court is considering the issue at present and the hope is that some definitive standard will be set.   19

According to Deputy Mayor Gibson, minorities represented 31 percent of the payroll, but suffered 44 percent of the cuts. Males, he said, were 70 percent of the payroll and were affected by 63 percent of the cuts.   20

Commissioner Norton said that even before the layoffs, Federal officials had warned the city from time to time that financing for various programs would be cut off because of noncompliance with equal opportunity standards. She said that Mayor Beame had signed an executive order in 1974 committing city agencies to specific improvement programs.   21

Thus far there have been no Federal threats of cutoffs during the fiscal crisis, she said, apparently because the city is on record as pledging to seek a more equitable system in the event it ever resumes full-scale hiring.   22

But Deputy Mayor Gibson feels the situation is becoming critical. "We're losing ground," he said.   23

Student Opinions

Lydia Allen: The performance of a job must be the primary focus in deciding layoffs. I feel that, as a whole, people with more seniority in a job would perform that job best. Therefore, seniority, not minority, rights must be the deciding vote.

Grace Burrows: I believe that both sides have validity. I do feel that because minorities have been held back for so long *some* concessions should be made in their favor. Minorities were just beginning to make progress and now they will be set back once again. A person who's been on the job for a number of years shouldn't be made to suffer either.

Marion J. Buskin: I believe that an individual should be dismissed according to his ability to produce. A person with more seniority should not be allowed to keep his job if someone with less time on the job is capable of performing it better.

Robert Fuhst: I believe in seniority for job protection. If seniority doesn't prevail, then your job is based on how well you are liked and your freedom to express yourself is hampered.

John Giannini: Minorities should have a say in matters of layoffs, especially when a large percentage of the minority is affected. Minorities and senior personnel should share layoffs equally.

Dorothy Humphrey: I think there should be equal employment in this country. If an individual is senior in a field and satisfactorily functioning, he should remain employed. On the other hand, if a member of a minority can function even better, why not employ him instead? Production of work is what counts, not who performs it.

Rosemary McAleer: I favor seniority in employment because it is a system that does not permit discrimination. Regardless of race, color, or creed, if you have acquired more time than another employee, your job should be secure.

Marc Page: The longer a man is yoked to a job and its connected financial position, the more severe are the effects of being sundered from it. Seniority is the overriding consideration.

Megan Phillips: I feel seniority of employment is important in the job crisis because it is the only way of ensuring good and efficient services. Second, I feel the more mature one is in a job, the more the job becomes a part of one's welfare, as opposed to a younger person or a novice in the job, who only performs the job for the money.

Alice Reich: I think seniority in employment is an important consideration for the major reason that the benefits of seniority are hard-earned over the years. It seems unjust for a person who has given perhaps seven-eighths of his working lifetime to a job to find himself "out in the cold." Worse yet, the time of life when seniority would count is the time, very often, when other employment is unobtainable.

Robert Rivera: I feel that minority groups should be protected from job cutbacks. The reason is that the minorities that were hired were hired to fulfill the employment clauses set up through government laws. This law deals with equal opportunity for sexes and minorities to hold jobs and offices. Since this law has been recently enforced (in the last five or six years), why should minorities then hired be affected so tremendously by unemployment?

Jesse Rogers: I feel that minority workers for the city government should be protected, because it does not seem fair that, after waiting so long to get in, they are so easily kicked out by the unions.

Peter Rossi: I believe the federal government should compensate the minority people who were fired because of budget cuts and lack of seniority. The compensation should be the creation of new jobs and not unemployment insurance.

John Seeback: Most jobs run on the idea that the last hired are the first fired, even if the jobs held by senior workers are costing the business millions of dollars. Also, the white majority of senior workers feels superior to the minority workers on a racial basis rather than on a performance basis. Many employers also feel the minority workers are expendable: they had to hire them because of the law; now they have a good reason to fire them.

Nancy Vitale: Men and women, after putting their time and effort (not to mention their skills) into a job for a great number of years, deserve the protection of their jobs in accordance with seniority. It is unfair to dismiss a person from a longstanding position to make a position for a minority member.

When you prepare to explore a variety of opinions about a complex and perhaps controversial subject, follow these steps:

1. Summarize the facts of the issue.

Write a brief, objective summary of the issue under discussion (in this case, the problem described in the article). Your summary of this article should convey both the situation and the two key ideas that are stressed. Try structuring your paragraph to contrast the conflicting opinions.

2. Establish your own point of view.

End your summary with a statement of your own reaction to suggest a possible direction for your essay.

This step is more important than it might at first seem. Once you begin to analyze a mass of contradictory opinion, you may find yourself being completely convinced by first one source and then another, or you may try so hard to stay neutral that you end up with no point of view of your own at all. You need to find a vantage point for yourself from which to judge the validity of the statements that you read. Of course, you can (and probably will) adjust your point of view as you become more familiar with all the arguments and evidence that your sources raise. *Do not regard your initial statement of opinion as a thesis to be proven, but rather as a hypothesis to be tested, modified, or even abandoned.*

3. Synthesize your evidence.

Label your set of opinions and establish categories. The statements follow-ing the article are all personal reactions to job layoffs and the issue of seniority protection versus equal employment opportunity. For each statement, follow these steps:

A. *Read each statement carefully and think about its exact meaning.* First, get a rough idea of what each statement says—do a mental paraphrase, if you like. You will naturally notice which "side" the author of each statement is on. There is a tendency to want to stop there, as if the authors' posi-tions are all that one needs to know. But your object is not only to find out which side of an issue each person prefers, but also to understand *why* that side was chosen.

B. *Try to pick out the chief reason put forth by each person, or, even better, the prin-ciple that lies behind each argument.* Sum up the reasoning of each person in a word or two, a phrase—invent a label, as if for a scientific specimen.

C. When you have labeled the statements, the final stage of synthesis be-comes easier. *Review your summarizing phrases to see if there is an abstract idea, used to describe several statements, that might serve as a category title.* (Some change in the wording may be necessary.) Once two or three cate-gories become obvious, consider their relationship to each other. Are they parallel? Are they contrasting? Then attempt to see how the smaller categories fit into the pattern that is beginning to form.

How the Three Steps Work

Following is one student's exploration of the article on New York City lay-offs and the fifteen student opinions.

1. **Summarizing.** Here the student identifies the article to which he and his sources are responding, summarizing the issue and the nature of the conflict.

> In the New York Times, Francis X. Clines reported that the budget crisis had substantially reduced the number of minorities—blacks, women, and His-panics—on New York City's payroll. The minority members laid off were the em-ployees most recently hired by the city to meet federal minority employment requirements. Eleanor Holmes Norton, who chairs the Commission on Human Rights, described the situation as a conflict between "two competing and legiti-mate interests"—the traditional principle of union seniority protection and equal opportunity employment.

2. **Hypothesizing** (stating your own point of view). Here the student ex-presses an opinion that suggests the possible direction for an essay. At

this point, the student has not studied the group of opinions that accompanies the article.

Both the competing interests are right in their claims, but there is a third principle that goes beyond both: in the name of fairness, the city should take the trouble to evaluate the performance of all its employees and dismiss those whose performance is inferior. Where a senior employee and a minority employee share the same performance rating but are competing for a single position, the city should help both employees and wait for retirements to make room for both.

3. **Labeling your set of opinions and establishing categories.** In this step, the student moves away from the article to examine the opinions of others who have read the article, determining first the position of each respondent and then the reasoning behind the position. Here, the statements of the fifteen respondents are repeated, with a summarizing label following each statement.

Lydia Allen: The performance of a job must be the primary focus in deciding layoffs. I feel that, as a whole, people with more seniority in a job would perform that job best. Therefore, seniority, not minority, rights must be the deciding vote.

Allen: seniority ensures performance

Grace Burrows: I believe that both sides have validity. I do feel that because minorities have been held back for so long *some* concessions should be made in their favor. Minorities were just beginning to make progress and now they will be set back once again. A person who's been on the job for a number of years shouldn't be made to suffer either.

Burrows: evades the issue—both approaches unfortunate

Marion J. Buskin: I believe that an individual should be dismissed according to his ability to produce. A person with more seniority should not be allowed to keep his job if someone with less time on the job is capable of performing it better.

Buskin: performance should be the only criterion

Robert Fuhst: I believe in seniority for job protection. If seniority doesn't prevail, then your job is based on how well you are liked and your freedom to express yourself is hampered.

Fuhst: seniority deserves protection (without it employment becomes a popularity contest)

John Giannini: Minorities should have a say in matters of layoffs, especially when a large percentage of the minority is affected. Minorities and senior personnel should share layoffs equally.

Giannini: minorities and senior personnel should share burden equally

Dorothy Humphrey: I think there should be equal employment in this country. If an individual is senior in a field and satisfactorily functioning, he should remain employed. On the other hand, if a member of a minority can function even better, why not employ him instead? Production of work is what counts, not who performs it.

Humphrey: performance should be the prevailing criterion

Rosemary McAleer: I favor seniority in employment because it is a system that does not permit discrimination. Regardless of race, color, or creed, if you have acquired more time than another employee, your job should be secure.

McAleer: seniority protection is fundamentally the only nondiscriminatory criterion

Marc Page: The longer a man is yoked to a job and its connected financial position, the more severe are the effects of being sundered from it. Seniority is the overriding consideration.

Page: seniority protection is the more humane policy

Megan Phillips: I feel seniority of employment is important in the job crisis because it is the only way of ensuring good and efficient services. Second, I feel the more mature one is in a job, the more the job becomes a part of one's welfare, as opposed to a younger person or a novice in the job, who performs the job only for the money.

Phillips: seniority protection leads to greater efficiency, i.e., performance

Alice Reich: I think seniority in employment is an important consideration for the major reason that the benefits of seniority are hard-earned over the years. It seems unjust for a person who has given perhaps seven-eighths of his working lifetime to a job to find himself "out in the cold." Worse yet, the time of life when seniority would count is the time, very often, when other employment is unobtainable.

Reich: seniority protection is the more humane policy (other employment often impossible for those laid off)

Robert Rivera: I feel that minority groups should be protected from job cutbacks. The reason is that the minorities that were hired were hired to fulfill the employment clauses set up through government laws. This law deals with equal opportunity for sexes and minorities to hold jobs and offices. Since this law has been recently enforced (in the last five or six years), why should minorities then hired be affected so tremendously by unemployment?

Rivera: the law requires that minorities be protected

Jesse Rogers: I feel that minority workers for the city government should be protected, because it does not seem fair that, after waiting so long to get in, they are so easily kicked out by the unions.

Rogers: minority protection is the more humane policy in the light of history

Peter Rossi: I believe the federal government should compensate the minority people who were fired because of budget cuts and lack of seniority. The compensation should be the creation of new jobs and not unemployment insurance.

Rossi: compensate laid-off minority employees with new jobs (implication that city should not lay off senior employees in order to accommodate minority employees)

John Seeback: Most jobs run on the idea that the last hired are the first fired, even if the jobs held by senior workers are costing the business millions of dollars. Also, the white majority of senior workers feels superior to the minority workers on a racial basis rather than on a performance basis. Many employers also feel the minority workers are expendable: they had to hire them because of the law; now they have a good reason to fire them.

Seeback: (implies that) minorities, as victims of union and employer prejudice, deserve protection

Nancy Vitale: Men and women, after putting their time and effort (not to mention their skills) into a job for a great number of years, deserve the protection of their jobs in accordance with seniority. It is unfair to dismiss a person from a long-standing position to make a position for a minority member.

Vitale: seniority protection is the more humane policy

From this list, the student can establish five categories that cover the range of answers. Here is the list of categories:

Category	Source	Note
1. Seniority ensures good performance.	Allen; Phillips	——

Category	Source	Note
2. Performance = vital criterion	Buskin; Humphrey	——
3. Seniority protection = vital criterion	Page	Financial and emotional hardship greatest for laid-off senior employees
	Reich; Vitale	——
	Fuhst	Employment would be popularity contest without it
	McAleer	Truly nondiscriminatory policy
4. Minority protection = vital criterion	Rivera	Legally
	Seeback	Compensation for past and present injustices
	Rogers	——
5. Each group should share the burden.	(Burrows); Giannini; Rossi	Federal gov't should hire laid-off minorities. Senior employees should retain city jobs

EVALUATING SOURCES

Although you are obliged to give each of your sources serious and objective consideration and a fair presentation, synthesis also requires a certain amount of selection. Certainly, no one's statement should be immediately dismissed as trivial or crazy; include them all in your chart. But do not assume that all opinions are equally convincing and deserve equal representation in your essay.

The weight of a group of similar opinions can add authority to an idea. If most of your sources hold a similar view, you will probably give that idea appropriate prominence in your essay. However, *majority rule should not govern the structure of your essay.* Your own perspective determines the thesis of your essay, and you must use your understanding of the topic to evaluate your materials, analyze the range of arguments provided by your sources, and determine for your reader which have the greatest validity.

- Review the hypothesis that you formulated before you begin to analyze the sources. *Decide whether that hypothesis is still valid* or whether, as a result of your full exploration of the subject, you wish to change it or abandon it for another.

■ Sift through all the statements and *decide which ones seem thoughtful and well-balanced, supported by convincing reasons and examples, and which seem to be thoughtless assertions that rely on stereotypes, catch phrases, and unsupported references.* Your evaluation of the sources may differ from someone else's, but you must assert your own point of view and assess each source in the context of your background, knowledge, and experience.

You owe it to your reader to evaluate the evidence that you are presenting, partly through what you choose to emphasize and partly through your explicit comments about flawed and unconvincing statements.

In synthesis, your basic task is to present the range of opinion on a complex subject. You need not draw final conclusions in your essay or provide definitive answers to the questions that have been raised. But you must have a valid thesis, an overall view of the competing arguments to present to your reader. Your original hypothesis, either confirmed or altered in the light of your increased understanding, becomes the *thesis* of your essay.

WRITING A SYNTHESIS ESSAY

Spend some time planning your sequence of ideas and considering possible arrangements and strategies. Do your topic and materials lend themselves to a cause-and-effect structure, or definition, or problem and solution, or comparison, or argument? In writing about the issue of job layoffs, you might want to use an overall *problem-solution* strategy, at the same time *arguing* for your preferred solution.

Next, before starting to write each paragraph, review your sources' statements. By now, you should be fully aware of the reasoning underlying each point of view and the pattern connecting them all. But because your reader does not know as much as you do, *you need to explain your main ideas in enough detail to make all the complex points clear.* Remember that your reader has neither made a list nor even read the original sources. It is therefore important to include some explanation in your own voice, in addition to quoting and paraphrasing specific statements.

If possible, you should present your sources by using all three methods of reference: *summary, paraphrase,* and *quotation.* (See the paragraph in Exercise 16 as an appropriate model.) Remember that, as a rule, paraphrase is far more effective than quotation. When you paraphrase someone's reaction in your own voice, you are underlining the fact that you are in charge, that the opinion you are citing is only one of a larger group, and that a full exploration of the topic will emerge from your presentation of *all* the evidence, not from any one source's quoted opinion. *The first sentence presenting any new idea (whether the topic sentence of a new paragraph or a shift of thought within a paragraph) should be written entirely in your own voice,* as a generalization, without any reference to your sources.

To summarize, your essay should include the following elements:

- *Topic sentence:* Introduce the category or theme of the paragraph, and state the idea that is the common element tying this group of opinions together.

- *Explanation:* Support or explain the topic sentence. Later in the paragraph, if you are dealing with a complex group of statements, you may need a connecting sentence or two, showing your reader how one reason is connected to the next. For example, an explanation might be needed in the middle of the "seniority protects the worker" paragraph, as the writer moves from financial and emotional hardship for laid-off senior employees to the prevention of discriminatory job conditions.

- *Paraphrase or summary:* Present specific ideas from your sources in your own words. In these cases, you must of course *acknowledge your sources* by citing names in your sentence.

- *Quotation:* Quote from your sources when the content or phrasing of the original statement justifies word-for-word inclusion. In some groups of statements, there may be several possible candidates for quotation; in others, there may be only one; often you may find no source worth quoting. For example, read the statements made by Page, Reich, and Vitale once again. Could you reasonably quote any of them? Although Reich and Vitale both take strong positions well worth presenting, there is no reason to quote them and every reason to use paraphrase. On the other hand, Page's briefer statement might be quoted, since the contrast between "yoked" and "sundered" is effective and difficult to paraphrase.

As you analyze the opinions of your sources in the body of your essay, you should remain neutral, giving a fair presentation of each point of view. It is also your responsibility to use the final paragraphs of your essay to present your own conclusions, in your own voice, about this issue—to argue for seniority or equal opportunity employment, or to recommend ways to accommodate both sides.

Guidelines for Citing Sources for Synthesis

- *Cite the source's full name,* whether you are quoting or not.

- *Try not to begin every sentence with a name,* nor should you introduce every paraphrase or quotation with "says."

- *Each sentence should do more than name a person;* don't include sentences without content: "Mary Smith agrees with this point."

- If possible, *support your general points with references from several different sources,* so that you will have more than one person's opinion or authority to cite.

- When you have several relevant comments to include within a single paragraph, *consider carefully which one should get cited first—and why.*

(continued)

(continued)

- You need not name every person who has mentioned a point (especially if you have several almost identical statements); however, *you may find it useful to sum up two people's views at the same time,* citing two sources for a single paraphrased statement:

    Mary Smith and John Jones agree that playing the lottery can be very enjoyable. She finds a particular pleasure in scratching off the numbers to see if she has won.

- *Cite only one source for a quotation,* unless both have used exactly the same wording. In the example above, the first sentence would not make sense if you *quoted* "very enjoyable."

- If an idea under discussion is frequently mentioned in your sources, *convey the relative weight of support* by citing "five people" or "several commentators." Then, after summarizing the common response, cite one or two specific opinions, with names. But try not to *begin* a paragraph with "several people"; remember that, whenever possible, the topic sentence should be a generalization of your own, without reference to the supporting evidence.

- *Discuss opposing views within a single paragraph as long as the two points of view have something in common.* Radically different ideas should, of course, be explained separately. Use transitions like "similarly" or "in contrast" to indicate the relationship between contrasting opinions.

EXERCISE 16: ANALYZING A PARAGRAPH BASED ON SYNTHESIS OF SOURCES

Read the following paragraph and decide which sentences (or parts of sentences) belong to each of the categories in the preceding list. Insert the appropriate category name in the left margin, and bracket the sentence or phrase illustrating the term. Be prepared to explain the components of the paragraph in class discussion.

Those who emphasize the upgrading of minority employment have pointed out that, since the hiring of minorities has been encouraged by governmental legislation only for the last few years, the seniority system will of necessity operate against those minorities. Thus, in the opinion of Robert Rivera, it is only fair that, during the present budget crisis, workers from minority groups be protected from cutbacks. One statement, by John Seeback, even suggests the possibility of a return to racial discrimination by white workers who have seniority and by employers, if equal opportunity laws are not enforced: "Many employers feel the minority workers are expendable: they had to hire them because of the law; now they have a good reason to fire them." In a related argument, Jesse

Rogers points out that, since minorities have waited such a long time for decent job opportunities, a certain amount of preferential treatment might serve as a concrete measure of compensation. Neither Seeback nor Rogers emphasizes the abstract principle of equal opportunity implemented by the law. Peter Rossi advocates a practical solution: the federal government should undertake "the creation of new jobs," so that, presumably, there would be enough to satisfy both groups.

ASSIGNMENT 9: WRITING AN ESSAY SYNTHESIZING MULTIPLE SOURCES

Read the following excerpt by Gene Maeroff on school promotion.

1. Write a summary of the point at issue, and then write a brief explanation of your opinion of this issue.
2. Use the statements that follow as a basis for a synthesis essay. These statements were written in response to the question: Should seventh-grade students who failed a reading test repeat the grade? Analyze each statement, label each kind of reason, and organize all the categories in a chart. Then write an essay that presents the full range of opinion, paraphrasing and, if desirable, quoting from representative sources.

from RULE TYING PUPIL PROMOTION TO READING SKILL STIRS WORRY

Gene I. Maeroff

A strict new promotion policy requires the public schools to hold back seventh-grade pupils until they pass the reading test. The difficulty will be compounded this year by a requirement that new seventh graders also pass a mathematics test.   1

"I am frightened that we may end up losing some of these kids, creating a whole new group of dropouts who leave school at junior high," said Herbert Rahinsky, principal of Intermediate School 293, on the edge of the Carroll Gardens section of Brooklyn.   2

Students like Larry, who is 16 years old and in the seventh grade at I.S. 293, are repeating the grade because they scored too low on the reading tests last June to be promoted. If Larry does not do well enough on the test this spring, he will remain in the seventh grade in the fall.   3

An analysis by the Board of Education has shown that about 1,000 of the 8,871 students repeating the seventh grade are already 16 years of age or older. At least one 18-year-old is repeating the seventh grade.   4

Normally, a seventh grader is 12 years old.   5

When the promotion policy, which threatened to hold back students with low reading scores in the fourth and seventh grades, was implemented in 1980, it was hailed by many observers as a welcome effort to tighten standards.   6

But as the program has continued, certain students have failed to show adequate progress. These youngsters are in jeopardy of becoming "double holdovers" in the seventh grade. Some were also held back at least once in elementary school. . . .   7

Authorities theorize that these youngsters form a hard core of poor readers for whom improvement is slow and difficult. Such students often were not held back in prior years because it was easier to move them along than to help them.   8

Educators now wonder whether repeated failure will simply lessen the likelihood of students persisting in school long enough to get a regular diploma.   9

Statements

Diane Basi: If these students are pushed through the system and receive a diploma, not being able to read beyond a seventh-grade level, we will be doing them and society a grave injustice. What good will it do to have a diploma if you cannot read or write? In the end, the students will be hurt more if they are just promoted through the system.

Jason Berg: A student should not be repeatedly held back on the basis of one test. A student's overall performance—such as classwork, participation, and attitude—should be taken into consideration. If a student is not up to par for some reason on the day of the test, all the work and effort that was put into school during the year goes down the drain.

Rafael Del Rey: This strict rule has unfortunate consequences. The students who are being forced out don't comprehend what is being taught to them. Exasperated and feeling like social outcasts and inferior beings, it is no wonder that many drop out without skills or goals. Educators should be interested in more than just test scores.

Anita Felice: It is extremely embarrassing to be a 16-year-old in a class of 12-year-olds. Such poor students should be promoted to a special program with other students who have the same problems. In time, there should be some improvement in their reading scores. Being held back will only cause frustration and eventually cause them to drop out. Test scores should be a lot less important than they are now.

Joe Gordon: By enforcing a rigid standard, the schools are actually promoting an increased dropout rate and, by doing so, are harming the student and society.

Margaret Jenkins: After two tries, a student should be able to pass a test. It's to the child's advantage to learn and keep learning while moving upward in school. Holding them back is for their own good.

Rachel Limburg: It isn't fair to those students who can do the work just to push these students along. It also isn't fair to the kids who can't pass the test because eventually they are going to have to earn a living.

Barbara Martin: It's a hard question, but I think you have to look at the cost in terms of money, as well as frustration and embarrassment. I'm sorry for kids who are left back, but it's only going to be a problem for everyone later when they can't get a job. Work today is increasingly technical, and everyone needs basic skills. This policy is tough love, and it's necessary.

Len McGee: This policy isn't good enough because it doesn't deal with the individual student; it deals with seventh graders as a whole. The individual's problems and motivation are not taken into consideration. Sometimes exam pressure defeats intelligence. If left back, the student is trapped in a revolving door and is likely to lose interest in school.

Tina Pearson: It's a mistake to pass students solely on the basis of the reading score. It may show they have learned to read well, but it doesn't mean they learned well in their other classes. Perhaps they worked especially hard on reading and English but just coasted along in their other subjects.

Julius Pena: Automatic promotion is a guarantee that the weak student will face future problems. Making the student repeat is for his own good. Imagine how frustrating it would be for someone who can't fill out a job application. Of course, you shouldn't just throw the student back into the class, but give as much encouragement as possible.

Mark Pullman: We must have certain standards in our educational system. This is a challenge for these students, and repeating the course may encourage them to try harder, making them smarter and better prepared to face life's challenges.

Anthony Raviggio: Strict standards are best for the student. In the long run, individuals who really want the college degree will be glad to remember the ordeal they went through in junior high. It's better to make them keep trying and succeed than to let them think it's okay to fail.

Vivian Ray: If a child has been held back in elementary and held back again in junior high school, it should become quite apparent to teachers and parents that the child has a problem. Being slow to learn is not sufficient reason to hold back a child. The child should be promoted and put in a slower class with more students like himself.

Bernice Roberts: I think there's too much concern for the feelings of the "poor" student and too little concern for the needs of society. Eighteen-year-olds who can't read are likely candidates for welfare. I don't want to have the responsibility of carrying some illiterate kid who couldn't be bothered to learn when he was in school.

Althea Simms: The tough standards are good for these students because they will be motivated to become more serious about doing well. There are kids who don't care whether or not they study for their exams since they know they're going to be promoted to the next grade anyway. Knowing that you may be held back is a strong motivator to study harder.

Patricia Sokolov: Not all students are intellectually gifted, nor is the progress of the nation solely dependent on the effort of intellectuals. Laborers and blue-collar workers have been credited throughout our history for their great contribution to the wealth and progress of our country. Educators should be more concerned with nurturing students' individual potential and less concerned with passing tests.

Matthew Warren: What's the point of promoting a student who won't be able to keep up in his new classes, much less perform his job properly when he's out in the working world? Standards should be enforced regardless of age. What's age? It's just a number.

Michael Willoughby: Educators should recognize that some students don't have the capacity, for whatever social, genetic, or psychological reasons, to fulfill the educators' traditional expectations. An alternative effort must be made, emphasizing vocational skills and also basic reading and math, that will permit students to progress at their own pace.

Betty Yando: I am concerned about the large number of dropouts and their dismal prospects. Why should a student, despite obvious learning disabilities, be forced to continue in an exasperating educational process in which he is making little or no progress? The standards by which we determine whether an individual will make a good worker and a good citizen are too high.

ASSIGNMENT 10: WRITING AN ARGUMENT FROM MULTIPLE SOURCES

Read "Marriage with No Easy Outs," and the Letters to the Editor that follow.

1. Write a brief summary of the issue raised by Amitai Etzioni, and list his arguments as well as the counterarguments in the Letters to the Editor.
2. Write an essay that explores the arguments on both sides of the issue and finally supports either Etzioni's position or that of his opponents. Make sure that you use summary, paraphrase, and quotation to represent the opinions of your sources.

MARRIAGE WITH NO EASY OUTS
Amitai Etzioni

Your local ice cream parlor, after selling only ice cream for years, suddenly starts offering frozen yogurt as well. Is this an imposition on customers, who are now "required" to make a choice? Are they being "coerced to think"?   1

This is the way some critics have characterized a new Louisiana law that, as of Friday, will allow couples to choose between the standard "no fault" marriage and a "covenant" marriage.   2

Couples choosing a covenant marriage pledge to enter matrimony only after serious deliberations. They agree to try to resolve potential marital conflicts through   3 counseling if either spouse requests it and to seek divorce only by a mutually agreed upon two-year separation or under a limited set of circumstances, like adultery, abuse, imprisonment for a felony and abandonment. The law also allows married couples to renew their vows and to recast their commitment as a covenant marriage.

Basically, the new Louisiana law provides couples with a ready-made contract 4 that, like all contracts, becomes enforceable by the state once it is entered into freely. In effect, Louisiana is providing a new form of prenuptial agreement, focused not on what happens to assets if the couple divorces, but on how to make divorce less likely.

The Louisiana Legislature, which is not widely known for social innovations, has 5 come under criticism for this imaginative act. Some critics have said that the law imposes new constraints on marrying couples because they are forced to make a choice between the old no-fault and the new covenant marriage.

The feminist writer Katha Pollitt has characterized the law as "forcing" couples 6 to make a choice. Margaret Carlson of Time magazine even suggested that the choice was "theoretical" because after Friday couples would no longer dare choose what she calls Marriage Lite over Marriage Plus. If only she would accept bets.

Most people would agree that allowing individuals to make choices is the exact 7 opposite of coercion. Indeed, the Louisiana legislation provides a model of how a state can foster what it considers a virtue—in this case, stronger marriages—by giving people the opportunity to be virtuous, but not penalizing them if they choose not to.

If this approach were extended to other areas, more teachers would allow pupils 8 to do extra schoolwork to improve a bad grade, rather than merely telling students they should do better next time. Anti-abortion forces might stop emphasizing a ban on abortion and instead offer even more pregnant women support services and help with adoption.

A state may favor some types of behavior over others, but it should promote 9 these by giving people expanded options, rather than forcing them to behave in a preordained manner. And Louisiana couples who are in a rush to marry or for any other reason refuse to deliberate their joint future will not need to elope; they will still be able to marry the old-fashioned, no-fault way.

We are all better off if those who tie the knot are prepared for the commitment. 10 Yes, divorce is sometimes called for. But most divorces are damaging, painful and costly for all involved. Moreover, studies show that about 20 percent of those who avail themselves of premarital counseling decide not to marry, thus perhaps sparing themselves from a bad marriage and a messy divorce.

Some critics of the Louisiana law have argued that slowing down divorce is poor 11 public policy because children are better off when feuding couples break up; they are no longer subject to incessant conflict or hostile silence.

Yet at issue here are not physically or psychologically abusive marriages, because 12 these can be dissolved without undue difficulty under the new law. But for two people who have simply grown apart or are otherwise discontent, a divorce will be delayed for at least two years rather than the standard six months. This time could give the couple a chance to work things out.

The issue is not whether our divorce laws should be tailored for the small percentage of marriages that are seriously abusive, but whether the legal system now makes divorce too easy or too difficult. Are there millions of couples for whom a delayed divorce would cause serious and irreparable harm? Or are millions of couples calling it quits too easily? 13

To put it differently, should only "disposable" marriages be available to couples—or should there also be an option that encourages them to work harder at sustaining their marriages? 14

Far from joining with those who would abolish no-fault divorce and replace it with vows that severely restrict divorce, Louisiana has left the choice completely to the couples. Do they prefer to start with the promise of an easy exit, or are they willing to slow down before they quit? 15

The fact that some critics object to this modest, moderate step speaks to what is wrong in our divorce-prone culture. 16

LETTERS TO THE EDITOR

To the Editor:

Amitai Etzioni assumes that divorce occurs because it is legally easy. This assumption is not supported by the social science data. Divorce rates were rising before—not after—no-fault divorce was implemented. A more reasonable interpretation of the data is that no-fault divorce represented the rising desire of citizens to have their divorces without finger-pointing. 1

Mr. Etzioni seems to believe that making divorce harder will make people work harder at their marriages. Again, there are no data to support that argument. An alternative scenario is that people would remain in unhappy marriages because it is too difficult to get a divorce. That can be shown to be damaging to both children and adults in the family. 2

JOSEPH LEVENSTEIN

To the Editor:

The major, insuperable problem with "covenant marriage" that Amitai Etzioni endorses is that the "covenant" is that of a particular set of religious notions found in conservative Christian circles. In other words, the state of Louisiana has passed a law that essentially enshrines religious dogma as law. Moreover, the state is being asked to do what the churches have not been able to do: keep people in marriages that fail. 3

This law says volumes about the inability of the churches to use moral suasion to encourage their adherents to stick to their marriages, if the churches find themselves having to resort to legislation to force people to do what they would not do otherwise. 4

DEANA MARIE HOLMES

To the Editor:

    Re "Marriage with No Easy Outs." While the "covenant" marriage is an option   5
that must be mutually agreed upon and is one that can be dissolved in instances of
abuse, the reality of family violence often defies unequivocal, free decision-making.

    Emotional, financial and physical coercion and intimidation make ending a rela-   6
tionship difficult for many women now under no-fault divorce laws; by extension, it
is safe to assume that those who once freely chose to enter the more highly regarded covenant marriage, with its inextricable binds, will have an even more difficult time leaving an abusive relationship.

NICOLE MELLOW

To the Editor:

    Classic liberalism would say that the law that governs best governs least. Why   7
should we assume that our laws contain the full force of our moral, ethical, emotional and psychological selves? Amitai Etzioni ("Marriage with No Easy Outs")
mistakenly assumes that only if a couple had chosen to be forced by law, as they
now can under the new Louisiana "covenant" marriage, would they wait two years
to divorce rather than doing so after six months.

    The underlying problem with social conservatives is that they don't trust people's   8
moral action to exceed what the law requires. Rather than allowing individuals the
most moral options that society can tolerate, social conservatives seek to limit
these options through government intervention into the private realm.

    Mr. Etzioni's comparison of marriage options to an ice cream parlor is disingenu-   9
ous. For the image to reflect more accurately his claim that Louisiana simply presents a couple with a ready-made contract that they might otherwise draft
themselves, the store would need to offer more than a choice between ice cream
and yogurt. Like Howard Johnson's, which offers 32 flavors, the state would offer
ready-made contracts for every kind of marriage people wanted, including same-
sex unions.

JOHN PULTZ

To the Editor:

    Several decades ago Margaret Mead suggested that couples should not need a li-   10
cense to be married, but only to have children. This desirable but impractical suggestion may have found new life in Louisiana's two-level marriage contract: one a
"no-fault" arrangement, the other a "covenant" that allows either party to veto a
divorce except under certain circumstances.

    Why not have every marriage start as a no-fault contract with an automatic con-   11
version to a covenant contract upon the conception of a child? The covenant contract would then remain for the duration of any child's life to majority.

    This arrangement would make conception a new stage in the deliberations of   12
any couple: Mead's original objective. There would be a greater awareness of the
responsibilities of this stage of life during the period the marriage contract has
been converted to a "child-bearing" contract.

JAMES J. WARFIELD

To the Editor:

Amitai Etzioni suggests that couples who choose to be married under Louisiana's   13
new "covenant" law, with its restrictive provisions on divorce, will have "no easy
outs" if they later decide to divorce.

Past experience with restrictive divorce laws suggests, however, that it is only   14
the poor who will be denied an easy out. The more well-to-do will find it quite
easy to establish a technical domicile in a state with a lenient divorce law and then
to obtain a valid divorce from that state. In other words, at least for those with
some money, what Louisiana may join together, Nevada may rend asunder.

WILLIAM L. REYNOLDS

SYNTHESIS AND COMPARISON

Synthesis is a method; it is not an end in itself. Some works do not lend themselves to synthesis, which tends to emphasize similarities at the expense of interesting differences between sources.

The academic writer should be able to distinguish between material that is
appropriate for synthesis and material whose individuality should be recognized and preserved. One example of the latter is fiction; another is autobiog-
raphy. Assume that three writers are reminiscing about their first jobs: one was
a clerk in a drugstore, the second a telephone operator, and the third plowed
his father's fields. In their recollections, the reader can find several similar
themes: accepting increased responsibility; sticking to the job; learning appropriate behavior; living up to the boss's or customers' or father's expectations.
But, just as important, the three autobiographical accounts *differ* sharply in
their context and circumstances, in their point of view and style. You cannot
lump them together in the same way that you might categorize statements
about the lottery or opinions about school uniforms, for they cannot be reduced to a single common experience. The three are not *interchangeable*; rather,
they are comparable.

Since *synthesis* does not always do justice to individual works, *comparison*
can be a more effective strategy for writing about several full-length essays
with a common theme. In many ways, comparison resembles synthesis. Both
involve analyzing the ideas of several sources and searching for a single vantage point from which to view these separate sources. However, there is an important difference. *The writer of a synthesis constructs a new work out of the
materials of the old; the writer of a comparison tries to leave the sources intact throughout the organizational process, so that each retains its individuality.*

When you are assigned an essay topic, and when you assemble several
sources, you are not likely to want to *compare* the information that you have
recorded in your notes; rather, you will *synthesize* that material into a complete presentation of the topic. One of your sources may be an encyclopedia;
another a massive survey of the entire subject; a third may devote several
chapters to a scrutiny of that one small topic. In fact, these three sources are
really not comparable, nor is your primary purpose to distinguish between

them or to understand how they approach the subject differently. You are only interested in the results that you can achieve by using and building on this information. In contrast, the appropriate conditions for comparison are more specific and rare.

For comparison, you must have two or more works of similar length and complexity that deal with the same subject and that merit individual examination.

Point-to-Point Comparison

Point-to-point comparison resembles synthesis. You select certain major ideas that are discussed in all the works being compared and then, to support conclusions about these ideas, describe the full range of opinion concerning *each* point, one at a time.

Because point-to-point comparison cuts across the source essays, as synthesis does, you must work hard to avoid oversimplification. If you are focusing on one idea, trying to relate it to a comparable reaction in another essay, don't forget that the two works are separate and whole interpretations of the topic. Otherwise, you may end up emphasizing similarities just to make your point.

Here is a paragraph taken from a *point-to-point comparison* of three movie reviews:

> None of the three reviewers regards Lady and the Tramp as a first-rate product of the Walt Disney studio. Their chief object of criticism is the sugary sentimentality, so characteristic of Disney cartoons, which has been injected into Lady in excessive quantities. Both John McCarten in the New Yorker and the Time reviewer point out that, for the first time, the anthropomorphic presentation of animals does not succeed because the "human" situations are far too broadly presented. Lady and the Tramp are a "painfully arch pair," says McCarten. He finds the dialogue given to the movie's human characters even more embarrassing than the clichés exchanged by the animals. Even Bosley Crowther of the Times, who seems less dismissive of feature cartoons, finds that Lady and the Tramp lacks Disney's usual "literate originality." Crowther suggests that its oppressive sentimentality is probably made more obvious by the film's use of the wide screen. McCarten also comments on the collision between the winsome characters and the magnified production: "Obviously determined to tug all heartstrings," Disney presents the birth of Lady's puppy "while all the stereophonic loudspeakers let loose with overwhelming barrages of cooings and gurglings." All the reviewers agree that the audience for this film will be restricted to dog lovers, and lapdog lovers at that.

Whole-to-Whole Comparison

In whole-to-whole comparison, you discuss each work, one at a time. This method is more likely to give the reader a sense of each source's individual qualities. But unless your sources are fairly short and simple, this method can be far more unwieldy than point-to-point. If you compare a series of long and complex works, and if you complete your entire analysis of one before you move on to the next, the reader may get no sense of a comparison and forget that you are relating several sources to each other. *Without careful structuring, whole-to-whole comparison becomes a series of loosely related summaries,* in which readers must discover for themselves all the connections, parallels, and contrasts.

There are two ways to make the structure of whole-to-whole comparison clear to the reader:

1. **Although each work is discussed separately and presented as a whole, you should nevertheless try to present common ideas *in the same order,* an order that will carry out the development of your thesis about the works being compared.**

   Thus, whichever topic you choose as the starting point for your discussion of the first work should also be used as the starting point for your treatment of each of the others. The reader should be able to find the same general idea discussed in (roughly) the same place in each section of a whole-to-whole comparison.

2. **Remind the reader that this is a comparison by frequent *cross-cutting* to works already discussed; you should make frequent use of standard transitional phrases to establish such cross-references.**

   Initially, you have to decide which work to begin with. The best choice is usually a relatively simple work that nonetheless touches on all the major points of comparison and that enables you to begin establishing your own point of view. Beginning with the second work, you should refer back to what you have said about the first writer's ideas, showing how they differ from those of the second. This process can become extremely complex when you are analyzing a large number of essays, which is one reason that whole-to-whole comparison is rarely used to compare more than three works.

Here is the second major paragraph of a *whole-to-whole comparison* that deals with critical reaction to the film *West Side Story*:

> Like the author of the <u>Time</u> review, Pauline Kael criticizes <u>West Side Story</u> for its lack of realism and its unconvincing portrayal of social tensions. She points out that the distinction between the ethnic groups is achieved through cosmetics and hair dye, not dialogue and actions. In her view, the characters are like Munchkins, stock figures without individual identities and recognizable motives. Natalie Wood as the heroine, Maria, is unfavorably com-

pared to a mechanical robot and to the Princess telephone. Just as the <u>Time</u> reviewer accuses the film of oversentimentalizing its teenage characters at society's expense, so Kael condemns the movie's division of its characters into stereotypical good guys and bad guys. In fact, Kael finds it hard to account for the popularity of <u>West Side Story</u>'s "frenzied hokum." She concludes that many may have been overwhelmed by the film's sheer size and technical achievements. The audience is persuaded to believe that bigger, louder, and faster has to be better. Her disapproval extends even to the widely praised dancing; like the rest of the movie, the choreography tries too hard to be impressive. In short, Pauline Kael agrees with the <u>Time</u> reviewer: <u>West Side Story</u> never rises above its "hyped-up, slam-bang production."

Whether you choose point-to-point or whole-to-whole comparison depends on your sources. Whichever you choose, begin planning your comparison (as you would begin synthesis) by *listing the important ideas discussed by several of your sources.*

- If you eventually choose to write a *point-to-point* essay, then your list can become the basis for your paragraph outline.
- If you decide to compare each of your essays *whole to whole,* your list can suggest what to emphasize and can help you to decide the order of topics within the discussion of each work.

These lists can never be more than primitive guidelines; but unless you establish the primary points of similarity or difference among your sources, your essay will end up as a series of unrelated comments, not a comparison.

ASSIGNMENT 11: WRITING A COMPARISON ESSAY

Write a comparison of three reviews of a film. Your first concern should be the reactions of the critics, not your own opinion of the work; you are not expected to write a review yourself, but to analyze and contrast each critic's view of the film. Try to describe the distinctive way in which each reacts to the film; each will have seen a somewhat different film and will have a different understanding of what it signifies.

For films reviewed before 1970, consult James Salem's *A Guide to Critical Reviews.* Don't commit yourself to a specific film until you have seen a sampling of reviews; if they are all very similar in their criticisms or all very short, choose a different film. If you have doubts about the reviews' suitability, let your teacher see a set of copies. *Be prepared to hand in a full set of the reviews with your completed essay.*

Part III

WRITING
THE RESEARCH
ESSAY

Most long essays and term papers in college courses are based on library research. Sometimes, an instructor will expect you to develop and present a topic entirely through synthesizing preassigned sources; but for many other assignments, you will be asked to formulate your own opinion and then to validate and support that opinion by citing authorities. Whether your essay is to be wholly or partly substantiated through research, you will still have to start your essay by choosing sources at the library.

Your research essay (or extended multiple-source essay) will present you with several new problems, contradictions, and decisions. On the one hand, you will probably be starting out with no sources, no thesis, and only a broad topic to work with. Yet as soon as you go to the library and start your research, you will probably find yourself with too many sources—books and articles in the library and on the Internet from which you will have to make your own selection of readings. Locating and evaluating sources are complex skills, calling for quick comprehension and rapid decision-making.

- At the *indexes* and *online computer catalogs*, you have to judge which books are worth locating.
- At the *shelves*, and on the *computer screen*, you have to skim a variety of materials rapidly to choose the ones that may be worth reading at length.
- At the *library table* and *on the Internet*, you have to decide which facts and information should go into your notes and which pages should be duplicated in their entirety.

In Chapters 5, 6, and 7, you will be given explicit guidelines for using the library, choosing sources, and taking notes.

As you have learned, in order to write a multiple-source essay, you have to establish a coherent structure that builds on your reading and blends together your ideas and those of your sources. In Chapter 8, you will find a stage-by-stage description of the best ways to organize and write an essay based on complex sources. But here, again, is a contradiction.

Even as you gather your materials and synthesize them into a unified essay, you should also keep in mind the greatest responsibility of the researcher—*accountability. From your first efforts to find sources at the library and at your computer, you must carefully keep track of the precise source of each of the ideas and facts that you may use in your essay.* You already know how to distinguish between your ideas and those of your sources and to make that distinction clear to your readers.

Now, you also have to make clear which source is responsible for which idea and on which page of which book that information can be found—without losing the shape and coherence of your own paragraphs.

To resolve this contradiction between writing a coherent essay and accounting for your sources, you will use a system that includes the familiar skills of *quotation, paraphrase,* and *citation of authors,* as well as the skills of *documentation* and *compiling a bibliography.* This system is explained in Chapter 9.

Finally, in Chapter 10, you will be able to examine the product of all these research, writing, and documenting techniques: three essays that demonstrate, respectively, how to write a successful persuasive, narrative, and analytical research essay.

·5·

Finding Sources

Knowing exactly what you want to write about is a great advantage when you are beginning your research. Your instructor may give you that advantage by assigning a precise topic. On the other hand, you may be asked to *narrow a broad subject* or to *develop a topic of your own choosing*, perhaps an idea that you wrote about in your single- or multiple-source essay to give you a head start.

TOPIC NARROWING

Topic narrowing should be a *practical* process. Here are some of the questions that you should ask yourself before you go to the library:

- How much time do I have?
- What resources are available to me?
- How long an essay am I being asked to write?
- How complex a project am I ready to undertake?

Choosing a good topic requires some familiarity with the subject and with the available resources, which is why topic narrowing should continue all through the early stages of your research. Even before you start your research, you should invest some time in analyzing your subject and considering your options. Here are some approaches to topic narrowing that have worked well for students starting their first research project.

Guidelines for Narrowing Your Topic

1. Whether your instructor assigns a broad topic for your research paper or you are permitted to choose your own topic, do some *preliminary reading* to get more background information.

2. As you start your reading, begin to *break down the broad topic into its components:* try thinking about a specific point in time or the influence of a particular event or person if your topic is *historical* or *biographical;* try applying the standard strategies for planning an essay if you're going to write about a *contemporary issue;* try formulating the reasons for and against if you're going to write an argument.

3. Consider *your own perspective* and what interests you about the person, event, or issue.

4. *Formulate a few questions* that might help you to structure your reading and research.

5. Think about the possible answers to these questions as you read, especially those questions and answers that might develop into a *thesis* for your essay.

Topic Narrowing: Biographical and Historical Subjects

Biographical and historical topics have an immediate advantage: they can be defined and limited by space and time. Events and lives have clear beginnings, middles, and ends, as well as many identifiable intermediate stages. You are probably not ready to undertake the full span of a biography or a complete historical event, but you could select *a specific point in time as the focus for your essay.*

Assume, for example, that by choice or assignment your broad subject is *Franklin Delano Roosevelt,* who was president of the United States for fourteen years—an unparalleled term of office—between 1932 and 1945. You begin by reading *a brief overview of FDR's life.* An encyclopedia article of several pages might be a starting point. This should give you enough basic information to decide which events in FDR's life interest you enough to sustain you through the long process of research. You might also read a few articles about the major events that formed the background to FDR's career: the Great Depression, the New Deal, the changing role of the president.

Now, instead of tracing *all* the incidents and related events in which he participated during his sixty-three years, you might decide to describe FDR at the point when his political career was apparently ruined by polio. Your focus would be the man in 1921, and your essay might develop a thesis drawing on any or all of the following topics—his personality, his style of life, his experiences, his idea of government—at *that* point in time. Everything that happened to FDR after 1921 would be relatively unimportant to your chosen perspective. Another student might choose a different point in time and describe *the new president in 1933 against the background of the depression.* Yet another might focus on an intermediate point in FDR's presidency and construct *a profile of the man as he was in 1940, when he decided to run for an unprecedented third term in office.*

The topic might be made even more specific by focusing on *a single event and its causes.* For example, the atomic bomb was developed during FDR's presidency and was used in Japan shortly after his death:

- What was FDR's attitude toward atomic research?
- Did he advocate using the bomb?
- Did he anticipate its consequences?

Or you might want to study Roosevelt in the context of an important political tradition:

- How did he influence the Democratic party?
- How did the party influence his personal and political decisions?
- What role did Roosevelt play in the establishment of the United States as a "welfare state"?

This kind of profile attempts to describe the subject and explore his or her motives and experiences. In effect, *your overriding impression of character or intention serves as the thesis, the controlling idea of the biographical profile.* You undertake to determine whether the available evidence supports your thesis, and present that thesis—if valid—to your readers, supported by facts and details.

You can also view a *historical event* from a similar specific vantage point. Your broad subject might be the Civil War, which lasted more than four years, or the Berlin Olympics of 1936, which lasted a few weeks, or the Los Angeles riots of 1991, which lasted a few days. To cover a long span of time, you might focus on an intermediate point or stage, which can serve to illuminate and characterize the entire event. The Battle of Gettysburg, for example, is a broad topic often chosen by those interested in the even broader topic of the Civil War. Since the three-day battle, with its complex maneuvers, can hardly be described in a brief narrative, you would want to narrow the focus even more. You might describe the battlefield and the disposition of the troops, as a journalist would, at a single moment in the course of the battle. In this case, your thesis might demonstrate that the disposition of the troops at this point was typical (or atypical) of tactics used throughout the battle, or that this moment did (or did not) foreshadow the battle's conclusion. In fact, always assuming that sufficient material is available, *you will find that it makes sense to narrow your focus as much as you can.*

In writing about history, you also have to consider your own point of view. If, for example, you set out to recount an episode from the Civil War, you first need to establish your perspective: Are you describing the Union's point of view? the Confederacy's? the point of view of the politicians of either side? the generals? the civilians? industrialists? hospital workers? slaves in the South? black freedmen in the North? If you tried to deal with *all* these reactions to a chosen event, you might have difficulty in settling on a thesis and, in the long run, would only confuse and misinform your reader.

The "day in the life" approach can also be applied to *events that had no specific date.*

- When and under what circumstances were primitive guns first used in battle?
- What was the psychological effect of gunfire on the opposing troops?
- What was the reaction when the first automobile drove down a village street?

Or, rather than describe the effects of a new invention, you might focus on *a social institution that has changed radically.*

- What was it like to shop for food in Paris in 1810?
- In Chicago in 1870?
- In any large American city in 1945?

Instead of attempting to write a complete history of the circus from Rome to Ringling, try portraying *the particular experience of a single person.*

- What was it like to be an equestrian performer in Astley's Circus in eighteenth-century London?
- A chariot racer in Pompeii's Circus Maximus in 61 B.C.?

Setting a tentative target date helps you to focus your research, giving you a practical way to judge the relevance and the usefulness of each of your sources. As you narrow your topic and begin your reading, *watch for your emerging thesis—a single, clear impression of the person or event that you wish your reader to receive.* Whether you are writing about a sequence of events, like a battle or a flood, or a single event or issue affecting the life of a well-known person, you will still need both a *thesis* and a *strategy* to shape the direction of your essay. *A common strategy for biographical and historical topics is the cause-and-effect sequence*—why a certain decision was made or an event turned out one way and not another.

Finally, do not allow your historical or biographical portrait to become an exercise in creative writing. Your evidence must be derived from and supported by well-documented sources, not just your imagination. The "Napoleon might have said" or "Stalin must have thought" in some biographies and historical novels is often a theory or an educated guess that is firmly rooted in research—and the author should provide documentation and a bibliography to substantiate it.

Topic Narrowing: Contemporary Subjects

If you chose to write about the early history of the circus, you would find an assortment of books describing many traditional kinds of circus activity, from the Roman arena to the turn-of-the-century Barnum and Bailey big top. But there has been an enormous increase in the amount of information published in this half of the twentieth century; reviews and features are printed—and preserved for the researcher—every time Ringling Brothers opens in a new city. Your research for an essay about the circus today might be endless and the results unmanageable unless, quite early, you focus your approach.

If your topic cannot be defined and narrowed through the perspective of time, you can analyze its component parts and select *a single aspect* as the tentative focus of your essay. If you do a computer search for information, you will scan a large number of "descriptors" for your broad topic. Reviewing all these subtopics may help you to find a narrow focus for your topic.

You will find that many of the guides, indexes, and online databases in the reference room contain not only lists of sources but also a useful breakdown of subtopics, suggesting possibilities for the direction of your essay. You will automatically narrow your perspective if you begin to ask questions about and apply different strategies to possible topics. For example, suppose that *food* is your broad topic. Your approach might be *descriptive,* analyzing *causes and effects*: you could write about some aspect of nutrition, discussing what we ought to eat and the way in which our nutritional needs are best satisfied. Or you could deal with the production and distribution of food—or, more likely, a specific kind of food—and use *process description* as your approach. Or you could analyze a different set of *causes:* Why don't we eat what we ought to? Why do so many people have to diet, and why aren't diets effective? Or you could plan a *problem-solution* essay: What would be the best way to educate the public in proper nutrition? Within the narrower focus of *food additives,* there are numerous ways to develop the topic:

- To what degree are additives dangerous?
- What was the original purpose of the Food and Drug Act of 1906?
- Would individual rights be threatened if additives like Nutrasweet were banned?
- Can the dangers of food additives be compared with the dangers of alcohol?

On the other hand, your starting point could be *a concrete object,* rather than *an abstract idea:* you might decide to write about the Big Mac. You could describe its contents and nutritional value; or recount its origins and first appearance on the food scene; or compare it to best-selling foods of past eras; or evaluate its relative popularity in different parts of the world. All of these topics require *research.*

It is desirable to have a few possible narrow topics in mind before you begin intensive reading. Then, as you start to compile your preliminary bibliography, you can begin to distinguish between sources that are potentially useful and sources that will probably be irrelevant. What you *cannot* do at this stage is formulate a definite thesis. *Your thesis will probably answer the question that you asked at the beginning of your research.* Although, from the first, you may have your own theories about the answer, you cannot be sure that your research will confirm your hypotheses. Your thesis should remain tentative until your reading has given your essay content and direction.

Topic Narrowing: Issues for Argument

Finding a topic can be easier when you set out to write an argument. Although it is possible to do well with a topic that is new to you, most people gravitate toward issues that have some significance for them. If nothing immediately occurs to you, try *brainstorming*—jotting down possible ideas in a list. Recall conversations, news broadcasts, class discussions that have made you feel interested, even argumentative. Prepare a list of possible topics over a few days, and keep reviewing the list, looking for one that satisfies the following criteria:

- *Your topic should allow you to be objective.* Your reader expects you to present a well-balanced account of both sides of the argument. Too much emotional involvement with a highly charged issue can be a handicap. If, for example, someone close to you was killed in an incident involving a handgun, you are likely to lose your objectivity in an essay on gun control.

- *Your topic should have appropriate depth.* Don't choose an issue that is too trivial: "Disney World is better than Disneyland." For a general audience, don't choose an issue that is too specialized: "The Rolling Stones were a more influential band than the Beatles," or "*2001: A Space Odyssey* is the most technically proficient science-fiction film ever made." And don't choose an issue that is too broad or too abstract: "Technology has been the bane of the twentieth century" or "A life without God is not worth living." Your topic should be definable in terms that your reader can understand and, perhaps, share. Finally, your topic should lend itself to a clear, manageable path of research. Using the keywords "god" and "life" in a database search will produce a seemingly unending list of books and articles. Where will you begin?

- *Your topic should have appropriate scope.* Consider the terms of your instructor's assignment. Some topics can be explored in ten pages; others require more lengthy development. Some require extensive research; others can be written using only a few selected sources. Stay within the assigned guidelines.

- *Your topic should have two sides.* Some topics are nonissues: it would be hard to get anyone to disagree about them. "Everyone should have the experience of work" or "Good health is important" are topics that aren't worth arguing. (Notice that they are also far too abstract.) Whatever the issue, your opponents must have a credible case for you to attack.

- *Your topic can be historical.* There are many issues rooted in the past that are still arguable. Should President Truman have authorized dropping the atomic bomb on Japan? Were there better alternatives to ending slavery than the Civil War?

- *Your topic should be practical.* It may be tempting to argue that tuition should be free for all college students, but, in the process, you would have to recommend an alternative way to pay for the cost of education—something that state and federal governments have yet to figure out.

- *Your topic should have sufficient evidence available to support it.* You may not know for sure whether you can adequately defend your argument until you have done some library research.

- *Your topic should be within your range of understanding.* Don't plan an argument on "the consequences of global warming" unless you are prepared to present scientific evidence, much of which is written in highly technical language. Evidence for topics in the social sciences can be equally difficult to comprehend, for many depend on surveys that are hard for a nonprofessional to evaluate.

Many of these criteria also apply to choosing either a historical narrative or a contemporary subject. What's important in writing any essay—especially one involving a commitment to research—is that the topic interest you. If you are bored while writing your essay, your reader will probably be just as bored while reading it.

EXERCISE 17: PROPOSING A TOPIC

The following topic proposals were submitted by students who had already spent two sessions at the library focusing their topics for an eight- to ten-page research essay. Consider the scope and focus of each proposal, and decide which ones suggest *practical* topics for an essay of this length. If the proposal is too broad, be prepared to offer suggestions for narrowing the focus.

Student A

Much of the interest in World War II has been focused on the battlefield, but the war years were also a trying period for the public at home. I intend to write about civilian morale during the war, emphasizing press campaigns to increase the war effort. I will also include a description of the way people coped with brown-outs, shortages, and rationing, with a section on the victory garden.

Student B

I intend to deal with the role of women in feudal life, especially the legal rights of medieval women. I would also like to discuss the theory of chivalry and its effects on women, as well as the influence of medieval literature on society. My specific focus will be the ideal image of the medieval lady.

Student C

I have chosen the Lindbergh kidnapping case as the subject of my essay. I intend to concentrate on the kidnapping itself, rather than going into details about the lives of the Lindberghs. What interests me is the planning of the crime, including the way in which the house was designed and how the kidnapping was carried out. I also hope to include an account of the investigation and courtroom scenes. Depending on what I find, I may argue that Hauptmann was wrongly convicted.

Student D

I would like to explore methods of travel one hundred and fifty years ago, and compare the difficulties of traveling then with the conveniences of traveling now. I intend to stress the economic and social background of the average traveler. My focus will be the Grand Tour that young men used to take.

Student E

I'd like to explore quality in television programs. Specifically, I'd like to argue that popular and critically acclaimed TV shows of today are just as good as comparable programs ten and twenty years ago and that there really hasn't been a decline in popular taste. It may be necessary to restrict my topic to one kind of television show—situation comedies, for example, or coverage of sports events.

Student F

I would like to do research on several aspects of adolescent peer groups, trying to determine whether the overall effects of peer groups on adolescents are beneficial or destructive. I intend to include the following topics: the need for peer acceptance; conformity; personal and social adjustment; and peer competition. I'm not sure that I can form a conclusive argument, since most of the information available on this subject is purely descriptive; but I'll try to present an informed opinion.

EXERCISE 18: NARROWING A TOPIC

A. Here are ten different ways of approaching the broad topic of *poverty in America.* Decide which questions would make good starting points for an eight- to ten-page research essay. Consider the practicality and the clarity of each question, the probable availability of research materials, and the likelihood of being able to answer the question in approximately nine pages. Try rewriting two of the questions that seem too broad, narrowing the focus.

  1. How should the nation deal with poverty in its communities?
  2. What problems does your city or town encounter in its efforts to make sure that its citizens live above the poverty level?
  3. What are the primary causes of poverty today?
  4. Whose responsibility is it to help the poor?
  5. What effects does a life of poverty have on a family?
  6. What can be done to protect children and the aged, groups that make up the largest proportion of the poor?

7. Does everyone have the right to freedom from fear of poverty?

8. Which programs for alleviating poverty have been particularly successful, and why?

9. Should all those receiving welfare funds be required to work?

10. What nations have effectively solved the problem of poverty, and how?

B. Make up several questions that would help you to develop the broad topic of *restricting immigration to America* for an eight- to ten-page research essay.

IDENTIFYING SOURCES FOR RESEARCH

> ### *Preliminary Research in the Library: Three Overlapping Stages*
>
> 1. Discovering and locating the titles of some possible sources.
> 2. Recording basic facts about each source.
> 3. Noting each source's potential usefulness—or lack of usefulness—to your topic.

These three stages of identifying sources for resources usually form a *continuous cycle.* You probably will not be able to locate *all* your sources at once, and then record *all* your basic information, and lastly take notes about *all* your sources. Rather, you will have to move back and forth from computer terminal to stacks to reference room. Even after you begin to plan and write your essay, you will probably find yourself back at the library, checking another potentially useful source.

Because you may be looking at a great many titles and because, in any one session at the library, you may be at a different stage of research with each of several different books and articles, you should thoroughly familiarize yourself with the three steps.

The Library

Even before your research essay is assigned, you should become acquainted with your college library. Every library has a different layout, with a different online (computerized) catalog, and stacks that use various kinds of numbering systems. *Find out how your library is organized, how the online catalog works, and what it contains.* Most libraries provide guided tours for groups of interested students. Ask the reference librarian about tour schedules; in fact, the librarian will probably provide you with pamphlets about the library, a map, and almost any other information you're likely to need.

If a tour is not available, make your own exploratory visit. Ask yourself some of the following questions:

- How are the books arranged?
- Are the collections for the different disciplines housed in separate buildings?
- Do you have access to all the stacks of books?
- Is there a map of the reference room on the wall?
- How are the guides and indexes arranged in the reference room? Do you have access to these online?
- Is there a list of all the periodicals owned by the library? Is this list online?
- What kinds of sources are available on microfilm and microcards? Where are the microfilm and microcard readers, and how do you locate and sign out the cards and spools of film?
- Are there computerized databases, and how do you get access to them?
- Does your library have a consortial arrangement with neighboring libraries, and do you have access to materials at these libraries, via a delivery system (interlibrary loan) or computer printout?
- Does your library provide access to the Internet? What special research services are available?

Get these questions answered before you start your research; then you will not lose time and impetus because of interruptions later on.

Online Databases and CD-ROMs

Until recently, libraries listed all their holdings on cards—one card per book—contained in narrow drawers: the *card catalog*. Sometimes, instead of cards in drawers, libraries used a series of bound volumes, with forty or more entries per page. Now, most libraries list their holdings in searchable *databases*, including online databases (often called Online Public Access Catalogs, or OPACs) and in databases stored on CD-ROMs (compact disk, read-only memory). These computerized catalogs enable you to sit at a computer terminal and, using a menu that appears on the screen, retrieve information about a topic or an author or a book. This information can consist of

- The holdings of your library.
- The holdings of other libraries that are part of a local group or libraries across the globe.
- General and specialized indexes and bibliographies that list the names of sources—books and periodicals—some of which may be owned by your library.
- Journals that are online—that is, that you can call up and read on your computer screen—and from which you can obtain printouts of specific articles.

Your library also has databases of electronic information sources available on CD-ROM. The database is stored on a computer disk, and is periodically updated. Once the disk is inserted in the library computer, you use a menu to search for information, just as you would look for sources in an online database.

Each online database or CD-ROM database has a set of commands that students can type in order to access information on the screen. You will usually find a set of instructions posted by each terminal indicating the basic steps to follow in order to find what you are looking for. Reference librarians can also assist you in using the library's computers.

Figure 5-1 shows a sample—one screen—of what's available to students on the twenty campuses of The City University of New York (CUNY). Here, you can choose between the CUNY on-line catalog—the holdings of the libraries of the university—or various online databases containing information about articles in newspapers and periodicals.

Searching a database is, in many ways, easier and more efficient than using a traditional card catalog. To check a number of possible topics or authors in the card catalog, you would have to move from drawer to drawer, pulling one out, thumbing through the cards, making notes, returning the drawer, and moving to a different section of the catalog for your next reference. It is physically easier to remain at a terminal, locating potential sources by making choices from a menu and typing in commands so that the information you want appears on the screen. What you see on the screen probably isn't much different from what you would find in the card catalog. But the process is faster and, once you become familiar with the library's system, much less tedious.

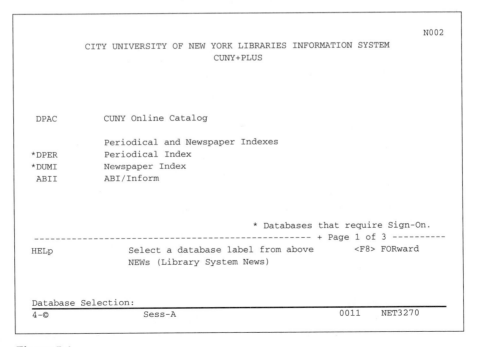

Figure 5-1

On-line databases and CD-ROMs have their limitations. Your library's on-line catalog may be restricted to its own holdings (or, if your college is part of a state university system or a consortium of universities, the combined holdings of all libraries in that system or consortium). Now, however, some online databases are linked to library databases throughout the state or even the nation. If you want to examine a range of all the possible sources on a particular topic, you will probably have to consult specialized databases that may include some titles that your library doesn't own. (See Computer Searches on pp. 254–258 for information on conducting computer searches in specialized databases.)

For decades, researchers have had access to a number of general and specialized indexes and bibliographies that they use to find articles (and sometimes books) related to their research topics. For example, *Applied Science and Technology Index* contains brief summaries of a large number of journal articles about topics in science and technology; *Human Resources Abstracts* lists articles about areas such as poverty, the workforce, and the distribution of human services. Appendix A contains an extensive list of these specialized indexes and bibliographies, the vast majority of which are now online (indicated by an asterisk).

The Internet

In addition to those resources already mentioned, the computer terminal in your library (or your dormitory room) can provide you with access to many other powerful electronic tools that will produce information of prodigious range and depth. To gain access to this information, you need access to the *Internet*—a huge worldwide network of smaller, interconnected computer networks. Currently used by 25 to 30 million people—and growing daily—the Internet is now one of the world's largest repositories of information.

Your university may provide you with free Internet access or may charge a small fee. Or your library's computers may give you access to the Internet. Or you might open an account with a local Internet service provider or subscribe to a *commercial information service*, such as America Online, CompuServe, or Microsoft Network; for a monthly fee, a subscription gives you access to the Internet and, therefore, to the kinds of services described here, as well as to other sources of information and entertainment. Whatever means of access you choose, the Internet is well worth exploring, for it has become an essential tool for anyone who engages in research.

Today, information on the Internet is accessible in three primary ways: E-mail, World Wide Web sites, and Usenet newsgroups.

E-Mail

E-mail enables people to communicate with each other and exchange information electronically all over the world, in minutes. It is as quick and easy as a telephone conversation, but expands your audience to, potentially, hundreds of thousands. Like using the postal mail ("snail-mail"), you write a message in your E-mail software, address it to one or more people, and send it through a computer network.

You can use E-mail to request assistance in exploring a research topic. If you know the E-mail address of an expert in that field, you can send the person an E-mail inquiry, asking questions or requesting specific information. (Make sure that you are courteous in making your request; some people don't have the time to answer unsolicited E-mail or may resent being asked to contribute to your "homework." Review the suggestions in Appendix C for approaching an interview subject.) Remember that any information obtained through E-mail that is subsequently used in an essay must have its source cited. (See Appendix B for the appropriate format.) E-mail also enables you to collaborate with other students on group projects by exchanging information electronically.

Another way to use E-mail is to subscribe to a *mailing list* or *list-serv* (sometimes spelled *listserve*). These are, basically, E-mail exchanges among people interested in a particular subject. When your E-mail address is added to the mailing list, you receive E-mail from members of the group and can send E-mail in return. Large mailing lists are usually automated, with a computer (or *list-serv*) receiving and distributing E-mail to and from you and the other group members. Not all list-servs are open to the public, and some are moderated: volunteers screen all E-mail to ensure that it is appropriate for distribution. You can search for mailing lists and list-servs on these web sites: www.liszt.com (Liszt) and www.tile.net (Tile.Net).

Mailing lists are potentially a source of information for research. For example, lists like TECHWR-L, TEKCOML, or TECHCOMM would provide you with opportunities for discussing technical communication. And subscribing to AAWOMLIT might help you obtain information about literature written by African-American women. Remember that material obtained through E-mail or, indeed, from the Internet in general, has not been validated for accuracy, as have works that have gone through the review and selection processes used by publishers of books and journals. See Chapter 6 for a discussion of evaluating materials on the Internet.

World Wide Web Sites

Of all the sources of information on the Internet, the fastest growing and most fluid is the World Wide Web, where files containing text, graphics, video, sound, and animation come together to form *web sites*. Web sites can vary from a text-only *web page* on a single screen to a complex, interconnected collection of web pages. Software called *web browsers* enables you to navigate the Internet and view web sites. Netscape Navigator and Microsoft Internet Explorer are web browsers that can display both text and graphics; Lynx is a web browser that displays only text.

A central concept of the Web is the *hypertext*, a system of codes that allow readers of web pages to navigate by clicking on *links* and moving to another web page, to a portion of a web page, or to another web site entirely. Clicking on a link may also allow you to see a graphic image, listen to music, or view a

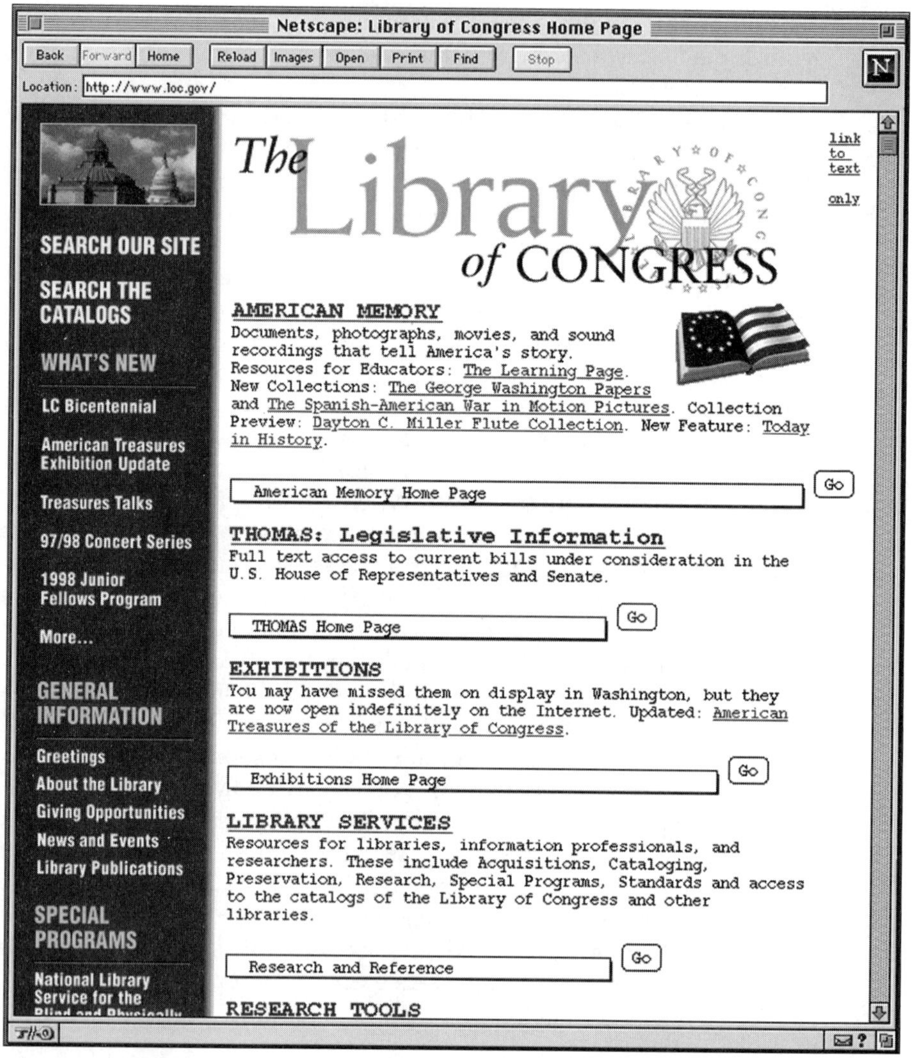

Figure 5-2

short video clip. Because links can point to anywhere on the web site or to other web sites, hypertext enables you to move through web-based documents in a nonlinear fashion. If you choose, you can read through a web-based document from beginning to end. If it isn't useful to you, at any point you can follow hypertext links to another part of the document, to another document, or to another web site. Another way to move from one web site to another is by typing in the URL (Uniform Resource Locator); the URL is the "address" of the web site you want to visit.

Web sites are created by governmental agencies, schools, businesses, nonprofit organizations, and individuals (Figure 5-2 shows the home page of the

Library of Congress). Your university probably maintains a web site; some of your instructors may also have created web sites with information about their courses. You and your friends might maintain *home pages* containing information about yourselves and your interests. Web sites are clearly ideal for distributing up-to-date information to a worldwide audience cheaply and easily. (Indeed, many corporations maintain web sites, partly for purposes of advertising.) That's why you need to make sure that information for research obtained through the Internet is accurate, reliable, and objective. It may be hard to distinguish between the web site of a leading authority on the Army of the North and a Civil War buff who's done a lot of reading. Not all web sites are equally valid. Before you take notes or print out material, check credentials, cited sources, dates, and facts.

The sheer size of the World Wide Web—and the Internet in general—can complicate the process of research. With millions of web sites available, you may have to scan a great many before you can find what you need. As the amount of information stored on the Internet grew, electronic tools were developed to assist Internet users in finding and locating information. One of the first such tools was called a *gopher:* software that allows users to "burrow" from one network to another and from one database to another, using key words and phrases to search for the information. Today, gophers are almost superseded by the faster *browsers,* which navigate the Internet, and by web-based *search engines,* which obtain information on a specific subject. Web search engines are huge databases containing indexes of key words and phrases gathered from various web sites. (See Compiling a Working Bibliography on p. 254 for a description of organizing subject headings.) Methods for searching vary among search engines; before using one that is unfamiliar to you, read the help files and learn about its specific processes. Some of the more popular search engines include

www.altavista.digital.com (AltaVista)

www.infoseek.com (InfoSeek)

www.yahoo.com (Yahoo!)

www.webcrawler.com (WebCrawler)

www.lycos.com (Lycos)

www.excite.com (Excite)

www.hotbot.com (HotBot)

Usenet Groups

Usenet groups provide another means of access to information, through a worldwide network of electronic *bulletin boards,* each devoted to a particular subject. Numbering in the tens of thousands, these *newsgroups* resemble a traditional bulletin board. Using your web browser or specialized news-reading software, you can post messages to one or more newsgroups, you can read messages other people have posted, and you can reply to those messages. So, if your research topic were the Civil War, you could read the newsgroup soc.history.war.us-civil war, or you could obtain information from participants in that or other newsgroups interested in the Civil War simply by posting your questions. Here's what such a question might look like:

> I know that in the North, men born between 1818 and 1843 had to register for the draft. What about aliens? Did they have to register? If not, did they have to prove that they were not citizens? Where would I obtain records?

Before posting that request for information, you might check to see if the question has already been answered on the newsgroup's FAQ: a document, posted by volunteers, that answers frequently asked questions about the newsgroup or the newsgroup's subject. You can find a newsgroup's FAQ and Usenet messages in searchable databases, such as DejaNews (www.dejanews.com), on the World Wide Web. Or you can search Usenet from such web-based search engines as AltaVista or Yahoo! The resources available to you are vast. For example, one recent search for the phrase *home automation* turned up over 1,500 Usenet messages containing the phrase, most of them posted to alt.home. automation and comp.home.automation. Of course, sometimes the sheer number of possibilities can create problems in sorting out which documents to check first. And the same concerns about reliability and accuracy of E-mail information and web-site information apply to Usenet groups.

COMPILING A WORKING BIBLIOGRAPHY

To use virtually all online databases—OPACs, gophers, standard research indexes, and databases provided by commercial services—you have to carry out a computer search, based on the principle of *cross-referencing*. When a new source—a book, for example—is being entered into a database, it would be foolish to include a separate entry for that book under every possible subject heading; that would create an overflowing database and an unmanageable system. Instead, just as libraries have done for decades in organizing their card catalogs, most online databases today use cross-referencing. First, *a standardized set of subject headings* is created to index information in the database. Then, the newly acquired book is scanned, and an entry for that book is placed *only* under those subject headings that are relevant to its content. The most commonly used set of subject headings for cross-referencing is the three-volume *Library of Congress Subject Headings* (LCSH), containing the standard set of cross-references found in all libraries using the Library of Congress system. Or a database may have a special list of descriptors relevant to its subject that can be found in a separate "thesaurus." Libraries generally have LCSH lists or other thesauruses available online or in books near the computer terminals.

Computer Searches

Suppose that you come to the library with a broad topic in mind: you plan to write an essay about *Prohibition,* the period between 1920 and 1933 when the

Eighteenth Amendment to the U.S. Constitution prohibited the manufacture and sale of all alcoholic beverages in the United States. You want to know why Prohibition was abandoned; you wonder whether the circumstances surrounding the institution of this ban on alcohol are relevant to the increasing limitations being placed on tobacco products today. How would you determine the available sources? How would you begin your search through all these databases that contain more information than you need or want?

A computer search usually begins by consulting the LCSH or other thesaurus to identify the appropriate *key words* (called *subject headings* or *descriptors*)—that describe your topic. The object is to find a group of descriptors that you can use, separately or together, to narrow down your topic. (This process is sometimes called *Boolean searching,* a term derived from mathematics, referring to questions limited in scope by combining two descriptors—for example, greater than, less than, x *and* y, x *and not* y—in order to narrow down a topic.) Figure 5-3 shows a listing of LCSH topics that you could look up in addition to Prohibition. Be aware that a key-word search may not always turn up relevant information. Some databases are organized rigorously; others are more haphazard, with odd articles, even promotional material, included in a grab bag of information that can appear on your screen.

Many other subject headings might lead to useful information about Prohibition, yet they don't appear on the cross-referencing list. Some preliminary reading on the topic might encourage you to look up "Organized Crime," for example, or "Smuggling of Illegal Substances."

If you can't find appropriate key words in LCSH, and your online catalog has the capacity to do a Keyword or Boolean search, you would consult the menu for Keyword Searching and then type in combinations of possible key words. Figure 5-4 shows two of the Help Screens, in sequence, in the CUNY Online Catalog that give students a choice of appropriate commands to do a Keyword Search.

If you wanted to do a Keyword Search for the topic "Prohibition," using the AND search, you would choose another appropriate term ("Temperance,"

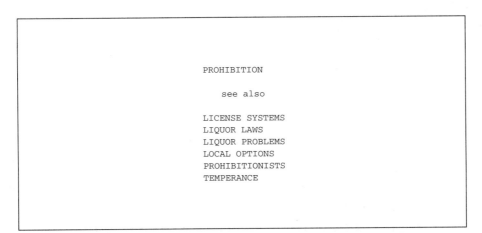

Figure 5-3

```
                                                   CUNY Online Catalog
                                                   Explain Keyword
        ------------------------------------------------------------------
                      Boolean and Positional Operators

    ADJ  -- ADJACENT searches for terms in the order typed in the search and
             immediately next to each other in the same record
                Example: k=abortion adj activists

    SAME -- searches for terms in the same group of fields in a record, but in
             any order and not necessarily next to each other
                Example: k=car same bomb

    AND  -- searches for the terms anywhere in the same record
                Example: k=ozone and atmosphere
                    Continued on the next screen, type for and <enter>
        -------------------------------------------------+ Page 5 of 12 ----------
    STArt over                                      <F8> FORward page
    OTHer options                                   <F7> BACk page


    NEXT COMMAND:

    ------------------------------------------------------------------------
    4-©              Sess-A                          0011    NET3270
```

Figure 5-4A

```
                                                   CUNY Online Catalog
                                                   Explain Keyword
        ------------------------------------------------------------------
                  Boolean and Positional Operators - continued

    NOT  -- Searches for occurrences of the first term and will match only if
             the second term is NOT in the same record
                Example: k=haymarket not riot

    NEAR -- Searches for the two terms next to each other, but in any order
                Example: k=mexico near trade

    OR   -- Searches for the first term or second term or both
                Example: k=hurricanes or typhoons


            For information on qualifying search terms press <enter>
        -------------------------------------------------+ Page 6 of 12 ----------
    STArt over                                      <F8> FORward page
    OTHer options                                   <F7> BACk page


    NEXT COMMAND:

    ------------------------------------------------------------------------
    4-©              Sess-A                          0011    NET3270
```

Figure 5-4B

for example), and, at the K= prompt, you would type in: Prohibition and Temperance.

Here is the result of a computer search in the ERIC database using a combination of *three* key words: the student typed in a request for articles about PROHIBITION and ALCOHOL and the UNITED STATES. Only two articles fulfilled those three descriptors. Figures 5-5 and 5-6 show the summaries of those two articles that appeared on the computer screen (and could, later on, be printed).

Either of these two articles might be interesting material for an essay on Prohibition in the United States. The Rorabaugh article seems to provide general background (but note that it is only three pages long), and the last section of the Wasserman article explicitly describes the period immediately before the passage of the Eighteenth Amendment. The printout contains information about the journal, volume, and date of publication, but does not use MLA or any other standard method of documentation.

The student tried another computer search, using the same three descriptors, this time in a database called DPAC (a book catalog database). The search resulted in the titles of one book and one book review. Unlike ERIC, DPAC provides no summaries, but does include a set of additional descriptors that might prompt you to enter a different combination of commands and produce a different group of titles from the database. In Figure 5-7, the information about the Blocker book review tells you the name of the work being reviewed, suggests that the length of the review is "medium," and assures you that the review is "favorable."

```
                                                       1 of 2
                                           Marked in Search: #6
   AN ACCESSION NUMBER: EJ449332
   AU PERSONAL AUTHOR: Rorabaugh, -W.-J.
   TI TITLE: Alcohol in America.
   PY PUBLICATION YEAR: 1991
   JN JOURNAL CITATION: OAH-Magazine-of-History; v6 n2 p17-19 Fall 1991
   AB ABSTRACT: Traces the history of alcohol use in the United States from
   the colonial period to the present. Discusses changes in public attitudes
   toward drinking. Explores attempts at prohibition, alcohol preferences,
   the relationship between alcohol consumption and economic prosperity, and
   the dichotomy of alcohol as a part of a European heritage that is also a
   destructive substance. (DK)
```

Figure 5-5

```
                                                            2 of 2
                                                Marked in Search: #6
AN ACCESSION NUMBER: EJ448301
AU PERSONAL AUTHOR: Wasserman,-Ira-M.
TI TITLE: The Impact of Epidemic, War, Prohibition and Media on Suicide:
United States, 1910-1920.
PY PUBLICATION YEAR: 1992
JN JOURNAL CITATION: Suicide-and-Life-Threatening-Behavior; v22 n2 p240-54
Sum 1992
AV AVAILABILITY: UMI
AB ABSTRACT: Estimated impact of exogenous social and political events on
suicide behavior in the United States between 1910 and 1920. Concluded that
World War I did not influence suicide; Great Influenza Epidemic caused suicide
to increase; and continuing decline in alcohol consumption from 1910 to 1920
depressed national suicide rates. (Author/NB)
```

Figure 5-6

Specialized Indexes

In addition to the larger online databases available through the Internet, a number of smaller indexes of periodicals and journals intended for research in specific disciplines are available online or through CD-ROMs that you can access yourself at a terminal. (Appendix A has a comprehensive listing.) Most library information systems have the most frequently used periodical indexes right in their online system as separate databases (usually limited to the last ten years). To continue your research on Prohibition, you might want to consult the *Social Sciences Index,* the *Readers' Guide to Periodical Literature,* or the *Times Index.*

The *Readers' Guide to Periodical Literature* is especially useful for research on contemporary issues. It contains listings of a number of popular magazines, but very few scholarly journals, so it should not be the *only* index that you consult in preparing an academic paper. For your essay on Prohibition, you would look at the *Readers' Guide* for the 1920s and early 1930s (available in bound volumes, but not online), and find titles such as "Why Repeal Will Be Coming Soon." Here is what a *Readers' Guide* entry for a 1932 article looks like:

After Prohibition, what? L. Rogers. New Repub. 73:91–99   D7 '32
[title]   [author]   [magazine]   [volume; pages]   [date]

As you can see, the title of the article comes first; then L. Rogers, the author's name, with the first name indicated only by the initial; then the title of the periodical (often abbreviated); then the volume number, followed by a colon and the

```
DPER [Periodical Database]
Sample Computer Screen entry
From search: k= prohibition and alcohol and United States

AUTHOR:      Blocker, Jack S. Jr.
ARTICLE TITLE: Book Reviews: Profits, Power, and Prohibition
SOURCE
DATE:          Journal of American History. Dec. 1990,
               v77n3, P.1010-1011
ABSTRACT:      J.S. Blocker, Jr. reviews "Profits, Power, and Prohibition:
               Alcohol Reform and the Industrializing of America,
               1800-1930," by John H. Rumbarger.
SUBJECT
DESCRIPTORS:   Nonfiction
               History
               Prohibition era
               Reforms
               United States
LENGTH:        Medium (10-30 col inches)
ARTICLE
TYPE:          Book Review Favorable

AUTHOR:      Rumbarger, John J.
TITLE:       PROFITS, POWER, AND PROHIBITION: ALCOHOL REFORM AND THE
             INDUSTRIALIZING OF AMERICA, 1800-1930.
PUBLISHER:   Albany: SUNY Press, 1989.
SUBJECTS:    Prohibition—United States—History
             Temperance—United States—History
             United States—Industries—History
```

Figure 5-7

pages (91–99) on which the article appears; then the month, day, and year (December 7, 1932) of publication. *Be aware that this citation is not the appropriate format for your bibliography.* It is merely the sequence of information used by *this* index.

Another popular source of information on contemporary life is the *Times Index*, which contains topical news articles from the *New York Times* on Prohibition, such as "Rise in Gangland Murders Linked to Bootlegging." Here is a typical *Times Index* listing for 1933:

25 Buffalo speakeasies and stills raided, S 24,   IV,   6:6

                                   [date] [section] [page: column]

The title of the article is followed by the date (24 September), the section of the newspaper (IV, indicated in Roman numerals to avoid confusion), the page (6), and the column (the sixth from left). Again, the format of this citation is peculiar to this index and is not to be used as a model for your bibliography.

Since these indexes have to cram a great deal of information into a relatively small space, they include only one entry for each book or article, and make extensive use of cross-referencing. In the *Readers' Guide* for 1932–1933, for example, you would find four columns of articles about Prohibition, first divided into regions and then into a series of headings that include "Economic Aspects," "Enforcement," "Political Aspects," "Repeal," and "Results." But at the very beginning of the list, the reader is referred to other subject headings to be found elsewhere in the *Readers' Guide:*

> *See also*
> alcohol
> liquor problem
> liquor traffic
> liquor

It is your job to check any of the other headings that seem relevant to your topic, and include some of them in your list of key words for additional computer searches in the larger databases.

Some indexes do not provide "See also" lists. In one year's listings of the *Social Sciences Index,* for example, the subject headings do not include "Prohibition," but under the broad heading of "Alcohol," you would find "Social Interaction in the Speakeasy of 1930." The Library of Congress Subject Headings can help you to identify possible topics for checking, but you also need to use your ingenuity and imagination to cross-reference your topic.

Using Your Library's Online Periodicals Database

Many campus libraries provide students with access to a *periodicals database* listing all the articles in all the newspapers, magazines, and journals available in *that* library (or group of libraries). A student searching the CUNY database—using the key word "Prohibition"—accessed the screen shown in Figure 5-8, which contains the first fourteen entries on that topic in the database.

The student wanted to know more about the first article and typed in #1 at the prompt to get a detailed description of "Carry from Kansas Became a Nation All Unto Herself." As Figure 5-9 shows, the article (which appeared in *Smithsonian*) deals with the more bizarre aspects of Carry Nation's life. Moreover, the temperance crusader died more than eight years before Prohibition became law. Before deciding whether to read the article, you should consider whether you are interested in exploring the historical background of the temperance movement, which was instrumental in bringing about Prohibition. "Lessons of Prohibition" (#6) might be more relevant to a comparison with a modern ban on tobacco.

Selecting Sources for Examination

Perhaps the most obvious source of information for an essay on Prohibition is the online catalog of the books available for borrowing in your library system.

```
Search Request: S=PROHIBITION                        General Periodical Ind
Search Results: 52 Entries Found  _____ Subject Index
       PROHIBITION
 1     CARRY FROM KANSAS BECAME A NATION ALL UNTO H <1989> (RG)
 2     DRINKING IN AMERICA <1990> (RG)
 3     FISH DRY AND VOTE WET <1987> (RG)
 4     GOOD BYE WHISKEY GOOD BYE GIN <1992> (RG)
 5     LAST UNTOUCHABLE <1987> (RG)
 6     LESSONS OF PROHIBITION <1988> (RG)
 7     PROHIBITIONS FAILURE LESSONS FOR TODAY <1992> (RG)
 8     REAL ELIOT NESS <1987> (RG)
 9     REAL MCCOY <1987> (RG)
10     REFLECTIONS ON THE DRY SEASON <1990> (RG)
11     SHOULD WE LEGALIZE DRUGS HISTORY ANSWERS <1993> (RG)
12     SHOULD WE LEGALIZE DRUGS HISTORY ANSWERS <1993> (RG)
13     WANTED CONSENSUS ON ABORTION <1989> (RG)
14     WHAT HAPPENED IN HINTON <1988> (RG)
---------------------------------------- CONTINUED on next page  ---
STArt over        Type number to display record        <F8> FORward page
HELp              GUIde
OTHer options


NEXT COMMAND:
4-©              Sess-A                         0011    NET3270
```

Figure 5-8

```
Search Request: S= PROHIBITION                       General Periodical Ind
WILSON RECORD -- 1 of 52 Entries Found  _____ Brief View
AUTHORS:        Day, Robert


ARTICLE TITLE: Carry from Kansas became a Nation all unto herself.


SOURCE/DATE:    20:147-8+ Apr '89 Smithsonian


SPECIAL FEATURES:
                il pors.


ABSTRACT:       Born Carry Amelia Moore in Kentucky in 1846, Carry Nation is
                remembered more for demolishing bars with hatchets than for
                her liberal beliefs on such issues as the homeless, battered
                women, smoking, and sex education. Nation had a strange
                upbringing: Her mother sometimes believed herself to be
                Queen Victoria, an aunt thought that she was a weathervane,
---------------------------------------------- + Page 1 of 3 ----------
STArt over        HOLdings            GUIde            <F8> FORward page
HELp              LONg view                            <F6> NEXt record
OTHer options     INDex
Held by library—type HOL for holdings information.
NEXT COMMAND:
4-©              Sess-A                         0011    NET3270
```

Figure 5-9

Using key words to search that catalog should be relatively simple and should turn up a list of several possible books. Figure 5-10 shows reproductions of three different computer screens accessed in response to such a subject search. How would you decide which book to examine first?

The first two titles in Figure 5-10 are both relevant to your paper topic; the third is probably not.

- *Ardent Spirits:* The topics at the bottom of the *Ardent Spirits* screen are listed in order of their importance in the book. Accordingly, Kobler's main emphasis is on Prohibition and its relation to American history; you would almost certainly find some useful information there. There is a sixteen-page bibliography.

- *Repealing National Prohibition:* Since there is only one topic listed under "Subject," *Repealing National Prohibition* is evidently concerned only with Prohibition. Judging from its title, the book focuses on the end of the period you would be concerned with. So you can conclude that its treatment of the topic will probably be more detailed than the first book's. It also has a longer bibliography—twenty pages—than *Ardent Spirits* does. However, for a broad overview of the subject, you might begin with *Ardent Spirits.*

- *Women's Suffrage and Prohibition:* If you were interested in the connection between the women's suffrage movement and the temperance movement, you might want to consult the third title. But Prohibition is not Paulson's primary subject; it is highlighted on the screen only because the book has been cross-referenced under that broad topic. Moreover, *Women's Suffrage and Prohibition* seems to consist largely of case studies; your interest would depend on what cases Paulson chooses to examine at length.

Figure 5-11 is not a reproduction of a computer screen, but a facsimile of the entry for *Ardent Spirits* found in a subject card catalog. Notice that the information about Kobler's book is almost identical to that on the computer screen and that it is organized in much the same way. Both the card and the screen provide you with a call number so that, if you wish, you can retrieve the book from the stacks. Unless your database provides you with a printout of the entire entry, remember to copy the book's call number from the screen or card, as well as other important information such as author, title, and the book's probable focus. If the stacks of your library are open to students, explore them until you find the books that you need. Otherwise, use the procedure for having the library staff find these books for you.

Using Bibliographies

Once you locate *Ardent Spirits* or *Repealing National Prohibition,* you check either book's bibliography for other books relevant to your project. This step allows you to add to your own bibliography some of the titles that these authorities used in researching their studies of Prohibition. Of course, you will

```
CALL #      HV 5089.K67  Location: 7th floor stacks   Status: not checked out
AUTHOR      Kobler, John.
TITLE       Ardent spirits : the rise and fall of prohibition / by John
              Kobler.
EDITION     1st Da Capo Press ed.
IMPRINT     New York : Da Capo Press, 1993.
DESCRIPT    386 p. : ill. ; 21 cm.
NOTE        Originally published: New York : Putnam, 1973.
            Includes bibliographical references (p. [358]-[373]) and index.
SUBJECT     Prohibition Party (U.S.)
            Prohibition--United States--History.
            Temperance--United States--History.
```

```
CALL #      HV 5089.K95  Location: 7th floor stacks   Status: not checked out
AUTHOR      Kyvig, David E.
TITLE       Repealing national prohibition / David E. Kyvig.
IMPRINT     Chicago : University of Chicago Press, 1979.
DESCRIPT    xix, 274 p. : ill. ; 24 cm.
NOTE        Bibliography: p. 245-266.
            Includes index.
SUBJECT     Prohibition--United States.
```

```
CALL #      JF 848.P3    Location: 7th floor stacks   Status: not checked out
AUTHOR      Paulson, Ross E.
TITLE       Women's suffrage and prohibition: a comparative study of
              equality and social control [by] Ross Evans Paulson.
IMPRINT     Glenview, Ill., Scott, Foresman [1973]
DESCRIPT    212 p. front. 23 cm.
NOTE        Includes bibliographical references.
SUBJECT     Woman--Suffrage--Case studies.
            Prohibition--Case studies.
            Equality--Case studies.
            Social control--Case studies.
```

Figure 5-10

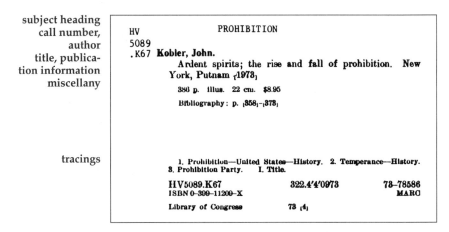

subject heading
call number,
author
title, publica-
tion information
miscellany

tracings

Figure 5-11

have to find and examine these other titles before you can decide whether to use them. Again, check the author or title database or catalog, record their call numbers, and then find them in the stacks. (They are probably shelved together.) If your library does not own these titles, you will have to decide whether any look interesting enough to warrant a visit to another library.

If you are unable to locate a vital source in any of the local libraries, you might consult your college librarian about the possibility of an *interlibrary loan,* in which books or copies of articles are sent to your library from the library that owns the source that you need. But remember that interlibrary loans may take some time, and allow for that as you plan your research schedule. Finally, some libraries have "shared systems" that facilitate the delivery of documents. If you want a printed copy of an article in a periodical index, you press a button at your terminal and then pick up the hard copy at a central desk. There may be a charge for this service.

Focusing Your Topic

After you look in catalogs, bibliographies, and indexes, you will probably have listed and located the following *kinds* of sources for an essay on Prohibition:

- Economic and social histories for a general background of the period
- Congressional reports, political analyses, and legal studies of the Eighteenth Amendment
- Contemporary newspaper accounts, magazine articles, and memoirs describing the everyday effects of the ban on liquor
- Exposés of bootlegging and other criminal activities associated with Prohibition
- Philosophy and psychology books and articles dealing with recurring forms of Puritanism

Using Databases to Focus Your Topic

- Become familiar with your library's information system.
- Use computer searches in the databases/indexes to help you to narrow the focus of your broad topic and to identify possible sources.
- Use your library's on-line databases to get information about available books and articles that might be worth exploring; on the basis of that information, decide which ones to obtain from the library.
- Examine the bibliography at the back of each book that you obtain at the library and note down information about other titles that seem useful to your topic.
- Throughout all the stages of this process, take *complete* notes about the books and articles you may be working with (unless the system provides you with a computer printout of information about each one).
- Exploring a topic at the library is an assisted form of brainstorming. The screen or card will provide you with ideas about your topic, and that will prompt you to come up with ideas of your own. Make sure that you note down interesting directions for your research as they occur to you.

At the beginning, uncertain about the precise scope and focus of your essay, you may find it difficult to decide which of these sources will ultimately be useful to you. What are you going to write about? Will you stress:

- The reasons for the movement toward Prohibition?
- The religious influence?
- The economic background?
- Prohibition as a consequence of social changes in the era after World War I?
- The link between Prohibition and organized crime?
- The effects of Prohibition on recreation and leisure?
- The constitutionality of the Eighteenth Amendment?
- The rituals of illegal drinking?

Or will you pursue your original idea and focus on the relationship between the prohibition of alcohol in the 1920s and the restriction on the use of tobacco decades later?

To make the most efficient use of your resources, you need to estimate the *amount of material that is available* and the approximate *amount of time that you will need to spend on library research.*

1. At the beginning, if you have an hour or two to spend in the library, you should spend that time at the terminal or in the reference room, rounding

out your list of possible sources and narrowing your topic. At this stage, you should not start to read extensively (and take notes) in any single work.

2. Later, after you have compiled a working bibliography, you will begin the reading part of your research, starting with the most comprehensive source.

Certainly, you will want to find out if the most likely titles are available in the stacks and, if they are, to check them out and take them home. *But, at this point, don't spend too much time with each book.* At the most, you will want to look at a book's table of contents, index, and bibliography, or flip through an article in order to gain a rough idea of its scope and relevance.

Writing a successful research essay depends on your doing your research thoroughly and checking a reasonable number of reference works, bibliographies, indexes, and other sources. If you wonder how many is a "reasonable" number, report your progress to your instructor or a librarian, and ask for comments.

RECORDING BASIC INFORMATION FOR YOUR BIBLIOGRAPHY

A *bibliography* is loosely defined as *a complete list of all the works that you use in preparing your essay.* In practice, however, there are really two kinds of bibliography, corresponding to the stages of your research.

Your **preliminary** or **working bibliography** consists of all the sources that you learn about and perhaps examine as you discover what material is available and as you develop your ideas about the topic.

Your **final bibliography** (sometimes called "Works Cited") consists of the material that you will actually use in the writing of your essay. (For a discussion of the final bibliography, see Chapter 9, pp. 388–392.)

You need to have very precise information for all the entries in your bibliography. If you have consistently used a computer database that has printed out lists of books or articles, then you may be able to work from those lists when you prepare your final bibliography. If you are working with a database that doesn't have a printer, or if you are relying entirely or partly on a card catalog and printed indexes from the reference room, you should, from the very beginning of your research, carefully copy down all facts that you may need later on in order to construct a complete and correct final bibliography. These notes can be written on *index cards,* in a separate section of your notebook, or in a separate file of your laptop.

It is important that your records be *accurate, readable, and reasonably consistent.* Several weeks later, when you are working on your list of "works cited" for submission with your essay, you should be able to transform your notes into the correct format without difficulty. (Some software programs, like Nota Bene, allow you to enter data about each source and then automatically prepare correct bibliographic entries in any of the standard formats.) In your early sessions at the library, even though you are at the beginning of your research and cannot be sure which sources will actually become important, *make your notes legible* and *do not abbreviate* unless you are aware of the significance of each symbol. If you cannot understand your notation, you will have to return to the library to check your references, probably when you can least spare the time.

As you work from the computer screen or the card catalog or from one of the indexes or from a bibliography, start a fresh card or a fresh line on the screen for each new item. It may help to assign a number to each new source. Since some indexes do not always provide complete information, indicate gaps in your notes that you can later fill when you are examining the article itself. If you are using a notebook page, remember to leave enough space for comments about the work's potential usefulness.

More likely than not, you will be using MLA style to document your essay. (See Chapter 9, pp. 373–381, for an explanation.) To prepare a final bibliography in MLA style, you should include the following facts in your preliminary notes:

For Books

- the author's full name
- the exact title, underlined
- the name of the editor(s) (for an anthology) or the name of the translator (for a work first written in a foreign language)
- the date and place of publication and the name of the publisher
- the original date of publication and the date of the new edition or reprint, if the book has been reissued
- the inclusive page numbers if you are planning to use only a single chapter or section of the book
- the call number, so that you will not need to return to the database/catalog if you decide to locate the book

For Articles

- the author's full name
- the title of the article, in quotation marks
- the exact title of the periodical, underlined
- the volume number and the date of the issue
- the inclusive page numbers of the article
- the call number of the periodical, so that you will not need to return to the database/catalog if you decide to locate the article

Later, when you locate the book or article itself, remember to check all these facts and supply missing information by examining the front and back of the title page of the book or the first page of the article and the title page of the periodical or newspaper. The *Readers' Guide* does not always include the author's name in its entries (especially the first name), so remember to note it down. Check the spelling of the author's name; find out if the book had an editor; find out whether the place of publication was, for example, Cambridge, Massachusetts, or Cambridge, England.

Figure 5-12 shows two sample note cards, each containing basic information about one of the works on Prohibition mentioned earlier in this chapter. Since these notes are part of a preliminary bibliography, prepared in the library under time pressure, the information is jotted down as a list, using no particular style of documentation. Notice that the first card contains a note questioning the book's relevance to the topic, and the second specifies the *Readers' Guide to Periodical Literature* as the source of the article.

To show you what information looks like when it is placed in the standard format, here is a *bibliography* for the Prohibition essay, with some of the works listed so far:

LIST OF WORKS CITED

Kobler, John. Ardent Spirits: The Rise and Fall of Prohibition. New York: Putnam, 1973.

Kyvig, David E. Repealing National Prohibition. Chicago: U of Chicago P, 1979.

Paulson, Ross E. Women's Suffrage and Prohibition: A Comparative Study of Equality and Social Control. Glenview: Scott, 1973.

Rogers, L. "After Prohibition, What?" New Republic 7 Dec. 1932: 91–99.

"25 Buffalo Speakeasies and Stills Raided." New York Times 24 Sept. 1933, sec. 4:6.

Research is open-ended. You cannot judge in advance how many sources will provide adequate documentation for your topic. *You need to include enough sources to support your thesis convincingly, yet not so many that you treat them superficially.* Your instructor may stipulate that you consult at least five authorities, or ten, or fifteen; but that is probably intended to make sure that each student in the class does a reasonable and roughly equal amount of research. Certainly, without guidelines, your preliminary list of sources could conceivably reach and exceed the dozens, even the hundreds. If you wished, you could copy whole sections of a database, or whole pages of an index, or whole rows of titles on the shelves; but you would have little knowledge of the contents or the relevance of your "Works Cited." It is not enough to have compiled the suggested number of source materials if the works on your list are minor or trivial or peripheral to the topic. An endless list of sources does not automatically demonstrate your competence in research. What is important is not quantity, but usefulness for your purpose.

A good grade for a research essay is likely to depend on the inclusion of a few crucial sources, the works of well-known authorities, whose evidence or points of view must be considered if your essay is to be thoroughly documented.

In Chapter 6, you will start learning how to distinguish those useful sources from the irrelevant ones.

Ross E. Paulson

JF
848
.P3

Women's Suffrage and Prohibition:
a comparative study of equality
and social control

Glenview, Illinois / Scott, Foresman

1973

212 pp.

Prohibition = Secondary Subject

L. Rogers

"After Prohibition, what?"

New Republic 7 Dec. 1932

pp. 91-9

(Readers' Guide)

Figure 5-12

TAKING NOTES ABOUT THE USEFULNESS OF EACH SOURCE

In addition to the factual information that you will need for your bibliography, you should write down a few preliminary notes about the probable usefulness of each work. This step takes place *after* you have *located* and briefly *examined* a source. These are not notes that you will use in writing your essay, but comments indicating which sources merit closer examination and notetaking at a later stage of your research. Simply jot down your initial assessment of the work's scope and contents, strong or weak points, and possible relevance to your topic, as well as any rough impressions about the author's reliability as a source. Often, you can write down such comments just by examining the table of contents and leafing through the pages. *Don't trust your memory.* If you forget to note your reaction, weeks later you may find yourself wondering whether to return to the library to check what seems to be a likely looking title.

Your preliminary comments also enable you to review the progress of your research. You can glance through your notes after each trip to the library to decide whether your sources are going to be numerous and thorough enough to support your essay or whether you should return to the computer terminal and reference room to add a few new authors to your list.

Finally, your preliminary notes will be useful when you assemble your final bibliography, especially if you are expected to *annotate* it.

> *Annotation means that you insert a short comment after each item in your bibliography, describing the work's scope and specific focus and suggesting its relevance and usefulness to the development of your topic.*

This is a more formal variation on annotating a text, which was the first topic in this book. The annotations in a bibliography are usually only a sentence or two, just enough to help your reader judge the importance of each source.

In the following annotated bibliography for an essay on politics and the Olympics, the notes for each entry were taken, with few changes, from the earlier working bibliography.

AN ANNOTATED LIST OF SOURCES CONSULTED

Espey, Richard. The Politics of the Olympic Games. Berkeley: U of California P, 1979. Espey spends 8 or so pages on each of the modern Olympics up to 1976, with an emphasis on political motivation and the shift of emphasis from the athlete to the nation.

Kieran, John, Arthur Daley, and Pat Jordan. The Story of the Olympic Games 776 B.C.–1960. Rev. ed. Philadelphia: Lippincott, 1977. Approximately 12 pages on each of the games up to 1976, with a concise and interesting narrative, but little interest in politics. The authors assume that the Olympics will always continue as they have.

Ludwig, Jack. Five Ring Circus. Toronto: Doubleday Canada, 1976. A lengthy account of the Montreal 1976 Olympics, with anecdotes. Most interesting on the Canadian commercial and political role in staging the Olympics.

Mandell, Richard D. The First Modern Olympics. Berkeley: U of California P, 1976. A detailed account of the reasons and preparations for reviving the Olympics in Athens in 1896, with an emphasis on Coubertin's personality and philosophy.

---. The Olympics of 1972: A Munich Diary. Chapel Hill: U of North Carolina P, 1991. Written in the form of a literary diary, provides an insider's views on the terrorist attacks during the 1972 Olympics. Examines the political context and ramifications of terrorism and sports.

"The Perseus Project." 2/21/97 HTTP://Olympics.Tufts.Edu/.10/25/97.
A study, carried out at Tufts University, comparing ancient and modern Olympic games.

Shaw, Russell. "Whistling Dixie: Professionalism and Politics Lure '96
Olympics to Atlanta." Sporting News 1 Oct. 1990: 8–10. An account
of Atlanta's campaign to court the International Olympic
Committee in order to host the 1996 games. Analyzes Atlanta's
political image.

Williams, Roger M. "Moscow '80, Playing for Political Points." Saturday
Review 1 Sept. 1979: 12–16. A detailed analysis of political and
nationalistic interests in the Moscow Olympics, with emphasis on
Soviet motivation.

EXERCISE 19: COMPILING A WORKING BIBLIOGRAPHY

The following is a list of four different topics for a research essay dealing with
the broad subject of *advertising,* followed by a bibliography of twenty articles,
arranged in order of their publication dates. Each item in the bibliography is
followed by a note giving a brief description of its contents.

Examine the bibliography carefully and choose a set of appropriate sources
for each of the four essay topics. You are not expected to locate and read these
articles; use the notes to help you make your decisions.

The bibliography is numbered to make the distribution process easier. List
the numbers of the articles that you select underneath each topic. You will notice that many of the articles can be used for more than one topic.

Topics

A. What is an appropriate role for advertising in our society? What are the
advertiser's responsibilities?

B. Feminists have argued that the image of women created by the advertising
industry remains a false and objectionable one. Is that claim valid?

C. How do advertising agencies go about manipulating the reactions of consumers?

D. To what extent does advertising serve the public? harm the public?

1. "The Sexism Watch." *US News & World Report* 27 Mar. 1989: 12. This short but
informative piece describes public reaction to sexism in advertising and the
advertising industry's responses to public attitudes with regard to campaign
design.

2. Eller, J. "The Era of the Big Blur." *Newsweek* 22 May 1989: 73. The author of this article presents a highly critical analysis of the increasing "blurring" of advertising and editorial content prevalent in many print media.

3. Kanner, B. "Mind Games." *New York* 8 May 1989: 34–40. This article is an overview of the psychological testing and research methods used by advertising firms to maximize the effectiveness of their campaigns.

4. Eder, Peter F. "Advertising and Mass Marketing: The Threat and the Promise." *The Futurist* May/June 1990: 38–40. This article describes alterations in mass media research techniques as advertisers employ market research to determine what consumers want. The shift considers the change from mass marketing to micro-marketing in order to better affect consumers' purchasing habits.

5. Landler, Mark. "Madison Avenue Is Getting a Lot Less Madcap." *Business Week* 29 Oct. 1990: 78+. This article examines the relationship between a decline in flamboyant advertising campaigns and shrinking marketing budgets. The new advertising style attempts to conjure links between images and values and the product in the minds of consumers.

6. Rudman, William J., and Patty Verdi. "Exploitation: Comparing Sexual and Violent Imagery of Females and Males in Advertising." *Woman & Health.* 1993: 1–14. This article attempts to trace the depiction of women in the mass media and link it to sexual violence to determine if advertising and sexual depictions can affect social interactions. The article raises the question of the responsibility of advertisers when they create images of women.

7. Madden, Patricia A. "The Frequency and Nature of Alcohol and Tobacco Advertising in Televised Sports, 1990 Through 1992." *American Journal of Public Health* Feb. 1994: 297–9. This article traces the advertising industry's attempts to link cigarettes and beer to television sports in the minds of sports viewers, so as to create an association of them with healthy activities.

8. Jolley, Reed. "The Condom War on Children." *Christianity Today* 7 Mar. 1994: 38. This article charges that the Clinton administration's public service ad campaign designed to prevent the spread of AIDS promotes casual sex between young unmarried couples, and it criticizes the manipulation of the young through advertising.

9. Ingrassia, Michele. "Going One Step Ogle the Line? (Diet Coke Ads Depict Ogling of Men by Women)." *Newsweek* 14 Mar. 1994. This article contends that gender depiction role reversal signifies a shift in the public's increasing resistance to the objectification of women.

10. Rich, Frank. "Gay Shopping Spree. (Reactions to IKEA Television Ad Featuring a Gay Male Couple; Op-Ed)." *New York Times* 3 Apr. 1994, sec. 4: 11. This article praises the first mainstream commercial featuring a gay couple, which marked a breakthrough in advertisers' depictions of society, possibly signalling a service to the audience by expanding the normal scope of images they are presented with.

11. Signorielli, Nancy. "Gender Stereotypes in MTV Commercials: The Beat Goes On." *Journal of Broadcasting & Electronic Media* Winter 1994: 91–101. This long article examines the presentation of gender roles through commercials to the typically adolescent viewer of MTV. The depiction of women as linked primarily to sexuality is also discussed.

12. Sengupta, Subir. "The Influence of Culture on Portrayals of Women in Television Commercials." *International Journal of Advertising* 1995: 314–333. This technical study compares Japanese and American television commercials and the way in which cultural influences affect the depiction of women in advertising.

13. Hitchon, Jacqueline C., and Chingching Chang. "Effects of Gender Schematic Processing on the Reception of Political Commercials for Men and Women Candidates." *Communication Research* Aug. 1995: 430–458. Another scholarly survey focusing on the appeal to gender in the marketing of commercials for political candidates.

14. Tauchi, Teresa. "Truth in Advertising." *HaasWeek Home* 30 Oct. 1995. Online. Internet. WWW.http://haas.berkeley.edu/~haasweek/issues/XXII_10/index.html. 13 Oct. 1997. A chatty little story about tasteless ads, often offensive to women, and the need for more responsible behavior on the part of advertising executives.

15. Elliott, Dorinda. "Objects of Desire." *Newsweek* 12 Feb. 1996: 41. This news story concerns the potentially big market for exotic underwear in Asia, and the ways in which advertising can sell more push-up bras to Asian women.

16. Lafky, Sue, Margaret Duffy, Mary Steinmaus, and Dan Berkowitz. "Looking through Gendered Lenses." *Journalism & Mass Communication Quarterly* Summer 1996: 379–388. Full of jargon, this article describes a study of gender-role stereotyping. High school students were given magazine ads to show how quickly they are influenced by stereotypes of gender.

17. Miller, Molly. "The Color of Money." *Mother Earth News* Feb. 1996: 78–89. The subject is environmental protection, and the false claims about their environmental policies that some companies have made in their advertisements.

18. LaTour, Michael S., Robin L. Snipes, and Sara J. Bliss. "Don't Be Afraid to Use Fear Appeals." *Journal of Advertising Research* Mar. 1996: 59–67. A video based on an appeal to the viewers' fears raised some ethical concerns; this article shows how potential criticism was avoided by trying out the video on a focus group.

19. Pratt, Charlotte A., and Cornelius B. Pratt. "Nutrition Advertisements in Consumer Magazines." *Journal of Black Studies* Mar. 1996: 504–523. The authors focus on claims made about potential benefits to health in advertisements for various foods.

20. McFadden, Daniel L., and Kenneth E. Train. "Consumers' Evaluation of New Products." *Journal of Political Economy* Aug. 1996: 683–703. This is a technical article about how people accept new products through their own or other people's experiences, and how that process can be word-of-mouth information; the authors map out a step-by-step process for evaluation that might be helpful to advertisers.

ASSIGNMENT 12: PREPARING A TOPIC PROPOSAL FOR A RESEARCH ESSAY

A. Choose a broad topic that, for the next few weeks, you will research and develop into an extended essay of eight or more pages.

- If you have a *person or an event* in mind, but do not have sufficiently detailed knowledge to decide on a focus and target date, wait until you have done some preliminary reading. Start with an encyclopedia article or an entry in a biographical dictionary; then use the online catalog and any databases and bibliographies that you find along the way. Decide whether your topic is recent enough to have been featured in available newspapers and periodicals, and consult the appropriate indexes.

- If you select a *contemporary subject or issue for argument,* examine some of the entries dealing with that topic in recent volumes of the *Readers' Guide* or the *New York Times Index;* then formulate a few questions that you might try to answer in your essay.

B. Compile a preliminary bibliography, consulting the relevant indexes and databases. At this point, you need not examine all the sources, take notes, or plan the organization of your essay. Your purpose is to assess the *amount* and, as much as possible, the *quality* of the material that is available. Whether or not your instructor asks you to hand in your preliminary bibliography, make sure that the publication information that you record is accurate and legible. Indicate which sources your library has available and which may be difficult to obtain.

C. Submit a topic proposal to your instructor, describing the probable scope and focus of your essay. (If you are considering more than one topic, suggest a few possibilities.) Be prepared to change the specifics of your proposal as you learn more about the number and availability of your sources.

·6·

Evaluating Sources

While compiling a preliminary bibliography, a student has located several promising sources. Her topic is *high school dropouts:* specifically, she wants to discuss the age at which adolescents should be allowed to leave school.

At the library, the student has consulted indexes and bibliographies, and has found a number of books and articles, all of which, judging by their titles, might be relevant. Some of these authors may have a better claim to being cited as authorities than others. Since all the names are unfamiliar to her, which should she read first? How can she weigh one source of evidence against another and decide whose ideas she should emphasize in her essay?

First of all, the student can try to find out something about each author's credentials. Is the writer a *teacher*? an *administrator*? an *educator*? a *journalist*, presenting secondhand information? Are the writer's qualifications appropriate for the subject? A *kindergarten teacher* may not be the best person to offer opinions about sixteen-year-olds. On the other hand, you might not think that an *economist* would be worth consulting on the topic of high school dropouts; yet, if one has made a study of the job market and the career prospects of workers without high school diplomas, then an economist's evidence and recommendations should be worth including in a research essay. Would a *social psychologist* be a useful source? That would depend on the nature of the work: a study of abnormal social behavior in adolescents might be unrelated to the problem of determining the minimum age for leaving high school; but a study of juvenile delinquency might suggest connections between teenage crime and teenage dropouts.

Chapter 3 included an article about strict attendance policies in grade school. What *are* Roger Sipher's qualifications for making such tough recommendations? Consider also "A Question of Degree" in Chapter 1. Who *is* Blanche Blank, and why should we believe her claim that we have grossly inflated the value of a college degree? Is Blank an employee denied promotion because she lacks a B.A.? Or is she a college graduate seeking a more interesting job? a homemaker eager to return to college? a college teacher who specialized in education (as, in fact, she is)? What difference would this information make to your understanding of her essay?

On the other hand, you may be asked to write about a writer or a group of writers (in an anthology, perhaps) whose names are all familiar to you. Why would you need to find out more about these authors? Would they have been chosen for inclusion in an anthology if their authority were questionable? Once again, how can information about the source help in the writing of your research essay?

LEARNING MORE ABOUT YOUR SOURCES

It is useful to know something about the mind, personality, and experience of the authors that you cite (as well as the times in which they lived), if only to provide a context for understanding their purpose and meaning. There may be some significant connection between an author's background—education, previous writings, professional interests, political leanings, life experience— and the ideas in the book or article that you may write about. Finding out about an author's credentials and background not only helps you to decide whether the source is trustworthy, but also enables you to make allowances for an individual approach to the subject and, occasionally, for bias.

In this sense, "bias" is not a bad word, nor is it quite the same thing as "prejudice." *Bias means special interest or personal angle: the line of thought that this person would be expected to pursue, which might affect his or her opinion about the subject that interests you.* Few knowledgeable people are entirely detached or objective, whether about their pet interests or about the area of learning that has been their life's work. The awareness of bias may weaken your belief in the author's credibility; it is the person who is both knowledgeable and with minimal bias whose opinions tend to carry the most weight. Nevertheless, you shouldn't discount a good idea just because you believe that the writer's ideas may reflect a special interest. Once you have identified a possible bias, you can either disregard it as harmless or adjust your judgment to allow for its influence.

Learning about an author's background does not always permit you to make assumptions about that person's probable point of view. For example, one of the authors whose writings are included in this book is a scholar whose interests are intellectual rather than popular. Yet, on the basis of that information, it would be foolish to try to trace a cause-and-effect connection between his academic background and the negative attitudes toward the media expressed in his essay. *In general, the purpose of inquiring about the author's life and work is to understand more about the wider context of the work that you are reading.*

Authors

Where do you go to find out about a writer's background? Possibly to the book itself. The *preface* may contain biographical information, and the *blurb* on the cover or jacket will probably describe the author (but frequently in such laudatory terms that you may have to discount much of the information). Periodicals may provide a *thumbnail biography* of an article's author at the bottom of its first page, or at the end of the article, or in a group of authors' biographies at the beginning or end of an issue.

What you should look for are details about the author's education, professional experience, and published works. These facts can tell you quite a bit about the writer's probable approach to the subject of your research. Look out for vague descriptions: "a freelance writer who frequently writes about this topic" can describe a recognized authority or an inexperienced amateur. You can also consult one of the many *biographical dictionaries, encyclopedias,* and *indexes.* Some of them are more informative than others. *Who's Who,* for example, provides some basic facts about positions held and works published; but you may need to know a good deal about the academic world to interpret this information, and you may not find out very much about the author's characteristic activities or interests. Good indexes to consult are *Biographical Index* and *Current Biography.*

To illustrate this evaluating process, let us look more closely at the author of one of the paragraphs in Exercise 5 on p. 46. Margaret Mead's name is very famous, yet you may have often read and heard that name without really knowing why she is famous. To find out something about her achievements and her credentials for writing about family relationships, you stop in the library and check one of the biographical reference works. (If you know where these books are shelved or you can call up the text on a computer terminal, this step can take less than ten minutes.) In the index to *Current Biography,* you find a listing for Margaret Mead's obituary in the 1978 volume; to supplement that brief paragraph, you can also look up the complete article on Mead in the 1951 volume. Here is the obituary, followed by an excerpt from the much longer 1951 article (which ends with references to twelve other sources of information about Margaret Mead).

1978 Volume

MEAD, MARGARET Dec. 16, 1901–Nov. 15, 1978. One of world's foremost anthropologists; pioneered in research methods that helped to turn social anthropology into a major science; curator emeritus (from 1969) of American Museum of Natural History, with which she had been associated since 1926; taught at Fordham, Columbia, and other universities; made many expeditions, to Samoa, New Guinea, Bali, and other parts of South Pacific; author of hundreds of articles and more than a score of books, including all-time best-seller *Coming of Age in Samoa* (1928); commented on American institutions in such books as *And Keep Your Powder Dry* (1942) and *Male and Female* (1949); promoted environmentalism, women's rights, racial harmony, and other causes; died in New York City. See *Current Biography* (May) 1951.

Obituary

NY Times A pl + N 16 '78

1951 Volume

Dr. Mead during World War II "wrote OWI pamphlets and interpreted GI's to the British" *(Saturday Review of Literature)* and also served (1942–5) as executive secretary of the committee on food habits, the National Research Council. She was a visiting lecturer at Teacher's College (1945–51) and has further served as consultant on mental health, as a member of the committee on research of the mental health division of the National Advisory Mental Health Council of the United States Public Health Service and as a member of the interim governing board of the International Mental Health Congress. . . .

What do you learn from this information?

- Margaret Mead was a *scientist,* thoroughly familiar with the rigorous methods and the complexities of scientific research; therefore, she is unlikely to be casual in her analysis of the sources of neurosis in children.

- Margaret Mead was a *social scientist,* specifically, an *anthropologist;* she was accustomed to studying the whole of a community or society, assessing its customs, its stability, its morale, its probable responses to challenges and emergencies; this training would make her acutely sensitive to and objective about the dynamics within the American family.

- Margaret Mead did not restrict her writing to anthropological studies of remote tribes; the article quoted in Exercise 5 is by no means her first comment on the American scene, and so her analysis and predictions gain the credibility that comes with *repeated observation.*

- Family relationships were among Margaret Mead's special concerns; thus, one can understand the *context* for her analysis of the neurotic child.

- Finally, the *popularity* of her best-selling scientific work suggests that her readers would be more likely to accept her conclusions than they would the ideas of an author who was less well known and whose background was exclusively academic.

On the other hand, the fact that Mead was a *popularizer*—one who takes dry and difficult ideas and makes them understandable to a wide public—helps to explain why her presentation may seem facile, with many of its assertions unsupported. In fact, the paragraph on p. 47 comes from an article written for *Redbook,* not for a scholarly journal; it can be important to consider the *audience* for which an author is writing. *The writings of Margaret Mead, the anthropologist, clearly differ from those of Margaret Mead, the social commentator.*

Finding out about your sources can enhance your understanding of what you read; however, getting this information should not dominate the research process. If your preliminary bibliography contains twenty books, and you are writing an essay in which no single source will be emphasized, don't waste your time looking up each author at length in the reference room.

But if you are building a paper around a subject for which there are clearly going to be only a few highly important sources, and if you feel uneasy about your ignorance of their qualifications, invest some time in reading a few articles about these authors and their writings.

Check the *Book Review Index* and read reviews of the books that you intend to cite, or look at articles cited in *Biographical Index.* If no other information is available, check the catalog and indexes to see what other books and articles these authors have published. In the end, however, you may have to rely on your research instincts, which will become remarkably accurate after you spend some time comparing the content and style of the sources that you find.

Dates of Publication

One indication of a work's usefulness for your purpose is its *date.* In your essay on high school dropouts, to survey past and present policy, you want to choose some representative works published over the last few decades. However, if you are focusing only on the present, using only material published in the fifties or sixties would be pointless (unless you wanted to include some predictions that might or might not have come true). An article about outdated school attendance laws or social conditions (like the draft) that have changed would be of little value in preparing an essay about contemporary dropouts. However, you may find older sources with theoretical content that is not dated, such as discussions of the role of education in the formation of personality.

Primary and Secondary Sources

To judge the usefulness of a work, you should know the difference between *primary* and *secondary sources.*

> *A primary source is a work that is itself the subject of your essay or (if you are writing a historical research essay) a work written during the period that you are writing about that gives you direct or primary knowledge of that period.*

"Primary source" is frequently used to describe an original document—such as the Constitution—or memoirs and diaries of historical interest, or a work of literature that, over the years, has been the subject of much written commentary.

> *A secondary source can be any commentary written both after and about the primary source. Thus, a history textbook is a secondary source.*

While you generally study a primary source for its own sake, the secondary source is important—often, it only exists—because of its primary source.

- If you are asked to write an essay about *Huckleberry Finn* and your instructor tells you not to use any *secondary sources,* you are to read *only* Mark Twain's novel and not consult any commentaries.

- Carl Sandburg's biography of Abraham Lincoln is a *secondary source* if you are interested in Lincoln, but a *primary source* if you are studying Sandburg.

- And if you read the *New York Times* in order to acquire information about life in America on a certain date, you are using the newspaper as a *primary source,* since it is your direct object of study; but when you look up a *Times* review of a book or a movie you want to write about, then you are locating a *secondary source* in order to learn more about your primary subject.

In the sciences and social sciences, the most recent secondary sources usually replace earlier ones. However, that rule does not always apply to secondary sources written about historical and biographical subjects. For example, Forster's biography of Charles Dickens, written in the nineteenth century, is still considered an interesting work, in part because Forster knew Dickens and could provide much firsthand information. Nevertheless, because research is always unearthing new facts about people's lives, Forster's work has been superseded by new biographies that feature the latest information. In fact, for a biographical or historical essay, you should consult some primary sources, a few secondary sources written at the time of the event or during the subject's lifetime, and the most recent and reliable secondary sources. It is the sources in the middle—written a few years after your target date, without the perspective of distance—that often lack authenticity or objectivity.

If you are in doubt about the credibility of a source, check to see whether the author has included documentation and a bibliography; *well-documented works tend to be the most reliable sources.* But the absence of documentation is not the only reason for distrusting a source. You can decide not to take a book seriously just by glancing through it. If it is written in a superficial, frivolous, or overly dramatic style, then you may be right to suspect its claim to authority.

Finally, try dividing the available sources into *three* groups: those you are sure that you will want to use, those you rejected on sight, and those you are doubtful about. *Indicate the reasons for your doubts in the notes for your bibliography.* Later in your research, you can check the qualifications of those sources with your instructor or (with the help of the reference librarian) in reference works; or you can simply annotate your bibliography to make your reader aware of your reasons for proceeding with caution.

EVALUATING SOURCES FROM THE INTERNET

No one doing research on the Internet can complain about a lack of sources. The profusion of material on every subject far exceeds the number of print articles and books listed in databases and indexes. Indeed, initially, you may feel spoiled for choice. With abundance, however, comes the need for decisions. When a random listing of over 5,000 titles appears in response to your keywords, which ones do you access and examine? Once you have a document on the screen, how can you make sure that the information is appropriate, accurate, and authoritative enough to include in your essay?

A crucial difference between publishing work on the Internet and publishing work in print is the presence or absence of a standard for publication. To get your book or article accepted by a reputable publishing house or journal, you must submit your manuscript to a lengthy process of peer review. Specialists in the field assess the quality, timeliness, and originality of your ideas, as well as the accuracy of your evidence, based on their knowledge of comparable works. The imprimatur—decision to print—means that the reader can assume that the book or article meets a reasonably high standard.

There is no comparable process for reviewing material appearing on the Internet. No one at AltaVista or Yahoo! is in charge of making choices or maintaining quality; every document listed is equal to the rest. So, you are on your own in deciding what is worth examining and what is worth using in your essay. What do you look for?

- *The author.* First, you have to locate the author's name, which can be hard to find. If it doesn't appear in the document (and there is no sponsoring organization), try doing a search, using the author's name as a keyword. Is a home page mentioned? You may need to keep on moving from one site to the next until you find out something about the author's background and credentials. Then you can check that person's claim to authority about this topic.

- *The sources cited in the document.* Are sources provided for the information contained in the document? The inclusion of appropriate documentation tells you that the author understands the basic requirements for academic scholarship and gives you some assurance that the information is reliable. You may decide to access some of those references to make sure that your author has presented them fairly. Also, check whether the information is consistent with what you have found in other sources.

- *The date of publication.* The absence of a date casts considerable doubt not only on the timeliness and currency of the information, but also on the validity of the source.

- *The writing and presentation.* Is the author's purpose clearly stated and then supported with evidence? The Internet contains a lot of self-serving material, propaganda for a cause or advertisement for a product. Is the tone of a document objective? Or is it ideological? Or frivolous?

To illustrate some of the problems of doing research on the Internet, let's continue to explore the topic *high school dropouts.* Typing those two key words in the search box of your browser results in 2,759 possible listings, with the "Top Ten List" of the best matches appearing on your screen first. Here, without access information (but with authors and sources, when they are listed), are the titles:

1. Joseph Campell [sic], cont'd: A high school dropout talks back

2. Madison's High School Dropout Rate Drops

3. High school dropout rate the lowest in two decades by Sharon Foster, Staff Writer

4. High School Dropout Gets a New Chance

5. State: Local high school dropout rate ranked second lowest in county

6. High School Dropout Rates Decline Over Two Decades Contact: Melinda Kitchell

7. Myth: The High school dropout rate is climbing

8. I'm a high school dropout! To Whom It May Concern: Chana Williford

9. Branson R-4 School District High School Dropout Rate

10. HISPANIC DROPOUT RATE HIGH. Excerpts from USA TODAY Written by HAYA EL NASSER

These ten are far from "top." A very mixed group, they appear to feature local statistics (2, 5, and 9) and human-interest stories (4 and 8), rather than issues and information useful for general research. (The grab-bag nature of Internet searching is evident in the inclusion of the "Joseph Campell" article—the noted anthropologist's name is misspelled—in the "dropout" category.) Of the four remaining articles, we access the one that has no author: "Myth: The High school dropout rate is climbing." Here is part of what appears on the screen:

> Summary: Statistics by the U.S. Census show that the high school graduate rate has been increasing for many decades now, and for all sub-groups of the population. This has occurred at a time when public educators are spending more money on programs designed to keep students in school. Their success is a vindication of that policy. Argument: The claim that more and more American students are dropping out of high school is false. According to the U.S. Census, more young people are graduating from high school than ever before—a trend [sic] has continued for decades, and among all sub-groups of the population. In 1970, 75 percent of young people aged 25–29 had graduated from high school. By 1990, that had risen to 86 percent.

This information is followed by several tables, and the article concludes:

> The above numbers refute conservative rhetoric that spending more on public education resulted in worst outcomes . . . [Public educators'] success in reducing the dropout rate would indicate that this policy is effective and conservatives have no case for arguing otherwise.

Endnotes follow, citing the U.S. Bureau of the Census as the source of the charts.

While the statistical information might be useful, you need to know who's responsible for the document before you can safely cite the text. (The statistics could be verified by checking the Census Bureau reports.) Embedded in the document is a hyperlink to another Internet document that, when accessed, produces a name—WELCOME TO STEVE KANGAS' WEB PAGE—and a title—THE LONG FAQ ON LIBERALISM—and a listing of "myths" about education, the environment, etc., that reflect Mr. Kangas' interests. Here is his introduction:

> Greetings, devils and peaceniks. I'm a college student who lives in Santa Cruz, California, a tourist/university town overlooking Monterey Bay. Besides admiring the local scenery, I'm into politics, tournament-level chess, Santa Cruz's thriving coffee shops and bookstores, writing my Great American Novel, running children's chess clubs, and movies of all types (Hollywood and foreign, young and old).

Kangas tells us that he maintains this Web site as a clearinghouse for his interests, focusing right now on liberal politics. So far, this seems a dubious prospect as a source of authoritative information about dropouts, but, just in case, we click on the listing on the Web site menu labeled "resumé," which begins:

> ABOUT ME
> I was born at a relatively young age in the first year of "Camelot"—no, not King Arthur's reign in the 6th Century, but President Kennedy's in 1961. You could say that I was literally a child of the 60s, but love, peace and understanding had no chance to pervert my young mind, since my family was strictly Christian conservative.

Now that you've found out something about Kangas, does he have any claim to be cited in your essay? His statistics are secondhand, and he has no demonstrable expertise in the field; moreover, he has a political agenda that may color his interpretation of facts. Kangas may be an interesting person to chat with; he appears sincere and amusing; but, as a source for a research essay, he is far from reliable.

Let's go back, then, and, still at random, choose a second "top ten" title for examination: "High School Dropout Rates Decline Over Two Decades." This turns out to be a press release (with Melinda Kitchell as contact person) describing a report released today—June 17, 1997—by the Department of Education. The summary includes quotations from Robert Riley, the Secretary of Education, mixed together with a variety of statistics. Here's an excerpt:

> "Many dropouts say they left school because they were failing or just didn't like it," Riley said as he released Dropout Rates in the United States: 1993. "Some will come back and finish, but too many find themselves unemployed or stuck in a job with no future. If we are to meet the national goal of a 90 percent high school graduation rate, we must all do more to keep our children connected to school, to teach them the value of learning, and to keep them engaged in school by making schools places where challenging courses interest and expand young minds."

The statistics correlate dropout rates with income, ethnicity, and gender, and there is a brief reference to reasons for dropping out. Since some of this information might be useful supporting evidence in your essay, it's important to verify the source. The U.S. Government Printing Office is cited as the place to obtain a copy of the report, but there is also an embedded hyperlink to access the home page of the U.S. Department of Education, which provides opportunities to find more information. This second attempt at locating a source has produced acceptable, if limited information.

It is certainly possible to carry on research in this haphazard way, following one lead after another. But the frequent digressions, characteristic of the Internet, may make it hard for you to stay on track, especially if you're not yet sure of your thesis.

Using the Internet for research becomes especially problematic if you expect to get *all* your sources from the Internet. This hit-or-miss process requires a great deal of patience; you need persistence to investigate each source, discarding many sources for every one that you can use. Persistence may not be enough: many important sources publish their work only in traditional print forms; their absence from your essay may skew the coverage of your topic, making it less complete and less objective. Another concern is length. Many Web articles are the spatial equivalent of soundbites. Their authors don't engage in the kind of complex analysis and interpretation of ideas that requires slow and careful development.

Will using the Internet exclusively make a difference to your instructor? In "How the Web Destroys the Quality of Students' Research Papers," Professor David Rothenberg says that "it's easy to spot a research paper that is based primarily on information collected from the Web," partly because no books are included in the bibliography. Most disturbing to Professor Rothenberg is the mindlessness of the research process:

> You toss a query to the machine, wait a few minutes, and suddenly a lot of possible sources of information appear on your screen. Instead of books that you have to check out of the library, read carefully, understand, synthesize and then tactfully excerpt, these sources are quips, blips, pictures, and short summaries that may be downloaded magically to the dorm-room computer screen. Fabulous! How simple! The only problem is that a paper consisting of summaries of summaries is bound to be fragmented and superficial, and to demonstrate more of a random montage than an ability to sustain an argument through 10 to 15 double-spaced pages.

There are no shortcuts to thorough research. Use the Internet as you would any tool available to you, but try to resist its facile charms.

SELECTING SOURCES THAT WORK WELL TOGETHER

In Chapter 4, when you learned how to work with multiple sources, the process was simplified to make your assignments easier: the sources were all of the same kind, homogeneous, and therefore relatively easy to synthesize. The statements in each group all came from sources with roughly the same skills and experience, whose opinions were therefore comparable. But in research at the library, the sources that you find may have nothing at all in common but their subject.

Periodicals provide a clear example, for most are published for specific audiences with well-defined interests, reading habits, and (in some cases) social and political views. Since readership varies so greatly, articles on the same subject in two different periodicals are likely to vary widely in their point of view and development. An article on dropouts in a well-known women's magazine is likely to be reassuring and helpful, filled with concrete advice to parents. It will not have the same purpose, nor cite the same kinds of evidence, nor be expressed in the same kind of vocabulary as an article of comparable length published the same year in *Psychology Today*. And that, in turn, will probably not resemble a scholarly essay on dropouts in the *Journal of the American Psychological Association* or the *American Journal of Sociology*. An equivalent article in *Newsweek* or *Time* will be shorter and livelier, filled with vivid, concrete illustrations.

Because of these differences, these periodicals will not be equally valuable as evidence for your essay:

- Newsmagazines provide factual information.
- Periodicals like *Psychology Today* popularize ideas in the social sciences, presenting them in a readable form for a wide audience.
- Scholarly journals usually contain a depth of analysis and a breadth of research that makes them comprehensive and convincing.

On the other hand, articles in scholarly journals are often written in a dense style, with a vocabulary comprehensible only to someone familiar with the discipline. Someone writing a freshman essay on a general topic may find these articles difficult to read and understand. Books can be even more difficult to synthesize since they vary so greatly in length, purpose, and presentation.

Suppose that in researching your paper on high school dropouts you have found three very different sources:

- The first is exclusively about dropouts; chapter after chapter is filled with statistical studies and case histories presented in dense detail and in an abstract language that requires concentration to absorb.
- The second book is a comprehensive study of decision-making in education; there is one lengthy chapter about the reasons why students may choose to drop out.
- The third source is a stirring speech, directed at educators and businesspeople, with one section devoted to the importance of making students stay in school. The issue is presented broadly and rhetorically.

Here are the excerpts from these three sources:

1. At the secondary school level the question of the impact of increased time requirements on student achievement has been examined through a series of

studies regarding the relationship between time spent on homework, a readily apprehensible form of student effort, and achievement. Coleman, Hoffer, and Kilgore, using data from the nationally representative sample of students in the High School and Beyond Survey found that differences in the time spent on homework by high school students accounted for a small but consistent part of the differences in achievement test scores between public and private sector schools. Using this same data set, Keith showed that the amount of time that students spent on homework contributed significantly and positively to their grades. A meta-analysis of 15 empirical studies of the relationship of time spent on homework to learning found a modest, positive effect of homework on learning.

> EDWARD L. MCDILL, GARY NATRIELLO, and
> AARON M. PALLAS, "A Population at Risk: Potential
> Consequences of Tougher School Standards for Student
> Dropouts," from *School Dropouts: Patterns and Policies*

2. There is indeed quite a high correlation between failure at school and the probability of dropping out. . . . (In one of the surveys analyzed here, 71 percent of the dropouts had at least one failure as opposed to an average of 44 percent over the whole sample.) There are, however, certain considerations which prevent one from concluding that dropping out is not a decision at all. First there is the fact that the correlation between repeating and dropping out is far from perfect and that more than one-quarter of those who left during high school had never been kept down. Moreover, only half of them declared that they had left as consequence of a failure.

> DIEGO GAMBETTA, from *Were They Pushed or Did They Jump:*
> *Individual Decision Mechanisms in Education*

3. In my parents' day, a child of thirteen more often than not would leave school to help support the family during the hard times of the "Great Depression." Getting a high school education ran a distant second to helping the family survive.

Today, I believe many students—and even some bitter educators—view dropping out as a viable alternative to completing school. The pressure to drop out isn't always economic any more. After all, there are many avenues of public assistance. . . .

As a citizen, I'm appalled that we'll waste the potential of so many of our young people. As a business leader, I'm shocked. We have to rely on the public schools to produce the people who will lead our businesses and our society. There are no "spare" people. Society needs us all.

> ANTON J. CAMPANELLA,
> from "Public Education Is Turning the Corner"

Can these three sources be integrated into the same essay? All three are relevant to the topic, and each may be interesting and useful in itself. But the difference in *depth* and *level of detail* among them is so great that it is hard to see how the three can be used together in a single essay. And, indeed, the only thing that you should not do is to plunk down excerpts from these three sources side by side, in adjoining sentences. If they are to be integrated at all, you must first recognize and then communicate to your reader that *the three sources are not equivalent or even similar.*

This does not mean that all of your sources should cover the same range of ideas, be roughly the same length, and employ the same vocabulary and depth of evidence. And certainly *you should avoid using a single book or journal as the sole source of supporting evidence for your essay.* Working with materials of the same order of difficulty may be convenient, but developing a balanced bibliography offering a variety of approaches to your topic is more important. The key is to become sensitive to the *kinds of sources* that you find in your research. As you glance through an article or a chapter in a book, ask yourself:

- Is the content primarily theoretical or practical?

- How often does the author offer evidence to support conclusions? What kind of evidence? Is it documented?

- Does the author's thesis depend on a series of broad propositions, linked together into an argument?

- What is the scope of the work?

- Is the focus narrow, with the entire work centered around one person's experience? Or does it sum up the work of others?

Finally, be alert to the kind of language that the author is using and make mental or written notes about its difficulty and your ability to understand it.

Guidelines for Choosing Sources

As you choose sources for your essay, consider the following:

- the author's background and qualifications to write on that subject;

- the date of the work, whether it is a primary or secondary source, and (if secondary) whether its information is still timely;

- the scope of the work and the extent to which it deals with your topic;

- the depth of detail, the amount and kind of evidence presented, citation and documentation of sources, and the level of analysis and theory;

- the degree to which you understand and feel comfortable with the author's language and style; and

- the way in which possible sources could be used together in your essay.

Understanding the differences among your sources will help you to determine your *research priorities.* You would not begin your research by taking notes from the book on dropouts; much of its contents would be irrelevant to your eventual thesis. Instead, you might begin with the single comprehensive chapter from the second source to give you an overview of the subject and help you to establish your own approach to the topic and your thesis. Once you have a list of specific points that you want to develop, you may not need to read every chapter of the first source; you could look up items of interest in the table of contents and the index. And don't forget the third work; the speech might provide you with a broader understanding of your topic, as well as provide you with an excellent quotation or two.

INTEGRATING YOUR SELECTED SOURCES

Once you have become familiar with your main sources, their differences, and their relative usefulness, how do you integrate them into your essay? You may simply decide to exclude those that do not mesh easily with the others. You may not want to confuse your reader by moving back and forth from extremely broad statements of policy to detailed citations of case studies or statistical evidence, especially if the different sources are expressed in a completely different vocabulary and style. The following excerpt comes from a paper in which the three sources on dropouts are lumped together through quotation. It's not clear that the writer understood the purpose of the "correlation" presented in Excerpt 1 or the relationship between higher academic standards and the decision to drop out. The writer tries to disguise this by working very hard on the transitions between quotations, leaving the reader to figure out what it all means. The transitional phrase "on the other hand" is not really contrasting anything.

> Educators find it difficult to solve the problem of dropouts. Diego Gambetta points out the "high correlation between failure at school and the probability of dropping out." On the other hand, higher standards, such as giving students more homework, can help students to achieve, not fail: "A meta-analysis of 15 empirical studies of the relationship of time spent on homework to learning found a modest, positive effect of homework on learning." It is important for efforts to be made to keep students in school because, as Anton Campanella has said, "we have to rely on the public schools to produce the people who will lead our businesses and society."

Even if you use your own style to integrate your sources through paraphrase, it would still be difficult to combine these three sources in a single paragraph. *In a short essay of less than ten pages, you would be wise to limit your sources to those that blend well together because they are of the same order of difficulty.* The writers you cite do not have to agree with each other; rather, their scope and approach should be roughly similar.

For a short essay, you would have to decide in the early stages of your research which kind of source would help develop your thesis. How sophisticated is your argument? Does it require support from complex case studies? If you intend to prove that dropouts come from a specific kind of family environment, you will probably need to cite such scholarly sources as the dropout book. On the other hand, you might want to argue that the dropout rate can be linked to a general decline in standards of education, drawing to some extent on your own high school experience. This thesis would be more "popular" in its approach to the subject and would require less rigorous sources. Remember that *a popularization is a simplification of a difficult subject; popular essays could not exist without the evidence found in longer and more complex works.* In a sense, a college research essay has to be "popular" since it is intended to be evidence of the student's understanding of the subject, rather than a contribution to scholarly knowledge.

In deciding whether or not to use the popular approach, remember to consider the level of your course. In an *introductory course,* you are expected only to grasp the broad concepts that are basic to the discipline; so your instructor will probably not expect you to go out of your depth in hunting scholarly sources for your essay. On the other hand, in an *advanced course,* you are preparing to do your own research; and so you need to demonstrate your understanding of the work of others as well as the methods that are commonly used in that field. In an advanced course, the popular approach can be regarded as superficial.

In a longer essay of ten pages or more, you should have much less trouble blending ill-assorted sources. With the opportunity for leisurely development, you can position each source in the place where it is most appropriate and where it will have the most convincing effect. Thus, for the dropout essay the quotations that you select from the speech might be placed in the introduction or conclusion of your essay; the theories relating students' decisions to drop out could be included in your preliminary presentation of your argument; and the detailed evidence of the longest source could be cited in support of your own ideas or as part of your survey of the work already done in this field. In short, these very different sources can be used together successfully, provided that you do not give your reader the impression that they are interchangeable in their usefulness. Unfortunately, a single paragraph cannot be included here to demonstrate the successful incorporation of the three excerpts on pp. 285–286 into a research essay; you would need to read the entire paper to see how each of the three sources was deployed.

Finally, in your search for a well-balanced bibliography, include only what you yourself understand. By all means, consult your instructor or librarian, or the staff of the writing center on your campus, to clarify the meaning of difficult sources that nevertheless seem important enough to include in your essay. However, *if you cite sources whose writing makes no sense to you, no matter how eminent and qualified these authorities may be, your essay will be a failure; for you will be pretending a mastery of the subject that you do not actually have.*

EXERCISE 20: CHOOSING SOURCES

Examine the following preliminary bibliography of articles for a research essay on the broad topic of *education*.

A. Make up two *narrow* topics, one focused on an issue in education that is presently being debated, the other suggesting a more historical approach that might include articles published during the last few decades. (Your instructor may ask the entire class to work on the same two topics.)

B. Carefully read the preliminary bibliography, and consider the probable contents of each article, as suggested by the *title*; the *kind of periodical* it appears in; the *length*; and the *date* of publication. What can you conclude about each article?

C. Determine your research priorities for each of your two topics by choosing a list of five articles that you believe ought to be located and consulted first. Record your two lists, and be prepared to explain your choices.

Abbott, John. "21st-Century Learning: Beyond Schools." *The Education Digest* 63 (Oct. 1997): 11–15.

Akande, B. "Six Ways to Save Our Schools." *USA Today* 122 Nov. 1993: 62–63.

"America's Schools: A Panorama of Excellence." *Today's Education* 1984–1985 Annual: 3–35.

"Are High-School Standards Too Low?" *Ladies Home Journal* Sept. 1956: 86–88.

"Are Schools Changing Too Much Too Fast?" *Changing Times* Sept. 1966: 6–10.

"Back to Basics in the Schoolhouse." *Readers Digest* Feb. 1975: 149–52.

Bailey, S. K. "Educational Planning: Purposes and Promise." *Public Administration Review* May 1971: 345–52.

Barber, B. R. "America Skips School." *Harper's* Nov. 1993: 39–46.

Bracey, G. W. "The 'Education Crisis': More Rhetoric than Reality." *The Education Digest* 57 (Fall 1992): 39–42.

Bracey, Gerald W. "75 Years of Elementary Education." *The Education Digest* 61 (Mar. 1996): 26–29.

Broudy, H. S. "Demand for Accountability: Can Society Exercise Control over Education?" *Education and Urban Society* Feb. 1977: 235–50.

Buckley, William F. "Disassembling Education." *National Review* 6 Mar. 1995: 78–79.

Burris, V. "Social and Political Consequences of Overeducation." *American Sociology Review* Aug. 1983: 454–67.

Clinchy, Evans. "Reforming American Education from the Bottom to the Top: Escaping Academic Captivity." *Phi Delta Kappan* Dec. 1996: 268–71.

Cuban, L. "Better Teaching or 'Just the Facts Ma'am'? [Flaws in Reform Agenda]." *The Education Digest* 58 (Spring 1992): 40–42.

Drucker, P. F. "How Schools Must Change." *Psychology Today* May 1989: 18–20.

Finn, Chester E., and Diane Ravitch. "Is Educational Reform a Failure?" *USA Today* 125 (Nov. 1996): 22–24.

Finnan, Christine, and Wendy Hopfenberg. "Accomplishing School Change." *Journal for a Just and Caring Education* 3.4 (Oct. 1997): 480–93.

Forbes, Steve. "Rays of Educational Sunshine." *Forbes* 13 Oct. 1997: 27–28.

Handl, J. "Educational Chances and Occupational Attitudes of Women: A Sociohistorical Analysis." *Journal of Social History* 17 (Spring 1984): 463–87.

Hechinger, Grace, and Fred M. Hechinger. "Report Card on Education." *Ladies Home Journal* Sept. 1985: 96.

Hershey, J. A. "How Schools Sabotage a Creative Work Force." *Business Week* 13 (July 1987): 16.

Hodgkinson, H. L. "Pinpointing the Failures in American Education." *The Education Digest* 57 (Fall 1992): 36–38.

Holcomb, J. H. "Can We—Should We Save the Public Schools?" *American Educator* June 1983: 34–37.

"Johnny Is Doing a Lot Better." *Life* Apr. 1961: 32.

Kirst, M. W. "How to Improve Schools without Spending Money." *Phi Delta Kappan* Sept. 1982: 6–8.

Klitgaard, R. E., and G. R. Hall. "Are There Unusually Effective Schools?" *Journal of Human Resources* 10 (Winter 1975): 90–106.

Lanier, H. B., and J. Byrne. "How High School Students View Women: The Relationship Between Perceived Attractiveness, Occupation, and Education." *Sex Roles* 7 (1981): 145–48.

Leonard, G. E. "The Great School Reform Hoax." *Esquire* Apr. 1984: 47–52.

Liazos, A. "School Alienation and Delinquency." *Crime and Delinquency* July 1978: 355–70.

Lieberman, M. "Why School Reform Isn't Working." *Fortune* 17 February 1986: 135–36.

Linton, C. D. "In Defense of a Liberal Arts Education." *Christianity Today* May 1974: 5–8.

"Low Marks for U.S. Education." *Saturday Evening Post* 20 Oct. 1962: 96.

Morris, J. P. "Principles of Education for a Free Society." *Bulletin of the National Association of Secondary School Principals* Dec. 1954: 99–100.

Petrie, M. A. "Education Without Schools." *Nation* 15 November 1971: 505–6.

Pipho, C. "Gridlock on the Road to Reform." *Phi Delta Kappan* June 1993: 750–51.

Poplin, M., and J. Weeres. "Listening at the Learner's Level: Voices from Inside the Schoolhouse." *The Education Digest* 59 (Spring 1993): 9–13.

Riesman, D. "Quixotic Ideas for Education Reform." *Society* Mar./Apr. 1993: 17–24.

Rossides, D. W. "What Is the Purpose of Education? The Worthless Debate Continues." *Change* Apr. 1984: 14–21.

Scully, M. A. "Some Hope for the Schools." *National Review* 9 March 1984: 47.

Silber, J. R. "Need for Elite Education." *Harper's* June 1977: 22–24.

Soder, Roger. "American Education: Facing Up to Unspoken Assumptions." *Daedalus* 124 (Fall 1995): 163–67.

Spock, B. "Coercion in the Classroom Won't Work." *Atlantic* Apr. 1984: 28–31.

Stafford, Tim. "Helping Johnny Be Good." *Christianity Today* Sept. 1995: 34–39.

Steller, Arthur. "Every Child, Every School: Success for All." *Educational Leadership* 55.2 (Oct. 1997): 88.

Szabo, J. C. "'Schools for the 21st Century' [G. Bush's Address on America 2000 Plan, January 1992]." *Nation's Business* 80 (Fall 1992): 22.

Tevis, C. "Why Local Schools Aren't Good Enough." *Successful Farming* Dec. 1986: 18N–18O.

Weiss, Michael J. "America's Best Elementary Schools." *Redbook* April 1995: 55–58.

"Why Our Schools Went Wrong." *Changing Times* May 1978: 25–28.

EXERCISE 21: EVALUATING SOURCES

Each of the following passages has been extracted from a longer article or book on the general subject of *boxing*. Most of these excerpts deal specifically with the dangers of the sport and the arguments for and against banning it.

A. Carefully examine the distinctive way in which each passage presents its information, noting especially:

- the amount and kind of evidence that is cited
- the expectations of the reader's knowledge and understanding
- the relative emphasis on generalizations and abstract thinking
- the characteristic tone and vocabulary
- the date of publication.

B. Take into consideration what you may already know about these publications and the audience for each. Then decide how—or whether—you would use these sources together in a single research essay exploring whether boxing should be banned.

C. Write a thesis for such an essay, and then decide which sources you would definitely use in writing your essay. Be prepared to justify your choice.

1. The action of one human striking another with the fists must date to about the time humans began to walk on two feet. Aggressive behavior is certainly a normal human trait. Defending oneself using any method available is at the top of Maslov's hierarchy, namely, survival. The use of a violent act to entertain others vicariously is also thousands of years old. Gladiatorial events, Christians being fed to lions, gunfights in the old American West, and other such events have been legendary. From time to time, however, society looks at its behavior in terms of both the effects on individual participants and the moral and ethical aspects of the events affecting society as a whole. Thus, Christians are no longer fed to lions, and gladiatorial combat, sword duels to the death, cockfights, dogfights, and gunfights have been outlawed, and, to some extent do not occur.

   Over many decades, boxing has come under public scrutiny, which has led to numerous reforms. In 1743, Broughton's rule put the testes off limits. In 1838, new rules for the London prize ring eliminated holding, butting, gouging, kicking, and the wearing of shoes with improper spikes. In 1866, the Marquis of Queensberry rules instituted gloves in all bouts and a 10-second count after a knockdown, and for the first time fighters were matched by weight. Such actions as limiting the number and length of rounds, having a referee with power, mandating medical evaluations, establishing athletic commissions, and requiring the wearing of mouthpieces have represented major efforts at reform.

On January 14, 1983, the *Journal of the American Medical Association* got the modern reform movement going with an Editorial entitled "Boxing Should Be Banned in Civilized Countries." We stated that "the principal purpose of a boxing match is for one opponent to render the other injured, defenseless, incapacitated, unconscious." We pointed out that boxing was wrong medically because of the very high frequency of brain damage being experienced by boxers and that it was wrong morally because a boxer could win by intentionally damaging the brain of an opponent. Thus, we believe that there are many excellent reasons why both professional and amateur boxing as we know them should be banned. The American Medical Association (AMA) has held a similar position since 1984, and it has been reaffirmed several times.

3

> Georgy Lundberg, from "Blunt Force Violence in
> America—Shades of Gray or Red," *The Journal of the
> American Medical Association* (1996)

2. Ego is driving a point through to a conclusion you are obliged to reach without knowing too much about the ground you cross between. You suffer for a larger point. Every good prizefighter must have a large ego, then, because he is trying to demolish a man he doesn't know too much about, he is unfeeling—which is the ground floor of ego; and he is full of techniques—which are the wings of ego. What separates the noble ego of the prizefighters from the lesser ego of authors is that the fighter goes through experiences in the ring that are occasionally immense, incommunicable except to fighters who have been as good, or to women who have gone through every minute of an anguish-filled birth, experiences that are finally mysterious. Like men who climb mountains, it is an exercise of ego which becomes like soul—just as technology may have begun to have transcended itself when we reached to the moon. So, two great fighters in a great fight travel down subterranean rivers of exhaustion and cross mountain peaks of agony, stare at the light of their own death in the eye of the man they are fighting, travel into the crossroads of the most excruciating choice of karma as they get up from the floor against all the appeal of the sweet swooning catacombs of oblivion—it is just that we do not see them this way, because they are not primarily men of words, and this is the century of words, numbers and symbols. Enough.

1

> Norman Mailer, from "King of the Hill," *Existential
> Errands* (1975), reprinted in *Reading the Fights* (1988)

3. There were just forty seconds of the twelfth round left when the horror story started to take shape. Owen was trying to press in on Pintor near the ropes, failed to prevent that deadly space from developing again and was dropped on his knees by a short right. After rising at three and taking another mandatory count, he was moved by the action to the other side of the ring and it was there that a ferocious right hook threw him on to his back. He was unconscious before he hit the canvas and his relaxed neck muscles allowed his head to thud against the boards. Dai Gardiner and the boxer's father were in the ring long before the count could be completed and they were quickly joined by Dr. Schwartz, who called for oxygen. Perhaps the oxygen might have come rather more swiftly than it did but only if it had been on hand at the ringside. Obviously that would be a sensible precaution, just as it might be sensible to have a stretcher immediately available. It is no easy job to bring such equipment through the jostling mass of spectators at an arena like the Auditorium, where Pintor's supporters were mainly concerned about cheering its arrival as a symbol of how comprehensive their man's victory had been. The outward journey to the dressing room, with poor Johnny Owen deep in a sinister unconsciousness, was no simpler and the indifference of many among the crowd was emphasized when one of the stretcher bearers had his pocket picked.

There have been complaints in some quarters about the delay in providing an ambulance but, in the circumstances, these may be difficult to justify. Dr. Ferdie Pacheco, who was for years Muhammad Ali's doctor and is now a boxing consultant with NBC in the United States, insists that the company lay on an ambulance wherever they cover fights, but no such arrangements exist at the Auditorium and the experienced paramedics of the Los Angeles Fire Department made good time once they received the emergency call. Certainly it was grief and not blame that was occupying the sick boy's father as he stood weeping in the corridor of the California Hospital, a mile from the scene of the knockout. A few hours before, I had sat by the swimming pool at their motel in downtown Los Angeles and listened to them joke about the calls Johnny's mother had been making from Merthyr Tydfil on the telephone they had recently installed. The call that was made to Mrs. Owen from the waiting room of the California Hospital shortly before 7 A.M. Saturday, Merthyr time (11 P.M. Friday in Los Angeles) had a painfully different tone. It was made by Byron Board, a publican and close friend of the family, and he found her already in tears because she had heard that Johnny had been knocked out. The nightmare that had been threatening her for years had become reality.

She can scarcely avoid being bitter against boxing now and many who have not suffered such personal agony because of the hardest of sports will be asking once again if the game is worth the candle. Quite a few of us who have been involved with it most of our lives share the doubts. But our reactions are bound to be complicated by the knowledge that it was boxing that gave Johnny Owen his one positive means of self-expression. Outside the ring he was an inaudible and almost invisible personality. Inside, he became astonishingly positive and self-assured. He seemed to be more at home there than anywhere else. It is his tragedy that he found himself articulate in such a dangerous language.

(The doctors' struggle to rescue Johnny Owen from deep coma proved to be   4
hopeless and he died in the first week of November 1980. His body was brought home to be buried in Merthyr Tydfil.)

> HUGH MCILVANNEY, from "Onward Virgin Soldier," *McIlvanney*
> *on Boxing* (1982), reprinted in *Reading the Fights* (1988)

4. Boxing's reputation is under fierce assault once more: Scottish bantamweight   1
James Murray was last night declared "clinically dead" after a title fight that ended in a riot.

The twin spectres haunting the sport—grave injury and crowd misbehavior—   2
came together in Glasgow late on Friday night, after Murray was knocked out in the 12th and final round of his title challenge to fellow Scot Drew Docherty.

While Murray was unconscious and being treated inside the ring, hooligans   3
were throwing bottles and chairs at commentators and spectators, who dived under tables or fled in terror.

The crowd violence, in the ballroom of Glasgow's Hospitality Inn hotel, where   4
the match followed a dinner, is thought to have hampered Murray's exit to the hospital, although both police and hospital authorities have denied that the rioting had worsened his condition. "As far as we are concerned, we received Mr Murray expeditely," said a spokesman for Glasgow's Southern General Hospital.

Surgeons carried out a two-hour emergency operation to remove a blood   5
clot from the brain of Murray, 25. Doctors last night told his family that he was "clinically dead," according to Murray's manager, Alex Morrison. "All I know is that there is virtually no hope," he said. . . .

The British Medical Association (BMA) has been trying since 1982 to outlaw   6
boxing. Yesterday a BMA spokeswoman asked: "How many more brain-damaged boxers do there have to be before boxing is banned?"

Yesterday one of boxing's leading figures seemed close to agreeing. The pro-   7
moter Frank Warren said it was "very difficult to justify" the sport in the light of Murray's injuries. "I could not look Jim's father and mother in the eye and say the sport should go on, but it is a very emotive subject at times like this, so we should all give it a few days," he said.

More than 500 boxers have died since the Queensberry Rules were intro-   8
duced in 1884.

> JOHN MCKIE, from "Fresh call for ban on boxing as fighter
> collapses," http://www.virgin.net/bv/havana/resources/
> sport/athlete/features/1995101500.html (1995)

5. If boxers were boxing's only victims, railing against it wouldn't be worth the trou-   1
ble. They're big boys, after all. The real tragedy is all the inner-city teenagers who gather to watch the fights on closed-circuit TV. Many of them were born tethered to a values system that bodes ill for economic success, and their worship of

boxers worsens the odds. Much has been said about the unhealthy fact that so few black role models are professors and lawyers, and so many are athletes. Of all professional athletes, none are less worthy of emulation than boxers. Boxers get rich without an education. They achieve status through violence. Their victories involve no teamwork. And they indulge in ritual self-promotion. Even Tyson—fairly mild-mannered, as these guys go—declared himself "the toughest man on the planet." If there's one thing worse for poor kids than wanting to be the toughest man on the planet, it's wanting to boast about it. Violent egomania just isn't a prescription for success in a post-industrial economy. (To say nothing of the more immediate effects of emulation. According to David Phillips, a sociologist at the University of California, homicides increase appreciably after every nationally broadcast heavyweight championship fight.)

There's no denying that boxing has its up side. If the sport didn't exist, a few hardworking millionaires, like Tyson, would be spending their lives washing dishes. On the other hand, thousands of poor kids wouldn't be enticed into dropping out of school to hang around dingy gyms and get pummeled for nickels and dimes. And hundreds of thousands of young, poor blacks and Hispanics would be spared the burden of idols like James ("Bonecrusher") Smith, Hector ("Macho") Camacho, and Adilson ("Maguila Gorilla") Rodrigues.

The standard argument against banning boxing is libertarian: people should be allowed to do whatever they want—pay people to punch each other, get paid to get punched, etc. But even in capitalist America there are circumstances under which commerce can rightly be restrained. Boxing's apologists sound quite principled when they defend Muhammed Ali's right to get his brains scrambled, but few of them would defend a drug addict's right to do the same. The question is whether boxing is pernicious enough to join drug use, prostitution, and several other "victimless" pastimes deemed illegal. It's a tough call, but we vote yes.

from "Ban Boxing," Editorial. *The New Republic* (1988)

6. I have no difficulty justifying boxing as a sport because I have never thought of it as a sport.

There is nothing fundamentally playful about it; nothing that seems to belong to daylight, to pleasure. At its moments of greatest intensity it seems to contain so complete and so powerful an image of life—life's beauty, vulnerability, despair, incalculable and often self-destructive courage—that boxing *is* life, and hardly a mere game. During a superior boxing match (Ali-Frazier I, for instance) we are deeply moved by the body's communion with itself by way of another's intransigent flesh. The body's dialogue with its shadow-self—or Death. Baseball, football, basketball—these quintessentially American pastimes are recognizably sports because they involve play: they are games. One *plays* football, one doesn't *play* boxing.

Observing team sports, teams of adult men, one sees how men are children in the most felicitous sense of the word. But boxing in its elemental ferocity cannot be assimilated into childhood. (Though very young men box, even professionally, and many world champions began boxing in their early or mid-teens. By the time he was sixteen Jack Dempsey, rootless and adrift in the West, was fighting for small sums of money in unrefereed saloon fights in which—in the natural course of things—he might have been killed.) Spectators at public games derive much of their pleasure from reliving the communal emotions of child-hood but spectators at boxing matches relive the murderous infancy of the race. Hence, the occasional savagery of boxing crowds—the crowd, largely Hispanic, that cheered as the Welshman Johnny Owen was pounded into insensibility by the Mexican bantamweight champion Lupe Pintor, for instance—and the excite-ment when a man begins to seriously bleed. . . .

Considered in the abstract the boxing ring is an altar of sorts, one of those legendary spaces where the laws of a nation are suspended: inside the ropes, during an officially regulated three-minute round, a man may be killed at his op-ponent's hands but he cannot be legally murdered. Boxing inhabits a sacred space predating civilization; or, to use D. H. Lawrence's phrase, before God was love. If it suggests a savage ceremony or a rite of atonement it also suggests the futil-ity of such gestures. For what possible atonement is the fight waged if it must shortly be waged again . . . and again? The boxing match is the very image, the more terrifying for being so stylized, of mankind's collective aggression; its ongo-ing historical madness.

JOYCE CAROL OATES, from *On Boxing* (1987)

7. Since 1950 more than 2500 studies have attempted to discover whether mass media violence triggers additional aggressive behavior (Comstock et al., 1978; Murray and Kippax, 1979; Roberts and Bachen, 1981; National Institutes of Men-tal Health, 1982). With few exceptions (reviewed in Phillips, 1982b), researchers have studied aggression *in the laboratory*, and there is consensus that media vio-lence can trigger additional aggression in the laboratory setting. However, policy makers, unlike researchers, have been primarily concerned with violence *outside* the laboratory, particularly with serious, fatal violence like homicide. Studies of media effects on homicide have been extremely rare and there is no systematic evidence to date indicating that mass media violence elicits additional murders.[1] As Andison has noted (1980:564), we do not know whether "there are deaths and violence occurring in society today because of what is being shown on the TV screen."

This paper presents what may be the first systematic evidence suggesting that some homicides are indeed triggered by a type of mass media violence. The cur-rent study builds on earlier research (Phillips, 1974, 1977, 1978, 1979, 1980, 1982a) which showed that: (1) U.S. suicides increase after publicized suicide sto-ries. This finding has been replicated with American (Bollen and Phillips, 1982) and Dutch (Ganzeboom and de Haan, 1982) data. (2) The more publicity given to the suicide story, the more suicides rise thereafter. (3) The rise occurs mainly in the geographic area where the suicide story is publicized. . . .

In reviewing the literature on media effects, Comstock (1977) concluded that violent stories with the following characteristics were most likely to elicit aggression: When the violence in the story is presented as (1) rewarded, (2) exciting, (3) real, and (4) justified; when the perpetrator of the violence is (5) not criticized for his behavior and is presented as (6) intending to injure his victim.[2]

One type of story that meets all of these criteria is the heavyweight prize fight, which is almost universally presented as highly rewarded, exciting, real, and justified. Furthermore, the participants are not criticized for their aggressive behavior and are presented as trying to injure each other.

In a well-known series of studies, Berkowitz and various associates (1963, 1966, 1967, 1973) examined the impact of a filmed prize fight in the laboratory. They found that angered laboratory subjects behaved more aggressively after seeing a filmed prize fight scene. In contrast, angered laboratory subjects exposed to a track meet film displayed a significantly lower level of aggression.

In sum, the heavyweight prize match is a promising research site because (1) it meets Comstock's criteria for stories most likely to elicit aggression, and (2) it is known to elicit aggression in the laboratory.

DAVID P. PHILLIPS, from "The Impact of Mass Media Violence
on U.S. Homicides," *American Sociological Review* (1983)

8. Even as boxing exploits, it also liberates and, like most sports, it has an aesthetic quality which has intrinsic appeal to those who step into the ring. In this regard it is mistaken to view boxing as a straightforward example of exploited wage labor. Boxers take up the sport and stay involved because, first and foremost, they enjoy it as an athletic experience and, secondly, because it gives them status within the ghetto and, if they are very successful, a semblance of respectability in the wider society. Interview managers, trainers and young boxers anywhere in the world, ask them to justify boxing and, whatever the language, the message will be the same: boxing is not just a sport, it is a savior of the oppressed and a theatre of their dreams. Colin McMillan (1991), former British featherweight champion, speaks for most boxers when he claims that:

> In a world cloaked in prejudice, the ring is the one place where all men are equal . . . to us pugilists the boxing arena is a place where we can raise our self esteem; where the short can stand tall, the weak become strong, and the shy become bold. It is a place to fulfil one's dreams, aim for the stars, and better one's future.

It is possible to interpret this and the many statements like it emanating from the boxing fraternity as evidence that boxing is a site for subcultural resistance against political and economic oppression and discrimination. In the 1970s, there were a significant number of theorists who focused on subcultures as sites for reaction against an imposed social order and the dominant value system (Hall and Jefferson, 1975; Robins and Cohen, 1978; Willis, 1978; Corrigan, 1979). According to this school of thought, subcultures did not just appear and languish in the cracks of society; rather, they were produced by structured inequalities and cohered around patterns of behavior and styles which, at least at a local level, enabled members to appear to be fighting back. However, it has been pointed out that this new wave of subculture theory failed to account for the ephemeral and transient nature of most subcultures and, perhaps more significantly, underestimated the extent to which subcultures which have the appearance of resistance, like, for instance, punk rock, are incorporated into dominant cultural forms (Brake, 1980).

In this respect boxing occupies an ambivalent position. Boxing clubs do offer 2 at least temporary sanctuary from the worst excesses of ghetto life, and a prolonged commitment to the sport often keeps "at-risk" young males on the straight and narrow. For the small minority, prolonged engagement within the subculture can lead to a successful professional career and economic, if not social, mobility. In short, it is possible to view boxing as a positively sanctioned mechanism (at least for the time being) through which young men in the ghetto, with few other opportunities, can fight back against the structures which define the poverty of their existence. It is hard for anybody who has spent time in the modern ghetto not to conclude that, given what else is on offer, boxing is an extremely positive option for the young men who have to live there.

However, a note of caution must be included. When questioned, none of the 3 professional boxers whom I met in the course of this study were eager to have any of their children embark on a career in the ring. For them boxing was the best way to exchange their 'body capital' for a livelihood, but they wanted better futures for their children. Moreover, as we have seen, even though boxing may be interpreted by fighters themselves as a form of resistance against layers of social, political and economic disadvantage, it is, nonetheless, an extremely exploitative medium. Furthermore, while boxing draws heavily on the working-class experience for participants and followers, it is a mistake to interpret the ring as a forum for ritualized class struggle against bourgeois hegemony. If anything, given the rational and proselytizing value system which characterizes this subculture worldwide, boxing supports rather than detracts from established society.

JOHN SUGDEN, from *Boxing and Society* (1996)

EVALUATING ELEVEN SOURCES ABOUT ERNEST HEMINGWAY

Assume that you are gathering information for an essay about *Ernest Hemingway's life in Paris in 1924 and 1925*. From your introductory reading, you have already become familiar with some of the basic facts. You know that the novelist Hemingway and his wife, Hadley, traveled to Paris with their infant son,

Bumby; that the Hemingways had very little money; that they associated with many of the literary figures who lived in Paris at the time; that they took occasional trips to Spain for the bull-running and to Austria for the skiing; and that Hemingway was working on a novel called *The Sun Also Rises.* Now, through research, you intend to fill in the details that will enable you to construct a portrait of Hemingway and his Paris experiences. You have selected a preliminary bibliography of eleven sources. Here is the *annotated preliminary bibliography;* the comments are based on a rapid examination of each source and are intended for your own use in completing research and organizing the essay.

Baker, Carlos. *Hemingway: A Life Story.* New York: Scribner's, 1969. 563 pages of biography, with 100 pages of footnotes. Everything seems to be here, presented in great detail.

Donaldson, Scott. *Hemingway: By Force of Will.* New York: Viking, 1977. The material isn't organized chronologically; instead, the chapters are thematic, with titles like "Money," "Sex," and "War." Episodes from Hemingway's life are presented within each chapter. The introduction calls this "a mosaic of [Hemingway's] mind and personality." Lots of footnotes.

Griffin, Peter. *Less Than a Treason: Hemingway in Paris.* New York: Oxford UP, 1990. Part of a multivolume biography. Covers Hemingway's life from 1921–1927, exclusively. Griffin says in the preface that his goal is not to "analyze this well examined life" but "to recreate it." Reads like a novel. A little bit choppy and anecdotal, and documentation format is unwieldy. Should probably be cautious about Griffin's preoccupation with EH's stories as autobiographical/psychological documents, but could be useful for speculations on connections between personal life and work.

Gurko, Leo. *Ernest Hemingway and the Pursuit of Heroism.* New York: Crowell, 1968. This book is part of a series called "Twentieth-Century American Writers": a brief introduction to the man and his work. After fifty pages of straight biography, Gurko discusses Hemingway's writing, novel by novel. There's an index and a short bibliography, but no notes. The biographical part is clear and easy to read, but it sounds too much like a summary.

Hemingway, Ernest. *A Moveable Feast.* New York: Scribner's, 1964. This is Hemingway's own version of his life in Paris. It sounds authentic, but there's also a very strongly nostalgic tone, so I'm not sure how trustworthy it is.

Hemingway in Paris. Home page. 13 Oct. 1997 <http://204.122.127.50/WSHS/Paris/HTM/>. Three photos of the Hemingways' apartment, with brief comments.

Hemingway, Leicester. *My Brother, Ernest Hemingway.* Cleveland: World, 1962. It doesn't sound as if the family was very close. For 1924–1925, he's using information from Ernest's letters (as well as commonly known facts). The book reads like a thirdhand report, very remote; but L. H. sounds honest, not as if he were making up things that he doesn't know about.

Hotchner, A. E. *Papa Hemingway.* New York: Random House, 1955. This book is called a "personal memoir." Hotchner met Hemingway in 1948, and evidently hero-worshiped him. Hemingway rambled on about his past, and Hotchner tape-recorded much of it. The book is their dialogue (mostly Hemingway's monologue). No index or bibliography. Hotchner's adoring tone is annoying, and the material resembles that of *A Moveable Feast,* which is better written.

Meyers, Jeffrey. *Hemingway: A Biography.* New York: Harper, 1985. 572 pages of bio. Includes several maps, and two chronologies: illnesses and accidents, and travel. Book organized chronologically, with every year accounted for, according to table of contents. Well documented, and seems less gossipy than Griffin.

Reynolds, Michael. *Hemingway: The Paris Years.* Cambridge, Mass.: Blackwell, 1989. Second of three-volume biography. Includes a chronology covering December 1921–February 1926, five very basic outline maps ("Hemingway's Europe 1922–26," "France," "Switzerland," "Italy," and "Key points for Hemingway's several trips through France and Spain"). Chapters grouped into sections by single years, from "Part One: 1922," to "Part Four: 1925."

Sokoloff, Alice Hunt. *Hadley, the First Mrs. Hemingway.* New York: Dodd, 1973. This is the Paris experience from Hadley's point of view, most of it taken from her recollections and from the standard biographies. (Baker is acknowledged.) It's a very slight book—102 pages—but there's an index and footnotes, citing letters and interviews that some of the other biographers might not have been able to use.

Examining the Sources

The preliminary notes describing these eleven sources seem to be the outgrowth of two separate processes. In the first place, the student is noting basic facts about each biography—the *length* of the book, the amount of *documentation,* the potential *bias* of the writer (if it is easily recognized), and the *organization* of the material. But there are also several comments on *tone,* impressions of the way in which the information is being presented: "sounds like . . ." or "reads like. . . ." How were these impressions formed?

Let's begin with the biography, which, according to the annotations, may be the most thorough and complete of the eleven. Here is Carlos Baker's account of Ernest and Hadley Hemingway immediately after their arrival in Paris:

The first problem in Paris was to find an apartment. Ezra's pavillon in the rue Notre Dame des Champs was too cold and damp for the baby, but there was another available flat on the second floor of a building farther up the hill. It was a pleasant street sloping down from the corner of the Avenue de l'Observatoire and the Boulevard du Montparnasse, an easy stroll from the Luxembourg Gardens, where Hadley could air the baby, a stone's throw from an unspoiled café called La Closerie des Lilas, and much closer to Gertrude Stein's than the former walk-up apartment in the rue du Cardinal Lemoine. The whole neighborhood was a good deal prettier and more polite than that of the Montagne Ste.-Geneviève, though not much quieter. The Hemingways' windows at Number 113 looked down upon a sawmill and lumberyard. It was owned and operated by Pierre Chautard, who lived with his wife and a small dog on the ground floor. The whine of the circular saw, the chuff of the donkey-engine that drove it, the hollow boom of newly sawn planks being laid in piles, and the clatter of the ancient camions that carried the lumber away made such a medley that Ernest was often driven to the haven of the Closerie des Lilas to do his writing.

In the apartment itself, a dark tunnel of a hall led to a kitchen with a stone sink and a two-ring gas burner for cooking. There was a dining room, mostly filled by a large table, and a small bedroom where Ernest sometimes worked. The master bedroom held a stove and double bed, with a small dressing room large enough for the baby's crib. Hadley quickly rehired the *femme de ménage,* Madame Henri Rohrback, who had worked for her off and on before. Marie was a sturdy peasant from Mur-de-Bretagne. She and her husband, who was called Ton-Ton, lived at 10 bis, Avenue des Gobelins. Her own nickname was Marie Cocotte, from her method of calling the chickens at home on the farm in Brittany. She took at once to the child and often bore him away in a carriage lent by the Straters to see Ton-Ton, who was a retired soldier with time on his hands. Madame Chautard, the wife of the owner of the sawmill, was a plump and childless woman with brassy hair and a voice so harsh that it made the baby cry. She seemed to be envious of Hadley's motherhood. Watching the child drink his daily ration of orange juice she could only say scornfully, "*Il sera un poivrot comme sa mère.*"* Of the baby's many nicknames—Gallito, Matt, and Joe—the one that stuck was Bumby, which Hadley invented to signify his warm, plump, teddy-bearish, arm-filling solidity which both parents admired and enjoyed.

*"He'll become a lush like his mother."

CARLOS BAKER

What makes Baker's description so effective is the *impressive amount of detail.* You cannot help believing a biographer who offers so much specific information about everyone and everything with even the remotest connection to his subject. You expect to be told what Hemingway ate for dinner and, indeed, in reporting the novelist's skiing trip to Schruns, Baker writes that the cook prepared "great roasts of beef, with potatoes browned in gravy, jugged hare with wine sauce, venison chops, a special omelette soufflé, and homemade plum pudding." On the other hand, you are sometimes told more than you want to know. There's a house-that-Jack-built effect in the sentences about the Hemingways' nursemaid who was a "sturdy peasant from Mur-de-Bretagne," who had a husband named Ton-Ton, who lived in the Avenue des Gobelins, whose nickname was the result of . . . and so on. Nevertheless, Baker tells a good story and his description of the apartment is effective: notice the description of the sounds that Hemingway must have heard from his windows.

Next, in sharp contrast to all this detail, we have a comparable passage from the biography by Leo Gurko (which the bibliography described as "a summary"). *Gurko* is dealing with the same material as *Baker*, in less than one-tenth the space, and naturally offers much less detail.

> Paris in the 1920s was everyone's catalyst. It was the experimental and fermenting center of every art. It was highly sophisticated, yet broke up naturally into small intimate quartiers. Its cafés were hotbeds of intellectual and social energy, pent up during the war and now released. Young people from all over the world flocked to Paris, drawn not only by the city's intrinsic attractions but by the devaluation of the franc. 1
>
> The young Hemingways settled on the Left Bank, and since they were short of money, rented modest rooms in an ancient walkup. They moved several times, taking flats that were usually on the top floor, five or six flights up, commanding good views of the roofs of Paris. This was somehow in tune with a passion to absorb the city. Hemingway did much of his writing in cafés, where he would sit for hours over a beer or *Pernod* with paper spread before him. He took long walks through the streets and gardens, lingered over the Cézannes in the Luxembourg Museum, and let the great city permeate his senses. 2
>
> LEO GURKO

Baker was trying as much as possible to draw the reader into the scene and to share the Hemingways' own experience of Paris. In contrast, *Gurko* is outside the scene, describing what he, the observer, has seen over the distance of time. He does not hesitate to tell his reader what to think—about Paris, about its expatriate population, and about the Hemingways. Notice in this short passage how *Gurko* moves from verifiable facts to his own hypotheses:

> The Hemingways put themselves on short rations, ate, drank, and entertained as little as possible, pounced eagerly on the small checks that arrived in the mail as payment for accepted stories, and were intensely conscious of being poor. The sensation was not altogether unpleasant. Their extreme youth, the excitement of living abroad, the sense of making a fresh start, even the unexpected joy of parenthood, gave their poverty a romantic flavor.
>
> LEO GURKO

Gurko's book does not document his sources; the reader is asked to accept Gurko's assertion that being poor in Paris was "not altogether unpleasant" for

Hemingway, because of its romantic connotations. Other biographers, however, may not agree with this statement. Remember that Gurko's hypothesis is one person's opinion and is not to be confused with fact or presented as such in a research essay. Acceptance of his opinion depends on Gurko's credentials as an authority on Hemingway and on what other established authorities have to say.

Here's a final excerpt from Gurko's biography, as a starting point for a second group of comparisons. Notice his tendency to generalize and summarize and, especially, to speak for Hemingway. Then contrast *Gurko's* approach with that of *Alice Sokoloff:*

> He was becoming increasingly devoted to imaginative writing, to the point where his newspaper assignments and the need to grind out journalistic pieces were growing more and more irksome. Another threat to his work was the "arty" atmosphere of Paris. The cafés of the city, he soon recognized, were filled with aesthetes of one kind or another who wanted to be artists, talked incessantly and even knowledgeably about art, but never really produced anything. There were a hundred of these clever loafers and dilettantes for every real writer. Hemingway developed a contempt and even fear of them, perhaps because there was in him, as in most genuine artists, a feeling of uncertainty about his own talent. He drove himself to hard work and avoided the café crowd as much as he could.
>
> LEO GURKO

> It was a worldly crowd, full of intellectual and artistic ferment, some of it real, some of it bogus, some of them obsessed with their own egos, a few of them deeply and sincerely interested in Ernest's talent. The Hemingways' finances were as restricted as ever, but these people "could offer them all the amenities, could take them anywhere for gorgeous meals," could produce any kind of entertainment and diversion. Although Ernest accepted it all, Hadley thought that he resented it and always kept "a very stiff upper front to satisfy himself." He did not want "simply to sink back and take all this," but the success and admiration was heady stuff and he could not help but enjoy it.[1] Hadley used to be wryly amused when Ernest and Gertrude Stein would talk about worldly success and how it did not mean anything to them.[2] The fact that this was true for a part of him, and that he despised anything false or pretentious, was a source of inner conflict which sometimes expressed itself in malice.
>
> [1]John Dos Passos. *The Best Times* (New York: New American Library, 1966), p. 143.
> [2]Interview with Hadley Richardson Hemingway Mowrer, January 18, 1972.
>
> ALICE SOKOLOFF

Sokoloff's conclusions differ from *Gurko's:* she points to a conflict in Hemingway's reaction to his Paris acquaintances, and offers *footnotes* to support her suggestion. In another sense, Sokoloff's commentary is limited: because the subject of her biography is Hadley Hemingway, she is describing events from Hadley's point of view. On the other hand, Sokoloff's presentation makes it fairly easy to figure out where Hadley's version leaves off and the biographer's account begins, and the story is told coherently.

Leicester Hemingway's account of his brother's life is far more confusing; most of his information comes from letters, and he makes little attempt to sort out the contents into a form that the average reader can follow easily:

> Things were going very well for Ernest, with his home life as well as with his writing. Bumby was beginning to talk and Ernest was learning that a child could be more fun than fret. With wife and son he took off for Schruns in the Vorarlberg when good skiing weather set in. For months they were deep in the snow up there, working and enjoying the sports, before returning to Paris in mid-March. [1]
>
> Ernest wrote the family that when they camped in the mountains, up above 2,000 meters, there had been lots of ptarmigan and foxes, too. The deer and chamois were lower down. [2]
>
> He said Bumby weighed twenty-nine pounds, played in a sand pile with shovel and pail, and was always jolly. His own writing was going very well. *In Our Time* was out of print and bringing high prices, he said, while his stories were being translated into Russian and German. . . . [3]
>
> Hadley added other details, thanking the family for the Christmas box which had been delayed more than two months in customs, but had arrived without damage to the fruit cake—Mother's one culinary triumph besides meat loaf. She wrote that Bumby had a wonderful nurse who had taken care of him while she and Ernest spent days at a stretch in mountain huts to be near good snow. [4]
>
> LEICESTER HEMINGWAY

Ernest's writing is mixed up with Bumby's pail and shovel and fruitcakes for Christmas. This is certainly raw material. The biography offers no interpretation at all for the reader to discount or accept. The material is stitched together so crudely that one has to spend time sorting out important details from trivia. Certainly, this biography would be a poor choice for the student who was beginning research on this topic; but the details might provide interesting background once the events of 1924–1925 were made more familiar by other biographies.

Next, here are three more recent biographies of Hemingway. How do they describe the apartment near the lumberyard?

> "Hemingway had then and has always a very good instinct for finding apartments in strange but pleasant localities," wrote Gertrude Stein, "and good femmes de menage and good food." They arrived in France on January 29, 1924, and soon found a flat above a noisy sawmill, near Pound's old studio, at 113 rue Notre Dame des Champs, where the street curves parallel to the Boulevard Montparnasse. [1]
>
> But the flat had more character than comfort. American friends, who were used to living well in France, were shocked by the squalor. Kitty Cannell said: "The Hemingways lived in a cold-water apartment that gave on[to] a lumber yard in the Montparnasse quarter. It had neither gas nor electric light." And the journalist Burton Rascoe wrote: "They lived, at the time, in an incredibly bare hovel, without toilet [2]

or running water, and with a mattress spread on the floor for a bed; it was in the court of a lumber yard, on the second floor, to which one climbed by a flight of rickety steps."

JEFFREY MEYERS

Meyers attempts to give some idea of what the Hemingways themselves were experiencing, not by piling on physical details, but by providing a kaleidoscope of eyewitness impressions, rather like interviews in a documentary film or the accumulation of evidence at a trial. An explicit interrogation of the testimony here and the speakers might be helpful, and reminiscences aren't always reliable (the other biographers mention the lack of electricity, but no one else says there was no running water), but this passage does alert us to some of the issues of class that colored Hemingway's experience of Paris, and words like "squalor" and "hovel" offer a contrast to the romantic picture drawn by Baker.

Just before he'd left New York, Ernest had heard from Ford Madox Ford. Ford had written that, since the Pounds were traveling, the Hemingways could spend a few weeks in the Pounds' flat at 70 Rue Notre Dames des Champs. But Ford had made a mistake. When Ernest arrived at Pound's apartment, he learned that, although Ezra was, as Ford said, traveling, he had left no key. Ernest, exhausted and desperate, trudged through the wet snow toward the noise of a band saw, a few buildings down the street. In a small square of black, dripping trees and narrow old wooden houses, he found Pierre Chautard, a carpenter. 1

When Ernest asked if the carpenter knew of a place to stay, Chautard showed him a five-room flat over the sawmill. The kitchen had a slimy slate sink and a gas stove, with piles of burnt matches beneath the two burners. The place was furnished, Chautard said. But Ernest saw little more than a big bed in one room and a big table in another. Still, there was the pleasant smell of fresh-cut lumber, and windows all around. Madame Chautard, a foulmouthed, henna-haired harridan, sneered at the young couple and suggested she was doing them a favor—especially with the baby. Though he wanted to, Ernest did not haggle over the rent. For himself, his wife, and his son, nothing mattered more than a good night's sleep. 2

PETER GRIFFIN

Griffin's entire book is devoted to Hemingway's experiences in Paris, so we should expect a level of detail to at least rival that of Baker. Griffin acknowledges in his preface his indebtedness to Baker, and we recognize here some of the same details we learned in Baker: the slate sink, the gas stove, the big table. Baker passed over why, specifically, the Hemingways were in the Montparnasse district; Griffin gives us some sense of how professional and personal lives were entangled, with messages from Pound being relayed by another literary luminary, Ford Madox Ford. Is this additional information useful?

On February 8, after much shopping, Ernest leased a second-floor apartment at 113 rue Notre-Dame-des-Champs, a stone's throw from Ezra's studio and directly behind Montparnasse. A month's rent was 650 francs, almost three times their Cardinal Lemoine rent, but the space was better, the location closer to their friends, and with the franc fluctuating at twenty-one to the dollar, the real cost was about $30 monthly. The apartment had no electricity, and the lumberyard buzz saw in the courtyard below whined steadily during working hours, but their old *femme de menage*, Marie Rohrbach, returned to help with the baby. As February rain mixed with snow, Hadley, sick and physically worn out, watched her furniture move once more into new quarters. "We have the whole second story," she told mother-in-law Grace, "tiny kitchen, small dining room, toilet, small bedroom, medium size sitting room with stove, dining room where John Hadley sleeps and the linen and his and our bath things are kept and a very comfortable bedroom . . . you're conscious all the time from 7 A.M. to 5 P.M. of a very gentle buzzing noise. They make door and window frames and picture frames. The yard is full of dogs and workmen[,] and rammed right up against the funny front door covered with tarpaulin is the baby's buggy." |

Despite the lumberyard's noise, the new apartment was an improvement over their first Paris home. Here they were only a few minutes walk from the Notre-Dame-des-Champs Metro station, the Luxembourg Gardens, Sylvia's bookshop and Gertrude Stein's place on the rue de Fleurus. The neighborhood was less working class, less down at the heels. At one end of the street stood the Clinique d'Accouchement, for which both Ernest and Hadley hoped they would have no use. (In his 1924 day book, mostly blank, Ernest was keeping careful track of Hadley's monthly periods.) Nearby, on the Boulevard Montparnasse, in good weather and bad, their American friends gathered to drink and talk at the Select, the Rotonde and the Dome where one could gossip, leave messages, borrow money, repay debts and keep generally abreast of local news. 2

MICHAEL REYNOLDS

Here is another full-length work devoted to the Paris years. Like *Griffin, Reynolds* professes his debt to Carlos Baker, and he sees the significance of the new flat in much the same light as did Baker: better, more convenient location, with the disadvantages of the apartment minimized. Like *Meyers,* Reynolds relies on eyewitness reports, in this case a letter written by Hadley, giving her own impressions of the new apartment and directly contradicting Burton Rascoe's assertion that there was no toilet (although in writing to her mother-in-law she might have minimized the "squalor").

In fact, an Internet source confirms the lack of a toilet. "Hemingway in Paris" provides three photographs: the circular stairway leading into the apartment, the window of Hemingway's room (with a plaque honoring him), and the outside of the building, including a café. The prose commentary is brief, indicating that there was no hot water and no toilet, "only a chamber pot located in a niche on each floor of the winding staircase."

Finally, here are five descriptions of Hemingway as a baby sitter, odd-job man, and scavenger, all dealing with similar experiences:

Ernest was working fairly hard. He awoke early in the spring mornings, "boiled the rubber nipples and the bottles, made the formula, finished the bottling, gave Mr. Bumby a bottle," and wrote for a time at the dining-room table before Hadley got up. Chautard had not begun his sawing at that hour, the street was quiet, and Ernest's only companions were Mr. Bumby and Mr. Feather Puss, a large cat given them by Kitty Cannell and named with one of Hadley's nicknames. But Ernest was truly domestic only in the early mornings. He took the freedom of Paris as his personal prerogative, roving as widely as he chose. There was a gymnasium in the rue Pontoise where he often went to earn ten francs a round by sparring with professional heavyweights. The job called for a nice blend of skill and forbearance, since hirelings must be polite while fighting back just enough to engage, without enraging, the emotions of the fighters. Ernest had befriended a waiter at the Closerie des Lilas and sometimes helped him weed a small vegetable garden near the Porte d'Orléans. The waiter knew that he was a writer and warned him that the boxing might jar his brains. But Ernest was glad enough to earn the extra money. He had already begun to save up to buy pesetas for another trip to Spain in July.

CARLOS BAKER

When there were the three of us instead of just the two, it was the cold and the weather that finally drove us out of Paris in the winter time. Alone there was no problem when you got used to it. I could always go to a café to write and could work all morning over a café crème while the waiters cleaned and swept out the café and it gradually grew warmer. My wife could go to work at the piano in a cold place and with enough sweaters keep warm playing and come home to nurse Bumby. It was wrong to take a baby to a café in the winter though; even a baby that never cried and watched everything that happened and was never bored. There were no baby-sitters then and Bumby would stay happy in his tall cage bed with his big, loving cat named F. Puss. There were people who said that it was dangerous to leave a cat with a baby. The most ignorant and prejudiced said that a cat would suck a baby's breath and kill him. Others said that a cat would lie on a baby and the cat's weight would smother him. F. Puss lay beside Bumby in the tall cage bed and watched the door with his big yellow eyes, and would let no one come near him when we were out and Marie, the *femme de ménage*, had to be away. There was no need for baby-sitters. F. Puss was the baby-sitter.

ERNEST HEMINGWAY

Ernest wanted me to see the neighborhood where he had first lived; we started on Rue Notre-Dame-des-Champs, where he had lived over a sawmill, and slowly worked our way past familiar restaurants, bars and stores, to the Jardin du Luxembourg and its museum, where, Ernest said, he fell in love with certain paintings that taught him how to write. "Am also fond of the Jardin," Ernest said, "because it kept us from starvation. On days when the dinner pot was absolutely devoid of content, I would put Bumby, then about a year old, into the baby carriage and wheel him over here to the Jardin. There was always a *gendarme* on duty, but I knew that around four o'clock he would go to a bar across from the park to have a glass of wine. That's when I would appear with Mr. Bumby—and a pocketful of corn for the pigeons. I would sit on a bench, in my guise of buggy-pushing pigeon-lover, casing the flock for clarity of eye and plumpness. The Luxembourg was well known for the classiness of its pigeons. Once my selection was made, it was a simple matter to entice my victim with the corn, snatch him, wring his neck, and flip his carcass under Mr. Bumby's blanket. We got a little tired of pigeon that winter, but they filled many a void. What a kid that Bumby was—played it straight—and never once put the finger on me."

A. E. HOTCHNER

. . . As he grew older (and *A Moveable Feast* was the last book he finished), Hemingway laid increasing stress on the poverty he suffered in Paris. Without question, Ernest and Hadley Hemingway lived on a relatively scant income during those years, but they were never so badly off as the writer, in retrospect, liked to believe.

In any case, poverty is virtually apotheosized in *A Moveable Feast*. As the title hints, a gnawing hunger for food and drink symbolizes Hemingway's indigence. According to the legend constructed in this book, Hemingway worked all day in his unheated garret, too poor to buy firewood or afford lunch. At least he does not tell here the unlikely yarn that appears in A. E. Hotchner's biography: the one about Hemingway catching pigeons in the Luxembourg Gardens in order to satisfy a rumbling stomach. But poverty, and its symbolic hunger, are nonetheless celebrated. "You got very hungry when you did not eat enough in Paris," Hemingway writes, because of the good things on display in the *pâtisseries* and at the outdoor restaurants. Mostly he and Hadley survived on leeks *(poireaux)*, but at least so frugal a diet enabled one to savor, truly, the joys of eating well when an unexpected windfall made it possible for them to dine out.

SCOTT DONALDSON

In the late spring of 1925, when the cold rains that ended the winter had come and gone and the warmth of the sun increased each day, Ernest loved to take his son in the stroller, "a cheap, very light, folding carriage, down the streets to the Closerie des Lilas." They would each have brioche and cafe au lait, Ernest pouring some of the hot coffee into the saucer to cool it, and to let Bumby dip his brioche before eating. Ernest would read the papers, now and then looking up to see his son attentive to everything that passed on the boulevard. After breakfast, Ernest would wheel Bumby across the street from the cafe and past the Place de l'Observatoire. Bumby loved to see the bronze horses rearing in the fountain spray that made the June air smell so clean.

PETER GRIFFIN

Characteristically, *Baker* describes exactly how the father tended his son, pausing to explain the full name and the origins of their cat. *Griffin* pays the same attention to detail, without being so exhaustive. *Hemingway* himself, years after the event, describes much the same relationship, but with a completely different emphasis and set of details. These three passages are not in conflict; but they are not at all the same kind of writing and, in fact, they provide an excellent illustration of the difficulties of combining sources written in different modes for different kinds of audience. The Hemingway who reminisced for *A. E. Hotchner* offers a somewhat different version of the same experience, a version criticized in *Donaldson*'s extract, which tries to distinguish between nostalgia and truth. Unlike *Gurko*'s, *Donaldson*'s presentation is detailed; unlike *Baker* and *Griffin*, he has an outsider's perspective, and the combination, backed up by documentation, is quite convincing.

In what order, then, would you consult these ten books for full-scale research? You might begin with Gurko's brief account, to establish the sequence of events, and then fill in the details by reading Baker's longer version or the more recent, comprehensive biographies by Meyers or Reynolds, which depend so much on Baker's earlier work. Donaldson gets pushed down the list to third or fourth, primarily because his biography is not chronological; gathering the scattered references to 1924 will be easier once the overall chronology has been made clear by Gurko, Baker, Meyers, or Reynolds. Now, you can also draw on the details to be found in the works by "interested" parties: wife, brother, friend, and the author himself. And, at intervals, you should stop reading and note-taking to compare these various versions of one life and determine which of the sources was in a position to know the truth—the man himself thirty years later? his correspondence at the time? records left by his wife (whom, in fact, he divorced in 1929)? his biographers, whose information is presented secondhand? a combination of all the sources?

EXERCISE 22: LEARNING ABOUT AUTHORS

Each of the following authors is represented by an essay or paragraph in this book. Choose one of the authors and:

A. Find out some information about the author's background and write a paragraph describing his or her qualifications for writing about this subject.

B. Think about the suggested research topics that accompany the references. Would you use this passage if you were writing an essay on that topic?

Bertrand Russell: "The Social Responsibility of Scientists" (Chapter 1, pp. 55–57)
  a. The arms race
  b. The power of the media

Robert Bork: "The Case for Censorship" (Chapter 3, pp. 137–146)
  a. The popularity of supermarket tabloids
  b. The decline of American culture

Shelby Steele: excerpt from "I'm Black, You're White, Who's Innocent?" (Appendix E, pp. 503–514)
  a. Are affirmative action programs justified?
  b. Should our curriculums be "politically correct"?

Margaret Mead: excerpt from *Some Personal Views* (Chapter 1, p. 47)
  a. Origins of neurosis
  b. Problems of the disabled child

EXERCISE 23: COMPARING SOURCES

In the middle of the night of November 29, 1942, a Boston nightclub called the Cocoanut Grove burned down, resulting in the deaths of at least 300 people. Read the following three accounts of this disaster, and be prepared to discuss the differences in content, organization, tone, purpose, and point of view. What is the thesis of each article? Consider how you would use the three articles in a single research essay dealing with the Cocoanut Grove disaster. Are these three variations interchangeable?

NEW YORK TIMES, 30 NOVEMBER 1942

300 KILLED BY FIRE, SMOKE AND PANIC IN BOSTON RESORT— DEAD CLOG EXITS—Terror Piles Up Victims as Flames Suddenly Engulf Nightclub—Service Men to Rescue—Many of Them Perish—Girls of Chorus Leap to Safety—150 Are Injured

BOSTON, Sunday, Nov. 29—More than 300 persons had perished early this morning in flames, smoke and panic in the Cocoanut Grove Night Club in the midtown theatre district. | 1

The estimate of the dead came at 2 A.M. from William Arthur Reilly, Fire Commissioner, as firemen and riggers searched the ruins for additional bodies. It was a disaster unprecedented in this city. | 2

The chief loss of life resulted from the screaming, clawing crowds that were wedged in the entrance of the club. Smoke took a terrific toll of life and scores were burned to death. | 3

At the Boston City Hospital officials said there were so many bodies lined up in corridors that they would attempt no identifications before daybreak. | 4

Commissioner Reilly stated that an eyewitness inside the club said the fire started when an artificial palm near the main entrance was set afire. | 5

Martial law was clamped on the entire fire area at 1:35 A.M. Sailors, Coast Guardsmen, shore patrolmen and naval officers dared death time and again trying to get at bodies that were heaped six feet high by one of the entrances. | 6

Firemen said that many bodies were believed to have fallen into the basement after the main floor collapsed. | 7

A chorus boy, Marshall Cook, aged 19, of South Boston, led three co-workers,   8
eight chorus girls and other floor show performers totaling thirty-five to an adjoining roof from the second-floor dressing rooms and from there they dropped to the
ground from a ladder.

Scores of ambulances from nearby cities, the Charlestown Navy Yard and the   9
Chelsea Naval Hospital poured into the area, but the need for ambulances became
so great that even railway express trucks were pressed into service to carry away
victims. At one time victims, many of them dead, lay two deep in an adjoining garage.

Many of the victims were soldiers, sailors, marines and Coast Guardsmen, some   10
of them junior officers, visiting Boston for a weekend of merrymaking. In the throng
were persons who had attended the Holy Cross–Boston College football game.

Scores of dead were piled up in the lobbies of the various hospitals as the doc-   11
tors and nurses gave all their attention to the 150 injured.

A "flash" fire, believed to have started in the basement, spread like lightning   12
through the dance floor area, and the panic was on. All available nurses and priests
were being called into the disaster area.

Among the dead were a marine and one who appeared to be a fireman. Casual-   13
ties were arriving at hospitals so rapidly that they were being placed in the corridors wherever a suitable place could be found.

It appeared probable that the greatest loss of life was in the newly opened lounge   14
of the night club in Broadway. Here, one policeman said, burned and suffocated
persons were heaped to the top of the doors, wedged in death.

The night club was a one-and-a-half story building with a stucco exterior. The   15
blaze was said to have broken out in the basement kitchen at 10:17 P.M. just as the
floor show performers were preparing for their next performance. Performers on
the second floor were met by terrific smoke and flame as they started downstairs.
Their stories were the only ones available, as those who had escaped the dance
floor and tables were too hysterical to talk.

A temporary morgue and hospital were set up in the garage of the Film Exchange   16
Transfer Company at the rear of the club in Shawmut Street. At least fourteen persons, suffocated and lying in grotesque positions, were lying on the garage floor at
one time, while scores of injuries were cared for by garage workers and others.

The city's Civilian Defense Workers were called to the scene to maintain order   17
and to give first aid to those suffering from burns and smoke inhalation. Every hospital in the area soon was loaded with the victims.

At least thirty-five performers and their friends were rescued by the quick actions   18
of Marshall Cook, a South Boston boy. He was met by a blast of flame as he started
down stairs, went back to the dressing room and organized those caught there.

He then smashed his way through a window, carrying away the casing. Through   19
this opening he led a group to an adjoining room, where a small ladder was found.
The ladder was not long enough to reach the street, but Cook and several other
male performers held the top end over the roof's edge and guided the women over
the side. They had to jump about 6 feet to reach the ground.

At the City Hospital bodies were piled on the floors, many so burned that there was no attempt to identify them immediately. Many service men were among the victims, many of whom were partly identified through their uniforms. 20

Buck Jones, the film star, was believed to be one of the victims. 21

Among the first at the scene was the Rev. Joseph A. Marcus of Cranwell School, Lenox, who administered the last rites for at least fifty persons. In the meantime, thirty or forty ambulances rushed to the fire, these coming from Lynn, Newton, and Brookline. Despite the hindrances caused by automobiles parked in the streets, some of the dead and injured were taken from nearby buildings, where they had been left covered only by newspapers. 22

Abraham Levy, a cashier at the Cocoanut Grove, said there were about 400 in the place, including many sailors. 23

Sailors saved many lives, pulling people through the doors and out of danger. A fireman said that he saw at least thirty bodies lying on the floor, and that he believed some of them were firemen. 24

Among the spectacular escapes were those of two of the eight chorus girls, who leaped from the second floor and were caught by two of the male dancers. They were Lottie Christie of Park Drive, Boston, and Claudia Boyle. They jumped into the arms of Andrew Louzan and Robert Gilbert. Louzan and Gilbert had climbed out of a window of their dressing room to an adjoining roof and then descended by ladder. 25

TIME, 7 DECEMBER 1942
CATASTROPHE: BOSTON'S WORST

Holy Cross had just beaten Boston College: downtown Boston was full of men & women eager to celebrate or console. Many of them wound up at Cocoanut Grove: they stood crowded around the dimly lighted downstairs bar, filled the tables around the dance floor upstairs. With them mingled the usual Saturday night crowd: soldiers & sailors, a wedding party, a few boys being sent off to Army camps. 1

At 10 o'clock Bridegroom John O'Neil, who had planned to take his bride to their new apartment at the stroke of the hour, lingered on a little longer. The floor show was about to start. Through the big revolving door, couples moved in & out. 2

At the downstairs bar, a 16-year-old busboy stood on a bench to replace a light bulb that a prankish customer had removed. He lit a match. It touched one of the artificial palm trees that gave the Cocoanut Grove its atmosphere; a few flames shot up. A girl named Joyce Spector sauntered toward the checkroom because she was worried about her new fur coat. 3

Panic's Start

Before Joyce Spector reached the cloakroom, the Cocoanut Grove was a screaming shambles. The fire quickly ate away the palm tree, raced along silk draperies, was sucked upstairs through the stairway, leaped along ceiling and wall. The silk hangings, turned to balloons of flame, fell on table and floor. 4

Men & women fought their way toward the revolving door; the push of bodies   5
jammed it. Nearby was another door; it was locked tight. There were other exits,
but few Cocoanut Grove patrons knew about them. The lights went out. There
was nothing to see now except flame, smoke and weird moving torches that were
men & women with clothing and hair afire.

The 800 Cocoanut Grove patrons pushed and shoved, fell and were trampled.   6
Joyce Spector was knocked under a table, crawled on hands & knees, somehow was
pushed through an open doorway into the street. A chorus boy herded a dozen
people downstairs into a refrigerator. A few men & women crawled out windows;
a few escaped by knocking out a glass brick wall. But most of them, including Bridegroom John O'Neil, were trapped.

Panic's Sequel

Firemen broke down the revolving door, found it blocked by bodies of the dead,   7
six deep. They tried to pull a man out through a side window; his legs were held tight
by the mass of struggling people behind him. In an hour the fire was out and firemen began untangling the piles of bodies. One hard bitten fireman went in to hys-
terics when he picked up a body and a foot came off in his hand. They found a girl
dead in a telephone booth, a bartender still standing behind his bar.

At hospitals and improvised morgues which were turned into charnel houses for   8
the night, 484 dead were counted; it was the most disastrous U.S. fire since 571
people were killed in Chicago's Iroquois Theater holocaust in 1903. One Boston
newspaper ran a two-word banner line: BUSBOY BLAMED. But the busboy had not
put up the Cocoanut Grove's tinderbox decorations, nor was he responsible for
the fact that Boston's laws do not require nightclubs to have fireproof fixtures,
sprinkler systems or exit markers.

BERNARD DEVOTO, *HARPER'S*, FEBRUARY 1943
THE EASY CHAIR

On the last Sunday morning of November, 1942, most inhabitants of greater   1
Boston learned from their newspapers that at about the time they had gone to bed
the night before the most terrible fire in the history of their city had occurred. The
decorations of a crowded night club had got ignited, the crowd had stampeded, the
exits had jammed, and in a few minutes hundreds of people had died of burns or
suffocation. Two weeks later the list of dead had reached almost exactly five hundred, and the war news was only beginning to come back to Boston front pages.
While the Allied invasion of North Africa stalled, while news was released that several transports engaged in it had been sunk, while the Russians and the Germans
fought monstrously west of Stalingrad and Moscow, while the Americans bombed
Naples and the RAF obliterated Turin and conducted the war's most widespread
raids over western Europe, while the Japs tried again in the Solomons and mowed
down their attackers in New Guinea, while a grave conflict of civilian opinion over

the use of Admiral Darlan developed in America and Great Britain, while the anniversary of Pearl Harbor passed almost unnoticed—while all this was going on the Boston papers reported it in stickfuls in order to devote hundreds of columns to the fire at the Cocoanut Grove. And the papers did right, for the community has experienced an angry horror surpassing anything that it can remember. For weeks few Bostonians were able to feel strongly about anything but their civic disaster.

There is irony in such preoccupation with a minute carnage. In the same fortnight thousands of men were killed in battle. Every day, doubtless, more than five hundred were burned to death, seared by powder or gasoline from bombed dumps, in buildings fired from the sky, or in blazing airplanes and sinking ships. If these are thought of as combatants meeting death in the line of duty, far more than five hundred civilians were killed by military action in Germany, Italy, France, Great Britain, Russia, China, Australia, and the islands of the Pacific. Meanwhile in two-thirds of the world civilians died of torture and disease and starvation, in prison camps and wire stockades and the rubble of their homes—they simply came to their last breath and died, by the thousand. At a moment when violent death is commonplace, when it is inevitable for hundreds of thousands, there is something grotesque in being shocked by a mere five hundred deaths which are distinguished from the day's routine only by the fact that they were not inevitable. When hundreds of towns are bombed repeatedly, when cities the size of Boston are overrun by invading armies, when many hundreds of Boston's own citizens will surely be killed in battle in the next few weeks, why should a solitary fire, a truly inconsiderable slaughter, so oppress the spirit? 2

That oppression provides perspective on our era. We have been so conditioned to horror that horror must explode in our own backyard before we can genuinely feel it. At the start of the decade our nerves responded to Hitler's murdering the German Jews with the outrage properly felt in the presence of cruelty and pain. Seven years later our nerves had been so overloaded that they felt no such outrage at the beginning of a systematic effort to exterminate an entire nation, such as Poland. By progressive steps we had come to strike a truce with the intolerable, precisely as the body develops immunity to poisons and bacteria. Since then three years of war have made the intolerable our daily bread, and every one of us has comfortably adapted to things which fifteen years ago would have driven him insane. The extinction of a nation now seems merely an integral part of the job in hand. But the needless death of five hundred people in our home town strikes through the immunity and horrifies us. 3

The fire at the Cocoanut Grove was a single, limited disaster, but it exhausted Boston's capacity to deal with an emergency. Hospital facilities were strained to the limit and somewhat beyond it. If a second emergency had had to be dealt with at the same time its victims would have had to wait some hours for transportation and a good many hours for treatment. If there had been three such fires at once, two-thirds of the victims would have got no treatment whatever in time to do them any good. Boston is an inflammable city and it has now had instruction in what to 4 expect if a dozen hostile planes should come over and succeed in dropping incendiary bombs. The civilian defense agencies which were called on justified themselves and vindicated their training. The Nurses' Aid in particular did a memorable job; within a few hours there was a trained person at the bed of every victim, many other Aids worked to exhaustion helping hospital staffs do their jobs, and in fact more were available than could be put to use. Nevertheless it was clearly demonstrated that the civilian agencies are nowhere near large enough to take care of bombings if bombings should come. There were simply not enough ambulances; Railway Express Company trucks had to be called on to take the injured to hospitals and the dead to morgues. The dead had to be stacked like cord wood in garages because the morgues could take no more; the dying had to be laid in rows in the corridors of hospitals because the emergency wards were full. The drainage of doctors into the military service had left Boston just about enough to care for as many victims as this single fire supplied. Six months from now there will be too few to handle an equal emergency; there are far too few now for one twice as serious. One planeload of incendiaries would start more fires than the fire department and its civilian assistants could put out. There would be more injured than there are even the most casually trained first-aiders to care for. Hundreds would be abandoned to the ignorant assistance of untrained persons, in streets so blocked by rubble and so jammed with military vehicles that trained crews could not reach them even when trained crews should be free. Boston has learned that it is not prepared to take care of itself. One doubts if any community in the United States is.

Deeper implications of the disaster have no direct connection with the war. An   5
outraged city has been confronting certain matters which it ordinarily disregards. As a place of entertainment the Cocoanut Grove was garish but innocuous and on the whole useful. It has been called "the poor man's Ritz"; for years people had been going there to have a good time and had got what they were looking for. With the naive shock customary in such cases, the city has now discovered that these people were not receiving the minimum protection in their pleasures to which they were entitled and which they supposed they were receiving.

The name of the night club suggests the kind of decorations that cluttered it; the   6
public supposed that the law required them to be fireproof; actually they burned like so much celluloid. The laws relating to them were ambiguous and full of loopholes; such as they were, they were not enforced. The public supposed that an adequate number of exits were required and that periodic inspections were made; they were not. There were too few exits for the customary crowds, one was concealed, another could not be opened, and panic-stricken people piled up before the rest and died there by the score. The public supposed that laws forbidding overcrowding were applied to night clubs and were enforced; on the night of the fire the place was packed so full that movement was almost impossible, and it had been just as crowded at least once a week throughout the years of its existence. The public supposed that laws requiring safe practice in electric wiring and machinery were enforced; the official investigations have shown that the wiring was installed by unlicensed

electricians, that a number of people had suspected it was faulty, and that in fact officials had notified the club that it was violating the law and had threatened to take action—but had not carried out the threat. Above all, the public supposed that an adequate building code taking into account the realities of modern architecture and modern metropolitan life established certain basic measures of protection. It has now learned that the Boston building code is a patched makeshift based on the conditions of 1907, and that though a revision which would modernize it was made in 1937, various reasons have held up the adoption of that revision for five years.

These facts have been established by five official investigations, one of them made   7
by the Commonwealth of Massachusetts in an obvious expectation that the municipal authorities of Boston would find convincing reasons to deal gently with themselves. They have turned up other suggestive facts. The Cocoanut Grove was once owned by a local racketeer, who was murdered in the routine of business. The present owners were so expertly concealed behind a facade of legal figureheads that for twenty-four hours after the fire the authorities were not sure that they knew who even one of them was and two weeks later were not sure that they knew them all. An intimation that financial responsibility was avoided by a technically contrived bankruptcy has not yet been followed up as I write this, and other financial details are still lost in a maze of subterfuges. It is supposed that some of the club's employees had their wagescale established by terrorism. Investigators have encountered, but so far have not published, the customary free-list and lists of those entitled to discounts. Presumably such lists contemplated the usual returns in publicity and business favors; presumably also they found a use in the amenities of regulation. Names and business practices of the underworld have kept cropping up in all the investigations, and it is whispered that the reason why the national government has been conducting one of them is the presence at the club of a large amount of liquor on which the latest increase in revenue taxes ought to have been paid but somehow had not been.

In short, Boston has been reminded, hardly for the first time, that laxity in mu-   8
nicipal responsibility can be made to pay a profit and that there can be a remunerative partnership between the amusement business and the underworld. A great many Bostonians, now writing passionate letters to their newspapers and urging on their legislators innumerable measures of reform, have gone farther than that. They conclude that one of the reasons why the modernized building code has not been adopted is the fact that there are ways of making money from the looser provisions of the old code. They suppose that one reason why gaps and loopholes in safety regulations are maintained is that they are profitable. They suppose that one reason why laws and regulations can be disregarded with impunity is that some of those charged with the duty of enforcing them make a living from not enforcing them. They suppose that some proprietors of night clubs find that buying immunity is cheaper than obeying safety regulations and that they are able to find enforcement agents who will sell it. They suppose that civil irresponsibility in Boston can be related to the fact that a lot of people make money from it.

But the responsibility cannot be shouldered off on a few small grafters and a few 9
underworld characters who have established business relations with them, and it
would be civic fatuousness to seek expiation for the murder of five hundred citizens in the passage of some more laws. The trouble is not lack of laws but public
acquiescence; the damaging alliance is not with the underworld but with a communal reverence of what is probably good for business. Five hundred deaths in a single
hour seem intolerable, but the city has never dissented at all to a working alliance
between its financial interests and its political governors—a partnership which daily
endangers not five hundred but many thousand citizens. Through Boston, as through
every other metropolis, run many chains of interests which might suffer loss if regulations for the protection of the public's health and life were rigorously enforced.
They are sound and enlightened regulations, but if they should be enforced then
retail sales, bank clearings, and investment balances might possibly fall off. The corner grocery and the downtown department store, the banks and the business
houses, the labor unions and the suburban housewife are all consenting partners in
a closely calculated disregard of public safety.

Since the system is closely calculated it usually works, it kills only a few at a time, 10
mostly it kills gradually over a period of years. Sometimes however it runs into another mathematical certainty and then it has to be paid for in blocks of five hundred lives. At such times the community experiences just such an excess of guilt as
Boston is feeling now, uncomfortably realizing that the community itself is the perpetrator of wanton murder. For the responsibility is the public's all along and the
certain safeguard—a small amount of alertness, civic courage, and willingness to
lose some money—is always in the public's hands. That means not the mayor's
hands, but yours and mine.

It is an interesting thing to hold up to the light at a moment when millions of 11
Americans are fighting to preserve, among other things, the civic responsibility of a
self-governing people. It suggests that civilians who are not engaged in the war effort, and who feel intolerably abased because they are not, could find serviceable
ways to employ their energies. They can get to work chipping rust and rot from the
mechanisms of local government. The rust and rot are increasing because people
who can profit from their increase count on our looking toward the war, not toward them. Your town may have a police force of no more than four and its amusement business may be confined to half a dozen juke joints, but some percentage of
both may have formed a partnership against your interests under cover of the war.

Certainly the town has a sewage system, a garbage dump, fire traps, a rudimen- 12
tary public health code, ordinances designed to protect life, and a number of Joe
Doakes who can make money by juggling the relationship among them. Meanwhile
the ordinary hazards of peace are multiplied by the conditions of war, carelessness
and preoccupation increase, and the inevitable war pestilence is gathering to spring.
The end-products do not look pleasant when they are seen clearly, especially when
a community realizes that it has killed five hundred people who did not need to die.

·7·

Taking Notes

Have copying machines and computers put an end to note-taking? Some sources, such as newspaper articles, are difficult to copy clearly; others contain only one or two useful sentences and are not worth the expense of copying. Still, there are other reasons why taking notes remains an important skill.

When you have found and copied some useful sources, what do you do with the stack of photocopied pages or the excerpts typed into your laptop computer? So far, you have only moved the raw materials from the library to your desk. How do you turn them into an essay? In order to take inventory and start working on your *essay* (as distinguished from your *research*), you must find the important points and discard the irrelevancies that surround them. Of course, you could plan the organization of your essay by cutting up each page and sorting the vital passages into separate piles; but unless you identify each source clearly on each bit of cut-up paper, you can easily lose track of its origin.

It therefore makes sense to *take notes as part of the research process* and to express as much of the information as you can *in your own words*. At the same time, you should make copies of the most important passages, so that you will have the originals to refer to if your notes let you down. *There is no substitute for good notes.*

TAKING GOOD NOTES

The following guidelines should help your note-taking:

1. **Try to complete your survey of the library's resources and work out a preliminary bibliography before you start to make copies or take notes.**

   You will get a good idea of what materials are available and the probable extent of your research, and you will also make sure that your preferred topic is a practical one. If you start taking notes before you are certain of your precise focus, you may waste a good deal of time. You may discover, for example, that there is very little documented information about the gunfight at the O.K. Corral, and decide to shift your focus to Wyatt Earp. Or the amount of technical material about Lindbergh's flight in the *Spirit of St. Louis* might overwhelm you, with the result that you switch to Lindbergh's opposition to America's entry into World War II.

2. **Use paraphrase and summary rather than quotation.**

   If you copy down sentence after sentence, word for word from your source onto index cards or a pad, or into a computer, you might as well save time and photocopy the page. Remember that using the language of the original author will make it more difficult for you to shift to your own writing style. If your first draft reads like an anthology of cannibalized quotations, then you will find it hard to make your final essay coherent and intelligible. The pasted-together sources will still be in control. Take the trouble *now* to master each new idea by putting it in your own words.

3. **Make sure that your notes make sense.**

   Remember that you will have read a vast number of similar pages by the time you begin to organize your essay and that you won't remember everything. In your notes, spell out the author's exact meaning.

4. **Include a certain number of facts to serve as your supporting evidence.**

   It is not enough to say that "X's father lost his job." What was his job? Why did he lose it? What did he do instead? Later, you may find that these details are irrelevant and will not fit into the shape of your essay; but if you do need supporting evidence, you will find it easier to look in your notes than to go back to the library.

5. **Differentiate your own ideas from those that you are paraphrasing.**

   Taking notes is often an intellectually stimulating experience, probably because it requires so much concentration and because your reading rate is slowed down. You may have plenty of comments about the source that you are paraphrasing. As you develop your own ideas and include them in your notes, be careful to separate them from those of your sources. Later, you will want to know exactly which ideas were yours and which were your source's. Using square brackets [like these] around your own ideas is a good way of making this distinction.

6. **Keep a running record of page references.**

In your essay, you will have to cite the correct page number for *each* reference, not an approximate guess. It is not enough to write "pp. 285–91" at the top of the note card or page. Three weeks later, or three hours later, how will you remember on *which* pages you found the point that you want to cite in your essay? If you are writing a lengthy set of notes that paraphrase your source, make a slash and insert a new page number to indicate exactly where you turned the page. Recording page numbers is especially important for *quotations*. Of course, it is vital that you immediately put quotation marks around all quotations.

7. **Keep a master list of the sources in your preliminary bibliography, assigning a code number or symbol to each one.**

As you take notes, use an abbreviation or code number to identify each new source. When you begin a new card or sheet, you won't have to repeat all the basic information.

Guidelines for Taking Good Notes

1. Try to complete your survey of the library's resources and work out a preliminary bibliography before you start to make copies or take notes.
2. Use paraphrase and summary rather than quotation.
3. Make sure that your notes make sense.
4. Include a certain number of facts to serve as your supporting evidence.
5. Differentiate your own ideas from those that you are paraphrasing.
6. Keep a running record of page references.
7. Keep a master list of the sources in your preliminary bibliography, assigning a code number or symbol to each one.

Using Note Cards—One Fact per Card

The traditional method of taking notes is to write *a single fact or piece of information on one three-by-five-inch index card.* These single-note cards are easily organized by topic into stacks; they can also be left at home when you go back to the library. Index cards, however, can stray from the pile and become lost. A stack of cards should be kept under control with a sturdy rubber band.

Certain topics lend themselves to note cards, topics that require the collection of small, fragmentary bits of information, like facts or brief descriptions, which fit easily on an index card. Eight-by-ten-inch cards or sheets of paper (written by hand or on the computer) may be more practical for an

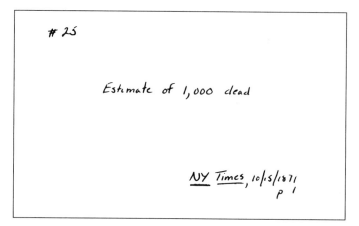

Figure 7-1. One-Fact-per-Card Method

abstract topic that depends on complex sources, with each one discussed at length. If you are typing notes into a computer, put a page break between each fact or each topic, so you can print out a separate sheet for each piece of information.

Whether you write on small cards or long sheets, make sure that you write on one side only. Whether you write by hand or use a computer, be careful to label each separate unit of information with its exact source and page number, using abbreviations, symbols, or numbers.

One student, taking notes for an essay describing the 1871 fire that devastated Chicago, used the one-fact-per-card method shown in Figure 7-1. The empty space left on this card may seem wasteful, but the method enables the writer, later on, to place all the cards that refer to the category *casualties* in a single pile. If the card contained information relating to two different categories—like *casualties* and *looting*—the same card would have to be placed in two separate piles, which would defeat the purpose of the organizational system. Notice that, to keep track of all the notes, the writer has assigned a number (#25) to the card. Of course, the source *and* page number are included.

Notes Grouped by Topic

A second student used a more sophisticated system combining note-taking and preliminary organization. Early in the note-taking process, the student decided that at least one card would be devoted only to notes about *fire-fighting*. Thereafter, every time the student came across a new point about fire-fighting—no matter what the source—it was added to that card. Students who take notes using a computer can start a new file for each topic or simply establish several topics within the same file, and scroll through searching

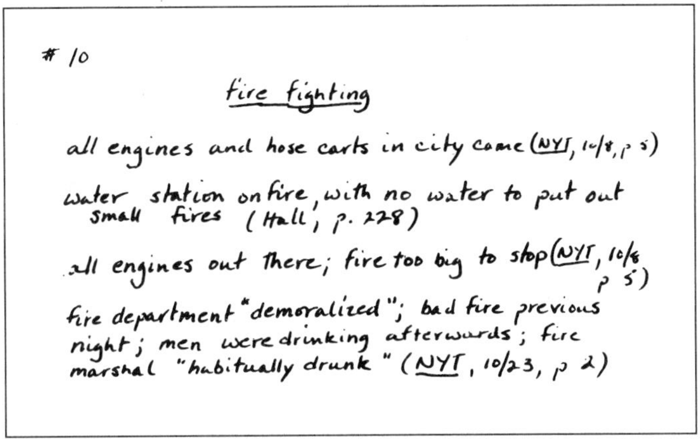

10

<u>fire fighting</u>

all engines and hose carts in city come (<u>NYT</u>, 10/8, p 5)

water station on fire, with no water to put out
small fires (Hall, p. 228)

all engines out there; fire too big to stop (<u>NYT</u>, 10/8
p 5)

fire department "demoralized"; bad fire previous
night; men were drinking afterwards; fire
marshal "habitually drunk" (<u>NYT</u>, 10/23, p 2)

Figure 7-2. Notes Grouped by Topic

for the topic name as each new piece of information is added. Such organization depends on making a list, either written or mental, of possible categories or note topics.

Because the notes in Figure 7-2 are grouped according to topic, this student will find organizing an outline easier than will the first student. But preliminary categorizing during the note-taking stage is practical only with relatively short items. A lengthy presentation of a theory can ruin this tidy system by forcing the note-taker to devote card after card to a single idea from a single source. (Notice that none of the sources on the "fire-fighting" card seems to offer any lengthy opinions about the fire.) For this reason, when you organize notes by topic, you may prefer to use long sheets of paper or a computer in order to be prepared for any kind of material and to have enough space.

Notes Grouped by Source

Instead of putting one point on each card or one topic on each card, a third student chose to use *one source per sheet*. This system, shown in Figure 7-3, "uses up" one source at a time and produces a long sheet of notes in which the information is presented in the order of its appearance in the source.

The disadvantage of this method is that it doesn't encourage you to start categorizing. This student, however, *numbered each item* on the sheet and also gave each sheet *a code letter*. When the time comes to synthesize these notes into paragraph topics, the student can establish a category dealing with, say, *food supplies,* find the relevant references to that topic, and place the code numbers under that heading. While writing the first draft, the writer will find H-11 under the heading *food supplies* and have immediate access to information about the price of bread after the fire. (For further explanation of this process, see Chapter 8, p. 335).

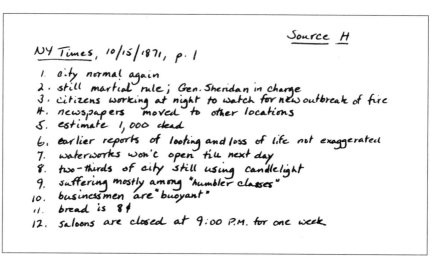

Figure 7-3. Notes Grouped by Source

TAKING NOTES FROM ABSTRACT SOURCES

As the sample notes suggest, research on the Chicago fire uncovered mostly factual information about incidents that occurred during and after the catastrophe. The notes are therefore brief, factual summaries. When the source consists of generalizations and evidence used to develop complex ideas, the note-taker must often struggle to understand and paraphrase abstract thinking.

To illustrate the difficulties, here is a brief extract from *Victorian Cities*, by Asa Briggs. Assume that the book is being consulted for an essay on "The City One Hundred Years Ago."

The industrial city was bound to be a place of problems. Economic individualism and common civic purpose were difficult to reconcile. The priority of industrial discipline in shaping all human relations was bound to make other aspects of life seem secondary. A high rate of industrial investment might mean not only a low rate of consumption and a paucity of social investment but a total indifference to social costs. Overcrowding was one problem: displacement was another. There were parts of Liverpool with a density of 1,200 persons to the acre in 1884: rebuilding might entail the kind of difficulties which were set out in a verse in *The Builder* of 1851:

> Who builds? Who builds? Alas, ye poor!
> If London day by day "improves,"
> Where shall ye find a friendly door,
> When every day a home removes?

The paragraph may seem hard to understand on first reading because Briggs is developing his image of the industrial city through *a series of abstract words combined into phrases*—"economic individualism," "common civic purpose," "industrial discipline," and "low rate of consumption."

These difficult abstractions, typical of the social sciences, are included in the paragraph as if everyone could easily understand them. Fortunately, the essential point is repeated in several different ways and supported by some straightforward facts about the density of population in Liverpool. The passage ends with quite a different kind of evidence: a verse-quotation suggesting that, earlier in the century, people were already aware of the dangers of unlimited expansion.

The figures below show attempts at note-taking based on Briggs's paragraph.

In Figure 7-4, the researcher has made a point of paraphrasing, rather than copying the original phrasing, and thus has avoided the danger of quoting the author's words without acknowledgment. The researcher's brief comments in square brackets, clearly distinguished from the notes on Briggs, suggest some points for development in the research essay.

If you don't expect to refer to Briggs in any detail, making a note that summarizes his basic point more briefly would be sufficient, as in Figure 7-5.

> Briggs, p. 491
>
> If capital is being used for industrial expansion and personal profit, the same money can't be used for social services. [This was before the welfare state.] Because production was paramount, no one worried that living conditions were impossibly crowded or that people were evicted or moved to allow for industrial expansion. Example: Liverpool -- 1,200 per acre in 1884. Fear of improvement ("If London day by day 'improves'") [sounds like urban renewal and the inner city cycle today -- renovating slum brownstones becomes fashionable]

Figure 7-4. Note A: Effective Summary, Using Paraphrase

> Briggs, p. 491
>
> Danger of industrialization: profit becomes more important than social values. Expansion results in a highly dense population and the need for relocating existing neighborhoods.

Figure 7-5. Note B: Effective Short Summary

In taking good notes, everything depends on achieving a clear understanding of the author's meaning. Figure 7-6, however, suggests that the researcher did not bother to puzzle out the complexities of the paragraph and, instead, tried a few wild guesses. With the possible exception of the first sentence, none of these points can be correctly attributed to Briggs, whose meaning has been entirely distorted. On the other hand, in Figure 7-7, the attempt to play it safe by copying out the phrases verbatim is equally unsuccessful. Although this information is beautifully laid out in outline form, with quotation marks carefully inserted, there is no evidence that the researcher has understood a word of Briggs's paragraph. Moreover, the outline format makes it hard to understand the relationship among these concepts. When the time comes to include a reference to Briggs in the research essay, this student will have no idea how the phrases fit together.

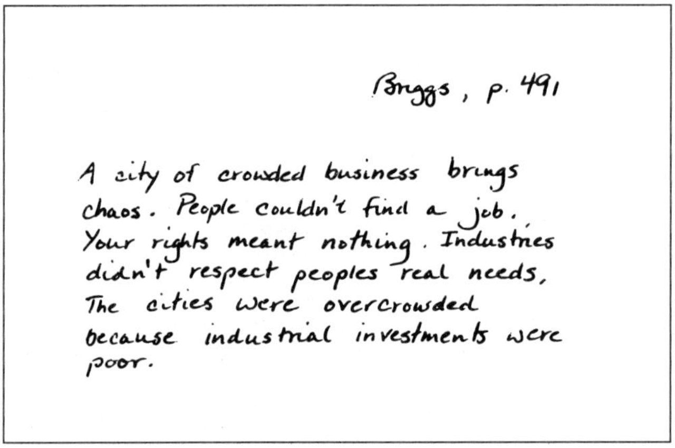

Briggs, p. 491

A city of crowded business brings chaos. People couldn't find a job. Your rights meant nothing. Industries didn't respect peoples real needs. The cities were overcrowded because industrial investments were poor.

Figure 7-6. Note C: Distortion of the Source

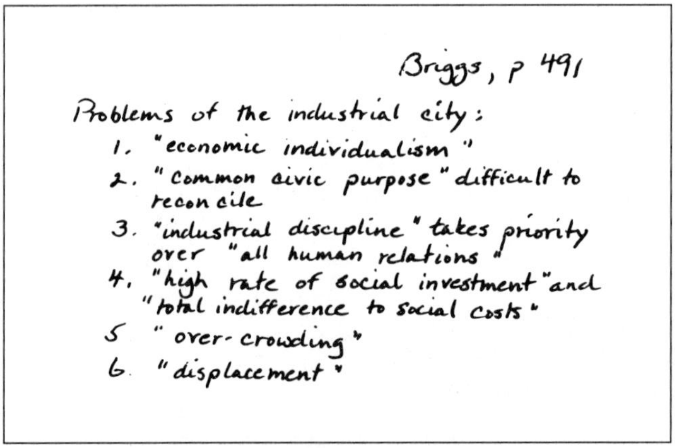

Briggs, p 491

Problems of the industrial city:
1. "economic individualism"
2. "Common civic purpose" difficult to reconcile
3. "industrial discipline" takes priority over "all human relations"
4. "high rate of social investment" and "total indifference to social costs"
5. "over-crowding"
6. "displacement"

Figure 7-7. Note D: Meaningless List

Even when a reading is much less abstract and densely argued than the excerpt from Briggs, it is possible to distort the author's meaning by selecting the wrong points to emphasize in your notes. Here are two paragraphs from *Shakespeare of London,* by Marchette Chute, followed by sample notes for an essay on "Shakespeare's Education as a Playwright."

Apart from teaching him Latin, Stratford grammar school taught Shakespeare nothing at all. It did not teach him mathematics or any of the natural sciences. It did not teach him history, unless a few pieces of information about ancient events strayed in through Latin quotations. It did not teach him geography, for the first (and most inadequate) textbook on geography did not appear until the end of the century, and maps and atlases were rare even in university circles. It did not teach him modern languages, for when a second language was taught at a grammar school it was invariably Greek.

What Shakespeare learned about any of these subjects he learned for himself later, in London. London was the one great storehouse in England of living, contemporary knowledge and in that city an alert and intelligent man could find out almost anything he wanted to know. It was in London, for instance, that Shakespeare learned French; and French was taught by Frenchmen who worked in competition with each other and used oral conversational methods that were designed to get colloquial French into the student's head as quickly as possible.

In Figure 7-8, the note-taker has made the essential contrast between Stratford and London, and the generalization is clearly distinguished from the evidence that Chute cites to support it. In Figure 7-9, the focus shifts from what Shakespeare did or did not learn to the deficiencies of schools in sixteenth-century England.

What the student is missing in Note F is the contrast between an ordinary, unsophisticated school in rural England and the resources available to an

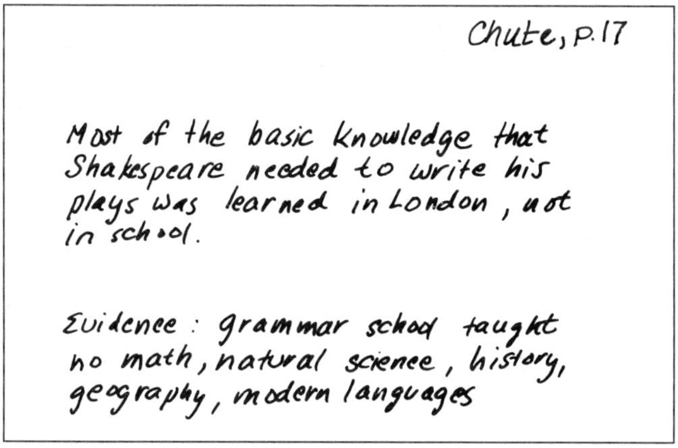

Chute, p. 17

Most of the basic knowledge that Shakespeare needed to write his plays was learned in London, not in school.

Evidence: grammar school taught no math, natural science, history, geography, modern languages

Figure 7-8. Note E: Summarizing the Main Point, with Supporting Facts

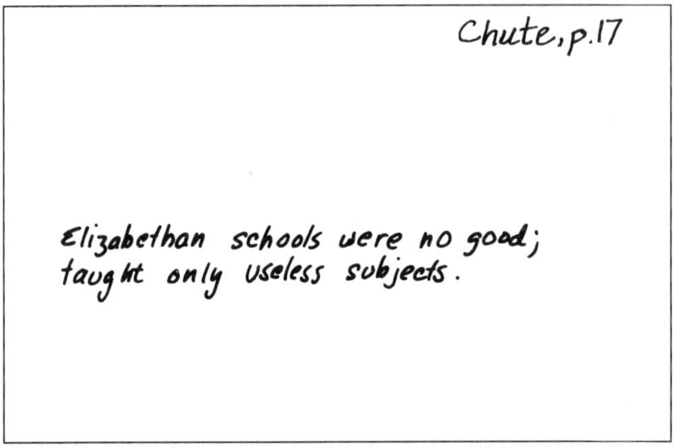

Figure 7-9. Note F: False Emphasis/Context Disregarded

inquiring young man (no longer a school boy) in the capital city. The note-taker has ignored the *context* of the two paragraphs and the material that surrounds them in the original source. Chute has previously explained the advantages that Shakespeare derived from learning Latin at school, and is now listing what he was unable to learn (partly because books and other teaching materials had not yet been developed). Chute is *not* condemning Stratford grammar school, but preparing the reader for the burst of learning that would occur when Shakespeare arrived in London. The context for the paper—Shakespeare's development—is ignored in favor of a narrower focus on the inaccurate statement that he was taught nothing at all.

EXERCISE 24: EVALUATING NOTES

In 1937, the German airship *Hindenburg* caught fire near Lakehurst, New Jersey, killing thirty-six people. Two of the many eyewitness accounts were by Leonhard Adelt and Margaret Mather, both passengers on the ship. Read these two passages (which begin on p. 329) and then evaluate the sets of notes that follow them prepared by students writing about the *Hindenburg* disaster. Consider the following criteria:

1. Does one get a good sense of the experience from reading the notes?
2. Which sets of notes are reliable? complete?
3. Do any of the notes omit anything important?
4. Which notes quote excessively?
5. Does the note-taker recognize that the two sources often confirm each other's testimony, and indicate when they agree?
6. Would the notes make sense to someone who had not read the original?
7. Which sets of notes would you prefer to work from if you were writing an essay on the *Hindenburg*?

Leonhard Adelt's Account

With my wife I was leaning out of a window on the promenade deck. Suddenly there occurred a remarkable stillness. The motors were silent, and it seemed as though the whole world was holding its breath. One heard no command, no call, no cry. The people we saw seemed suddenly stiffened. | 1

I could not account for this. Then I heard a light, dull detonation from above, no louder than the sound of a beer bottle being opened. I turned my gaze toward the bow and noticed a delicate rose glow, as though the sun were about to rise. I understood immediately that the airship was aflame. There was but one chance for safety—to jump out. The distance from the ground at that moment may have been 120 feet. For a moment I thought of getting bed linen from the corridor in order to soften our leap, but in the same instant, the airship crashed to the ground with terrific force. Its impact threw us from the window to the stair corridor. The tables and chairs of the reading room crashed about and jammed us in like a barricade. | 2

"Through the window!" I shouted to my fellow passengers, and dragged my wife with me to our observation window. | 3

Reality ceased with one stroke, as though fate in its cruelty was yet compassionate enough to withdraw from its victims the consciousness of their horror. I do not know, and my wife does not know, how we leaped from the airship. The distance from the ground may have been 12 or 15 feet. I distinctly felt my feet touch the soft sand and grass. We collapsed to our knees, and the impenetrable darkness of black oil clouds, shot through with flames, enveloped us. We had to let go of each other's hands in order to make our way through the confusion of hot metal pieces and wires. We bent the hot metal apart with our bare hands without feeling pain. | 4

We freed ourselves and ran through a sea of fire. It was like a dream. Our bodies had no weight. They floated like stars through space. | 5

Margaret Mather's Account

I was leaning out of an open window in the dining saloon with many others including the young aviator, who was taking photographs. He told me that he had taken eighty during the trip. When there were mysterious sounds from the engines I glanced at him for reassurance. | 1

At that moment we heard the dull muffled sound of an explosion. I saw a look of incredulous consternation on his face. Almost instantly the ship lurched and I was hurled a distance of fifteen or twenty feet against an end wall. | 2

I was pinned against a projecting bench by several Germans who were thrown after me. I couldn't breathe and thought I should die suffocated, but they all jumped up. | 3

Then the flames blew in, long tongues of flame, bright red and very beautiful. | 4

My companions were leaping up and down amid the flames. The lurching of the ship threw them repeatedly against the furniture and the railing, where they cut their hands and faces against the metal trimmings. They were streaming with blood. I saw a number of men leap from the windows, but I sat just where I had fallen, holding the lapels of my coat across my face, feeling the flames light on my back, my | 5

hat, my hair, trying to beat them out, watching the horrified faces of my companions as they leaped up and down.

Just then a man—I think the man who exclaimed "Mein Gott" as we left the   6
earth—detached himself from the leaping forms, and threw himself against a railing
(arms and legs spread wide) with a loud terrible cry of "Es ist das Ende."

I thought so too but I continued to protect my eyes. I was thinking that it was   7
like a scene from a medieval picture of hell. I was waiting for the crash landing.

Suddenly I heard a loud cry: "Come out, lady!" I looked and we were on the ground.   8

Student A

All of a sudden there was complete silence and not a sound from the
motors of the airship. Everybody in the airship "stiffened." Leonhard Adelt suddenly "heard a dull detonation from above, no louder than a beer bottle being
opened." L.A. knew that the "airship was aflame." The only way to save one's life
was to jump. This meant the jump was for 120 feet. All of a sudden, "the airship
crashed to the ground with terrific" speed. The force was so high that Margaret
Mather "was hurled a distance of fifteen to twenty feet against an end wall."

Student B

"At that moment we heard the dull and muffled sound of an explosion.
Almost suddenly the ship lurched and I was hurled a distance of 15 or 20 feet
against an end wall." This is the beginning described by two passengers that
were on the Hindenburg of 1937. After a long voyage over the Atlantic and being
so close to their destiny, this was too much of a shock for them to handle. All
the passengers had to escape death. Some were fortunate, others weren't. "I was
pinned against a projecting bench by several Germans who were thrown after
me. I couldn't breathe, and thought I should die, suffocated, but they all jumped
up." Everyone ran for their life.

Student C

Adelt: "The motors were silent"

Mather: "Dull muffled sound of an explosion"

Adelt: "I turned my gaze toward the bow and noticed a rose glow. . . ."

Mather: "The ship lurched and I was hurled a distance of fifteen or twenty feet
against an end wall."

Adelt: "Its impact threw us from the window to the stair corridor."

Mather: "Then the flames blew in"

Mather: "I saw a number of men leap from the windows."

Adelt: "We leaped from the airship."

Student D

before crash:

Adelt: "The motors were silent" "I heard a light, dull detonation from above. . . ."
"I turned my gaze toward the bow and noticed a delicate rose glow"

Mather: "Mysterious sounds from the engine" . . . "dull muffled sound of an explosion" . . . "then the flames blew in, long tongues of flame, bright red and very beautiful"

after crash:

Adelt: "'Through the window!' I shouted to my fellow passengers. . . ." ". . . how we leaped from the airship. The distance from the ground may have been 12 or 15 feet," . . . "impenetrable darkness of black oil clouds, shot through with flames" . . . "a sea of fire."

Mather: ". . . where they cut their hands and faces against the metal trimmings. They were streaming with blood."

Student E

"I turned my gaze toward the bow and noticed a delicate rose glow, as though the sun were about to rise." The blimp catches on fire: the only means of escape is jumping to the ground. Distance from the ground approximately 12 or 15 feet when couple jumped out of "airship." People "beat the hot metal apart with our bare hands without feeling pain." How mind works when in life and death situation. No pain. People had to run through fire one at a time.

Mather: "mysterious sounds from the engine." She was leaning out of the dining saloon, heard sounds of explosion. People thrown 15 or 20 feet after hearing explosion. Flames came into room after people thrown. "lurching of ship threw them repeatedly across furniture and the railings."

Student F

There was an inexplicable silence followed by a "light, dull detonation from above, no louder than the sound of a beer bottle being opened." Then it was discovered that the airship was on fire looking like "the sun were about to rise." There was the realization that the only chance for survival was to abandon the ship. By the time the decision to jump and the action itself was implemented, the ship had crashed (from 120 feet). Upon impact, everything in the ship (chairs, tables, people) was tossed about. Reality became suspended "as though fate in its cruelty was yet compassionate enough to withdraw from its victims the consciousness of their horror."

EXERCISE 25: TAKING NOTES ON TWO TOPICS

Reread the three articles dealing with the Cocoanut Grove fire of 1942 at the end of Chapter 6. Head one group of cards or one sheet of paper "The Causes of the Fire," and take a set of notes on that topic. Head another group of cards or sheet of paper "The Fire's Intensity and Speed," and take a second set of notes on the second topic. Each set of notes should make use of all three sources.

EXERCISE 26: TAKING NOTES ON THREE TOPICS

Assume that you are doing research on the Indian Wars and that you have come across the following source in the library. After doing a preliminary evaluation of the passage, take a set of notes for an essay entitled "The Native American Ideal of Honor," a second set of notes for an essay entitled "War Atrocities," and a third set of notes for an essay entitled "White Attitudes toward Native Americans."

from *KILLING CUSTER*
James Welch

Most tribal battles involved a lot of skirmishing, a lot of coup counting, with very few casualties. Indians were not out to annihilate each other, but to exact revenge or cover themselves with war honors. In most instances, it was better to humiliate the enemy than to kill him. A Blackfeet account tells of a party of horse raiders who stole into an enemy camp one night and made off with some buffalo runners. One of the raiders found a sentry sleeping at the base of a ledge near the edge of camp. The warrior pissed on the sentry from the ledge, then stole off into the darkness. This feat was talked about in the Blackfeet camps for years to come. The Blackfeet got off with the horses, and the drenched sentry had to explain to his chiefs what happened. It was almost better than counting coup. It gave the whole tribe a chuckle.

Of course, warfare was more serious than that. It was important to lift the enemy's hair, both as a warning to the enemy and as a morale-booster to the scalper, his party, and other tribesmen. Nothing delighted a waiting camp more than to see scalps on the lances of returning warriors. These scalps were passed around, talked about, laughed at, sometimes thrown into the fire or given to the dogs in disdain. Often the hair decorated a lodge or was sewn onto a war shirt. White men's hair was taken but was less desirable because it was usually short. Some of the white men were balding and weren't worth scalping. But scalping was an institution among the Plains tribes. A scalp was a trophy of war, just as it became for the whites.

Torture, and the mutilation of bodies dead and alive, was, and is, more problematic, if only because it is odious to civilized society. Throughout the years, those cultures which have "seen the light" have been horrified by the desecration of bodies committed by barbarians of other cultures. We think of the Nazis in World

War II who justified torture and mutilation of live bodies for "scientific" purposes. The communists in Russia, especially under Stalin, committed similar atrocities on ethnic groups. The Khmer Rouge beheaded and chopped the limbs from innocent people and left them by the thousands in the killing fields of Cambodia. The military did the same in El Salvador. Thousands of Moskito Indians died in such a horrible fashion. African leaders, in their beribboned military costumes and with their weapons supplied by the United States, Russia, France, and Israel, continue to kill and mutilate their tribal enemies.

European tribes beheaded their foes, posting the heads along roads or at the   4
town gates as a grisly warning to those who would oppose them. The Catholic Church in Europe, especially Spain, during the Inquisition tortured and mutilated those who it thought were possessed by the devil—or those it simply wanted to get rid of for political reasons. The Puritans in America burned, crushed, and drowned people almost gratuitously in their effort to root out witchery. Thousands, probably millions, of people have been treated in a similar fashion by the religious right of all cultures.

Soldiers who go to war commit unspeakable acts to their enemies. Homer tells   5
us that in the Trojan War, Achilles dragged Hector's mutilated body behind his chariot for twelve days. From the time of the Slaughter of the Innocents to My Lai in Vietnam, war has created a callousness toward human life to such a degree that torture and mutilation have become accepted practices. Witness the Serbs in their treatment of the Muslims, torturing and mutilating men, raping women to death— all in the name of ethnic and religious purity. Virtually all warfare has been conducted for such contrived principles as ethnic and religious purity.

On November 29, 1864, a former Methodist preacher and Civil War officer,   6
Colonel John Chivington, led two regiments of Colorado militia in a dawn attack on a sleeping camp of Southern Cheyennes at Sand Creek. This group of Indians was led by Black Kettle, who survived the attack only to be killed four years later in another dawn surprise led by General George A. Custer on the Washita River in Oklahoma.

The reason given for Chivington's attack was a familiar one. Indians had been   7
raiding, stealing horses and cattle, killing settlers. Whether the attack by Chivington's hundred-day volunteers caught the right Indians is not even debatable. They did not. It has been stated that these Colorado volunteers' enlistment was about up and they wanted some action. Because of their inefficiency in punishing Indians they were derisively called the "Bloodless" 3rd Cavalry.

Black Kettle had been given an American flag at a treaty council in 1861 by the   8
Commissioner of Indian Affairs. The chief had been told at that time that as long as the flag flew over his village his people would be safe.

It is known that some of Chivington's junior officers reminded him of this   9
promise. Evan S. Connell, in *Son of the Morning Star,* quotes the violent Chivington as replying: "I have come to kill Indians, and believe it is right and honorable to use any means under God's heaven to kill Indians!" He is reported to have added: "Scalps are what we are after. . . . I long to be wading in gore!"

And soon he was. Even after Black Kettle himself came out of his lodge waving   10
the American flag, Chivington's troopers shot men, women, and children indiscrim-
inately. There are many accounts, not only those of Indian survivors but also those
of the troopers themselves, of soldiers taking deliberate aim at fleeing children. A
Major Scott Anthony remembered the murder of a three-year-old: "I saw one man
get off his horse at a distance of about seventy-five yards and draw up his rifle and
fire. He missed the child. Another man came up and said, 'Let me try the son of a
bitch. I can hit him.' He got down off his horse, kneeled down, and fired at the little
child, but he missed him. A third man came up and made a similar remark, and
fired, and the little fellow dropped."

When the killing ended, soldiers went from body to body, scalping them, cutting   11
off ears and fingers to get at jewelry, cutting out the genitals of men, women, and
children, arranging the bodies in suggestive postures. A Lieutenant James Connor
stated in testimony that he did not find a single body that had not been mutilated.
He went on: "I also heard of numerous instances in which men had cut out the private parts of females and stretched them over the saddlebows and wore them over
their hats while riding in the ranks."

By way of justification for such acts, several men said they found scalps, which   12
they identified as belonging to whites by the color of the hair, hanging from lodge-
poles, a couple of them fresh. "The skin and flesh attached to the hair appeared to
be yet quite moist," one said. It doesn't appear that there were many of these scalps,
but by the time the militia got back to Denver the number had grown to dozens of
white scalps—as well as a blanket woven from white women's hair.

Chivington's troop's last act of heroism was to display a hundred Indian scalps on   13
the stage of a Denver theater. They were greeted by thunderous applause. The
Bloodless 3rd became celebrated as the "Bloody Thirdsters."

The Indians committed their share of atrocities, of torture and mutilation. There   14
had been many accounts in the eastern newspapers of such acts, but they were isolated, small instances, quickly forgotten in the bustle of the industrializing nation.
The frontier newspapers were more alarmed. These killings were happening too
close for comfort. In 1869, the *Helena Weekly Herald* reported: "That we are on
the verge of a general Indian outbreak no sensible man who understands the situation can deny. The pleasant and innocent amusement of butchering and scalping the
pale-faces is believed by some likely soon to begin in good earnest."

But the Plains Indians were equally outraged by the notion that an invasion force   15
of whites was seeking to conquer them, perhaps annihilate them, certainly take
their land, kill all their buffalo, and reduce them to prisoners on reservations where
they would be forced to deny their religion, their culture, their traditional methods
of supporting themselves—in short, take away their way of life as they had practiced it for centuries. They had learned at Sand Creek, the Marias, and the Washita
that the whites would stop at nothing to bend the Indians to their will. The arrogant invaders would not stop until the Indians were forced to adopt the ways of
the white man—or were executed.

·8·

Organizing and Writing the Research Essay

You should plan and write your research essay in exactly the same way that you would work on any other essay. Whatever the topic, you will probably start out with written notes—facts, ideas, comments, opinions—that serve as the raw materials for your synthesis. From these notes, you form a sequence of separate generalizations to be used as the focus of each of your paragraphs. These steps help you to work out the basic structure of your essay.

The difference between organizing the research essay and organizing the other essays that you have previously written comes from the unusually large quantity of *notes.* The term "notes" here refers to any of the products of your research, including your own *summaries* and *paraphrases, quotations, Xeroxed copies* of pages and articles, class *lecture notes,* and stories clipped from *newspapers,* as well as *your own ideas* about the topic.

TAKING INVENTORY AND
DEVELOPING A LIST OF TOPICS

You search for ideas worth developing by reviewing all the major points that you have learned and thought about during your research. These ideas form the core of your essay.

You select the main ideas of your research by:

1. Carefully reading through all your notes;
2. Looking for and writing down any points that seem especially important to understanding and explaining your topic.

In other words, *you take a new set of notes from your old set.* In this way, you can reduce the accumulated mass of information to a more manageable size. The new list of generalizations can be rearranged, tried out in different versions, and eventually converted into an outline of topic sentences.

Organizing your essay involves:

- reading lists of notes,
- thinking about them,
- making new lists,
- deleting and adding items,
- rearranging the order.

You follow these steps until the list of topics—and the paragraphs of your essay—form a sequence that both makes sense and makes your point. This process is actually a more elaborate version of the synthesis that you practiced in Chapter 4.

Guidelines for Taking Inventory of Your Notes and Forming Your Paragraph Topics

1. *Do write down in any order* the important ideas that you find in your notes. At this point, the items don't have to be related to each other in sequence.

2. *Don't* try to *summarize* all your notes or even summarize each of your notes. At this point, you are working on a paragraph outline, not a summary of your research.

3. *Don't try to link* the ideas that you write down to specific sources. At this point, there is no special reason to place the names of the sources next to your new list of ideas; not every statement in your new list will be included in your essay. Later, you will decide which source to use in support of which topic sentence.

4. *Do think about your own reactions* to the information that you have collected. At this point, the many strands of your research begin to become the product of your own thinking. Now you are deciding what is worth writing about.

5. *Do use your own words.* At this point, even if you only jot down a phrase or a fragment, it should be *your* version of the source's idea. Even if the point has appeared in ten different articles (and has been noted on ten different index cards), you are now, in some sense, making it your own.

6. *Do evaluate your list* of important ideas that are worth writing about. At this point, notice which ideas are in the mainstream of your research, discussed by several of your sources, and which ones appear in only one or two sources. Consider whether you have enough evidence to support these ideas or whether you should exclude them from your master outline. Think about eliminating the ones that seem minor or remote from the topic. Remember to look for and combine similar statements. If you are developing an argument essay, make sure that each of the key points supporting your side, as well as your counterarguments to the opposition, is supported by your research.

7. *Do think about the sequence of ideas* on your final list and the possible *strategies* for organizing your essay. At this point, consider how these ideas relate to the topic with which you began your research:

   - How does your list of ideas help to establish a thesis?

   - Are you working with a collection of reasons? consequences? problems? dangers?

   - What kind of essay are you writing: cause and effect? problem and solution? explanation of a procedure? evaluation of reasons for an argument?

   If you are developing a historical or biographical topic:
   - Did the event fall into distinct narrative stages?

   - What aspects of the scene would an observer have noticed?

   - Which of your subject's activities best reveals his or her personality?

   If you are developing an argument:
   - Does your issue lend itself to a cause-and-effect or a problem-and-solution essay?

   - Do your main reasons require deductive or inductive support?

   - Which are your most compelling arguments?

8. *Do arrange your list of topics* in a sequence that has meaning for you, carries out your strategy, and develops your thesis in a clear direction.

PLANNING A STRATEGY FOR ARGUMENT

In Chapter 1, you learned that most arguments are based on a combination of two kinds of logical reasoning:

- *deductive* reasoning: you provide a series of linked premises, based on assumptions that you and your reader share, that leads to a logical conclusion.
- *inductive* reasoning: you provide a range of evidence from which you construct a logical conclusion.

In practice, these two basic logical tools—the use of linked premises and the use of evidence—are often used to develop the most common patterns of argument: cause-and-effect and problem-and-solution.

The *cause-and-effect* essay establishes a causal linkage between two circumstances. The argumentative thesis is usually derived from answering the question "why?" Why is the high school dropout rate as high as it is today? Here are a few typical answers: because class sizes are too large; because students are poorly prepared to handle the work; because many students are foreign-born and can't speak English well; because local governments are not providing sufficient funding; because family life is breaking down, leaving students without support and discipline.

Clearly, there are many possible causes. If you try to give equal weight to every one of them, your essay will be long and unmanageable, with a thesis that pulls the reader in many contrary directions. If, however, you focus on only one cause, you run the risk of oversimplifying your argument. First, *consider whether a specific cause actually accounts for its effect and whether other circumstances also have a contributing influence.* Also consider which causes work together: the problem of class size is probably linked to—caused by—the problem of funding. Here you have a smaller cause-and-effect embedded within the larger one. It's these links that you have to point out in the deductive part of your argument.

Notice how most of the causes listed above lend themselves to *inductive support.*

You should expect to find factual evidence, including statistics, about class sizes, student preparedness, language difficulties, and diminished funding. (Whether or not that evidence supports your causal point about student dropouts will emerge from your research.) The last point on the list is more abstract; you would need to develop a series of deductive premises to make a strong causal linkage between the decline of family life and the incidence of high school dropouts.

What kinds of counterarguments would you have to anticipate and rebut? This may be a question of weight and emphasis. You believe that the poor educational environment, resulting from inadequate funding, makes it hard for students to learn so they drop out. While your research supports this thesis, you also find authorities who argue that students from strong family backgrounds perform well and stay in school even in periods of economic hardship. You must defend your preferred thesis, while acknowledging the more limited validity of your opponent's.

The *problem-and-solution* essay often incorporates the cause-and-effect essay in five stages:

1. *Establish that a problem exists.* Explain why it is a problem, and anticipate the negative consequences if nothing is done.

2. *Analyze the causes of the problem.* Here you can include a modified version of the cause-and-effect strategy: emphasize the major causes, but remind your reader that this is a complex issue, with a number of contributory influences working together. Provide some evidence, but not the full range of your research on causes.

3. *Assert the best solution.* Using the evidence of your research, demonstrate its benefits, and indicate how you would go about implementing it.

4. *Anticipate counterarguments and answer them.* Your research has turned up authorities who have recommended different solutions. What are the advantages and disadvantages of those solutions? Is your solution better? Why?

5. *Conclude in a spirit of accommodation.* Assert your solution once again, but also consider acknowledging the complexity of the problem and making room for some of your opponents' ideas. Sometimes the arguments on either side of an issue are too evenly balanced for certainty, and you need to find a solution within common ground.

As an example of such accommodation, here is the beginning of the last paragraph of Sanford Levinson's "The Court's Death Blow," a defense of assisted suicide in the context of the 1997 Supreme Court decision:

> So, on balance, what should "liberals" believe in regard to assisted suicide? With fear and trembling, we should, as a political matter, support enhancing the choices available to people (including, ultimately, to us) as death begins to overtake life. But we should also recognize that people of undoubted good faith, committed no less than we are to protecting the vulnerable and to criticizing optimistic assumptions about "free markets" and "untrammeled choice," are on the other side of this issue. It is a true judgment call, balancing important autonomy interests against the possibility of exploitation.

ARRANGING THE ORDER OF TOPICS

At some point in the process of organizing your essay, your initial list of ideas becomes an outline. After you make new lists out of old ones, adding and deleting topics, you finally decide on a sequence that will correspond to the sequence of paragraphs in your essay. In a historical essay, the ordering principle is frequently time: the deployment of troops has to be described before the actual battle. In a personality portrait, dominant qualities will take precedence over minor quirks. Problems get described before solutions; causes before effects.

When you organize, you are determining priorities and prerequisites, based on the relationships between ideas. What does your reader need to know first? What information does your reader need in order to understand a second, more complex point? How does one idea lead into another?

In determining the sequence of reasons for an argument essay, first assess the degree of support that you have provided for each one through your research. At the same time, consider the strength of the arguments against each reason, as presented by your opponents. You will probably find that some points are naturally linked to others and that stronger, well-supported points take precedence over more tenuous ones. One rationale for your sequence is "most compelling" to "least compelling" reason. But a stronger rationale is "most fundamental" to "most complex" or "most peripheral." Your earlier arguments become a platform on which your later arguments can rest.

USING THE COMPUTER TO ORGANIZE YOUR ESSAY

One advantage of taking notes on a computer is that you can move the items around experimentally as you develop a new sequence of key ideas. Even if you have only a limited knowledge of word processing, you'll soon find it easy to pull a quotation or a paragraph out of your notes and add it to your outline, or to place a concrete example next to the general idea that it illustrates. A more sophisticated knowledge of "windows" and other software allows you to shift back and forth from one file to another or see two screens simultaneously, giving you even more flexibility in trying out different organizational strategies.

As you work with your notes on the computer, remember to *make a duplicate file of your notes,* keeping one file intact as a resource should you, later on, want to abandon a half-completed outline and start over or—worst case—lose your working file completely. Above all, *save your work at regular and frequent intervals*—and back up your files on a disk—or your notes and outline may suddenly dissolve into an empty screen.

The computer can make organizing, writing, and revising a research paper very easy. You can electronically manipulate notes, sentences, and paragraphs with miraculous speed. But you should apply the same thoughtfulness and care to working out your strategies for organization on the computer as you would if you were rearranging a stack of index cards and cutting and pasting a typed draft.

CROSS-REFERENCING

When you have developed a list of major topics that will roughly correspond to the paragraphs of your essay, you are ready to link your tentative outline to your research notes. Remember to:

- Leave plenty of space between the items on your outline; and
- Assign a number or a letter to each item.

Now, once again, *slowly reread all your research notes, this time keeping your list of topics in front of you.* Every time you come across a point in your notes that might be cited in support of a topic on your outline, immediately:

1. Place the number or letter of the topic in your outline next to the reference in your notes.

2. Place the source's name (and the number of the notecard, if you have used that system, or the page number of your notes) under the item on your outline.

For the system to work, you must complete both stages: notes must be keyed to the outline, and the outline must be keyed to each item in your research notes. The notes and the outline criss-cross each other; hence the term, *cross-referencing.*

To illustrate cross-referencing, here are three paragraph topics taken from an outline for an essay on the *Chicago Fire.* The outline for the essay is divided into three main sections: the *causes* of the fire, the *panic* during the fire, and *restoring order* after the fire. The three paragraph topics come from the last section of the outline. Figure 8-1 shows an excerpt from the notes for the essay. Both paragraph topics and notes have cross-references in the margins. Notice that, to avoid confusion, the paragraph topics have Roman numerals, and the notes have arabic numerals.

Paragraph Topics

IX. Feeding the homeless G6/G7

X. Providing basic services G4

XI. Protecting life and property G3/G8

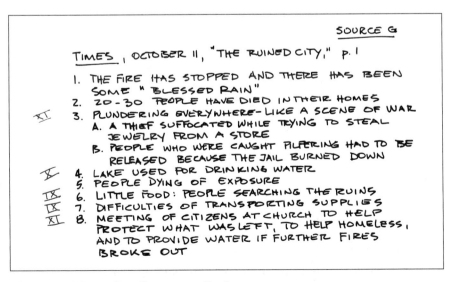

Figure 8-1. Notes: One Source per Card

Cross-referencing helps you to make full use of your notes and avoids time-consuming searches for references later on when you are writing the essay. At the end of this procedure:

- Your outline will have a list of sources to be cited for each main point, *and*

- Your research notes will have code numbers in most (but not necessarily all) of the margins.

Notice that a few items on the note card for Source G have no cross-references next to them. Some will be cross-referenced to other topics in this outline, and they have not yet been given their reference numbers. Items 2 and 5 in the notes, for example, would probably come under the heading of Casualties, in the section on panic during the fire. On the other hand, *not all the notes will necessarily be used in the essay;* some items will simply not fit into the topics chosen for the outline and will be discarded.

Figure 8-1 illustrates a method of note-taking that put all the material taken from a single source on a single card. Cross-referencing can also be used to organize *one-fact-per-card* notes, which can be sorted into piles corresponding to your topics. If you use this method, remember to put an identifying number on *each* card. In Figure 8-2, notice that:

- The code letter identifying the *source* (G) is in the upper right-hand corner.

- The code number identifying the *card* (32) is placed in the upper left-hand corner.

- The code number identifying the *outline topic* (XI) that this fact will be used to illustrate is indicated on the bottom of the card.

When you use the one-fact-per-card system, you put the relevant card number after each topic on your outline, but it is not necessary to identify the source.

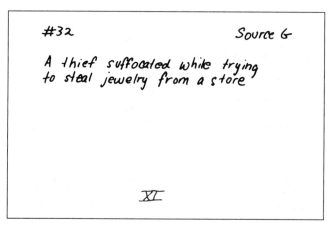

Figure 8-2. Notes: One Fact per Card

Paragraph Topics

IX. Feeding the homeless

X. Providing basic services

XI. Protecting life and property

#32, #38

The third kind of notes—*one-topic-per-card/sheet*—already incorporates the cross-referencing process by planning topics at the same time that notes are taken. Since you have already grouped your materials by topic, using a special card or sheet for each topic, you need only review your notes and shift those points (usually by cutting and pasting) that have inadvertently been placed under the wrong topic. In the next stage, as you prepare to write about each topic on your outline, you will be able to refer to the exact points in your notes that you need to cite.

Of course, if you are using a computer to organize your notes, your "cutting and pasting" will be done much more quickly on the screen. But the cross-referencing process is still important. In developing a complex research topic, it is helpful to print out your outline and your notes, to identify outline topics and sections of your notes through numbers and letters, and to match up your notes with your outline by cross-referencing using numbers and letters in the margins. When you are satisfied with your organization, and the topics in your outline are fully supported by information from your notes, then you turn to the computer and "cut and paste" on the screen.

The more notes that you have collected, the more important it is to be thorough during the preliminary organization. *Don't start to write your essay, and don't even start to sort your notes or "cut and paste" your sheets, until you have completed both your basic outline and your cross-referencing.*

EXERCISE 27: WRITING AN OUTLINE WITH CROSS-REFERENCING

Read the following set of notes, organized by source, for an argument essay on immigration.

1. Write an outline of topics for an essay to be called "The Economic and Social Consequences of Immigration in the United States Today."

2. Cross-reference the notes with your outline.

As you consider the information in these notes, remember that, if this exercise were preparation for an assigned essay, you could return to any of the sources, if you wished, and add details or examples to develop a topic that does not have enough supporting information.

Source A

Borjas, George J. "Tired, Poor, On Welfare." *National Review* 13 (Dec. 1993): 40–42.

1. It's true that immigrants contribute more in taxes to the nation's economy than they consume in welfare payments.

2. But the cost of living in this country and of using services and facilities adds an enormous amount to the cost of their support. That isn't being considered in most pro-immigration arguments. In this regard, immigrants do potentially take more than they give.

3. In 1990, a greater percentage of immigrants than natives received welfare. Immigrants comprise 8% of the population; they receive 13% of the cash benefits distributed.

4. Recent immigrants are less skilled than their counterparts 100 years ago. (B. says he's not saying that immigrants come to this country expressly to live on welfare.)

5. Whether immigrants want to work or not isn't the point; they don't have the skills, so they go on welfare.

6. B. fears creation of a new underclass of the unskilled. "A welfare state cannot afford the large-scale immigration of less-skilled persons." (42)

Source B

Brimelow, Peter. "Time to Rethink Immigration?" *National Review* 22 (June 1992): 30–46.

1. Cites large numbers of recent immigrants. Between 1951 and 1990, about one-fifth of the population of Jamaica had immigrated to the U.S.

2. 85% of legal immigrants between 1971 and 1990 were from the Third World.

3. Consequence: "The American ethnic mix *has* been upset." (31) White population of U.S. fell by 13% from 1960–90. The projection: by 2020, whites would only be 61% of population.

4. U.S. birthrate has declined since big waves of immigration at turn of century; therefore, new immigrants now have greater opportunity to dominate.

5. Major historical influence on U.S. culture has been British and German.

6. Proponents of present immigration policy are urging "Americans to abandon the bonds of a common ethnicity and instead to trust entirely to ideology to

hold together their state." (35) Historically, this bond of ideology hasn't been successful (e.g., USSR).

7. Melting pot tradition: "cultural synthesis . . . a pattern of swallowing and digestion" of immigrant groups (e.g., Irish immigrants eventually abandoned antisocial tendencies like dysfunctional families, alcoholism, disease). (36)

8. Economic argument: immigrants needed to perform jobs no one else will do. Instead, why not force unemployed Americans to work for their welfare? Or encourage a higher birth rate?

9. Cultural characteristics of each immigrant group predict whether that group will thrive or fail in new country. Cultural qualities of current major immigrant groups include unfortunate antisocial tendencies (like violence); this will have "economic consequences" for U.S.

10. Cites Borjas: welfare benefits to immigrants cost $1 billion more than they pay in taxes.

11. Hispanics in particular aren't being urged to assimilate; their tendency to support bilingualism and multiculturalism is deplorable.

Source C
Custred, Glynn. "Country Time." *National Review* 16 (June 1997): 39–40.

1. To maintain an orderly society, our country needs common cultural values, including "shared meanings, myths, and values conveyed in a common language, realized in national symbols, and supported by formal institutions, especially public education." (39)

2. Immigration can easily disturb this sense of community.

3. Earlier waves of immigration weren't a threat to national stability because those immigrants assimilated easily and willingly.

4. Immigrants in the last three decades aren't content to assimilate. They demand multiculturalism, which "drives [the nation] apart." (39) Multiculturalists attack the very concept of linguistic and cultural unity, which they regard as simply a way of oppressing ethnic and racial minorities. Custred depicts multiculturalists as whining for their rights.

5. The nation is becoming increasingly divided without any effort by our business and government leaders to prevent it.

6. The more immigrants allowed in, the more likely the newcomers will remain in their "ethnic enclaves" and this divisive multicultural attitude will grow.

7. Example: 86 languages spoken in California schools.

8. Disregard the argument that U.S. needs new workers. The danger of social tension resulting from immigration would be just as serious an economic threat.

Source D
Fukuyama, Francis. "Immigrants and Family Values." *Commentary* May 1993: 26–32.

1. "The symptoms of cultural decay are all around us, but the last people in the world we should be blaming are recent immigrants." (26)

2. Rejects Brimelow's argument that culture determines economic success for immigrants.

3. American identity doesn't derive from a specific culture; it's rooted in (a) ideals of democracy that transcend ethnicity, and (b) a consumer culture. Both are available to any immigrant group.

4. Do non-European immigrant groups threaten basic American values (e.g., nuclear family, success through hard work)? Decline of family structure and work ethic results from our declining postindustrialist society, not from values of new immigrants, who tend to have strong family loyalties (e.g., Asian immigrants: large families, economically successful).

5. Fear of immigration really directed at Hispanics: some Hispanics have had social problems, and many Americans lump together Hispanics with blacks as "a vast threatening underclass." (29)

6. F. cites diversity of Hispanics: some good, some bad. Problems really arise from poverty.

7. Reason for cultural disruption in U.S. has to do with economic and social change. Newly arrived immigrants didn't create sexual revolution, feminism, alienating workplace, single-parent households.

8. Clamor for multiculturalism comes more from leaders than from the average immigrant, for whom preserving ethnicity is not a primary goal.

9. Real issue: do we believe so strongly in our cultural heritage that we insist that all immigrants assimilate, or do we "carry respect for other cultures to the point that Americans no longer have a common voice with which to speak to one another?" (31)

Source E

Glazer, Nathan. "The Closing Door." *The New Republic* 27 Dec. 1993. Rpt. in *Arguing Immigration*. Ed. Nicolaus Mills. New York: Simon and Schuster, 1994. 37–47.

1. Some immigrants (mostly Asians) come with better education and work skills than most Americans have. Some are less qualified than Americans (mostly Hispanics and Caribbean blacks).

2. Even within these groups, ability to work and support themselves varies.

3. The economic argument isn't the crucial one. Whether we import cheap labor or not isn't the point (Japan thrives on a low immigration rate).

4. Those who use the economic argument to propose restrictions are really responding to the perceived threat of a more diverse nation. But they shouldn't be called bigots or racists. The preference for people of one's own culture is natural. "There is a difference between recognizing those who are in some sense one's own, with links to a people and a culture, and a policy based on dislike, hostility, or racial antagonism." (44)

5. Why doesn't U.S. assimilate immigrants the way it used to? "It is a different country: less self-confident, less willing to impose European and American customs and loyalty as simply the best in the world." (44)

6. G. is very tolerant of the movement to restrict immigration. "They ask why the stream of immigration should be so unrepresentative of the nation that already exists." (45)

Source F

McCarthy, Kevin. "Immigration by the Numbers." *New York Times* 15 Oct. 1997: 28.

1. McC. is a demographer who produces studies of the impact of immigrants on the California economy. Such statistics are used and sometimes distorted by proponents and opponents of present immigration policy. The issue is: does immigration have a positive effect on the national economy?

2. "No matter what ideologues on both sides say, immigration is neither absolutely good or evil."

3. On balance, California has gained more than it has lost from the availability of a low-wage immigrant work force.

4. But low-skilled workers (immigrant and native) are earning less and less.

5. Immigrants without skills aren't thriving.

6. The state is burdened by providing services to immigrants.

7. McC. suggests "modest" changes in policy: (a) scale back the number of immigrants admitted to halfway between present number and the number in the 1960s; and (b) try for a formula that favors immigrants with education and skills, rather than low-skilled immigrants who are being admitted to join family members already here.

Guidelines for Constructing Paragraphs in a Research Essay

1. *Each paragraph should possess a single main idea, usually expressed in the topic sentence.* That topic or design controls the arrangement of all the information in the paragraph. Everything that is included should develop and support that single idea, without digressions.

2. *The body of the paragraph should contain a combination of information taken from a variety of sources.* The number of different sources that you include in any one paragraph depends partly on the number of authors in your notes who have touched on its main idea and partly on the contribution each can make to the development of your topic.

3. *The topic sentence of each paragraph should support the development of your essay's thesis.*

INTEGRATING YOUR SOURCES INTO PARAGRAPHS

Writing a research essay resembles putting together a *mosaic*. Each paragraph has its basic design, determined by its topic sentence. To carry out the design, a paragraph might contain a group of reasons or examples to illustrate its main idea, *or* an extended explanation to develop that idea in greater detail, *or* a comparison between two elements introduced in the first sentence. These are the same paragraphing patterns that you use in all your writing. What makes the research essay different is the fact that the materials are assembled from many sources, *not* the way that they are organized or presented.

Imagine that the notes that you have taken from several different sources are boxes of tiles, each box containing a different color. You may find it easier to avoid mixing the colors and to work *only* with red tiles or *only* with blue, or to devote one corner of the mosaic to a red pattern and another to a blue. In the same way, you may find it both convenient and natural to work with only one source at a time and to avoid the decisions and the adjustments that must be made when you are combining different styles and ideas. But, of course, it is the design and only the design that dictates which colors should be used in creating the pattern of the mosaic, and it is the design or outline of your essay that dictates which evidence should be included in each paragraph.

When you decide to discuss a topic in a given paragraph, you must work with all the relevant information that you have gathered about that topic, whether it comes from one source or from many. Of course, you may have *too much material;* you may find it impossible to fit everything into the paragraph without overloading it with repetition. These rejected pieces may not fit into another part of the essay; instead, they will go back into their boxes as a backup or reserve fund of information.

The criteria for judging the quality of a paragraph remain the same—*clarity, coherence,* and *unity.*

- Do integrate your materials so that your reader will not be distracted by the differing sources or made aware of breaks between the various points.
- Don't integrate your materials so completely that you forget to provide appropriate acknowledgment of your sources.

Here is a paragraph from an essay about the novelist F. Scott Fitzgerald, in which four different explanations of an incident are presented, each at suitable length. Formal documentation of the sources has been omitted; but, to emphasize the variety and complexity of the research, the names of the sources and the attributing verbs and phrases have been underlined. The writer is describing an affair between Fitzgerald's wife, Zelda, and Edouard Jozan, a young Frenchman.

There is a lack of agreement about the details of the affair as well as its significance for the Fitzgeralds' marriage. According to one of Fitzgerald's biographers, Jozan and Zelda afterwards regarded it as "nothing more than a summer flirtation." But Ernest Hemingway, in his memoirs, wrote much later that Scott had told him "a truly sad story" about the affair, which he repeated many times in the course of their friendship. Gerald and Sara Murphy, who were present that summer and remembered the incident very well, told of being awakened by Scott in the middle of a September night in order to help him revive Zelda from an overdose of sleeping pills. The Murphys were sure that this incident was related to her affair with Jozan. Nancy Milford, Zelda's biographer, believes that the affair affected Zelda more than Scott, who, at that time, was very engrossed in his work. Indeed, Milford's account of the affair is the only one that suggests that Zelda was so deeply in love with Jozan that she asked Scott for a divorce. According to an interview with Jozan, the members of this triangle never engaged in a three-way confrontation; Jozan told Milford that the Fitzgeralds were "the victims of their own unsettled and a little unhealthy imagination."

This paragraph gives a brief but adequate account of what is known about the events of that summer of 1924. The writer does not try to rush through the four accounts of the affair, nor does he reduce each one to a phrase, as if he expected the reader to have prior knowledge of these people and their activities. In the context of the whole essay, the paragraph provides enough information for the reader to judge whose interpretation of the affair is closest to the truth.

ACCOMMODATING ARGUMENT IN YOUR PARAGRAPHS

When you write a paragraph based on *induction,* the topic sentence should clearly summarize the range of evidence being cited. Here is an example from Edward Tenner's *Why Things Bite Back,* a book about the dangers of technological progress:

> The startling wartime successes of penicillin created the dangerous myth of an antibiotic panacea. Even after the U.S. Food and Drug Administration began to require prescriptions in the mid-1950s, an antibiotic injection or prescription remained for many people the payoff of a medical encounter. They resisted the medical fact that antibiotics can do nothing against colds and other viral diseases. In many other countries, antibiotics are still sold legally over the counter to patients who may never get proper instructions about dosage or the importance of completing a course of treatment. Dr. Stuart B. Levy of Boston cites an Argentinian businessman who was cured of leukemia but died of an infection by the common bacterium *E. coli.* Ten years of self-medication had produced plasmids in his body that were resistant to every antibiotic used. Governments, too, have unintentionally promoted resurgence. Indonesian authorities have literally ladled out preventive doses of tetracycline to 100,000 Muslim pilgrims for a week at a time. Since the Mecca pilgrimage has historically been one of the great mixing bowls of microorganisms, it is especially disturbing to learn that half of all cholera bacilli in Africa are now resistant to tetracycline.

Paragraphs presenting inductive evidence tend to be long. Tenner makes his point about the "dangerous myth" of penicillin in the topic sentence, but he doesn't immediately cite evidence. He first explains the "danger" in the second sentence, and the "myth" in the third. Only then does he introduce his first supporting point—self-medication in countries without drug regulation—with Dr. Levy's example of the antibiotic-resistant Argentinian businessman. Signalled by the transitional word "too," Tenner's second example—the Mecca pilgrimage—increases the scale of potential danger.

In contrast to the specifics of induction, an article on "Methods of Media Manipulation" starts in a deductive mode, with a series of premises:

> We are told by people in the media industry that news bias is unavoidable. Whatever distortions and inaccuracies found in the news are caused by deadline pres-

sures, human misjudgment, budgetary restraints, and the difficulty of reducing a complex story into a concise report. Furthermore—the argument goes—no communication system can hope to report everything, selectivity is needed.

I would argue that the media's misrepresentations are not at all the result of innocent error and everyday production problems, though such problems certainly do exist. True, the press has to be selective, but what principle of selectivity is involved?

Media bias usually does not occur in random fashion; rather, it moves in the same overall direction again and again, favoring management over labor, corporations over corporate critics, affluent whites over low-income minorities, officialdom over protesters. . . . The built-in biases of the corporate mainstream media faithfully reflect the dominant ideology, seldom straying into territory that might cause discomfort to those who hold political and economic power, including those who own the media or advertise in it.

The initial presentation of Michael Parenti's argument is based on a dichotomy—contrast—between the media's view of news bias and his own. There is a disputed primary premise (bias is or is not avoidable) and a disputed secondary premise (one can't print everything vs. one prints what pleases one's corporate masters). Parenti's premises are developed in more detail, and the article goes on to support those premises through induction, by citing evidence of such manipulative tactics as "suppression by omission" and "framing."

While the opening of Parenti's article presents the opposition's argument as well as his own, the tone is grudging, even hostile. He leaves no room for accommodation between the two points of view. Yet, whenever possible, it is useful to acknowledge some merit in one's opponents or in their argument. Here are excerpts from two essays supporting opposite sides of the "wilderness preservation" issue. In the first, John Daniel is arguing that the advancement of science, if uncontrolled, can do harm to unspoiled land. He is careful, however, to distinguish between his allies and his enemies:

I don't mean to indict science in general. Many of the foremost champions of wild nature are scientists, and their work has done much to warn us of the environmental limits we are transgressing. I am arguing only against interventionist science that wants to splice genes, split atoms, or otherwise manipulate the wild—science aimed more at control than understanding, science that assumes ownership of the natural mysteries. When technological specialists come to believe that nature is answerable to their own prerogatives, they are not serving but endangering the greater community.

In William Tucker's view, society has more compelling interests, to which the wilderness movement must sometimes defer. But, before stating his argument, he pays his dues to nature:

I am not arguing against wild things, scenic beauty, pristine landscapes, and scenic preservation. What I am questioning is the argument that wilderness is a value against which every other human activity must be judged and that human beings are somehow unworthy of the landscape. The wilderness has been equated with freedom, but there are many different ideas about what constitutes freedom. . . .

Interestingly enough, Tucker then proceeds to move from his impeccably fair presentation to an argument that approaches *ad hominem*—a personal attack:

It may seem unfair to itemize the personal idiosyncrasies of people who feel comfortable only in wilderness, but it must be remembered that the environmental movement has been shaped by many people who literally spent years of their lives living in isolation.

Citing John Muir, David Brower, and Gary Snyder, leaders of the Sierra Club who spent much time alone in the mountains, Tucker continues:

There is nothing reprehensible in this, and the literature and philosophy that emerge from such experiences are often admirable. But it seems questionable to me that the ethic that comes out of this wilderness isolation—and the sense of ownership of natural landscapes that inevitably follows—can serve as the basis for a useful national philosophy.

Whatever his disclaimers, Tucker is rooting one of his key arguments against the wilderness movement in the personal preferences of three men. He does not, however, resort to using slanted, exaggerated, or dismissive language about his opponents. In contrast, here is Robert W. McChesney's attack on commercialism in the media:

The commercial blitzkrieg into every nook and cranny of U.S. culture, from schools to sport to museums to movie theaters to the Internet, has lessened traditional distinctions of public service from commercialism.

The word "blitzkrieg"—literally, lightning battle—originally referred to the German army in World War II. It immediately conjures up an image of a mechanized, pitiless army rolling over everything in its path, a reference reinforced by the domestic, vulnerable image of "nook and cranny," used to describe U.S. culture, the victim. Without even articulating his point, McChesney has created a lingering association between corporations and Nazis. This is a clever use of language, but is it a fair argument? In the next example, Leslie Savan also uses emotionally charged language to attack a similar target:

Advertising now infects just about every organ of society, and wherever advertising gains a foothold it tends to slowly take over, like a vampire or a virus.

The brutal swiftness of the blitzkrieg has been replaced by the slow insinuation of an infection, but both images are deadly and unyielding. (The allusion to a vampire must have been tempting—advertising leaves viewers bloodless and brainwashed—but it should not be placed in tandem with the insidious, slowly creeping image of infection.) Interestingly enough, McChesney and Savan are both adopting the tactics of the commercial media that they condemn: using powerful images in an attempt to force their readers into agreement.

PRESENTING ARGUMENTS FAIRLY

Perhaps the greatest disservice that you can do your sources is to distort them so that your reader is left with a false impression of what they have said or written. Such distortion is most likely to happen when you are writing an argumentative essay.

Mistakes to Avoid When Summarizing an Argument

1. Don't be one-sided; present *both* sides of an argument.

2. Don't omit crucial parts of the source's reasoning; provide a complete account of the argument.

3. Don't quote ideas out of context: make sure that you—and your reader—understand whether the source really supports the idea that you are citing.

4. Don't twist the source's ideas to fit your own purpose; provide a fair presentation.

---

1. **Present both sides of the argument.**

    One way of shading an argument to suit your own ends is to *misrepresent the strength of the opposition.* Let us assume that you are working with a number of articles, all of which are effectively presented and worth citing. Some clearly support your point of view; others are openly opposed; and a few avoid taking sides, emphasizing related but less controversial topics. If your essay cites only the favorable and neutral articles, and avoids any reference to the views of the opposition, you have presented the issue falsely. Using ostrich tactics will not convince your reader that your opinions are right; on the contrary, your unwillingness to admit the existence of opposing views suggests that your point of view has some basic flaw. A one-sided presentation will make you appear to be either biased or sloppy in your research. If the sources are available and if their views are pertinent, they should be represented and, if you wish, refuted in your essay.

2. **Provide a complete account of the argument.**

    Sometimes, distortions occur accidentally, because you have presented only a *partial* account of a source's views. In the course of an article or a book, authors sometimes examine and then reject or accept a variety of views before making it clear which are their own conclusions. Or an author may have mixed opinions about the issue and see merit in more than one point of view. If you choose to quote or paraphrase material from only one section of such a work, then you must find a way to inform your reader that these statements are not entirely representative of the writer's overall views.

3. **Make sure that you—and your reader—understand whether the source really supports the idea that you are citing.**

   Ideas can get distorted because of the researcher's misunderstanding, careless note-taking, or hasty reading. Remember to check the entire section of the article or all your notes before you attribute an opinion to your source, to make sure that you are not taking a sentence out of context or ignoring a statement in the next paragraph or on the next page that may be more typical of the writer's thinking. Writers often use an argumentative strategy that sets up a point with which they basically disagree in order to shoot it down shortly thereafter. Don't confuse a statement made for the sake of argument with a writer's real beliefs.

4. **Provide a fair presentation.**

   Occasionally, you may be so eager to uphold your point of view that you will cite any bit of material that looks like supporting evidence. To do so, however, you may have to twist the words of the source to fit your ideas. This is one of the worst kinds of intellectual dishonesty—and one of the easiest for a suspicious reader to detect: one has only to look up the source. *If you cannot find sufficient arguments and if your sources' evidence does not clearly and directly support your side, then you should seriously consider switching sides or switching topics.*

Here is a fairly clear instance of such distortion. In an essay on the need for prison reform, Garry Wills is focusing on the *deficiencies of our society's penal system;* he is not directly concerned with the arguments for or against the death penalty. But the student citing Wills in a research essay is writing specifically in support of capital punishment. To make Wills's argument fit into the scheme of this essay, the student must make some suspiciously selective references. Here is a paragraph from the research essay (on the left), side by side with the source.

Although the death penalty may seem very harsh and inhuman, is this not fair and just punishment for one who was able to administer death to another human being? A murderer's victim always receives the death penalty. Therefore, the death penalty for the murderer evens the score, or, as stated in the Bible, "an eye for an eye, and a tooth for a tooth." According to	The oldest of our culture's views on punishment is the *lex talionis*, an eye for an eye. Take a life, lose your life. It is a very basic cry—people must "pay" for their crimes, yield exact and measured recompense. No one should "get away with" any crime, like a shoplifter taking something unpaid for. The desire to make an offender suffer equivalent pain (if not compensatory excess of pain) is very

Garry Wills, "take a life, lose your life." Throughout the ages, society has demanded that man be allowed to right his wrongs. Revenge is our culture's oldest way of making sure that no one "gets away with" any crime. As Wills points out, according to this line of reasoning, the taking of the murderer's life can be seen as his payment to society for his misdeed.

deep in human nature, and rises quickly to the surface. What is lynching but an impatience with even the slightest delay in exacting this revenge? It serves our social myth to say that this impatience, if denied immediate gratification, is replaced by something entirely different—by an impersonal dedication to justice. Only lynchers want revenge, not those who wait for a verdict. That is not very likely. Look at the disappointed outcry if the verdict does not yield even delayed satisfaction of the grudge.

In the essay, the writer is citing only *part* of Wills's argument and thus makes him appear to support capital punishment. Wills is being misrepresented because (unlike the writer) he considers it fair to examine the views of the opposing side before presenting his own arguments. The ideas that the student cites are not Wills's, but Wills's presentations of commonly accepted assumptions about punishment. It is not entirely clear whether the writer of the research essay has merely been careless, failing to read past the first few sentences, or whether the misrepresentation is intentional.

INTEGRATING YOUR SOURCES: AN EXAMPLE

To illustrate the need for careful analysis of sources before you write your paragraphs, here is a group of passages, all direct quotations, which have been gathered for a research essay on college athletics. The paragraph developed from these sources must support the writer's *thesis:*

Colleges should, in the interests of both players and academic standards, outlaw the high-pressure tactics used by coaches when they recruit high school players for college teams.

The first three statements come from college coaches describing recruiting methods that they have observed and carried out; the last four are taken from books that discuss corruption in athletics.

I think in the long run, every coach must recognize this basic principle, or face the alumni firing squad. Recruiting is the crux of building a championship football team.

STEVE SLOAN, Texas Tech

Athletics is creating a monster. Recruiting is getting to be cancerous.

DALE BROWN, Louisiana State University

> You don't out-coach people, you out-recruit them.
>
> PAUL "BEAR" BRYANT, University of Alabama

> It is an athletic maxim that a man with no special coaching skills can win games if he recruits well and that a tactician without talented players is a man soon without a job.
>
> KENNETH DENLINGER

> There is recruiting in various degrees in every intercollegiate sport, from crew to girls' basketball and from the Houston golf dynasty that began in the mid-50's to Southern California importing sprinters and jumpers from Jamaica.
>
> J. ROBERT EVANS

> The fundamental causes of the defects in American college athletics are too much commercialism and a negligent attitude towards the educational opportunity for which the college exists.
>
> CARNEGIE FOUNDATION, 1929

> [*Collier's* magazine, in 1905, reported that] Walter Eckersall, All-American quarterback, enrolled at Chicago three credits short of the entrance requirement and his teammate, Leo Detray, entered the school before he even graduated high school. In addition the University of Minnesota paid two players outright to play in a single game (Nebraska: 1902). A quarterback and an end also from Minnesota admitted shaving points during the 1903 Beloit game.
>
> JOSEPH DURSO

Examining the Sources

Your paragraph will focus on *recruiting high school stars,* as opposed to developing students who enter college by the ordinary admissions procedure. Which of these ideas and observations might help to develop this paragraph? In other words, which statements should be represented by *paraphrase* or perhaps by *direct quotation?*

> I think in the long run every coach must recognize this basic principle, or face the alumni firing squad. Recruiting is the crux of building a championship football team.
>
> STEVE SLOAN

This very broad generalization seems quotable at first, largely because it sums up the topic so well; but, in fact, because it does no more than sum up the topic, it does not advance your argument any further. Therefore, you need not include it if your topic sentence makes the same point. (In general, you should write your own topic sentences rather than letting your sources write them for you.) The phrase "alumni firing squad" might be useful to quote in a later paragraph, in a discussion of the specific influence of alumni on recruiting.

Athletics is creating a monster. Recruiting is getting to be cancerous.

DALE BROWN

Coach Brown's choice of images—"cancerous" and "monster"—is certainly vivid; but the sentence as a whole is no more than a *generalized opinion about recruiting,* not an explanation of why the situation is so monstrous. To be lured into quoting Brown for the sake of two words would be a mistake.

You don't out-coach people, you out-recruit them.

PAUL "BEAR" BRYANT

This is the first statement that has advanced a specific idea: the coach may have a *choice* between building a winning team through recruiting and building a winning team through good coaching; but recruiting, not coaching, wins games. Coach Bryant, then, is not just making a rhetorical point, as the first two coaches seem to be. His seven-word sentence is succinct, if not elaborately developed, and would make a good introduction to or summation of a point that deserves full discussion.

The remaining four statements suggest a wider range of approach and style.

Walter Eckersall, All-American quarterback, enrolled at Chicago three credits short of the entrance requirement and his teammate, Leo Detray, entered the school before he even graduated high school. In addition, the University of Minnesota paid two players outright to play in a single game (Nebraska: 1902). A quarterback and an end also from Minnesota admitted shaving points during the 1903 Beloit game.

JOSEPH DURSO

This passage is as much concerned with corruption as recruiting and indicates that commercialism is nothing new in college athletics. Although the information is interesting, it is presented as a list of facts, and the language is not worth quoting. You may, however, want to summarize the example in your own words.

The fundamental causes of the defects in American college athletics are too much commercialism and a negligent attitude towards the educational opportunity for which the college exists.

CARNEGIE FOUNDATION

This extract from the 1929 Carnegie Foundation study is phrased in *abstract* language that is characteristic of foundation reports and academic writing in general. This style can be found in most textbooks (including this one) and in many of the sources that you use in college. The foundation presents its point clearly enough and raises an important idea: an athlete recruited to win games (and earn fame and fortune) is likely to ignore the primary reason for going to college—to acquire an education. Nevertheless, there is no compelling reason to *quote* this statement. *Remember that you include quotations in your essay to enhance your presentation; the quotation marks automatically prepare the reader for special words and phrasing.* But the prose here is too colorless and abstract to give the reader anything to focus on; a paraphrase is preferable.

> There is recruiting in varying degrees in every intercollegiate sport, from crew to girls' basketball and from the Houston golf dynasty that began in the mid-50's to Southern California importing sprinters and jumpers from Jamaica.
>
> J. ROBERT EVANS

This statement presents a quite different, more *detailed* level of information; it lists several sports, including some not known for their cutthroat recruiting practices. But details do not necessarily deserve quotation. Will these references be at all meaningful to the reader who is not familiar with the "Houston golf dynasty" or Jamaican track stars? To know that recruitment is not limited to cash sports, such as football, is interesting, but such specifics date quickly: in a few years, they may no longer be a useful frame of reference for most readers.

> It is an athletic maxim that a man with no special coaching skills can win games if he recruits well and that a tactician without talented players is a man soon without a job.
>
> KENNETH DENLINGER

Largely because of parallel construction, the last comment sounds both sharp and solid. In much the same way as Coach Bryant's seven words, but at greater length, Kenneth Denlinger sums up the contrast between coaching and recruiting, and suggests which one has the edge. Because the statement gives the reader something substantial to think about and because it is well phrased, Denlinger is probably worth quoting.

Should the writer include the statements by Bryant and by Denlinger, both of which say essentially the same thing? While Bryant's firsthand comment is commendably terse and certainly authoritative, Denlinger's is more complete and self-explanatory. A solution might be to include both, at different points in the paragraph, with Bryant cited at the end to sum up the idea that has been developed. Of course, the other five sources need not be excluded from the paragraph. Rather, if you wish, all five may be referred to, by paraphrase or brief reference, with their authors' names cited.

Here is *one* way of integrating this set of statements into a paragraph. (Note that, in this version, there is no documentation: none of the sources—except those quoted—is cited.)

In college athletics, what is the best way for a school to win games? Should a strong team be gradually built up by training ordinary students from scratch, or should the process be shortened and success be assured by actively recruiting players who already know how to win? The first method may be more consistent with the traditional amateurism of college athletics, but as early as

1929, the Carnegie Foundation complained that the focus of college sports had shifted from education to the material advantages of winning. Even earlier, in 1903, there were several instances of players without academic qualifications who were "hired" to guarantee victory. And in recent years excellence of recruiting has become the most important skill for a coach to possess. Kenneth Denlinger has observed, "It is an athletic maxim that a man with no special coaching skills can win games if he recruits well and that a tactician without talented players is a man soon without a job." It follows, then, that a coach who wants to keep his job is likely to concentrate on spotting and collecting talent for his team. Coaches from LSU, Alabama, and Texas Tech all testify that good recruiting has first priority throughout college athletics. According to Bear Bryant of Alabama: "You don't out-coach people, you out-recruit them."

One problem that can arise as you are crafting your paragraph is what to do with material that casts doubt on or flatly contradicts the point you're making. (Frequently, you come across that material *after* you have worked out your thesis and structure.) Here, for example, is an excerpt from *College Sports Inc.* by Murray Sperber. How does it fit with the paragraph on recruiting to win?

> Coaches who cheat do so for the same reasons that some gamblers try for an illegal advantage. They are extremely competitive, obsessed with winning, and will bend or break the rules to obtain the winning edge. They subscribe to the dictum that "winning is the only thing," that losing is not merely defeat but also a loss of self-worth. When gamblers or coaches cheat and succeed, they consider themselves "smart" and they show no remorse or inclination to stop. Only when caught do recriminations and blame—"Pressure from the school made me do it"—appear.

> Richard "Digger" Phelps, head of Notre Dame's men's basketball program, has long argued that external pressure is not the main source of coaches' cheating. He says of himself and his colleagues, "You choose the job you want to take. You decide who you want to recruit—the type of person. You also decide who you want to have surround that program as far as alumni, boosters, and friends. . . ."

The coaches referred to in the earlier student paragraph about recruiting assume that winning is the point of college athletics. The author of the paragraph is focusing on the best way to win—recruiting—and the only criticism of the primacy of winning is a slight complaint by the Carnegie Foundation about the materialism of college athletics. Now, not only does Sperber denigrate the "win at all costs" philosophy, but he (and Phelps, his source) suggests that the impetus to win and cheat (and, presumably, recruit at the expense of good sportsmanship) comes from the egoism of the coaches themselves, rather than the pressure from college officials and alumni.

What do you do with this excerpt from Sperber? Should you rewrite your paragraph on recruiting to include Sperber's (and Phelps's) opinions and attempt to reconcile them with the material provided by your other sources? In this situation, do two things:

1. **Examine the new source more completely to see if the author provides a broader context for these contradictory opinions.**

    In fact, Sperber also has a good deal to say about the commercialism of college sports, pointing out that athletic departments resemble business enterprises, with program directors who are in the "entertainment business." His book indicates that the "winning is everything" philosophy derives as much from institutional (and media) expectations as from the competitive obsessions of individual coaches.

2. **If the point made by the new source is worth developing, it may be preferable to do so in a separate paragraph.**

    The "recruiting" paragraph focuses on *what* coaches do to win, not why they do it. Sperber, however, is more concerned with motivation—quite a different topic and an equally interesting one. Your essay may benefit from an exploration of this point, but to develop and support it properly, you will probably have to find more sources that deal with the pressures to compete to win. The more you read, the more new directions you are likely to find for the development of your essay.

SELECTING QUOTATIONS

Now that you are working with a great variety of sources, you may find it difficult to limit the number of quotations in your essay and to choose quotable material. If you are doubtful about when and what to quote, review the sections on quotation in Chapter 2 and Chapter 4, starting on pp. 73 and 189. As a rule, the more eminent and authoritative the source, the more reason to consider quoting it.

Are the quoted phrases in the following excerpt worth quoting? Charles Dickens is describing the house that he has rented, the Chateau des Moulineux:

Excessive Use of Quotation

Dickens rattled off a list of phrases in his attempt to describe this idyllic

place. It was to become his "best doll's house," "our French watering place,"

and "this abode of bliss." More than anything else it would become a "happy,

happy place."

Such a list of separately quoted phrases creates an awkward, disconnected effect, which, if used too often, becomes tedious to read.

Descriptions are often more difficult to paraphrase than ideas; as a result, they tend to be presented in such a sequence of quoted phrases. If your source states that the walls of the room were painted sea-green and the furniture was made out of horsehair and covered with light-brown velvet, you may find it

---

Guidelines for Quoting

1. *Never quote something just because it sounds impressive.* The style of the quotation—the level of difficulty, the choice of vocabulary, and the degree of abstraction—should be compatible with your own style. Don't force your reader to make a mental jump from your own characteristic voice and wording to a far more abstract, flowery, or colloquial style.

2. *Never quote something that you find very difficult to understand.* When the time comes to decide whether and what to quote, stop and observe your own reactions. Rapidly reread the quotation. If you find it difficult to understand on the first try, then either attempt to paraphrase the point or leave it out entirely. If you become distracted or confused, your reader will be, too.

3. *Primary sources are often worth quoting—if they are clear and understandable.* When you are working on a biographical or historical research essay, you may encounter special problems in deciding whether or not to quote. Primary sources often have a special claim to be quoted. For example, you would be more likely to quote one of Hemingway's own descriptions of Paris in 1925 than a comparable sentence by one of his biographers. A person who witnessed the Chicago Fire has a better claim to have his original account presented verbatim than does a historian decades later.

4. *Use single and double quotation marks to differentiate between primary and secondary sources.* When quoting primary sources, it is essential to make the exact source of the quotation clear to your reader.

---

next to impossible to find appropriate synonyms to paraphrase these descriptive terms. "Crin de cheval" covered with fuzzy beige fabric? Mediterranean colors decorating the walls? The result is hardly worth the effort. If the man's eyes are described as dark blue, don't alter the phrase to "piercing blue" or "deep azure" or "ocean pools." If you place "dark blue" in a sentence that is otherwise your own writing, you may omit the quotation marks.

EXERCISE 28: INCORPORATING SOURCES INTO A PARAGRAPH

The following unfinished student paragraph is followed by brief excerpts from sources.

1. Decide which excerpt contains the most appropriate sentence for quotation. (It is not necessary to quote the entire excerpt.) For the purposes of this exercise, assume that all the sources are qualified authorities.

2. Paraphrase the other excerpts.

3. Complete the paragraph by using both paraphrase and quotation, citing two *or* three sources. Maintain a consistent tone and (except for the quotation) a single voice. Do not digress too far from the topic sentence.

Student Paragraph

Today, old people are often shunted aside into nursing homes as if they were useless vegetables. Fearful of contact with those so close to death, many people avoid their company. . . .

Sources

An old person who accepts mental and physical deterioration, illness, death, and dying is closer to wisdom than one who rejects it.

ADOLF GUGGENBUHL-CRAIG

I've been called senile. Senility is a convenient peg on which to hang nonconformity. . . . A new set of faculties seems to be coming into operation. I seem to be awakening to a larger world of wonderment—to catch little glimpses of the immensity and diversity of creation. More than at any other time in my life, I seem to be aware of the beauties of our spinning planet and the sky above. I feel that old age sharpens my awareness.

FRANCES [A NURSING-HOME RESIDENT, AGED 91]

Being old is just as beautiful and holy a task as being young, learning to die and dying are just as valuable functions as any other—assuming that they are carried out with reverence toward the meaning and holiness of life.

HERMANN HESSE

It is to be assumed that if man were to live this life like a poem, he would be able to look upon the sunset of his life as his happiest period, and instead of trying to postpone the much feared old age, be able actually to look forward to it, and gradually build up to it as the best and happiest period of his existence.

LIN YUTANG

ASSIGNMENT 13: ORGANIZING AND WRITING THE RESEARCH ESSAY

1. Read through all the essays in Appendix E. (In a full-scale research project, these readings would form a substantial part, but not all, of your sources. Check with your instructor about whether you may use additional sources.) Develop a topic for a research essay using most or all of these sources.

2. Write down a tentative list of main ideas, based on these sources, that should be discussed in an essay dealing with your subject. Also include your own ideas on the subject.

3. Develop an outline based on your list of ideas, and consider possible theses for the essay and the strategy that will best fit your thesis and sources.

4. After you have compiled a substantial list of topics and developed a tentative thesis, reread the passages, cross-referencing the topics on your list with the relevant material from the essays. While you do not have to use up everything in all of the readings, you should include all relevant points.

5. Develop this outline into an eight- or ten-page essay.

▪9▪

Acknowledging Sources

When you engage in research, you continually come into contact with the ideas and the words of other writers; as a result, the opportunities to plagiarize—by accident or by intention—increase tremendously. You must therefore understand exactly what constitutes plagiarism.

Plagiarism is the unacknowledged use of another person's work, in the form of original ideas, strategies, and research, or another person's writing, in the form of sentences, phrases, and innovative terminology.

- Plagiarism is the equivalent of *theft,* but the stolen goods are intellectual rather than material.

- Like other acts of theft, plagiarism is against the law. The copyright law governing publications requires that authorship be acknowledged and (if the borrowed material is long enough) that payment be offered to the writer.

- Plagiarism violates the moral law that people should take pride in, as well as profit from, the fruits of their labor. Put yourself in the victim's place. Think about the best idea that you ever had, or the paragraph that you worked hardest on in your last paper. Now, imagine yourself finding exactly the same idea or exactly the same sentences in someone else's essay, with no mention of your name, with no quotation marks. Would you accept the theft of your property without protest?

- Plagiarists are not only robbers, but also cheats. People who bend or break the rules of authorship, who do not do their own work, will be rightly distrusted by their classmates, teachers, or future employers, who may equate a history of plagiarism with laziness, incompetence, or dishonesty. One's future rarely depends on getting a better grade on a single assignment; on the other hand, one's lifelong reputation may be damaged if one resorts to plagiarism in order to get that grade.

But plagiarism is a bad risk for a more immediate and practical reason. As you observed in Exercise 10, an experienced teacher can usually detect plagiarized work quite easily. *If you are not skilled enough to write your own essay, you are unlikely to do a good enough job of adapting someone else's work to your needs.* Anyone can learn to write well enough to make plagiarism an unnecessary risk.

Finally, you will not receive greater glory by plagiarizing. On the contrary, most instructors believe that students who understand the ideas of their sources, apply them to the topic, and put them in their own words deserve the highest grades for their mastery of the basic skills of academic writing. There are, however, occasions when your instructor may ask you not to use secondary sources. In such cases, you would be wise to do no background reading at all, so that the temptation to borrow will not arise.

ACKNOWLEDGING YOUR SOURCES

Acknowledging your sources—or *documentation*—means telling your reader that someone other than yourself is the source of ideas and words in your essay. Acknowledgment can take the form of *quotation marks* and *citation of the author's name*—techniques that are by now familiar to you—or more elaborate ways to indicate the source, which will be explained later in this chapter. There are guidelines to help you decide what can and what cannot safely be used without acknowledgment, and these guidelines mostly favor complete documentation.

DOCUMENTING INFORMATION

By conservative standards, *you should cite a source for all facts and evidence in your essay that you did not know before you started your research.* Knowing when to acknowledge the source of your knowledge or information largely depends on common sense. For example, it is not necessary to document the fact that there are fifty states in the United States or that Shakespeare wrote *Hamlet* since these facts are common knowledge. On the other hand, you may be presenting more obscure information, like facts about electric railroads, which you have known since you were a child, but which may be unfamiliar to your readers. Technically, you are not obliged to document that information; but your audience will trust you more and will be better informed if you do so. *In general, if the facts are not unusual, if they can be found in a number of standard sources, and if they do not vary from source to source or year to year, then they can be considered common knowledge, and the source need not be acknowledged.*

Let's assume that you are writing an essay about *Lawrence of Arabia* for a course in film studies. The basic facts about the film—the year of release, the cast, the director, the technicians, the Academy Awards won by the film—might be regarded as common knowledge and not require documentation. But the cost of the film, the amount grossed in its first year, the location of the premiere, and the circumstances of production are relatively unfamiliar facts that you would almost certainly have to look up in a reference book. An authority on film who includes such facts in a study of epic films is expected to be familiar with this information and, in most cases, would not be expected to provide documentation. But a student writing on the same subject would be well advised to do so.

Similarly, if you are writing about the most recent World Cup and know who won a specific match because you witnessed the victory on television, then it would probably not be necessary to cite a source. Issues surrounding the World Cup—such as the use of steroids—are less clearly in the realm of common knowledge. You may remember news broadcasts about which athletes may or may not have taken steroids before a match, but the circumstances are hardly so well defined—or so memorable in their details—that you would be justified in writing about them from memory. The articles that you consult to jog your memory would have to be documented.

Documenting Ideas Found in Your Source

Your objective is both to acknowledge the source and to provide your reader with the fullest possible background. Let us assume that one of the ideas that you are writing about was firmly in your mind—the product of your own intellect—long before you started to work on your topic. Nevertheless, if you come across a version of that idea during your research, you should cite the source, *even though the idea was as much your own as the author's*. Of course, in your acknowledgment, you might state that this source is confirming *your* theories and indicate that you had thought of the point independently.

Documenting the Source of Your Own Ideas

Perhaps, while working on an essay, you develop a new idea of your own, stimulated by one of your readings. You should make a point of acknowledging the source of inspiration and, perhaps, describing how and why it affected you. (For example: "My idea for shared assignments is an extension of McKeachie's discussion of peer tutoring.") The reader should be made aware of your debt to your source as well as your independent effort.

PLAGIARISM: STEALING IDEAS

If you present another person's ideas as your own, you are plagiarizing *even if you use your own words*. To illustrate, the paragraph on the left, by Leo Gurko, is taken from a book, *Ernest Hemingway and the Pursuit of Heroism;* the paragraph on the right comes from a student essay on Hemingway. Gurko is listed in the student's bibliography and is cited as the source of several quotations elsewhere in the essay. But the student does not mention Gurko anywhere in *this* paragraph.

Source	Student Essay
The Hemingways put themselves on short rations, ate, drank, and entertained as little as possible, pounced eagerly on the small checks that arrived in the mail as payment for accepted stories, and were intensely conscious of being poor. The sensation was not altogether unpleasant. Their extreme youth, the excitement of living abroad, the sense of making a fresh start, even the unexpected joy of parenthood, gave their poverty a romantic flavor.	Despite all the economies that they had to make and all the pleasures that they had to do without, the Hemingways rather enjoyed the experience of being poor. They knew that this was a more romantic kind of life, unlike anything they'd known before, and the feeling that everything in Paris was fresh and new, even their new baby, made them sharply aware of the glamorous aspects of being poor.

The *language* of the student paragraph does not require quotation marks, but unless Gurko is acknowledged, the student will be guilty of plagiarism. These impressions of the Hemingways, these insights into their motivation, would not have been possible without Gurko's biography—and Gurko deserves the credit for having done the research and for having formulated the interpretations. After reading extensively about Hemingway, the student may have absorbed these biographical details so thoroughly that he feels as if he had always known them. But the knowledge is still secondhand, and the source must be acknowledged.

PLAGIARISM: STEALING WORDS

When you quote a source, remember that the quoted material will require *two* kinds of documentation:

1. *The acknowledgment of the source of the information or ideas* (through a system of documentation that provides complete publication information about the source and possibly through the citation of the author's name in your sentence), and

2. *The acknowledgment of the source of the exact wording* (through quotation marks).

It is not enough to supply the author's name in parentheses (or in a footnote) and then mix up your own language and that of your sources. The author's name tells your reader nothing at all about who is responsible for the choice of words. Equally important, borrowing language carelessly, perhaps in an effort to use paraphrase, often garbles the author's meaning.

Here is an excerpt from a student essay about Henrik Ibsen, together with the relevant passage from its source:

Source

When writing [Ibsen] was sometimes under the influence of hallucinations, and was unable to distinguish between reality and the creatures of his imagination. While working on *A Doll's House* he was nervous and retiring and lived in a world alone, which gradually became peopled with his own imaginary characters. Once he suddenly remarked to his wife: "Now I have seen Nora. She came right up to me and put her hand on my shoulder." "How was she dressed?" asked his wife. "She had a simple blue cotton dress," he replied without hesitation. . . . So intimate had Ibsen become with Nora while at work on *A Doll's House* that when John Paulsen asked him why she was called Nora, Ibsen replied in a matter-of-fact tone: "She was really called Leonora, you know, but everyone called her Nora since she was the spoilt child of the family."

P. F. D. TENNANT,
Ibsen's Dramatic Technique

Student Essay

While Ibsen was still writing *A Doll's House,* his involvement with the characters led to his experiencing hallucinations that at times completely incapacitated his ability to distinguish between reality and the creations of his imagination. He was nervous, distant, and lived in a secluded world. Gradually this world became populated with his creations. One day he had the following exchange with his wife:

Ibsen: Now I have seen Nora. She came right up to me and put her hand on my shoulder.

Wife: How was she dressed?

Ibsen: (without hesitation) She had a simple blue dress.

Ibsen's involvement with his characters was so deep that when John Paulsen asked Ibsen why the heroine was named Nora, Ibsen replied in a very nonchalant tone of voice that originally she was called Leonora, but that everyone called her Nora, the way one would address the favorite child in the family (Tennant 26).

The documentation at the end of the student's passage may refer the reader to Tennant's book, but it fails to indicate the debt that the student owes to Tennant's *phrasing* and *vocabulary*. Phrases like "distinguish between reality and the creatures of his imagination" must be placed in quotation marks, and so should the exchange between Ibsen and his wife. Arranging these sentences as dialogue is not adequate acknowledgment.

In fact, the problem here is too complex to be solved by inserting a few quotation marks. The student, who probably intended a paraphrase, has substituted some of her own words for Tennant's; however, because she keeps the original sentence structure and many of the original words, she has only succeeded in obscuring some of her source's ideas.

At times, the phrasing distorts the original idea: the student's assertion that Ibsen's hallucinations "incapacitated his ability to distinguish between reality and the creations of his imagination" is very different from "[Ibsen] was sometimes under the influence of hallucinations and was unable to distinguish between reality and the creatures of his imagination." Many of the substituted words change Tennant's meaning: "distant" does not mean "retiring"; "a secluded world" is not "a world alone"; "nonchalant" is a very different quality from "matter-of-fact." Prose like this is neither quotation nor successful paraphrase; it is doubly bad, for it both *plagiarizes* the source and *misinterprets* it.

EXERCISE 29: UNDERSTANDING WHEN TO DOCUMENT INFORMATION

Here are some facts about the explosion of the space shuttle *Challenger*. Consider which of these facts would require documentation in a research essay—and why.

1. On January 28, 1986, the space shuttle *Challenger* exploded shortly after takeoff from Cape Canaveral.
2. It was unusually cold in Florida on the day of the launch.
3. One of the *Challenger*'s booster rockets experienced a sudden and unforeseen drop in pressure 10 seconds before the explosion.
4. The explosion was later attributed to the failure of an O-ring seal.
5. On board the *Challenger* was a $100 million communications satellite.
6. Christa McAuliffe, a high school social studies teacher in Concord, New Hampshire, was a member of the crew.
7. McAuliffe's mission duties included conducting two classroom lessons taught from the shuttle.
8. After the explosion, classes at the high school were canceled.
9. Another crew member, Judith Resnick, had a Ph.D. in electrical engineering.
10. At the time of the explosion, President Ronald Reagan was preparing to meet with network TV news correspondents to brief them on the upcoming State of the Union address.
11. The State of the Union address was postponed for a week.

EXERCISE 30: ACKNOWLEDGING SOURCES

Here are two excerpts from two books about the Industrial Revolution in England. Each excerpt is followed by a passage from a student essay that makes use of the ideas and the words of the source without any acknowledgment at all.

1. Compare the original with the plagiarized passage.
2. Insert the appropriate quotation marks.
3. Underline the paraphrases.

Source A

Materially the new factory proletariat was likely to be somewhat better off [than domestic workers who did light manufacturing work in their own homes]. On the other hand it was unfree, under the strict control and the even stricter discipline imposed by the master or his supervisors, against whom they had virtually no legal recourse and only the very beginnings of public protection. They had to work his hours or shifts, to accept his punishments and the fines with which he imposed his rules or increased his profits. In isolated areas or industries they had to buy in his shop, as often as not receiving their wages in truck (thus allowing the unscrupulous employer to swell his profits yet further), or live in the houses the master provided. No doubt the village boy might find such a life no more dependent and less impoverished than his parents'; and in Continental industries with a strong paternalist tradition, the despotism of the master was at least partly balanced by the security, education, and welfare services which he sometimes provided. But for the free man entry into the factory as a mere "hand" was entry into something little better than slavery, and all but the most famished tended to avoid it, and even when in it to resist the draconic discipline much more persistently than the women and children, whom factory owners therefore tended to prefer.

E. J. HOBSBAWM, *The Age of Revolution 1789–1848*

Student Essay

The new factory proletariat was likely to be better off materially than those who did light manufacturing in their homes, but it was unfree. There was strict control and discipline imposed by the owner and his supervisors. They had no legal recourse and only the very start of public protection. The despotism of the master was at least a little bit set off by the security, education, and welfare services that he sometimes provided. But entry into the factory as a hand wasn't much better than slavery.

Source B

Most of the work in the factories was monotonously dreary, but that was also true of much of the work done in the homes. The division of labor which caused a workman to perform over and over only one of the several processes needful for the production of any article was intensified by the mechanical inventions, but it had already gone so far in the homes that few workers experienced any longer the joy of creation. It was, indeed, more of a physical strain to tend a hand loom than a power loom. The employment of women and children in the factories finally evoked an outcry from the humanitarians, but the situation was inherited from the domestic system. In the homes, however, most of the children worked under the friendly eyes of their parents and not under the direction of an overseer. That to which the laborers themselves most objected was "the tyranny of the factory bell." For the long hours during which the power kept the machines in motion, the workers had to tend them without intermission, under the discipline established by the employer and enforced by his foreman. Many domestic laborers had to maintain equally long hours in order to earn a bare subsistence, but they were free to begin, stop and rest when they pleased. The operatives in the factories felt keenly a loss of personal independence.

W. E. LUNT, *History of England*

Student Essay

Factory work was monotonous and dreary, but that was also true of work at home. Humanitarians cried out against the employment of women and children, but that was inherited from the domestic system. What annoyed the laborers the most was the dictatorship of the factory bell. The workers had to stay at the machines without intermission, maintaining long hours to earn a bare subsistence. Those who worked in their homes were free to begin, stop, and rest whenever they felt like it. Factory workers keenly felt a loss of personal freedom.

EXERCISE 31: IDENTIFYING PLAGIARISM

In 1995, the *Chronicle of Higher Education* reported that Stanley N. Ingber, a professor of law at Drake University, had recently been accused of plagiarizing the content and language of portions of three works by Michael J. Perry, a professor of law at Northwestern University. Professor Ingber had used ten passages without attribution in two articles. Other evidence suggested that Professor Ingber might have previously plagiarized passages from an article written by Mark G. Yudof, of the University of Texas at Austin.

Here, side by side, as published in the *Chronicle,* are parallel excerpts from Perry's 1982 *The Constitution, the Courts, and Human Rights* (on the left) and Ingber's 1994 "Judging Without Judgment: Constitutional Irrelevancies and the Demise of Dialogue." Examine them and determine whether, in your opinion, Ingber has plagiarized Perry's work.

I want to emphasize that I am *not* claiming that the Court always gives right answers. Of course it does not. . . . My basic point is simply this: In the constitutional dialogue between the Court and the other agencies of government—a subtle, dialectical interplay between Court and polity—what emerges is a far more self-critical political morality than would otherwise appear. . . .	I want to emphasize that I am *not* claiming that the Court always gives right answers, because of course it does not. My basic point is simply that from the constitutional dialogue between the Court and the other agencies of government—a subtle, dialectical interplay between Court and polity—a far more self-critical political morality emerges than would otherwise appear.

USING DOCUMENTATION

In addition to using quotation marks and citing the author's name in your text, you also need to provide your reader with more detailed information about your sources. This documentation is important for two reasons:

1. By showing where you found your information, you are providing *proof that you did your research.* Including the source's *publication history* and the *specific page* on which you found the information assures your reader that you have not made up fictitious sources and quotations. The systems of documentation that are described in this chapter and in Appendix B enable your reader to distinguish your ideas from those of your sources, to know who was responsible for what, by observing the parenthetical notes or numbered notes.

2. Documentation also enables your readers to *learn more about the subject of your essay.* Methods of documentation originally developed as a way for serious scholars to share their findings with their colleagues—while making it entirely clear who had done the original research. The reader of your research essay should be given the option of going back to the library and locating the materials that you used in writing about the topic. Of course, the essay's *bibliography* can serve this purpose, but not even the most carefully annotated bibliography guides readers to the book and the precise page that will provide the information that they need. Documentation, then, provides a direct link between an interesting sentence in the paper and the source in the library that will satisfy your readers' interest.

Using Parenthetical Notes

The most widely accepted system of documentation is based on the insertion directly into your essay of the author's name and the page on which the information can be found, placed in parentheses. This style of documentation is called the Modern Language Association (MLA) style. It has replaced footnotes and endnotes as the most common form of documentation, and it will probably be the style you use in writing general research essays, especially those in the humanities. Documenting through parenthetical notes is much less cumbersome than preparing an additional page of endnotes or placing footnotes at the bottom of the page. MLA style also allows your reader to see the source's name while reading the essay, instead of having to turn to a separate page at the back. Readers who want to know more about a particular source than the author's name and the number of the page containing the information can turn to the "Works Cited" page, which provides all the necessary details of publication.

Another frequently used kind of parenthetical documentation is the one recommended by the American Psychological Association (APA) for research in the social and behavioral sciences. APA style is described on pp. 452–461 of Appendix B.

For those writing essays on a computer, many software packages (especially those, like Nota Bene, specializing in academic writing) provide documentation automatically, in a choice of styles—provided that basic information about each work cited has been entered into the computer.

MLA Format

Here is what an excerpt from a biographical essay about Ernest Hemingway would look like using MLA style. Notice that the parenthetical notes are meaningless unless the reader can refer to an accurate and complete bibliography placed at the end of the essay on a page titled "Works Cited."

> Hemingway's zest for life extended to women also. His wandering heart seemed only to be exceeded by an even more appreciative eye (Hemingway 102). Hadley was aware of her husband's flirtations and of his facility with women (Sokoloff 84). Yet, she had no idea that something was going on between Hemingway and Pauline Pfeiffer, a fashion editor for Vogue magazine (Baker 159). She was also unaware that Hemingway delayed his return to Schruns from a business trip in New York, in February 1926, so that he might spend more time with this "new and strange girl" (Hemingway 210; also, Baker 165).

Works Cited

Baker, Carlos. Ernest Hemingway: A Life Story. New York: Scribner's, 1969.

Hemingway, Ernest. A Moveable Feast. New York: Scribner's, 1964.

Sokoloff, Alice Hunt. Hadley: The First Mrs. Hemingway. New York: Dodd, 1973.

Many of the basic rules for using MLA style are apparent in the previous example. Here are some points to observe.

1. **Format and Punctuation.**

   The placement of the parenthetical note within your sentence is governed by a set of very precise rules, established by conventional agreement. Like rules for quotation, these must be followed without any deviation.

   a. *The parenthetical note is intended to be a part of your sentence, which should not end until the source has been cited.* For this reason, terminal punctuation (period or question mark) should be placed *after* the parenthetical note.

   Incorrect

   Unlike most American writers of his day, Hemingway rarely came to New York; instead, he spent most of his time on his farm near Havana. (Ross 17).

Correct

Unlike most American writers of his day, Hemingway rarely came to New York; instead, he spent most of his time on his farm near Havana (Ross 17).

b. *If the parenthetical note follows a quotation, the quotation should be closed before you open the parentheses.* Remember that the note is not part of the quotation and therefore has no reason to be inside the quotation.

Incorrect

Hemingway's farm consisted of "a domestic staff of nine, fifty-two cats, sixteen dogs, a couple of hundred pigeons, and three cows (Ross 17)."

Correct

Hemingway's farm consisted of "a domestic staff of nine, fifty-two cats, sixteen dogs, a couple of hundred pigeons, and three cows" (Ross 17).

c. *Any terminal punctuation that is part of the quotation* (like a question mark or an exclamation point) *remains inside the quotation marks.* Remember also to include a period at the end of the sentence, *after* the parenthetical note.

Incorrect

One critic reports that Hemingway said of The Old Man and the Sea, "Don't you think it is a strange damn story that it should affect all of us (me especially) the way it does" (Halliday 52)?

Correct

One critic reports that Hemingway said of The Old Man and the Sea, "Don't you think it is a strange damn story that it should affect all of us (me especially) the way it does?" (Halliday 52).

d. *When you insert the parenthetical note, leave one space before it and one space after it*—unless you are ending the sentence with terminal punctuation (period, question mark), in which case you leave no space between the closing parenthesis and the punctuation, and you leave the customary one space between the end of that sentence and the beginning of the next one.

Incorrect

Given Hemingway's intense awareness of literary tradition, style, and theory, it is strange that many critics and readers have found his work primitive(Cowley 47).

Correct

Given Hemingway's intense awareness of literary tradition, style, and theory, it is strange that many critics and readers have found his work primitive (Cowley 47).

2. Placement.

The parenthetical note comes at the end of the material being documented, whether that material is quoted, paraphrased, summarized, or briefly mentioned. By convention, your reader will assume that the *parenthetical note signals the end of the material from that source.* Anything that follows is either your own idea, independently developed, or taken from a new source that will be documented by the next parenthetical note later in the text.

> One critic has remarked that it has been fashionable to deride Hemingway over the past few years (Cowley 50). However, though we may criticize him, as we can criticize most authors when we subject them to close scrutiny, we should never forget his brilliance in depicting characters having grace under the pressure of a sterile, valueless, painful world (Anderson 1036).

3. Frequency.

Each new point in your essay that requires documentation should have its own parenthetical note. Under no circumstances should you accumulate references to several different sources for several sentences and place them in a single note at the end of the paragraph. All the sources in the Hemingway paragraph cannot be covered by one parenthetical note at the end.

Incorrect

> The sources of Hemingway's fiction have been variously named. One critic has said he is driven by "personal demons." Another believes that he is occupied by a desire to truly portray reality, with all its ironies and symbols. Finally, still another has stated that Hemingway is interested only in presenting "fragments of truth" (Cowley 51; Halliday 71; Levin 85).

Correct

> The sources of Hemingway's fiction have been variously named. One critic has said he is driven by "personal demons" (Cowley 51). Another believes that he is occupied by a desire to truly portray reality, with all its ironies and symbols (Halliday 71). Finally, still another has stated that Hemingway is interested only in presenting "fragments of truth" (Levin 85).

4. Multiple Notes in a Single Sentence.

If you are using a large number of sources and documenting your essay very thoroughly, you may need to cite two or more sources at separate points in the same sentence.

> Even at this early stage of his career, Hemingway seemed to have developed a basic philosophy of writing. His ability to perceive situations

clearly and to capture the exact essence of the subject (Lawrence 93–94; O'Faolain 113) might have stemmed from a disciplined belief that each sentence had to be "true" (Hemingway 12) and that a story had to be written "as straight as you can" (Hemingway 183).

The placement of notes tells you where the writer found which information. The reference to Lawrence and O'Faolain must be inserted in mid-sentence because they are responsible only for the information about Hemingway's capacity to focus on his subject and capture its essence; Lawrence and O'Faolain are not responsible for the quoted material at the end of the sentence. The inclusion of each of the next two parenthetical notes tells you that a reference to "true" sentences can be found on page 12 of the Hemingway book and a reference to "straight" writing can be found on page 183.

5. Multiple Sources for the Same Point.

If you have two sources to document the same point, you can demonstrate the completeness of your research by placing both in the same parenthetical note. The inclusion of Lawrence and O'Faolain in the same note—(Lawrence 93–94; O'Faolain 113)—tells you that much the same information can be found in both sources. Should you want to cite two sources but emphasize only one, you can indicate your preference by using "also."

Hemingway's ability to perceive situations clearly and to capture the exact essence of the subject (Dos Passos 93–94; also O'Faolain 113) may be his greatest asset as a writer.

There is, of course, a limit to how many sources you can cram into a single pair of parentheses; common sense will tell you what is practical and what is distracting to the reader. Usually, one or two sources will have more complete or better documented information; those are the ones to cite. If you wish to discuss the quality of information in your various sources, then you can use an explanatory endnote to do so (see p. 384 on explanatory notes).

6. Referring to the Source in the Text.

In the previous examples, the writer of the Hemingway essay has chosen not to cite any sources in the text itself. That is why each parenthetical note contains a name as well as a page number. *If, however, you do refer to your source as part of your own presentation of the material, then there is no need to use the name twice; simply insert the page number in the parenthetical note.*

During the time in Paris, Hemingway became friends with the poet Ezra Pound, who told Hemingway he would teach him how to write if the younger novelist would teach him to box. Noel Stock reports what Wyndham Lewis saw when he walked in on one of their boxing sessions:

> A splendidly built young man [Hemingway] stript to the waist,
> and with a torso of dazzling white, was standing not far from me.
> He was tall, handsome, and serene, and was repelling with his
> boxing gloves—I thought without undue exertion—a hectic as-
> sault of Ezra's. (88)

Because Stock's name is cited in the text, it need not be placed in parentheses; the page number is enough. Stock's book would, of course, be
included in the list of "Works Cited." Also notice that the parenthetical
note works just as well at the end of a lengthy, *indented* quotation; but
that, because the quotation is indented, and there are no quotation marks
to signify its end, it terminates with a period placed *before* the parenthetical note, which follows separated by *two* spaces.

7. **Including the Source's Title.**

*Occasionally, your bibliography will include more than one source by the same
author or sources by different authors with the same last name. To avoid confusion and to specify your exact source, use an abbreviated title inside the parenthetical note.* Had the author of the Hemingway essay included more than
one work by Carlos Baker in the bibliography, the parenthetical note
would look like this:

> Yet, she had no idea that something was going on between Hemingway
> and Pauline Pfeiffer, a fashion editor for Vogue magazine (Baker, Life Story
> 159).

If you are working from a newspaper or periodical article that does not
cite an author, use an abbreviation of the article's title in your parenthetical note (unless you have referred to the title in your text, in which case
you need only include the page number in your note).

8. **Referring to a Whole Work.**

*Occasionally, you may refer to the overall theme of an entire work, citing the ti-
tle and the author, but no specific quotation, idea, or page. If you refer to a work
as a whole, no page numbers in parentheses are required.*

> Hemingway's The Sun Also Rises focuses on the sterility and despair per-
> vading modern culture.

9. **Referring to a Source by More Than One Author.**

*Occasionally, you will need to refer to a book that is by two, or three, or even
more authors. (If you have mentioned the authors' names in your text, just include a page reference in parentheses.) If you refer to a text by more than three
authors and you have not mentioned them in your text, it is acceptable (and saves
space) to cite the name of the first author followed by* et al., *unitalicized, and
then the page number, all within parentheses.* Et al. *is Latin for "and others."*

Two Authors

We may finally say of the writer Hemingway that he was able to depict the turbulent, often contradictory, emotions of modern man in a style as starkly realistic as that of the sixteenth century painter Caravaggio, who, art historians tell us, seems to say, "Here is actuality . . . without deception or pretence. . . . " (Janson and Cauman 221).

More than Three Authors

Hemingway did what no other writer of his time did: he captured the plight and total disenchantment of his age in vivid intensity (Spiller et al. 1300).

10. **Referring to One of Several Volumes.**

   You may use a single volume from a set of several volumes. If so, refer to the specific volume by using an arabic numeral followed by a colon. In your "Works Cited," be sure to list all the volumes. (See Appendix B for proper bibliographic entry of a set of volumes.)

   Perhaps Hemingway's work can be best summed up by Frederick Coppleston's comment concerning Camus: both writers prove that human greatness is not shown in escaping the absurdity of modern existence, but "in living in the consciousness of the absurd and yet revolting against it by . . . committing . . . [one]self and living in the fullest manner possible" (3:393).

11. **Referring to a Work of Literature.**

   If you refer to specific passages from a well-known play, poem, or novel, then you need not cite the author; the text's name is sufficient recognition. Use arabic numerals separated by periods for divisions such as act, scene, and line in plays and for divisions like books and lines in poems. For novels, cite the page number followed by a semicolon, "ch.," and the chapter number.

   Play

   Hemingway wished to show reality as truly as he could, even if he found man, as did King Lear, nothing but "a poor, bare, fork'd animal . . . " (3.4.106–7).

   Poem

   Throughout his career as a writer, Hemingway struggled to make sense of the human condition so powerfully and metaphorically presented in The Waste Land: "Son of man/ . . . you know only/ A heap of broken images" (2.21–23).

   Novel

   In The Sun Also Rises, toughness is an essential for living in the modern age, but even toughness has its limits in the novel; as Jake says, "It is

awfully easy to be hard-boiled about everything in the daytime, but at
night it is another thing" (34; ch. iv).

12. **Referring to a Quotation from an Indirect Source.**

*When you quote a writer's words that you have found in a work written by
someone else, you begin the citation with the abbreviation "qtd. in." This form*
shows the reader that you are quoting from a secondhand source, not the
original.

> In "Big Two-Hearted River," Hemingway metaphorically captures the
> pervasive atmosphere of his time in the tersest of descriptions: "There
> is no town, nothing . . . but the burned over country" (qtd. in Anderson
> 1027).

13. **Referring to Sources That Do Not Appear in Print.**

Sometimes you may cite information from nonprint sources such as interviews, films, or radio or television programs. If you do, be sure that
the text mentions (for an interview) the name of the interviewer and/or
the person being interviewed or (for a film) the name of the producer,
director, and/or scriptwriter; these names should also appear in your
list of "Works Cited." (For proper bibliographic form of nonprint sources,
including the Internet, see Appendix B.)

Interview

> In an unpublished interview conducted by the writer of this essay, the
> poet Phil Arnold said that a lean style like Hemingway's may be just as
> artificial as an elaborate one.

Preparing to Document Your Essay

- Whether you take notes or use photocopies of your sources, remember always to write down the information that you will need for
  your notes and bibliography.
- Look at the front of each book or periodical and jot down the publication information.
- As you work on the first draft of your essay, include the author's
  name and the relevant page number in parentheses after every reference to one of your sources, to serve as a guide when you document your essay. Even in this early version, your essay will resemble
  the finished product, with MLA documentation.
- Finally, when the essay is ready for final typing, read through it
  again, just to make sure that each reference to a source is covered
  by a parenthetical note.

MLA Style: A Sample Page

Reference to quotation, author mentioned in text

Michelle A. Cawley defines passive euthanasia as "cooperating with the patient's dying" (959). Failing to resuscitate a patient who has suffered a massive heart attack is one example of passive euthanasia. Another is deciding not to feed a terminally ill patient who is unable to feed himself. In contrast, removing the feeding tube from a patient who is being fed that way would be considered active euthanasia. Similar to passive euthanasia is "assisted suicide," in which a doctor or other person provides a terminally ill person with the means—pills, for example—and the medical knowledge necessary to commit suicide (Orentlicher 1844).

Reference to an entire work, no page reference required

Derek Humphrey's 1991 book *Final Exit,* which describes ways to painlessly commit suicide, and the organization Compassion in Dying, which helps terminally ill patients end their lives, are both recent examples of "assisted suicide" (Belkin 50; also Elliott 27).

Reference to two sources in which same information can be found, emphasis on "Belkin"

The professional people who care for the sick and dying think there is a great difference between active and passive euthanasia, or "assisted suicide." A recent panel of distinguished physicians declared themselves in favor, by a margin of 10 to 2, of doctor-assisted suicide for hopelessly ill patients who request it (Orentlicher 1844). In a survey taken in 1975, 73% of the nurses questioned were in favor of withholding treatment that would prolong the lives of dying patients who don't want their lives sustained in that way—in other words, passive euthanasia. But only 17% were in favor of using active means to end lives of dying patients who request euthanasia ("Taking Life" 40).

Standard reference, author mentioned in note

Reference to an article with no author listed

Constructing a "Works Cited" Page

None of the parenthetical notes explained above would make complete sense without a "Works Cited" page. The technical forms for bibliographic entries according to MLA style are described in Appendix B. Following is a sample "Works Cited" page for all of the parenthetical notes about Hemingway found earlier in this chapter.

Works Cited

Anderson, Charles W. Introduction. "Ernest Hemingway." American Literary Masters. Ed. Charles W. Anderson. New York: Holt, 1965. 1023–114.

Arnold, Philip. Telephone interview. 3 Nov. 1993.

Baker, Carlos. Ernest Hemingway: A Life Story. New York: Scribner's, 1969.

Coppleston, Frederick. Maine de Biran to Sartre. New York: Doubleday, 1974. Vol. 9 of A History of Philosophy. 9 vols. 1946–1974.

Cowley, Malcolm. "Nightmare and Ritual in Hemingway." Hemingway: Twentieth Century Perspectives. Ed. Robert P. Weeks. Englewood Cliffs: Prentice, 1962. 40–51.

Halliday, E. M. "Hemingway's Ambiguity: Symbolism and Irony." Hemingway: Twentieth Century Perspectives. Ed. Robert P. Weeks. Englewood Cliffs: Prentice, 1962. 52–71.

Hemingway, Ernest. A Moveable Feast. New York: Scribner's, 1964.

---. The Sun Also Rises. 1926. New York: Scribner's, 1964.

Janson, H. W., and Samuel Cauman. A Basic History of Art. New York: Abrams, 1971.

Lawrence, D. H. "In Our Time: A Review." Hemingway: Twentieth Century Perspectives. Ed. Robert P. Weeks. Englewood Cliffs: Prentice, 1962. 93–94.

Levin, Harry. "Observations on the Style of Ernest Hemingway." Hemingway: Twentieth Century Perspectives. Ed. Robert P. Weeks. Englewood Cliffs: Prentice, 1962. 72–85.

Ross, Lilian. "How Do You Like It Now, Gentlemen?" Hemingway: Twentieth Century Perspectives. Ed. Robert P. Weeks. Englewood Cliffs: Prentice, 1962. 17–39.

Shakespeare, William. King Lear. Ed. Frank Kermode. The Riverside Shakespeare. Boston: Houghton, 1974. 1249–305.

Spiller, Robert E., et al. Literary History of the United States. 3rd ed., rev. London: Macmillan, 1963.

Stock, Noel. The Life of Ezra Pound. New York: Pantheon, 1970.

Signaling the Transitions between Sources

If you go to considerable trouble to find and select the right materials to support your ideas, you will want to paraphrase and to use your sources' names in your sentences as a way of keeping them before your reader's eye. Of course, the sources' names should appear only when necessary so that the reader is not distracted by their constant appearance.

*In general, the citation of the author's name signals to your reader that you are starting to use **new** source material; the parenthetical note signals the* **point of termination** *for that source.*

If the name is not cited at the beginning, readers may not be aware that a new source has been introduced until they reach the parenthetical note. Here is a brief passage from an essay that illustrates this kind of confusion:

> The year 1946 marked the beginning of the postwar era. This meant the de-mobilization of the military, creating a higher unemployment rate because of the large number of returning soldiers. This also meant a slowdown in industry, so that layoffs also added to the rising rate of unemployment. As Cabell Phillips put it: "Motivation [for the Employment Act of 1946] came naturally from the searing experience of the Great Depression, and fresh impetus was provided by the dread prospect of a massive new wave of unemployment following demobiliza-tion" (292–3).

Here, the placement of the citation—"As Cabell Phillips put it"—creates a problem. The way in which the name is introduced into the paragraph firmly suggests that Cabell Phillips is responsible for the quotation and only the quo-tation. (The fact that the quotation is nothing more than a repetition of the first three sentences, and therefore need not have been included in the essay, may also have occurred to you.) Anyone reading the essay will assume that the ref-erence to Phillips covers only the material that starts with the name and ends with the page number. The coverage is not expected to go back any farther than the beginning of the sentence. Thus, in this passage, *the first three sentences are not documented.* Although the writer probably took all the information from Phillips, his book is not being acknowledged as the source. "Probably" is not an adequate substitute for clear documentation. Phillips's name should be cited somewhere at the beginning of the paragraph (the second sentence would be a good place); alternatively, an "umbrella" note could be used (see pp. 387–388).

You may need to insert a parenthetical note in midsentence if that single sen-tence contains references to *two* different sources. For example, you might want to place a note in midsentence to indicate exactly where the source's opinion leaves off and your own begins:

> These examples of hiring athletes to play in college games, cited by Joseph Durso (6), suggest that recruiting tactics in 1903 were not as subtle as they are today.

If the page number were put at the end of the sentence, the reader would as-sume that Durso was responsible for the comparison between 1903 and the present; but he is not. Only the examples must be documented, not the con-clusion drawn from these examples. In this case, the *absence* of a parenthetical note at the end of the sentence signals to the reader that this conclusion is the writer's own.

Here is a passage in which *the techniques of documentation have been used to their fullest extent* and *the transitions between sources are clearly indicated.* This example is taken from Jessie Bernard's "The Paradox of the Happy Marriage," an examination of the woman's role in American marriage. At this point, Bernard has just established that more wives than husbands acknowledge that their marriages are unhappy:

> These findings on the wife's marriage are especially poignant because marriage in our society is more important for women's happiness than for men's. "For almost all measures, the relation between marriage, happiness and overall well-being was stronger for women than for men," one study reports (Bradburn 150). In fact, the strength of the relationship between marital and overall happiness was so strong for women that the author wondered if "most women are equating their marital happiness with their overall happiness" (Bradburn 159). Another study based on a more intensive examination of the data on marriage from the same sample notes that "on each of the marriage adjustment measures . . . the association with overall happiness is considerably stronger for women than it is for men" (Orden and Bradburn 731). Karen Renne also found the same strong relationship between feelings of general well-being and marital happiness: those who were happy tended not to report marital dissatisfaction; those who were not, did. "In all probability the respondent's view of his marriage influences his general feeling of well-being or morale" (64); this relationship was stronger among wives than among husbands (Renne 63).[2] A strong association between reports of general happiness and reports of marital happiness was also found a generation ago (Watson).
>
> [2]Among white couples, 71 percent of the wives and 52 percent of the husbands who were "not too happy" expressed marital dissatisfaction; 22 percent of the wives and 18 percent of the husbands who were "pretty happy" expressed marital dissatisfaction; and 4 percent of the wives and 2 percent of the husbands who were "very happy" expressed marital dissatisfaction.

This paragraph contains *six parenthetical notes* to document the contents of *seven sentences.* Four different works are cited, and, where the same work is cited twice consecutively (Bradburn and Renne), the reference is to a different page. The material taken from page 64 of Renne covers a sentence and a half, from the name "Karen Renne" to the parenthetical note; the remainder of the sentence comes from page 63. Finally, there is no page reference in the note citing Watson, since Bernard is referring the reader to the entire article, not to a single part of it. Notice also that:

- Bernard quotes frequently, but she never places quotations from two different sources together in the same sentence.
- She is careful to use her own voice to provide continuity between the quotations.
- The reader is never in doubt as to the source of information.

Although Bernard does not always cite the name of the author, we are immediately told in each case that there is a source—"one study reports"; "the author wondered"; "another study based on a more intensive examination of the data on marriage from the same sample"; "Karen Renne also found." These phrases not only acknowledge the source but also provide vital transitions between these loosely related points.

EXERCISE 32: USING PARENTHETICAL NOTES

The following paragraph, taken from a research essay about the Industrial Revolution, is based on the source materials in Exercise 30 on p. 369. Compare the paragraph with its sources, and then decide where the parenthetical notes should be placed. Insert the notes, making sure that you distinguish the source material from the writer's own contributions to the paragraph.

The Industrial Revolution caused a major change in the working environment of most people in England. Historians have described the painful transition from working in the home and on the farm to working in the factory. E. J. Hobsbawm points out that most factory employees were at the mercy of the master and his foremen, who controlled their working hours with "draconic discipline." According to W. E. Lunt, those who previously did spinning and weaving in their homes had worked as long and as hard as the workers in the new textile factories, but they had been able to maintain more control over when and how they performed their tasks. It was the male workers who especially resented their loss of freedom and tended to be more resistant to discipline, and so manufacturers found it desirable to hire women and children, who were more passive and obedient. The long hours and bleak and unhealthy environment of the factories must have been particularly hard on the women and children who worked in them. Indeed, Lunt observes that it was their plight that "finally evoked an outcry from the humanitarians." Ultimately, then, an improvement in working conditions came about because of respect for the frailty of women and children, not because of respect for the rights of all workers.

Using Explanatory Notes

You will have noticed that, in the excerpt from Bernard on p. 383, following the second parenthetical reference to Renne, there is a number. This calls the reader's attention to a separate note appearing at the bottom of the paragraph. (In the actual essay, the note would appear either at the bottom of the page or, together with other notes, on a separate sheet at the end of the essay.) Jessie Bernard is using an *explanatory note* as a way of including information that does not quite fit into the text of her essay.

If your research has been thorough, you may find yourself with more material than you know what to do with. It can be tempting to use up every single point on your note cards and cram all the available information into your essay. But if you include too many extraneous points, your reader will find it hard to concentrate on the real topic of your paragraph. To illustrate this point, here are two paragraphs dealing with the domestic life of Charles Dickens: one is bulging; the other is streamlined. The first contains an analysis of Dickens's relationship with his sister-in-law; in the second, he decides to take a holiday in France.

Paragraph 1

Another good friend to Charles Dickens was his sister-in-law. Georgina had lived with the family ever since they had returned from an American tour in June 1842. She had grown attached to the children while the couple was away (Pope-Hennessy 179–80). She now functioned as an occasional secretary to Dickens, specifically when he was writing A Child's History of England, which Pope-Hennessy terms a "rather deplorable production." Dickens treated the history of his country in a very unorthodox manner (311). Dickens must have felt close to Georgina since he chose to dictate the History to her; with all his other work, Dickens always worked alone, writing and correcting it by himself (Butt and Tillotson 20–21). Perhaps a different woman would have questioned the relationship of her younger sister to her husband; yet Kate Dickens accepted this friendship for what it was. Pope-Hennessy describes the way in which Georgina used to take over the running of the household whenever Kate was indisposed. Kate was regularly too pregnant to go anywhere. She had ten children and four miscarriages in a period of fifteen years (391). Kate probably found another woman to be quite a help around the house. Pope-Hennessy suggests that Kate and her sister shared Charles Dickens between them (287).

Paragraph 2

In 1853, three of Dickens's closest friends had died (Forster 124),[5] and the writer himself, having become even more popular and busy since the publication of David Copperfield (Maurois 70), began to complain of "hypochondriacal whisperings" and also of "too many invitations to too many parties" (Forster 125). In May of that year, a kidney ailment that had plagued Dickens since his youth grew worse (Dickens, Letters 350), and, against the advice of his wife, he decided to take a holiday in Boulogne (Johnson 757).[6]

[5]The friends were Mr. Watson, Count d'Orsay, and Mrs. Macready.

[6]Tillotson, Dickens's doctor, who had been in Boulogne the previous October, was the one to encourage him to go there.

The first paragraph obviously contains too much information, most of which is unrelated to this topic. Pope-Hennessy's opinion of the history of England and the history of Kate's pregnancies are topics that may be worth discussing, but not in this paragraph. This extraneous material could be shifted to other paragraphs of the essay, placed in explanatory notes, or simply omitted. Its placement depends on the shape and structure of the entire essay.

The second, much shorter paragraph suggests that related but less important detail can usefully be put into explanatory notes where, if wanted, it is always available. Readers of the second paragraph are being given a choice: they can absorb the essential information from the paragraph alone, or they can examine the topic in greater depth by referring also to the explanatory notes.

Explanatory notes should be reserved for information that, in your view, is useful and to some degree relevant to the topic; if it is uninteresting and way off the point, simply omit it. If you indulge too often in explanatory notes, your notes may be longer than your essay. Also remember to find out whether including explanatory notes is acceptable to your instructor.

Avoiding Excessive Notes

Complex research was needed to gather the numerous details found in the biographical essays about Ernest Hemingway and Charles Dickens, and the writers of these essays use numerous parenthetical notes to document their sources. Here is a brief example:

> Dickens's regular work habits involved writing at his desk from about nine in the morning to two in the afternoon (Butt and Tillotson 19; Pope-Hennessy 248), which left a good deal of time for other activities. Some of his leisure each day was regularly spent in letter-writing, some in walking and riding in the open air (Pope-Hennessy 305, quoting Nathaniel Sharswell). Besides this regular routine, on some days he would devote time to reading manuscripts which Wills, his sub-editor on Household Words, would send to him for revision and comment (Forster 65; Johnson 702).

In this passage, three parenthetical notes are needed for three sentences because a different biographer is the source for each piece of information. To combine all the sources in a single note would confuse, rather than simplify, the acknowledgments. In addition, the writer of this essay is not only making it clear where the information came from, but is also providing the reader with a *choice of references*. The writer has come across the same information in more than one biography, has indicated the duplication of material in her notes, and has decided to demonstrate the thoroughness of her research by citing more than one reference. Since the sources are given equal status in the notes (by being placed in alphabetical order and separated by a semicolon), the reader can assume that they are equally reliable. Had the writer thought that one was more thorough or more convincing than another, she would either have omitted the secondary one or indicated its status by placing it after "also" (Johnson 702; also, Forster 65).

But an abundance of parenthetical notes does not always indicate sound research. As the following example demonstrates, excessive documentation only creates clutter.

> In contrast to the Dickenses' house in London, this setting was idyllic: the house stood in the center of a large garden complete with woods, waterfall, roses (Forster 145), and "no end of flowers" (Forster 146). For a fee, the Dickenses fed on the produce of the estate and obtained their milk fresh from the landlord's cow (Forster 146). What an asset to one's peace of mind to have such a cooperative landlord as they had (Pope-Hennessy 310; Johnson 758; Forster 147) in the portly, jolly Monsieur Beaucourt (Forster 147)!

Clearly, this entire passage is taken from three pages in Forster's biography of Dickens, and a single note could document the entire paragraph. What information is contained in the sentence leading up to the triple parenthetical note that justifies citing three sources? And what does the last note document? Is it only Forster who is aware that Monsieur Beaucourt is portly and jolly? To avoid tiring and irritating his readers, the writer here would have been well advised to ignore the supporting evidence in Pope-Hennessy and Johnson, and use a single reference to Forster. The writer was undoubtedly proud of his extensive research, but he seems more eager to show off his hours in the library than to provide a readable text for his audience.

Using Umbrella Notes

As in the previous example, sometimes the logical sequence of your ideas or information requires you to cite the same source for several sentences or even for several paragraphs at a stretch. Instead of repeating "Forster 146" again and again, you can use a single note to cover the entire sequence. These notes are sometimes called *umbrella notes,* because they cover a sequence of sentences as an umbrella might cover more than one person. Umbrella notes are generally used in essays where the sources' names are not often cited in the text, and so the reader cannot easily figure out the coverage by assuming that the name and the parenthetical note mark the beginning and ending points. An umbrella simply means that you are leaving the reader in no doubt as to how much material the note is covering.

An umbrella note consists of an explanation of how much material is being covered by a source. Such a note is too long to be put in parentheses within the text and generally takes the form of *an explanatory note placed outside the body of your essay.* Here is an example:

> [2]The information in this and the previous paragraph dealing with Dickens's relationship with Wilkie Collins is entirely derived from Hutton, Dickens-Collins Letters 41-49.

Inside your essay, the superscript number 2 referring the reader to this note would follow right after the *last* sentence that uses material from Hutton to discuss Dickens and Wilkie Collins.

Of course, umbrella notes work only when you are using a single source for a reasonably long stretch. If you use two sources, you have to distinguish between them in parenthetical notes, and the whole point of the umbrella—to cut down on the number of notes—is lost.

Umbrella notes must also be used with caution when you are quoting. Because the umbrella provides the reference for a long stretch of material, the citation usually includes several pages; but how will the reader know on which page the quotation appears? Sometimes you can add this information to the note itself:

> [2]The information in this and the previous paragraph is entirely derived from Hutton, Dickens-Collins Letters 41-49. The two quotations from Dickens's letters are from pages 44 and 47, respectively.

However, if you use too many umbrella notes, or if you expect a single note to guide your reader through the intricacies of a long paragraph, you will have abused the device. Your essay will have turned into a series of summaries, with each group of paragraphs describing a single source. That is not what a research essay is supposed to be.

THE FINAL BIBLIOGRAPHY

While the bibliography is always an essential part of the research essay, it becomes especially important when you use MLA documentation, since *it is the only place where your reader can find publication information about your sources.* Which works you include in your final bibliography may depend on the wording and intention of your assignment. There is an important difference between a list of works that you have *consulted* or *examined* and a list of works that you have *cited* or actually *used in writing your essay.* Many instructors restrict the bibliography to "Works Cited," but you may be asked to submit a list of "Works Consulted." Remember that one purpose of a "Works Consulted" bibliography is to help your readers to find appropriate background information, not to overwhelm them with the magnitude of your efforts. Don't present a collection of thirty-five titles if you actually cite only five sources in your essay.

An appropriate final bibliography of "Works Consulted" for an undergraduate essay consists of all the sources that you examined (in other words, actually read) that proved to have a clear bearing on your topic, whether or not you actually used them in your essay.

If you consulted a book in the hope that it contained some relevant information, and if it provided nothing useful, should you include it in your final bibliography? You might do so to prevent your readers from repeating your unnecessary research and attempting to consult works with misleading titles in the belief that they might be useful, but only if your bibliography is *annotated* and the book's lack of usefulness can be pointed out. Finally, if you have been unable to locate a source and have thus never examined it yourself, you may not ordinarily include it in your final bibliography, however tempting the title may be.

THE ANNOTATED BIBLIOGRAPHY

Annotating your bibliography (which was described in Chapter 5, pp. 269–271) is an excellent way to demonstrate the quality of your research. But, to be of use, your brief annotations must be informative. The following phrases do not tell the reader very much: "an interesting piece"; "a good article"; "well-done"; "another source of well-documented information." What is well done? Why is it interesting? What is good about it? How much and what kind of information does it contain? A good annotated bibliography will answer some of these questions.

Examine the bibliography on p. 391 carefully, noting the way it presents the basic facts about the author, title, and publication, as well as some *evaluative information.* If the annotations were omitted, these entries would still be perfectly correct, for they conform to the standard rules for bibliographical format. Without the annotation, one would simply have to change the heading to "Works Consulted" or "Works Cited."

Guidelines for Bibliographical Entries

(Additional models can be found in Appendix B, p. 442)

1. The bibliography is always listed on a *separate sheet* at the *end* of your research essay. The title should be centered, one-half inch from the top of the page.

2. Each entry is *double-spaced,* with double spacing between entries.

3. Each bibliographical entry starts with *the author's last name at the margin;* the second line of the entry (if there is one) is indented *five spaces.* This format enables the reader's eye to move quickly down the list of names at the left-hand margin.

4. The bibliography is in *alphabetical order,* according to the last name of the author.

(continued)

(continued)

- If there are two authors, only the first has the last name placed first: "Woodward, Robert, and Carl Bernstein."
- If an author has more than one work included on your list, do not repeat the name each time: alphabetize or arrange chronologically by publication date the works by that author; place the name at the margin preceding the first work; for the remaining titles, replace the name with three hyphens, followed by a period and one space.

  Freud, Sigmund. Civilization and Its Discontents. London: Hogarth, 1930.

  ---. Moses and Monotheism. New York: Knopf, 1939.

- A work that has no author should be alphabetized within the bibliography according to the first letter of the title (excluding "The"); the title is placed at the margin as the author's name would be.

5. A bibliographical entry for a book is read as a list of three items—author, title (underlined), and publication information—with *periods between each piece of information.* Each period is followed by *one* space. All the information should always be presented in exactly the same order that you see in the model bibliography on p. 391. Place of publication comes first; a colon separates place and name of publisher; a comma separates publisher and date.

6. A bibliographical entry for a *periodical* starts with the author's name and the article title (in quotation marks), each followed by a period and one space. Then comes the name of the periodical, followed by one space (and no punctuation at all). What comes next depends on the kind of periodical you are citing.

   - For *quarterly and monthly journals,* include the volume number, followed by a space, and then the year in parentheses, followed by a colon.
   - For *weekly or biweekly journals,* include only the full date—day, month, and year—followed by a colon.

   All periodical entries end with the inclusive pages of the article, first page to last, followed by a period.

   Tobias, Sheila, and Carol Weissbrod. "Anxiety and Mathematics: An Update." Harvard Educational Review 50 (1980): 61-67.

   Winkler, Karen J. "Issues of Justice and Individual's Rights Spur Revolution in Political Philosophy." Chronicle of Higher Education 16 April 1986: 6-8.

7. Each entry of the bibliography ends with a period.

HEMINGWAY: AN ANNOTATED BIBLIOGRAPHY

Baker, Carlos. Hemingway: A Life Story. New York: Scribner's, 1969. 563 pages
of biography, with 100 pages of footnotes. Everything seems to be here,
presented in great detail.

Donaldson, Scott. Hemingway: By Force of Will. New York: Viking, 1977.
The material isn't organized chronologically; instead, the chapters are
thematic, with titles like "Money," "Sex," and "War." Episodes from
Hemingway's life are presented within each chapter. The introduction
calls this "a mosaic of [Hemingway's] mind and personality."

Griffin, Peter. Less Than a Treason: Hemingway in Paris. New York: Oxford UP,
1990. Part of a multivolume biography. Covers Hemingway's life from
1921–1927, exclusively. Griffin says in the preface that his goal is not
to "analyze this well examined life" but "to recreate it." Not surprisingly,
it reads like a novel, with an omniscient narrator with access to
Hemingway's emotions.

Gurko, Leo. Ernest Hemingway and the Pursuit of Heroism. New York: Crowell,
1968. This book is part of a series called "Twentieth-Century American
Writers": a brief introduction to the man and his work. After fifty pages of
straight biography, Gurko discusses Hemingway's writing, novel by novel.
There's an index and a short bibliography, but no notes. The biographical
part is clear and easy to read, but it sounds too much like summary.

Hemingway, Ernest. A Moveable Feast. New York: Scribner's, 1964. This is
Hemingway's own version of his life in Paris. It sounds authentic, but
there's also a very strongly nostalgic tone, so it may not be trustworthy.

Hemingway in Paris. Home page. 13 Oct. 1997 <http://204.122.127.50/WSHS/
Paris/HTM/>. Three photos of the Hemingways' apartment, with brief comments.

Hemingway, Leicester. My Brother, Ernest Hemingway. Cleveland: World, 1962.
For 1924–1925, L.H. uses information from Ernest's letters (as well as
commonly known facts). The book reads like a third-hand report, very
remote; but L.H. sounds honest, not as if he were making up things that
he doesn't know about.

Hotchner, A. E. Papa Hemingway. New York: Random, 1955. This book is
called a "personal memoir." Hotchner met Hemingway in 1948, evidently
hero-worshiped him, and tape-recorded his reminiscences. The book is
their dialogue (mostly Hemingway's monologue). No index or bibliography.
Hotchner's adoring tone is annoying, and the material resembles that of
A Moveable Feast, which is better written.

Meyers, Jeffrey. <u>Hemingway: A Biography</u>. New York: Harper, 1985. Includes several maps, and two chronologies: illnesses and accidents, and travel. Book organized chronologically, with every year accounted for, according to table of contents. Well-documented critical biography, with personal anecdotes taking a back seat to literary. Less gossipy, more circumspect in claims than Griffin.

Reynolds, Michael. <u>Hemingway: The Paris Years</u>. Cambridge, Mass.: Blackwell, 1989. Second of three-volume biography. Includes a chronology covering December 1921–February 1926 and five maps ("Hemingway's Europe 1922–26," "France," "Switzerland," "Italy," and "Key points for Hemingway's several trips through France and Spain").

Sokoloff, Alice Hunt. <u>Hadley, the First Mrs. Hemingway</u>. New York: Dodd, 1973. This is the Paris experience from Hadley's point of view, most of it taken from her recollections and from the standard biographies. (Baker is acknowledged.) It's a very slight book—102 pages—but there's an index and footnotes, citing letters and interviews that some of the other biographers might not have been able to use.

Weeks, Robert P., ed. <u>Hemingway: Twentieth Century Perspectives</u>. Englewood Cliffs: Prentice, 1965. Contains many important essays on Hemingway's life and art. Offers a selected annotated bibliography.

Young, Philip. <u>Ernest Hemingway</u>. Minneapolis: U of Minnesota P, 1959. A short psychobiography of Hemingway's life. Offers stimulating insights, but suffers from the limitations of psychoanalysis.

EXERCISE 33: PREPARING THE BIBLIOGRAPHY

Correct the errors of form in the following bibliography:

Becker, Howard S, Geer, Blanche, and Everett C. Hughes. Making the Grade: New York (1968) Wiley.

Dressel, Paul L.. College and University Curriculum, Berkeley (California): McCutcheon, 1971

(same)----Handbook of Academic Evaluation. San Francisco (California): Jossey-Bass: 1976.

J. F. Davidson, "Academic Interest Rates and Grade Inflation," Educational Record. 56, 1975, pp. 122–5

(no author). "College Grades: A Rationale and Mild Defense." AAUP Bulletin, October 1976, 320–1.

New York Times. "Job Plight of Young Blacks Tied to Despair, Skills Lack," April 19, 1983: Section A page 14.

Milton Ohmer, Howard R. Pollio and James A. Eison. GPA Tyranny, Education Digest 54 (Dec 1988): 11–14.

Leo, John. "A for Effort". Or for Showing Up. U.S. News & World Report, 18 Oct, 1993: 22.

Kennedy, Donald. What Grade Inflation? The New York Times June 13, 1994: All.

Bretz, Jr., Robert D. "College Grade Point Average as a Predictor of Adult Success: a Meta-analytical Review and Some Additional Evidence" Public Personnel Management 18 (Spring 1989): 11–22.

PRESENTING YOUR ESSAY

A well-presented research essay must conform to a few basic mechanical rules:

1. Type your essay on a computer or typewriter. Make sure that you use a letter-quality printer.
2. Double-space throughout the essay.
3. Use 8½-by-11-inch paper; leave 1½-inch margins.
4. Use only one side of the page.
5. Number each page.
6. Proofread your essay, make minor corrections, and print out the revised version. If necessary, make minor corrections in ink.
7. Do not include graphics or illustrations unless your instructor requests them.
8. Include your name, the name of the course, the date, and the title of the essay, either on a separate title page, or on the first page of the essay.

Check with your instructor for any other special rules that may apply to the assignment.

A CHECKLIST FOR REVISION

As you read and re-read your essay, keep the following questions in mind.

1. Does the essay have a single focus that is clearly established and maintained throughout?

2. Does the essay have a thesis or a consistent point of view about the events or issues being described?

3. If it is a narrative essay, does the narration have a beginning, middle, and end? If it is an argument essay, are all assumptions explained and defended, and are all obvious counterarguments accommodated or refuted?

4. Does the essay begin with an informative introduction?

5. Does the essay end on a conclusive note?

6. Does each paragraph have a clear topic sentence?

7. Does each paragraph contain one and only one topic? Should any paragraphs be merged or deleted?

8. Are the paragraphs long enough to be convincing? Is each point supported by facts and information?

9. Does the development of the essay depend entirely on a dry listing of facts and examples, or do you offer explanations and relevant commentary? Is there a good balance between generalization and detail?

10. Do you use transitions to signal the relationship between separate points?

11. Is there unnecessary repetition? Are there any sentences that lack content or add nothing to the essay?

12. Does the reader get a sense of the relative importance of the sources being used?

13. Do you use one source for very long stretches at a time?

14. Is there an appropriate number of notes rather than too many or too few?

15. Is it clear how much material is covered by each note?

16. In essays containing endnotes, do notes provide important explanatory information?

17. Are the quotations well chosen?

18. Is paraphrase properly used? Is the style of the paraphrase consistent with your style?

19. Do you use enough citations? Does the text of the essay make it clear when you are using a specific source, and who that person is?

20. Is the essay convincing? Will your reader accept your analysis, interpretation, and arguments?

▪10▪

Three Research Essays

The following three student research papers, on three very different subjects, use three different kinds of documentation.

The first writer is analyzing an issue and constructing an *argument*. In presenting some of the reasons why some people advocate and others condemn the practice of euthanasia, the writer hopes to persuade his readers that terminally ill people should have the right to choose the time of their deaths. The writer documents his sources with MLA documentation. He summarizes, paraphrases, or quotes one source at a time, which makes it practical to use brief and unobtrusive parenthetical notes at the ends of the sentences. Almost everything that the writer wants to say is said within the body of the essay, so there are only a few endnotes.

The second writer uses a *narrative* structure, with a great deal of precise detail, to describe a real event—the aftermath of a plane crash in the Andes Mountains in 1972. This essay will help you to understand why many history instructors—and also instructors in some other humanities disciplines—still prefer the traditional footnote or endnote and bibliography form of documentation. The writer frequently refers to a group of sources to support specific points; she also presents a great deal of background information that cannot be included in the body of her paper. The separate endnotes provide enough room to cite all the sources and explain some of the points that they are making.

The third writer combines *narrative and analysis* by describing the aftermath of the strange event that happened in 1908 at Lake Tunguska, Siberia, and then analyzing some of the many theories that have been used to explain that event over the last seventy years. The bibliography for this essay contains relatively few sources, which are cited less frequently than the sources are in the first two essays. The writer's purpose is to help his readers understand what might have happened at Lake Tunguska and to clarify the scientific explanations. He is not using numerous sources to reconstruct the event in complete detail, or trying to convince his readers, by citing authorities, that his conclusions are the right ones. Like many essays in the behavioral sciences, this paper uses the author-year variation of parenthetical note documentation. (This method, often called APA after the American Psychological Association, is described in Appendix B, on pp. 452–461.) Having the date, as well as the author, included within the body of the essay is especially useful when you are reading about scientific theories developed over a span of eighty years.

Jorge Catto

English 102

Spring, 1997

Euthanasia: The Right to Die

Someone you love is suffering from terminal cancer. He asks you to inject a lethal drug into him so that he can die without prolonged agony. Would you do it? Should you? Incidents such as this one, in which one person asks another for help to die, are called euthanasia. At the center of this problem is the right of a person to die with the least suffering and the most dignity and comfort. In this essay, I will consider some of the reasons why euthanasia is so vigorously opposed, and why, in spite of that opposition, we must insist on our right to decide for ourselves when to end our own lives.

Euthanasia is usually divided into two kinds: active and passive. According to Michelle Anne Cawley's definition in The American Journal of Nursing, active euthanasia involves directly causing the death of another person through an intended action (859). Administering a fatal drug to a dying person, injecting an air bubble into the bloodstream, or giving him some other means to shorten his life constitute active euthanasia. The most famous recent example of active euthanasia is Dr. Jack Kevorkian, the doctor from Michigan who helps patients to die with the help of his "suicide machine," a tank of carbon monoxide and a mask (McHugh 15–21; Belkin 50; Elliott 27).

Passive euthanasia can be described as helping someone to die by doing nothing, which, according to The Economist, "happens in hospitals all the time" ("Euthanasia War" 22). It is also called, Cawley writes, "cooperating with the patient's dying" (959). Failing to resuscitate a patient who has suffered a massive heart attack is one example of passive euthanasia. Another is deciding not to feed terminally ill patients who are unable to feed themselves. In contrast, removing the feeding tube from a patient who is being fed that way would be considered active euthanasia. Dr. David Orentlicher, in the Journal of the American Medical Association, categorizes "assisted suicide" as a form of passive euthanasia. In assisted suicide, a doctor or other person provides a terminally ill person with the means--pills, for example--and the medical knowledge necessary to commit suicide (1844). Derek Humphrey's 1991 book Final Exit, which describes ways to commit suicide painlessly, and the organization Compassion in Dying, which helps terminally ill patients to end their lives, are both recent examples of instruction in "assisted suicide" (Belkin 50; also Elliott 27).

The professional people who care for the sick and dying think that there is a great difference between active euthanasia and passive euthanasia or "assisted suicide." A panel of distinguished physicians declared themselves in favor, by a margin of 10 to 2, of doctor-assisted suicide for hopelessly ill patients who request it (Orentlicher 1844). In a 1975 survey, 73% of the nurses questioned were in favor of withholding treatment that would prolong the lives of dying patients who don't want their lives sustained in that way--in other words, passive euthanasia. But only 17% were in favor of using active means to end the lives of dying patients who request euthanasia ("Taking Life" 40).

In the past, euthanasia was not such a topic for public speculation and censure. In part, this was because death did not usually take place in a public place, and therefore no one except family members or a doctor was likely to know whether the patient was or wasn't helped to die. Also, doctors lacked the knowledge and the means to try to prolong a dying person's life. But, as Sonia Rudikoff points out in Commentary, this acceptance that death was inevitable and not to be avoided may also have been related to the idea that death was a significant and sacred event and even a welcome one, because it was the prelude to a better existence in the afterlife (62).

Today, as a result of advances in medical science, it has become both possible and, many say, desirable to try to prolong a dying person's life. Indeed, it is considered criminal not to try to do so. Twenty years ago, Peter Hammerli, a doctor in Switzerland, was arrested for "murdering" his patients. He was accused of not taking steps to prolong the lives of the terminally ill people that he was treating.[1] Thus, most controversies over euthanasia center around the issue of who, if anyone, has the right to end a sick person's life. Those concerned in this issue include the patient, the patient's family, and the doctor and nursing staff, all of whom may be affected by their differing conceptions of God or divinity or fate.

Catto 3

In a Gallup poll in 1975, slightly over 50% of Americans said that they do not believe that an individual has the right to end his or her own life ("Taking Life" 40). Most of these people probably share the belief that life is a gift from God and that our bodies and lives are not our private possessions, but are held in trust (Cawley 869). As Rudikoff puts it, they believe that "the breath of life in each of us is a part of a spirit or life, or a community of spirit over which we do not exert ultimate control" (63). To these people, only God has enough knowledge and power to have the right to take away life. They associate euthanasia with murder, and quote Biblical phrases such as "Thou shalt not kill" and "The Lord giveth and the Lord taketh away" as the basis for their belief (Rudikoff 66). They argue that no human being--not even the dying person--can ever be certain when death is about to happen or whether euthanasia is really necessary. So, they want to turn the matter over to God, to whom they attribute perfect objectivity and omniscience.

Advocates of euthanasia think that this argument is a way of avoiding human responsibility. The ideals of our society include the belief that we are all individuals capable of self-determination. A Catholic theologian has observed that, in this respect, man is different from the rest of living creation, because he is "the only animal who knows he is going to die and who also knows he can bring about his own death" (Maguire 57). Before becoming ill, most patients were free to choose their style of life, to decide when to eat, when to sleep, and how to take care of themselves. Why, then, should they not have the right to choose whether to live or to die? (Rudikoff 63). Writing in the New York Times about a decision he once made to end his life if his illness grew more serious, Edward M. Brecher makes the point that it is perfectly acceptable for veterinarians to put extremely sick animals out of their misery, but the same privilege is not usually extended to human beings (72). It is as if one's ability to reason and make moral choices no longer matters when someone is dying.

This issue is made even more painful by the fact that, very often, the dying person is experiencing great suffering. Peter Hammerli became a practitioner of euthanasia because he could not bear to prolong the misery of the patients whom he saw suffering ("Hammerli Affair" 1273). Similarly, a licensed practical nurse reported that she had "seen an elderly terminal patient bite through his I.V. tubing to prevent prolonging of the inevitable. I think it was horrible that we drove that man to such extremes" ("Taking Life" 40). On the other hand, such incidents may be the exceptions, and these reactions may, to some extent, be extreme and unnecessary. According to a report made by the British Medical Association, most people, no matter how serious their illnesses are, do not die in agony, but rather peacefully and with dignity ("Against Euthanasia" 220).

The right to die with dignity is regarded as almost as important as the right to die without suffering excessive pain. In earlier times, people of all ages died at home, in a natural and familiar setting, with their loved ones about them. According to a survey in Time, 50 years ago, more than half the deaths that took place in the United States occurred at home (Tifft 68). In our time, however, four out of five Americans die in institutions ("Right to Choose" 22). Kathy Fackelmann points out in Science News that patients and their families are especially frightened by "the frantic commotion and turmoil that surround a dying patient." Those who aren't used to the new equipment and the hospital procedures intended to prolong lives think that what goes on is a form of torture inflicted on helpless victims (232).

The person making unpleasant decisions about euthanasia is often not the patient nor one of the patient's relatives, but rather the patient's doctor. The majority of doctors are strongly opposed to both passive and active euthanasia, arguing that the Hippocratic Oath, which they must swear when they receive their medical degrees, pledges them to save lives, not to end them. Few would approve of Dr. Walter W. Sackett, a general practitioner in Miami, who has publicly stated that he has prescribed euthanasia for hundreds of his patients during thirty years of medical practice (Maguire 64).[2] Most doctors tend to share the attitude of the British Medical Association: "No doctor or nurse should be asked to hold responsibility for deciding when euthanasia may properly be administered, or for administering it" ("Against Euthanasia" 220).

One reason that doctors frequently cite for their refusal to accept any form of euthanasia is that an error may have been made, that the case may not be hopeless, and that, as the British Medical Association puts it, "errors

Catto 5

of judgment in euthanasia cases would be irreversible" ("Against Euthanasia" 220). Some patients with symptoms that suggest a terminal illness have been known to survive for months or years. If euthanasia were an accepted practice, how could such patients be protected from a possible premature death? By prolonging life and postponing death, doctors are also buying time in the hope that a cure might soon be found for a disease that appears to be hopeless (St. John-Stevas 422; Fackelmann 233). To some extent, this concern over possible errors and possible cures may be connected to a fear of being sued. Each year, more and more lawsuits are being brought against doctors who have supposedly failed to use every possible means to ensure that the dying live as long as possible ("Right to Choose" 23). As Richard Lamm notes in his New Republic article, if it can be proven that a doctor has failed to do everything possible to prolong life, then she may be faced with a malpractice suit, and the resulting bad publicity could seriously affect her future career (21).[3]

     Another strong professional objection to euthanasia is based on the special relationship that is supposed to exist between doctor and patient. Doctors have traditionally promoted and preserved human life; euthanasia may change the doctor's role, some fear, to that of a hired hand who simply caters to the whims of one person's individual idea of the good life (Callahan, "Euthanasia Debate" 15). More important, people trust doctors because they assume that a doctor's sole object is to save lives. Daniel C. Maguire makes the point that doctors are not supposed to differentiate between good death and bad death: "As medicine has developed, it is geared to promoting life under all circumstances. Death is the natural enemy of the healing science" (59). According to the British writer Norman St. John-Stevas, it is vital that patients continue to regard doctors as a force for life, not as a potential giver of death (422). This argument informs the American Medical Association's vehement opposition to the work of Dr. Jack Kevorkian, a leading practitioner of active euthanasia: "By invoking the physician-patient relationship to cloak his actions, Jack Kevorkian perverts the idea of the caring and committed physician, and weakens the public's trust in the medical profession" (Johnson, par. 1). The British Medical Association confirms that "to be a trusted physician is one thing; to appear as a potential executioner is quite another" ("Against Euthanasia" 220). But there are those who criticize this attitude, suggesting that doctors get considerable personal satisfaction from their almost godlike ability to keep people from dying.[4] Some nurses have criticized the almost proprietary attitude of doctors and other health-care professionals toward their patients:

> In a sense aren't we playing God? If God has called a patient to meet his Maker, what right does a nurse or doctor have to prolong his suffering if there is no hope?

> A patient does not belong to the nurses or to the physician.

> We saved him, if you can call it that. What it amounts to is an ego trip for us. ("Taking Life" 41)

These statements suggest that doctors and nurses may be reluctant to practice or even permit any form of euthanasia because of their own fear of failing to carry out their mission (Fackelmann 232). Conversely, conscientious physicians may find the ethical ramifications of euthanasia too disturbing to accept, for, as Leon Kass of the University of Chicago asks, "How easily will they be able to care wholeheartedly for patients when it is always possible to think of killing them as a 'therapeutic option'?" (35).

Cases of comatose or irreversibly vegetative patients, or of infants born with terminal diseases or generally fatal malformations, present additional ethical problems. In theory, these patients have little to live for, yet they are, of course, unable to request euthanasia for themselves. Who will determine whether euthanasia is appropriate in such instances? Opponents of euthanasia argue that it is impossible for anyone to determine what any individual's "likely quality of life" will be regardless of that individual's present condition (Koop 3), and that "it will be difficult--if not impossible--to develop the requisite calculus of degradation or to define the threshold necessary for ending life" (Kass 33).

One important point is that the mission of the medical profession may have changed as a result of new advances in medical science and technology. The Hippocratic Oath was relatively simple to maintain centuries, even decades ago, before drugs, equipment, and techniques were invented that could prolong the natural course of a patient's life. An article in Science

News describes "the high-tech atmosphere" existing in most hospitals today, especially in intensive care units, that supports the idea that science is stronger than death, and that encourages doctors to think of death as "an unacceptable outcome of medical therapy" (Fackelmann 232). Some hospital teams seem to regard patients as the objects of scientific experiment: Lamm cites the case of a dying woman who was resuscitated 70 times in one 24-hour period (22). Professor George J. Annas of the Boston University School of Medicine considers whether patients have the right to refuse to have their lives prolonged and concludes that "the proper role of medical technology" is at the center of the debate over euthanasia: "Is technology going to be our master or our servant? Is technology going to take on a life of its own such that we give it rights of its own? Or are we going to reassert our dominant role in controlling technology and using it for human ends?" ("Symposium").[5]

An important factor here is the high cost of these technological miracles. Maintaining a comatose patient can cost hundreds of thousands of dollars. Even if much of the financial burden is placed on health insurance agencies or the government, the gain may not be worth the cost. Noting that, in 1983, the national bill for health care was $355 billion, Lamm observes that "the time is not far off when there will be a direct conflicts [sic] between the health of the individual and the health of the society" (21). Given the limited amount of money available to pay for chronic and terminal illnesses, it may be necessary to make some unpleasant choices. Opponents of euthanasia argue that, "because death is cheaper than treatment," hospitals, concerned with costs, might be tempted to practice euthanasia without patients' consent ("Euthanasia War" 22). In contrast, those who advocate some kind of euthanasia policy point out that providing the latest medical equipment for one comatose or terminally ill patient may drain resources that might be used to pay for more nursing personnel and a more pleasant environment for other patients. There are also those who believe that available resources should be spent on preventive medicine: according to one doctor writing in The New England Journal of Medicine, "the costs of trying to preserve the life of one cirrhotic patient with bleeding esophageal varices might be used to treat and prevent alcoholism in many persons" (Lamm 21).

The final argument against euthanasia that must be given serious consideration is that it is dangerous for any society to legalize the killing of a certain class of its citizens. Daniel Callahan of the Hastings Center argues that a society that condones euthanasia condones a fundamental moral wrong, namely to give one individual

> ultimate power over another. It is to create the wrong kind of relationship between people, a community that sanctions private killings amongst its members in pursuit of their individual goals. (5)

In the Hastings Report Special Supplement, Richard Fenigsen further cautions that the line between voluntary and involuntary euthanasia--between euthanasia and "crypthanasia"--is inherently impossible to distinguish and that members of some societal groups, the elderly for instance, may submit to euthanasia against their will if they feel pressured to do so by relatives, doctors, or society at large (25). Furthermore, according to those who reject euthanasia, it is too easy to enlarge the category of people marked for euthanasia to include the handicapped, the mentally ill and retarded, those convicted of serious crimes, and other groups rejected by society. Eventually, once the barriers begin to break down, the whole attitude of a society toward its members may undergo an "ominous shift":

> Instead of the message a humane society sends to its members--"Everybody has the right to be around, we want to keep you with us, every one of you"--the society that embraces euthanasia, even the "mildest" and most "voluntary" forms of it, tells people: "We wouldn't mind getting rid of you."
> (Fenigsen 26)

In light of Washington State's 1991 Initiative 119, a narrowly defeated referendum that would have made it legal for doctors in Washington to help terminally ill patients commit suicide (Belkin 51), opponents of euthanasia believe they have even more reason to fear the "slippery slope" syndrome: once a society makes it legal to kill one patient, then what's to stop it from unfairly killing many (Elliott 26)?

Some critics of euthanasia express concern about its implications as a social policy. St. John-Stevas points to the terrible precedent of Nazi Germany and the eugenics movement, which attempted to eliminate everyone who did not meet a certain standard of social excellence and desirability (421). Rudikoff fears that we will create "euthanasia mills," which would make the termination of life a routine matter (66). It is true that, as one psychiatrist put it, euthanasia can never be "a logical decision. It is not one that you can make by a computer model" (Fackelmann 233). It is important to have some degree of personal involvement in each decision, to consider each case individually, and to assert, as Dr. Peter Hammerli did, that "I have never done anything to my patients that I would not do for my own mother and father . . . if they were in such a position" ("Hammerli Affair" 1272).

If euthanasia is going to become acceptable social policy, it is important to have some guidelines so that hospitals and nursing homes will understand when and by whom each decision will be made. Otherwise, John Ladd observes in Ethics, euthanasia will eventually take place at random: "Sometimes someone, no one knows who it is, will turn off the ventilator or will turn it on again after it has been turned off, because he thinks that one ought to let the patient die or ought not to let him die." These communication breakdowns can happen easily enough when everyone thinks it is his or her particular duty to intervene--or to stop someone else from intervening. Eventually, Ladd continues, "the patient becomes a football tossed around among those with different and competing interests and ideologies" (138).

One solution to this problem is, whenever possible, to allow individuals to assume the responsibility for deciding when they are ready to die (Modell 908). The report of the Presidential Commission in 1983 determined that a dying patient, if competent to make a decision, should be informed of all the available options and that "those who decline life-prolonging therapy should not be denied other forms of care needed to relieve pain and to maintain dignity" ("Right to Choose" 23). But doctors may not always be sure when patients are competent to make a responsible decision or whether they may have been coerced by family members for whom a lingering illness may be a continued burden (Rudikoff 66–67). For this reason, supporters of the right to euthanasia frequently recommend that each individual write a "living will" relatively early in life while still healthy and undeniably competent to make decisions (Rudikoff 64; "Hammerli Affair" 1272). Such a legal document would state that, should the person be incapable of making such a decision, he or she is establishing certain preferences among the options that might be available for his or her care. Typically, such wills, which have been authorized by numerous states, instruct doctors not to start or to stop any procedures intended to sustain life if the condition is terminal (Modell 908).

Of course, a living will is no assurance that the patient would still choose euthanasia. What if the patient has changed his mind since he wrote the living will? (Fackelmann 233; Rudikoff 66). A nurse who frequently cares for the dying notes that many patients do change their minds--sometimes more than once--as death approaches: "Since the patient may be unresponsive by this time, and since hearing is the last thing to go, I have wondered if it wouldn't be a terrible thing to be laying [sic] there and each time someone came in, wondering if they were coming to kill you" ("Taking Life" 42). That is, of course, a horrifying picture. But so, too, is the picture of a patient lying there longing for death and unable to convince anyone to carry out that wish.

Today, for most of us, the dread of death is so great that we go to any lengths to avoid it for those we love, as well as for ourselves. However, death in the right circumstances is everyone's right. It may be that the right to choose euthanasia would never have become a vital issue if death were a more integral part of our lives and if the circumstances in which death took place were easier to bear. St. John-Stevas argues against euthanasia by asserting that "dying can be a vital period in a person's life, reconciling him to life and death and giving an interior peace" (422). But this kind of ideal acceptance of death is possible only if there is a lot of care and love provided by all those in charge of the patient. At present, we seem to be more concerned with keeping people alive than with the quality of the lives that are being prolonged. Until we can have some assurance of a compassionate death--without unbearable cost to others and to society--we should not be intimidated by the church, the law, or the medical profession. Just as we choose the way we live, so should we be able to choose the way we die.

Note: According to MLA guidelines, quotations more than four lines in length should start on a new line, indented either one inch or ten spaces. The first line of each note indents one-half inch or five spaces. In the "Works Cited" list, the first line of each entry should be flush left and additional lines should indent one-half inch or five spaces.

Notes

[1] When there seemed to be no hope at all of a return to consciousness for those elderly people who were being kept alive by artificial feeding, Hammerli and his staff decided against continued treatment. Defending his actions, Hammerli insisted that he did not "believe in giving extensive treatment to a patient who is hopelessly ill: sometimes it is better to allow a person to die in peace" (26).

[2] Sackett suggests that, whether they admit it or not, 75% of all doctors have acted similarly at some point in their careers.

[3] The president of a Presidential Commission on the question of euthanasia is concerned that this fear of legal action may affect doctors' medical judgment. He imagines "a future horror scene in which a dying patient looks up from his deathbed to see the doctor flipping through a thick docket of legal cases" (Fackelmann 233).

[4] Of those few (17%) nurses who favored active euthanasia, only half would allow patients themselves the means to end their own lives; the other half believe that only professionals should be allowed to make and carry out that decision ("Taking Life" 40).

[5] The case of Elizabeth Bouvia is a good illustration. A quadriplegic who is regarded as mentally competent, Bouvia has been prevented from carrying out her expressed wish to end her own life by hospital staff, who insist on force-feeding her. Ernest van den Haag compares this with force-feeding convicts who go on hunger strikes, and argues that it is acceptable to force food on convicts since they are not entitled to the same liberties that free people are. "A hospital . . . may be liable for failing to artificially feed patients who cannot eat by normal means, or are incompetent. But not a patient who will not eat. He has a perfect right to decline food, or medicine, or an operation, if he so wishes and is competent to understand the consequences" (45–46).

Works Cited

"Against Euthanasia." The Lancet 30 Jan. 1971: 220.

Belkin, Lisa. "There's No Simple Suicide." New York Times Magazine 14 Nov. 1993: 48–55+.

Brecher, Edwin. "Opting for Suicide." New York Times Magazine 18 Mar. 1979: 72–80.

Callahan, Daniel. "Can We Return Disease to Death?" Hastings Center Report Special Supplement Feb. 1989: 4–6.

---. "The Euthanasia Debate: A Problem with Self-Determination." Current Oct. 1992: 15–19.

Cawley, Michelle Anne. "Euthanasia: Should It Be a Choice?" American Journal of Nursing May 1977: 859–61.

Elliott, Carl. "Dying Rites: The Ethics of Euthanasia." New Scientist 20 June 1992: 25–27.

"The Euthanasia War." The Economist 21 June 1997: 21–24.

Fackelmann, Kathy. "A Question of Life or Death." Science News 9 Oct. 1982: 232–33.

Fenigsen, Richard. "Euthanasia: How It Works: The Dutch Experience." Hastings Center Report Special Supplement Feb. 1989: 22–30.

"The Hammerli Affair: Is Passive Euthanasia Murder?" Science 26 Dec. 1975: 1271–74.

Humphrey, Derek. Final Exit: The Practicalities of Self-Deliverance and Assisted Suicide for the Dying. Eugene: Hemlock Society, 1991.

Johnson, Kirk. "The AMA's Response to Jack Kevorkian." Ohio Right to Life. 21 Nov. 1995. 2 May 1997 <http://www.infinet.com/~life/euth/amaltr.htm>.

Kass, Leon R. "Neither for Love or for Money: Why Doctors Must Not Kill." Public Interest Winter 1989: 25–26.

Koop, C. Everett. "The Challenge of Definition." Hastings Center Report Special Supplement Feb. 1989: 2–15.

Ladd, John. "Euthanasia, Liberty, and Religion." Ethics Oct. 1982: 129–38.

Catto 13

Lamm, Richard D. "Long Time Dying." New Republic 27 Aug. 1984: 20–23.

Macguire, Daniel C. "Death By Chance, Death By Choice." Good
Housekeeping Jan. 1975: 57–65.

McHugh, Paul R. "The Kevorkian Epidemic." *The American Scholar* Winter
1997: 15–27.

Orentlicher, David. "Physician Participation in Assisted Suicide." Journal of
the American Medical Association 262 6 Oct. 1989: 1844–45.

"The Right to Choose." Economist 26 March 1983: 22–23.

Rudikoff, Sonia. "The Problem of Euthanasia." Commentary Feb. 1974:
62–68.

St. John-Stevas, Norman. "Euthanasia: A 'Pleasant Sounding Word.'"
America 31 May 1975: 421–22.

"Symposium: When Sophisticated Medicine Does More Harm Than Good."
New York Times 30 Mar. 1986: E6.

"Taking Life Away." Nursing 75 Oct. 1975: 4050.

Tifft, Susan. "Debate on the Boundary of Life." Time 11 Apr. 1983: 68–70.

van den Haag, Ernest. "A Right to Die?" National Review 4 May 1984: 45–46.

Walzen, Michael. "Feed the Face." *The New Republic* 9 June 1997: 29.

Joan Smith

History 101

December 10, 1997

The Quest for Survival in the Andes Mountains

What was meant to be a pleasure trip for forty-five people flying from Montevideo, Uruguay, to Santiago, Chile, on October 13, 1972, turned into the horror of instant death for some and of slow starvation in the freezing Andes temperatures for others. The Old Christian Rugby Team and families and friends of the team--forty-five in all--flew out of Montevideo with nothing more on their minds than a rugby match with a Chilean team and a few days of skiing. But a terrifying plane crash in the rugged peaks of the Andes changed everything. What ensued for those who survived first the crash of their plane and then a crushing avalanche a short time later was a long ordeal of hunger and cold. The events that took place during these seventy-two days high in the icy Andes remain a fascinating story of the tenacity of the human will to survive at almost any cost, even the cost of eating human flesh.

According to a comprehensive newspaper account, the rugby team departed from Montevideo on October 12, 1972, in a propeller-driven Fairchild F-227, a Uruguayan Air Force plane, and after a night in Mendoza because of bad weather, they resumed their flight on Monday, October 13, at midday. The plane would cross an Andes mountain range that had peaks up to 21,000 feet in a blizzard.[1] As Piers Paul Read describes it, though the weather was inclement, everyone was assured that the flight was perfectly safe because the plane would be able to stay above the clouds. As the plane approached Santiago, the co-pilot Lagurara radioed Air Traffic Control at 3:35 to announce the plane's location and altitude. The controllers authorized him to lower the plane to 10,000 feet as he neared the airport of Pudaheul. However, when he brought the plane down 3,000 feet, it began to shake as it entered the clouds. The plane continued to jump and shake more vigorously as it entered other cloudbanks; the passengers began to panic and pray.[2]

Apparently, as the plane continued through clouds, it got caught in an air pocket, sank quickly in seconds, and broke apart against the side of

Smith 2

an 11,500-foot mountain.[3] According to Benales's account, the tail section somersaulted down a mountain slope, killing those in the back of the plane immediately, while some still in their seats were swept out of the front of the plane because of the force of the air. The front section of the aircraft, or fuselage, slammed onto an area between peaks in the Hilario range of the Andes. José Luis Inciarte, one of the survivors interviewed by Benales, later described the scene as the fuselage slid over the snow: "Blood spurted all over me, people were screaming and I could smell fuel and cold air rushing in from outside, when suddenly with one big bump we came to rest."[4] Twelve of the forty-five people on board were killed in the crash.[5]

The first twenty-four hours were the worst for the survivors of the crash. Many were seriously or fatally injured, almost all were in a state of shock, and all of them froze in subfreezing temperatures of an Andes blizzard. Gustavo Zerbino, another survivor, remembers the first night as a nightmarish series of the "injured screaming, crying, dying. . . . "[6] Those who survived the first night did so by wrapping up in the ski clothes they had brought for their holiday[7] and by covering up in the seat covers they ripped from the seats of the plane. The group was almost totally exposed to the cold air, with only a makeshift barrier of seats and luggage protecting them. Worse than the cold was the hysteria.[8] It is miraculous that any survived that first night; the day after the crash, Chilean authorities said the chance for survival was "virtually nil" because those who hadn't died in the crash would die in the freezing blizzard.[9]

Suffering through the first night was the first of many trials for the sixteen who would live to tell the story. All of those who survived the crash had sustained some type of injury. In fact, three more people died during that first night. The wounded had to be attended to; fortunately, the survivors had among them an innovative medical student named Robert Canessa. Under Canessa's supervision, the survivors fought to keep their wounded alive. With the few makeshift medical tools they had, they tried several surgical operations. Cologne was the only disinfectant they had, and the harsh environment simply would not let the wounded heal properly.[10] Some would suffer from gangrene.[11] The fuselage also had to be made livable. The men of the rugby team worked tenaciously to pack the open back of the plane with whatever they could find to block the wind; they continued to rip the covers off the seats for more blankets; they made hammocks for the wounded out of cable and cord and metal plates ripped from the side of the plane.[12]

And they worried about how to get food and water. For ten days after the crash, the survivors lived off the meager rations that were found on the wrecked plane. During that period, each of the twenty-seven who survived the initial ordeal lived on a daily ration of one square of chocolate, one teaspoon of jam, a bit of toothpaste, and a small mouthful of wine in a deodorant cap.[13] Thirst was a big concern. In temperatures often descending to 25°C below zero, melting snow for water was a problem. Eating snow was no substitute for drinking water, as it burned the survivors' chapped lips and gave them stomach cramps.[14] They used the metal sheets from the wreck to rig up reflectors that tediously melted the snow into bottles. This process was slow, however, and the survivors were forced to carefully ration water.[15]

Meanwhile, the survivors had hope of rescue. A transistor radio was found in the wreckage, and Carlos Rosque, the plane's mechanic and only surviving crew member, said that batteries for it could be found in the other half of the plane. Three of the strongest survivors, including Canessa and Fernando Parrado, the two who would eventually succeed in hiking out of the mountains, went in search of the lost tail. After a strenuous hike, they located it, but the batteries were too heavy to carry back to the wreck. The three returned and the next day found it easier to carry the relatively light radio back to the tail. Roy Haley, who was knowledgeable about radios, went with them, and eventually figured out a way for them to listen to Radio Spectator in Montevideo. Listening to the radio, however, may have turned out to be more tragic than hopeful. On October 21, eight days after the crash, Haley heard that the rescue mission had been called off because there was little reason to believe anyone could survive the crash and the cold.[16]

After hearing that the search had been called off, the survivors knew that they would have to discover another source of food if they were going to live. Their meager rations were quickly running out, and the men were beginning to feel the effects of starvation.[17] They considered all possible options for sustenance. No plant life that might provide food survived in the harsh weather of the Andes; they found only lichen on the exposed rocks, which was worthless as sustenance.[18] For several days, many of the men had been silently concluding that the only way they would survive was to eat the bodies of those who had died. Canessa, the medical student, finally had the courage to openly suggest the possibility of consuming human flesh. He urged that, since the rescue had been called off, the only way the group would live was by rescuing themselves, and they could only do this if they had food. Further, he admonished that they had the moral duty to stay alive, that they had been given the gift of life and were responsible for sustaining it. Though many had serious reservations about eating the flesh of their families and friends, they felt the force of Canessa's arguments.[19] Several others supported Canessa, clothing their arguments more and more in religious language. God wanted them to live, they argued; He had spared them from the crash and had given them the bodies to eat. It would be wrong to reject this gift on the grounds of squeamishness.[20]

On the tenth day after the crash and the second day after the crushing news about the cancellation of rescue efforts, after much heated discussion, Canessa, with the support of most of the twenty-six other survivors, cut into a corpse with a shard of glass and ate the flesh.[21] The group calculated that each corpse would last five days if they carefully rationed their intake.[22] Two metaphors helped them to justify their actions. The group compared their consumption of flesh to a heart transplant; just as a heart is taken from one person at death to keep another alive, so the dead bodies sustained the breath of the living. But the most powerful metaphor for the survivors, most of whom were Catholic, was the sacrament of the Holy Communion.[23] Survivor Eduardo Deigrado later said, concerning their decision, "We thought of Jesus and how in the Last Supper He had divided his body and blood to all the apostles. We understood that we had to do the same, to take His body and blood which had been reincarnated and that was an intimate communion among us. It was what helped us to subsist."[24] Catholic priests would later support the survivors' decision. Two priests said that the men had "acted justifiably" and within the bounds of religious morality; a person is permitted to eat human flesh, they said, if there is no other means for survival. They called the Communion metaphor "not unreasonable."[25]

        In fact, the group's shared religious beliefs helped them through the
many life-threatening difficulties they faced. As José Luis Inciarte said later,
"When we got really low in spirits, we said our rosary together and we were
overcome with such strong faith that it bubbled up inside of us."[26] Carlos
Paez led the men in a nightly rosary throughout the ordeal.[27] But it was not
only religion that kept them alive; their youthful good health, as well as the
teamwork and discipline developed on the rugby field, also worked to sustain them.[28] As Claudia Dowling describes it, the survivors, all aged from
nineteen to twenty-six, worked together unselfishly, making rules and organizing chores. Adolfo Staunch, Eduardo Staunch, and Daniel Fernandez, all
cousins, initially took charge of apportioning labor and of the unpleasant
task of flaying the bodies. Others, like Canessa and Parrado, also emerged
as leaders. The men knew that to survive they must construct and follow
communal rules. Their discipline and teamwork kept them from consuming
too much food too quickly and encouraged them to look after each other's
needs. They knew that any selfish behavior might lead to death. The fact
that the men were friends from the same town definitely made their community more harmonious than it might have been in other circumstances. Inciarte remembers that when he was down to half of his body weight and
barely able to move, Adolfo Staunch gave him an entire bottle of his precious
water. Such unselfish behavior, generated by both religious belief and friendship, kept the men alive.[29] Dowling points out that the survivors "never degenerated into Lord of the Flies primitivism, never turned on one another.
They worked together as a tribe so all might survive."[30]

        Not all groups have behaved so harmoniously under the duress of
cold and starvation. The comparable incident of the Donner Party, trapped
in the Sierra Nevada mountains of California in the winter of 1846–47, provides a gruesome foil to the ordeal of the Uruguayan rugby team. The party,
comprised of ten unrelated families and sixteen other individuals and
headed by the Illinois farmer George Donner, was snowbound in the Sierra
Nevadas as they were making their way west. What ensued during that winter shares with the Andes incident the same tenacious struggle to survive
under similar conditions, but greed, selfishness, and possibly murder taint
the story.[31] As hunger overtook the party, families with food often refused

to help those with less, or charged them exorbitant prices for meager portions[32] and then seized their goods when they could not pay.[33] After the food ran out, the party agreed that cannibalism was the only means of survival. They waited impatiently for someone to die. When a bachelor in the group accidentally caught his hand on fire, they refused to save him; he died and they ate him.[34] As one member of the party wrote in his journal, certain people then began to talk freely about shooting and eating those who were probably going to die anyway.[35] Later, a woman, after eating a corpse, shot, killed, and ate the two Native Americans in the party. Finally, after some of the party had finally hiked out of the mountains and returned to rescue the others, a man named Keseberg was found alone, surrounded by several mutilated corpses and incredible filth. Though he said they had died naturally, he was frank about eating their flesh and enjoying it, and valuables of the dead were found on his person.[36]

Though physically taxed to the same limit as the Donner Party was, the Andes survivors maintained a sense of charity and morality. It is testimony to the group's fortitude that they held together in relative harmony and survived. As the days passed, their ordeal only became more dire. One week after eating their first flesh, they were struck by another tragedy. The group of twenty-seven was reduced to nineteen after an avalanche crashed into the fuselage in the middle of the night, and killed eight while wrecking the carefully arranged barrier against the cold.[37] The avalanche struck suddenly; the men all felt a push on the plane, and then all were buried, giving themselves up to die. Again, only the strength of those lucky enough not to be fully buried prevented the number of deaths from increasing. They worked vigorously to pull others from the snow and revive them with mouth-to-mouth resuscitation.[38] Those who did survive did so miraculously. Inciarte recalls his good fortune: "It [the avalanche] got me with my hand in front of my face, so I managed to make a little cavity and breathe a bit. I heard screaming. . . . I moved my hand about a bit but couldn't get out. I think it was the worst moment of all because I really gave myself up for lost."[39] But he was finally pulled out.

Though the group had found a way to sustain themselves and made rules for running an efficient community, the days after the avalanche threatened their morale. Not only did the men grieve over the deaths of their friends, but they also had to witness the slow deaths of three others due to starvation or injuries suffered in the crash or the avalanche. Among these was Numa Turcatti, one of the strongest and most fit of the group. During the days after the avalanche, he had suddenly lost the will to live; he refused food to the point that he essentially let himself die in early December.[40] Others seemed to follow Turcatti's lead, as despair set in for the group. Strife over cigarette rations was a constant irritation; discord started to threaten the group's harmony.[41]

A numbing boredom made matters worse. The men were well aware that they were miles from civilization, and that almost impassable mountains separated them from the nearest village.[42] In the face of such slim odds for survival, the group often had bouts with apathy. Through the long cold days and nights of November, they underwent long periods of silence.[43] They tried various ways to invigorate their spirits. Aside from the daily routine of melting snow for water and eating their sparse meals, they engaged in group discussions on pre-arranged topics,[44] planned what they would do when they returned to Montevideo, listed the best restaurants in their town, and held small birthday celebrations with red wine for the three men whose birthdays came during their ordeal.[45]

The survivors also continued to consider how they might rescue themselves. After several failed attempts to use the radio to call for help, they decided that the only chance for survival lay in hiking out of the mountains.[46] Throughout their stay in the mountains, the group had been sending out small scouting parties on trial expeditions. These short excursions allowed them to determine who the strongest of the group were and what clothing and methods for carrying food were the most effective.[47] As December approached, the weather began to warm as spring approached in the seasonal cycle of the Southern Hemisphere. Canessa, Parrado, and Antonio Vizintin were selected to make the trek out of the mountains.[48] The group began gathering food and the best clothing for the expeditioners, and tore felt covers from the heating tubes in the aircraft to make sleeping bags for them.[49] But the scouting trips did not provide much information on the group's exact location. They knew Chile was to the west, and had the aircraft compass to point them in that direction. Otherwise, the three knew they would be wandering blindly through the rugged, freezing peaks of the Andes.[50]

At the end of the first week of December, after the group had been trapped on the mountain for fifty-six days, two condors appeared and circled the sky. These were the first of several signs of spring. The weather warmed; the group heard from the radio that the search had resumed. They had planned for Canessa, Parrado, and Vizintin to leave as soon as the weather improved; the preparations for the journey were almost finished. However, the normally strong-willed Canessa began to procrastinate. As Read's account and the film based on it illustrate, strife broke out between Canessa and the others when he began finding excuses for not going on the journey. The others knew the effort would fail without him and felt that he was letting them down for the first time. Just before their greatest attempt to overcome their plight, the group seemed to be falling apart.[51]

It took another death to persuade Canessa that he must go. Turcatti finally breathed his last on December 10, reducing the number of survivors to sixteen. Canessa realized that he could wait no longer; the group's morale could stand little more. Others were on the verge of death as well.[52] Many had dropped in weight from two hundred to one hundred pounds.[53]

On December 11, the three set out, loaded with as many clothes and as much food as they could carry. On the third day of strenuous travel, during which the hunger-weakened travellers averaged only four miles a day,[54] they reached the top of a high mountain; there they saw a distant valley between the only two mountains that weren't snow-covered. They realized then that there was not enough food for the three of them to reach the valley. They decided that Vizintin must return to the plane so that Canessa and Parrado would have enough food to complete the journey.[55]

The two resumed a journey that would end seven days later. Of the many hard-fought victories over death during the ordeal, this ten-day trek was the most triumphant and the most difficult. Canessa recalls those "unending days of travel--intense cold at night, intolerable heat at midday. We rationed the water and the food and said, 'if we don't walk so far, then no food for us.'"[56] The two were near death from exhaustion and hunger when they saw a rancher's hut in Chile on December 20. The hut belonged to Sergio Catalan Martinez, a forty-four-year-old cattle hand, living in San Fernando, who at 9 p.m. heard the faint shouts of the men across the roaring Tinguiririca River. He saw what seemed to be two tramps shouting at him on the other side of the water. When he still couldn't hear them, he threw over a stone with a paper and pen attached. Parrado quickly wrote,

> I come from the plane that crashed in the mountains. I am Uruguayan. We have been walking like this for 10 days. My friend is injured [from the hike]. There are still 14 injured people in the plane. We have to get out of here quickly because we have nothing to eat. We can walk no more.[57]

He threw the rock back to Sergio, who immediately went for help; patrols reached them by 12 p.m.

Canessa and Parrado made it out just in time. By the time the men back at the plane heard the message on the radio that they would be rescued, they had almost given up hope. Each day brought the prospect of death by starvation. Christmas was approaching, and their pessimism grew each day that they heard no news of Canessa and Parrado. Only the remnants of their incredible will to stay alive kept them from sinking totally into despair like Turcatti.[58] But everything changed on the morning of December 20. As the men heard the news, euphoria spread through their camp. They abandoned their daily tasks; they made their remaining cigarettes into Havana-style cigars. Two days later, on the afternoon of December 22, most of the men were taken out by helicopter; the rest were removed the following day.[59] The seventy-two-day ordeal was over. They had survived.

The aftermath of the ordeal caused a major stir in Uruguay. As the survivors revealed their story and their methods of survival, the reaction from the media was one of admiration and sympathy. Experts were amazed that the men could walk and remain mentally lucid after such starvation.[60] People were moved by the religious metaphors the men used to describe their consumption of flesh. But the dead were not forgotten. The twenty-nine victims were given a Christian burial in a common grave near the snow-covered wreckage.[61]

The survivors' celebrity status has not waned in their home country, and now it is international in the wake of the film Alive. Dowling suggests that, while the survivors cannot forget their great victory for the force of life, they also won't forget the sacrifice and the pain. They were made soberer and wiser from the ordeal, with striking insights into what a human is capable of. Many survivors felt a religious depth on the mountain they have never again experienced.[62] As Canessa said in a recent interview about his reaction to the film Alive, "I think it's a family film because it values religion and friendship, if in a touching and different way."[63] This remark perhaps best sums up what the victory of the survivors can mean for us; life and friendship are precious and powerful gifts, and not to be taken lightly.

Notes

[1] Carlos Benales, "70 Days Battling Starvation and Freezing in the Andes: A Chronicle of Man's Unwillingness to Die," New York Times, 1 Jan. 1973: A3. This article was the first comprehensive one on the Andes story. It was issued from the South American news agency LATIN.

[2] Piers Paul Read, Alive (New York and Philadelphia: Lippincott, 1974), 36–37. Of the many books written about this Andes mountain incident, Read's is considered the most authoritative, so I have chosen to use it to elucidate certain points of the story. The survivors of the group authorized this book so that the truth could be known about the many rumors surrounding their story. The other books on the subject did not receive authorization and Frank Marshall chose Alive as the most accurate basis for his 1993 film portraying the story. The book is written in the form of a novel; it is based on actual events that Read has brought to life in more detail. Read's book contains all information that appears in this essay; I have specifically drawn on it to elucidate certain scenes that the periodical articles either did not cover or dealt with only briefly. Other unauthorized, novelistic accounts of the story may be found in Enrique Hank Lopez's The Highest Hell (New York: Pocket Books, 1973), Clay Blair Jr.'s Survive! (Berkeley: Berkeley Books, 1973), and Richard Cunningham's The Place Where the World Ends (New York: Sheed and Ward, 1973).

[3] Claudia Glenn Dowling, "Still Alive," Life, 16 Jan. 1993: 50.

[4] Benales.

[5] Several of the survivors later blamed the crash on a pilot's error. Terry Clifford, "Staying Alive," Chicago Tribune, 15 Jan. 1993: 5:3.

[6] Don Podesta, "Echoes of a Crash Unheard of: The Tales of 16 Uruguayans Are Still as Chilling as Their Survival 20 Years Ago," Washington Post, 21 Dec. 1992: C1. Benales reported that the co-pilot spent the entire night groaning for water and for his revolver.

[7] Benales.

[8] Read, 47.

[9] "Uruguayan Plane with 45 Is Missing on Andes Flight," New York Times, 14 Oct. 1972: A9.

[10] The information in this paragraph up to this point comes from "Cannibalism After Air Crash Reported," New York Times, 27 Dec. 1972: D2. Canessa extracted a steel bar, for example, from the intestines of a wounded person, who nevertheless died, as did two others who died over the next few days.

[11] Rick Miller, "A Nightmare Revisited: 20 Years Later, with the Film's Release, Andes Survivors Recall Ordeal," Boston Globe, 21 Jan. 1993: 1:2.

[12] Benales.

[13] Dowling, 50. Also, "8 Survivors of Crash Picked Up in Andes," New York Times, 24 Dec. 1972: A9.

[14] Benales.

[15] Benales; Podesta.

[16] This account of finding the batteries and listening to the radio is taken from Benales. Though official searches were called off, the parents of those on the plane continued to search throughout the ordeal. Most notably, Carlos Paez Vilaro, the father of Carlitos Paez, searched diligently for his son, plotting clairvoyants' visions of maps, hounding the authorities, and searching by means of airplanes, on a mule, and on foot. Dowling, 58.

[17] Read, 81. Read describes their hunger: "Starvation was taking its effect. They were becoming weaker and more listless. When they stood up they felt faint and found it difficult to keep their balance. They felt cold, even when the sun rose to warm them, and their skin started to grow wrinkled like that of old men."

[18] Read, 82. Benales reports that the group also tried to make a soup out of the lichens and water.

[19] Miller.

[20] Read, 84–85.

[21] Dowling, 51.

[22] Benales.

[23] "Cannibalism." Both metaphors are described in this article.

[24] "Survivors of Andes Air Crash Admit Dead Saved Their Lives," New York Times, 29 Dec. 1972: A9. Canessa also justified their actions later when he said, "I've . . . thought that if I were dying, I would be proud that a friend could use my body." Clifford, 5:3.

[25] "Two Catholic Aides Defend Cannibalism in Chilean Air Crash," New York Times, 28 Dec. 1972: A8.

[26] Benales.

[27] Podesta.

[28] Benales.

[29] Dowling, 50, 55.

[30] Dowling, 50. Dowling goes on to aptly link the men's friendship, religion, and consumption of flesh:

> At the most basic level, friendship is founded on the sharing of food; the word companion comes from the Latin "he with whom one shares bread." Sharing flesh has even more resonance. In primitive agricultural societies, the sacrifice of animals was often a sacred celebration of tribes. Jewish Passover and Christian Communion are based on such traditions.

[31] Eric Linklater, Preface, Ordeal By Hunger, by George R. Stewart (London: Jonathan Cape, 1936), p. 9. Stewart's book offers a thorough and riveting account of the Donner Pass incident.

[32] Jared Diamond, "Reliving the Donner Party," Discover 13 March 1992: 103.

[33] Patrick Breen, The Diary of Patrick Breen, One of the Donner Party, ed. Frederick J. Terrgart, Academy of Pacific Coast History Publications, Vol. 1 (Berkeley: University of California Press, 1910), p. 280. Breen's diary provides a terse day-by-day account of the ordeal; he briefly alludes to the dissension and the cannibalism.

[34] Diamond, 103.

[35] Breen, 284.

[36] Diamond, 105.

[37] Dowling, 50; Benales.

[38] "Cannibalism."

[39] Benales.

[40] Benales. Another of the group, Bobby Francois, was also reluctant to preserve himself. He refused to do his chores, and often just sat around smoking. The others told him if he didn't work, he couldn't eat. He said that sounded fair. The survivors fed him anyway, and kept him alive. Dowling 57.

[41] Read, 204–205.

[42] Podesta. The group learned how isolated they were when some men on an early scouting excursion ascended a 14,000-foot slope and saw only 100 miles of snow-covered mountains in every direction.

[43] Benales.

[44] "Cannibalism."

[45] Benales.

[46] Read, 204–208.

[47] Benales.

[48] Dowling, 51.

[49] Read, 213.

[50] Benales.

[51] All information in this paragraph comes from Read, 213–215, and the film Alive, directed by Frank Marshall (Touchstone and Paramount, 1993), which was adapted by Patrick Stanley from Read's novel. The box-office success of the film proves the story's lasting interest.

[52] Read, 218.

[53] Benales.

[54] Dowling, 51.

[55] Read, 227–228.

[56] Benales.

[57] Benales. Read, 271, reports an expanded version of the encounter with Martinez and the note.

[58] Read, 244.

[59] All information after note 58 to this point comes from Benales.

[60] Benales. Weathered mountaineers especially were amazed at the survivors' relative good health after such wear and tear on their minds and bodies.

[61] "29 Victims in Andes Crash to Receive Common Burial," New York Times 26 Dec. 1972: E12.

[62]Dowling, 58.

[63]Clifford, 5:3.

Bibliography

Benales, Carlos. "70 Days Battling Starvation and Freezing in the Andes: A Chronicle of Man's Unwillingness to Die." New York Times 1 Jan. 1973: A3.

Breen, Patrick. Diary of Patrick Breen, One of the Donner Party. Academy of Pacific Coast History Publications, Vol. 1. Ed. Frederick J. Terrgart. Berkeley: U of California P, 1910. 269–84.

"Cannibalism After Air Crash Reported." New York Times 27 Dec. 1972: D2.

Clifford, Terry. "Staying Alive." Chicago Tribune 15 Jan. 1993: 5:3.

Diamond, Jared. "Reliving the Donner Party." Discover 13 Mar. 1992: 100–105.

Dowling, Claudia Glenn. "Still Alive." Life Feb. 1993: 48–59.

"8 Survivors of Crash Picked Up in Andes." New York Times 24 Dec. 1972: A9.

Linklater, Eric. Preface. Ordeal By Hunger. By George R. Stewart. London: Cape, 1936.

Marshall, Frank, dir. Alive. Touchstone and Paramount, 1993.

Miller, Rick. "A Nightmare Revisited: 20 Years Later, with the Film's Release, Andes Survivors Recall Ordeal." Boston Globe 21 Jan. 1993: A2.

Podesta, Dan. "Echoes of a Crash Unheard of: The Tales of 16 Uruguayans Are Still as Chilling as Their Survival 20 Years Ago." Washington Post 21 Dec. 1992: C1.

Read, Piers Paul. Alive: The Story of the Andes Survivors. Philadelphia and New York: Lippincott, 1974.

"Survivors of Andes Air Crash Admit Dead Saved Their Lives." New York Times 29 Dec. 1972: A9.

"29 Victims in Andes Crash to Receive Common Burial." New York Times 26 Dec. 1972: E12.

"Two Catholic Aides Defend Cannibalism in Chilean Air Crash." New York Times 28 Dec. 1972: A8.

David Morgan

Natural Science I

December 15, 1998

Explaining the Tunguskan Phenomenon

The Tunguska River Valley in Siberia has always been an area of swamps and bogs, forests and frozen tundra, sparsely populated, and remote and inaccessible to most travelers. It was at dawn on June 30, 1908, that witnesses in the Tungus observed a light glaring more brightly than anything they had ever seen. This cosmic phenomenon, they said, was bluish-white in color and gradually became cigarlike in shape. Just as terrifying to the few people inhabiting that part of Siberia was the tremendous noise that accompanied the light, a noise that was reported to have been heard 1,000 kilometers from the site (Parry, 1961). Some who were in the vicinity were deafened, while others farther away apparently became speechless and displayed other symptoms of severe trauma. The Tungus community refused to go near the site or speak of the occurrence, and some even denied that it had ever happened (Crowther, 1931). The event was so frightening to these simple peasants that many believed it had been an act of divine retribution, a punishment by a god demanding vengeance (Baxter & Atkins, 1976).

Since 1921, when the first perilous expedition to the Tungus region confirmed that a remarkable event had indeed taken place, scientists have attempted to explain what it was and why it happened. Almost 80 years later, the various theories developed to explain the explosion in the Tunguska Valley have become almost as interesting a phenomenon as the original occurrence. Like doctors trying to diagnose a disease by examining the symptoms, scientists have analyzed the fragmentary evidence and published theories that supposedly account for it. However, no theory has been entirely convincing. The purpose of this essay is to provide a brief description of some of the major interpretations of the Tunguska occurrence and to suggest that, in their efforts to substantiate their theories, scientists can be fallible.

At dawn on that day in June 1908, a huge object evidently came from space into the earth's atmosphere, breaking the sound barrier, and, at

7:17 a.m., slammed into the ground in the central Siberian plateau. Moments before the collision, a thrust of energy caused people and animals to be strewn about, structures destroyed, and trees toppled. Immediately afterward, a pillar or "tongue" of fire could be seen in the sky several hundred miles away; others called it a cylindrical pipe. A thermal air current of extremely high temperature caused forest fires to ignite and spread across forty miles, melting metal objects scattered throughout the area. Several shock waves were felt for hundreds of miles around, breaking windows and tossing people, animals, and objects in the air. Finally, black rain fell from a menacing-looking cloud over a radius of 100 square miles. It is no wonder that the peasants of the Tunguska River Valley thought that this was the end of the world (Krinov, 1966; Baxter & Atkins, 1976).

For a variety of reasons, this devastating occurrence remained almost unknown outside Russia--and even outside central Siberia--for many years. The Tungus was extremely remote, even for Russia, which is such a vast country that transportation and communication between places can be slow and difficult. The few people living in the area who actually witnessed what happened were mostly peasants and nomadic tribesmen, and did not have much opportunity or inclination to talk about what they had seen. There was little publicity, and what there was was limited to local Siberian newspapers (Krinov, 1966). During that summer, there was a lot of discussion in the newspapers of the European capitals about peculiar lights and colors seen in the northern skies, unusually radiant sunsets, some magnetic disturbances, and strange dust clouds (Cowan, Atluri, & Libby, 1965). But, since news of the events at the Tungus River had hardly yet been heard even in Moscow, there was no way for scientists in other countries to see a connection between these happenings.

It was only in 1921, when Russia was relatively stable after years of war, revolution, and economic problems, that the first expedition to investigate the event at Tunguska actually took place (Crowther, 1931). That it occurred then at all was largely because an energetic Russian scientist, Leonid Kulik, had become fascinated by meteorites. He read in an old Siberian newspaper that, in 1908, a railway train had been forced to stop because a meteorite fell in its path--a story that was quite untrue. Kulik thought that

Morgan 3

he might become the discoverer of the greatest meteorite ever found on earth and determined to search for evidence that such a meteorite existed. Authorized by the Soviet Academy, Kulik led a series of expeditions to the Tungus River. In 1921, he did not even reach the site, for the route was almost impassable. In 1927, and annually for the next few years, Kulik did, indeed, explore the devastated area and was able to study the evidence of what had happened and listen to the oral accounts of the event provided by those inhabitants who were still alive and who were willing to talk to him. Finally, in 1938–39, Kulik traveled to the Tungus for the last time, for the purpose of taking aerial photographs that might confirm his meteorite theory (Baxter & Atkins, 1976).

Kulik and his fellow investigators believed that whatever had happened at the Tungus River had been caused by a meteorite. So, what they expected to find was a single, vast crater to mark the place where the meteorite had landed. Such a crater, however, was simply not there (Cowan, Atluri, & Libby, 1965). Instead, he found a vast devastated and burned area, a forest of giant trees with their tops cut off and scattered around (Crowther, 1931). In 1928, without the benefit of an aerial view of the region, Kulik concluded from his various vantage points on the ground that, around the circumference of the area where the meteorite had landed, there was a belt of upright dead trees, which he named the "telegraph pole forest." Scattered around the perimeter of the frozen swamp, which he called the "cauldron," were groups of fallen trees, with their tops all pointing away from the direction of where the blast had occurred (Cowan, Atluri, & Libby, 1965). None of this was consistent with Kulik's meteorite theory, and he could only attribute the odd pattern of upright and fallen trees to a shock wave or "hot compressed-air pockets," which had missed some trees and affected others (Baxter & Atkins, 1976). The account of his discovery in the Literary Digest of 1929 states that "each of the falling meteoric fragments must have worked, the Russian scientists imagine, like a gigantic piston," with compressed air knocking trees down like toothpicks (What a meteor, 1929, p. 34). Kulik continued to insist that the fire and the resultant effect on the trees was the result of a meteorite explosion. But the Russian scientist V. G. Fesenkov estimated that such destruction could only have been caused by an object of at least several hundred meters, and that, if anything of this size or force had hit the ground, it would have left a crater (Baxter & Atkins, 1976).

Kulik found other evidence that could not easily be explained by the meteorite theory. Although there was no trace of a single large crater (Cowan, Atluri, & Libby, 1965), there were numerous shallow cavities scattered around the frozen bog (Olivier, 1928). For several years, Kulik attempted to bore into the ground, seeking evidence that these pits and ridges were formed by lateral pressure caused by gases exploding from the meteorite's impact. Kulik described the scene as "not unlike a giant duplicate of what happens when a brick from a tall chimney-top falls into a puddle of mud. Solid ground actually must have splashed outward in every direction." In this account, the supposed meteorite became "the great swarm of meteors" that "must have traversed" the atmosphere for several hundred miles, pushing ahead of it a "giant bubble of superheated atmosphere" that was "probably responsible" for the burned countryside (What a meteor, 1929, p. 33). All the "must have's" and "probably's" make a good narrative, but are not scientifically convincing.

Similarly, Kulik endeavored to explain eyewitness accounts of the huge fireball in the sky that burned one observer's shirt off his back and threw him off his porch (Cowan, Atluri, & Libby, 1965). Such extreme heat waves had never before been known to have accompanied the fall of a meteorite, but Kulik decided that this meteorite was much larger than those previously recorded and that therefore it would have released much more energy upon impact and that would account for such radiant heat (Baxter & Atkins, 1976). So obsessed was Kulik with the idea that somewhere buried in the Tungus swamp was a phenomenal meteorite that he focused the efforts of all the expeditions to the area during his lifetime on digging beneath the frozen tundra and to some extent neglected the examination of other evidence that might have further threatened the theory that he was determined to prove (Parry, 1961). Initially, he was successful in convincing the scientific community that his theory was correct. It is most interesting to read excerpts from The American Weekly of 1929 flatly asserting that a meteorite had fallen in Siberia and that Professor Kulik had brought back photographs of the giant crater that he found, as well as small samples of meteoric materials. The article is accompanied by a photograph of Professor Kulik measuring "the main crater, where the largest mass of this celestial visitor buried itself in the earth" (Quoted in What a meteor, p. 34).

While Kulik's expeditions were still searching for evidence of a meteorite, other scientists were hypothesizing that the Tunguska explosion might have been caused by a small comet, which would account for the absence of a crater. Comets are composed of ice, frozen gases, and dust, and as they travel around the sun, they develop a long tail. Upon impact, a comet might give off a trail of gases and dust which would create a bright and colorful night sky similar to that observed after the explosion. This would not be true of a meteorite, which has no gaseous trail and thus leaves no trace in the atmosphere. It has also been suggested that the observed direction of the object's travel was more typical of a comet than a meteorite (Florensky, 1963). If the comet had blown up approximately two miles above the site, that would explain why some trees survived while others did not (Parry, 1961). On the other hand, there is no evidence that a comet had ever crashed on earth before, or caused a comparable change in magnetic and atmospheric phenomena, or even come so close without being sighted (Baxter & Atkins, 1976). Those scientists supporting the comet theory have suggested that, although it is unusual for any comet to come that close to earth without anyone sighting it, the one landing at Tunguska might have been small enough to go by unnoticed. But that idea is contradicted by Fesenkov's estimate that, to cause such destruction, the nucleus of the Tunguskan comet--if there was one--would have been only slightly smaller than those of well-documented comets that were visible at great distances (Cowan, Atluri, & Libby, 1965).

The next major explanation for the cosmic phenomenon at Tunguska could only have been formulated after World War II, when the scientific community had learned how to make atomic explosions and had become familiar with their aftermath. Aleksander Kazantsev, a Russian scientist and (equally important) science-fiction writer, had visited Hiroshima after the atom bomb explosion and had studied the data describing its impact and aftermath. Because of certain similarities in the blast effects--the burnt yet upright trees, the mushroom cloud, the black rain--Kazantsev and other

scientists concluded that the blast of 1908 was an atomic explosion estimated at a minimum of ten times the strength of the one at Hiroshima
(Parry, 1961). Witnesses had described the blinding flash and withering heat
at Hiroshima in much the same way that the Siberian peasants described
the frightening blast at Tunguska. The melting heat that Kulik found so inconsistent with his meteorite theory was more consistent with an atomic explosion (Baxter & Atkins, 1976). It is worth pointing out that scientists went
on to develop the hypothesis that a nuclear explosion had occurred at
Tunguska even though their theorizing was largely based on stories told by
ignorant peasants, believers in devils and wrathful gods, who could quite
easily have exaggerated what had actually happened to improve their stories.
Even though these eyewitness accounts were gathered twenty or more years
after the actual event, and had quite possibly entered the folklore of the
countryside (Krinov, 1966), they were still regarded as the purest evidence.

To test whether a nuclear explosion might have occurred, scientists
examined the trees for radioactivity and for any unusual increase in normal
growth patterns, shown by greater spacing between the age lines, that might
have been the result of radioactivity. What they found was that some trees at
the site grew to be four times greater than what would normally have been
expected. Similarly, scabs that appeared on the hides of local reindeer were
explained as being the result of radioactive contamination (Baxter & Atkins,
1976). This evidence, by no means conclusive (Florensky, 1963), was cited
as proof that such an atomic explosion had taken place, just as Kulik had
cited the existence of shallow pits in the terrain as proof that a meteorite
had exploded.

Assuming that what happened at Tunguska was the result of an
atomic blast, and faced with the fact that nuclear fission was not within
man's grasp before the 1940s, Kazantsev and his colleagues concluded that
the phenomenon must have involved extraterrestrial beings and that the
explosion was caused by a UFO, propelled by atomic energy, that crashed
(Parry, 1961). The pattern of devastation on the ground, as seen from the
air, suggested that the object took a zigzag path, changing its direction as it
came closer and closer to earth. Advocates of the UFO theory argue such a
change in direction would not have been possible with a natural object like a

meteorite or comet, and that the object--a spacecraft--was driven by intelligent beings who were trying to land without hitting a more densely populated area. They hypothesize that the craft had some mechanical problem that made it necessary to land but that the initial angle of its trajectory was too shallow for landing and would only have bounced the craft back into space. So the navigators tried to maneuver and correct the angle, but swerved, came down too sharply, and exploded (Baxter & Atkins, 1976). On the other hand, it seems just as possible that a natural object swerved or that debris from a nonatomic explosion was thrown in zigzag directions than that navigators from outer space ran into mechanical troubles and crash-landed. If probability is going to be disregarded in order to support one theory, then the same suspension of the natural order of things can be used to confirm an equally unlikely theory.

In the late 1950s, an exploratory team examined the Tunguska site with an advanced magnetic detector and, in 1962, scientists magnified the soil and found an array of tiny, colored, magnetic, ball-shaped particles, made of cobalt, nickel, copper, and germanium (Baxter & Atkins, 1976). According to extraterrestrial-intelligence specialists, these could have been the elements used for electrical and technical instruments, with the copper used for communication services and the germanium used in semiconductors (Parry, 1961). However, controlled experiments would be necessary to make this atomic-extraterrestrial argument convincing.

Scientists who find the UFO and extraterrestrial explanations less than credible have turned to the most recent theories of physics and astronomy to explain what might have happened in the Tungus. Some (including Kazantsev) argue that such an explosion might have been caused by debris from space colliding with the earth (Morrison & Chapman, 1990), or by antimatter, which exploded as it came in contact with the atmosphere (Parry, 1961). Alternatively, the explosion might have been caused by a "black hole" hitting the earth in Siberia and passing through to emerge on the other side. Those opposing these theories point, again, to the absence of a crater and to the numerous eyewitness accounts that describe the shape of the object and the sound of the blast, all of which would be inconsistent with antimatter or black-hole theories (Baxter & Atkins, 1976). However, a 1973 article in

Nature asserts that a black hole would not, in fact, leave a crater, but would simply enter the earth at a great velocity and that a shock wave and blast might possibly accompany its entrance (Jackson & Ryan).

What is most fascinating about the Tunguska Valley phenomenon is that, despite all the advances in science over the past 80 years, investigators cannot now be any more certain of the cause of the blast than they were in 1921, when Kulik first came near the site. None of the theories presented is wholly convincing, for all of them rely to some extent on human observers, whose accounts of events are notoriously unreliable, or hypotheses based on ambiguous evidence, without the support of controlled tests and experiments. The formulation of a radically new body of scientific knowledge might provide a new theoretical context for examining the evidence and establishing a more convincing explanation. But, as it is, with the trail getting colder, finding a solution to this mystery seems to become more and more unlikely.

Examining these explanations about what did or did not land and explode in Siberia does teach us that scientific theories are sometimes based on the selective interpretation of evidence and that scientists, like everyone else, tend to believe their own theories and find the evidence that they want to find. Although the language that they use is very different, the accounts of what happened at Tunguska according to Kulik, Kazantsev, and their other scientific colleagues are not so very different from what the local peasants say that they saw. Both have a closer resemblance to science fiction than science fact.

References

Baxter, J., & Atkins, T. (1976). The fire came by: The riddle of the great
    Siberian explosion. Garden City, NY: Doubleday.

Cowan, C., Atluri, C. R., & Libby, W. F. (1965, May 29). Possible antimatter
    content of the Tunguska meteor of 1908. Nature (London), 861–865.

Crowther, J. G. (1931). More about the great Siberian meteorite. Scientific
    American, 144(5), 314–317.

Florensky, K. P. (1963, November). Did a comet collide with the earth in
    1908? Sky and Telescope, 268–269.

Jackson, A. A., & Ryan, M. P. (1973, September 14). Was the Tungus event
    due to a black hole? Nature (London), 88–89.

Krinov, E. L. (1966). Giant meteorites. London: Pergamon.

Morrison, D., & Chapman, C. R. (1990). Target earth: It will happen. Sky
    and Telescope, 261–265.

Olivier, C. P. (1928). The great Siberian meteorite. Scientific American,
    139(1), 42–44.

Parry, A. (1961). The Tungus mystery: Was it a spaceship? In Russia's
    Rockets and Missiles (pp. 248–267). London: Macmillan.

What a meteor did to Siberia. (1929, March 16). Literary Digest, 33–34.

Appendix A

Some Useful Reference Sources

GUIDELINES FOR USING REFERENCE WORKS

1. You can find sources for your essays by looking
   - in the library's *online database of books* or *card catalog;*
   - in the *bibliographies of standard works* on your subject;
   - in the brief bibliographies at the end of *encyclopedia articles;*
   - under the broad subject headings in *general-interest bibliographies* and *periodical indexes;* and
   - in the *indexes and abstract collections* that deal with the specific subject of your research.

2. Some reference sources are entirely bibliography: they consist of long lists of articles and (sometimes) books, each followed by the essential publication information. These indexes are usually arranged by topic. You may have to check several broad headings before you find the articles that you need. If, for example, you are doing research on educational television, you would look up "education," "television," and the names of some of the programs that you intend to write about. Most indexes are cross-referenced.

3. Some reference sources are called "abstracts" because they contain abstracts or paragraph summaries of many (but not all) of the articles published each year in that discipline. Abstracts often have two sections: the first contains a series of summaries of articles, chosen for their special in-

terest or excellence and arranged by subject; the second contains a list of all the articles published in that field in that year. (Occasionally, you will find a modified form of abstract, in which several articles are each given a one-sentence summary.) First you look up the specific subject that you are interested in and glance at the summaries. Then you get the publication information about the articles relevant to your research by looking up their *authors* in the second section of the reference work. Although abstracts give you a convenient preview, you will find that many of the articles are highly technical and may therefore be difficult to read and write about.

4. Some of the periodical articles that you want to consult may be available only on microfiche or microcards. Ask the reference librarian to help you to use the system and its apparatus.

5. Many bibliographies and indexes are available online. Ask the reference librarian to show you the commands that you need to use at the computer monitor. *Reference sources that are available online and/or on CD-ROM are asterisked.*

GENERAL ENCYCLOPEDIAS

Collier's Encyclopedia. 24 vols. with annual supplements and revisions. 1995. Easier to read and understand than the old *Britannica* or *Americana*.

Encyclopaedia Britannica. 15th ed. 24 vols. with annual supplements and periodic revisions. 1998. *Britannica Online* is constantly being updated.

Encyclopedia Americana. 30 vols. with annual supplements and revisions. 1995. Use the index volume to locate your subject within the longer encyclopedia.

New Columbia Encyclopedia. 5th ed. 1993. A single-volume encyclopedia, especially good as a starting point.

New Encyclopaedia Britannica. 15th ed. 32 vols. with annual supplements and periodic revisions. 1994.

SPECIALIZED ENCYCLOPEDIAS

Encyclopedia of American Art. New York: Dutton, 1981.

Encyclopedia of Biological Sciences. Ed. Peter Gray. 2nd ed. New York: Van Nostrand, 1981.

Encyclopedia of Computer Science and Technology. 37 vols. New York: Dekker, 1997.

The Encyclopedia of Education. Ed. Lee C. Deighton. 10 vols. New York: Macmillan, 1971.

The Encyclopedia of Human Behavior: Psychology, Psychiatry, and Mental Health. Ed. Robert M. Goldenson. 2 vols. New York: Doubleday, 1974.

Encyclopedia of Psychology. Ed. Raymond J. Corsini. 2nd ed. 4 vols. New York: Wiley, 1994.

Encyclopedia of Sociology. Ed. Edgar F. Borgatta and Marie L. Borgatta. 4 vols. New York: Macmillan, 1991.

Encyclopedia of World Art. 17 vols. New York: McGraw, 1959–87.

An Encyclopedia of World History: Ancient, Medieval, and Modern Chronologically Arranged. Ed. William L. Langer. 5th ed. Boston: Houghton, 1972.

International Encyclopedia of the Social Sciences. Ed. D. L. Sills. 17 vols. New York: Macmillan, 1977.

McGraw-Hill Encyclopedia of Physics. Ed. Sybil Parker. 2nd ed. New York: McGraw, 1993.

McGraw-Hill Encyclopedia of Science and Technology. 7th ed. 20 vols. New York: McGraw, 1996.

McGraw-Hill Encyclopedia of World Drama. 2nd ed. 5 vols. New York: McGraw, 1983.

The New Grove Dictionary of Music and Musicians. Ed. Stanley Sadie. 20 vols. New York: Macmillan, 1980.

VNR Concise Encyclopedia of Mathematics. Ed. S. Gottwald et al. 2nd ed. New York: Van Nostrand, 1989.

GENERAL INDEXES

*Book Review Digest. New York: Wilson, 1905–present. Includes excerpts from reviews as well as lists of references.

*Book Review Index. Detroit: Gale Research Co., 1965–present. Lists reviews of books on literature, art, business, economics, religion, and current affairs.

*Books in Print Plus. Lists books currently in print in the United States, with prices. Full text of book reviews is available for some titles.

*British Newspaper Index. 1990–present. Indexes major British newspapers.

*Editorials on File. New York: Facts on File, 1970–present. Selected editorials on subjects of contemporary interest, with each editorial preceded by a summary of the issue being discussed.

*Facts on File. New York: Facts on File, 1941–present. Summaries of issues and events, with selected bibliographies.

Milner, Anita Check. *Newspaper Indexes: A Location and Subject Guide for Researchers,* Metuchen, N.J., and London: Scarecrow, 1982.

*National Newspaper Index. 1990–present. Combined indexing of five major newspapers: *The New York Times, The Wall Street Journal, Christian Science Monitor, Washington Post,* and *The Los Angeles Times.*

*New York Times Full-text. Indexes the most recent years of *The New York Times,* as well as providing the text of the articles.

*New York Times Index. New York: New York Times, 1851–present.

*Periodical Abstracts Ondisc. 1986–present. Indexes and abstracts over 950 general-interest periodicals from the United States, Canada, and the United Kingdom.

Popular Periodical Index. Camden, N.J.: Popular Periodical Index, 1971–present. Includes magazines such as *New York, Playboy, Rolling Stone,* and *TV Guide.*

*Proquest Image. Indexes and abstracts articles from hundreds of news and general-interest magazines and some scholarly journals, with text for many articles.

*Readers' Guide to Periodical Literature. New York: Wilson, 1905–present. Includes listings of articles in many general-interest magazines.

Vertical File Index. New York: Wilson, 1932/1935–present. Lists pamphlets on all subjects.

BIOGRAPHICAL SOURCES

Annual Obituary. New York: St. Martin's, 1980–present. Annual collection of profiles of prominent individuals who died during the year, arranged by month of death date.

*Biography Index. New York: Wilson, 1947–present. Organized like the *Readers' Guide,* listing articles about contemporary celebrities.

Current Biography. New York: Wilson, 1940–present. Consists of full-scale articles (like encyclopedia entries) about prominent people. Use the index to find the right year for the person that you are researching.

Dictionary of American Biography. 10 vols. New York: Scribner's, 1980. Articles contain basic information about notable figures in American history. (Do not use this source for contemporary figures.)

New York Times Obituary Index 1858–1990. New York: New York Times.

SEMISPECIALIZED INDEXES AND ABSTRACTS

Humanities

*Art Index. New York: Wilson, 1929–present. Covers the literature of art and art history in periodicals, yearbooks, and museum bulletins. Subjects include architecture; archaeology; art history; fine arts; crafts and folk art; film and photography; graphic arts; industrial design.

*Humanities Index. New York: Wilson, 1974–present. Annual volumes include reviews of books and performances as well as a listing of articles on issues and new developments in all the humanities.

*MLA International Bibliography of Books and Articles in the Modern Languages and Literature. New York: MLA, 1921–present. Indexes critical documents on literature, language, linguistics, and folklore. Articles from more than 3,000 journals, serials published worldwide, conference papers and proceedings, handbooks, dictionaries, and bibliographies are indexed.

*The Music Index. Detroit: Information Coordinators, 1949–present. Includes reviews listed under composer and title.

*The Philosopher's Index. Bowling Green, Ohio: Bowling Green State U, 1967–present. Articles on philosophy and its relation to art, religion, the humanities in general, and history.

Physical and Biological Sciences

*Applied Science and Technology Index. New York: Wilson, 1958–present. Includes references to a large number of scientific and technological periodicals.

*Biological and Agricultural Index. New York: Wilson, 1964–present.

*Chemical Abstracts. Washington: Amer. Chemical Soc., 1907–present. The online and CD-ROM databases are called *CA Search.*

*Engineering Index. New York: Engineering Information, 1906–present. The online and CD-ROM databases are part of *Compendex.*

*General Science Index. New York: Wilson, 1978–present. Includes articles in 109 English-language science periodicals of general interest.

*Science Abstracts. London, Eng.: Inst. of Electrical Engineers, 1898–present. Summaries of articles about physics.

Science Citation Index. Philadelphia: Inst. for Scientific Information, 1945–present. Includes citations to the literature of science, technology, medicine, and related disciplines from 3,300 science journals worldwide. The online and CD-ROM databases are part of *SciSearch.*

Social Sciences

Almanac of American Politics. Ed. Michael Barone. Boston: Gambit, 1972–present. Lists sources for information about local and national public affairs.

America: History and Life. Santa Barbara, Calif.: ABC-Clio, 1964–present. Includes references to 2,000 publications dealing with past, recent, and present history. Part A consists of abstracts; Part B consists of one-sentence summaries of articles, grouped under topic headings.

Ethnic Newswatch. Stamford, Conn: Sofline Info. Indexes and provides full text of articles from ethnic and minority newspapers and magazines across the United States. Subjects include current events covered with a specific ethnic focus.

Guide to U.S. Government Serials and Periodicals. McLean, Va.: Documents Index, 1964–present. A cumulative index directs the user to the correct volume.

Historical Abstracts. Santa Barbara, Calif.: ABC-Clio, 1955–present. Part A deals with modern history from 1450 to 1940; Part B deals with mid-twentieth-century history. The index is in the Winter issue.

International Bibliography of Economics. Paris: UNESCO, 1952–present.

International Political Science Abstracts. Paris: International Pol. Sci. Assn., 1951–present. Summaries of articles on political science and international relations.

Psychological Abstracts. Washington: American Psychological Assn., 1927–present. Use the three-year cumulative subject and author indexes; for example, the years 1978–1980 are indexed together. The online database is called *PsycInfo,* and the CD-ROM database is called *PsycLit.*

Public Affairs Information Service Bulletin. New York: PAIS, 1915–present. Includes pamphlets and government documents and reports as well as periodical articles. Covers an unusually large number of periodicals. Emphasizes factual and statistical information.

Sage Public Administration Abstracts. Beverly Hills, Calif.: Sage, 1979–present. Summaries of books, articles, government publications, speeches, and research studies.

Social Sciences Index. New York: Wilson, 1974–present.

Sociofile. A cumulation of *Sociological Abstracts* and *Social Planning, Policy and Development Abstracts.* Indexes over 1,500 serials published worldwide in sociology and its related disciplines.

INDEXES AND ABSTRACTS FOR PROFESSIONAL STUDIES

Business

ABI/INFORM. Ann Arbor: UMI, 1971–present. Provides abstracts from more than 800 business and trade journals. Subjects include accounting and auditing, banking, data processing and information management, economics, finance, health care, human resources, labor relations, public administration, and telecommunications.

Accountants' Index. New York: Amer. Inst. of CPAs, 1944–present. Lists articles about accounting, data processing, financial management, and taxation.

*Business Periodicals Index. New York: Wilson, 1958–present. Lists articles from more than 100 periodicals dealing with new developments and methods in business management.

*Corporate Text. Current. Copies of annual reports for companies traded on the New York Stock Exchange, American Stock Exchange, and NASDAQ exchange and over the counter.

Personnel Literature. Washington: U.S. Civil Service Commission, 1969–present. Lists articles about administration, supervision, management relations, and productivity.

Education

*CIJE: Current Index to Journals in Education. Phoenix: Oryx, 1969–present. The online and CD-ROM databases are part of *ERIC.*

*Education Index. New York: Wilson, 1929–present.

*ERIC. Indexes and abstracts journal and technical literature in education and related fields, including psychology and sociology. Information is compiled from *Resources in Education (RIE)* and *Current Index to Journals in Education (CIJE).*

Law

*Index to Legal Periodicals. New York: Wilson, 1908–present. In addition to listing articles by subject and author, there is a table of cases and a group of book reviews.

Library Science

Library and Information Science Abstracts. London: The Library Assn., 1970–present. Materials about information dissemination and retrieval.

Nursing and Health

*Aidsline. Provides detailed coverage of all aspects of the AIDS crisis, focusing on clinical aspects but including health-planning implications and cancer research. Information is derived from the U.S. National Library of Medicine's *Medline, Health Planning and Administration,* and *CancerLIT* databases.

*Chem-Bank. Indexes descriptions of and toxicity information on thousands of chemical substances in the form of lists prepared by four government agencies: RTECS (Registry of Toxic Effects of Chemical Substances), from the Department of Health and Human Services; OHMTADS (Oil and Hazardous Materials Technical Assistance Data System), developed by the Environmental Protection Agency; CHRIS (Chemical Hazard Response Information System), produced by the Coast Guard; and HSDB (Hazardous Substance Databank), from the National Library of Medicine.

Cumulative Index to Nursing and Allied Health Literature. Glendale: CINAHL Information Services, 1977–present. Articles listed include health education and social services as they relate to health care. The online and CD-ROM databases are called *Nursing and Allied Health Database.*

Index Medicus. Bethesda: National Lib. of Medicine, 1960–present. Lists articles of medical interest and includes a bibliography of medical book reviews. The online and CD-ROM databases are part of *Medline.*

International Nursing Index. New York: Amer. Journal of Nursing, 1966–present.

Medline. Database of the U.S. National Library of Medicine; contains bibliographic citations and abstracts of biomedical literature. Indexes articles from approximately 3,400 journals published in more than 70 countries.

OSH-ROM. Produced by the National Institute for Occupational Safety and Health; provides citations and abstracts from journals, books, and technical reports dealing with occupational health and safety. Subjects include environmental health, toxicology, safety engineering, and industrial pollution.

Social Work

Human Resources Abstracts. Beverly Hills, Calif.: Sage, 1965–present. Covers developments in areas such as poverty, employment, and distribution of human resources.

Journal of Human Services Abstracts. Rockville, Md.: Project Share, 1976–present. Summarizes articles concerning public administration, education, psychology, environmental studies, family studies, nutrition, and health services.

Sage Family Studies Abstracts. Beverly Hills, Calif.: Sage, 1979–present.

Social Work Research and Abstracts. Albany, N.Y.: National Assn. of Social Workers, 1965–present. Selected research articles as well as abstracts of other articles in the field of social welfare. Computer database is called *Swab Plus.*

INDEXES TO STATISTICAL COMPILATIONS

American Statistics Index: A Comprehensive Guide and Index to the Statistical Publications of the U.S. Government. Washington: Congressional Information Service, 1973–present.

County and City Plus. Indexes statistical information for counties, cities, and other designated places. Subjects include population, age, race, income, labor force and unemployment, hospitals, crime, climate, and more.

Statistical Yearbook. New York: UN Dept. of Economic and Social Affairs, 1949–present. International statistics.

STATMASTER. Indexes statistical publications issued by the U.S. government, U.S. state governments, international governmental organizations, professional and trade associations, business organizations, commercial publishers, and university and independent research organizations.

Appendix B

Some Basic Forms for Documentation: MLA, APA, and Endnote

MODELS OF MLA BIBLIOGRAPHICAL ENTRIES AND PARENTHETICAL DOCUMENTATION

The following is a list of model bibliographical and parenthetical entries for MLA style. The proper bibliographical form that will appear in alphabetical order on your "Works Cited" page is followed by a sample parenthetical documentation that might appear in the text. The sample documentation in this list will always contain the author's name; but remember that in your essay you will often mention the author's name in your text, thus making necessary only the parenthetical documentation of the page(s) of your source. You can find guidelines for preparing MLA documentation in Chapter 9, on pp. 373–381. See also the list of "Works Cited" in the student essay "Euthanasia: The Right to Die" in Chapter 10.

Book by a Single Author

Veysey, Laurence R. The Emergence of the American University. Chicago: U of
Chicago P, 1965.

(Veysey 23)

Book by Two Authors

Postman, Neil, and Charles Weingartner. Teaching as a Subversive Activity. New

York: Dell, 1969.

(Postman and Weingartner 34–36)

Book by More Than Three Authors

Spiller, Robert E., et al. Literary History of the United States. London:

Macmillan, 1946.

(Spiller et al. 67)

Edited Collection Written by Different Authors

Wheelwright, Philip, ed. The Presocratics. New York: Odyssey, 1966.

(Wheelwright 89)

Essay from a Collection Written by Different Authors

Webb, R. K. "The Victorian Reading Public." From Dickens to Hardy. Ed. Boris

Ford. Baltimore: Penguin, 1958. 205–26.

(Webb 209)

Book Published in a Reprinted Edition

Orwell, George. Animal Farm. 1946. New York: Signet, 1959.

(Orwell 100)

Book Published in a New Edition

Baugh, Albert C. A History of the English Language. 2nd ed. New York:

Appleton, 1957.

(Baugh 21)

Work in Translation

Lorenz, Konrad. On Aggression. Trans. Marjorie Kerr Wilson. 1966. New York:

Bantam, 1969.

(Lorenz 45)

Book Published in Several Volumes

> Tocqueville, Alexis de. Democracy in America. Ed. Phillips Bradley. 2 vols. New
> York: Knopf, 1945.
> (Tocqueville 2: 78)

One Volume in a Set or Series

> Granville-Barker, Harley. Prefaces to Shakespeare. Vol. 2. London: Batsford,
> 1963.
> Gaff, Jerry G. Institutional Renewal through the Improvement of Teaching. New
> Directions for Higher Ed. 24. San Francisco: Jossey-Bass, 1978.
> (Granville-Barker 193)
> (Gaff 45)

Book in an Edited Edition

> Kirstein, Lincoln. By With To & From. Ed. Nicholas Jenkins. New York: Farrar,
> 1991.
> Jenkins, Nicholas, ed. By With To & From. By Lincoln Kirstein. New York:
> Farrar, 1991.
> (Kirstein 190)
> (Jenkins xiii)

The second entry indicates that you are citing the work of the editor (not the author); therefore, you place the editor's name first.

Introduction, Preface, Foreword, or Afterword

> Spacks, Patricia Meyer. Afterword. Sense and Sensibility. By Jane Austen. New
> York: Bantam, 1983. 332–43.
> (Spacks 338)

Article in an Encyclopedia

> "American Architecture." Columbia Encyclopedia. 3rd ed. 1963.
> ("American Architecture")

Notice that no page numbers are needed for either the bibliographical entry or the parenthetical reference when the source is an encyclopedia. If the article is signed by an author, list the author's name at the beginning of the bibliographical entry and identify the source in your parenthetical documentation by using the author's name. If you are citing a little-known or specialized encyclopedia, provide full publication information.

Publication of a Corporation, Foundation, or Government Agency

Carnegie Council on Policy Studies in Higher Education. Three Thousand
Futures: The Next Twenty Years for Higher Education. San Francisco:
Jossey-Bass, 1980.

United States. Bureau of the Census. Abstract of the Census of Manufactures.
Washington: GPO, 1919.

Coleman, James S., et al. Equality of Educational Opportunity. U.S. Dept. of
Health, Education, and Welfare. Washington: GPO, 1966.

(Carnegie Council 34)

(Bureau of the Census 56)

(Coleman et al. 88)

Pamphlet or Brochure

The entry should resemble the entry for a book. If the author's name is missing, begin the entry with the title; if the date is missing, use the abbreviation *n.d.*

More, Howard V. Costa de la Luz. Turespana: Secretaria General de Turismo, n.d.

(More 6)

Classic Work

Job. The Jerusalem Bible. Reader's Edition. Ed. Alexander Jones. Garden City:
Doubleday, 1968.

Homer. The Odyssey. Trans. Robert Fitzgerald. Garden City: Doubleday, 1963.

(Job 3:7)

(Odyssey 7.1–16)

Article in a Scholarly Journal with Continuous Pagination

Shepard, David. "Authenticating Films." The Quarterly Journal of the Library of
Congress 37 (1980): 342–54.

(Shepard 350)

The four journals comprising Volume 37 are treated as a single continuous work for purposes of pagination. The first journal in Volume 38 will start again with page 1.

Article in a Scholarly Journal without Continuous Pagination

Burnham, Christopher C. "Expressive Writing: A Heretic's Confession." Focuses
2.1 (1989): 5–18.

(Burnham 7–8)

Article in a Monthly Periodical

Loye, David. "TV's Impact on Adults." Psychology Today Apr. 1978: 87+.

(Loye 87)

The plus sign after the page number indicates that the article is not printed on consecutive pages, but skips to later pages.

Article in a Weekly Periodical

Meyer, Karl E. "Television's Trying Times." Saturday Review 16 Sept. 1978: 19–23.

(Meyer 21)

Article in a Newspaper

Goldin, Davidson. "In a Change of Policy, and Heart, Colleges Join Fight Against
Inflated Grades." New York Times 4 July 1995, late ed.: 8.

(Goldin)

No page number is required in a parenthetical citation of a one-page article. If the issue of the *Times* or another newspaper is divided into separate sections, the page number in both the bibliographical entry and the citation should be preceded by the section, e.g., *B6*.

Article without an Author

"How to Get Quality Back into the Schools." US News & World Report 12 Sept.
1977: 31–34.

("How to Get Quality" 33)

Letter to the Editor

Kropp, Arthur J. Letter. <u>Village Voice</u> 12 Oct. 1993: 5.

(Kropp)

Editorial

"Justice Berger's Contradictions." Editorial. <u>New York Times</u> 27 June 1995, late
    ed.: A16.

("Justice Berger's Contradictions")

Review

Appiah, K. Anthony. "Giving Up the Perfect Diamond." Rev. of <u>The Holder of</u>
    <u>the World</u>, by Bharati Mukherjee. <u>New York Times Book Review</u> 10 Oct.
    1993: 7.

(Appiah)

Personal or Published Letter

Hans, James S. Letter to the author. 18 Aug. 1991.

Keats, John. "To Benjamin Bailey." 22 Nov. 1817. <u>John Keats: Selected Poetry</u>
    <u>and Letters</u>. Ed. Richard Harter Fogle. New York: Rinehart, 1952. 300–303.

(Hans)

(Keats 302)

Unpublished Dissertation

Eastman, Elizabeth. "'Lectures on Jurisprudence': A Key to Understanding
    Adam Smith's Thought." Diss. Claremont Grad. School, 1993.

(Eastman 34)

Previously Printed Source Accessed from CD-ROM

Burke, Marc. "Homosexuality as Deviance: The Case of the Gay Police Officer."
    <u>British Journal of Criminology</u> 34.2 (1994): 192–203. <u>PsycLit</u>. CD-ROM.
    SilverPlatter. Nov. 1994.

(Burke 291)

Personal Interview (Conducted by the Researcher)

Nussbaumer, Doris D. Personal interview. 30 July 1988.

Albert, John J. Telephone interview. 22 Dec. 1989.

(Nussbaumer)

(Albert)

Broadcast or Published Interview

Kennedy, Joseph. Interview with Harry Smith. This Morning. CBS. WCBS, New
York. 14 Oct. 1993.

Berger, John. Interview with Nikos Papastergiadis. American Poetry Review.
July–Aug. 1993: 9–12.

(Kennedy)

(Berger 10)

Lecture

Auchincloss, Louis, Erica Jong, and Gloria Steinem. "The 18th Century Woman."
Symposium at the Metropolitan Museum of Art, New York. 29 Apr. 1982.

(Auchincloss, Jong, and Steinem)

Live Performance

Tommy. By Pete Townshend. Dir. Des McAnuff. St. James Theater, New York. 3
May 1993.

(Tommy)

Film

Dr. Strangelove. Dir. Stanley Kubrick. Columbia Pictures, 1963.

Kubrick, Stanley, dir. Dr. Strangelove. Columbia Pictures, 1963.

Put the film first if you wish to emphasize material from the film; however, if
you are emphasizing the work of the director, list that name first.

(Dr. Strangelove)

(Kubrick)

Television or Radio Program

> Serge Pavlovitch Diaghilev 1872–1929: A Portrait. Prod. Peter Adam. BBC.
>
> > WNET, New York. 12 July 1982.
>
> (Diaghilev)

A radio program is entered the same way, with a listing of the program, the director or producer, the producing network, the local station and city, and the date. In citing television or radio programs, if you wish to emphasize the work of the producer or director, enter that name first.

Audio Recording

> Tchaikovsky, Piotr. The Tchaikovsky Collection. Audiocassette. CBS Special
>
> > Products, 1989.
>
> (Tchaikovsky)

Videocassette

> Wuthering Heights. Dir. William Wyler. 1939. Videocassette. Embassy, 1987.
>
> (Wuthering)

Work of Art

> Brueghel, Pieter. The Beggars. Louvre, Paris.
>
> (Brueghel)

Map or Chart

> Spain, Portugal, and North Africa. Map. American Automobile Association,
>
> > 1993–4.
>
> (Spain)

Cartoon

> Trudeau, Garry. "Doonesbury." Cartoon. Charlotte Observer 23 Dec. 1988: B12.
>
> (Trudeau)

MODELS OF MLA BIBLIOGRAPHICAL ENTRIES
FOR CITING INTERNET SOURCES

The models for citing sources on the World Wide Web are based on guidelines provided by the MLA. These guidelines can be found online at <www.mla.org> and in the second edition of the *MLA Style Manual and Guide to Scholarly Publishing* (1998). Using the sample below as a general guide, you should attempt to ascertain as many of the elements of citation as are appropriate to your source:

> Author's last name, First name, Middle initial. "Title of Article or Chapter."
>
> Title of Book, Periodical, or Web Site. Name of editor or translator of text.
>
> Original print publication information if available. Date of electronic publication or most recent update. Page numbers or number of paragraphs.
>
> Name of sponsoring institution or organization. Date of access <URL>.

Book

> Skene, Felicia. Penitentiaries and Reformatories. Edinburgh: Edmonston and
> Douglas, 1865. Victorian Women Writers Project. Ed. Perry Willett. 10 Dec.
> 1996. Indiana U. 11 Mar. 1998 <http://www.indiana.edu/~letrs/vwwp/
> skene/skene~reform.html>.

Poem

> Yeats, W. B. "The Wild Swans at Coole." Home page. 1998. 5 Mar. 1998 <http://
> www.geocities.com/Athens/5379/yeats_TheWildSwansAtCoole.html>.

Article in a Journal

> Osborne, Lawrence. "A Pirate's Progress: How the Maritime Rogue Became a
> Multicultural Hero." Linguafranca 8.2 (March 1998): 47 pars. 17 Mar.
> 1998 <http://www.linguafranca.com/>.

Article in a Magazine

> Cloud, John. "Harassed or Hazed?" Time 16 Mar. 1998. 19 Mar. 1998
> <http://www.pathfinder.com/time/magazine/1998/dom/980316/
> law.harassed_or_hazed.whll.html>.

Article in a Newspaper

Passacantado, John. "A Pothole in the Ozone Layer." Washingtonpost.com
15 Mar. 1998. 17 Mar. 1998 <http://www.washingtonpost.com/wp-srv/
WPlate/1998-03/15/130I-031598-idx.html>.

Article in a Reference Database

Staples, Brent. "Common Ground." Rev. of One Nation, After All, by Alan
Wolfe. New York Times Book Review 8 Mar. 1998. The New York
Times on the Web. 1998. The New York Times Company. 12 April 1998
<http://www.nytimes.com/books/98/03/08/reviews/
980308.08staplet.html>.

Scholarly Project

Gifts of Speech: Women's Speeches from Around the World. Mar. 1998. Sweet
Briar College. 21 Mar. 1998 <http://gos.sbc.edu/>.

E-mail or an Online Posting

Wittreich, Joseph. E-mail to the author. 12 Dec. 1997.

Porter, Don. "Inverted Pyramids." 12 Mar. 1998. Online posting. Society for
Professional Journalists. 16 Mar. 1998 <SPJL@LISTS.PSU.EDU>.

Professional Web Site

UC Berkeley Film Studies Web Page. U of California at Berkeley. 22 Jan. 1998
<http://cinemaspace.berkeley.edu/Film_Studies/index.html>.

Personal Web Site

Wong, James. Home page. 12 May 1998 <http://logic.simplenet.com/
jameswong/>.

AMERICAN PSYCHOLOGICAL ASSOCIATION (APA) PARENTHETICAL AUTHOR-YEAR DOCUMENTATION

The format for documentation recommended by the American Psychological Association is used primarily in the social and behavioral sciences, especially sociology and psychology. It is also often employed in subjects like anthropology, astronomy, business, education, linguistics, and political science.

Like MLA style, APA documentation is based on parenthetical references to author and page. The chief difference is that, in the APA system, you include the work's *date of publication* after the author's name, both within parentheses.

MLA

Primitive religious rituals may have been a means for deterring collective violence (Girard 1).

Brain Theory suggests two extremes of writing style, the appositional and the propositional (Winterowd and Williams 4).

APA

Primitive religious rituals may have been a means for deterring collective violence (Girard, 1972, p. 1).

Brain Theory suggests two extremes of writing style, the appositional and the propositional (Winterowd & Williams, 1990, p. 4).

As with MLA style, if you cite the author's name and/or the date of publication in your sentence, it is not necessary to repeat them in the parentheses.

In 1972, Girard suggested that primitive religious rituals may have been a means for deterring collective violence (p. 1).

According to Winterowd and Williams (1990), Brain Theory suggests two extremes of writing style, the appositional and the propositional (p. 4).

Here is what the bibliography for these two entries would look like in MLA style and in the style recommended by APA for student papers.

MLA

WORKS CITED

Girard, René. Violence and the Sacred. Baltimore: Johns Hopkins UP, 1972.

Winterowd, W. Ross, and James D. Williams. "Cognitive Style and Written Discourse." Focuses 3 (1990): 3–23.

APA

REFERENCES

Girard, R. (1972). Violence and the sacred. Baltimore: Johns Hopkins University Press.

Winterowd, W. R., & Williams, J. D. (1990). Cognitive style and written discourse. Focuses, 3, 3–23.

These are some of the ways that APA bibliographical style for student papers differs from MLA style:

- Authors' first and middle names are designated by initials. When there are multiple authors, all are listed last name first, and an ampersand (&) is used instead of *and*.

- Two or more works by the same author are listed chronologically. Instead of using a dash for repeated names (as in MLA style), you start each entry with the author's full name.

- The date of publication (in parentheses) is placed immediately after the author's name.

- In the title of a book or article, only the first word and the first word of the subtitle are capitalized.

- The title of a section of a volume (e.g., an article in a periodical or a chapter of a book) is neither underlined nor surrounded by quotation marks.

- The volume number of a journal is underlined.

Since the identification of sources greatly depends on the dates that you cite, you must be careful to clarify the dating, especially when a single author has published two or more works in the same year. Here, for example, is an excerpt from a bibliography that distinguishes among three sources published in 1972:

Carnegie Commission on Higher Education. (1972a). The campus and the city: Maximizing assets and reducing liabilities. New York: McGraw-Hill.

Carnegie Commission on Higher Education. (1972b). The fourth revolution: Instructional technology in higher education. New York: McGraw-Hill.

Carnegie Commission on Higher Education. (1972c). The more effective use of resources: An imperative for higher education. New York: McGraw-Hill.

And here is how one of these sources would be documented in the essay:

In its report The More Effective Use of Resources, the Carnegie Commission on Higher Education recommended that "colleges and universities develop a 'self-renewal' fund of 1 to 3 percent each year taken from existing allocations" (1972c, p. 105).

For an example of the use of APA author-year documentation, look at "Explaining the Tunguskan Phenomenon," the third research essay in Chapter 10.

MODELS OF APA BIBLIOGRAPHICAL ENTRIES AND PARENTHETICAL DOCUMENTATION

The following is a brief list of model entries for APA style. Each bibliographical form that will appear in alphabetical order on the "Works Cited" page is followed by a sample parenthetical reference as it might appear in your text. Whenever there is an author, the sample parenthetical references in this list will contain the author's name; remember that, in your essay, you will often mention the author's name (and the date) in your text, with only the page of the source needed in the parenthetical reference.

Book by a Single Author

Veysey, L. R. (1965). The emergence of the American university. Chicago: University of Chicago Press.

(Veysey, 1965, p. 45)

Book by More Than One Author

Postman, N., & Weingartner, C. (1969). Teaching as a subversive activity. New York: Dell.

(Postman & Weingartner, 1969, p. 143)

When a source has three to five authors, name them all in the first text reference or parenthetical note; then, in all subsequent references or notes, list only the first author's name followed by "et al." For sources with six or more authors, use "et al." in the first reference or note as well. Always list all authors in bibliographical entries.

Edited Collection Written by Different Authors

Wheelwright, P. (Ed.). (1966). The presocratics. New York: Odyssey.

(Wheelwright, 1966, pp. 2–3)

Essay from a Collection Written by Different Authors

Webb, R. K. (1958). The Victorian reading public. In B. Ford (Ed.), From Dickens to Hardy (pp. 205–226). Baltimore: Penguin.

(Webb, 1958, pp. 210–212)

Work in Translation/Work Published in a Reprinted Edition

Lorenz, K. (1969). On aggression. (M. K. Wilson, Trans.). New York: Bantam.
(Original work published 1966.)

(Lorenz, 1966/1969, p. 75)

Work Published in a New Edition

Baugh, A. C. (1957). A history of the English language. (2nd ed.). New York:
Appleton-Century-Crofts.

(Baugh, 1957, p. 288)

Book with No Author

World atlas. (1984). New York: Simon and Schuster.

(World atlas, 1984)

Article in an Encyclopedia

American architecture. (1963). Columbia encyclopedia. (3rd ed.). New York:
Columbia University Press.

(American architecture, 1963)

Publication of a Corporation, Foundation, or Government Agency

Carnegie Council on Policy Studies in Higher Education. (1980). Three thousand
futures: The next twenty years for higher education. San Francisco:
Jossey-Bass.

(Carnegie Council, 1980, p. 110)

Article in a Periodical Numbered by Volume

Plumb, J. H. (1976). Commercialization of childhood. Horizon, 18, 16–29.

(Plumb, 1976, p. 20)

Article in a Monthly Periodical

Loye, D. (1978, April). TV's impact on adults. Psychology Today, 87+.

(Loye, 1978, p. 87)

Article in a Weekly Periodical

Meyer, K. E. (1978, September 16). Television's trying times. Saturday Review, 19–23.

(Meyer, 1978, pp. 19–20)

Article in a Newspaper

Goldin, D. (1995, July 4). In a change of policy, and heart, colleges join fight against inflated grades. The New York Times, late ed., p. 8.

(Goldin, 1995)

Article without an Author

How to get quality back into the schools. (1977, September 12). US News & World Report, 31–34.

(How to get, 1977, p. 32)

Unpublished Dissertation

Eastman, E. (1993). "Lectures on jurisprudence": A key to understanding Adam Smith's thought. Unpublished doctoral dissertation, Claremont Graduate School.

(Eastman, 1993)

Film

Kubrick, S. (Director). (1963). Dr. Strangelove. [Film]. Columbia Pictures.

(Kubrick, 1963)

Material from an Electronic Information Service or Database

Belenky, M. F. (1984). The role of deafness in the moral development of hearing impaired children. In A. Areson & J. De Caro (Eds.), Teaching, learning and development. Rochester, NY: National Institute for the Deaf. (ERIC Document Reproduction Service No. ED 248 646)

(Belenky, 1984)

MODELS OF APA BIBLIOGRAPHICAL ENTRIES FOR CITING INTERNET SOURCES

Official APA citation guidelines for Internet sources are currently being developed. The citation models below are based on the guidelines provided in *Online!: A Reference Guide to Using Internet Sources,* by Andrew Harnack and Eugene Kleppinger (New York: St. Martin's Press, 1998), and are consistent with the principles of APA style. Using the sample below as a general guide, you should attempt to include as many of the elements of citation as are appropriate to your source:

> Author's last name, First initial, Middle initial. (Publication date). Title of document. Title of complete work. <URL> (Date of access).

Book

> Skene, F. (1865; 1996, December 10). Penitentiaries and reformatories. Victorian Women Writers Project. Ed. Perry Willett. Indiana U. <http://www.indiana.edu/~letrs/vwwp/skene/skene~reform.html> (1998, March 11).

Article in a Journal

> Osborne, L. (1998). A pirate's progress: how the maritime rogue became a multicultural hero. Linguafranca, 8(2). <http://www.linguafranca.com/> (1998, March 17).

Article in a Magazine

> Cloud, J. (1998, March 16). Harassed or hazed? Time. <http://www.pathfinder.com/time/magazine/1998/dom/980316/ law.harassed_or_hazed.whll.html> (1998, March 18).

Professional Web Site

> Cohen, A. J. (1997, January 4). Clockwork orange and the aestheticization of violence. UC Berkeley Film Studies Web Page. <http://cinemaspace.berkeley.edu/Cinema_Beyond/C_B.lectures/ ClockworkOrange/Benj_CultIndustr_Clckwrk.html> (1998, April 28).

Personal Web Site

> Wong, J. Home page. <http://logic.simplenet.com/jameswong/>
> (1998, May 12).

E-mail

> Phillips, S. <sphillips@ucb.edu>. (1997, December 19). Subject line of message
> [Personal email]. (1998, January 2).

NUMBERED BIBLIOGRAPHY

In this method, used primarily in the abstract and engineering sciences, you number each entry in your bibliography. Then, each citation in your essay consists of only the number of the work that you are referring to, placed in parentheses. Remember to include the page number if you quote from your source.

> Theorem 2 of Joel, Shier, and Stein (2) is strengthened in the following theorem:

> The following would be a consequence of the conjecture of McMullen and
> Shepher (3, p. 133):

Depending on your subject, you arrange your bibliography in alphabetical order (biology or mathematics) or in the order in which you cite the sources in your essay (chemistry, engineering, or physics). Consult your instructor or a style sheet that contains the specific rules for your discipline.

ENDNOTE/FOOTNOTE DOCUMENTATION

Until about ten years ago, documentation for most research essays was provided by *footnotes* or *endnotes.* In this system, a sequence of numbers in your essay is keyed to a series of separate notes containing publication information, which appear either at the bottom of the page (footnotes) or on a separate page at the end of the essay (endnotes). It also includes a standard bibliography as part of the essay. Many authors still use footnotes or endnotes, and some of your instructors may ask you to use this system of documentation.

This brief excerpt from a biographical essay about Ernest Hemingway shows you what the endnote/footnote system looks like.

> Hemingway's zest for life extended to women also. His wandering heart seemed
> only to be exceeded by an even more appreciative eye.[6] Hadley was aware of
> her husband's flirtations and of his facility with women.[7] Yet, she had no

idea that something was going on between Hemingway and Pauline Pfeiffer, a fashion editor for <u>Vogue</u> magazine.[8] She was also unaware that Hemingway delayed his return to Schruns from a business trip to New York, in February 1926, so that he might spend some more time with this "new and strange girl."[9]

> [6]Ernest Hemingway, <u>A Moveable Feast</u> (New York: Scribner's, 1964) 102.
>
> [7]Alice Hunt Sokoloff, <u>Hadley: The First Mrs. Hemingway</u> (New York: Dodd, Mead, 1973) 84.
>
> [8]Carlos Baker, <u>Ernest Hemingway: A Life Story</u> (New York: Scribner's, 1969) 159.
>
> [9]Hemingway 210. Also Baker 165.

If your instructor asks you to use endnotes or footnotes, do not put parenthetical source references, as in MLA or APA style, anywhere within the text of the essay. Instead, at each place where you would insert a parenthetical reference, put a number to indicate to your reader that there is a corresponding footnote or endnote.

When *inserting the numbers,* follow these rules:

- The note number is raised slightly above the line of your essay. To do this with a typewriter, move the roller up one half-turn. Many word processing programs have provision for various styles of documentation, including inserting footnotes/endnotes. If yours does not, leave two spaces in the line and insert the number neatly by hand in the first space, slightly above the line, once the essay is finished.

- The notes are numbered consecutively: if you have twenty-six notes in your essay, the number of the last one should be 26. There is no such thing as "12a." If "12a" appears at the last moment, then it becomes "13," and the remainder of the notes should be renumbered.

- Every note should contain at least one separate piece of information. Never write a note that states only, "See footnote 3." The reader should be told enough to make it unnecessary to consult footnote 3.

- While a note may contain more than one piece of information (for example, the source reference as well as some additional explanation of the point that is being documented), the note should have only one number. Under no circumstances should two note numbers be placed together, like this: [6,7].

When you prepare the documentation for your essay, you will have two lists to make: the list of works cited, and the list of notes.

The *format of the bibliography* closely resembles the "Works Cited" format for parenthetical documentation that was described in Chapter 5 and Chapter 9: the sources are alphabetized by last name, with the second and subsequent lines of each entry indented. The entries themselves closely resemble the forms for MLA bibliographical entries listed at the beginning of this appendix.

The *format of the list of notes* resembles the bibliography in reverse: the first line of the note is indented five spaces, with the second and subsequent lines at the margin; the note begins with a raised number, corresponding to the number in the text of the essay; the author's name is in first name/last name order; author and title are separated by commas, not periods; publication information is placed in parentheses; and the note ends with the page reference and a period. Notes should be double-spaced throughout.

Here is a list of five notes, illustrating the most common forms, followed by a bibliography consisting of the same five sources:

NOTES

[1]Helen Block Lewis, Psychic War in Men and Women (New York: New York UP, 1976) 43.

[2]Gertrude Himmelfarb, "Observations on Humanism and History," in The Philosophy of the Curriculum, ed. Sidney Hook (Buffalo: Prometheus, 1975) 85.

[3]Harvey G. Cox, "Moral Reasoning and the Humanities," Liberal Education 71.3 (1985): 196.

[4]Lauro Martines, "Mastering the Matriarch," Times Literary Supplement 1 February 1985: 113.

[5]Carolyn See, "Collaboration with a Daughter: The Rewards and Cost," New York Times 19 June 1986, late ed.: C2.

WORKS CITED

Cox, Harvey G. "Moral Reasoning and the Humanities." Liberal Education 71.3 (1985): 195–204.

Himmelfarb, Gertrude. "Observations on Humanism and History." In The Philosophy of the Curriculum. Ed. Sidney Hook. Buffalo: Prometheus, 1975. 81–88.

Lewis, Helen Block. Psychic War in Men and Women. New York: New York UP, 1976.

Martines, Lauro. "Mastering the Matriarch." Times Literary Supplement 1 February 1985: 113.

See, Carolyn. "Collaboration with a Daughter: The Rewards and Cost." New York Times 19 June 1986, late ed.: C2.

Another kind of endnote or footnote, known as the *short form,* should be used when you are citing the same source more than once in your essay. The first time you cite a new source, you use the long form, as illustrated above, which contains detailed information about publication history. The second time you cite the same source, and all subsequent times, you write a separate note, with a new number, but now you use a shorter form, consisting of the author's name and a page number:

> [6]Lewis 74.

The short form can be used here because there is already a long-form entry for Lewis on record in a previous note. If your bibliography contained two works by Lewis, then you would have to include an abbreviated title in the short form of the note:

> [6]Lewis, Psychic War 74.

The short form makes it unnecessary to use any Latin abbreviations, like *ibid.* or *op. cit.,* in your notes.

For an example of the use of endnote documentation in a full-length essay, see "The Quest for Survival in the Andes Mountains," in Chapter 10.

NOTES PLUS PAGE NUMBERS IN THE TEXT

If you are using only one or two sources in your essay, it is a good idea to include one footnote at the first reference and, thereafter, cite the page number of the source in the text of your essay.

For example, if your essay is exclusively about Sigmund Freud's *Civilization and Its Discontents,* document your first reference to the work with a complete note, citing the edition that you are using:

> *Sigmund Freud, Civilization and Its Discontents (Garden City:
> Doubleday, 1958) 72. All further citations refer to this edition.

This single note explains to your reader that you are intending to use the same edition whenever you cite this source. All subsequent references to this book will be followed by the page reference, in parentheses, usually at the end of your sentence.

> Freud has asserted that "the greatest obstacle to civilization [is] the
> constitutional tendency in men to aggression against one another . . . " (101).

This method is most useful in essays on literary topics when you are focusing on a single author, without citing secondary sources.

Remember: The choice of documentation for your essay is not really yours. Ask your instructor which method is appropriate for your course and your paper topic.

Appendix C

Interviewing and Field Research

As well as the books, articles, films, videos, and other research materials available at your library, personal interviews and field research can provide worthwhile information for your research essay. A well-conducted interview with an expert in the field, if it is carefully focused on your topic, can give you information unavailable from any other source. A personal interview can also enrich your essay with details, based on actual experience, that will capture and hold your audience's interest. Similarly, your own observation of an event or environment can be a source of valuable information. Through close observation of the river flowing past a sewage treatment plant or of the behavior of people during a political demonstration, you can collect data to support your thesis, to supplement the texts you have read, and to suggest alternative interpretations of the issues and ideas developed in your essay.

As you progress through your college's general education curriculum, you will probably find that some professional fields and academic disciplines, such as literature or history, depend most on library research, while others, such as sociology or science, often call for direct observation and interviewing by the researcher. For many of the topics that you explore across the curriculum, your essays will benefit from a combination of both library and personal investigation.

INTERVIEWING

Sources for Interviews

You will want to interview experts or authorities who are both knowledgeable and appropriate sources of information about your specific topic. First, consider the faculty on your campus, not only as direct sources of information but as sources of referrals to other experts in the field at nearby colleges and universities. If your general topic is the Holocaust, for example, you may want to interview a faculty member with that specialization in your college's history, sociology, or Judaic studies department. You may, in fact, come across the names of appropriate faculty at your college in the course of your library research.

An entirely different source of direct information is a person who has had personal experience with some aspect of your essay topic. As you talk about your research on the Holocaust, one of your friends might tell you about an aunt living nearby, someone who, for example, survived the concentration camps at Auschwitz. That woman's recollections can be just as appropriate and important an addition to your essay as a professor's more theoretical comments, lending it human drama or highlighting a particular issue that interests you.

Some essays can be enhanced by interviewing several sources. For example, if you were preparing a report on an environmental issue in your town—let's say the purity of its water supply—you would want to learn about the impact of the new sewage treatment plant on the local environment. Of course, you would want to talk to the plant's manager; but you might also consult the managers of local businesses to determine some of the economic implications, and to some public health officials to learn about the kinds of health hazards the plant is intended to avoid. In this case, a single source would not cover the possible spectrum of responses.

Interviews can be time-consuming, and direct information derived from interviews will probably have to be combined with notes taken from your reading. You need to know in advance what kinds of interview will be most useful and appropriate—if any—and, thus, not waste your time and that of your source.

Planning an Interview

Whether in person or on the telephone, interviews require careful planning and preparation. First, you have to establish a courteous and professional relationship with your subject (that is what the person you are interviewing is generally called). Most potential interview subjects will be pleased to participate in your research. Your interest enhances the value of their knowledge and experience, and they are likely to enjoy being cited as authorities and having their ideas quoted and read.

You are more likely to get someone to consent to an interview if you write or phone first to make an appointment. Arrange your appointments as soon as possible once you have focused your topic and identified candidates for interviews. Since your potential subjects are likely to have busy schedules, allow enough time to make initial contact and then to wait a week or two, if necessary, until the person has enough time to speak with you at length. This way you can avoid having your initial conversation turn into an interview before you are quite prepared for it—which can be awkward if you don't have your questions ready.

When you call or write to those whom you hope to interview, politely identify yourself; then briefly describe your topic and the special focus of your essay. Ask for an interview of 20 to 30 minutes at a later time convenient for the subject. If appropriate, mention the name of the person who suggested this source, or refer to the publication in which you saw the subject's name. Your objective is to convey your own serious interest in the topic and in your subject's knowledge of the topic. Be friendly, but professional. If someone is reluctant to be interviewed, you should retreat gracefully. At the same time, don't hesitate to ask for a referral to someone else who might be in a better position to provide helpful information.

Preparing for an Interview

Because your interview, whether in person or on the phone, will probably be brief, you need to plan in advance what you intend to say and ask so that you can use the time effectively. Careful preparation is also a compliment to your interview subjects and shows respect for their expertise.

Reviewing your research notes, make a focused list of questions in writing beforehand, tailoring them to your specific paper topic and to your source's area of knowledge. If, for example, you are going to interview the manager of a sewage treatment plant on the Hudson River about the effective removal of PCBs from the water, you don't want to use up ten minutes asking about plant management. It can be helpful to prepare a questionnaire, leaving space between the questions for you to take notes. You can use the same questionnaire, with variations, for a whole series of personal interviews.

Recording Information during an Interview

During the actual interview, you will be listening intently to your subject's responses and thinking about your next question. But as a researcher, you have another challenge. You need to take away with you a comprehensive record of the interview so that you can quote your expert accurately and cite information authoritatively. Most successful interviewers use one of two techniques to record the interview, or a combination of both: tape-recording and note-taking.

Tape-recording

If you plan to use a tape-recorder, make sure you ask your subject's permission in advance; test the equipment beforehand (especially if it's borrowed for the occasion); and know how to operate it smoothly. Bring it to the interview with the tape already loaded in the machine, and be sure the batteries are fresh. (Bring along a second tape in case the first one jams or breaks, and carry extra batteries.) When the interview is about to begin, check again to see if your subject has any objection to your recording the conversation. Then, to avoid making your subject self-conscious, put the tape recorder in an unobtrusive place. After that, don't create a distraction by fiddling with the machine.

Note-taking

Even if you plan to tape-record the interview, come prepared to take careful notes; bring notebook and pens, as well as your list of questions or questionnaire. One way of preparing for detailed note-taking—the kind that will provide you with accurate direct quotations to use in your essay—is to rehearse. Pair off with a classmate who is also preparing for an interview, and practice interviewing and note-taking (including handling the tape recorder). Also review the instructions for Assignment 7 and Assignment 8 in Chapter 4 (pp. 200–202, 208–210). If your subject presents a point so well that you know you'll want to quote it, write it down rapidly but carefully, and—then and there—read it back to make sure that you have transcribed the statement correctly.

Conducting the Interview

Arrive on time (not late and not early)! Once you've been invited to sit down and your equipment is set up, *briefly* remind your subject of the essay topic and your reason for requesting the interview. Then get right down to your "script": ask each question clearly, without hurrying; be alert to recognize when the question has been fully answered (there is usually a pause); and move briskly on to the next question. Otherwise, let your subject talk freely, with minimum interruption. Remember that you are the receiver, not the provider, of information, and let your subject do almost all the talking.

Sometimes, a particular question will capture your subject's interest, and you will get a more detailed answer than you expected. Be aware of the time limit for the interview; but if you see a promising line of questioning that you didn't anticipate, and your subject seems relaxed and willing to prolong the conversation, take advantage of the opportunity and ask follow-up questions. What if your subject digresses far away from the topic of your essay? At the first opportunity, ask whether there is a time constraint. If there is, politely indicate that you have three or four more questions to ask and you hope that there will be enough time to include them.

No matter how careful your preparations, a good interview won't go exactly as you planned. You should aim to participate in a conversation, not direct an interrogation. At the end, your subject should feel that the time has passed too quickly and, ideally, offer to speak with you again, if necessary, to fill up any gaps. To maintain that good impression, be sure to send a brief note of thanks to your subject no longer than a day or two after the interview. Later on, you may want to send a copy of the completed essay.

Using Interview Sources in Your Essay

Since the purpose of the interview is to gather information (and to provide yourself with a few apt quotations), you need to have clear notes to work from as you organize your essay. If you used a tape recorder, you should transcribe the interview as soon as you can; if you took notes, you should go over them carefully, clarify confusing words, and then type a definitive version. Otherwise, you may find yourself deciphering your almost-illegible notes at a later time or searching through the entire tape to find a specific sentence that you want to quote. Transcribe the interview accurately, without embroidering or revising what your subject actually said. Keep the original notes and tapes; your instructor may want to review them along with your essay.

Working with notes from an interview is almost exactly the same as working with notes from library research. As you organize your essay (following the process described in Chapter 8), you cross-reference your notes with a list of the topics for your essay, choosing information from the interview that might be cited to support the major points in your outline. When you begin to choose quotations, you may want to review the section on "Selecting Quotations," pp. 360–361. Remember that it is the well-chosen and carefully placed source that carries authority, not the number of words quoted. Finally, document each use of material taken from your interview, whether it is ideas or words, with a parenthetical reference. (See Appendix B for the appropriate bibliographical entry.)

FIELD RESEARCH

Like interviewing, field research is a way of supplementing the material you take from texts and triggering new ideas about your topic. When you engage in field research, you are gathering information directly, acting as an observer, investigator, and evaluator within the context of an academic or professional discipline. If you are asked by your anthropology instructor to describe and analyze a family celebration as an ethnographer would, your observations of Thanksgiving dinner at home would be regarded as field research.

In many of your college courses, you will be expected to engage in field research. When, for example, the nursing program sends students to a nearby hospital for their clinical practice and asks for a weekly report on their work with patients, these students are doing field research. Other students may participate in a cooperative education program involving professional internships in preparation for potential careers; the reports these interns prepare on their work experiences are based on field research. Whatever the course, your instructor will show you how to connect your field research activities to the theories, procedures, and format characteristic of that discipline. Still, there are certain practices common to most kinds of field research that you need to know from the beginning. Let's follow that process from assignment to essay as you develop a simple topic based on field research.

Your sociology professor has suggested that, although college students like to think of themselves as unique individuals, certain patterns clearly underlie their characteristic behavior. As an example, he asserts that both male and female students prefer to work and relax with members of the opposite sex. He is asking each of you to test this hypothesis by choosing a place on campus to observe students as they go about their daily routine, keeping in mind two questions: are there patterns one can observe in these students' behavior? what might be the significance of these patterns? If you were assigned this project, your work would fall into three stages: gathering the information, analyzing that information, and writing the essay.

Gathering Information

According to your instructor's guidelines for this essay based on field research, you will need to perform at least six separate observations for 20 to 30 minutes each at a site of your choice and, later, be prepared to hand in copies of your accumulated observation notes along with your essay. So your first important decision concerns the location for gathering information about students' behavior: the cafeteria? the library? a particular class? the student union? the college bookstore? a classroom or another place on campus where students congregate? You decide to observe students gathered at the row of benches outside Johnson Hall, the busiest classroom building, extending from the bookstore on the right to the student union building on the left; these benches also face a field where gym classes meet and the baseball team practices. Since this area is an important junction on the campus, you can assume that enough students will appear to provide basic information for your field research.

Planning the Observations

To conform to your instructor's requirements and obtain all the information you need for your essay, you should prepare for your observation sessions quickly and carefully. First, establish a schedule that will fulfill the guidelines for the assignment. Since your first class in Johnson Hall is at 11 A.M., and you are free before that, you decide to schedule your observations for the half hour before class, that is, from 10:30 to 11:00 A.M. on Monday, Wednesday, and Friday, for the next two weeks.

You will need to set aside a separate notebook for recording your observations. For each session, start a fresh page, and indicate the date and the times when you begin and end your sessions. Such specific information is what establishes your authority as a field researcher. Before your first session, consider making a diagram of the site, roughly sketching in the location of the buildings, placing the seven benches correctly, and assigning each a number.

As with interviewing, a list of prepared questions will help you to spend your time profitably. This time, however, your object is not to ask for information, but to set up a framework for your observations and, possibly, a potential structure for your essay. For this assignment, you are basically trying to find out:

- How many students are spending time at this site?
- Where are they and what are they doing?
- Do they stay for the whole observation period, or do they come and go?

Engaging in Observation

Your work consists of careful observing and precise note-taking. You are not trying to write a narrative or, at this point, understand the significance of what you are seeing; you are only trying to record your subjects' activities accurately to provide notes for future reflection.

Some people may feel self-conscious to have an observer watching them closely and writing down everything they do. To avoid potential questions or confrontations, try to do your observing and note-taking unobtrusively, without staring too hard at any one person. If someone asks what you are doing, be prepared to say that you are working on an assignment for a college class, that you aren't going to identify anyone by name, and that you would be grateful for the person's cooperation. As with interview subjects, you will find that most subjects of field research are sympathetic and helpful. If someone speaks to you, take advantage of the opportunity to combine observations with a little formal interviewing, and possibly gain a useful quotation for your essay. If someone objects to being included in your study, however, you should immediately turn your attention elsewhere, or move on and try again at another time.

A portion of your notes for one session might look like that shown in Figure C-1.

After a couple of sessions, you may feel that you have a general idea of the range of students' behavior at the site, so you can begin to look specifically for repeated instances of certain activities: studying together or individually, eating, relaxing. But you will need to keep an open mind and eye about what you might observe. Again as with interviewing, your subjects' behavior may not absolutely conform to your planned questions, so you may need to add new questions as the sessions progress. For example, you may not have realized until your third session that students sitting on the benches closest to the playing field are focusing on the sports activities there; from then on, you will be looking for that behavior.

For this assignment, you would continue observing until you complete the number of observations specified; but for your own field research in a project for a course in your major field, you might conduct observations for most of a semester. As a professional researcher (like Margaret Mead when she was observing Pacific Island adolescents for her classic book *Coming of*

> Monday, April 3; 10:30 am.
>
> 3 students at bench 3 -- 1 male & 2 females. Females sitting on bench. Male, between them, standing with 1 foot up on bench, smoking. They're talking quietly. About 5 minutes later, another male arrives on bike & stands, straddling bike, in front of the bench. Conversation continues, now with 4 participants. At 10:50, females get up & walk into Johnson, along with 1st male. 2nd male rides off toward library.
>
> At benches 4 & 5, 2 people at each. At 4, 1 male reads book, stopping now and then to use a highlighter. 1 female has bunch of 3×5 cards, & she looks at each one for a second, then flips it, then goes to next one. At 10:35, another male comes over to her, she gets up, & they both go to bench 6, where no one is sitting. There she continues going through her cards, but now she seems to read something from each card, as male responds with a word or 2. They continue to do this for another 10 minutes.

Figure C-1

Age in Samoa), you might even live with a tribe, studying their culture for a year or more.

Analyzing Your Information

When you have all your observations recorded, you are ready to move on to the next stage: reviewing your notes to understand what you have seen, and analyzing what you have learned. You have probably noticed that this overlaps with the previous observation stage; as you watched students in front of Johnson Hall, you were already beginning to group their activities into several categories: studying, casual conversations, watching sports, eating, sleeping.

Once you establish these categories, you pull out of your notes the specific references that match the category, noting the date and time of each instance. So now you have several new pages that look like those shown in Figure C-2.

Studying

girl and guy with flash cards 4/6   10:35
group of 5 with science notes 4/8   10:30 - 10:58
   (they told me about their 11 am quiz --
   all in same class)
guy with book and highlighter 4/6
   10:30 - 10:45

Sports watching

observations 2, 4, 5, 6: groups of 2 - 5 guys at
   benches 1, 2, 3 (facing sports field).
   Groups generally talked, pointed,
   laughed, while gym classes did
   aerobics.

observations 4, 5: during baseball team
   practice, guys in small groups
   cheered, pointed; several stood up
   and walked over to edge of path
   that overlooks field.

female pairs watching sports
   during 4, 5, but no groups.

observations 1, 2: no sports scheduled
   then; few people on benches 1, 2,
   and 3.

Figure C-2

You may want to chart your observations to represent at a glance such variables as these: how many students studied, or watched sports, or socialized? Which activities were associated with males or with females? If your sessions took place during different times of the day, the hour would be another variable to record on your chart.

As you identify categories, you need to ask yourself some questions to help you characterize each one and define the differences among some of your subjects' behaviors. For example: are these differences determined by gender, as with the sports watchers, or by preferred methods of learning, like solitary or group study? As you think through the possible conclusions to be drawn from your observations, record them in your notebook, for these preliminary analyses will later become part of your essay.

Writing the Essay

An essay based on field research generally follows a format appropriate to the particular discipline. Your instructor will provide detailed guidelines and, perhaps, refer you to an article in a professional journal to use as a model. For the essay analyzing student behavior, you might present your findings according to the following outline:

Purpose: In the first section, you state the problem—the purpose of your field research—clearly indicating the question(s) you set out to investigate.

Method: Here, you explain your choice of site, the times and number of your observation sessions, and the general procedure for observation that you followed, including any exceptions to or deviations from your plan.

Observations: Next, you record the information you gathered from your observations, not as a list of random facts, but as categories or groupings that make the facts coherent to the reader. In many disciplines, this kind of information can be presented through charts, graphs, or tables.

Analysis: The heart of your essay, here is where you explain to your readers the significance of your observations. If, for example, you decided that certain activities were gender-related, you would describe the basis for that distinction. Or you could discuss your conclusion that students use the benches primarily as a meeting place to socialize. Or you might make the connection between studying as the most prevalent student activity outside Johnson Hall and the scheduling of midterms during the time of your observations.

Conclusions: At the end of your essay, you remind your readers—and the instructor who is evaluating your work—that your purpose throughout has been to answer the questions and clarify the problems posed in the first paragraph. What did you discover that can illuminate your response to your professor's assertions about students' behavior?

Using Field Research

There are several important points to remember about using field research:

1. In actual practice across the curriculum, field research is usually combined with library research. As part of your investigation, you will often be asked to include in an early section of your essay a "literature search," that is, a summary of some key articles on your topic. This summary shows that you are familiar with an appropriate range of information and, especially, the major work in the field.

2. Whether you emphasize library or field research depends on the purpose and nature of your essay. If field research is integral to your

(continued)

(continued)

topic, you will be acting as the principal investigator and interpreter of new data, and the library research will serve only as a supplement to your field research. Otherwise, you should integrate your field research into your essay as you would any other source of information.

3. For field research, careful documentation is especially important since you are asking your reader to trust the data that you yourself have gathered and upon which your speculations and conclusions are based. You can create this trust by making careful and repeated observations, recording them in detail and accurately, and presenting them in a clear and logical manner.

4. The methods of analyzing data obtained through field research are, in most cases, specific to particular disciplines. So you should indicate to your readers, by reference to authorities or models, that you are observing the conventions of the field you are working in. It is especially important that, after consultation with your instructor, you use the appropriate method of documenting both your field research and your library research, so that a reader can clearly distinguish the work of the previous investigators who are your secondary sources from your own primary contributions.

Appendix D

Writing Essay Examinations

Instructors give essay examinations for three reasons:

- To make sure that you have read and understood the assigned reading;
- To test your analytical skills;
- To find out if you can integrate what you have read with the ideas and information that you have learned in lectures and class discussion.

Since your instructor is usually not trying to test your memory, essay examinations are often open-book, allowing you to refer freely to the source. But in any exam, even a take-home assignment, there is likely to be some time pressure. To prepare, you should have read all the material carefully in advance and outlined, underlined, or annotated the text.

READING THE QUESTION

You determine your strategy by carefully examining the wording of the question before you begin to plan and write your essay. First, you must accept that someone else is providing the topic for your essay. The person who wrote the question wants to pinpoint a single area to be explored, and so you may have very little scope. However restrictive it may seem, you must stay within the boundaries of the question. If you are instructed to focus on only a small section of the text, summarizing the entire work from beginning to end is inappropriate. If you are asked to discuss an issue that is raised frequently throughout the work, paraphrasing a single paragraph or page is pointless. Do not include extraneous information just to demonstrate how much you know. Most teachers are more impressed with aptness and conciseness than with length.

The controlling verb of the question will usually provide you with a key. Different verbs will require different approaches. You are already familiar with the most common terms:

summarize; state; list; outline; condense; cite reasons

What is sometimes forgotten under pressure is that you are expected to carry out the instructions literally. *Summarize* means condense: the reader expects a short but complete account of the specified subject. On the other hand, *list* should result in a sequence of short entries, somewhat disconnected, but not a fully developed series of paragraphs.

Other directions may be far broader:

describe; discuss; review; explain; show; explore; determine

Verbs like these give you a wide scope. Since they do not demand a specific strategy, be careful to stay within the set topic, so that you do not explain or review more than the readers want to know about.

Still other verbs indicate a more exact method of development, perhaps one of the strategies that you have already worked with in Assignment 5 in Chapter 3:

compare and contrast; illustrate; define; show the reasons; trace the causes; trace the effects; suggest solutions; analyze

Notice that none of the verbs so far has provided an opportunity for personal comment. You have been asked to examine the text, to demonstrate your understanding of its meaning and its implications, but you have not been asked for your opinion. However, several verbs do request commentary:

evaluate; interpret; criticize; justify; prove; disagree

Although these verbs invite a personal response, they do not give you freedom to write about whatever you choose. You are still confined to the boundaries of the set subject, and you should devote as much of your essay as possible to demonstrating your understanding of what you have read. *A brilliant essay that ignores the topic rarely earns the highest grade.* If you have worked hard to prepare for the essay, you would be foolish to ignore the question. Don't reinterpret the directions in order to write about what is easiest or what would display your abilities to best advantage or what you figured out earlier would be asked. Just answer the question.

PLANNING AND DEVELOPING THE ESSAY

Even when you have worked out what you are expected to write about, you are still not ready to start writing. Your reader will also judge the way in which your essay is constructed, so organize your thoughts before you begin to write. No elaborate outline is necessary.

Guidelines for Planning and Developing Your Essay

1. *List some of the main points that come into your head, reduce the list to a manageable number, and renumber the sequence.* This process does not take very long and it can prevent unnecessary repetition, unintentional omissions, mixed-up sequences, and overemphasis.

2. *Develop each point separately.* Don't try to say everything at the same time. Consult your list, say what is necessary about each item, and then move on to the next.

3. *Develop each point adequately.* Each reason or cause or criticism deserves convincing presentation. Unless you are asked for a list, don't just write down one sentence and rush away to the next item. You will write a more effective essay by including some support for each of your points. Do not make brief, incomplete references to ideas because you assume that the reader will know all about them. It is your responsibility to explain each one so that it makes sense by itself.

4. *Refer back to the text.* Whenever possible, demonstrate that you can cite evidence or information from the assigned reading. If you think of two possible examples or facts, one from the source and one from your own experience or knowledge, and if you haven't enough time to include both, the safe choice will come from the source. However, you must always mark the transition between your own presentation of ideas and your reference to the source by citing its title, or the name of its author, or both.

ANALYZING AN ESSAY
AND AN ESSAY QUESTION

Carefully read through George Stade's "Football—The Game of Aggression." Assume that you have previously read this essay and that you have between forty-five minutes and an hour to answer the following question:

Although he acknowledges that it can be violent, George Stade suggests that football may serve a constructive social function. Considering some of his descriptive comments about the sport, explain why football may not be as healthy for society as Stade implies.

FOOTBALL—THE GAME OF AGGRESSION
George Stade

There are many ways in which professional football is unique among sports, and as many others in which it is the fullest expression of what is at the heart of all sports. There is no other major sport so dependent upon raw force, nor any so dependent on a complex and delicate strategy; none so wide in the range of specialized functions demanded from its players; none so dependent upon the undifferentiated athletic *sine qua non*, a quickwitted body; none so primitive; none so futuristic; none so American.

Football is first of all a form of play, something one engages in instinctively and only for the sake of performing the activity in question. Among forms of play, football is a game, which means that it is built on communal needs, rather than on private evasions, like mountain climbing. Among games it is a sport; it requires athletic ability, unlike croquet. And among sports, it is one whose mode is violence and whose violence is its special glory.

In some sports—basketball, baseball, soccer—violence is occasional (and usually illegal); in others, like hockey, it is incidental; in others still, car racing, for example, it is accidental. Definitive violence football shares alone with boxing and bullfighting, among major sports. But in bullfighting a man is pitted not against another man, but against an animal, and boxing is a competition between individuals, not teams, and that makes a great difference. If shame is the proper and usual penalty for failures in sporting competitions between individuals, guilt is the consequence of failing not only oneself and one's fans, but also one's teammates. Failure in football, moreover, seems more related to a failure of courage, seems more unmanning than in any other sport outside of bullfighting. In other sports one loses a knack, is outsmarted, or is merely inferior in ability, but in football, on top of these, a player fails because he "lacks desire," or "can't take it anymore," or "hears footsteps," as his teammates will put it.

Many sports, especially those in which there is a goal to be defended, seem enactments of the games animals play under the stimulus of what ethologists, students of animal behavior, call *territory*—"the drive to gain, maintain, and defend the exclusive right to a piece of property," as Robert Ardrey puts it. The most striking symptom of this drive is aggressiveness, but among social animals, such as primates, it leads to "amity for the social partner, hostility for the territorial neighbor." The territorial instinct is closely related to whatever makes animals establish pecking orders; the tangible sign of one's status within the orders is the size and value of the territory one is able to command. Individuals fight over status, groups over *lebensraum*[1] and a bit more. These instincts, some ethologists have claimed, are behind patriotism and private property, and also, I would add, codes of honor, as among

[1] Literally, living space. The word is often most associated with the territory thought by the Nazis to be essential to Germany's political and economic security.

ancient Greeks, modern Sicilians, primitive hunters, teen-age gangs, soldiers, aristo-
crats, and athletes, especially football players.

The territorial basis of certain kinds of sports is closest to the surface in foot-   5
ball, whose plays are all attempts to gain and defend property through aggression.
Does this not make football *par excellence* the game of instinctual satisfactions, especially among Americans, who are notorious as violent patriots and instinctive de-
fenders of private property? . . . Even the unusual amity, if that is the word, that
exists among football players has been remarked upon. . . . And what is it that cor-
responds in football to the various feathers, furs, fins, gorgeous colors by means of
which animals puff themselves into exaggerated gestures of masculine potency?
The football player's equipment, of course. His cleats raise him an inch off the
ground. Knee and thigh pads thrust the force lines of his legs forward. His pants
are tight against his rump and the back of his thighs, portions of the body which
the requirements of the game stuff with muscle. . . . Even the tubby guard looks
slim by comparison with his shoulders, extended half a foot on each side by padding.
Finally, the helmet, which from the esthetic point of view most clearly expresses
the genius of the sport. Not only does the helmet make the player inches taller and
give his head a size proportionate to the rest of him; it makes him anonymous, in-
scrutable, more serviceable as a symbol. The football player in uniform strikes the
eye in a succession of gestalt[2] shifts; first a hooded phantom out of the paleolithic
past of the species; then a premonition of a future of spacemen.

In sum, and I am almost serious about this, football players are to America what   6
tragic actors were to ancient Athens and gladiators to Rome: models of perennially
heroic, aggressive, violent humanity, but adapted to the social realities of the times
and places that formed them.

[2]I.e., perceptual.

ANSWERING THE QUESTION

At first, you may have some difficulty determining the focus of your essay
since the question includes more than one key word to help you work out your
strategy. The main verb in this question is *explain.* You are being asked to account for something, to help your reader understand what may not be entirely
clear. *Explain* also implies persuasion: your reader must be convinced that your
explanation is valid.

- If the question asked you to explain *something that is confusing* in Stade's
  essay, your task would be to provide an interpretive summary of some
  part of the text. For example, you might have been asked to explain the
  differences, with illustrations, between violence that is occasional, incidental, and accidental, discussing the implications of these distinctions
  for sports in general.

- If the question asked you to explain *some related point that Stade omits* from his discussion, your task would be to extend his reasoning, perhaps to discuss causes or effects, or to contrast and compare. For example, you might have to explain why football lends itself to a greater degree of violence than other sports, or explain the parallel between the way football players and animals defend their territory.

- If the question asked you—as it does—to *evaluate the author's reasoning* in forming his conclusions, you would then examine Stade's "almost serious" conclusions and demonstrate—explain—the limitations of his arguments and examples; in other words, argue against his position.

The essay question raises the point that Stade may have underestimated the harmful effects of football, a sport so violent that it could undermine the social benefits that it otherwise provides. To answer the question, then, you must accept the assumption that Stade may be overenthusiastic about football, *whether or not you agree,* and proceed to point out the implications and the shortcomings of his analysis. In a sense, writing a good essay depends on your willingness to allow your views to be shaped by the examiner's, at least for the duration of the exam.

The question defines the *limits* as well as the strategy of your essay. It does not permit you to dispute Stade on grounds that are entirely of your choosing. You are firmly instructed to focus your attention on the conflict between violence and social benefit. It would be foolish to ignore these instructions and write only about the glories of football or to condemn the sport for reasons unrelated to the violence of its play.

What should you be evaluating in your essay, and how many comments are "some"? Stade makes the following points in support of his view that football can be a useful social ritual:

- It fosters individual strength and determination.
- It develops cooperation and teamwork.
- It teaches players how to acquire and defend territory and thus encourages nationalism and the patriotic defense of one's country.
- It provides players and spectators with the opportunity to act out their aggressions in a controlled and relatively harmless way.

These points should certainly be on the list of paragraph topics that you jot down as you plan your essay. Since these ideas are embedded within the paragraphs of Stade's essay, you should use your own ordering principle—least violent to most (potentially) violent might be a good choice. Each of your paragraphs should begin with a description of one characteristic of the sport as Stade presents it, followed by your own explanation of the social disadvantages or benefits that might result.

Resist the temptation to devote too much space to a single aspect of the sport. For example, if you spend too much time discussing Stade's comments about uniforms and the extent to which the football player is magnified and dehumanized by his padding and his helmet, you may not be able to develop your discussion of whether football encourages patriotism or a more divisive and dangerous nationalism. Stade's essay is based on his belief that people participate in sports as a way of expressing passions and impulses that have no place in our normal daily occupations. He implies that, if this outlet is eliminated, our instincts for violence may spill over into activities where they would be far more dangerous. This argument has often been used to justify violence as depicted on television and in the movies. While you are not expected to analyze the issue with the expertise of a trained psychologist or sociologist, your essay should reflect your awareness of and your views on Stade's conception of football as a way of controlling our aggressive instincts.

INTRODUCING YOUR TOPIC

Examination essays, like all essays, require an introduction. Before beginning to explore some of the issues inherent in George Stade's analysis, you should provide a short introduction that defines the author's topic and your own. Your later references to his ideas will need a well-established context; therefore, try to define Stade's conception of football (which might differ from someone else's) right at the outset of your essay. Although the introduction need not be longer than two or three sentences, *cite your source*—the name of the author and the name of the essay, both properly spelled—and state exactly what it is that you and your author are concerned about. To demonstrate the frustration of reading an introduction that is shrouded in mystery, look at the first paragraph from a student essay answering the question that has just been analyzed:

> The attitude of the author of this essay is highly supportive of a sport that may be the most violent in the world. It is true that players acquire a lot of skills and learn about teamwork, as well as receiving huge sums of money and becoming public idols. However, there are also risks and dangers that result, for spectators and those watching on television, as well as for those on the field wearing team uniforms, which he fails to point out in this brief essay.

"He," of course, is George Stade, and the sport under discussion is football. The student had read and understood the source essay, but is so eager to begin commenting on Stade's ideas that she fails to establish a context for her arguments. Here is a more informative introduction:

> In "Football--The Game of Aggression," George Stade presents the game of football as a necessary evil and a useful social ritual. He does not deny that the game, more than most sports, is based on a potentially lethal kind of aggression. But, contrasting football with other sports, he finds that it also encourages a sense of teamwork and an instinct for patriotism, which can be valuable both to the individual and to society. Left unclear is whether ritualizing violence through

sports does, in fact, result in a less violent society, or whether watching football players maul each other in weekly combat only encourages spectators to imitate their heroes.

PRESENTING YOUR ESSAY TO THE READER

Students often choose to divide their time into three parts. For example, if you have forty minutes during which to write an essay, try the following timetable:

- ten minutes to analyze the question and plan a strategy
- twenty minutes to write the essay
- ten minutes to proofread and correct it

During in-class examinations, students often waste vital minutes by painstakingly transcribing a new copy from their rough drafts. While *your handwriting must be legible,* it is not necessary to hand in a clean copy. Teachers expect an exam essay to have sentences crossed out and words inserted. They are used to seeing arrows used to reverse sentences and numbers used to change the sequence of paragraphs. It makes no sense to write the last word of your first draft and then, without checking what you have written, immediately take a clean sheet of paper and start transcribing a copy to hand in. Because transcription is such a mechanical task, the mind tends to wander and the pen makes errors that were not in the original draft. Take time to proofread your essay, to locate grammatical errors, and to fill in gaps in continuity. As long as your corrections and changes are fairly neat and clear, your instructor will not mind reading the first draft and will probably be pleased by your efforts to improve your writing.

Appendix E

Readings for a Research Essay

The essays in this appendix are sources for you to work with if your instructor asks you to write a research essay based on Assignment 13 (pp. 362–363). These ten readings (including one in another part of this book) could form the entire bibliography for your research essay. Or (with your instructor's permission) you may wish to supplement these essays with additional sources of your own choosing.

Henderson, Cinqué. "Myths of the Unloved." *The New Republic* 25 Aug. 1997.

Kennedy, Randall. "My Race Problem—and Ours." *The Atlantic Monthly* May 1997.

*Paley, Grace. "Travelling." *The New Yorker* Aug. 1997.

Sleeper, Jim. "Toward an End of Blackness: An Argument for the Surrender of Race Consciousness." *Harper's* May 1997. [With three "Letters to the Editor." *Harper's* Aug. 1997.]

Steele, Shelby. "I'm Black, You're White, Who's Innocent?" *Harper's* June 1988. Rpt. in *Voices in Black and White: writings on race in America from Harper's Magazine.* Eds. Katharine Whittemore and Gerald Marzorati. New York: Franklin Square Press, 1992.

Taylor, Jared. "Middle-Class Solutions." *Paved with Good Intentions: The Failure of Race Relations in Contemporary America.* New York: Carroll & Graf, 1992.

Williams, Patricia J. "Pansy Quits." *The Rooster's Egg.* Cambridge, Mass: Harvard UP, 1995.

*See Chapter 1, pp. 16–19.

DeMott, Benjamin. "Visions of Black-White Friendship." *The Trouble with Friendship: Why Americans Can't Think Straight about Race.* New York: Atlantic Monthly Press: 1995.

Wicker, Tom. "Expanding the Center." *Tragic Failure: Racial Integration in America.* New York: Morrow, 1996.

Early, Gerald. "Whatever Happened to Integration?" Rev. of *The Trouble with Friendship* and *Tragic Failure. The Atlantic Monthly* February 1997.

MYTHS OF THE UNLOVED

Cinqué Henderson

The Ku Klux Klan owns Church's Chicken and poisons blacks with addictive, deadly ingredients. Tropical Fantasy puts chemicals in its soda to sterilize black men. The CIA runs drugs in South Central Los Angeles.   1

It is difficult to hear myths like these—myths that have gained surprisingly wide   2
acceptance in the black community—and not realize something is dreadfully wrong with race relations in the United States. When the Kerner Commission concluded nearly thirty years ago that America was "moving towards two societies, one black, one white, separate and unequal," it failed to point out that the gross material disparities would be attended by equally vast psychological ones. In this context, Bill Clinton's national dialogue on race actually seems like a hopeful idea: What is psychology, after all, if not the therapy of curing neuroses through conversation?

But don't be surprised if the conversation leads off in some unexpected direc-   3
tions. Even though the persistence of these theories defies logic (the CIA myth, for example, has been largely disavowed by the very newspaper that started it), the "paranoid style," as Richard Hofstadter calls it, has a long, sometimes distinguished history in this country—particularly among those who, as he says, see only the consequences of power, and not the inner workings. As the historian Bernard Bailyn argued thirty years ago, the "fear of a comprehensive conspiracy against liberty throughout the English-speaking world . . . lay at the heart of the Revolutionary movement." America, in other words, was founded by conspiracy nuts.

The Eso Won bookstore sits in the heart of black L.A. One block west of Martin   4
Luther King Boulevard, just south of Magic Johnson Theaters, it is California's largest black-owned bookstore. At the back of the store, next to the shelf on black health care, there is an entire shelf devoted to conspiracies, some 200 books in all. The best is Patricia Turner's *I Heard It Through the Grapevine*, which, despite some of its more questionable conclusions, provides a fascinating survey of the unlikely and sometimes bizarre beliefs that manifest themselves in the black community. As Turner notes, no myth has enjoyed more durability than the rumor of CIA drug-running in South Central Los Angeles. (Small wonder, given what crack has done to black communities.)

The crucial point, which she makes only glancingly, is described this way: "About   5
80 percent of my informants reported [belief in] what I call 'malicious intent,'" but

when questioned more directly, "most professed greater belief in what I call 'benign neglect.'" Maxine Waters, South Central's representative in Congress, invokes similar language when it comes to the CIA-crack theory: "It confirmed many of the suspicions about some plot or some negligence on the part of the government. . . ." Yet what an odd statement to make so offhandedly: "some plot or some negligence." Trussed together as these words are, it is easy to overlook the fact that "plot" and "negligence" describe fundamentally different things. How you get from one to the other tells a lot about being black in America.

I have a friend who believes the CIA did what everyone says it did. Her brother is in jail for crack possession. He won't speak to her because she prayed for him to be arrested, and, as far as she is concerned, God heard and answered. She worries about her brother still, but knows of no decent drug rehab program in the county where she lives, so she is content to let him stay in jail. At first, she said she thought the government just didn't care about blacks and crack. She was "fed up" with the police's unwillingness to fight the drug sales where she lives. "They [crack addicts] come and go big as day, and the police just sit there." Recalling her family's attempt to get her brother into a program, she despaired, "We tried and tried. Didn't nobody lift a finger. They didn't care whether we lived or died." And then the despair turned to anger. "I believe what they say," she says, her voice rising. "I wouldn't put it past none of them. They out to get black people." Belief in the CIA myth gives my friend a measure of peace. She had considered the possibility of neglect and found the argument wanting, deciding, ultimately, that conspiracy was more plausible. This may have to do with an overestimation of the government's power, but I think the switch, as sudden and surprising as it was, was occasioned by something more powerful than reason: love.

Black Americans, despite themselves, are deeply patriotic; and the popularity of conspiracy theories is, in its own odd way, a heartfelt expression of this patriotism. Strange as it sounds, black conspiracy theories remain popular precisely because so few of us are willing to believe the alternative: that our depressed stature in the American hierarchy is due in large part to America's indifference to black suffering. We contrive elaborate ways of concealing it, but the idea that this country and only this country is ours, that, at the last, there is no place for us but here, is impossible to deny.

In 1963, Maya Angelou came to this realization while in Ghana. She and a band of fellow black expatriates, calling themselves the "Revolutionist Returnees," were there during the historic March on Washington, doing what most black radicals were doing: dressing like Africans, eating like Africans, calling themselves African. The Returnees had long since abandoned King's nonviolent philosophy for more radical postures. After word spread among them that W. E. B. DuBois, the great black nationalist, had died, the Returnees, in a powerful show of transatlantic solidarity, staged a march against the U.S. Embassy. When two soldiers came out the door, carrying a folded American flag, the crowd began to jeer, "This isn't Iwo Jima. . . . You haven't taken Bunker Hill, you know. This is Africa!"

The two soldiers, one black, one white, nervously fumbled the flag, and it began   9
to sag toward the ground. The black man hurriedly caught the cloth and "folded it
lovingly into the White soldier's arms." Angelou later concluded, "I shuddered to
think that while we wanted that flag dragged into the mud and sullied beyond repair we also wanted it pristine, its white stripes, summer cloud white. Watching it
wave in the breeze of a distance made us nearly choke with emotion. It lifted us up
with its promise and broke our hearts with its denial."

Glenn Loury echoed this theme in [The New Republic] after the Million Man   10
March. (See "One Man's March," November 6, 1995.) In the midst of the single
most extravagant display of black nationalism in American history, the real story,
Loury wrote, was the "young black guys . . . scrambling up the steps and lounging
between the columns of the National Gallery building . . . sharing an excited ex-
pectancy with Japanese tourists and rural whites as we all waited in line to tour the
White House . . . this is their country, too. So, embarrassed that I needed to remind myself of this fact, I wept."

Some will tell you that the persistence in the black community of speculation   11
over whether Thomas Jefferson sired black heirs is due to the fact that blacks are
less likely than whites to idolize Jefferson and therefore have no trouble facing the
truth of his paternity. But it really derives from an opposite impulse: the fact that,
quietly and mostly secretly, blacks do revere Thomas Jefferson quite as much as
whites, and they want to lay claim to the legacy of America as much as whites,
too. No less a purveyor of proper bourgeois norms than *Ebony* magazine has
heaped coverage on the issue of the Hemings-Jefferson family tree, all of whom
are reportedly tony members of black society in Virginia. So, too, conventional
wisdom holds that the switch from "black" to "African American" was occasioned
by the need to assert black peoples' African identity, but, again secretly, I think it
was to bind us, roundabout, to America. In that formulation, "African" is an adjective, "American" the supporting noun. It is the fear that America does not return
this powerful, if often concealed, devotion that drives blacks to embrace theories of
race-conspiracy.

John Edgar Wideman, commenting on his new novel canvassing four centuries of   12
black history, says "one way of visualizing African-American peoples' relationship to
America is a story of unrequited love . . . a love that has never been fully answered
or accepted." Black Americans have been engaged in a 300-year lover's quarrel with
their country; the fear that we are losing that quarrel drives us toward the madness and fevered speculations that every scorned lover knows.

Given the choice between neglect and conspiracy, black people will always   13
choose conspiracy. To be the victim of a constant, unchanging indifference is a far
greater torment than to be the object of obsession, no matter how warped. The
move from neglect to obsession is also a move from despair to rage, from a kind of
loneliness to righteous indignation. But that emotional move purchases more than
it bargains for.

And this is where the trouble starts. Anger, Aristotle argued a thousand years   14
ago, is the only passion that must be justified by speech and reason. In the anger of

the conspiracists, speech and reason take wild, unseemly, sometimes horrific, forms: outrageous theories about sun and ice people, blue-eyed evils, and big-headed scientists named Yakub; dreams of lives lived by numbers, and Egyptian miracles plundered by Greek pirates. It is a debilitating fantasy, because the anger we embrace has a chimera at its source. There are no ice people, no ravaging Greeks, no murderous Jews tainting our blood. But wrongs demand villains of equal stature—and only blue-eyed devils could conspire so wickedly against us.

This entire phenomenon rests on the acceptance of the racist assumption that   15
blacks are separate from the whole of society, even as we are part of it—a limb that may be easily amputated. As long as black people continue to accept (and white racists and black racialists continue to perpetuate) the idea that we are ancillary members of this country, that we can be ghettoized or segregated out of existence, we will forever doubt our place here. There is no "America" that exists outside of, separate and above, its citizens. Black Americans, as Ralph Ellison insisted his entire life, carry inside themselves the country's "most stringent testing and the possibility of its greatest human freedom." If America is indeed obsessed with black people, it is because it is obsessed with itself. It is not so much that "We are Americans" but, rather, "We are America."

MY RACE PROBLEM—AND OURS
Randall Kennedy

What is the proper role of race in determining how I, an American black, should   1
feel toward others? One response is that although I should not dislike people because of their race, there is nothing wrong with having a special—a *racial*—affection for other black people. Indeed, many would go further and maintain that something would be wrong with me if I did not sense and express racial pride, racial kinship, racial patriotism, racial loyalty, racial solidarity—synonyms for that amalgam of belief, intuition, and commitment that manifests itself when blacks treat blacks with more solicitude than they do those who are not black.

Some conduct animated by these sentiments has blended into the background   2
of daily routine, as when blacks who are strangers nonetheless speak to each other—"Hello," "Hey," "Yo"—or hug or give each other a soul handshake or refer to each other as "brother" or "sister." Other manifestations are more dramatic. For example, the Million Man March, which brought at least 500,000 black men to Washington, D.C., in 1995, was a demonstration predicated on the notion that blackness gives rise to racial obligation and that black people should have a special, closer, more affectionate relationship with their fellow blacks than with others in America's diverse society.

I reject this response to the question. Neither racial pride nor racial kinship of-   3
fers guidance that is intellectually, morally, or politically satisfactory.

* * *

I eschew racial pride because of my conception of what should properly be the   4
object of pride for an individual: something that he or she has accomplished. I can
feel pride in a good deed I have done or a good effort I have made. I cannot feel
pride in some state of affairs that is independent of my contribution to it. The color
of my skin, the width of my nose, the texture of my hair, and the various other signs
that prompt people to label me black constitute such a state of affairs. I did not
achieve my racial designation. It was something I inherited—like my nationality and
socio-economic starting place and sex—and therefore something I should not feel
proud of or be credited with. In taking this position I follow Frederick Douglass, the
great nineteenth-century reformer, who declared that "the only excuse for pride in
individuals . . . is in the fact of their own achievements." If the sun has created curled
hair and tanned skin, Douglass observed, "let the sun be proud of its achievement."

It is understandable why people have often made inherited group status an hon-   5
orific credential. Personal achievement is difficult to attain, and the lack of it often
leaves a vacuum that racial pride can easily fill. Thus even if a person has little to
show for himself, racial pride gives him status.

But maybe I am misconstruing what people mean by racial pride; perhaps it   6
means simply that one is unashamed of one's race. To that I have no objection. No
one should be ashamed of the labeling by which she or he is racially categorized,
because no one chooses her or his parents or the signs by which society describes
and sorts people. For this very same reason, however, no one should congratulate
herself on her race insofar as it is merely an accident of birth.

I suspect, however, that when most black people embrace the term "racial pride,"   7
they mean more than that they are unembarrassed by their race. They mean, echo-
ing Marcus Garvey, that "to be [black] is no disgrace, but an honor." Thus when
James Brown sings "Say It Loud—I'm Black and I'm Proud," he is heard by many
blacks as expressing not just the absence of shame but delight and assertiveness in
valuing a racial designation that has long been stigmatized in America.

There is an important virtue in this assertion of the value of black life. It combats   8
something still eminently in need of challenge: the assumption that because of their
race black people are stupid, ugly, and low, and that because of their race white
people are smart, beautiful, and righteous. But within some of the forms that this
assertiveness has taken are important vices—including the belief that because of
racial kinship blacks ought to value blacks more highly than others.

* * *

I reject the notion of racial kinship. I do so in order to avoid its burdens and to   9
be free to claim what the distinguished political theorist Michael Sandel labels "the
unencumbered self." The unencumbered self is free and independent, "unencumbered by aims and attachments it does not choose for itself," Sandel writes. "Freed
from the sanctions of custom and tradition and inherited status, unbound by moral
ties antecedent to choice, the self is installed as sovereign, cast as the author of the
only obligations that constrain." Sandel believes that the unencumbered self is an
illusion and that the yearning for it is a manifestation of a shallow liberalism that

"cannot account for certain moral and political obligations that we commonly recognize, even prize"—"obligations of solidarity, religious duties, and other moral ties that may claim us for reasons unrelated to a choice," which are "indispensable aspects of our moral and political experience." Sandel's objection to those who, like me, seek the unencumbered self is that they fail to appreciate loyalties and responsibilities that should be accorded moral force partly because they influence our identity, such that living by these attachments "is inseparable from understanding ourselves as the particular persons we are—as members of this family or city or nation or people, as bearers of that history, as citizens of this republic."

I admire Sandel's work and have learned much from it. But a major weakness in   10
it is a conflation of "is" and "ought." Sandel privileges what exists and has existed so much that his deference to tradition lapses into historical determinism. He faults the model of the unencumbered self because, he says, it cannot account for feelings of solidarity and loyalty that most people have not chosen to impose upon themselves but that they cherish nonetheless. This represents a fault, however, only if we believe that the unchosen attachments Sandel celebrates should be accorded moral weight. I am not prepared to do that simply on the basis that such attachments exist, have long existed, and are passionately felt. Feelings of primordial attachment often represent mere prejudice or superstition, a hangover of the childhood socialization from which many people never recover.

One defense of racial kinship takes the shape of an analogy between race and   11
family. This position was strikingly advanced by the nineteenth-century black-nationalist intellectual Alexander Crummell, who asserted that "a race *is* a family," that "race feeling, like the family feeling, is of divine origin," and that the extinction of race feeling is thus—fortunately, in his view—just as impossible as the extinction of family feeling.

Analogizing race to family is a potent rhetorical move used to challenge those   12
who, like me, are animated by a liberal, individualistic, and universalistic ethos that is skeptical of, if not hostile to, the particularisms—national, ethnic, religious, and racial—that seem to have grown so strong recently, even in arenas, such as major cosmopolitan universities, where one might have expected their demise. The central point of the challenge is to suggest that the norms I embrace will, or at least should, wobble and collapse in the face of claims on familial loyalty. Blood, as they say, is thicker than water.

One way to deal with the race-family analogy is to question its aptness on the   13
grounds that a race is so much more populous than what is commonly thought of as a family that race cannot give rise to the same, or even similar, feelings of loyalty. When we think of a family, we think of a small, close-knit association of people who grow to know one another intimately over time. A race, in contrast, is a conglomeration of strangers. Black men at the Million Man March assuredly called one another brothers. But if certain questions were posed ("Would you be willing to lend a hundred dollars to this brother, or donate a kidney to that one?"), it would have quickly become clear that many, if not most, of those "brothers" perceived one another as strangers—not so distant as whites, perhaps, but strangers nonetheless.

However, I do not want to rest my argument here. Rather, I want to accept the   14
race-family analogy in order to strengthen my attack on assumptions that privilege
status-driven loyalties (the loyalties of blood) over chosen loyalties (the loyalties of
will). In my view, many people, including legislators and judges, make far too much
of blood ties in derogation of ties created by loving effort.

A vivid illustration is provided by the following kind of child-custody decision. It   15
involves a child who has been separated from her parents and placed with adults
who assume the role of foster parents. These adults nurture her, come to love her,
and ultimately seek legally to become her new parents. If the "blood" parents of
the child do not interfere, the foster parents will have a good chance of doing this.
If, however, the blood parents say they want "their" child back, authorities in many
jurisdictions will privilege the blood connection and return the child—even if the
initial separation is mainly attributable to the fault of the blood parents, even if the
child has been with the foster parents for a long time and is prospering under their
care, even if the child views the foster parents as her parents and wants to stay
with them, and even if there is good reason to believe that the foster parents will
provide a more secure home setting than the child's blood parents. Judges make
such rulings in large part because they reflect the idolatry of "blood," which is an
ideological cousin to the racial beliefs I oppose.

Am I saying that, morally, blood ties are an insufficient, indeed bad, basis for pre-   16
ferring one's genetic relatives to others? Yes. I will rightly give the only life jacket on
the sinking ship to my mother as opposed to your mother, because I love my
mother (or at least I love her more than yours). I love my mother, however, not
because of a genetic tie but because over time she has done countless things that
make me want to love her. She took care of me when I could not take care of myself. She encouraged me. She provided for my future by taking me to the doctor
when appropriate, disciplining me, giving me advice, paying for my education. I love
her, too, because of qualities I have seen her exhibit in interactions with others—
my father, my brother, my sister, neighbors, colleagues, adversaries. The biological
connection helped to create the framework in which I have been able to see and
experience her lovable qualities. But it is deeds, not blood—doing, not being—that
is the morally appropriate basis for my preference for my mother over all other
mothers in the world.

* * *

Some contend, though, that "doing" is what lies at the foundation of black racial   17
kinship—that the reason one should feel morally compelled by virtue of one's
blackness to have and show racial solidarity toward other blacks is that preceding
generations of black people did things animated by racial loyalty which now benefit
all black people. These advocates would contend that the benefits bestowed—
for instance, *Brown* v. *Board of Education,* the Civil Rights Act of 1964, the Voting
Rights Act of 1965, and affirmative-action programs—impose upon blacks cor-
relative racial obligations. That is what many are getting at when they say that all

blacks, but particularly affluent ones, have a racial obligation to "give back" to the black community.

I agree that one should be grateful to those who have waged struggles for racial justice, sometimes at tremendous sacrifice. But why should my gratitude be racially bounded? Elijah Lovejoy, a white man murdered in Alton, Illinois, in 1837 for advocating the abolition of slavery, participated just as fervently in that great crusade as any person of my hue. The same could be said of scores of other white abolitionists. Coming closer to our time, not only courageous black people, such as Medgar Evers, Vernon Dahmer, and James Chaney, fought white supremacy in the shadow of death during the struggle for civil rights in the Deep South. White people like James Reeb and Viola Liuzzo were there too, as were Andrew Goodman and Michael Schwerner. Against this history I see no reason why paying homage to the struggle for racial justice and endeavoring to continue that struggle must entail any sort of racially stratified loyalty. Indeed, this history suggests the opposite.

18

* * *

Thus far I have mainly argued that a black person should not feel morally bound to experience and show racial kinship with other blacks. But what do I say to a person who is considering whether to *choose* to embrace racial kinship?

19

One person who has made this choice is Stephen L. Carter, a professor at Yale Law School and a well-known author. In a contribution to an anthology titled *Lure and Loathing: Essays on Race, Identity, and the Ambivalence of Assimilation,* Carter writes about his racial love for black people, declaring at one point that "to love one's people is to crave a kind of familyhood with them." Carter observes that this feeling of racial kinship influences his life concretely, affecting the way in which he values people's opinions of him. "The good opinions of black people . . . matter to me more," he writes, than the good opinions of white people. "That is my choice, and I cannot imagine ever making another." In *Reflections of an Affirmative Action Baby,* Carter gives another example of how racial kinship affects his life.

20

> Each December, my wife and I host a holiday dessert for the black students at the Yale Law School. . . . our hope is to provide for the students an opportunity to unwind, to escape, to renew themselves, to chat, to argue, to complain—in short, to relax. For my wife and myself, the party is a chance to get to know some of the people who will lead black America (and white America, too) into the twenty-first century. But more than that, we feel a deep emotional connection to them, through our blackness: we look at their youthful, enthusiastic faces and see ourselves. There is something affirming about the occasion—for them, we hope, but certainly for us. It is a reminder of the bright and supportive side of solidarity.

I contend that in the mind, heart, and soul of a teacher there should be no stratification of students such that a teacher feels closer to certain pupils than to others on grounds of racial kinship. No teacher should view certain students as his racial

21

"brothers and sisters" while viewing others as, well, mere students. Every student should be free of the worry that because of race, he or she will have less opportunity to benefit from what a teacher has to offer.

Friends with whom I have debated these matters object to my position, charging   22
that I pay insufficient attention to the complexity of the identities and roles that individuals assume in society, and that I thus ignore or minimize the ability of a black professor to be both a good teacher who serves all his students well *and* a good racial patriot who feels a special, racial affection for fellow blacks. These friends assert that I have no valid basis for complaint so long as the professor in his official duties is evenhanded in his treatment of students. By "official duties" they mean his conduct in the classroom, his accessibility during office hours, and his grading of students' academic performance. If these duties are met, they see no problem if the black professor, paying homage to his feelings of racial kinship, goes beyond what is officially required in his dealings with black students.

I see a variety of problems. For one thing, I find it inconceivable that there would   23
be no seepage from the personal sphere into the professional sphere. The students invited to the professor's home are surely being afforded an opportunity denied to those who are not invited—an opportunity likely to be reflected in, for instance, letters of recommendation to Judge So-and-So and Law Firm Partner Such-and-Such.

Another problem is that even in the absence of any tangible, dollars-and-cents   24
difference, the teacher's racial distinctions are likely to make a difference psychologically to the students involved. I have had the great benefit of being taught by wonderful teachers of various races, including white teachers. I never perceived a racial difference in the way that the best of these teachers treated me in comparison with my white classmates. Neither John McCune nor Sanford Levinson nor Eric Foner nor Owen Fiss ever gave me reason to believe that because of my color I took a back seat to any of my classmates when it came to having a claim on their attention. My respect for their conduct is accompanied by disappointment in others who seemed for reasons of racial kinship to invest more in white than in black students—who acted, in other words, in a way that remains unfortunately "normal" in this society.

Am I demanding that teachers make no distinctions between pupils? No. Distinc-   25
tions should be made. I am simply insisting that sentiments of racial kinship should play no role in making them.

Am I demanding that teachers be blind to race? No. It seems to me bad policy to   26
blind oneself to any potentially useful knowledge. Teachers should be aware of racial differences and differentiations in our society. They should be keenly aware, for instance, that historically and currently the dominant form of racial kinship in American life, the racial kinship that has been best organized and most destructive, is racial kinship mobilized in behalf of whites. This racial kinship has been animated by the desire to make and keep the United States "a white man's country." It is the racial kinship that politicians like Patrick Buchanan and Jesse Helms openly nurture and exploit. This is also the racial kinship that politicians take care to avoid chal-

lenging explicitly. A teacher should be aware of these and other racial facts of life in order to satisfactorily equip students with knowledge about their society.

The fact that race matters, however, does not mean that the salience and conse-
quences of racial distinctions are good or that race must continue to matter in the future. Nor does the brute sociological fact that race matters dictate what one's response to that fact should be.

Assuming that a teacher is aware of the different ways in which the race problem
bears down upon his students, how should he react? That depends on the circumstances.

Consider a case, for instance, in which white students were receiving consider-
able attention from teachers while black students were being widely ignored. In this case it would be morally correct for a professor, with his eyes focused on race, to reach out with special vigor to the black students. In this circumstance the black students would be more in need than the white students, whose needs for mentorship were already being abundantly met. This outreach, however, would be based not on racial kinship but on distributive justice.

* * *

The distinction is significant. For one thing, under the rationale of giving priority
of attention to those most in need, no racial boundary insulates professors from the obligation to attend to whatever maldistributions of mentorship they are in a position to correct. White professors are at least as morally obligated to address the problem as are black or other professors.

This is a point with ramifications that reach far beyond the university. For it is
said with increasing urgency by increasing numbers of people that the various so-
cial difficulties confronting black Americans are, for reasons of racial kinship, the moral responsibility of blacks, particularly those who have obtained some degree of affluence. This view should be rejected. The difficulties that disproportionately afflict black Americans are not "black problems" whose solutions are the special responsibility of black people. They are *our* problems, and their solution or amelio-
ration is the responsibility of us all, irrespective of race. That is why it is proper to object when white politicians use the term "you people" to refer to blacks. This happened when Ross Perot addressed the NAACP annual convention during the 1992 presidential election campaign. Many of those who objected to Perot's reference to "you people," however, turned right around and referred to blacks as "our people," thereby replicating the racial boundary-setting they had denounced.

A second reason why the justification for outreach matters is that unlike an appeal to racial kinship, an appeal to an ideal untrammeled by race enables any per-
son or group to be the object of solicitude. No person or group is racially excluded from the possibility of assistance, and no person or group is expected to help only "our own." If a professor reaches out in response to student need, for instance, that means that whereas black students may deserve special solicitude today, Latino

students or Asian-American students or white students may deserve it tomorrow. If Asian-American students have a greater need for faculty mentorship than black students, black professors as well as other professors should give them priority.

Some will argue that I ignore or minimize the fact that different groups are differently situated and that it is thus justifiable to impose upon blacks and whites different standards for purposes of evaluating conduct, beliefs, and sentiments. They will maintain that it is one thing for a white teacher to prefer his white students on grounds of racial kinship and a very different thing for a black teacher to prefer his black students on grounds of racial kinship. The former, they will say, is an expression of ethnocentrism that perpetuates racist inequality, whereas the latter is a laudable expression of racial solidarity that is needed to counter white domination.   33

Several responses are in order.   34

First, it is a sociological fact that blacks and whites are differently situated in American polity. But, again, a brute fact does not dictate the proper human response to it. That is a matter of choice—constrained, to be sure, but a choice nonetheless. In choosing how to proceed in the face of all that they encounter, blacks should insist, as did Martin Luther King Jr., that acting with moral propriety is itself a glorious goal. In seeking to attain that goal, blacks should be attuned not only to the all too human cruelties and weaknesses of others but also to the all too human cruelties and weaknesses in themselves. A good place to start is with the recognition that unless inhibited, every person and group will tend toward beliefs and practices that are self-aggrandizing. This is certainly true of those who inherit a dominant status. But it is also true of those who inherit a subordinate status. Surely one of the most striking features of human dynamics is the alacrity with which those who have been oppressed will oppress whomever they can once the opportunity presents itself. Because this is so, it is not premature to worry about the possibility that blacks or other historically subordinated groups will abuse power to the detriment of others.   35

Moreover, at long last blacks have sufficient power to raise urgent concerns regarding the abuse of it. Now, in enough circumstances to make the matter worth discussing, blacks are positioned to exploit their potential racial power effectively. Hence black attorneys wonder whether they should seek to elicit the racial loyalties of black jurors or judges in behalf of clients. Black jurors and judges face the question of whether they should respond to such appeals. Black professors face the question of whether racial loyalty should shape the extent to which they make themselves available to their students. Black employers or personnel directors face the question of whether racial loyalties should shape their hiring decisions. Were blacks wholly bereft of power, as some commentators erroneously assert, these and similar questions would not arise. Thus I evaluate arguments in favor of exempting blacks from the same standards imposed upon whites and conclude that typically, though perhaps not always, such arguments amount to little more than an elaborate camouflage for self-promotion or group promotion.   36

A second reason I resist arguments in favor of asymmetrical standards of judgment has to do with my sense of the requirements of reciprocity. I find it difficult   37 to accept that it is wrong for whites to mobilize themselves on a racial basis solely for purposes of white advancement but morally permissible for blacks to mobilize themselves on a racial basis solely for purposes of black advancement. I would propose a shoe-on-the-other-foot test for the propriety of racial sentiment. If a sentiment or practice would be judged offensive when voiced or implemented by anyone, it should be viewed as prima facie offensive generally. If we would look askance at a white professor who wrote that on grounds of racial kinship he values the opinions of whites more than those of blacks, then unless given persuasive reasons to the contrary, we should look askance at a black professor who writes that on grounds of racial kinship he values the opinions of blacks more than those of whites.

38   In some circumstances it is more difficult for blacks to give up the consolations of racial kinship than for whites to do so, insofar as whites typically have more resources to fall back on. But that should not matter, or at least should not matter decisively, if my underlying argument—that the sentiments and conduct of racial kinship are morally dubious—is correct. After all, it is surely more difficult for a poor person than for a rich one to give up the opportunity to steal untended merchandise. But we nevertheless rightly expect the poor person to give up that opportunity.

39   A third consideration is prudential. It is bad for the country if whites, blacks, or any other group engages in the politics of a racial kinship, because racial mobilization prompts racial countermobilization, further entrenching a pattern of sterile racial competition.

* * *

40   I anticipate that some will counter that this is what is happening, has happened, and will always happen, and that the best that blacks can expect is what they are able to exact from the white power structure through hard bargaining. In this view, racial unity, racial loyalty, racial solidarity, racial kinship—whatever one wants to call it—is absolutely essential for obtaining the best deal available. Therefore, in this view, my thesis is anathema, the most foolhardy idealism, a plan for ruination, a plea for unilateral disarmament by blacks in the face of a well-armed foe with a long history of bad intentions.

41   This challenge raises large issues that cannot be exhaustively dealt with here. But I should like to conclude by suggesting the beginning of a response, based on two observations.

42   First, it is noteworthy that those who have most ostentatiously asserted the imperatives of black racial solidarity—I think here particularly of Marcus Garvey, Elijah Muhammad, and Louis Farrakhan—are also those who have engaged in the most divisive, destructive, and merciless attacks on "brothers" and "sisters" who wished to follow a different path. My objection to the claims of racial pride and kinship stems in part from my fears of the effect on interracial relations. But it stems

also in large part from my fears of the stultifying effect on intraracial relations. Racial pride and kinship seem often to stunt intellectual independence. If racial loyalty is deemed essential and morally virtuous, then a black person's adoption of positions that are deemed racially disloyal will be seen by racial loyalists as a supremely threatening sin, one warranting the harsh punishments that have historically been visited upon alleged traitors.

Second, if one looks at the most admirable efforts by activists to overcome racial   43
oppression in the United States, one finds people who yearn for justice, not merely for the advancement of a particular racial group. One finds people who do not replicate the racial alienations of the larger society but instead welcome interracial intimacy of the most profound sorts. One finds people who are not content to accept the categories of communal affiliation they have inherited but instead insist upon bringing into being new and better forms of communal affiliation, ones in which love and loyalty are unbounded by race. I think here of Wendell Phillips and certain sectors of the abolitionist movement. I also think of James Farmer and the early years of the Congress of Racial Equality, and John Lewis and the early years of the Student Nonviolent Coordinating Committee. My favorite champion of this ethos, however, is a person I quoted at the beginning of this article, a person whom the sociologist Orlando Patterson aptly describes as "undoubtedly the most articulate former slave who ever lived," a person with whose words I would like to end. Frederick Douglass literally bore on his back the stigmata of racial oppression. Speaking in June of 1863, only five months after the Emancipation Proclamation and before the complete abolition of slavery, Douglass gave a talk titled "The Present and Future of the Colored Race in America," in which he asked whether "the white and colored people of this country [can] be blended into a common nationality, and enjoy together . . . under the same flag, the inestimable blessings of life, liberty, and the pursuit of happiness, as neighborly citizens of a common country." He answered: "I believe they can."

I, too, believe we can, if we are willing to reconsider and reconstruct the basis of   44
our feelings of pride and kinship.

TOWARD AN END OF BLACKNESS: AN ARGUMENT FOR THE SURRENDER OF RACE CONSCIOUSNESS

Jim Sleeper

Last January, not long after the national furor over the decision by an Oakland   1
school board to recognize "Ebonics," I happened upon a C-SPAN telecast of the awarding of seven Congressional Medals of Honor to black World War II veterans, each of whose "gallantry and intrepidity at the risk of his life" had been ignored for more than fifty years. President Clinton strode across the East Room of the White House to present the medals to Vernon Joseph Baker, seventy-seven, the only recipient still living, and to the others' families. "History has been made whole today,"

the President told the assembly. The honorees, he said, had "helped us find a way to become a more just, more free nation . . . more worthy of them and more true to its ideals."

History has not been made whole for American blacks, of course, and yet something almost archaic in the recipients' bearing and in the ceremony itself reminded me that none of us in the younger generations can say with certainty what an American wholeness might be or, within any such presumed wholeness, what blackness and whiteness might mean. If we have trouble thinking about race, possibly it's because we no longer know how to think about America itself.

At least Second Lieutenant Baker seemed to have less trouble fifty-two years ago than we do now. In April 1945, he single-handedly wiped out two German machine-gun nests in Viareggio, Italy, drew fire on himself to permit the evacuation of wounded comrades, and led his segregated battalion's advance through enemy minefields. Asked by reporters after the East Room ceremony whether he had ever given up hope of winning the medal, he "sounded surprised . . . as if the question presumed arrogance," said one report. "I never thought about getting it," Baker said. Asked why he had joined the army in the first place, Baker responded, "I was a young black man without a job." Ah, yes, *that.* Prodded to comment on having risked his life for his country while in a segregated unit, he answered, "I was an angry young man. We were all angry. But we had a job to do, and we did it. . . . My personal thoughts were that I knew things would get better, and I'm happy I'm here to see it."

Asked what the ceremony meant to her, Arlene Fox, widow of First Lieutenant John Fox, who died in Italy in 1944, said, "I think it's more than just what it means to this family. I think it sends a message . . . that when a man does his duty, his color isn't important."

Even in the prime of their anger, Baker and Fox, as well as the black leaders and writers of their generation, such as A. Philip Randolph, Bayard Rustin, Richard Wright, and Ralph Ellison, did not urge the importance of color as much as they found color imposed on them in ways that affronted something in them that wasn't "of color" at all. Proud though they were of what blacks had endured and would overcome (as Baker "knew" they would), they believed, before most of the rest of us, that after a long dalliance with a white manifest destiny the American republic would recognize no black or white sanction from God. In Baker's black 92nd Infantry Division, in Randolph's Brotherhood of Sleeping Car Porters, and in countless churches, blacks found it within themselves to treat society torn by racism not as inherently, eternally damned but as nevertheless worth joining and redeeming. Blacks who thought and acted that way shared with whites an important belief: not, alas, a consensus that racism was wrong but a deep certainty that, despite it, they were all bound passionately to the promise of the nation.

But what was that promise? It seems a long time now since the Smothers Brothers crooned "The Lord is colorblind" to what CBS must have assumed was a reasonably receptive national audience in the late 1960s. Today many of us would think such an audience naive or hypocritical, if not racist; it is almost as if any assertion that color isn't important insults what has come to be known as black pride. It is almost as if we fear that if race lost all weight in our social equations or disappeared entirely through interracial marriages and offspring, we would have nothing of value to say or give to one another. The problem is not that racism has grown stronger; it is that American civic life has become weaker—and not primarily because of racism. If we find it difficult to say that a black person's color isn't important, that is because we no longer know how to say that being an "American" is important—important enough to transcend racial identity in a classroom, in a jury room, or at the polls.

"An individual's moral character is formed by narrative and culture," writes the   7
sociologist Alan Wolfe. "Contracts between us are not enforced by laws or economic incentives; people adhere to social contracts when they feel that behind the contract lies a credible story of who they are and why their fates are linked to those of others." But what is America's story, when Vernon Baker's and Arlene Fox's descendants can climb to the very summit of the American Mt. Parnassus only to find there Dick Morris, *Vanity Fair,* Dennis Rodman, Time Warner Inc., and a retinue of dancing pollsters? The old American story of white manifest destiny, thankfully gone, was coherent enough to give blacks enough moral footing and traction to undo its moral affronts. By comparison, our new stories (the space shuttle *Challenger? Forrest Gump?* curricular gardens of multicultural delight?) are incoherent—much like Bill Clinton, truly a man of our time. In 1963, James Baldwin wondered aloud why any black American would want "to be integrated into a burning house." Obviously, he was not proposing resegregation. What, then? How were black Americans to think about themselves? Baldwin's emigration to France left the question open. And so have we all.

For a short while twenty years ago, Alex Haley's *Roots* seemed to offer an an-   8
swer. Turning on an intrepid black American's report of an astonishing encounter with his African past, it promised to weave a recovered, emblematic black story into the American national narrative, whose promise, whatever it was, would become more coherent for resolving the contradictions in its black story line. The story of Haley's story is worth retracing, because *Roots* wound up demonstrating both that blackness has no reliable myth of its own and that the summit of the American Parnassus is bare.

Published late in 1976, *Roots* became the next year's top nonfiction bestseller   9
(selling some 1.5 million copies in one year) after a record 130 million Americans saw the twelve-hour ABC miniseries it inspired. At least 250 colleges began offering credit courses based significantly on *Roots.* Travel agencies packaged back-to-Africa "*Roots*" tours. Even before TV had anointed Haley, I watched him tell a rapt audience of Harvard undergraduates, many of them black, of his meeting with the *griot,* or oral historian, of a village in Gambia from which, Haley said, his ancestor Kunta Kinte had been abducted to America in 1767. When he noted, as he had in the book, that the *griot* "had no way in the world to know that [his story's particu-

lars] had just echoed what I had heard all through my boyhood years on my grandma's front porch in Henning, Tennessee," there were gasps, and then the packed Quincy House dining hall was awash in tears.

With this unprecedented return by a black American to the scene of the primal   10
crime against his West African forbears—"an astonishing feat of genealogical detective work," Doubleday's original dust jacket had called it—the long, tortuous arc of black dispossession and yearning for a historic reckoning seemed, at last, to come home. *Roots* wasn't just Haley's own story; it was "a symbolic history of a people," he told a British reporter who raised doubts about its accuracy. "I, we, need a place called Eden. My people need a Pilgrim's Rock."

Indeed they did. The sudden lurch toward integration in the 1960s had disrupted   11
old black coping strategies, scrambling the coordinates of an uneasy racial coexistence and confounding pious hopes for a smooth transition to the integration envisioned by so many of Baker and Fox's generation. Some white-ethnic Roman Catholics and Jews, who had resisted their own assimilation into Anglo-Saxon norms, now intensified the subcultural revivals of "unmeltable ethnics." Responding to these assertions and, at the same time, to the equally unsettling prospect of black dissolution into whiteness through integration, a retaliatory black parochialism surfaced in public life for the first time in decades, assailing blacks whom it deemed too accommodating and forcing even assimilationist whites to acknowledge their own hyphenated Americanism.

Appearing amid the confusion, *Roots* at first startled, then relieved, pessimists on   12
both sides of the color line. By the grace of Haley's pilgrimage, it seemed, blacks could recover and share the true story of their dispossession. His mythopoetic triumph tugged at people's hearts, strengthening hopes for a decorous pluralism of peoples and a decent integration of persons. Americans of all colors were transfixed, even as charges emerged that Haley had taken too many folkloric and fictional liberties with material he'd claimed was historically true. (He settled out of court for $650,000 with author Harold Courlander, passages of whose novel *The African* Haley had pretty much copied.) Yet while *Roots* was denounced as a scholarly "fraud" by the historian Oscar Handlin, it was defended as an irresistible historical novel and pedagogical tool by other historians, including David Brion Davis, who told the *New York Times*, "We all need certain myths about the past, and one must remember how much in the myths about the Pilgrims or the immigrants coming here has been reversed." Haley received a "special" Pulitzer Prize and a rare "Citation of Merit" from a National Book Awards panel. ABC produced a second miniseries, *Roots: The Next Generations*, based on his new book *Search*, which chronicled his family's later tribulations and triumphs, including Haley's own work on *The Autobiography of Malcolm X*. "Now, as before," wrote Frank Rich in *Time*, "*Roots* occupies a special place in the history of our mass culture: it has the singular power to reunite all Americans, black and white, with their separate and collective pasts."

Today *Roots* is seldom mentioned. The History Channel's twentieth-anniversary   13
broadcast in February was little remarked by viewers or print commentators. The

book is still in stores—Doubleday calls it "an important title on the Dell backlist"—but it's not much read in college or high school courses. Few books on American racial matters mention Haley (who died in 1992). "*Roots?*" laughs the black religion scholar C. Eric Lincoln. "It's disappeared! Alex Haley was my friend, and I can tell you, he was a journeyman freelance writer, not a political writer or historian. He was given a status he didn't expect."

Roots's virtual disappearance can't be explained with the observation that it accomplished its mission by transforming the consciousness of a generation. Nor is it enough to say that *Roots* shortchanged women by portraying them as passive helpmates; Haley's misconstruals have been redressed by Alice Walker, Toni Morrison, Maya Angelou, and others. What drained *Roots* of its power with blacks as well as whites was a disillusionment in at least three dimensions. First, Haley idealized an Africa and a blackness that had been so overwhelmed (indeed, defined) by European invasion that they flourished only as negations of whiteness. Second, so complete was this submergence that Haley himself idealized American blacks' white abductors, if only implicitly, by telling blacks' own story in Western terms. In doing so he met his third pitfall: he tried to skirt Western mythology's tragic sense of life by telling an upbeat story for the mass market. *Roots* became the next "myth for a day," turning immense historical pain into immense profit. That was what slavery had done, and it was what *Roots* was meant to counter. But Haley's TV-friendly, docudramatic tale of black dispossession subtly reinforced the moral neutrality of classical liberalism, where markets are stronger than myths and history is not so much falsified as tamed.

In Africa, Haley depicted a precolonial Eden that hadn't existed, created his account of Kunta Kinte's youth there more out of current anthropology than history, paired all of this with the tale of his own communion with village elders in *post*-colonial Gambia, and inflated black Americans' expectations of sub-Saharan Africa, past and present. For American blacks, there was no there there: "Whatever Africans share," writes the Ghanaian intellectual Kwame Anthony Appiah, "we do not have a common traditional culture, common languages, a common religious or conceptual vocabulary. . . . [W]e do not even belong to a common race . . ." When Americans making visits inspired by Haley's epiphanies got past their African hosts, they found strangers as indifferent or hostile to them as "fellow whites" in my grandparents' native Lithuania might be to me were I to visit there now—strangers who may resemble me racially but whose religion, myths, and current interests have little in common with those of my Jewish "tribe," which they drove out or exterminated in the 1940s. American Afrocentrists (and liberal whites) seeking a romantic, Pan-African foil to a racist America found the same "ethnic cleansing" furiously under way in Nigeria, Rwanda, Zaire, and the Sudan. The very designation "black" was no more useful a moral, political, or cultural identification than is "white" in Lithuania or the Balkans. . . .

By assigning two white men to kidnap Kunta Kinte, Haley wasn't just distorting African history (in which the majority of slaves were captured and sold to whites by blacks); he was juggling European archetypes, borrowing Western literary themes meant to appeal to whites as well as blacks. He formulated sub-Saharan Africa's diffuse cultural attitudes into a Western myth of "exile" or "pilgrimage" for a black American audience that had internalized such notions from the Old Testament and for other Americans who needed to understand, in both Christian and Enlightenment terms, what their own forebears had perpetrated or suborned. But the African slaves had no signs that an African god was punishing them for their sins with an exile like that of the Jews, or blessing their "errand into the wilderness" like that of the Puritans. *Roots* wasn't a product of its protagonists' own mother culture; it was the work of a thoroughly Western, Christian, *American* writer who took as much from Hebrews and Puritans as from Africans. The novel is a Western account of a monstrous Western crime—a crime only according to Western religious and political standards that triumphed later to abolish slavery, as no African authority had done and as the Sudan hasn't done yet.

The irony, of course, is that the Western Enlightenment principles that supported African colonial liberation failed to prevent colonialism in the first place. And the ghastly, bloody misadventures in Europe since 1914 remind us that Western "values" often only ratchet up the human struggle with evil into unprecedented levels of barbarity. Even the notion that skin color is destiny derives from the ignorant scientific and cultural prejudices that draped nineteenth-century European imperialist states in all their clanking, blundering glory. 17

If there *is* any glory for the West in all this, it lies not in Western power but in Western thought, which projects triumphs out of tragedies and which, for all its misuses, nourishes the capacity for rational self-contradiction that alone has put such words as "democracy," "liberation," and "human rights" into the minds and hearts of peoples on all five continents. The West's true Eden is not Haley's bucolic African village but the garden in which a serpent corrupted two human beings with the apple of knowledge. Haley's distortions—like those of countless Western writers before him—misrepresented the West as much as they did Africa. When people of any color imagine their origins as racially pure and their heroes as morally infallible, they shrink from the tragic Western truth rooted in the story of The Fall. 18

They also misunderstand that if the West has any hope of improving on its work, that hope is in America. *Roots* showed, yet could not quite proclaim, that blacks brought as slaves into the American national experiment were so thoroughly uprooted from African sources that they were obliged to accept—for lack of anything else—the transcending liberal and Christian promises of their newfound land. Blacks internalized those promises and rehearsed their implementation long before Vernon Baker joined the 92nd Infantry Division in Italy. Precisely because they had not chosen to join this society, could not dominate it, and could not leave it, they had the highest possible stakes in redeeming its oft-stated, oft-violated ideal. 19

In that sense, surely, blacks became, for better or worse, the most "American" of us all. In a nation born of fraught departures, clean breaks, and fresh starts on new frontiers, they had to construct their moral universe, . . . in the words of Glenn 20

Loury, "almost out of nothing, almost heroically, in the cauldron of slavery. Or, as my friend Nathan Huggins puts it, 'We're not an alien population, we're the alienated population We're after getting our birthright. We're the son who hasn't been acknowledged.' See, *that binds you.* You can't turn back from it. Part of what I want is an acknowledgment of my place, my legitimacy, my belonging." The special depth of this need is what makes blacks "America's metaphor," as Richard Wright called them—moral witnesses to a self-creating America, as well as the country's harshest, sometimes most nihilist, assailants.

No wonder whites at first felt relieved by the *Roots* story: it had an ending happy   21
enough to make whites as well as blacks feel better about themselves. Although Haley didn't make much of the point in the book, white Americans had responded to black fortitude and resistance not only with cross burnings and guns but with the Abolitionist crusade, the great pedagogical project that sent W. E. B. Du Bois and hundreds of New England schoolteachers South during and after Reconstruction to "uplift" freed slaves. Despite all of their cruelties, condescensions, and overweening moral self-regard, white Americans participated in a civil-rights movement that combined black Baptist communalism with a race-transcendent, New England Calvinist theology of personal responsibility and justification by a faith beyond color.

So, if there was any real nobility in Haley's effort to weave blacks more vividly   22
into the American tapestry—to make Kunta Kinte a mythic American like Paul Revere—it consisted of the tragic but potentially redemptive fact that the author had to use the abductors' language and metaphysical looms. If *Roots* hasn't helped a new generation of American blacks to fit itself into the national tapestry, we must find something else that can, for separating the black thread would harm all of us even more than hiding it deep in the weave, as we've done in the past. Even Louis Farrakhan knows this, no matter how strenuously he insists on the separatist claims of the Nation of Islam. Not for nothing did he hold his march on the Washington Mall, amid all those white monuments, rather than in the part of the Mississippi Delta that the enthusiasts of his predecessor, Elijah Muhammad, once designated as the provisional seat of the Republic of New Africa. Had Farrakhan gone there, many fewer black men would have followed.

Yet *Roots* failed to forestall the ascendancy of Farrakhan not only because Haley   23
dissembled about Africa and juggled tragic Western myths to tell a black story but also because those myths are losing their traction against the forces of a global market that employs the techniques of mass marketing to guarantee the liquidity of collective amnesia. The relentless logic of the market overwhelms not only the worst racist pretensions, white as well as black, but also the best American civic cultural traditions. Commitments to reason, individual rights, and freedom of contract aren't "Eurocentric" ruses meant to co-opt and subordinate nonwhites; they embody historic human gains, and it would be folly to abandon them for fantasies of racial destiny.

When Vernon Baker said, "I knew things would get better," surely he did not think   24
they would get "blacker" in the sense that blacks would become so protective of

blackness that whites' enthusiasm at the prospect of Colin Powell's running for president would engender marked black ambivalence about it. Nor, surely, did Baker's "better" characterize extenuated rationalizations of Ebonics, gangsta-rap celebrations of black self-immolation, or widespread black support for O. J. Simpson's acquittal and the "black" jurisprudence and epistemology invoked to excuse it.

Similarly, when Arlene Fox said, "When a man does his duty, his color isn't important," she was not applauding some recent efforts to redefine "duty" in ways that make one's skin color one's destiny all over again. Three years ago, while defending race-norming in college admissions and a dizzying array of campus "diversity" programs that transform everyone with a dark skin into a walking placard for disadvantage, Rutgers University president Francis Lawrence slid, infamously, into lingo about blacks' "genetic hereditary background." It was an all too emblematically liberal Freudian slip, born of believing that the best way to overcome racism's legacies is to create separate, remedial tracks for blacks while denying that one is doing anything of the sort by enshrining and embellishing disparities as cultural "differences."   25

On the other hand: Colin Powell could yet become president, and Oprah Winfrey could own a movie studio; black candidates keep winning in white-majority districts, and more blacks and nonblacks are marrying, which explains why many of the novels in black bookstores are about multiracial relationships. Many blacks, in fact, have anticipated and met a challenge now facing everyone else in the country; we are all being "abducted" from our ancient ethnic moorings by powerful currents we no longer control or fully comprehend. Thanks significantly to blacks, who started from "nothingness" here, other Americans have a better start on what now has become a more general problem. Europeans sometimes say that white Americans walk and talk "black." The observation fits neatly with the feeling among some Africans that black Americans are not "black" at all. America needs blacks not because it needs blackness but because it needs what they've learned on their long way out of blackness—what others of us have yet to learn on the journeys we need to take out of whiteness.   26

For all its wrong turns and dead ends, the quest by black Americans for acknowledgment and belonging in our national life is the most powerful epic of unrequited love in the history of the world. "Afrocentism," Gerald Early has written, "is a historiography of decline, like the mythic epic of the [lost, antebellum] South. The tragedy is that black people fail to see their 'Americanization' as one of the greatest human triumphs of the past 500 years." Even if every broken heart could be mended and every theft of opportunity be redressed, there would remain a black community of memory, loss, and endurance. Yet the country's special debt to blacks cannot be paid by anything less than an inclusion that brings the implosion of the identity of blackness—and, with it, of whiteness. The most that blacks can expect of the rest of us (and the most that Vernon Baker and Arlene Fox have expected) is that we will embrace and judge blacks—and let ourselves in turn be embraced and judged by them—as individual fellow participants in our common national experiment. As brothers, some used to say.   27

Letters to the Editor

I was both dismayed and offended by Jim Sleeper's essay "Toward an End of Blackness" [May], which informs us that race is a social construction, an idea that is not exactly news to black people in the United States. We happen to know that we are not stupid, that we are not lazy, and that we are not bent toward criminality. We know that we will succeed if we are given the opportunity, because, as Sleeper rightly comments, the success of the "American experiment" is founded on the presence and participation of Africans. Sleeper is absolutely right when he says that we black Americans are as American as you can get. Unfortunately, he perpetuates the racism that created "blackness" in the first place. It's not blackness that's the problem, but "whiteness."

In his writings on race and identity, James Baldwin reiterated time and again that to be "white" in America is, essentially, to be "not-black." Witness the "wigger" fad among some of America's disaffected white youths. They wear "colors" and baggy pants that fall off their hips, and speak what they perceive to be black English. And the wigger phenomenon isn't new; generations of rebellious white American youths have aspired to an image of blackness that would repel their white elders.

An unwillingness to recognize and value difference is the source of the American problem with race. And it's a problem rooted in mainstream America, not in black America.

DAVID WRIGHT

Albion, Mich.

Jim Sleeper's essay on blackness is an amazing example of white conservatives' penchant for criticizing African-American behavior. It blatantly violates one of the unwritten but well-known rules of ethnic-group etiquette: members of one ethnic community should not comment publicly on what might be called the "organic patterns" of behavior found within another ethnic community. Commentators such as Sleeper justify their effrontery to blacks by arguing that the black intelligentsia should just quiet down and defer to a newly emerging "colorblindness." This is simply another attempt to silence black dissent.

Sleeper also expends considerable energy on a critique of Alex Haley's 1976 bestseller, *Roots*. Well, *Roots* got too damn much attention in the first place. Even though other ethnic groups' quasi-mythical stories have been similarly hyped and commercialized, Sleeper's shallow understanding of the political and cultural patterns among black Americans leads him to the bizarre conclusion that *Roots* was actually the canonical text for black Americans that the media claimed it to be. His thimbleful of knowledge of black history leads him to believe that although black folks have been on American shores since the seventeenth century, they waited until the appearance of Haley's book before they could proclaim a viable understanding of their tragic history.

Sleeper and other conservatives who trash African-American reality blithely ignore the rich world of black meanings found in traditional African-American music and in the oral tales and spirituals that have been handed down from our ancestors. These deep cultural sources are the true context of black American experience and represent a massive historical counterweight to the central falsehood of Sleeper's article.

MARTIN KILSON
Committee on African Studies
Harvard University
Cambridge, Mass.

Jim Sleeper's essay is itself an ambiguous example of his thesis that black people are an integral part of the great experiment that is America. Sleeper, a non-black writing for a non-black audience, and I, a black man, are participants in his literary experiment. But I am the specimen in the petri dish, and my participation is not at the same level as that of Sleeper and his audience. Thus the writer-reader relationship excludes me, trapping me in my petri dish. I, the specimen, am helpless, as the writer pretends to capture the sentiments of my people, whose heart he does not know. He is unable to convey what my second-class American citizenship means to me; nor does he understand my need to feel connected to the elsewhere-land of my racial heritage, even if that connection is as mythical as a St. Patrick's Day parade.

Sleeper tells a story about blackness that is not true, a story that will not change the day-to-day reactions of my purported compatriots to my attempts to live my own African-American dream. Sleeper has not discovered a hidden secret to race relations in the United States. He has propagated an old lie in a clever new disguise.

D. JOSEPH WHITTEN
New York City

I'M BLACK, YOU'RE WHITE, WHO'S INNOCENT?
Shelby Steele

It is a warm, windless California evening, and the dying light that covers the red-brick patio is tinted pale orange by the day's smog. Eight of us, not close friends, sit in lawn chairs sipping chardonnay. A black engineer and I (we had never met before) integrate the group. A psychologist is also among us, and her presence encourages a surprising openness. But not until well after the lovely twilight dinner has been served, when the sky has turned to deep black and the drinks have long since changed to scotch, does the subject of race spring awkwardly upon us. Out of nowhere the engineer announces, with a coloring of accusation in his voice, that it bothers him to send his daughter to a school where she is one of only three black children. "I didn't realize my ambition to get ahead would pull me into a world where my daughter would lose touch with her blackness," he says.

Over the course of the evening we have talked about money, infidelity, past and present addictions, child abuse, even politics. Intimacies have been revealed, fears named. But this subject, race, sinks us into one of those shaming silences where eye contact terrorizes. Our host looks for something in the bottom of his glass. Two women stare into the black sky as if to locate the Big Dipper and point it out to us. Finally, the psychologist seems to gather herself for a challenge, but it is too late. "Oh, I'm sure she'll be just fine," says our hostess, rising from her chair. When she excuses herself to get the coffee, the two sky gazers offer to help.

With three of us now gone, I am surprised to see the engineer still silently hold- 3
ing his ground. There is a willfulness in his eyes, an inner pride. He knows he has said something awkward, but he is determined not to give a damn. His unwavering eyes intimidate me. At last the host's head snaps erect. He has an idea. "The hell with coffee," he says. "How about some of the smoothest brandy you ever tasted?" An idea made exciting by the escape it offers. Gratefully we follow him back into the house, quickly drink his brandy, and say our good-byes.

An autopsy of this party might read: death induced by an abrupt and lethal injec- 4
tion of the American race issue. An accurate if superficial assessment. Since it has been my fate to live a rather integrated life, I have often witnessed sudden deaths like this. The threat of them, if not the reality, is a part of the texture of integra-tion. In the late 1960s, when I was just out of college, I took a delinquent's delight in playing the engineer's role, and actually developed a small reputation for playing it well. Those were the days of flagellatory white guilt; it was such great fun to pin-ion some professor or housewife or, best of all, a large group of remorseful whites, with the knowledge of both their racism and their denial of it. The adolescent im-pulse to sneer at convention, to startle the middle-aged with doubt, could be indulged under the guise of racial indignation. And how could I lose? My victims—earnest liberals for the most part—could no more crawl out from under my accu-sations than Joseph K. in Kafka's *Trial* could escape the amorphous charges brought against him. At this odd moment in history the world was aligned to facilitate my immaturity.

About a year of this was enough: the guilt that follows most cheap thrills caught 5
up to me, and I put myself in check. But the impulse to do it faded more slowly. It was one of those petty talents that is tied to vanity, and when there were ebbs in my self-esteem the impulse to use it would come alive again. In integrated situa-tions I can still feel the faint itch. But then there are many youthful impulses that still itch, and now, just inside the door of mid-life, this one is least precious to me.

In the literature classes I teach, I often see how the presence of whites all but 6
seduces some black students into provocation. When we come to a novel by a black writer, say Toni Morrison, the white students can easily discuss the human motivations of the black characters. But, inevitably, a black student, as if by reflex, will begin to set in relief the various racial problems that are the background of these characters' lives. This student's tone will carry a reprimand: the class is afraid to confront the reality of racism. Classes cannot be allowed to die like dinner par-ties, however. My latest strategy is to thank that student for his or her moral vigi-lance, and then appoint the young man or woman as the class's official racism

monitor. But even if I get a laugh—I usually do, but sometimes the student is particularly indignant, and it gets uncomfortable—the strategy never quite works. Our racial division is suddenly drawn in neon. Overcaution spreads like spilled paint. And, in fact, the black student who started it all does become a kind of monitor. The very presence of this student imposes a new accountability on the class.

I think those who provoke this sort of awkwardness are operating out of a black identity that obliges them to badger white people about race almost on principle. Content hardly matters. (For example, it made no sense for the engineer to expect white people to sympathize with his anguish over sending his daughter to school with *white* children.) Race indeed remains a source of white shame; the goal of these provocations is to put whites, no matter how indirectly, in touch with this collective guilt. In other words, these provocations I speak of are *power* moves, little shows of power that try to freeze the "enemy" in self-consciousness. They gratify and inflate the provocateur. They are the underdog's bite. And whites, far more secure in their power, respond with a self-contained and tolerant silence that is, itself, a show of power. What greater power than that of non-response, the power to let a small enemy sizzle in his own juices, to even feel a little sad at his frustration just as one is also complimented by it. Black anger always, in a way, flatters white power. In America, to know that one is not black is to feel an extra grace, a little boost of impunity.

I think the real trouble between the races in America is that the races are not just races but competing power groups—a fact that is easily minimized perhaps because it is so obvious. What is not so obvious is that this is true quite apart from the issue of class. Even the well-situated middle-class (or wealthy) black is never completely immune to that peculiar contest of power that his skin color subjects him to. Race is a separate reality in American society, an entity that carries its own potential for power, a mark of fate that class can soften considerably but not eradicate.

The distinction of race has always been used in American life to sanction each race's pursuit of power in relation to the other. The allure of race as a human delineation is the very shallowness of the delineation it makes. Onto this shallowness—mere skin and hair—men can project a false depth, a system of dismal attributions, a series of malevolent or ignoble stereotypes that skin and hair lack the substance to contradict. These dark projections then rationalize the pursuit of power. Your difference from me makes you bad, and your badness justifies, even demands, my pursuit of power over you—the oldest formula for aggression known to man. Whenever much importance is given to race, power is the primary motive.

But the human animal almost never pursues power without first convincing himself that he is *entitled* to it. And this feeling of entitlement has its own precondition: to be entitled one must first believe in one's innocence, at least in the area where one wishes to be entitled. By innocence I mean a feeling of essential goodness in relation to others and, therefore, superiority to others. Our innocence always inflates us and deflates those we seek power over. Once inflated we are entitled; we are in fact licensed to go after the power our innocence tells us we deserve. In this sense, *innocence is power*. Of course, innocence need not be genuine or real in any objective sense, as the Nazis demonstrated not long ago. Its only test is whether or not we can convince ourselves of it.

I think the racial struggle in America has always been primarily a struggle for in-   11 nocence. White racism from the beginning has been a claim of white innocence and, therefore, of white entitlement to subjugate blacks. And in the 1960s, as went innocence so went power. Blacks used the innocence that grew out of their long subjugation to seize more power, while whites lost some of their innocence and so lost a degree of power over blacks. Both races instinctively understand that to lose innocence is to lose power (in relation to each other). Now to be innocent some-one else must be guilty, a natural law that leads the races to forge their innocence on each other's backs. The inferiority of the black always makes the white man su-perior; the evil might of whites makes blacks good. This pattern means that both races have a hidden investment in racism and racial disharmony, despite their good intentions to the contrary. Power defines their relations, and power requires inno-cence, which, in turn, requires racism and racial division.

I believe it was this hidden investment that the engineer was protecting when he   12 made his remark—the white "evil" he saw in a white school "depriving" his daugh-ter of her black heritage confirmed his innocence. Only the logic of power ex-plained this—he bent reality to show that he was once again a victim of the white world and, as a victim, innocent. His determined eyes insisted on this. And the whites, in their silence, no doubt protected their innocence by seeing him as an un-gracious troublemaker—his bad behavior underscoring their goodness. I can only guess how he was talked about after the party. But it isn't hard to imagine that his blunder gave everyone a lift. What none of us saw was the underlying game of power and innocence we were trapped in, or how much we needed a racial im-passe to play that game.

When I was a boy of about twelve, a white friend of mine told me one day that   13 his uncle, who would be arriving the next day for a visit, was a racist. Excited by the prospect of seeing such a man, I spent the following afternoon hanging around the alley behind my friend's house, watching from a distance as this uncle worked on the engine of his Buick. Yes, here was evil and I was compelled to look upon it. And I saw evil in the sharp angle of his elbow as he pumped his wrench to tighten nuts, I saw it in the blade-sharp crease of his chinos, in the pack of Lucky Strikes that threatened to slip from his shirt pocket as he bent, and in the way his concen-tration seemed to shut out the human world. He worked neatly and efficiently, wiping his hands constantly, and I decided that evil worked like this.

I felt a compulsion to have this man look upon me so that I could see evil—so   14 that I could see the face of it. But when he noticed me standing beside his toolbox, he said only, "If you're looking for Bobby, I think he went up to the school to play baseball." He smiled nicely and went back to work. I was stunned for a moment, but then I realized that evil could be sly as well, could smile when it wanted to trick you.

Need, especially hidden need, puts a strong pressure on perception, and my need   15
to have this man embody white evil was stronger than any contravening evidence.
As a black person you always hear about racists but never meet any. And I needed
to incarnate this odious category of humanity, those people who hated Martin
Luther King, Jr., and thought blacks should "go slow" or not at all. So, in my mental
dictionary, behind the term "white racist," I inserted this man's likeness. I would
think of him and say to myself, "There is no reason for him to hate black people.
Only evil explains unmotivated hatred." And this thought soothed me; I felt innocent. If I hated white people, which I did not, at least I had a reason. His evil com-
manded me to assert in the world the goodness he made me confident of in myself.

In looking at this man I was *seeing for innocence*—a form of seeing that has more   16
to do with one's hidden need for innocence (and power) than with the person or
group one is looking at. It is quite possible, for example, that the man I saw that
day was not a racist. He did absolutely nothing in my presence to indicate that he
was. I invested an entire afternoon in seeing not the man but my innocence through
the man. *Seeing for innocence* is, in this way, the essence of racism—the use of others as a means to our own goodness and superiority.

The loss of innocence has always to do with guilt, Kierkegaard tells us, and it has   17
never been easy for whites to avoid guilt where blacks are concerned. For whites,
seeing for innocence means seeing themselves and blacks in ways that minimize white
guilt. Often this amounts to a kind of white revisionism, as when President Reagan
declares himself "color-blind" in matters of race. The President, like many of us, may
aspire to racial color blindness, but few would grant that he has yet reached this
sublimely guiltless state. The statement clearly revises reality, moves it forward into
some heretofore unknown America where all racial determinism will have vanished.
I do not think that Ronald Reagan is a racist, as that term is commonly used, but
neither do I think that he is capable of seeing color without making attributions,
some of which may be negative—nor am I, or anyone else I've ever met.

So why make such a statement? I think Reagan's claim of color blindness with   18
regard to race is really a claim of racial innocence and guiltlessness—the precondi-
tions for entitlement and power. This was the claim that grounded Reagan's campaign against special entitlement programs—affirmative action, racial quotas, and so
on—that black power had won in the Sixties. Color blindness was a strategic assumption of innocence that licensed Reagan's use of government power against
black power.

I do not object to Reagan's goals in this so much as the presumption of inno-   19
cence by which he rationalized them. I, too, am strained to defend racial quotas
and any affirmative action that supersedes merit. And I believe there is much that
Reagan has to offer blacks. His emphasis on traditional American values—individual
initiative, self-sufficiency, strong families—offers what I think is the most enduring
solution to the demoralization and poverty that continue to widen the gap between blacks and whites in America. Even his de-emphasis of race is reasonable in
a society where race only divides. But Reagan's posture of innocence undermines

any beneficial interaction he might have with blacks. For blacks instinctively sense that a claim of racial innocence always precedes a power move against them. Reagan's pretense of innocence makes him an adversary, and makes his quite reasonable message seem vindictive. You cannot be innocent of a man's problem and expect him to listen.

I'm convinced that the secret of Reagan's "teflon" coating, his personal popularity apart from his policies and actions, has been his ability to offer mainstream America a vision of itself as innocent and entitled (unlike Jimmy Carter, who seemed to offer only guilt and obligation). Probably his most far-reaching accomplishment has been to reverse somewhat the pattern by which innocence came to be distributed in the Sixties, when outsiders were innocent and insiders were guilty. Corporations, the middle class, entrepreneurs, the military—all villains in the Sixties—either took on a new innocence in Reagan's vision or were designated as protectors of innocence. But again, for one man to be innocent another man must be bad or guilty. Innocence imposes, *demands,* division and conflict, a right/wrong view of the world. And this, I feel, has led to the underside of Reagan's achievement. His posture of innocence draws him into a partisanship that undermines the universality of his values. He can't sell these values to blacks and others because he has made blacks into the bad guys and outsiders who justify his power. It is humiliating for a black person to like Reagan because Reagan's power is so clearly derived from a distribution of innocence that leaves a black with less of it, and the white man with more. 20

Black Americans have always had to find a way to handle white society's presumption of racial innocence whenever they have sought to enter the American mainstream. Louis Armstrong's exaggerated smile honored the presumed innocence of white society—I will not bring you your racial guilt if you will let me play my music. Ralph Ellison calls this "masking"; I call it bargaining. But whatever it's called, it points to the power of white society to enforce its innocence. I believe this power is greatly diminished today. Society has reformed and transformed— Miles Davis never smiles. Nevertheless, this power has not faded altogether; blacks must still contend with it. 21

Historically, blacks have handled white society's presumption of innocence in two ways: they have bargained with it, granting white society its innocence in exchange for entry into the mainstream; or they have challenged it, holding that innocence hostage until their demand for entry (or other concessions) was met. A bargainer says, *I already believe you are innocent (good, fair-minded) and have faith that you will prove it.* A challenger says, *If you are innocent, then prove it.* Bargainers *give* in hope of receiving; challengers *withhold* until they receive. Of course, there is risk in both approaches, but in each case the black is negotiating his own self-interest against the presumed racial innocence of the larger society. 22

Clearly the most visible black bargainer on the American scene today is Bill Cosby. His television show is a perfect formula for black bargaining in the Eighties. The remarkable Huxtable family—with its doctor/lawyer parent combination, its 23 drug-free, college-bound children, and its wise yet youthful grandparents—is a blackface version of the American dream. Cosby is a subscriber to the American identity, and his subscription confirms his belief in its fair-mindedness. His vast audience knows this, knows that Cosby will never assault their innocence with racial guilt. Racial controversy is all but banished from the show. The Huxtable family never discusses affirmative action.

The bargain Cosby offers his white viewers—I will confirm your racial innocence if you accept me—is a good deal for all concerned. Not only does it allow whites to enjoy Cosby's humor with no loss of innocence, but it actually enhances their innocence by implying that race is not the serious problem for blacks that it once was. If anything, the success of this handsome, affluent black family points to the fair-mindedness of whites who, out of their essential goodness, changed society so that black families like the Huxtables could succeed. Whites can watch *The Cosby Show* and feel complimented on a job well done.

24

The power that black bargainers wield is the power of absolution. On Thursday nights, Cosby, like a priest, absolves his white viewers, forgives and forgets the sins of the past. (Interestingly, Cosby was one of the first blacks last winter to publicly absolve Jimmy the Greek for his well-publicized faux pas about black athletes.) And for this he is rewarded with an almost sacrosanct status. Cosby benefits from what might be called a gratitude factor. His continued number-one rating may have something to do with the (white) public's gratitude at being offered a commodity so rare in our time; he tells his white viewers each week that they are okay, and that this black man is not going to challenge them.

25

When a black bargains, he may invoke the gratitude factor and find himself cherished beyond the measure of his achievement; when he challenges, he may draw the dark projections of whites and become a source of irritation to them. If he moves back and forth between these two options, as I think many blacks do today, he will likely baffle whites. It is difficult for whites to either accept or reject such blacks. It seems to me that Jesse Jackson is such a figure—many whites see Jackson as a challenger by instinct and a bargainer by political ambition. They are uneasy with him, more than a little suspicious. His powerful speech at the 1984 Democratic convention was a masterpiece of bargaining. In it he offered a Kinglike vision of what America could be, a vision that presupposed Americans had the fair-mindedness to achieve full equality—an offer in hope of a return. A few days after this speech, looking for rest and privacy at a lodge in Big Sur, he and his wife were greeted with standing ovations three times a day when they entered the dining room for meals. So much about Jackson is deeply American—his underdog striving, his irrepressible faith in himself, the daring of his ambition, and even his stubbornness. These qualities point to his underlying faith that Americans can respond to him despite his race, and this faith is a compliment to Americans, an offer of innocence.

26

But Jackson does not always stick to the terms of his bargain—he is not like Cosby on TV. When he hugs Arafat, smokes cigars with Castro, refuses to repudiate Farrakhan, threatens a boycott of major league baseball, or, more recently, talks

27

of "corporate barracudas," "pension-fund socialism," and "economic violence," he looks like a challenger in bargainer's clothing, and his positions on the issues look like familiar protests dressed in white-paper formality. At these times he appears to be revoking the innocence so much else about him seems to offer. The old activist seems to come out of hiding once again to take white innocence hostage until whites prove they deserve to have it. In his candidacy there is a suggestion of protest, a fierce insistence on his *right* to run, that sends whites a message that he may secretly see them as a good bit less than innocent. His dilemma is to appear the bargainer while his campaign itself seems to be a challenge.

There are, of course, other problems that hamper Jackson's bid for the Demo-   28
cratic presidential nomination. He has held no elective office, he is thought too flamboyant and opportunistic by many, there are rather loud whispers of "charac-ter" problems. As an individual he may not be the best test of a black man's chances for winning so high an office. Still, I believe it is the aura of challenge surrounding him that hurts him most. Whether it is right or wrong, fair or unfair, I think no black candidate will have a serious chance at his party's nomination, much less the presidency, until he can convince white Americans that he can be trusted to pre-serve *their* sense of racial innocence. Such a candidate will have to use his power of absolution; he will have to flatly forgive and forget. He will have to bargain with white innocence out of a genuine belief that it really exists. There can be no faking it. He will have to offer a vision that is passionately raceless, a vision that strongly condemns any form of racial politics. This will require the most courageous kind of leadership, leadership that asks all the people to meet a new standard.

Now the other side of America's racial impasse: How do blacks lay claim to their   29
racial innocence?

The most obvious and unarguable source of black innocence is the victimization   30
that blacks endured for centuries at the hands of a race that insisted on black infe-riority as a means to its own innocence and power. Like all victims, what blacks lost in power they gained in innocence—innocence that, in turn, entitled them to pursue power. This was the innocence that fueled the civil rights movement of the Sixties, and that gave blacks their first real power in American life—victimization metamorphosed into power via innocence. But this formula carries a drawback that I believe is virtually as devastating to blacks today as victimization once was. It is a formula that binds the victim to his victimization by linking his power to his sta-tus as a victim. And this, I'm convinced, is the tragedy of black power in America today. It is primarily a victim's power, grounded too deeply in the entitlement de-rived from past injustice and in the innocence that Western/Christian tradition has always associated with poverty.

Whatever gains this power brings in the short run through political action, it un-   31
dermines in the long run. Social victims may be collectively entitled, but they are all too often individually demoralized. Since the social victim has been oppressed by society, he comes to feel that his individual life will be improved more by changes *in* society than by his own initiative. Without realizing it, he makes society rather than himself the agent of change. The power he finds in his victimization may lead him

to collective action against society, but it also encourages passivity within the sphere of his personal life.

This past summer I saw a television documentary that examined life in Detroit's 32
inner city on the twentieth anniversary of the riots there in which forty-three people were killed. A comparison of the inner city then and now showed a decline in the quality of life. Residents feel less safe than they did twenty years ago, drug trafficking is far worse, crimes by blacks against blacks are more frequent, housing remains substandard, and the teenage pregnancy rate has skyrocketed. Twenty years of decline and demoralization, even as opportunities for blacks to better themselves have increased. This paradox is not peculiar to Detroit. By many measures, the majority of blacks—those not yet in the middle class—are further behind whites today than before the victories of the civil rights movement. But there is a reluctance among blacks to examine this paradox, I think, because it suggests that racial victimization is not our real problem. If conditions have worsened for most of us as racism has receded, then much of the problem must be of our own making. But to fully admit this would cause us to lose the innocence we derive from our victimization. And we would jeopardize the entitlement we've always had to challenge society. We are in the odd and self-defeating position where taking responsibility for bettering ourselves feels like a surrender to white power.

So we have a hidden investment in victimization and poverty. These distressing 33
conditions have been the source of our only real power, and there is an unconscious sort of gravitation toward them, a complaining celebration of them. One sees evidence of this in the near happiness with which certain black leaders recount the horror of Howard Beach and other recent (and I think over-celebrated) instances of racial tension. As one is saddened by these tragic events, one is also repelled at the way some black leaders—agitated to near hysteria by the scent of victim-power inherent in them—leap forward to exploit them as evidence of black innocence and white guilt. It is as though they sense the decline of black victimization as a loss of standing and dive into the middle of these incidents as if they were reservoirs of pure black innocence swollen with potential power.

Seeing for innocence pressures blacks to focus on racism and to neglect the individual initiative that would deliver them from poverty—the only thing that finally 34
delivers anyone from poverty. With our eyes on innocence we see racism everywhere and miss opportunity even as we stumble over it. About 70 percent of black students at my university drop out before graduating—a flight from opportunity that racism cannot explain. It is an injustice that whites can see *for innocence* with more impunity than blacks can. The price whites pay is a certain blindness to themselves. Moreover, for whites *seeing for innocence* continues to engender the bad faith of a long-disgruntled minority. But the price blacks pay is an ever-escalating poverty that threatens to make the worst off of them a permanent underclass. Not fair, but real.

Challenging works best for the collective, while bargaining is more the individual's suit. From this point on, the race's advancement will come from the efforts of 35
its individuals. True, some challenging will be necessary for a long time to come.

But bargaining is now—today—a way for the black individual to *join* the larger society, to make a place for himself or herself.

"Innocence is ignorance," Kierkegaard says, and if this is so, the claim of innocence amounts to an insistence on ignorance, a refusal to know. In their assertions of innocence both races carve out very functional areas of ignorance for themselves—territories of blindness that license a misguided pursuit of power. Whites gain superiority by *not* knowing blacks; blacks gain entitlement by *not* seeing their own responsibility for bettering themselves. The power each race seeks in relation to the other is grounded in a double-edged ignorance, ignorance of the self as well as the other.   36

The original sin that brought us to an impasse at the dinner party I mentioned at the outset occurred centuries ago, when it was first decided to exploit racial difference as a means to power. It was the determinism that flowed karmically from this sin that dropped over us like a net that night. What bothered me most was our helplessness. Even the engineer did not know how to go forward. His challenge hadn't worked, and he'd lost the option to bargain. The marriage of race and power depersonalized us, changed us from eight people to six whites and two blacks. The easiest thing was to let silence blanket our situation, our impasse.   37

I think the civil rights movement in its early and middle years offered the best way out of America's racial impasse: in this society, race must not be a source of advantage or disadvantage for anyone. This is fundamentally a *moral* position, one that seeks to breach the corrupt union of race and power with principles of fairness and human equality: if all men are created equal, then racial difference cannot sanction power. The civil rights movement was conceived for no other reason than to redress that corrupt union, and its guiding insight was that only a moral power based on enduring principles of justice, equality, and freedom could offset the lower impulse in man to exploit race as a means to power. Three hundred years of suffering had driven the point home, and in Montgomery, Little Rock, and Selma, racial power was the enemy and moral power the weapon.   38

An important difference between genuine and presumed innocence, I believe, is that the former must be earned through sacrifice, while the latter is unearned and only veils the quest for privilege. And there was much sacrifice in the early civil rights movement. The Gandhian principle of non-violent resistance that gave the movement a spiritual center as well as a method of protest demanded sacrifice, a passive offering of the self in the name of justice. A price was paid in terror and lost life, and from this sacrifice came a hard-earned innocence and a credible moral power.   39

Non-violent passive resistance is a bargainer's strategy. It assumes the power that is the object of the protest has the genuine innocence to morally respond, and puts the protesters at the mercy of that innocence. I think this movement won so many concessions precisely because of its belief in the capacity of whites to be moral. It did not so much demand that whites change as offer them relentlessly the opportunity to live by their own morality—to attain a true innocence based on the sacrifice of their racial privilege, rather than a false innocence based on presumed   40 racial superiority. Blacks always bargain with or challenge the larger society; but I believe that in the early civil rights years, these forms of negotiation achieved a degree of integrity and genuineness never seen before or since.

In the mid-Sixties all this changed. Suddenly a sharp *racial* consciousness emerged to compete with the moral consciousness that had defined the movement to that point. Whites were no longer welcome in the movement, and a vocal "black power" minority gained dramatic visibility. Increasingly, the movement began to seek racial as well as moral power, and thus it fell into a fundamental contradiction that plagues it to this day. Moral power precludes racial power by denouncing race as a means to power. Now suddenly the movement itself was using race as a means to power, and thereby affirming the very union of race and power it was born to redress. In the end, black power can claim no higher moral standing than white power. 41

It makes no sense to say this shouldn't have happened. The sacrifices that moral power demands are difficult to sustain, and it was inevitable that blacks would tire of these sacrifices and seek a more earthly power. Nevertheless, a loss of genuine innocence and moral power followed. The movement, splintered by a burst of racial militancy in the late Sixties, lost its hold on the American conscience and descended more and more to the level of secular, interest-group politics. Bargaining and challenging once again became racial rather than moral negotiations. 42

You hear it asked, why are there no Martin Luther Kings around today? I think one reason is that there are no black leaders willing to resist the seductions of racial power, or to make the sacrifices moral power requires. King understood that racial power subverts moral power, and he pushed the principles of fairness and equality rather than black power because he believed those principles would bring blacks their most complete liberation. He sacrificed race for morality, and his innocence was made genuine by that sacrifice. What made King the most powerful and extraordinary black leader of this century was not his race but his morality. 43

Black power is a challenge. It grants whites no innocence; it denies their moral capacity and then demands that they be moral. No power can long insist on itself without evoking an opposing power. Doesn't an insistence on black power call up white power? (And could this have something to do with what many are now calling a resurgence of white racism?) I believe that what divided the races at the dinner party I attended, and what divides them in the nation, can only be bridged by an adherence to those moral principles that disallow race as a source of power, privilege, status, or entitlement of any kind. In our age, principles like fairness and equality are ill-defined and all but drowned in relativity. But this is the fault of people, not principles. We keep them muddied because they are the greatest threat to our presumed innocence and our selective ignorance. Moral principles, even when somewhat ambiguous, have the power to assign responsibility and therefore to provide us with knowledge. At the dinner party we were afraid of so severe an accountability. 44

What both black and white Americans fear are the sacrifices and risks that true racial harmony demands. This fear is the measure of our racial chasm. And though fear always seeks a thousand justifications, none is ever good enough, and the 45 problems we run from only remain to haunt us. It would be right to suggest courage as an antidote to fear, but the glory of the word might only intimidate us into more fear. I prefer the word *effort*—relentless effort, moral effort. What I like most about this word are its connotations of everydayness, earnestness, and practical sacrifice. No matter how badly it might have gone for us that warm summer night, we should have talked. We should have made the effort.

MIDDLE-CLASS SOLUTIONS
from *Paved with Good Intentions: The Failure*
of Race Relations in Contemporary America
Jared Taylor

Fortunately, despite their urgency, the problems of the underclass affect only a minority of blacks. In the other black America, what is needed is the realization that the bounty of this nation is not wrung from the reluctant, racist bosom of the white man but is won through individual responsibility and hard work. A recent book on the psychology of successful blacks includes a list of the ingredients of what the black authors call the psychology of black success. At the top of the list is personal responsibility. Another characteristic the authors found in successful blacks was that "they neither expect the Man to save them, nor blame the Man for all the problems and injustices of society."

Seminars on racism and mandatory college courses in ethnic studies are precisely what we do not need. Their ostensible purpose is to "sensitize" whites to the needs of minorities, but their real effect is to hammer at the old theme that whites are responsible for everything that goes wrong for blacks. This does nothing to help blacks, and whites have been so thoroughly "sensitized" that they are sick of it. College-age whites, especially, who have had no hand in shaping society, are increasingly confused and angry about constant harping on guilt they do not feel. What are they to make of the preposterous idea, propounded with the blessings of the university, that the Ivy League may be a subtle form of genocide? Ultimately, the very notion that Americans must be "sensitized" to race flies in the face of what we are presumably trying to achieve: a society in which race does not matter.

Moreover, there are limits to the patience with which whites will listen to appeals to a guilt they no longer feel. In the past, the best way to get whites to help blacks may have been to try to make them feel guilty. Increasingly, that will only make them angry. Blacks who seek the help and genuine goodwill of whites will not get it by dwelling on white racism and white guilt.

Something else that does no good is the constant proliferation of black subgroups. As soon as blacks join an organization, they band together into a racially exclusive subgroup. The doors of mainly white organizations are open to them, but their organizations are closed to whites. By any definition, this is racial discrimination.

There is a certain logic to this that few acknowledge. Mainly-white colleges must be integrated, but black colleges must stay black because they provide role models. Mainly-white fraternities must be integrated, but exclusively black fraternities will nurture the "black identity." The Miss America contest must be open to blacks, but blacks must have their own, racially exclusive beauty contest. There is black English and a black learning style, and they must be recognized. Job preferences for blacks are a civil right, but job preferences for whites are racism. "Black pride" is healthy and necessary, but "white pride" is bigotry. Standardized tests work for other races, but they are biased against blacks. All-black interest groups must be established to fight the racism within every American organization. Blacks should patronize black-owned stores and vote for black candidates. Blacks feel closer to Africans than to white Americans. Black students must have black teachers or they will not learn properly.

all more than skin color struggle understand one another because of

One man who understands where all this leads is Louis Farrakhan, leader of the Nation of Islam. The logic of black pride, black caucuses, and black role models leads straight to black nationhood. That, of course, is Mr. Farrakhan's stated objective. For him, whites are "devils" and "evil by nature." Blacks can expect nothing from them, and should carve out an independent black nation for themselves. He already has a national anthem for them. Citizens of a black nation would certainly escape the "racism" they claim to find at every turn in the United States.   6

Is Mr. Farrakhan's whites-are-devils theory any different from that of the equal employment officer who wrote that in America all whites are racist and only whites can be racist? Is it any different from the whites-are-always-responsible theory of black failure? Is the black nation that Mr. Farrakhan would carve out for himself so very different from the black caucuses that blacks so frequently carve out for themselves? → *many blacks don't agree*   7

Whether they mean to or not, when blacks set up racially exclusive groups, when they demand special privileges, when they state black goals that are different from America's goals, they are widening the racial fault lines that divide this country. *Main point* They cannot go on forever demanding special treatment in the name of equality, or practicing racism in the name of ethnic pride, or rebuilding segregation in the name of black identity. The "black agenda" all too often means nothing more than patronage, handouts, double standards, and open hostility to whites.   8

White Americans will eventually lose patience. The White Student Union at Temple University, the National Association for the Advancement of White People, the popularity in Louisiana of former Klansman David Duke—these are all disquieting signs that whites are tired of double standards. Only for so long will whites watch blacks use race as a weapon before they forge racial weapons of their own. *Main point*   9

Of course, race matters in America. It may always matter. But if we really are trying to build a color-blind society, our methods are not merely wrong but perverse. The entire apparatus of government, industry, and education is painfully conscious of race and treats the races differently at every turn. Blacks now demand special *examples* ← treatment as a matter of course. In its befuddled way, society is trying to do what is right. But to favor blacks systematically and then call this sorry charade "equal opportunity" is self-delusion of the worst kind.   10

If anything brings down the American experiment, it will be the notion that deliberate race consciousness can lead to racial harmony, that reverse racism can   11 eliminate racism.) Affirmative action, minority set-asides, and double standards are well-meant folly. If America really were boiling with white racism and the nation's most urgent task were to stamp it out, what more insanely inflammatory policy could one invent than to discriminate against whites because of their race? When the occasional ragtag band of placard-waving Ku Kluxers is outnumbered, not only by hecklers but also by police sent to protect them from outraged citizens, can white racism really be the crippling evil it is made out to be?

Racial distinctions replace the principle of individual merit with that of group re-   12
wards. If blacks get favors simply because they are black, it encourages them to think of themselves neither as individuals nor as Americans, but as blacks. How can blacks help but think of themselves as a separate people when society, at every turn, treats them as a separate people? In turn, how can we expect whites not to respond in kind to "ethnic aggressivity"? And finally, how can blacks be expected to believe in ability and hard work when society rewards them for being black instead? They must listen to the words of Booker T. Washington, the former slave who went on to found Tuskeegee Institute:

> No greater injury can be done to any youth than to let him feel that because he belongs to this or that race he will be advanced regardless of his own merit or efforts.

Unlike the problems of the underclass, the folly of affirmative action could quickly   13
be cured. We need only to interpret the laws on our books exactly as they were written. Nothing could be clearer than a prohibition against discrimination by race, creed, color, or national origin. The layman's understanding of these laws is precisely what their authors meant. Future generations will shake their heads in wonder at the mental acrobatics of our most learned judges, who have stood justice on its head.

Of course, judges cannot, by themselves, change the way America thinks. Even if   14
all race-based preferences were thrown out tomorrow, the job would be only half done until the double standards that first justified them were discredited. For that, all Americans will have to believe that blacks can and must take hold of their own destinies. They must realize that America will cease to be America if race becomes more important than nation. Only then can we begin to heal the hidden wound.

De Tocqueville feared that white America's relations with its freed slaves would   15
be the greatest social crisis the young democracy would face. He was right. Many great Americans—Abraham Lincoln, Thomas Jefferson, James Madison, John Marshall, Henry Clay, and Daniel Webster, to name just a few—did not believe that black and white could live peaceably in the same society.

We have not yet proven that they can. But if we do, it will be because we faced   16
the truth unflinchingly. We will have to shun the shakedown artists and guiltmongers. Whites will have to turn their backs on cowardly, dishonest behavior designed solely to escape charges of "racism." They must reject wholesale, off-the-shelf accusations and search for explanations that go deeper than the sloganeering, grandstanding, and buffoonery that now control the field.

The men who founded this country and established the first modern democracy believed that in the marketplace of ideas, the truth would always prevail. It was a belief that the common man would have the courage of his convictions and that society would always honor the truth that made "the land of the free and the home of the brave" something more than an empty slogan. When whites submit to accusations they know are untrue, they are the silent accomplices of falsehood. They must have the courage to say what they know to be true.

Blacks have the harder but more inspiring task of shucking the old excuses and finally taking possession of their lives. They must learn, just as Asians have, that whites can thwart them only if they permit themselves to be thwarted, and that society can help them only if they are able to help themselves. They must recognize that the weapon of race consciousness, which they are so tempted to wield, is a sword that cuts in every direction. Blacks who understand this, and say so publicly, will be reviled by other blacks who are still looking for excuses and handouts. Brave, clear-sighted black men and women carry a heavy burden, for no one else can even hope to touch the desolated generations that are ravaging our cities.

One hundred thirty years ago, this nation very nearly tore itself apart because of race. It could do so again. Policies based on white guilt and reverse racism have failed. Policies based on the denial of individual responsibility have failed. We must have the courage to admit that they have failed, and forge new policies that will succeed.

PANSY QUITS
from *The Rooster's Egg*
Patricia J. Williams

> *"Help me out of these wet things, Pansy," Scarlett ordered her maid. "Hurry." Her face was ghostly pale, it made her green eyes look darker, brighter, more frightening. The young black girl was clumsy with nervousness. "Hurry, I said. If you make me miss my train, I'll take a strap to you."*
>
> *She couldn't do it, Pansy knew she couldn't do it. The slavery days were over, Miss Scarlett didn't own her, she could quit any time she wanted to.*
>
> Alexandra Ripley, *Scarlett: The Sequel to Margaret Mitchell's* Gone with the Wind

Despite the enormous social, political, and legal fluctuations of twentieth-century American life, there has been a remarkable stasis in race relations, an intractability of gender hierarchy, an entrenched power dynamic that has resisted the reorderings of the very best rhetoricians and theoreticians. When Frederick Douglass described his own escape from slavery as a "theft" of "this head" and "these arms" and "these legs," he employed the master's language of property to create the unforgettable paradox of the "owned" erupting into the category of a speaking subject whose "freedom" simultaneously and inextricably marked him as a "thief." That this disruption of the bounds of normative imagining is variously perceived as dangerous as well as liberatory is a tension that has distinguished racial politics in America from the Civil War to this day. Scarcely thirty years after Martin Luther King's dream of a day when his children would be judged by the content of their character alone, the Reagan-Bush presidencies were able to reverse the metaphor of the Freedom Train into a commodity with a high-priced ticket whose fare must be earned in the marketplace.

The transformation of the rationales for enslavement or oppression from one discourse to another is perhaps a more familiar one than we in the United States would at first be comfortable acknowledging. As Walter Benn Michaels has observed:

> Imagining the slave as a buyer and seller, the contract at the same time defeudalizes slavery, replacing a social fact that exists independent of the desires of master or slave with a market agreement that insists on and enacts the priority of those desires . . . Hence the "new feudalism" that Progressives . . . feared . . . can never come into being not because conditions as bad as and even worse than those obtaining under "old-fashioned" slavery cease to exist but because the intervention of the market, even when it leaves these conditions intact, alters their meaning. In other words, the apologists for "modern slavery" defended it not by appealing to the usual paternalist ideals but by appealing to freedom, in particular freedom of contract.

Political appeals to "liberty," popular references to "freedom," and legal discussions of "equality" have always been weighted and authorized by very powerful images culled from hotly contested fields of symbolic reference. Who is really included in the notion of "national unity"? What is being negotiated when mass violence is labeled a "war," as opposed to a revolution, a rebellion, a riot, or the hold of some cult leader over innocent followers? When did affirmative action become reverse discrimination? How did we get to the point where no one puts black bodies on the auction block anymore, only healthy white babies? Against what social backdrop is sexual harassment transformed into high-tech lynching? And how on earth did we end up in the best-selling world of *Scarlett: The Sequel,* in which ex-slaves comfort themselves, as the whip descends, with the thought that they can quit at any time?

As the civil rights movement has made claims on the civic circle of participation, those resources located in the public sphere (including not just wealth but such intangibles as political responsibility and general idealism) have been spirited out of reach, as in a shell game between the walnut halves of public and private; as in a shell game among a welter of legal nuts. The debate about equality has shifted to one of free speech; legal discussions involving housing, employment, and schooling have shifted from the domain of civil rights to that of the market and thus have become "ungovernable," mere consumption preference. It serves us well, I think, to observe the ironies as well as the consistencies, the currents of desired investment and unintended disenfranchisement that flow on and on and on beneath the surface of our finest aspirations.

It is useful to attempt to unravel the degree to which powerful negative stereotypes of race and gender play against one another, first in negotiating the subtle, sometimes nearly invisible boundaries of social life, of citizenship, and of entitlement; and then, ultimately, in dictating the very visible limits of the law itself. To study the unreflective resurrection and recirculation of the metaphors of disregard in the United States is to reveal a powerful ideological pattern, a semantic of racism that is nurtured in the hidden spaces of cognitive blind spots. As Professors Nancy Fraser and Linda Gordon have written about the genealogy of the notion of "welfare dependence," the use of overdetermined and taken-for-granted images and keywords "serve[s] to enshrine certain interpretations of social life as authoritative and to delegitimate or obscure others, generally to the advantage of dominant groups in society and to the disadvantage of subordinate ones."

The degree to which such images are influential raises the question of the degree to which they may be manipulated for better or worse ends. Thus the scope of my concern includes the rhetorical strategies by which borders are drawn and community marked, including the cultural theorist Eduardo Cadava's question of "how one's rhetoric may see its way home to the mark when the figures one uses may include, within their history, connotations that lead one's argument away from its intended end," as well as the function of the media in shaping "American" identity—in particular the currently popular configuring of "whites as victims" in the shaping of civic identity and legal outcome.

As I write, it is the fortieth anniversary of *Brown v. Board of Education,* the case that shaped my life's possibilities, the case that, like a stone monument, stands for just about all of the racial struggles with which this nation still grapples. I cite it as a watershed moment, but the *Brown* case was part of a larger story that couldn't, shouldn't be made into private property; it was an exemplary story but far from unique.

My family, like so many black families, worked in the civil rights movement, joined the NAACP, took me to march out in front of Woolworth's before I could read—not because of a great event in their lives but because of all the ordinary daily grinding little events that made life hard in the aggregate. Even though I was raised in Boston during the 1950s and 1960s, I grew up knowing the back-of-the-bus stories, the peanut gallery stories, the having-to-go-the-bathroom-in-the-woods stories, the myriad mundane nearly invisible yet monumentally important constraints that circumscribed blacks, and not only in the South. My father, who grew up in Savannah, Georgia, during the 1920s and 1930s, remembers not only the inconveniences but the dangers of being black under Jim Crow: "You had to be careful of white people, you got out of the way, or you'd get hurt, immediately. If you saw a white person coming, you got off the sidewalk. Don't make too much noise. Know which side of the street to walk on. You were always conscious of the difference. The big conversation in all 'colored' homes was just that, color. It affected everybody."

"But that's exactly why *Brown* is indeed, 'our' story," cautioned a friend of mine,   8
who being fifteen or so years older than I was old enough to have gone on enough
marches to have worn out many pairs of shoes:

> The civil rights movement was all about ordinary people who weren't neces-
> sarily on the road to Damascus. If some lent their names, others lent their backs,
> or their expertise or their lives. It was life-threatening work after all, so nobody
> did it to get their name up in lights; you did it because there was no alternative.
> Neither fame nor anonymity existed as issues per se—that's come later, as the
> country seems to have sorted out who it's going to remember for fifteen sec-
> onds and what it will forget. It was about group survival. You were always think-
> ing about what would make it better for the children.

Perhaps part of the difficulty in reviewing the years since *Brown* with anything like   9
a hopeful countenance is that we as a nation have continued to underestimate the
complicated and multiple forms of prejudice at work in the United States. Segregation did not necessarily bar all forms of racial mixing; its odd, layered hierarchies of
racial attitude were substantially more complicated than that. My grandfather, for
example, was a doctor who owned several of the houses in the neighborhood where
he lived. "Dad's tenants were white, Irish," says my father, "but I never even thought
about where they went to school. We all lived kind of mixed up, but the whole system made you think so separately that to this day I don't know where they went to
school." There is an old story that speaks to the profundity of these invisible norms:
Three men in the 1930s South set out to go fishing in a small boat. They spent the
morning in perfectly congenial and lazy conversation. At lunchtime they all opened
their lunch buckets and proceeded to eat, but not before the two white men put an
oar across the middle of the boat, dividing themselves from their black companion.

The continuing struggle for racial justice is tied up with the degree to which seg-   10
regation and the outright denial of black humanity have been *naturalized* in our civilization. An aunt of mine who is very light-skinned tells of a white woman in her
office who had just moved from Mississippi to Massachusetts. "The North is much
more racist than the South," she confided to my aunt. "They don't give you any
credit for having white blood." This unblinking racial ranking is summarized in the
thoughts of James Kilpatrick, now an editor of the *National Review,* who stated the
case for southern resistance in a famous and impassioned plea:

> For this is what our Northern friends will not comprehend: The South, agree-
> able as it may be to confessing some of its sins and to bewailing its more mani-
> fest wickednesses, simply does not concede that at bottom its basic attitude is
> "infected" or wrong. On the contrary, the Southerner rebelliously clings to what
> seems to him the hard core of truth in this whole controversy: Here and now, in
> his own communities, in the mid-60s, the Negro race, as a race, plainly is not
> equal to the white race, as a race; nor, for that matter, in the wider world be-
> yond, by the accepted judgment of ten thousand years, has the Negro race, as a
> race, ever been the cultural or intellectual equal to the white race, as a race.

This we take to be a plain statement of fact, and if we are not amazed that our Northern antagonists do not accept it as such, we are resentful that they will not even look at the proposition, or hear of it, or inquire into it.

Dealing with the intractability of this sort of twisted social regard is what the years since *Brown* have been all about. Legal remedy after legal remedy has been challenged on the basis of assertions of not being able to "force" people to get along, assertions that "social equality" (or, these days, "market preference") is just not something that can be legally negotiated. Jack Greenberg, a Columbia University law professor and one of the attorneys who worked on the original *Brown* case, dismisses these arguments concisely: "You have to wonder how it is that *Plessy v. Ferguson,* which made segregation the law for almost seventy years, didn't come in for the same kinds of attacks, as 'social engineering.' " 11

Jerome Culp, a Duke University law professor, has observed that the litigators and activists who worked on *Brown* in the early 1950s assumed at least three things that have not come to pass: (1) that good liberals would stand by their commitment to black equality through the hard times; (2) that blacks and whites could come to some kind of agreement about what was fair and just—that there *was* a neutral agreed-upon position we could aspire to; and (3) that if you just had enough faith, if you just wished racism away hard enough, it would disappear. 12

"Growing up," says my father, "we thought we knew exactly what integration meant. We would all go to school together; it meant the city would spend the same money on you that they did on the white students. We blacks wouldn't be in some cold isolated school that overlooked the railroad yards; we wouldn't have to get the cast-off ragged books. We didn't think about the inevitability of a fight about whose version of the Civil War would be taught in that utopic integrated classroom." 13

The *Brown* decision itself acknowledged the extent to which educational opportunity depended on "intangible considerations" and relied "in large part on 'those qualities which are incapable of objective measurement but which make for greatness.' " Yet shaking the edifice sometimes brings home just how enormous the edifice really is. Moreover, the task of education in general has become vastly more complicated by the influence of television, and the task of learning racial history has been much confounded by the power of mass media. 14

"We've become a nation of sound bites," says Cheryl Brown Henderson, the daughter of the late Oliver Brown—the named plaintiff in *Brown*—and the founder of the Brown Foundation, an organization dedicated to teaching the history of the civil rights movement. 15

That millisecond of time to determine our behavior, whether it's behavior toward another individual, or behavior toward a product we might purchase, or our behavior with regard to what kind of housing or community we want to live in—I really think we allow that [millisecond] to determine far too much of our lives . . . When you take something that short and infuse it with a racial stereotype, and no other information is given, the young person looking at that—even the older person who spends most of his time watching television—that's all they know. How can you expect them to believe anything else? They're not going to pick up a book and read any history, do any research, or talk to anybody that may in fact be able to refute the stereotype.

In addition to stereotypes, perhaps the media revolution has exacerbated the very American tendency to romanticize our great moments into nostalgia-fests from which only the extremes of Pollyannaish optimism or Malthusian pessimism can be extracted. For all the biblical imagery summoned to inspire the will to go on with the civil rights struggle in this century, if the waters have parted at any given moment, perhaps it has been more attributable to all those thousands of busy people working hard to make sure Exodus occurred one way or another—just people, just working and just thinking about how it could be different, dreaming big yet surprised most by the smallest increments, the little things that stun with the realization of the profundity of what has not yet been thought about.

My father muses:

> It's funny . . . we talked about race all the time, yet at the same time you never really thought about *how* it could be different. But after *Brown* I remember it dawning on me that I *could* have gone to the University of Georgia. And people began to talk to you a little differently; I remember [the white doctor who treated my family in Boston, where I grew up] used to treat us in such a completely offhand way. But after *Brown,* he wanted to discuss it with us, he asked questions, what I thought. He wanted my opinion and I suddenly realized that no white person had ever asked what I thought about anything.

Perhaps as people like my father and the doctor have permitted those conversations to become more and more straightforward, the pain of it all, the discomfort, has been accompanied by the shutting down, the mishearing, the turning away from the euphoria of *Brown.* "It has become unexpectedly, but not unpredictably hard. The same thing will probably have to happen in South Africa," sighs my father.

Perhaps the legacy of *Brown* is as much tied up with a sense of national imagination as with the pure fact of its legal victory; it sparked our imagination, it fired our vision of what was possible. Legally it set in motion battles over inclusion, participation, and reallocation of resources that are very far from over. But in a larger sense it committed us to a conversation about race that we must move forward with, particularly in view of a new rising Global Right.

We must get beyond the stage of halting conversations filled with the superficialities of hurt feelings and those "my maid says blacks are happy" or "whites are devils" moments. If we could press on to a conversation that takes into account the devastating legacy of slavery that lives on as a social crisis that needs generations more of us working to repair—if we could just get to the enormity of that unhappy acknowledgement, then that alone might be the source of a genuinely revivifying, rather than a false, optimism.

I think that the crisis in universities over what is so snidely referred to as "political correctness" must be viewed as part of the attempt to have such a conversa-

16

17

18

19

20

tion. The much-publicized campus tensions are an unfortunate but perhaps predictable part of the institutional digestive process of the beneficiaries or demographic heirs of the civil rights movement. The battle for equal rights that is symbolized by the landmark integration of grammar schools in Topeka, Kansas, that was waged also with the integration of high schools and colleges, then professional and graduate schools, then workplaces—that battle is now just about forty years old. The generation of children who entered white schools as a result of the transformative legacy of the Supreme Court's opinion in *Brown v. Board of Education* has grown up, become middle-aged, attained the time of life when careers make their lasting mark. It is not surprising, therefore, that the bitter resistance and powerful backlash that have met every step of integrationist vision should have flowed to their current loci, those Steven Carter calls "affirmative action babies." It is not surprising, as more blacks, women, gays, Hispanics, Jews, Muslims, and wheelchair-bound people have entered the workplace, gotten tenure in universities, and risen to political office, that the new generation of fire-hosing tomato-throwers have shifted their aim and their tactics accordingly.

No longer are state troops used to block entry to schools and other public 21
institutions—segregation's strong arm, states' rights, has found a new home in an economic gestalt that has simply privatized everything. Whites have moved to the suburbs and politicians have withdrawn funds from black to white areas in unsubtle redistricting plans. No longer is the law expressly discriminatory (as to race and ethnicity at any rate; this is not yet the case in terms of sexual orientation)—yet the phenomenon of laissez-faire exclusion has resulted in as complete a pattern of economic and residential segregation as has ever existed in this country.

Most of all, the moral currency of the civil rights movement's vocabulary has 22
been under attack. "Integration" itself has been transformed in meaning, now used glowingly by former segregationists like Jesse Helms and Strom Thurmond—and rejected by many former civil rights activists—as having come to mean a form of assimilation that demands self-erasure rather than engagement of black contributions and experience.

This facile deflection has historical precedents in the 1950s incantations of "free- 23
dom of association" and "contract," which were used to block discussions of integration. Then, as now, civil rights activists had to respond with lawsuits focusing on substantive equality as a constitutional objective, on the premise that certain groups need not suffer unrestrained stigmatization of their humanity and of their citizenship. In today's world, such efforts have focused on harassment in the workplace, the academic freedom to include or exclude the histories of minority groups in curricula, the redefinition of citizenship to encompass the extraordinary linguistic, ethnic, religious, racial, and physical variety of those of us who are American Citizens Too.

While this particular battle resounds in every aspect of American life, there is 24
no place it has been more visible than in universities; there is no fiercer entrenchment than the line drawn around the perceived property in culture. It is a battle remarkable for the persistence of prejudice: as women are still trying to overcome

presumptions that they really *like* getting fondled in the back office, blacks are trying to overcome presumptions that they really *deserve* to be on the bottom of the
heap. It is a battle complicated not just by ignorance and denial but by disastrous
yet well-intentioned experiments—such as the slavery lesson described in this
news item:

> A White first-grade teacher in Atglen, Pa., who asked her only two Black pupils
> to pretend they were slaves during a class discussion on slavery, recently apolo-
> gized to the youngsters' parents.
>
> "Teacher put us up on a table," said Ashley Dixon, 6, describing the history
> lesson by teacher Mary Horning. Ashley said Horning told her that, as a slave,
> she would be sold for about $10 as a house cleaner.
>
> Zachary Thomas, also 6, said Horning used him to demonstrate how shirtless
> slaves were chained to a post before flogging.
>
> Horning apologized the next day to the children's mothers and asked them to
> speak to her class on Black heritage. "I did not view it as racial," she said, adding,
> "I wanted to teach the children about prejudice. I did not do it with malice or to
> embarrass anyone."

Such well-meaning but thoughtless scenarios reenact and reinforce a power dynamic in which some people get to *imagine* oppression, and others spend their lives
having their bodies put through its most grotesque motions. Reference to "good
intentions," moreover, however blunderingly destructive their impact, tends to end
all further discussion. The merest whisper of the possibility that a little education, a
little history, a little forethought might improve things is too often crudely and immediately translated into electrical blizzards of fear of "fascism," "thought control,"
"hypersensitivity," and "lowered standards."

I can't help wondering what is implied when the suggestion of more knowledge,   25
more history is so persistently misunderstood and devalued as unscientific unknowl-
edge, as untruthful unhistory. In fact, the upside-downness of meaning has become a
major threat to the ability to address educational inequality in a whole range of contexts. "*Inter*culturalism," said a Swarthmore undergrad firmly and disapprovingly
when I used the word "multiculturalism" at a tea given in my honor not long ago.
"Huh?" said I, through a mouthful of chocolate cream and crumbs. "Intercultural-
ism," she repeated. "Multiculturalism has too much negative meaning these days."

I guess she was right. Every generation has to go through a purging of language,   26
an invention of meaning in order to exist, in order to be seen. Renaming as fair
turnaround; renaming as recapture from the stereotypes of others. Yet . . . somehow . . . it seems I am running out of words these days. I feel as if I am on a linguistic treadmill that has gradually but unmistakably increased its speed, so that no
word I use to positively describe myself or my scholarly projects lasts for more
than five seconds. I can no longer justify my presence in academia, for example,
with words that exist in the English language. The moment I find some symbol of
my presence in the rarefied halls of elite institutions, it gets stolen, co-opted, filled

with negative meaning. As integration became synonymous with assimilation into whiteness, affirmative action became synonymous with pushing out more qualified whites, and of course multiculturalism somehow became synonymous with solipsistically monocultural privilege.

While constant rejuvenation is not just good but inevitable in some general sense, the rapid obsolescence of words even as they drop from our mouths is an increasingly isolating phenomenon. In fact, it feels like a form of verbal blockbusting. I move into a large meaningful space, with great connotations on a high floor with lots of windows, and suddenly all the neighbors move out. My intellectual aerie becomes a known hangout for dealers in heresy and other soporific drugs, frequented by suspect profiles (if not actual suspects) and located on the edge of that known geological disaster area, the Slippery Slope.   27

The roadblock that the moral inheritance of the civil rights movement has encountered in the attack on "political correctness" strikes me as just such rhetorical robbery—it is a calculated devaluation of political property values no less than the "white flight" organized by the National Association of Realtors a few decades ago, which left us with the legacy of the "inner city." It seems to me that the ability to talk about diversity (now synonymous with balkanization) depends therefore on a constant clarification of terms, a determination to leave nothing to presupposition, and a renewed insistence upon the incorporation of multiple connotative histories into our curricula, our social lives, our politics, and our law.   28

I worry that while the happy universalism of assimilative "neutrality" is a fine ideal, we will never achieve it by assuming away the particularity of painful past and present inequalities. The creation of a false sense of consensus about "our common heritage" is not the same as equality. As the example of the first-grade slave auction demonstrates, the ignorant (or innocent) perpetuation of oppression, even as we purport to be challenging it, can result in situations where empowered people imagine they are learning and even end up feeling pretty good about themselves, yet the disempowered end up feeling pretty awful, bearing the burden of the lessons imparted to the more powerful while learning nothing themselves that is new or helpful. Thus powerful inequities and real social crises are ignored, are made invisible, and just get worse.   29

Does this mean we eliminate the topic of slavery or sexism or homophobia from our classrooms as too "dangerous" or "divisive" or "controversial"? Do we really want to avoid controversy in education? Or is that even the issue?   30

I am concerned that the noisy rush to discuss the legalities of censorship and the First Amendment preempts more constructive conversations about how we might reinfuse our pedagogy with dignity and tolerance for all. As I have remarked a number of times before, it is as if the First Amendment has become severed from any discussion of the actual limits and effects of political, commercial, defamatory, perjurious, or any other of the myriad classifications of speech. It is as if expressions that carry a particularly volatile payload of hate become automatically privileged as political and, moreover, get to invoke the First Amendment as a bludgeon of   31 paradox—"I have my First Amendment right to call you a monkey, so you shut up about it." As the legal anthropologist Richard Perry observes, hatred thereby gets to cross-dress as Virtue Aggrieved.

In a much-publicized incident at Harvard University a few years ago, a white stu-   32
dent hung a Confederate flag from her dormitory window, saying that to her it symbolized the warmth and community of her happy southern home. This act produced a strong series of public denunciations from many other students, blacks in particular, who described the symbolic significance of the Confederacy as a *white* community forged against a backdrop of force, intimidation, and death for blacks. Eventually one black student hung a sheet with a swastika painted on it out her window, with the expressed hope that the university would force both her and the white student to remove such displays. The university did not, and eventually the black student removed her flag voluntarily because it was creating tension between black and Jewish students.

While the entire debate about this incident predictably focused on free speech   33
issues, what seemed strange to me was a repeated and unexamined imbalance in how the two students' acts were discussed. On the one hand, there was a ubiquitous assumption that the white student's attribution of meaning to the Confederate flag was "just hers," so no one else had any "business" complaining about it. The flag's meaning became a form of private property that she could control exclusively and despite other assertions of its symbolic power. (Those other assertions are just "their opinion"; all's fair in the competitive marketplace of meaning.)

At the same time, there was an assumption that the swastika's meaning was fixed,   34
transcendent, "universally" understood as evil. The black student's attempt to infuse it with "her" contextualized meaning (that of the translated power of what the Confederate flag meant to her) was lost in the larger social consensus on its historical meaning. This larger social consensus is not really fixed, of course, but its monopoly hold on the well-educated Harvard community's understanding is a tribute both to the swastika's overarchingly murderous yet coalescing power in the context of Aryan supremicist movements and to our having learned a great deal of specific history about it. The power of that history understandably overshadowed not only that black student's attempt at a narrower meaning but also the swastika's meaning in aboriginal American religion or in Celtic runes.

The questions remains, however, how some speech is so automatically put be-   35
yond comment, consigned to the free market of ideas, while other expressions remain invisibly regulated, even monopolized by the channels not merely of what we have learned but of what we have not learned. I do not want to be misunderstood: I do not question our consensus on the image of genocide embodied in the swastika; I wonder at the immovability of the comfy, down-home aura attending the Confederate flag—the sense that as long as it makes some people happy, the rest of us should just butt out. The limits of such reasoning might be clearer if applied to the swastika: without having to conclude anything about whether to censor it, the fact remains that we usually don't cut off discussions of Nazism with the conclusion that it was a way of creating warm and happy communities for the German bourgeoisie.

Let me be clearer still in this thorny territory: I wish neither to compare nor to relativize the horrors of the Holocaust and of the legacy of slavery in the United States. This is not an appropriate subject for competition; it is not a sweepstakes anyone could want to win. I do worry that it is easier to condemn that which exists at a bit of cultural distance than that in which we may ourselves be implicated. And it is easier to be clear about the nature of the evils we have seen in others an ocean away than about those whose existence we deny or whose history we do not know. The easy flip-flopping between "free" and "regulated" signification is a function of knowledge; it underscores the degree to which we could all stand to educate ourselves, perhaps most particularly about the unpleasantnesses of the past. We should not have to rely upon the "shock" shorthand of campus crises, for example, to bring to our public consciousness the experience of black history in the good old days of legalized lynching. . . .

I remember when I was a little girl, in the late 1950s, two or three black families moved into our neighborhood where for fifty years my mother's family had been the only blacks. I remember the father of my best friend, Cathy, going from house to house, warning the neighbors, like Paul Revere with Chicken Little's brain, that the property values were falling, the values were falling. The area changed overnight. Whites who had seen me born and baked me cookies at Halloween and grown up with my mother now fled for their lives. ("We'd have to hold our breath all the time because colored people smell different," said Cathy with some conviction. Cathy, who was always a little slow about these things, had difficulty with the notion of me as "colored": "No, you're not" and then, later, "Well, you're different.")

The mass movement that turned my neighborhood into an "inner city" was part of the first great backlash to the civil rights movement. I think we are now seeing the second great backlash, disguised as a fight about reverse discrimination and "quotas" but in truth directed against the hard-won principles of equal opportunity in the workplace and in universities as feeders for the workplace. Universities are pictured as "fortresses" of enlightened and universal values under "siege" by those who are perceived to be uncivilized heathen. (Wherever 3 percent or more of us are gathered, it's a siege, I guess.) The cry has been sounded: The standards are falling, the standards are falling.

The story of my inner-city neighborhood would have been vastly different if Cathy and her family had bothered to stick around to get to know the two nice black families who moved in. Similarly, the future of the U.S. universities—particularly in the hoped-for global economy—could be a fascinating one if campus communities chose to take advantage of the rich multiculturalism that this society offers. We face a quite disastrous intellectual crisis, however, if our universities persist in the culture-baiting that has brought us the English-only movement, the brazen assumption that any blacks on campus don't deserve to be there, and the mounting levels of verbal and physical violence directed against anyone perceived to be different or marginal.

This situation makes it easy to spend a lot of time being defensive. We've all heard the lame retorts into which these attacks box us: "I am too qualified!" "Vote for me but not because I'm a woman!" But they don't work. You simply can't dispel powerful cultural stereotypes by waving your degrees in people's faces. (That's precisely the premise of ultraconservative Dinesh D'Souza's much-touted book *Illiberal Education:* that an Ivy League degree just isn't worth what it used to be now that the riffraff has moved in.)

It's hard not to be defensive, of course—talking about race in any other posture   41
is extremely difficult. I recently guest-lectured in the class of a constitutional law professor who was teaching disparate impact cases (cases that consider what if any remedies might correct the racially disparate impact of rules that on their face are race-neutral). As I spoke about shifting demographics and the phenomenon of "white flight," the class grew restless, the students flipping pages of newspapers and otherwise evidencing disrespect. Afterward, the two or three black students congratulated me for speaking so straightforwardly, and for using the words "black" and "white." I later asked the professor: How is it possible to teach cases about racial discrimination without mentioning race? "I just teach the neutral principles," he replied; "I don't want to risk upsetting the black students." (And yet it was clear that those most upset were the white students.)

This tendency to neutralize is repeated throughout the law school curriculum: 42
"core" classes carve off and discard some of their most important parts, such as welfare and entitlement programs from tax policy, consumer protection law from commercial contract. And even though the civil rights movement was one of the most singularly transformative forces in the history of constitutional law, very little of it is taught in basic constitutional law classes. (When I took constitutional law, we spent almost no class time on civil rights.) Some schools—by no means all— pick up the pieces by offering such optional courses as Poverty Law, Law and Feminism, or Race and the Law. It is no wonder that the Rehnquist court has been able to cavalierly undo what took so many lives and years to build: the process of legal education mirrors the social resistance to antidiscrimination principles. Subject matter considered to be "optional" is ultimately swept away as uneconomical "special" interests—as thoughtlessly in real life as it has been in law schools.

Ironically, the smooth conceptual bulwark of "neutral principles" has been turned   43
to the task of evading the very hard work that moral reflection in any sphere requires, the constant balancing—whether we act as voters, jurors, parents, lawyers, or laypeople—of rules, precepts, principles, and context. I have always considered developing the ability to engage in such analytical thought to be the highest goal of great universities. Yet even this most traditional of educational missions is under attack. "Should [parents] be paying $20,000 a year to have their children sitting there, figuring out how they feel about what they read?" asks James Barber, founder of the neoconservative National Association of Scholars at Duke University. His question underscores the degree to which the supposed fear of balkanized campuses is in fact the authoritarian's worst nightmare of a world in which people actually think for themselves.

The necessity of thinking long and hard and aloud about the nature of prejudice   44
was exemplified for me when I was visiting Durham, North Carolina, during the

1990 senatorial race between Jesse Helms and Harvey Gantt (the first black to run for that office since Reconstruction). A friend of mine said she wanted me to see something. Without any explanation, she drove me over to Chapel Hill and dragged me to the center of the University of North Carolina campus. There, right in front of the student union, was a statue entitled *The Student Body*. It was a collection of cast bronze figures, slightly smaller than life-size. One was of an apparently white, Mr. Chips–style figure with a satchel of books on his back, pursuing his way. Another was of a young woman of ambiguous racial cast, white or maybe Asian, carrying a violin and some books and earnestly pursuing her way. A third figure was of a young white woman struggling with a load of books stretching from below her waist up to her chin. Then two white figures: a young man holding an open book with one hand; his other arm floating languidly downward, his hand coming to casual rest upon a young woman's buttocks. The young woman leaned into his embrace, her head drooping on his shoulder like a wilted gardenia. In the center of this arrangement was a depiction of an obviously black young man. He was dressed in gym shorts and balanced a basketball on one finger. The last figure was of a solemn-faced young black woman; she walked alone, a solitary book balanced on her head.

It turned out I was about the only one in the state who hadn't heard about this   45
statue. A gift from the class of 1985, it had been the topic of hot debate. Some students, particularly black and feminist students, had complained about the insensitivity of this depiction as representative of the student bod(ies). Other students said the first students were just "being sensitive" (invoked disparagingly as though numbskulledness were a virtue). At that point the sculptor, a woman, got in on the act and explained that the black male figure was in honor of the athletic prowess of black UNC grads like Michael Jordan, and that the black female figure depicted the grace of black women. The university, meanwhile, congratulated itself publicly on how fruitfully the marketplace of ideas had been stimulated.

As I stood looking at this statue in amazement, I witnessed a piece of the   46
debate-as-education. Two white male students were arguing with a black female student.

"You need to lighten up," said one of the men.   47

"But . . ." said the black woman.   48

"Anyway, black women *are* graceful," said the other.   49

"But," said the black woman as the white men kept talking.   50

In the end the black woman walked off in tears, while the white men laughed.   51
There is a litany of questions I have heard raised about scenarios like this: Why should the university "protect" minority students against this sort of thing? Don't they have to learn to deal with it?

Let me pose some alternative questions of my own: Why should universities be   52
in the business of putting students in this sort of situation to begin with? Since when is the persistent reduction of black men and all women to their physical traits "educational" about anything? How is it that these sorts of ignorant free-for-alls are smiled upon by the same university officials who resist restructuring curricula to teach the actual histories of women and people of color?

There is a popular insistence that the solution to the struggle over campus multi-   53
culturalism is to just talk about it, one-on-one, without institutional sanction or interference. Free speech as free enterprise zone. But this solution makes only certain
students—those who are most frequently the objects of harassment—the perpetual
teachers, not merely of their histories, but of their very right to be students. This is
an immense burden, a mountainous presumption of noninclusion that must be constantly addressed and overcome. It keeps them eternally defensive and reactive.

This denial of legitimacy is not merely an issue for students. The respect accorded   54
any teacher is only in small—if essential—part attributable to the knowledge inside
the teacher's head. (If that were all, we would have much more respect for street-
corner orators, the elderly, and the clear uncensored vision of children.) What
makes one a teacher is the force lent to one's words by the collective power of institutional convention. If faculty members do not treat women as colleagues, then
students will not treat women as members of the faculty.

I think that the ability to be, yes, *sensitive* to one another is what distinguishes   55
the joy of either multiculturalism or willing assimilation from the oppression of either groupthink or totalitarianism. Empathic relation is at the heart of diplomacy,
and a little well-deployed diplomacy can keep us from going to war with one another. But the dilemma many people of color face at this moment in the academic
and employment world is this: if we respond to or open discussion about belliger-
ent or offensive remarks—that is, if we pursue the much-touted path of responding to hate speech with "more speech"—we are called "PC" and accused of forcing
our opinions down the throats of others. If we respond with no matter what degree of clear, dignified control, we become militant "terrorists" of the meek and
moderate middle. If we follow the also-prevalent advice to "just ignore it," then we
are perceived as weak, humiliated, ineffectual doormats who ought to have told off
our harassers on the spot.

It's great to turn the other cheek in the face of fighting words; it's probably even   56
wise to run. But it's not a great way to maintain authority in the classroom or self-
respect in the workplace—particularly in a society that abhors "wimps" and considers "kicking ass" a patriotic duty. In such a context, "just ignoring" verbal
challenges is a good way to deliver oneself into the category of the utterly power-
less. If, moreover, all our colleagues pursue the same path (insult, embarrassed
pause, the world keeps on moving as though nothing has happened), then we have
collectively created that peculiar institutional silence known as a moral vacuum.

One of the subtlest challenges we face, if we are not to betray the hard-won   57
gains of the last forty years, is how to relegitimate the national discussion of racial,
ethnic, and gender tensions so that we can get past the Catch-22 in which merely
talking about it is considered an act of war, in which not talking about it is complete capitulation to the status quo, and in which not talking about it is repeatedly
covered up with a lot of high-volume substitute talk about the legalities of censorship and the First Amendment. In the long run, taking refuge in such excuses preempts more constructive conversations about how we might reinfuse our pedagogy
with dignity and tolerance for all.

The most eloquent summary of both the simplicity and the complexity of that   58
common task remains W. E. B. Du Bois's essay "On Being Crazy":

> After the theatre, I sought the hotel where I had sent my baggage. The clerk
> scowled.
>   "What do you want?"
>   Rest, I said.
>   "This is a white hotel," he said.
>   I looked around. Such a color scheme requires a great deal of cleaning, I said,
> but I don't know that I object.
>   "We object," he said.
>   Then why, I began, but he interrupted.
>   "We don't keep niggers here," he said, "we don't want social equality."
>   Neither do I, I replied gently, I want a bed.

VISIONS OF BLACK-WHITE FRIENDSHIP
from *The Trouble with Friendship:*
Why Americans Can't Think Straight about Race
Benjamin DeMott

At the heart of today's thinking about race lies one relatively simple idea: the race   1
situation in America is governed by the state of personal relations between blacks
and whites. Belief in the importance of personal relations reflects traits of national
character such as gregariousness, openness, down-to-earthness. It also reflects
American confidence that disputes can be trusted to resolve themselves if the parties consent to sit down together in the spirit of good fellowship—break bread,
talk things out, learn what makes the other side tick.

But there's rather more to faith in black-white friendship than off-the-rack Ro-   2
tarianism. There are convictions about the underlying sameness of black and white
ways of thinking and valuing, and about the fundamental causes of racial inequity
and injustice, and about the reasons why the idea of addressing race problems
through political or governmental moves belongs to time past.

One leading assumption is that blacks and whites think and feel similarly because   3
of their common humanity. (Right responsiveness to racial otherness and full access to black experience therefore require of whites only that they listen atten-
tively to their inner voice.) Another assumption is that differences of power and
status between whites and blacks flow from personal animosity between the
races—from "racism" as traditionally defined. (White friendship and sympathy for
blacks therefore diminishes power differentials as well as ill feeling, helping to produce equality.) Still another assumption is that bureaucratic initiatives meant to
"help" blacks merely prolong the influence of yesteryear. (The advent of good interpersonal feeling between blacks and whites, on the other hand, lessens yesteryear's dependency.)

Each of these closely related assumptions surfaces regularly in print media treat-   4
ment of the friendship theme—material promoting interracial amity and weaving
together concern for "the disadvantaged" and the "underclass," anecdotal evidence
of the mutual affection of blacks and whites, and implicit or explicit disparagement
of politics and politicians. And traces of the same assumptions appear in fraternal
gestures favored by campaigning political candidates.

White candidates attend services at black churches, socialize at black colleges,   5
play games with blacks (as when, during Campaign '92, Jerry Brown took gang leaders rafting). And candidates speak out in favor of black-white friendships, venturing
that such ties could be the answer to race riots. On the second day of the Los Angeles riots, Candidate Clinton declared: "White Americans are gripped by the isolation of their own experience. Too many still simply have no friends of other races
and do not know any differently."

But fantasies about black-white friendship are dramatized most compellingly for   6
large audiences in images. Movies, TV, and ads spare us abstract generalizing about
the isolation of the races. They're funny and breezy. At times, as in *Natural Born
Killers,* they deliver the news of friendship and sympathy in contexts of violence and
amorality. At times they deliver that news through happy faces, loving gestures,
memorable one-liners. Tom Hanks as Forrest Gump loses his beloved best buddy, a
black (Mykelti Williamson), in combat and thereafter devotes years to honoring a
pledge made to the departed (*Forrest Gump,* 1994). A rich white lady (Jessica Tandy)
turns to her poor black chauffeur (Morgan Freeman) and declares touchingly:
"Hoke, you're my best friend" (*Driving Miss Daisy,* 1989). Michael Jackson pours his
heart into a race-dismissing refrain: "It doan matter if you're black or white" (1991).
Scene and action hammer home the message of interracial sameness; mass audiences *see* individuals of different color behaving identically, sometimes looking alike,
almost invariably discovering, through one-on-one encounter, that they need or
delight in or love each other. . . .

A key, early contribution to the mythology of black-white friendship was that of   7
The Cosby Show. Without actually portraying blacks and whites interacting, and without preaching directly on the subject, this sitcom lent strong support to the view
that white friendship and sympathy could create sameness, equality, and interchangeability between the races. Under the show's aegis an unwritten, unspoken,
felt understanding came alive, buffering the force both of black bitterness and resentment toward whites and of white bitterness and resentment toward blacks.
*Race problems belong to the passing moment. Race problems do not involve group inter-
ests and conflicts developed over centuries. Race problems are being smoothed into nothingness, gradually, inexorably, by goodwill, affection, points of light.*

The Cosby family's cheerful at-homeness in the lives of the comfortably placed   8
middle class, together with the fond loyalty of their huge audience, confirmed
both the healing power of fellow feeling and the nation's presumably irreversible
evolution—as blacks rise from the socioeconomic bottom through the working
poor to the middle class—toward color blindness. In the years before the show,

black-white themes, in film as well as TV, had passed through several stages of development. One of a half-dozen milestones was the introduction, in *The Jeffersons,* of the first blacks to achieve middle-class affluence via entrepreneurship. Another milestone was the introduction, by adoption, of charming black children into white families—as in *Webster* and *Diff'rent Strokes.* (The "white foster parents," wrote Jannette Dates, "could then socialize the youngsters into the 'real' American way.")

And in the wake of the success of *The Cosby Show,* the eradication of race difference by friendship became an ever more familiar on-camera subject. Closeness between the races ceased to be a phenomenon registered indirectly, in surveys documenting the positive reaction of white audiences to the Huxtables; it moved to the center of mass entertainment. Everywhere in the visual media, black and white friendship in the here and now was seen erasing the color line. Interracial intimacy became a staple of mass entertainment story structures. 9

Consider *White Men Can't Jump* (1992), a movie about a white quester—a dropout eking a living on basketball courts in Los Angeles—surviving, with black help, on ghetto turf. Working first as a solitary, the young white hustles black ballplayers on their own turf, trading insults with blacks far more powerful, physically, than himself. He chides black athletes to their faces for being showboats, concerned about looking good, not about winning. He flashes rolls of bills and is never mugged. Accompanied only by his girlfriend, he walks the most dangerous ghetto streets at night, once making his way uninvited into an apartment filled with black ballplayers. He mocks black musical performers to their faces in a park, describing the hymns they sing as "shit." That an arrogant, aggressive, white wiseass can do all this and more and emerge unscathed means partly that his behavior is protected under the laws of comedy. 10

But the armor that counts more, here as in numberless black-white friendship tales, is provided by the black buddy. The acquaintance of white Billy Hoyle (Woody Harrelson) and black Sidney Deane (Wesley Snipes) begins badly: each hoaxes the other. Later they communicate through taunts. Black taunts white for incapacity to appreciate the black musicians whom white claims to admire. "Sure, you can listen to Jimi [Hendrix]. Just, you'll never hear him." Black taunts white for dreaming he can slam-dunk: "White men can't jump." Black mockingly offers technical aid to white: pumping up his Air Jordans for dream-flight. White jabs back hard, charging black with exhibitionism and sex obsession. 11

Yet the two make it as friends, form a team, work their scams in harmony. More than once the buddies save each other's tails, as when a black ballplayer whom they cheat turns violent, threatening to gun them down. (The two make a screaming getaway in the white quester's vintage ragtop.) And the movie's climax fulfills the equation—through sympathy to sameness and interchangeability. During a city-wide, high-stakes, two-on-two tournament, Billy, flying above the hoop like a stereotypical black player, scores the winning basket on an alley-oop from his black chum, whereupon the races fall into each other's arms in yelping, mutual, embracing joy. Cut to the finale that seals the theme of mutual need and interdependency; 12

black Sidney agrees to find quasi-honest work for white Billy at the floor-covering "store" that he manages:

Billy (helpless): I gotta get a job. Can you give me a job?

Sidney (affectionately teasing): Got any references?

Billy (shy grin): You.

Like many if not most mass entertainments, *White Men Can't Jump* is a vehicle of wish fulfillment. What's wished for and gained is a land where whites are unafraid of blacks, where blacks ask for and need nothing from whites (whites are the needy ones; blacks generously provide them with jobs), and where the revealed sameness of the races creates shared ecstatic highs. The precise details of the dream matter less than the force that makes it come true for both races, eliminating the constraints of objective reality and redistributing resources, status, and capabilities. That force is remote from political and economic policy and reform; it is, quite simply, personal friendship.   13

Another pop breeding ground of delusion is the story structure that pairs rich whites and poor blacks in friendship—as in *Regarding Henry* (1991), a Mike Nichols film about a white corporation lawyer and a black physical therapist. The two men meet following a holdup during which a gunman's stray bullet wounds the lawyer, Henry Turner (Harrison Ford), in the head, causing loss of speech, memory, and physical coordination. The therapist, Bradley (Bill Nunn), labors successfully at recovering Henry's faculties.   14

In outline, *Regarding Henry*—a video store hit—is a tale of moral transformation. Henry Turner is a corporate Scrooge who earns a fortune defending insurance companies against just suits brought by the injured and impecunious. Between the time of the gunshot wound and his return to his law firm, he experiences a change of heart—awakens to the meanness and corruption of his legal work and begins a movement toward personal reform. The sole influence on this transformation is Bradley, who shows the lawyer a persuasive example of selfless concern for others.   15

Bradley is called upon, subsequently, to give further guidance. Back in his luxo apartment and offices, Henry Turner, aware finally of the amoral selfishness of his professional life and of his behavior as husband and father, sags into depression—refuses to leave his bed. His wife, Sarah (Annette Bening), summons the black therapist, the only man Henry respects. Over beer in Henry's kitchen, Bradley tells his host of a crisis of his own—a football injury which, although it ended his athletic career, opened the prospect of the more rewarding life of service he now leads.   16

But does Bradley really believe, asks Henry Turner, that he's better off because of the accident? His black friend answers by citing the satisfactions of helping others, adding that, except for his football mishap, "I would never have gotten to know you."   17

The black man speaks as though fully convinced that his own turning point—his 18
unwanted second choice of life—and Henry Turner's are precisely similar. Nothing
in his voice hints at awareness either of the gap between riches and privation or of
the ridiculousness of the pretense that race and class—differences in inherited
property, competencies, beliefs, manners, advantages, burdens—don't count.
Wealthy white lawyer and humble black therapist speak and behave as though both
were Ivy League clubmen, equally knowledgeable about each other's routines,
habits, tastes. The root of Bradley's happiness as he sings his song of praise to his
white buddy is that, for Henry Turner, difference doesn't exist.

The predictable closer: a new Henry Turner launches an effort at restitution to 19
the poor whom his chicanery has cheated; black-white friendship not only makes
us one but makes us good.

When crime enters, fellow feeling should in theory exit. But visions of the force 20
of friendship challenge this rule, too. They thrust characters and audiences into
hitherto unexplored passages of self-interrogation and self-definition, obliging
whites to clarify, for themselves, the distinction between humane and racist responses to troubling black behavior. And they present the process of arriving at a
humane response—i.e., one that doesn't allow a criminal act to derail black-white
sympathy and friendship—as an act of personal reparation. . . .

Incessantly and deliberately, the world of pop is engaged in demonstrating, 21
through images, that racism has to do with private attitudes and emotions—with
personal narrowness and meanness—not with differences in rates of black and
white joblessness and poverty, or in black and white income levels, or in levels of
financing of predominantly black and white public schools. The images body forth
an America wherein some are more prosperous than others but all—blacks as well
as whites—rest firmly in the "middle income sector" (the rising black middle class
encompasses all blacks), where the free exchange of kindness should be the rule.

This America is of course remote from fact. One out of every two black chil- 22
dren lives below the poverty line (as compared with one out of seven white children). Nearly four times as many black families exist below the poverty line as
white families. Over 60 percent of African Americans have incomes below $25,000.
For the past thirty years black unemployment rates have averaged two to three
times higher than those of whites.

But in the world of pop, racism and fraternity have to do solely with the condi- 23
tions of personal feeling. Racism is unconnected with ghetto life patterns that abstractions such as income and employment numbers can't dramatize. Racism has
nothing to do with the survival strategies prudently adopted by human beings without jobs or experience of jobs or hope of jobs. It has no link with the rational re-
jection, by as many as half the young black men in urban America, of such dominant
culture values as ambition, industry, and respect for constituted authority. Pop
shows its audiences that racism is *nothing but* personal hatred, and that when
hatred ends, racism ends. The sweet, holiday news is that, since hatred is over, we—
black and whites together, knit close in middleness—have already overcome.

EXPANDING THE CENTER
from *Tragic Failure: Racial Integration in America*
Tom Wicker

The precipitate loss of decent jobs and decent wages was the most important factor in the explosive growth of the underclass in the 1970s and its continuing, blighting presence. To make income-earning jobs generally available to what are now inner-city residents, therefore, and to equip them to get and keep such jobs are important corollaries to the overall goal of full employment. It might even prove an effective anticrime program.

No one can pretend, however, that putting jobs into the inner city for its residents to fill would be an easy task. Quite the opposite. The frequently touted panacea of "job training" certainly is not enough. Even if in the era of technology adequate training programs for ill-educated persons could be devised, and if they could be made attractive to undisciplined ghetto youth, they would do little good if they only spewed jobless people back to the mean streets whence they came. Jobs, good jobs, have to be available at the end of the training pipeline.

If no such jobs await, the trainees are likely to believe that only a placebo has been offered in the few weeks of training—not a real remedy for a real malady. All too often, unfortunately, that has been the truth of well-intended job-training programs.

Even affluent, entrepreneurial blacks with the best will in the world can bring few jobs to the ghetto. The almost entirely white lords of the U.S. economy might—if they would. But bottom-line considerations make it unlikely that even the most public-spirited corporations actually will put major operations into the ghetto. More willing and skilled workers, at the same or lower wages, in better social and working conditions, can be found almost anywhere outside the big-city ghetto—foreign countries included. Nor would middle management and skilled technologists be likely to want to go to work every day in the dismal and dangerous South Bronx or any other inner-city neighborhood.

Substantial incentives might—or might not—lure owners and managers of job-providing enterprises to set up shop in the ghetto, finding and training their workers from among those available nearby. But such incentives are not in the political cards. President Clinton has proposed nothing of the sort. In a time of budget constraint and animosity toward racial integration, neither Congress nor any state, much less the taxpayer, seems willing to take such costly, problematical steps.

The idea of "ghetto renewal" may be illusory in any case. One who thinks so is Nicholas Lemann, the chronicler of the great post–World War II black migration out of southern cotton fields and into American cities:

> Of all the dramatic solutions to the problems of the ghettos, probably the most common and persistent for the past quarter century has been the idea that they can be "developed" into thriving ethnic enclaves. . . . Such proposals

have a powerful emotional attractiveness. They envelop the ghettos in the romanticized aura that Americans attach to small-town life.

Lemann believes, however, that "the clear lesson of experience" is that this kind of "ghetto development hasn't worked." Nor does he think it *can* work: "[T]he reality is that our ghettos bear the accumulated weight of all the bad in our country's racial history, and they are now among the worst places to live in the world."   7

Why should blacks or anyone be expected to work or live in such areas? Lemann asks, pointing out that European immigrants of a century ago "had no intention of making the ghetto their permanent residence."   8

In a panel discussion at Harvard's Kennedy School of Government, Margaret Weir of the Brookings Institution advocated instead a federal effort to "promote the mobility of the urban poor," in much the same way that government policies have helped whites to move out of cities into suburbs. Such mobility would increase what she called "access to prosperity" for the underclass and "help poor people as well as poor places."   9

That approach also presents numerous difficulties. White suburbanites as well as working-class whites and middle-class blacks in better urban neighborhoods will not welcome inner-city blacks. They fear the lawlessness some might bring along, and they would resent feared newcomers being imposed on often close-knit areas by government policy.   10

Ghetto "dispersal," moreover, is not always a popular idea even among blacks concerned about the inner city. Dispersal smacks too much of "forced removal" or, more cynically, "Negro removal." African-Americans learned to be wary of such plans from the old "slum clearance" programs that made urban land available for many a luxurious apartment building only whites could afford. And dispersal would make little allowance for the solid working-class families that somehow have remained in the inner city.   11

Some black elected officials would object, even if selfishly, to diminution of their inner-city political bases. Other African-Americans, accustomed to doubting white motives, might believe that was the real objective: to diminish black voting strength in the cities. In some cases it might be.   12

If "ghetto renewal" and "ghetto dispersal" are unpromising approaches to redeeming the inner city, what's left? The range of approaches to the problems of the underclass are certainly limited. But that's not a reason for giving up, for writing off generations of African-Americans who, as things now appear, will be forever lost to productive citizenship and the good American life.   13

Part of the answer is that nationwide public works program—rebuilding streets, highways, bridges, railways—and the business and industrial expansion it would spark. Such a renewal of the national infrastructure would symbolize, perhaps even inspire a larger national renewal.   14

Another vital part of the answer is improved public education, in general and in the inner city. Too many of today's schoolchildren are being shortchanged by public   15 and taxpayer apathy; by crime- and fear-ridden schools in the inner city that teach little more than survival; by schools elsewhere that focus on driver training and sports; by shortsighted, selfish, sometimes corrupt unions; by legislative indifference and political hostility to "spending" and taxes; by an imbalance of resources favoring affluent over poor school districts.

Privatization of some public schools, competition between these and remaining public schools, vouchers to enable parents to choose more promising schools for their children—such conservative proposals deserve comprehensive testing and adoption where proved effective. They do *not* justify a precipitate turn from the public education that has been vital to the nation's development.　16

However it's done, the rejuvenation of public education is vital to the redemption of the ghetto. And for this purpose too, economic gains for the poor are all-important, tending, as they would, to improve the social and physical environment of families, upgrade student behavior and performance, and—not least—yield more political "clout" to those who now have little.　17

Perhaps more important than any specific proposal would be the fact of a new party [built by African-Americans]—the political pressure it would bring, win or lose, on the mainstream parties. Such a party would make it impossible for the Democrats to court middle-class white votes while depending on the votes of poor blacks. Republicans could no longer slight the interests of more than forty million Americans living in poverty.　18

A new party's activities and votes would focus public attention on the needs of the poor and disadvantaged, including the African-Americans for so long victimized by American society, and on the attitudes of those who no longer believe in the promise of democracy. These, rather than the supposed miseries of the relatively well-off white middle class, are the gravest threats to the national future. These are the proper objects of an enlightened politics.　19

The major parties, however, are not going to recognize that, the Republicans because their interest is in the middle class and white communities, the Democrats because they are trying to compete with the Republicans. Both parties' political pitch is to the middle class, not to an underclass that hangs like a dark cloud over the future of American cities and American life.　20

"We all know [the underclass] is the principal problem in American domestic life," Nicholas Lemann has written, "a problem that poisons not just race relations but also our attitudes toward education, law enforcement, and city life itself."　21

"We all" may *know* that; unfortunately we all—most particularly the Democratic and Republican parties—neither admit it nor want to do anything effective about it. Consequently those parties will not think, much less do anything useful, about the problems of the underclass or the unemployed or the nonvoters.　22

Only a new party, formed for that purpose, made up principally of those to be redeemed, will take up the cause of these virtually forgotten Americans. Only a new party will devote its best minds and its best efforts to their cause. And only a new party's political determination and dedicated votes can see to it that the rest of us pay attention.　23

WHATEVER HAPPENED TO INTEGRATION?
Gerald Early

In the ideological warfare between liberals and conservatives, African-Americans exist as a kind of Rorschach test, an enigma to be solved in the context of their disturbing exceptionalism in a country obsessed with its own exceptionalism. Blacks have been in this country as long as its earliest European settlers. Why haven't they, well, for lack of a better phrase, quite measured up? Why do they lag behind whites and seemingly behind all the other immigrant groups to have come here? To white liberals like Tom Wicker and Benjamin DeMott, African-Americans are incorruptible victims, sanctified by their long history of suffering at the hands of whites, and stigmatized by the legacy of slavery and a virulent, unending white racism. As many conservatives see it, all the problems of blacks are essentially caused by an inability to fit in to the culture in which they live and an inability to stop seeing themselves as victims—an attitude that white liberals encourage them to maintain.

In short, the liberal believes that whites are the problem, the conservative that blacks are the problem. Any thinking black person must sit between these contesting categorizations, which have existed since antebellum days, feeling something between bemusement and contempt. Although blacks at various times, under various circumstances, may prefer one explanation to the other (usually, though certainly not always, the liberal's to the conservative's), the truth about blacks is to be found not in the middle ground but, paradoxically, in both views simultaneously, and in neither of them. The race problem is not really understood if it is seen as a white problem or a black problem. It is an American conundrum.

Americans do not like protracted problems or problems that suggest a limit to their power. Part of this is bound up with the belief of both blacks and whites in American exceptionalism—the idea of this country as a redeemer nation, a New Jerusalem. Americans also do not like to face the liberating possibilities of the profound historical tragedy within themselves; hence white neo-conservatism on the one hand, Afrocentrism on the other—ideologies of tragedy avoidance or sheer escapism.

Tom Wicker, a southerner and thus more believable as a sincere white liberal because he was reared amid the worst kind of racism, has in essence written a defense of the moral and political superiority of the welfare state, apparently the only kind of state in which blacks can thrive. (Conservatives assert that the welfare state has been the utter ruination of blacks.) His book argues that white America has reneged on its promise of integration and full justice and economic parity for black Americans in the 1960s and 1970s—a promise implicit in the *Brown* school-desegregation decision of 1954 and explicit in the Civil Rights Act of 1964—as it reneged on full citizenship and political parity for black Americans during Reconstruction. What has happened, Wicker asserts, from the time of Richard Nixon through the time of Ronald Reagan, has been a steady retreat on the question of civil rights and black advancement, for reasons of expediency on the part of white politicians at best, or of wretched cowardice on the part of white civic leadership at worst. The country

is as racist as it ever was, and the white population is still selfishly, even pathologi-
cally, venting its anger at and fashioning its scapegoats from the least among us—
African-Americans. Now, this thesis is hardly new. Andrew Hacker and Derrick
Bell are among the latest to sell a great number of books having anguish and outrage about the black condition as a theme. Of course, no one is very happy with
race relations in the United States, the sorry state of which was supposedly revealed, according to Wicker, by the public response to the O. J. Simpson verdict. In
fact, Wicker's indictment has a measure of merit and truth in it. Nonetheless, there
are a great number of problems with this book.

"If racial integration is to be revived as essential to a secure future for America,   5
an effective new political party forthrightly working for economic justice will be
necessary," Wicker writes in *Tragic Failure: Racial Integration in America*. "African-
Americans," he says explicitly, "must build a new political party." (Who could be
more expert on the issue of economic justice or a better advocate for it than the
very group that has suffered the greatest economic injustice? is, I think, Wicker's
reasoning.) Then we would have the usual populist assemblage of poor whites,
other racial minorities (after all, Wicker reminds us, whites themselves will be a
minority come 2050), and the like—that is, people who are "likely to encounter
some degree of economic and racial disadvantage."

Frankly, it is incomprehensible to me how black people could solve the problems   6
of isolation and alienation they face in the political realm (Republicans and Democrats are chary about a black political agenda and even, to some degree, about the
black vote itself) by forming their own political party, which would seem to do nothing more than institutionalize their isolation and alienation as a disaffected minority.

Tragic Failure wishes to be an accusatory book (against whites), but it is in essence   7
a lazy book. For instance, Wicker says that "the growth of the black middle class
was largely lost to view [of whites] in the lurid new visibility of the underclass remaining in the ghetto." Yet how does one explain the impact of people like Bill
Cosby, Oprah Winfrey, and Michael Jordan, and of the barrage of images on television and in advertising of a seemingly happy and broad black middle class—images
that have encouraged whites to believe that some blacks have indeed made it?

Blacks strike the white imagination in largely contradictory ways: as huge success   8
stories and as the underclass of criminals and welfare cheats. An analysis of this
contradiction is needed, but the book does not provide one. Wicker states, "It's
plain now that those inner-city blacks noticed mostly when they appear on the
nightly television news as perpetrators or victims of crime will be with us for years
to come." But since most nightly news shows, both local and national, have black
reporters and even black news anchors, why won't their images stay with "us" just
as long? And if inner-city blacks are seen largely as criminal, how much have they
participated in their own degradation through the marketing and commercialization of their cultural expressions, hip-hop and rap? These exploit the image of the
black male as outlaw and deviant to titillate the white suburban mind and to give
black culture, for the black consumers of this product, some supposedly subver-

sive, radical edge. Changing crime into political resistance, marginalization into a broad expression of humanity and liberation, has been a romantic preoccupation of the bourgeois intellectual since long before Foucault and the postmodern sensibility. In other words, blacks have historically been far too willing to accept distortions of themselves, because they see themselves culturally as whites see them: in intensely romantic terms.

In speaking of the connection between the black image and criminality Wicker does not mention that Danny Glover, Morgan Freeman, Whoopi Goldberg, Denzel Washington, Eddie Murphy, Martin Lawrence, Wesley Snipes, Laurence Fishburne, Jim Brown, Sidney Poitier, Paul Winfield, Yaphet Kotto, and Will Smith have all played cops or government agents in movies or on television. What impact has this had on the image of the black as criminal? If it has had none, why? 9

The book suffers greatly from this lack of consideration of the difficult contradictions in American culture. There is no serious thinking here. In a footnote Wicker suggests that although Lincoln thought that blacks should be sent back to Africa, he never suggested that whites go back to Europe. But Lincoln would have thought that sending blacks back to Africa was humane because they had been brought here against their will (unlike whites) and may very well have wanted to go back. (Of course they did not.) Also, Lincoln believed that as a recently freed people with no education and what appeared to him to be servile habits, they stood little chance of surviving in direct competition with whites. . . . 10

In speaking about sellouts, Wicker writes, "An African-American clearly would have a difficult task succeeding materially in American society (save perhaps in sports or show biz) without joining, to some extent, in the values and attitudes of that society—as a minor example, without dressing conventionally." Surely many whites, too, feel that they must "sell out," not be themselves, in order to get a job or pursue a career in the mainstream. That is what all the talk of conformity in the 1950s and surely the countercultural revolt of the 1960s was about. Selling out in order to make it is an issue that transcends race. Obviously it is even more difficult for blacks, in part because the opportunities to sell out are fewer and the demand for conformity is more charged. Dressing conventionally, Wicker suggests, is a white custom. Yet blacks have a long history of manners, etiquette, dressing well. What Ralph Ellison referred to as "elegance" is not foreign to black experience. 11

The overall problem with this book is that Wicker chose not to provide a deeply focused look at race relations and liberalism in this country. He did not interview dozens of people from various walks of life and in various locations to give their perspectives on integration and liberalism. He did not read—or at least did not provide evidence that he had read—all the books, conservative and liberal, about race and the pros and cons of integration that have come out in the past ten or fifteen years. If he had done this, *Tragic Failure* might have been an important book, instead of a sloppy, ill-considered one that says nothing new and does not condemn the failure of the national will to effect integration or defend liberalism nearly as well as the work of Jonathan Kozol and William Julius Wilson, for instance. This 12 book largely turns on the fact that a white southerner wrote it and in a rather bellicose way calls other whites incorrigible racists—which they may very well be, but that does not solve much of anything. And, of course, he charitably excuses black folk of all complicity after the fact, which is a form of rank patronization. Even the oppressed are not immune to stupidity, opportunism, greed, demagoguery, and a complex form of connivance in their own suffering.

Benjamin DeMott's *The Trouble With Friendship: Why Americans Can't Think Straight About Race* is more interesting, in part because DeMott's concerns are largely centered in the cultural realm, where most people find the real heat and light about race. It is also a more interestingly reasoned and argued book than Wicker's. DeMott's basic case is that through films, television, advertising, and other cultural products a "friendship orthodoxy" has arisen, in which the relationship between the races has become intensely personalized, the persistent dogma is that the races are essentially the same, and racism is regarded as the viewpoint of a psychotic fringe, a marginal expression that whites, once they are awakened, fight and defeat through their good will. Racism thus has no connection to power relations, to the purpose and coherence of American institutions, to the very sense of the nation as a political and social entity. In these dramatizations blacks bring no brutal history of oppression to the table and whites no sense of advantage from having had them to oppress. Everyone is more or less innocent, and after a few rough moments a kind of recognition of common humanity is achieved and we all go off together into that great, gettin' up, biracial morning. As far as it goes, this thesis about the representation of race relations and racial history in American popular culture is correct. But, alas, it does not go very far.

DeMott's marks are too easy. To condemn as fantasies most current Hollywood films with major black characters misses two points. First, Hollywood films are always about fantasy human relationships, whether they deal with man against the dark forces of society (film noir), marriage and sex (the romantic comedy, the screwball comedy, the domestic drama), or so-called social realism (the "problem" film, the protest film). Few American films have ever shown "power relations," "institutional influence on the formation of character," or other Marxist constructs. The fact is that race fits in with all these other relationships and gets dramatized in pretty much the same way. I am not sure that white America is trying to avoid anything more with race films than it is trying to avoid with films on any other subject. What is important is how race fits into this larger overall pattern; but DeMott simply describes the pattern, very incompletely and without the kind of historical rigor that would have given his argument value. A consideration of the careers of Harry Belafonte and Sidney Poitier in the 1950s alongside the careers of Hattie McDaniel, Stepin Fetchit, Clarence Muse, Willie Best, and the cohort of black comic actors of the 1930s and 1940s would have made his point far more powerfully and vividly. Poitier thought what he was doing was a matter of dignity, although DeMott would complain that his films were early versions of the black-white friendship fantasy. But McDaniel thought that what she was about concerned dignity as well, which is why she said she'd rather play a maid than be one.

Second, DeMott picks films like *White Men Can't Jump* and *Regarding Henry,* which are easy to analyze in the way he chooses, as friendship fantasies—but these are not expected to be anything more, politically, than, say, *The Terminator* or *Casino.* And, of course, why should they be anything more? What about a look at, for example, the blaxploitation movies of the late 1960s and early 1970s, which many blacks believe saved Hollywood financially and claimed, at times, some sort of social relevance? What about an examination of the black filmmaker in Hollywood and how he or she dealt with the "friendship orthodoxy"? Why are American films generally disposed not to deal with personal problems as having political and economic origins? Is it because of the ideology of individualism that so permeates the culture and that everyone—black and white—believes? 15

Another historical and cultural point DeMott misses is that, as David Riesman described in his classic work, *The Lonely Crowd,* post-industrial society, in particular America after the Second World War, is other-directed—that is to say, concerned with personal relationships. The prevalence of the other-directed social character goes a long way toward explaining why the race problem is depicted as it is in our cultural products and why many blacks and whites are satisfied with that form of depiction. Why does DeMott not talk about any of this? 16

The racial friendship fantasy is not some recent Hollywood invention; it dates back to Mark Twain's *The Adventures of Huckleberry Finn* (1884) and Harriet Beecher Stowe's *Uncle Tom's Cabin* (1852), both premised on intense friendships between people of different races. The friendship fantasy is deeply entwined with our concept of slavery itself—with one of the nation's worst political and social crimes. Herman Melville's "Benito Cereno" brilliantly explodes the idea of interracial friendship as a delusion. What lies behind the utopia of racial fusion is the horror of race war, Melville tells us. DeMott does not talk about any of this; he does not show that he is especially learned in the details of race in this culture. Those who are interested in this subject should read Melville. 17

Acknowledgments *(continued from copyright page)*

McCullough, Fran. "Ice Cream: Giving in to Rich Temptation." *The New York Times,* August 13, 1997, pp. C1, C6. Copyright © 1997 by The New York Times Company. Reprinted by permission.

Schwartz, Harry. "Must Doctors Serve Where They're Told?" *The New York Times,* 1942, Copyright © 1975 by The New York Times Company. Reprinted by permission.

Raab, Selwyn. "Holdup Man Tells Detectives How to Do It." *The New York Times,* March 5, 1975, p. A1+. Copyright © 1975 by The New York Times Company. Reprinted by permission.

"School Uniforms Growing in Favor in California." *The New York Times,* September 3, 1994. Copyright © 1994 by The New York Times Company. Reprinted by permission.

Russell, Bertrand. "The Social Responsibility of Scientists." Extract taken from *Fact and Fiction* by Bertrand Russell. Reproduced by the kind permission of Unwin Hyman Ltd.

Easterbrook, Gregg. "The Case Against Nature." Extract taken from pages 140–149 in *A Moment on Earth* by Gregg Easterbrook. Copyright © 1995 by Gregg Easterbrook. Used by permission of Viking Penguin, a division of Penguin Books USA Inc.

Tabor, James D. and Gallagher, Eugene V. "Waco and Religious Freedom in America." Excerpt from pages 173–186 in *Why Waco? Cults and the Battle for Religious Freedom in America* by James D. Tabor and Eugene V. Gallagher. Copyright © 1995 The Regents of the University of California. By permission of The University of California Press.

Rieff, David. "Multiculturalism's Silent Partner: Global Capitalism." Copyright © 1993 by *Harper's Magazine.* Reproduced from the August issue by special permission. All rights reserved.

O'Brien, Conor Cruise. "Violence—and Two Schools of Thought." Reprinted by permission of The Observer News Service.

Shea, Chris. "A Prominent Scholar's Plan for the Inner Cities Draws Fire." *The Chronicle of Higher Education* (September 5, 1997): A21. Copyright © 1997 The Chronicle of Higher Education. Reprinted with permission.

Sipher, Roger. "So That Nobody Has to Go to School If They Don't Want To." *The New York Times,* December 19, 1977. Copyright © 1977 by The New York Times Company. Reprinted by permission.

Singleton, Carl. "What Our Education System Needs Is More F's." *The Chronicle of Higher Education,* 1984. Reprinted by permission of the author.

Bork, Robert H. "The Case for Censorship" from Chapter 8 in *Slouching Towards Gomorrah* by Robert H. Bork. Copyright © 1996 by Robert H. Bork. Reprinted by permission of HarperCollins Publishers, Inc.

Henry III, William A. "The Museum of Clear Ideas." Extract taken from *In Defense of Elitism* by William Henry III. Copyright © 1994 by William Henry III. Used by permission of Doubleday, a division of Bantam Doubleday Dell Publishing Group, Inc.

Strossen, Nadine. "'Sex' Is also a Dirty Word." Extract from pages 19–25 in *Defending Pornography: Free Speech, Sex and the Fight for Women's Rights* by Nadine Strossen. Copyright © 1995 by Nadine Strossen. Reprinted with the permission of Scribner, a division of Simon & Schuster.

Rubin, Gayle. Quote from *Pleasure and Danger* by Carole S. Vance, editor. By permission of Routledge & Kegan Paul (1986).

tasy. But McDaniel thought that what she was about concerned dignity as well, which is why she said she'd rather play a maid than be one.

Second, DeMott picks films like *White Men Can't Jump* and *Regarding Henry,* which are easy to analyze in the way he chooses, as friendship fantasies—but these are not expected to be anything more, politically, than, say, *The Terminator* or *Casino.* And, of course, why should they be anything more? What about a look at, for example, the blaxploitation movies of the late 1960s and early 1970s, which many blacks believe saved Hollywood financially and claimed, at times, some sort of social relevance? What about an examination of the black filmmaker in Hollywood and how he or she dealt with the "friendship orthodoxy"? Why are American films generally disposed not to deal with personal problems as having political and economic origins? Is it because of the ideology of individualism that so permeates the culture and that everyone—black and white—believes?

Another historical and cultural point DeMott misses is that, as David Riesman described in his classic work, *The Lonely Crowd,* post-industrial society, in particular America after the Second World War, is other-directed—that is to say, concerned with personal relationships. The prevalence of the other-directed social character goes a long way toward explaining why the race problem is depicted as it is in our cultural products and why many blacks and whites are satisfied with that form of depiction. Why does DeMott not talk about any of this?

The racial friendship fantasy is not some recent Hollywood invention; it dates back to Mark Twain's *The Adventures of Huckleberry Finn* (1884) and Harriet Beecher Stowe's *Uncle Tom's Cabin* (1852), both premised on intense friendships between people of different races. The friendship fantasy is deeply entwined with our concept of slavery itself—with one of the nation's worst political and social crimes. Herman Melville's "Benito Cereno" brilliantly explodes the idea of interracial friendship as a delusion. What lies behind the utopia of racial fusion is the horror of race war, Melville tells us. DeMott does not talk about any of this; he does not show that he is especially learned in the details of race in this culture. Those who are interested in this subject should read Melville.

Angier, Natalie. "The Other Side of Suicide." Extract from pages 243–249 in *The Beauty and the Beastly: New Views on the Nature of Life*. Copyright © 1995 by Natalie Angier. Reprinted by permission of Houghton Mifflin Co. All rights reserved.

Lindholm, Charles. "Love as an Experience of Transcendence." Extract from pages 57–69 in *Romantic Passion: A Universal Experience* by William Jankowiak, ed. Copyright © 1995 by Columbia University Press. Reprinted with permission of the publisher.

Postman, Neil and Powers, Steve. "Getting Them into the Electronic Tent." Extract from pages 27–39 in *How to Watch TV News* by Neil Postman and Steve Powers. Copyright © 1992 by Neil Postman and Steve Powers. Used by permission of Viking Penguin, a division of Penguin Books USA Inc.

Clines, Francis X. "City Layoffs Hurt Minorities Most." *The New York Times*, February 20, 1990. Copyright © 1990 by The New York Times Company. Reprinted by permission.

Maeroff, Gene I. "Rule Tying Pupil Promotion to Reading Skill Stirs Worry."

Etzioni, Amitai. "Marriage with No Easy Outs." *The New York Times* (Op-ed page), August 13, 1997. Copyright © 1997 by The New York Times Company. Reprinted by permission. Responses from readers: Joseph Levenstein, Ph.D., Deana Marie Holmes, Nicole Mellow, John Pultz, James Warfield, and William L. Reynolds. Reprinted by permission.

Extracts from *Reader's Guide to Periodical Literature, 1905–1997*. Copyright © 1997 by the H. W. Wilson Company. Material reprinted by permission of the publisher.

Extract from *New York Times Index, 1851–1997*. Copyright © 1997 by The New York Times Company. Reprinted by permission.

Current Biography, 1978 and 1951 volumes. Obituary for Margaret Mead. Copyright © 1978, 1951 by the H. W. Wilson Company. Material reprinted by permission of the publisher.

McIlvanney, Hugh. "Onward Virgin Soldier." Combines two extracts: from "Onward Virgin Soldier" from the *Observer,* February 25, 1979 and "Johnny Owen's Last Fight" from the *Observer,* September 19, 1980. Copyright © 1979, 1980 by Hugh McIlvanney. Both articles were later published in *On Boxing: An Anthology* by Hugh McIlvanney (1980). Reprinted by permission of API Personality Management Ltd. on behalf of the author.

"Ban Boxing." *The New Republic,* August 8 & 15, 1988. © 1988, The New Republic, Inc. Reprinted by permission of *The New Republic*.

Oates, Joyce Carol. Extract from *On Boxing* by Joyce Carol Oates. Copyright © 1985 by The Ontario Review, Inc. Published by Doubleday, a division of Bantam Doubleday Dell Publishing Group, Inc. This article originally appeared in *The Ontario Review.* Reprinted by permission of John Hawkins & Associates, Inc.

Sugden, John. Extract from *Boxing and Society* by John Sugden. Copyright © 1997 by John Sugden. Reprinted by permission of Manchester University Press.

Baker, Carlos. Extract from *Ernest Hemingway: A Life Story*. Copyright ©1969 by Carlos Baker and Mary Hemingway. Reprinted with permission of Charles Scribner's Sons, an imprint of Macmillan Publishing Company.

"300 Killed by Fire, Smoke and Panic in Boston Resort." *The New York Times,* November 30, 1942. Copyright © 1942 by The New York Times Company. Reprinted by permission.

Index

causes in, 196
chart of commonly held views for, 203–5
citing sources in, 223
consequences in, 196
definition essays, 200–202
distinguishing between reasons in, 205
drawing conclusions for, 190–92
establishing own point of view (hypothesis) for, 214, 215–16
evaluating sources for, 219–20
generalizing from examples for, 195–97
narrow range of research for, 190
organizing sources for, 210–19
selecting information for, 189–92
sequence of topics in, 206
summarizing facts for, 214, 215
synthesis essays, 220–21
synthesis in, 202–6, 215, 216–19, 223
"Museum of Clear Ideas, The" (Henry), 146–55
"Must Doctors Serve Where They're Told?" (Schwartz), 35–37
My Brother, Ernest Hemingway (Hemingway), 300–301, 305
"My Race Problem—and Ours" (Kennedy), 485–94
"Myths of the Unloved" (Henderson), 482–85

Natriello, Gary, 285–86
New Republic, The, 295–96
newsgroups, 253–54
New York Times, 52, 259, 311–13
nonprint sources, 379
Nota Bene, 266, 373
note cards, 321–22
notes
    analyzing, 469–70
    cross-referencing, 340–43
    explanatory, 384–86, 387
    grouping by source, 323
    grouping by topic, 322–23
    organizing, 335–37
    parenthetical. *See* parenthetical notes
    umbrella, 387–88
note-taking, 319–34
    from abstract sources, 324–28
    appropriate emphasis in, 327–28
    for field research, 467–70
    guidelines for, 320–21
    for interviews, 465
    for making summaries, 55, 57–58
    one-fact-per-card method, 321–22, 342
    one-topic-per-card/sheet method, 322–23, 343
    paraphrasing for, 320, 325
    on potential usefulness of sources, 269–71
    for single-source essays, 162–63
    by source, 342
    summaries for, 320
numbered bibliographies, 458
nursing subjects indexes, 440–41

Oates, Joyce Carol, 296–97
O'Brien, Conor Cruise, 115–16
observations, for field research, 467–69

obsolete language, quoting, 75–76
On Boxing (Oates), 296–97
online databases and CD-ROMs, 248–64, 436
    bibliographies, 262–64
    cross-referencing, 254
    Internet, 250–54
    periodicals, 260
    searching, 254–57
    selecting sources to examine, 260–62
    specialized indexes, 258–60
    subject headings, 254, 255
    See also catalogs
Online Public Access Catalogs (OPACs), 248, 254
"Onward Virgin Soldier" (McIlvanney), 294–95
opinions
    labeling, 216–18
    placing, in categories, 218–19
Osler, Sir William, 90
"Other Side of Suicide, The" (Angier), 168–72
outlining, 34–43
    by categories, 40–43
    consistency in, 35, 42
    defined, 34, 121
    format for, 34–35, 41–42
    language used in, 35, 38
    levels of, 35, 38
    vs. paraphrasing, 102
    purpose of, 35
    rewording ideas in, 42
    single-source essays, 164–65
    thesis, 39

page references, including, in notes, 321
Paley, Grace, 16–19
Pallas, Aaron M., 285–86
"Pansy Quits" (Williams), 517–31
Papa Hemingway (Hotchner), 301, 308–9, 310
"Paradox of the Happy Marriage, The" (Bernard), 383
paragraphs
    accommodating argument in, 350–53
    guidelines for constructing, 348
    integrating quotations into, 96–98
    integrating sources into, 348–50
    for single-source essays, 166
    summarizing, 44–48
paraphrasing, 73, 79, 99–121
    accuracy of, 106–8
    defined, 2, 100, 121
    in essays, 100–101
    free, 103–4, 110, 112–13
    guidelines for, 102–3, 106–8, 113
    integrating, into essays, 115–21
    literal, 110, 111–13
    in note-taking, 320, 325
    vs. outlining, 102
    plagiarizing and, 102, 117–19, 368–69
    in preparing for reading and writing essays, 101–2
    selecting quotations for, 117
    vs. summarizing, 100, 105–6
    in synthesis essays, 220, 221
    in two stages, 110–13

THE
ULTIMATE
MICROSOFT
WINDOWS 95
BOOK

JOANNE WOODCOCK

Microsoft *Press*

PUBLISHED BY
Microsoft Press
A Division of Microsoft Corporation
One Microsoft Way
Redmond, Washington 98052-6399

Library of Congress Cataloging-in-Publication Data
Woodcock, JoAnne.
    The ultimate Microsoft Windows 95 book / JoAnne Woodcock.
        p.   cm.
    Includes index.
    ISBN 1-55615-670-7
    1. Microsoft Windows 95.   2. Operating systems (Computers)
I. Title.
QA76.76.O63W6633   1995
005.4'469--dc20   95-30710
                                                                        CIP

Printed and bound in the United States of America.

1 2 3 4 5 6 7 8 9 MLML 0 9 8 7 6 5

Distributed to the book trade in Canada by Macmillan of Canada, a division of Canada
Publishing Corporation.

A CIP catalogue record for this book is available from the British Library.

Microsoft Press books are available through booksellers and distributors worldwide.
For further information about international editions, contact your local Microsoft
Corporation office. Or contact Microsoft Press International directly at fax (206) 936-7329.

PostScript is a trademark of Adobe Systems, Inc. Apple, LaserWriter, Macintosh, and
TrueType are registered trademarks of Apple Computer, Inc. Banyan is a registered
trademark of Banyan Systems, Inc. CorelDRAW is a registered trademark of Corel Systems
Corporation. GEnie is a trademark of General Electric Corporation. Hayes is a registered
trademark of Hayes Microcomputer Products, Inc. Hewlett-Packard and LaserJet are
registered trademarks of Hewlett-Packard Company. Intel and Pentium are registered
trademarks of Intel Corporation. IBM and OS/2 are registered trademarks of International
Business Machines Corporation. 1-2-3 and Lotus are registered trademarks of Lotus
Development Corporation. DoubleSpace, Microsoft, MS-DOS, and Windows are registered
trademarks and DriveSpace and Windows NT are trademarks of Microsoft Corporation.
Arial is a registered trademark of The Monotype Corporation PLC. DR DOS, NetWare,
Novell, and WordPerfect are registered trademarks of Novell, Inc. Norton Utilities is a
registered trademark of Peter Norton Computing. SunSoft is a trademark of Sun
Microsystems, Inc.

Acquisitions Editor: Casey Doyle
Project Editor: Ron Lamb
Technical Editor: Kurt Meyer
Manuscript Editor: Marianne Moon
Visuals Editor: Ina Chang

Contents

PART 5: Road Signs 265

Acknowledgments

Acknowledgments filled with superlatives tend to be unbelievable. Yet it's also true that a book does not just happen and that there are many people whose efforts deserve such recognition. At the top of this list is Kyle Martin—sports fan and author of the troubleshooting chapter—whose own acknowledgments appear below. Thanks, Kyle, for taking on this book in addition to your real work with Windows 95.

Equally important are the members of the book team, all of whom believe that "less than best" is not worth doing. Those most closely involved with this book were: Ron Lamb, project editor; Marianne Moon, manuscript editor; Kurt Meyer, technical editor; Deborah Long and backups Cheryl Penner, Lisa Theobald, Stephanie Marr, and Pat Forgette, copy editors and proofreaders all; Peggy Herman, electronic publishing and layout artist; David Holter, technical and creative illustrator; Ina Chang, photo editor; Michael Victor, digital imaging and photo color correction; and David Mighell, digital imaging coordinator. No superlatives, everyone, even though you deserve them. But...*thanks*. And finally, for many reasons, thanks to Kate and Mark, and to Greg Schultz, Craig Stinson, Carl Seichert, Jim Fuchs, and John Pierce for companionship on the road to "Chicago."

—*JoAnne Woodcock*

Special thanks to the following people, who provided excellent feedback and technical insight: John Akers, Rob Beard, Michael Dunn, Faron Faulk, Don Ferguson, Geoff Gray, Robert Greenwell, Brian Gregor, Bill Jupena, William Keener, Scott McArthur, Richard McConnell, Dana Ratchford, David Reeck, Mitch Tate, Charles Teague, Richard Thomason, Charles Walker, Jeff Williams, and, of course, the rest of the Windows 95 Beta Team.

—*Kyle Martin*

①Getting Ready

Chapter 1

Starting Off

About This Book

This book aims to be your one-stop, plain-English guide to the ins and outs of Microsoft Windows 95, a powerful and exciting new operating system. The book's "ultimate" goal is to provide you with the "ultimate" trip through Windows 95—a trip that will help you understand and use your computer and your software intelligently and well without becoming a computer scientist in the process and without feeling that not knowing a lot about computers somehow makes you less intelligent than you ought to be. If the book can do this, it will have succeeded in *its* goal. The power and the achievement will be yours, however, and that's as it should be.

This chapter tells you about the book: what it covers, the hardware and software you need to use it, and what you can expect to gain from reading it. This is where you find out how the book presumes it can enrich your life and— especially important—what it assumes about you.

WHAT'S AN OPERATING SYSTEM?

It's the set of programs that control the way your computer behaves and, on a more personal level, that determine how you interact with your favorite machine. Thanks to its operating system, your computer shows a friendly face and does all the work you ask it to do... and more.

You First

If you're looking at this book, Windows 95 obviously is (or soon will be) a part of your computing life. Perhaps Windows 95 was preinstalled on your new computer, perhaps Aunt Matilda is trying to (or actually did) talk you into buying it, or perhaps you arrived at work one day to find that some gremlin had installed Windows 95 on your desktop machine. However you and Windows 95 joined forces, you now need to find out what it is and how you can make it work for you instead of feeling that *you* are working for *it* (a not-uncommon feeling among some computer users).

This book is for people who want practical advice on using Windows 95. But there are many books about Windows 95. Is this one appropriate for you? Well, it is or can be if you agree with statements like the following:

- Computers are good, but ice cream's better.

- I have no plans to build a shrine to microprocessors in the corner of my bedroom.

- The information superhighway sounds terrific, but I'll wait until someone else builds it.

- Basic, C, and Pascal are *not* legitimate answers on forms that ask "How many languages do you know?"

If you agree, you're *tuned* in but not *plugged* in. And that's the kind of person this book is looking for.

POWER PLAY

Chicago, Chicago...

If you've been following news reports for the past year or so, you probably know that "Chicago" was Windows 95's code name during the days of its development. But why would anyone name a computer operating system, even temporarily, after a city? You would think that software engineers seeking a pet name for their product would at least gravitate toward something "techno" sounding.

Well, even though Windows 95 *is* sleek, sophisticated, and (for those who see things that way) "sexy" enough to be a cybernaut's dream, the primary goal of its designers was to produce a *mainstream* (comfortable, easy-to-use) operating system for *mainstream* personal computers. Windows 95 was never meant for technical wizards using exotic machines for exotic purposes; hence the name "Chicago"—a constant reminder that Windows 95's real destiny was not to become a technological

showpiece (which it is anyway) but to become a functional and usable operating system as thoroughly mainstream in computing country as the city of Chicago is central to the United States.

Like Chicago, Windows 95 is both elegant and muscular, hardworking and yet fun. It's your personal environment, but one from which you can reach out to the world. It is, as advertised, friendly and mainstream. You'll like it.

(Ahh...there *is* one other point of similarity between Windows 95 and the city in Illinois. Remember Mrs. O'Leary's cow, the one that kicked over a lantern and started the Great Chicago Fire? Don't be surprised if Windows 95 takes over computing desktops as quickly and completely—though certainly not as destructively—as that famous fire swept across Chicago.)

Where You're Going and How You'll Get There

This book makes one assumption: "If at first you don't succeed" is a great attitude when you're trying to overcome an obstacle, but it's a lousy way to learn how to use Windows 95. "Try, try again" is for lab rats in mazes. Sure, when your goals become a little more advanced than searching your hard disk for ThatFileISavedButNowDontKnowWhereToFind, experimenting might well give you a lot of pleasure. But when you're trying to master the basics, the trial-and-error treadmill mostly produces frustration.

What (and How Much) You'll Learn

For the most part, this book covers information for beginning to intermediate computer users. This does not mean, however, that the book is superficial (even though some of the photographs might give it a rather...well...breezy air). Three-hundred-some pages about an operating system is quite enough to dig in a little, and so you shall. Sure, you'll find instructions of the "click this, drag that" variety that will explain how you use Windows 95 to manage your computer, your applications, your documents, and your printer. But you'll also push a little beyond the basics to see how to use Windows 95 with computers and printers on a network, and you'll see how Windows 95 can help you merge painlessly onto the much-touted information superhighway. Toward the end of the book, you'll check out ways to take the show on the road, and you'll find out how to use Windows 95 to keep your system neat, clean, and under control. And hopefully you'll have come to appreciate the underlying complexity of Windows 95—complexity that you never see but that is exactly what makes Windows 95 so robust and easy to use.

FILENAMES

MS-DOS and Windows 3 users: note that you really can name a document something like ThatFileISavedBut-EtcEtcEtc.... Windows 95 supports filenames up to 255 characters long. At last you can be as verbose on a PC as you can on a Mac.

Where to Start

Your starting point is easy: at the beginning, meaning here and in the next few chapters. Telling you where to start might seem silly, but think a moment. Computer books—and other nonfiction books—are not like favorite novels. Most people don't feel compelled to start at page 1 and read every word. Very often, readers turn directly to a part of the book that covers some topic they want or need to know about. Unfortunately, most nonfiction books must present information logically, so their coverage of a subject like Windows 95 tends to evolve from simple(r) to more complex as the chapter numbers grow larger.

This is not to say that you must read this book from cover to cover. Not at all. In fact, you're invited to skip around, especially in Part 3 and beyond, where the chapters cover different topics of interest, some of which might intrigue you while others might bore you to tears.

Regardless of your level of expertise, however, the first two parts of the book are meant to be used by everyone—yes, even those who have some experience with computers and with earlier versions of Windows. Why? Because Windows 95 is *different*.

Part 1 of the book shows and tells just how different it is. Part 1 is where you'll find the basic information you need, whether you're learning to use a computer for the first time or you're making the transition from MS-DOS, Windows, or (don't cringe) a Macintosh. Chapter 2 in particular tells you about Windows 95 and explains where it stands in relation to other operating systems, especially to those others also named Windows.

Part 2 (Chapters 3, 4, and 5) builds on this introductory information by taking you on a hands-on, guided tour of Windows 95. When you finish these chapters, you'll be able to use Windows 95 for most common computing tasks, such as starting applications, copying files, and arranging things nicely on screen.

Once you have these basics under your belt, you can use the rest of the book when, and as, the mood takes you. Browse chapters out of order, if you want, because the chapters in Part 3 and, especially, in Part 4 provide an up-close-and-personal look at individual Windows 95 features. Those later chapters are designed to help you not only use Windows 95 but also understand why you do what you do with it.

Traveling Light

To use this book, you need only a few things:

- A computer with an 80386DX or better microprocessor and at least 4 megabytes (MB) of random access memory, or RAM. (*Better,* by the way, means 80486 or Pentium microprocessors.)

- Windows 95, which can be either installed or still sitting in its box. Guidance and troubleshooting tips both for new installations and for upgrades are in the book.

- A mouse and printer—the usual stuff—and, optionally, add-ons such as a CD-ROM drive and a sound card (which are standard on multimedia machines).

However…

Readme

You'll see, over and over, that Windows 95 is nothing if not flexible and customizable. Windows 95's adaptability extends even to the Setup program used to install the operating system on your hard disk. As you read through this book, particularly in the beginning tutorial chapters, please keep the following in mind:

- Every effort has been made to ensure that you can try out most, if not all, of the practice sessions. There is, however, no guarantee that a particular feature has been installed on your computer.

The examples in this book were checked against Windows 95 as installed from CD-ROM onto a desktop computer. Some of these examples might not work if you install Windows 95 from floppies or if you opt for a relatively lean Windows 95 installation. Such "iffy" situations are noted for you in the margins, but do remember that if you can't seem to get Windows 95 to behave as advertised here, the capability might not be installed on your computer, at least not yet.

Why "yet"? With Windows 95, just because you can't do something right away doesn't mean you'll never be able to. You—yes, you—can install new Windows 95 features at any time. All you need are your original Windows 95 CD-ROM or floppies and the guidelines in Chapter 12. So if you want a feature, such as a game or a screen saver, that you don't seem to have, don't get mad. Skip the example for the time being, get comfortable with Windows 95, and when you're ready to install the feature, turn to the heading "Add/ Remove Programs" in Chapter 12.

Getting Your Bearings

And finally, what about all the boxes and colors and little pictures (icons) you see as you flip through the book? Much of this design is meant to pique and hold your interest, but there's method to this madness too, as the picture on page 8 explains. Basically, if you want "just the facts, ma'am," read the text and refer to the screen illustrations and diagrams. If you don't mind wandering off on tangents every now and then, check out the tips and troubleshooting

items. And if you want to go a little beyond the basics, spend some quality time with the Power Play topics.

However you approach this book, good luck, and may you enjoy the trip.

Chapter 3: The Start Button and My Computer

Hands-On!

Looking at Some Properties

You can familiarize yourself with several properties sheets by trying the following:

1. Right-click My Computer and choose Properties from the popup menu. Click the tabs, one after the other, for a Windows 95–eye view of your computer.
2. For a less dazzling technological display, open My Computer and request the properties sheet for your hard disk.
3. Double-click the Printers folder in your My Computer window.
4. Right-click a blank part of the taskbar and choose Properties.

Cleaning House

Barring disaster, extreme misfortune, or disk failure (which is rare, despite the horror stories that sometimes circulate), every file and folder and shortcut and scrap you create or save remains on disk in perpetuity, at least as far as Windows 95 is concerned. If there is any rule that a good operating system must follow, it's that every single character of every single piece of work you do must be remembered accurately, safely, and for as long as you want to keep it around. Such concern is admirable in the extreme, and computers certainly could not have become as valuable as they are if data storage were a hit-and-miss affair.

What this unswerving devotion to the well-being of each and every file cannot cope with, however, is human productivity and, face it, human foible. They've created tons of files. Some are indispensable.

DRAG
Place the mouse pointer on an object, press and hold a mouse button (left or right), move the mouse, and then release the button. You drag to move an object from one place to another. In text, you'll be told when to use the left button and when to use the right.

POWER PLAY
Where They Go

If you're familiar with Windows 3, scraps probably remind you of items you used to cut or copy to the Clipboard. In some respects, they are. In one important way, however, they are not. Remember that the Clipboard was designed for temporary storage of reusable information. Although you were able to save Clipboard contents with the help of the Clipbook Viewer, an item you placed on the Clipboard normally remained in memory only until it was replaced by new information.

When you create a scrap, Windows 95 creates a file for it—one that, if you're familiar with Windows 3 and MS-DOS filenames—has the extension SHS. Although Windows 95 doesn't ask when, whether, or where you want to save a scrap, a scrap file is as real as any you create with an application program. If the scrap is sitting on your desktop, Windows 95 places the SHS file in a folder named Desktop, which is stored within your Windows 95 folder.

Tip!
WHAT KEY WAS THAT AGAIN? Windows 95 supports a lot of mouse/key combinations. Sometimes, it's easy to forget which key you're supposed to use: Was it Ctrl or Shift that lets you use drag and drop to copy?

101

Hands On sections are step-by-step examples that let you try out what you've been reading about in the text.

Definitions provide on-the-spot explanations of terms and acronyms.

Tabs let you turn instantly to the section you need.

Getting Your Bearings sections help you keep track of what you should see on screen as you work through the tutorial chapters in Part 2.

Power Play topics take you a little beyond the basics; read them or skip them as you wish.

Tips give you practical advice.

Chapter 2

Windows 95

From the Ground Up

In the next chapter, you're going to start off on a tour of Microsoft Windows 95. This chapter is your orientation session, so to speak—an introduction to computers in general and to Windows 95 in particular. If you already know a lot about computers and operating systems, feel free to skip ahead. If you're stepping out for the first time (or almost the first time), this chapter should help you overcome any shyness you might feel toward your computer or Windows 95.

The Computer

Your computer is the hardware that you expect will perform miraculous feats at the touch of a key or the click of a mouse button. You know, of course, that a computer can support many different types of hardware, such as a modem, a microphone, a joystick, speakers, a printer, and so on. But what makes your computer different from your toaster? Why is it that your toaster simply makes toast, while your computer can help you write a letter, chart your investments, send electronic mail (e-mail) to a friend, or draw a picture?

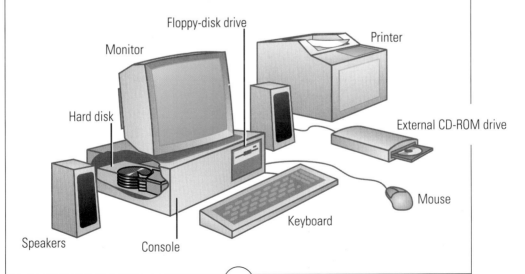

What makes it smart enough to play chess with you and probably beat you in the process?

The whole concept of computing boils down to three stages: input, processing, and output. What happens during these stages is, of course, extremely complex, but you don't have to know anything about that. What you should know is how these stages differ.

Input   Input is whatever information you enter into your computer. Traditionally, input has been defined as keystrokes—typing. That's still the most common form of input, but mouse clicks are input, too. So are lines and circles you produce with mouse, keyboard, or drawing tablet in a drawing or painting program. These days, input also often includes images you "read" into a computer with a scanner, voice commands you speak into a microphone, and information you pull into the machine with a modem or a fax/modem. Whatever its source, input represents the data and commands you ask your computer to act upon.

Processing   Processing, more than either input or output, is what you mean when you talk about *computing*. This is the act of taking input and manipulating it in some way to produce the results you want. Processing is what your computer does so quickly and so well. To perform this work, your computer relies on an unbelievably complex silicon chip (which is *not* made of compressed beach sand). This chip, your microprocessor, works with a number of other special-purpose chips to act upon the input you provide.

But, you might think, sometimes I input numbers, sometimes words, sometimes sounds, and sometimes pictures. How does the microprocessor distinguish among and process all these different forms of input? The answer is simple: to the microprocessor, there is no difference between numbers and letters or sounds and pictures. Why? Because all information inside your computer is stored and manipulated as blips, the 1s and 0s that give meaning to the words

HARDWARE

The touchable— "Are you sure I won't break it?"—console, monitor, keyboard, mouse, printer, and other mechanical and electronic parts of the system you paid a lot for.

digital and *binary*, both of which define *computer*. *Digital*, meaning numerical, tells you that all processing is done on information represented as numbers; *binary*, which refers to a number system, tells you that all processing is based on two digits, 1 and 0. Hard as it is to believe that so much can be made of so little, those 1s and 0s are what computing is all about. The magic lies in the fact that the microprocessor—and your computer's memory and disk drives and screen and so on—manipulate those digits in so many remarkable ways.

Output   After the input and the processing comes the output—the product of your microprocessor crunching your input. Often, output goes to your printer. Not always, though. When you save an edited document, the output goes to a file on disk. When you send e-mail, the output goes to your network connection or to your modem. When you play a stored video clip, the output goes to your screen. And when you play a sound bite, the output goes to your speakers. Regardless, output is the result of the work you've told your computer to perform.

Types of Software

When you set up a computer, your hardware is only the most visible part of the system. To make that hardware work, you need software: the programs that contain the myriad detailed instructions that tell the computer what to do and, at your command, when to do it. Software is what makes your computer *interactive* and, therefore, immediately responsive to your commands.

There are three main types of programs: system software, application software, and language software (programming languages, that is).

- System software controls the hardware. Windows 95 is system software.

- Application software, via the system software, makes the computer do useful work. Your word processor is application software.

SOFTWARE

The programs—sets of coded instructions —that reside on disk and make your computer do work.

LIVEWARE, AKA WETWARE

You.

- Language software helps create the system and application software you use. Unless you're a programmer, this type of software lies in the realm of "I doubt very much I'll ever buy *that*."

Windows 95, then, is system software, and it controls the hardware. Terrific, but what does that mean to you?

The answer is simple:

- Windows 95 makes all the parts of your computer work together without conflict. *Something* has to keep the peace so that your keyboard, display, disk drive, mouse, and assorted other hardware don't drive you crazy by fighting for attention at the same time. That *something* is Windows 95 (or any other operating system for that matter).

- Windows 95 supports your applications by doing basic housekeeping chores such as fetching documents from disk and making sure that commands like Print and Save interact with your hardware the way they're meant to. Because Windows 95 takes over these basic chores, it guarantees a constant environment for applications to work in, and it also frees applications to concentrate on what they do best.

- Most visibly, Windows 95 acts as an "interpreter" for you, providing you with a way to make your computer and your applications do what you want them to do. This part of Windows 95 is generally known as the *shell* or the *user interface,* and it is the part that will be most important to you. It's also the part you'll investigate most thoroughly throughout this book.

Although all these tasks seem straightforward, there's a lot of work involved in actually carrying them out—work that you don't see but that goes on constantly while your computer is active. As you learn more about the kinds of things operating systems do, you'll come to appreciate the scope and power of Windows 95's involvement with you, your hardware, and your applications. You'll realize that your operating system takes on a lot of work and a lot of responsibility.

FIRMWARE

Everybody knows about hardware and software. Fewer people know about something called *firmware,* which is kind of a "tweener" halfway between hardware and software. Like hardware, firmware is physical. It is, in fact, a special kind of chip called a ROM (read-only memory) that does not lose its contents when the power goes off. Like software, however, firmware is a set of instructions, but which have been "burned" into the ROM. What's firmware good for? Oh, just little things like the very, very basic instructions that help your computer start up and use its disk drives. Sometimes it's the little things that mean a lot.

POWER PLAY

Between You and the Machine: Windows 95

Of all the many parts of Windows 95—and there *are* many—the interface is the part that most directly concerns you, because its job is to give you a means of controlling your computer. Actually, the interface is your *only* means of controlling the machine, so the job's a critical one. After all, computers are, at heart, alien creatures that speak a strange, strange language.

Suppose you want to start your word processor. If the computer understood English, you could just type *start my word processor.* But, of course, the computer doesn't understand human language at all. In fact, even if all you had to do was simply translate the command *start my word processor* into the computer's native language of numbers, the command in its most readable form (for both you and the machine) would look something like this:

```
73 74 61 72 74 20 6D 79 20 77 6F 72 64 20 70 72 6F 63 65 73 73 6F 72
```

Inside the computer, however, even this instruction would be mashed into long strings of 1s and 0s. In this inner world, the *s* in *start* would actually become changes in voltage that can be expressed on paper like this:

```
0111 0011
```

As you can see, there's not a whole lot of common ground between you and the machine. If you personally had to translate all your instructions into 1s and 0s (as people once did by flipping switches), you'd probably chisel letters onto stone tablets before you'd use such a demonic machine. Thankfully, however, Windows 95 sits between you and the computer's innards, and like any other operating system, it steps in to handle the details for you. Because of Windows 95, all you need to do to make your wishes known is click here, drag there, drop somewhere else, and type this or that. Windows 95 takes over the job of translating your mouse and keyboard activity into computer-readable instructions that quickly reach the microprocessor, where command turns into action.

Now that you know about the tools—yes, tools—you'll be working with, it's time to move on to a closer look at Windows 95: what's new, what's exciting, what came before, and what's running alongside but on a different track.

What's New

The two illustrations on the next page show Windows as it was and as it is now in Windows 95. Quite a difference—and what you see on the outside is only the beginning. If you want the highlights, refer to the shaded box headed "Warning…" If a slower pace and less computerspeak are more your speed, skip over the shaded box and read on.

A thumbnail description of Windows 95 must include at least these three facts: it is *32-bit*, it is *preemptively multitasking*, and it runs in *protected mode*. Simply put, *32-bit* means that Windows 95 handles information in large chunks for faster, more effective computing; *preemptive multitasking* means that Windows 95 can run more than one program at a time and can schedule running programs in a highly efficient manner; and *protected mode* means that Windows 95 kicks your computer's microprocessor into highest gear, where the processor can work with the largest amounts of memory and information to give you peak performance.

EQUALS

You've no doubt heard the statement "less is more." The two illustrations on this page prove that point. The upper picture shows Windows 3; the lower picture shows Windows 95. Even though the lower illustration is far less cluttered than the upper one, its few simple elements provide easy access to everything shown in the Windows 3 illustration—more, in fact, as you'll see for yourself in the next chapter.

Didactics aside: Know who came up with "less is more"? Victorian poet Robert Browning. ☺

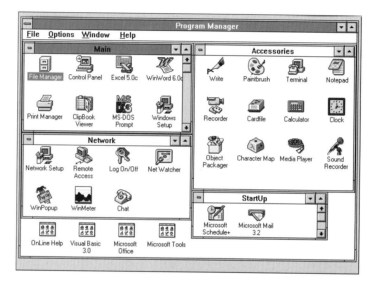

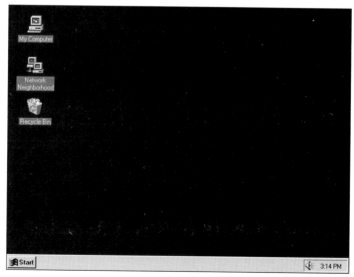

POWER PLAY

Warning: The Following May Be Hazardous…

Whether or not you're fluent in "computerese," the following paragraphs give a quick overview of Windows 95's main features. If you're new to computing, you might find some of this interesting, and for sure you'll pick up a few buzzwords to throw around, but don't expect to understand everything you read here. (Don't, by the way, let this computer-speak throw you into the Slough of Despond; it's just here for a little fun and a change of pace.)

Windows 95 is a *32-bit, preemptively multitasking, protected-mode operating system* with an *object-based graphical user interface.* The system is designed to work with *Plug and Play hardware* and contains built-in support for networking, mail, and mobile computing. Internally, Windows 95 relies on a "ringmaster" called the Virtual Machine Manager, or VMM, to ensure that resources are managed wisely and well and that programs run smoothly and without conflict. To deal with hardware, Windows 95 relies on *virtual device drivers* that fool multiple applications into believing that each has exclusive ownership of a particular device, such as the screen. These drivers can also be dynamically loaded and unloaded as needed to make Windows 95 as lean and efficient as possible.

On the functionality front, Windows 95 has a *32-bit print subsystem* that

spools documents as *enhanced metafiles* so that you can return to your application as quickly as possible, and it uses a 32-bit Installable File System (IFS) manager that supports (on your hard disk) a 32-bit file system called the VFAT. The VFAT allows you to create filenames as long as 255 characters and to track not only the date and time you create a document but also the date you last used it. If your computer is part of a network, Windows 95 can support a number of networks and network protocols, all of which make using shared resources as simple as looking up a number in the phone book. In addition, Windows 95's logon and password security help guarantee your privacy.

Memorywise, Windows 95 has cast aside *segmented memory addressing* (at least wherever possible) and treats computer RAM as a flat, *linearly addressable space* of 0 to 4 gigabytes—that's in the region of 4 billion characters—most of which isn't really even there. And (this really *is* interesting) Windows 95 runs MS-DOS programs in their own individual virtual machines, runs 16-bit Windows-based programs in a single common *virtual address space,* and will—when lots of 32-bit applications come along—run each 32-bit "app" in its own *protected address space.*

Had enough? Back to the real world.

To you, as a person who *uses* computers, however, other aspects of Windows 95's personality are of more immediate concern. *Bitness,* multitasking, and *processor modes* are fascinating for computer professionals, and as mentioned, they make Windows 95 the powerful operating system that it is. But real life is less analytical. After all, most people admire Porsches for their performance (and price) rather than for the actual engineering that produces their performance (and price).

Similarly, even though its technical underpinnings are remarkable, Windows 95 will work its way into your heart not because of its digital wizardry but because:

- It is easy to use, thanks to a simpler and more intuitive interface than the Program Manager/File Manager offering in previous versions of Windows.

- It can run existing MS-DOS and Windows-based applications in addition to programs specifically designed to take advantage of its speed and power.

- It easily lets you run several applications—even Windows-based and MS-DOS programs—at the same time.

- It is tougher than earlier versions of Windows, meaning that it provides a more stable environment for non-Windows 95–based applications—even MS-DOS games, some of which are remarkably single-minded about the way they run and the way they use your computer's hardware and memory.

- It offers strong support for communications, network connections, mobile computing, and—increasingly important to many people—multimedia.

- It is designed for Plug and Play (PNP), which eventually will make installing new hardware as simple as plugging it in and restarting the computer.

- It lets you use the *right* mouse button (yes!) to request lists of actions appropriate to whatever you're currently doing.

- It doesn't need to use MS-DOS as a stepping-stone to awareness.

- And, if you choose to install and use the Microsoft Network, Windows 95 even becomes a fun and easy ticket to a world of news, chats, bulletin boards, and general electronic fellowship.

The Windows Family Tree

It all started back in 1982, with a tiny little operating system named MS-DOS and the first of the 80x86 computers, the IBM PC. MS-DOS, which many people know quite well, grew from a small operating system to a rather sizable (and capable) one over the course of a dozen years. For the most part, however, the MS-DOS interface works from a command prompt that looks like this:

```
C:\>
```

NEW TO COMPUTERS?

If you've never used a computer or Microsoft Windows, you might feel you don't properly appreciate people's enthusiasm for some of Windows 95's most talked-about features, such as its friendly interface. Don't worry about this. You just haven't developed a "world view" that puts such things in perspective. Give yourself a year or two, and when the next version of some popular software comes along, you'll be right in there discussing the benefits and drawbacks of each new bell and whistle. For now, assume that enthusiasm about Windows 95 means it's a winner—which it is.

POWER PLAY

Getting Bitwise

Everybody's talking 32 bits these days. All right, want to byte? Thirty-two bits of what?

Here's a primer.

Start with the concept of a binary number, a number made up of nothing but 1s and 0s, like this: 1111011. That's the binary equivalent of decimal 123. Neat, isn't it? To your computer, each one of those *binary* digits is one bit. The only thing you have to know about bits is that they're a computer's food for thought. Everything, but everything, goes through the processor as bits. And how do those bits travel to and from the processor? On circuitry known as *buses* (basically, internal freeways connecting the processor with memory and various other hardware within the computer).

Now, some freeways—the car kind—are three lanes wide; others are four; and still others are six. If you were to think of each lane as capable of carrying a stream of individual bits, you could say that a 3-lane freeway would be 3 bits wide, a 4-lane freeway would be 4 bits wide, and so on. Apply that thinking to the processor and the buses inside your computer, and voilà, you've got it. In olden days (about 12 years ago), computers handled information in groups of 8 or 16 bits, meaning that some information traveled along 8-lane freeways and other information was routed along 16-lane jobs.

As processors and computers became more powerful and more sophisticated, the "chunk size" and the bus size grew, until today, with the 80386, 80486, and Pentium processors, you have chips and hardware that shuttle information in groups of 32 bits. (Actually, the Pentium goes one better: it handles references to memory in 32-bit chunks but can shift data in 64-bit pieces.)

Anyway, what has all this got to do with Windows 95? Well, earlier versions of Windows handled information in 16-bit parcels. Except for tasks that require 16-bit maneuvers to maintain compatibility with older programs, Windows 95 takes advantage of the 32-bit "freeways" in your computer by moving everything 32 bits at a time. The result for you is an operating system that can do more and do it faster, an operating system that can handle complicated internal procedures and so open up a host of new ways of working. Most visibly, Windows 95's 32-bitness means that it can easily reach—and make use of—an enormous amount of memory.

Many people, for some inexplicable reason, have found this command prompt rather…cold. In addition, they've been put off by MS-DOS commands that look something like this:

```
xcopy a:\*.doc c:\mydocs /d:01-01-95 /s /v /w
```

Looks simple enough, doesn't it? Well, doesn't it?

Windows

To make computers friendlier and to make using them easier for people, Windows came along in 1985. Although it was graphical, mouse-oriented, and friendlier than MS-DOS, Windows in its first incarnation (version 1) didn't exactly take the world by storm. To people with 20/20 hindsight, however, it did show the world where computing on 80x86 machines was headed. (Popular wisdom says this vision appeared sooner and better on the Apple Macintosh. True, perhaps, but Windows these days has a significant advantage over the Macintosh: sheer volume.)

Over the years between 1985 and 1990, Windows grew in speed and power and in its ability to overcome some of the limitations—such as the use of more than 1 MB of memory—that were imposed by MS-DOS. In its most recent form (prior to Windows 95), Windows version 3 accomplished what version 1 could not: it did, indeed, take the world by storm. With the release of this version of Windows (actually, versions 3.0, 3.1, and 3.11), software developers also began to produce a slew of applications that eventually led more and more people to the Windows way of working. Not coincidentally, it was version 3 of Windows, in both its stand-alone and networking Windows for Workgroups forms, that began to push MS-DOS aside as *the* operating environment for 80x86 computers.

During the time that Windows and Windows for Workgroups were establishing their dominance, hardware developers were also pumping electronic steroids into computers, video, and add-ons such as CD-ROM drives and sound boards. The result: high-performance hardware just itching for a high-performance operating system—which just happens to be either your Windows 95 or the Wonder Windows known as Windows NT in both its Workstation and Advanced Server models.

Windows NT

Windows NT is an operating system for a computer with a lot of horsepower under the hood. Although Windows NT runs nicely on an 80486 system, it can also run on computers built around RISC (pronounced "risk") chips and those that contain more than one processor. These are high-end systems indeed. In keeping with its muscular nature, Windows NT needs more memory than Windows 95 does, and it includes security and other features that are

RISC-Y BUSINESS

The acronym RISC stands for Reduced Instruction Set Computing and refers to a type of processor that carries out a limited number of simplified instructions but does so extremely quickly. The type of processors in the 80x86/ Pentium family are known as CISC (pronounced "sisk") chips. CISC is short for Complex Instruction Set Computing and covers processors that carry out complicated and powerful instructions. CISC chips have typically been the processors of choice in general-purpose computers like yours. Who knows, however, what the future holds, given the rapid development of new and ever more powerful processors.

really not needed on a desktop computer, especially one that does not run demanding high-end applications of the sort that produce models of DNA molecules or act as overseers of networks supporting hundreds of business machines and workstations.

Windows 95—My Kind of GUI

In comparison to earlier versions of Windows, the most noticeable feature of Windows 95 is the highly visible transformation its graphical user interface, or GUI (pronounced "gooey"), has undergone. Although the GUI is the means by which all versions of Windows have interacted with their users, the Windows 95 GUI is startlingly different—cleaner, simpler, and more intuitive—from the one used by even its closest relatives, Windows and Windows for Workgroups version 3.11.

An operating system's user interface is nothing more— and certainly nothing less—than the connection between you and the parts of the program that carry out your commands. To make your work as simple as possible, Windows 95, like earlier versions of Windows, uses pictures, called *icons,* and *menus* (lists of choices) to help you communicate your needs quickly and easily. In Windows 95, though, there's a big difference that can be summed up in one word: objects. Sound too technical? Nah.

For Every Object, an Action

Everyone knows what an object is: it's a thing, an item, an individual some-thing that you can identify, pick up, move, toss at the cat, put away, or throw away. In addition—and this is important in understanding the Windows 95 interface—an object can also be something that you can put inside other objects. You can, for example, take a scattering of marbles and treat each marble individually, or you can put one or more marbles inside another object, such as a box. It's the same with Windows 95, even though you handle Windows 95's objects with a mouse.

Buddy, Can You Paradigm?

What makes Windows 95 very different from its predecessors really boils down to a refinement of one simple concept:

• Choose it and do it.

Every version of Windows has emphasized "point and click" (with the mouse) as a much more natural way to work with a computer than typing strange commands that contain strange characters. Windows 95 takes point and click one giant step further by categorizing everything in its world as an object of some type. That is, Windows 95 assumes that the easiest way to work with a computer is not only to be able to see and point to onscreen items but to actually manipulate those items as if they were real, for-true, physical objects of the type you handle all the time in the real world.

This concept of "choose an object and do something to it" is known as Windows 95's "noun-verb" or "object action" paradigm—a fancy name for the conceptual model that describes the view of computing that, in turn, drives the way Windows 95 behaves and the way you work with it. In other words, Windows 95 is all about...

Doing What Comes Naturally

What's the first thing a small child does with a new object— food, toy, whatever? He or she picks it up and, probably, tries to eat it. You're a little older and a little wiser, and you're not about to try to eat your com-puter, but that instinct to handle objects still remains a basic part of you. You pick up and exam-ine items in a store, fill your pockets with shells at the beach, poke pillows to see how soft they are, and lob empty soda cans at the trash bin (oops, sorry, the recycling bin). Because this inclination to manipulate items in your environment is so ingrained, Windows 95's inclination to treat everything as an object makes it particularly easy for anyone, beginner or old pro, to figure out what to do.

Because Windows 95 works with hardware, programs, and documents as objects, you can drag them, drop them (on screen, of course), and otherwise manipulate them much as you do with real-life books, folders full of docu-ments, or telephones. For example, you can print a document (an object) by dragging it to the printer (another object). You can create a folder (again, an object) and place documents (objects) inside it. If you want, you can also move or copy documents from one folder to another.

If all those mentions of objects sound kind of airy, put them in perspective by thinking of objects as being comparable to teddy bears, basketballs, or bushel baskets. Bears, balls, and baskets can all be picked up, moved, and otherwise handled. Furthermore, bears and balls can easily be put inside baskets. It's the same with Windows 95 objects, except that these objects are on screen.

With that in mind, consider the illustration at the right, which shows several objects in Windows 95—including the My Computer icon that Windows 95 uses to represent on screen your real, touchable computer system.

Just as you can move your real computer around, you can move the My Computer object on the screen.

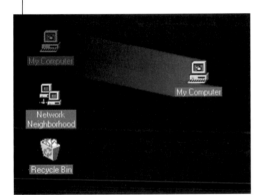

And just as you can work with disks on your real computer, you can "open" My Computer to view the drives and other objects that make up your system.

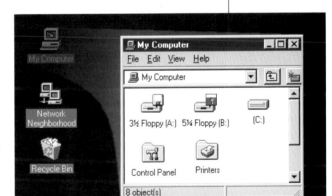

As you probably noted, My Computer is not *exactly* equivalent to your real computer. The physical machine, for instance, is connected to a printer by a cable; the printer isn't in a manila folder labeled *Printers*. Overall, though, the relationship should be fairly obvious: My Computer is equivalent to your hardware. At a minimum, your (real) hardware consists of one or more floppy-disk drives, a hard disk, and possibly a printer; so does My Computer. Easy, isn't it? Remember that onscreen objects:

- Represent the items you work with and

- Can be handled just as you handle real objects

and you'll have Windows 95 bowing to your wishes in no time, as you'll see in the next chapter.

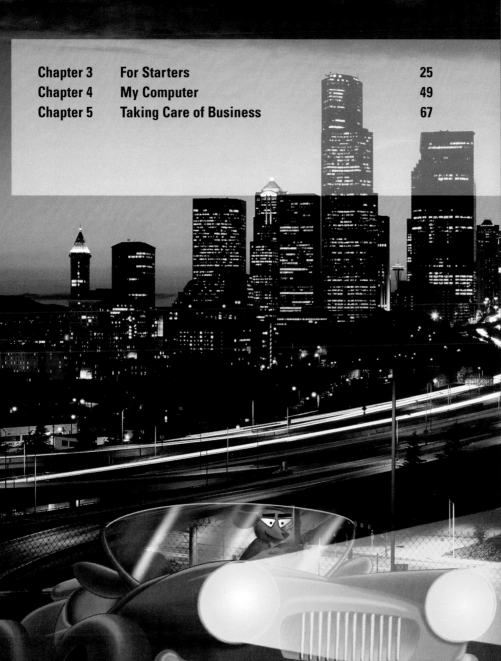

Taking Off

Chapter 3

For Starters

Taking Off

This chapter begins your hands-on look
at Microsoft Windows 95. If you're a
newcomer to Windows or to computers
in general, by the end of this chapter
you will be feeling comfortable with the
idea of dominating a machine that can
"talk" back to you. If you're a seasoned
Windows hand, some of this information
will seem familiar, but skim the material even if you don't think you need it.
Windows 95 resembles its predecessors, but it *is* different, and you'll be pleased
to find welcome new features tucked inside old familiar ones. (If you're new to
mousing, by the way, take note of the definitions on pages 28 and 29.)

The remainder of the chapter leads you through practice sessions that build
on one another, but you don't have to work straight through. Start and stop
when you want or when you reach one of the breakpoints noted in the text. If
you want to shut down Windows 95 for a while, follow the steps on page 46,
under the heading "Calling It Quits." To pick up where you left off, check for
the icon shown in the margin of this paragraph. That icon appears next to
text that explains what you should see on screen as you march into the next
fun-filled activity.

Tuning In

Before you can do anything with Windows 95, you obviously have to get it
started. How to do this?

• Turn on your computer.

Because Windows 95 is your operating system, the simple act of turning on
(booting) your computer is enough to get the show on the road. During startup, your computer beeps and burps, lights flash, and Windows 95 takes over
your display. That's all normal behavior, so sit back, watch, and wait as your
system, with the help of Windows 95, steps through the remarkable process
of transforming itself from inert machine to fully interactive computer.

Logging On

At startup, Windows 95 might prompt you to *log on* by displaying a message like the following.

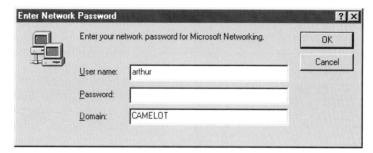

If you're not asked to log on, skip this section. If you are asked to log on, read on.

When you log on, you identify yourself to Windows 95 by providing a *user name* and a *password.* (A domain name or a server name like *CAMELOT,* as shown above, appears only when your computer is part of a network; if so, this box should already be filled in for you.) Although it's easy to log on, the actual procedure does vary from one situation to another because Windows 95 supports two different ways of logging on. Depending on your computer setup, you might see either or both of two prompts. Here's what to do:

- If you see a network logon prompt, which looks like the one illustrated above, type the user name assigned by your network administrator, press the Tab key, type your password (which you should also know), and then click the OK button. Logging on to a network lets you join the network community and gain access to the files, printers, and other shared resources you're permitted to use. If you have any questions, contact your network administrator. Don't play guessing games.

- Whether or not you're part of a network, you might also be asked to log on to Windows 95 itself. This "local" logon identifies you to Windows 95 on your computer so that it can distinguish you from others who use the computer. Why? So Windows 95 can customize itself to your preferences. This "local" prompt looks like the one above, without the Domain entry. If you see a local logon prompt, either type a name and password you've chosen or press the Esc key to tell Windows 95 not to bother verifying your identity for now. (If you want some tips on choosing a user name and password, refer to the shaded box, "Who Goes There?")

LOGON TIP

If you log on both to a network and to Windows 95, you can shorten your logon time by 50 percent simply by using the same password for both your network and Windows 95 logons. If both passwords are the same, Windows 95 displays only the network logon prompt. After you log on to the network, Windows 95 uses the same password to automatically carry out your local Windows 95 logon, too. Simple, effective, and easy on your memory. (There's more about passwords in Chapter 10, "Networks and *The* Network.")

POWER PLAY

Who Goes There?

If you've never had to vouch for yourself to a piece of software, don't worry about logging on. Windows 95 doesn't expect you to be a letter-perfect typist, so if you make a mistake you can either backspace and try again or wait until Windows 95 tells you of the error and then try again.

If you have to come up with a user name or password on your own, the following guidelines should help:

- **User name.** Choose any name you want, up to 20 characters (and presumably within the limits of taste and decency). Capitalization does not matter, nor do spaces and certain special characters such as ! and @. Do, however, try to choose a name that's uniquely you—for example, combine initials, use both your first and last names, or go by a nickname. Even if you're one of seven J. Does in

your organization, you can try using a middle initial, several letters from your first name, or a number, such as Jdoe2.

- **Password.** Choose a string of up to 14 characters, but omit spaces. Pick a password that's easy to remember and easy to type but unusual enough that others are unlikely to guess it. Skip the obvious, such as your first name, but forgo the exotic, such as *quetzalcoatlus* (unless you love dinosaurs) or *szgmp940xb* (unless you love finger aerobics).

For both your user name and password, Windows 95 insists on exact spelling but is cavalier about capitalization. So, for example, if your name or password were *Sherlock*, Windows 95 would refuse to acknowledge *Surelock* when you checked in, but it would happily accept either *sherlock* or *SHERLOCK*.

CHOOSING A PASSWORD

Don't choose *sex, love, money,* or *chicago.* You wouldn't believe how many other people will be clever that way, too.

Windows Welcome

Whether or not you end the startup process by logging on, your first look at Windows 95 is a display like the one in the illustration at the right.

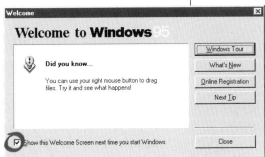

The box titled Welcome To Windows 95 is actually your first look at a *window*, the type of place in which you will work with Windows 95. This particular window is preset to appear whenever you start Windows 95 and is designed to help you familiarize yourself with what the Windows 95 designers knew could be a new and unknown environment. You can tell Windows 95 not to show you this window every time you start Windows by clicking the check box circled in the preceding illustration—but consider leaving the box checked for the time being. Each time you start up, Windows 95 will display one of 50 useful tips in the box, under the words *Did you know,* so leaving this Welcome window turned on gives you an effortless and memorable way to pick up some Windows 95 highlights.

If you want to explore the buttons in the Welcome window, refer to the shaded box titled "A Closer Look at the Welcome Window" or wait until later in this chapter, when you reach the section on Windows 95 Help. For now, to move on:

• Click the button labeled Close at the bottom of the window.

POWER PLAY

A Closer Look at the Welcome Window

You can use the top three buttons at the right of the Welcome window to request help in starting off on the right foot with Windows 95. The following list tells you what to expect:

• The Windows Tour button, if it appears in the Welcome window, takes you to a 10-minute interactive introduction to using Windows 95. (If you do not see this button, the tour is not installed on your computer but you can install it—CD-ROM only—as described under the heading "Add/Remove Programs" in Chapter 12.)

• The What's New button, primarily for people moving from Windows 3 to Windows 95, takes you to a series of question-and-answer screens that help make the switch from Windows Old to Windows New as easy as possible.

• The Online Registration button, which requires a modem, starts one of a number of Windows 95 programs known as *wizards.* This particular wizard prompts you for registration information and helps

you send that information directly to Microsoft. (Do remember to register your copy of Windows 95, either online or through "snail mail"—the postal system. Being a registered user means being able to call on Microsoft for support and other good things.)

If you'd really like to see all the tips the Welcome window has to offer but you'd just as soon not see the window each time you start up, use the Next Tip button in the window to click your way through all 50 tips and then turn off the window as described on page 27. All gone.

(You can get the Welcome window back, by the way. As you'll soon see, all you have to do is find and double-click a file named WELCOME, which is on your hard disk in a folder with the rest of Windows 95. Open the window, click to restore the check mark, and the window will return at every startup. You might not feel comfortable enough to do this now, but keep the tip in mind for later.)

MOVING THE MOUSE POINTER

Roll the mouse on your desk or mouse pad. As you move the mouse, the arrow-shaped onscreen pointer moves the same relative distance and direction. If you reach the edge of the desk or pad, don't keep going and going. Pick up the mouse, and move it back onto the playing field; the pointer moves only when you roll the little ball inside the mouse.

Home Base: The Desktop

With the Welcome window out of the way, you can see what Windows 95 really looks like. What you're gazing at is the *desktop*, the workspace on which Windows 95 displays and arranges all the windows you open. No matter what brand of computer you have, what hardware you use, or what software you've installed, the Windows 95 desktop always includes at least the four items labeled in the following illustration.

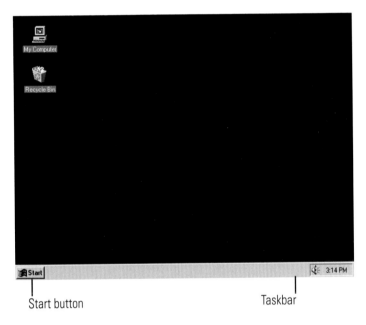

Start button   Taskbar

CLICK

Quickly press and release the left mouse button.

DOUBLE-CLICK

Press and release the left mouse button twice—quickly and without moving the mouse. It's easier than it sounds.

DRAG

Place the mouse pointer on an object, press and hold a mouse button (left or right), roll the mouse, and then release the button. You drag to move an object from one place to another. In this book, you'll be told when to use the left button and when to use the right.

- My Computer is an *icon* (small graphic) that represents your computer— its disk drives, attached printer, and so on. As you'll soon see, you can "open" the icon to work with disks and files.

- The Recycle Bin is a container in which Windows 95 deposits all the files you throw away (delete). Because the Recycle Bin actually saves deleted files on your hard disk, you have the ability to retrieve—recycle—a file you accidentally tossed away. As with real recycling, however, you periodically dispose of the contents for good by emptying the bin.

- The Start button, like the ignition in your car, gets you going. When you click the Start button, you open a series of menus that list programs, documents, and special commands that help you start programs, customize your computer, find files, and do other essential tasks.

- The taskbar is a "tray" of sorts on which Windows 95 places a button for each window you open. Because buttons for all open windows appear on the taskbar, you can easily switch from one program to another by clicking the button you want.

RIGHT-CLICK

Quickly press and release the right mouse button (the rightmost button if you have a three-button mouse). Yes. The right mouse button is no longer as useless as your appendix.

The desktop can, as you'll see throughout this book, be home to a number of other objects. Some of these might have been installed when you (or someone else) set up Windows 95. So you might, for example, see an icon labeled Network Neighborhood or My Briefcase. Other desktop objects, known as *shortcuts*, are icons that you, yourself, can place on your desktop at any time to customize Windows 95 and the way it works for you. Right now, however, concentrate on the basic desktop objects. What you learn about *them* will easily spill over into other areas.

This is a good breakpoint if you need a rest. If you shut down Windows 95, restart your computer and close the Welcome window when you return.

The Start Button

In the lower left corner of the screen, you've no doubt noticed the Start button begging to be pushed. This button, like much in Windows 95, resembles great architecture by being deceptively simple. Just a button? Not at all. Push it:

• Point to the Start button and click.

Up pops a colorful menu that, like a restaurant menu, is divided into categories. You don't have anything tasty here, but you do have entries named Programs, Documents, Settings, Find, Help, Run, and Shut Down. Notice the small triangle at the right of each of the first four items. Each triangle is Windows 95's way of telling you that choosing the entry will lead you to a secondary menu containing more choices, like this:

• Move the mouse so that the dark highlight is on Programs.

Now Windows 95 expands the Programs entry to show you a number of more specific choices, among them yet another group item, named Accessories, as well as "end-of-the-line" items that take you to the MS-DOS Prompt and the Windows Explorer. Enticing as these are, for now, take the offering that's the most fun:

• Highlight Accessories.

Yet another submenu opens, and as you can see, this one contains even more groups, as well as a number of Windows 95 accessory programs—miniature (and not so miniature) applications with which you can write, draw, calculate, and if you have a modem, even communicate. These applications, sometimes called *applets*, are a kind of bonus that everyone gets with Windows 95.

No doubt when you open a menu, you'll have a goal in mind. Sometimes, however, people open the wrong menus or they change their minds. Closing an unwanted menu is simple:

• Move the mouse pointer to an empty part of the desktop and click.

SEE SOMETHING DIFFERENT?

That's OK. The items on your Start menu, including those on the Programs and Accessories submenus, vary according to the components chosen when Windows 95 was installed on your computer. You might, therefore, see an item that is not shown here or, conversely, you might not see one that is shown here. Don't worry about such discrepancies. If you see an option you'd like on your computer, you can install it whenever you choose, as described in "Add/Remove Programs" in Chapter 12.

POWER PLAY

Using the Keyboard

If you're an inveterate keyboard fancier, you don't have to use the mouse to work with the Start button and its menus:

- Press Ctrl+Esc to open the Start menu. (Ctrl+Esc means press both keys at the same time.)

- Use the Up and Down direction keys to move the highlight to the item (command) you want, and then press Enter. Or press the

underlined letter, known as the *access key,* in the command name. Pressing this key immediately carries out the command.

- To open a submenu, such as Programs or Accessories, press Enter or press the Right direction key.

- To close a submenu, press the Left direction key.

- To close the Start menu, press Esc.

As Long As You're Here...

Even though some people, such as those who write computer books, spend inordinate amounts of time digging into operating systems, most people simply want to use their operating system as a springboard to specific tasks: creating documents, drawing pictures, calculating figures, playing games, and so on. Presumably, those are your goals too, so now is as good a time as any to start a program:

1. Reopen the Accessories submenu.

2. To choose from a menu, highlight the command or item you want and click. Try it by clicking the WordPad option to start Windows 95's compact word processor. Be patient. The program might take a few seconds to start up.

When the WordPad window opens, choose from the Start menu again and start another program so that you can practice managing windows:

1. Reopen the Accessories submenu.

2. This time, choose Paint.

Your screen should look like the one in the illustration at the right.

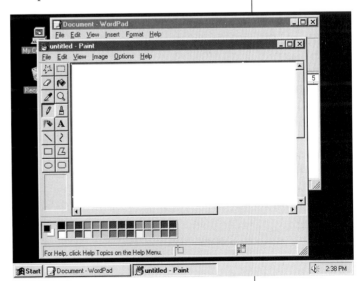

By the way, this ability of Windows 95 to hold more than one application open at the same time is not new, but it is just as welcome as in earlier versions of Windows. Remember that Windows 95 is capable of multitasking—working on more than one job at the same time. One important key to this multitasking is Windows 95's ability to maintain each program in its own usually inviolate and usually inviolable workspace, represented on screen by a window just like the two you're looking at right now.

The Taskbar

Now that you have some programs running, notice that your formerly barren taskbar now sports two buttons in addition to the Start button: one for WordPad and one for Paint. Notice too that the Paint button is "pushed in." That's Windows 95's way of telling you that the Paint window is the *active* window, the one Windows 95 is currently prepared to work in. Your WordPad window is *inactive*, meaning it's open and available but it's not the one Windows 95 assumes you'll be working in.

Switching Windows and Thereby Switching Tasks   It's almost axiomatic in Windows—and in many Windows-based applications—that for every task you can think up, you can choose among several ways to carry it out. So it is in going from one window to another as you move from one task to another. Since you're looking at the taskbar, try the easiest method:

• Click the WordPad button.

Several things happen: the WordPad button is pushed in; the WordPad window comes to the fore; and the title bar in the WordPad window becomes dark blue. All three results tell you that you are now experienced in *task switching*. You have switched from one active task (Paint) to another (WordPad). All at the click of a button.

If you were actually working with these programs, you would now have exchanged your Picasso paintbrush for a smart digital typewriter. To return to your canvas:

• Click the Paint button on the taskbar.

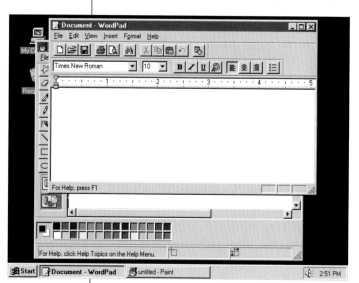

POWER PLAY

Can't Forget Program Manager?

If Windows or Windows for Work-groups version 3 feels as natural to you as breathing, you *can* still use Program Manager.

If Windows 95 is not yet installed, you can set it up to run the Windows 3.1 interface. To do so, choose a Custom installation. When Setup displays a window titled Computer Settings, scroll to the end of the list, click User Interface, and click the Change button. In the new window that opens, click Windows 3.1 (Program Manager). Click OK to return to the main Setup window, and continue the installation by clicking Next. (For more information on Setup, refer to Appendix B, "Setting Up.")

If Windows 95 is already installed or if you want to be able to "fall back" on Program Manager now and then, use the following instructions. Note, however, the instructions assume you know how to find your way around Windows 3.

1. Double-click the My Computer icon on your desktop.

2. Double-click the icon for your hard disk in the My Computer window.

3. Double-click the icon for your Windows 95 folder in the hard-disk window.

4. Scroll to Progman (the one with the icon representing three over-lapping windows) and double-click.

When Program Manager starts, you'll see a window for your desk-top and a window for each major group listed on your Windows 95 Start menu. You will not see group windows for installed applications, such as Microsoft Office, but you can start those programs easily enough in any of the following ways:

- Choose File Run, click the Browse button, find the folder that con-tains your program, and then double-click the program name.

- Choose File Run, and type the path and program name in the edit box.

- Double-click the Windows Ex-plorer icon in the Programs group, and work your way to the pro-gram folder with the help of the Windows Explorer (which looks and acts much like File Manager).

- Use the File New command to create a new program item for an installed application. You can then run the application by double-clicking the new icon.

If you want, drag Progman from your Windows 95 folder window and drop it on the Start button. The next time you start Windows 95, Program Manager will appear at the top of the Start menu.

Or, of course, you can read this chapter and the next few chapters. They won't take long, and you'll probably settle in a lot faster than you thought you would.

ACTIVE VS. INACTIVE

In addition to the state of the buttons on the taskbar, you can use two other prominent visual cues to tell you which of several open windows is currently the active one. The active window is always the one with a dark blue title bar (the band across the top of the window). Also, if windows overlap, the active window is always the one on top of the pile.

And what about those other ways to switch tasks? They can come in handy at times, so give them a try:

- Click in any clear area in the WordPad window or the WordPad title bar. You're a person of letters once again.

- Hold down the Alt key and press Tab a couple of times. These keys, as you can see, bring up a small window that helps you cycle through active programs. Use Alt+Tab to make Paint the active window by releasing the Alt key when Paint is named in the window.

(Historical sidelight: the Alt+Tab key combination was popular with many Windows 3 users as an always-reliable means of finding and switching to an open window. Windows 3, you see, didn't have a taskbar, so open windows sometimes had a way of getting lost behind other windows....)

Arranging Windows and Thereby Changing the View Switching from one window to another is handy, but sometimes you'll want to be able to arrange your open windows so that you can see them all at the same time, especially if you want to work with the contents of two or more windows. Windows 95, like its predecessors, offers two window arrangements: *cascading* and *tiling*. Try them both, and at the same time see how Windows 95, unlike its predecessors, handles the right mouse button:

1. Place the mouse pointer on a blank part of the taskbar, and *right-click* by quickly pressing and releasing the right (or rightmost) mouse button.

2. Click Cascade on the popup menu that appears.

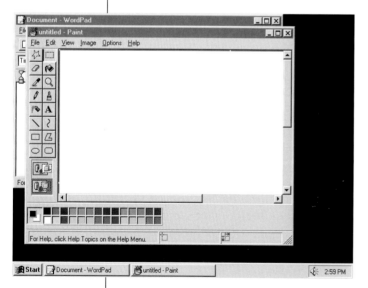

The result is shown in the illustration at the left.

As you can see, cascading starts in the upper left corner and spills windows down and across the screen so that the title bar of each is visible. As a window arrangement, cascading is nice for tidying up the desktop, especially because, as you can see, it generally results in same-size windows. Only the contents of the topmost window are visible, however, so cascading isn't particularly useful for viewing or working with information in multiple windows.

In addition, because the taskbar contains buttons for all open windows, cascading isn't as necessary as it was in Windows 3 for seeing which windows you have open.

If you cascade (or tile) windows, you can always undo the arrangement if you want to return either your desktop or your windows to their earlier state. Before you take a look at tiling, try an undo:

1. Right-click on a blank part of the taskbar.

2. Choose Undo Cascade from the popup menu.

Now for tiling, which places windows like, well, the tiles in your bathroom:

1. Right-click on a blank part of the taskbar to open the popup menu again.

2. Choose Tile Horizontally if you want your windows arranged one above the other; choose Tile Vertically if you want your windows set side by side, as in the following illustration. The only difference between these two options is the arrangement that results.

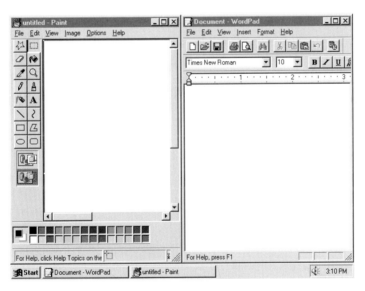

This time, you can see that Windows 95 arranged your windows so that you can see the blank workspace in each window. Tiling is the way to go when you want to work with documents in several windows. Notice, however, that tiling means each open window receives an equal share of your onscreen workspace. If you've opened many windows (say, four or more), tiling them all might result in windows that are smaller than you'd like. As a rule of thumb, close unneeded windows before tiling. That way, you maximize your workspace and minimize distraction from "clutter" you won't be using.

THE RIGHT MOUSE BUTTON

As you work with Windows 95, keep the right mouse button firmly in mind. Right-clicking an object in Windows 95 opens a *popup menu* that lists only those commands that are applicable to that particular object. Because the contents of a popup menu are limited to "legal" actions, the right mouse button is an ever-handy means not only of performing a task but also of determining what, exactly, you can and cannot do with a particular object at any given time. As you learn your way around Windows 95 and the applications developed for Windows 95, the right mouse button can help you keep your cool and develop an almost subconscious feel for the program as you work.

To return your screen to its prior state:

1. Right-click on a blank part of the taskbar.

2. Undo your tiling.

One Click Makes It Larger...

Aside from cascading and tiling windows, you can also temporarily close a window while keeping the program in it active and ready to return at a moment's notice. *Minimizing* a window in this way "collapses" the program into its taskbar button. You can minimize a single window by clicking the Minimize button, shown in the following illustration.

For example:

1. Make WordPad the active window if it is not already active.

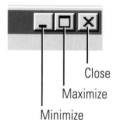

Close
Maximize
Minimize

2. Now click the Minimize button in the WordPad window.

Immediately Windows 95 shrinks the window to a dark bar that glides down onto the taskbar. To restore the window to its former shape and size:

• Click the WordPad button on the taskbar.

Quick and easy. And for those times when you want a clean desktop, you can minimize all currently open windows by right-clicking the taskbar, as you'll see now:

• Right-click on a blank part of the taskbar, and choose Minimize All Windows from the popup menu.

All open windows disappear into buttons on the taskbar. To reopen the windows:

• Right-click on a blank part of the taskbar again, and this time choose Undo Minimize All from the popup menu.

Finally, with no more than a click, you can also switch an open window back and forth between full-screen size and its current (less than full-screen) size. To do this, you use the middle button in the upper right part of the window— the button labeled Maximize in the preceding illustration:

• Click the Maximize button in the WordPad window. Immediately, Windows 95 expands the window to full-screen size.

Now you have lots of room for creative writing, but does this mean Paint is lost to you for the time being? Not at all. Notice that the Paint button still sits, nicely visible, on the taskbar. A single click on that button, and Paint will immediately overlay the WordPad window.

THOSE BUTTONS

If you're an experienced Windows 3 user, you'll notice that Windows 95 gives you three control buttons at the right end of the title bar instead of the two you're familiar with in Windows 3. In particular, notice that the Close button takes the place of Windows 3's Maximize button. Pay attention when you click. It's easy to inadvertently let old habits take over and thus close a window that you meant to maximize or restore.

Oh, and if you often work in an MS-DOS window, here's another tip: you can click the Close button to end an MS-DOS session. No more typing *exit* to close the MS-DOS window.

Restore

Notice also that Windows 95 has changed WordPad's Maximize button. When the middle button shows two overlapping "windows" as shown at the left, it has become a Restore button, which returns the window to its former size:

- Click the Restore button. Windows 95 shrinks the WordPad window back to its former size and shape.

Docking the Taskbar   You've seen what the taskbar can do for you, but you haven't yet seen that the taskbar itself is like a cargo ship: you can *dock* it at any of the four points of your onscreen compass—north, south, east, or west— simply by dragging with the mouse, like this:

1. Move your mouse pointer to a blank part of the taskbar.

2. Press and hold down the left mouse button.

3. Keeping the mouse button down, move the mouse pointer to the top or side of your screen. As you move the pointer, the outline of the taskbar will tag along and then suddenly jump to the top or edge of the screen when the pointer moves above or to the side of "ground zero," which is the midpoint of the screen. Release the mouse button when the outline settles at the top or side, and then return things to normal by dragging the taskbar back to the bottom of the screen.

Docking the taskbar is, of course, more than entertainment. Depending on how you work best and how you eventually organize your desktop, you might well find that you prefer to see the taskbar at the top or side of the screen rather than at the bottom. When the time comes, remember that the taskbar is a movable beast and represents just one of many ways in which you can customize Windows 95.

MORE FUN WITH THE TASKBAR

You can do more with the taskbar than simply drag it around. You can also hide it, and you can make it "float" on top of open windows. These capabilities are described in Chapter 7, "The Metaphorical Desktop."

Working in Windows

Now that you've played with windows a little, you can get down to the real nitty-gritty and actually get some work done. If you've been following along on your computer, you should still have the WordPad and Paint windows open. Although you won't be using Paint in the next example, just leave it open for a few minutes. You won't hurt anything. If you've shut down your computer in the meantime, restart WordPad only.

Creating a Document

Although the word *computer* tends to be near-synonymous with *game* to many people of the under-16 persuasion, more "productive" members of society know well that *computer* more often than not means *document.* The type of document, of course, depends on the software you use and the work you want to do. Regardless, there are three activities you can count on when working with documents: creating them, saving them, and reopening them.

Word processing is probably the most intuitive and popular computer application, so to keep matters simple, use WordPad to create a document:

1. If necessary, make WordPad the active window by clicking in the window itself or by clicking the WordPad button on the taskbar.

2. Type the following, pressing the Enter key where you see *[Enter]* in text:

    It's an open-and-shut case, Doc.[Enter]
    This is Windows 95.

Menu bar

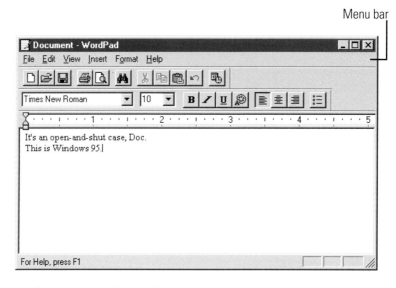

For straight text entry, that's about all there is to creating a WordPad document. You, of course, will produce more dynamic prose, but this will do as an example.

Saving a Document

Once you've created a document, the only way to keep it for reuse is to save it on disk. The reason you must save boils down to three letters: RAM. *RAM,* as you probably know, is short for random access memory, which is the type of computer memory you talk about when you tell the folks at the country club that you just bought a machine with 32 megs (megabytes, or MB) of RAM. Lucky you…nice toy.

ADDING EXCITEMENT

WordPad has a lot more to offer than just the black-and-white, typewriter-emulation mode you see in the text example. You can use color, boldfacing, and italics. You can change fonts (typefaces). You can realign paragraphs. And because Windows 95 and its accessories support a feature called *OLE* (pronounced "olay"), you can create mix-and-match documents that combine text with objects such as graphics, animation, and even sound. For more on this, refer to Chapter 9, "OLE!"

POWER PLAY

What's Random About It?

RAM is such a common shorthand for computer memory that people don't often stop to think about its full name—*random access* memory. Random access is an important part of what makes RAM so special (and your computer so fast).

Think of RAM as a wall or bank of numbered boxes very much like the boxes in a post office. Imagine what service would be like if a letter carrier had to open every box, starting at box 1, each and every time while delivering hundreds of pieces of mail to the hundreds of different boxes. And imagine what it would be like if you had to sift through mail one box at a time, starting at box 1, in order to collect your mail in box 376. Slow and inefficient.

The same situation applies to RAM, except that the "boxes" making up your RAM number in the millions. If the microprocessor had to start counting from box 1 each time it needed to fetch data, find an instruc-tion, or save the result of a calcula-tion, you'd be better off using an abacus and painting on papyrus. (Well, maybe not exactly, but bear in mind that information in a com-puter is handled in small quantities, including single characters.)

Given what the situation *could* be, you can see why random access is so valuable and efficient. The micro-processor and, by extension, your programs never have to start at the beginning of memory and work sequentially to any particular desti-nation. They can go directly to the box or boxes they need—which is to say, they can *randomly access* any portion of memory. Further-more, they can do all their deliver-ing and retrieving flawlessly and at incredibly high speeds so that you end up with a computer that "thinks" in thousands of instruc-tions per second. Impressed? There's a lot to be learned, even about so common a term as *RAM.*

RAM is as necessary to a computer as air is to you. RAM's primary function is to serve as the microprocessor's "knowledge base." That is, RAM is where your computer temporarily stores all data, program instructions, and even Windows 95 itself so that the microprocessor has facts and figures to process and instructional blueprints to tell it what to do. The problem with RAM is that it is electrically charged, so it holds information only as long as your computer is turned on. Turn off the computer or experience a power failure and—as many sadder but wiser people can tell you—RAM goes BAM. It loses every last scrap of information you entrusted to it. And if that information included the draft report you've been working on all night but didn't stop to save, well…join the sadder but wiser crowd. The report's gone, and the only way to get it back is to re-create it from scratch.

Now that you have deep appreciation for the act of saving your work, save your sample document:

1. Point and click to open the File menu on the WordPad *menu bar* (labeled in the illustration on page 38).

2. Choose the Save As command.

(This two-step procedure, so simple and intuitive, chooses the Save As command from the File menu. To simplify the text as well, from here on this book will often use a kind of shorthand for choosing menu commands that consists of the menu name followed by the command name. So, for example, the preceding steps would be "choose File Save As." OK? Now back to saving.)

When you chose File Save As, WordPad opened the small window shown below. This window is a *dialog box,* so called because the program uses it to carry on a dialog with you.

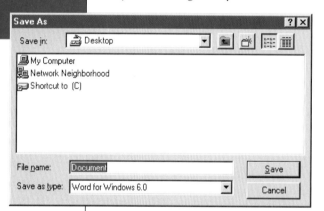

In this case, WordPad is asking you what to name the file and (as you can see at the top of the window) where to save it. In your real work, you'll want to organize your document files in folders, but since you'll soon be deleting this sample, go ahead and save it in WordPad's *default* suggestion, which is directly on your desktop, where the document will appear as a new icon.

Now tell Windows 95 what you want to call your literary achievement:

1. The word *Document* in the box labeled File Name should be highlighted. Whatever you type will replace the highlighted characters, so name the file by typing:

    My Sample WordPad Document

2. Click the Save button at the right of the dialog box to complete the save.

Your disk drive briefly spins into action, and WordPad changes its title bar to show you the name of your current—and newly saved—document.

Closing a Program

Although you can switch among windows at will, there will come a time when you will want to finish with a program. Finishing means saving your work (which you've just learned how to do) and then exiting. When you exit a program, you not only ensure that you've put everything away neatly but you also release memory that Windows 95 can reassign to other programs and data. It's a win-win situation for both you and Windows 95.

You've finished with WordPad for now, so close it (and Paint if it's still open). As usual, you can take any of several exits. Choose the one you like best from the following options:

- Click the Close button (the button marked with an X) in the upper right corner of the program window.

- Double-click the title-bar icon in the upper left corner of the program window. (In WordPad, the icon is the notepad at the left of the document name. In other programs, the title-bar icon reflects the program's specialty. In Paint, for example, the icon is a bucket of paint and brushes.)

- Press Alt+F4.

- Choose the File Exit command.

However you go about it, the program and its associated taskbar button disappear, to wait patiently on the disk for your next summons.

Reopening a Document

Now that you've closed your program, you can see how to restart a program and, at the same time, reopen a particular document. If the document is sitting right on your desktop, as your sample file is doing now, all you do is double-click the document icon. That's quick and easy, and you could take that route

POWER PLAY

Microsoft Word?

When you save WordPad documents, WordPad saves them, by default, as Microsoft Word version 6 documents. If you've installed Word on your hard disk and you use the Document list to reopen such a document, Windows 95 opens the document in Word rather than in the less powerful WordPad. This handing over of the baton does not mean, however, that you are forever locked into Word. You *can* open or reopen a Word 6 document in WordPad simply by

starting WordPad and opening the file in either of the following ways:

- Choose the file's name from the list of recently used documents at the bottom of WordPad's File menu.

- Use the Open command on WordPad's File menu to find and open the document you want.

(Related information, including more about document types, is in Chapter 8, "Workout: Exploring Files.")

here, but try a different way instead. Why? Because as you create many documents and learn how to organize them in *folders,* you won't want to keep all your work on the desktop. Take the time now to learn how to find and open a document tucked away somewhere on disk. Most times, all you need is the Start button:

1. Click the Start button to open the Start menu.

2. Choose Documents. This opens an ever-changing submenu in which Windows 95 lists the names of the last 15 documents you worked with. For people who work with a lot of different documents, this feature will no doubt rank high on the Windows 95 whizbang list.

3. Click the item labeled My Sample WordPad Document.

Within a few seconds, WordPad will start up and display the document you requested. If, instead of WordPad, you see Microsoft Word, don't be distressed. The explanation is in the shaded box on page 41 titled "Microsoft Word?"

This is a good breakpoint if you want a rest. Close WordPad (or Word). When you come back, restart Windows 95 and close the Welcome window.

Help!

As you saw earlier, when you start Windows 95, the Welcome window might display one button that takes you to help for new users and another button that takes you to help for prior Windows users. After you close the Welcome window, you can access these and other forms of help whenever you want. Once again, the doorway is the Start button:

1. Open the Start menu.

2. Click the Help command.

Whenever you request this help, you see the window shown at the left.

The three tabbed "cards" you see here let you search for help in different ways:

- The Contents tab lets you search through Help categories. As you can see from categories such as Introducing Windows and Tips And Tricks, this tab, like a book's table of contents, can be especially useful when you're in a browsing mood.

- The Index tab lets you search for specific topics, such as help in saving files or in resetting your computer's clock. When you know the name of what you want help with and you want to find it quickly, this is the tab to use.

- The Find tab lets you customize Help so that it can search not only for topics but also for specific words, word forms, or phrases within Help topics. The Find tab, new in Windows 95, is a fine and worthwhile addition to Help. Unlike the other tabs, this one becomes usable only after you've run a Find Setup wizard that helps Windows 95 build a database of terms gleaned from the Help topics themselves. The wizard is mighty easy to run. Simply click the Find tab, and when the wizard appears, click the Next and Finish buttons. From that point on, all you have to do is type or select "key" words and let Windows 95 do the searching for related topics. For the most part, however, plain old "uncustomized" Help is just fine.

Tabs aside, you can request either of two kinds of help: interactive guided tours, which provide the same assistance you can request by using the buttons in the Welcome window, and "mission-specific" Help screens, which give you step-by-step how-to instructions. First stop: the guided tours.

Interactive Help

Windows 95's guided tours present hands-on, interactive Help that familiarizes you with Windows basics. The easiest way to get to this Help (other than through the Welcome window) is to use the Contents tab, as follows:

1. If the Help window isn't open, click the Start button and choose Help.

2. If you're a new Windows 95 user and you see a topic titled Tour: Ten Minutes To Using Windows, double-click the "page" icon bearing a question mark at the left of the topic heading. You should see a colorful window like the one at the right. (If the topic does not appear, the tour is not installed on your computer. As mentioned earlier, you can either refer to Chapter 12 for help installing the tour or you can simply keep chugging through this and the next few chapters. Either way, you'll learn to use Windows 95, so don't feel that the choice is a monumental one.)

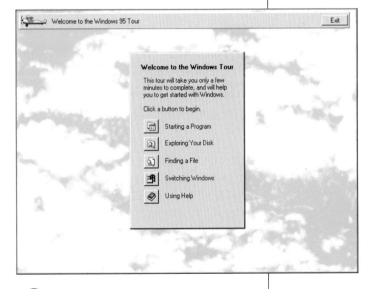

A WINDOWS 95 SUMMARY

If you open the topic titled A List Of What's New under Welcome on the Contents tab, you'll find six sub-topics, each of which takes you to a screen containing push buttons that walk you through hot new Windows 95 features. Browse these when you have a spare minute or two, either to see Windows 95 as a whole or to reinforce what you learn from this book and from your own Windows 95 experiences.

If you have the tour, click the button next to a topic that interests you and follow the (self-explanatory) instructions on your screen. If you want to quit before going through the complete set of lessons, click the Exit button at the top right of the window and then click the Exit Tour button in the next window that appears. Have fun.

3. If you're a former Windows user, set off on your own tour by double-clicking If You've Used Windows Before. Windows 95 will take you to the first of a set of question-and-answer screens that cover the most common questions about the move from Windows 3 to Windows 95. When you've had enough, click the Close button at the top right of the window.

Even if you never use either of these introductions to Windows 95 again, it's nice to know they both exist. It's better than wishing you could post a Help Wanted ad somewhere.

No matter which tour you took, reopen the main Help window when you're ready to continue in this chapter.

Step-by-Step Help

The Help you've just seen gently familiarizes you with the Windows 95 environment, but sometimes you want the how-tos that help you with a particular task. That's where Windows 95's mission-specific Help comes in. You can request this type of Help from any tab in the Help window. Since you've already seen the Contents tab, give the Index tab a whirl. You'll like it:

1. Click the Index tab. What you see looks like the following. As you can see from the labels in the illustration, the blank rectangular *text box* at the top is where you type all or part of a word you want to look up. As you type, the display in the *list box* below jumps to the first index entry that matches the letters you're typing.

Type a few letters here...

...and Help jumps to that part of the alphabet here.

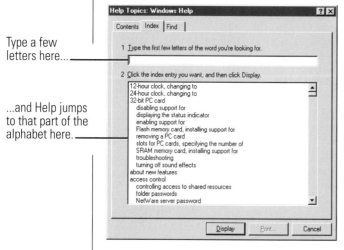

2. Choosing a Help topic is easy, so give it a try. The blinking vertical *insertion point* should already be in the text box, so type a letter to send Help on its way. Type the letter *s*, and the highlight in the list box immediately jumps to the first *s* entry, *safe mode*.

3. You're going to go a little further, so now type *p*. This time, the highlight jumps to the first *sp* entry, *space on disks*.

4. One more time. Now type *eed.* This is a good place to be—*speed.* All right, what kind of speed should you look for Help on? Mouse speed is fun, so double-click the topic *mouse double-click speed, adjusting.* The main Help window disappears, and a new, step-by-step window opens up.

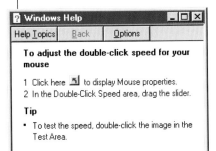

Take a moment to scan the window contents, and then turn your attention to the square button with an arrow in step 1 in the window. This is called a *shortcut button,* and it is to you what "Beam me up, Scotty" was to Captain Kirk. The button takes you directly to whatever program or part of Windows 95 you need in order to continue with Help. So…

5. Click the shortcut button. Now you see another window, this one a *properties sheet,* which is a fancy name for a window that lists (and lets you customize) the characteristics of a particular object—in this case, your mouse.

6. Refer back to the Help window. Step 2 in the window tells you how to change the rate at which you double-click. If you want, experiment with the slider—or leave it alone. Regardless, have a little fun while you're here.

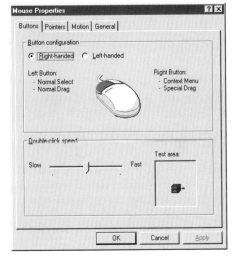

7. Point to the animated jack-in-the-box in the part of the properties sheet labeled Test Area, and double-click. If Windows 95 registers the two mouse clicks as a double-click, the Test Area lets you know. When you finish, click the Close button on the Mouse Properties sheet.

8. You've finished with Help for now, so click the Close button in the Help window.

Now it's time for one valedictory lesson to close the window (so to speak) on window basics: shutdown.

JUMPING AROUND IN THE INDEX

You can jump around in the index list. If an entire entry—such as *graphics, creating*—is highlighted, press the Del key or type the letter(s) you want to jump to. If the blinking bar is still in the box and the entry is not highlighted, use the Backspace key to erase letters and then type the one(s) you want.

HELP WANTED

When you're working with a properties sheet, you can ask for help with options you don't understand. Either right-click the option and then click the small box labeled What's This that appears, or click the question mark (?) in the upper right corner of the properties sheet and then click the option. Both approaches display a brief explanation that should help you figure things out.

Calling It Quits

Unless you plan to leave your computer running all the time—not a very "green" choice—knowing how to shut down is just as important as knowing

how to start up. Whether or not you've ever used a computer before, here's the first and most important rule: *don't* shut down by turning off the machine. That drastic action might be called for someday if an unruly program "hangs" your computer to the point that you, Windows 95, and the computer are all equally helpless to do anything, but under normal circumstances, you should do it Windows 95's way.

Here's what to do:

1. Save all unsaved documents and close open programs. Although you can leave an open program on screen, it's better to pack up everything when you shut down.

2. Choose Shut Down from the Start menu. The dialog box shown at the right appears.

3. The default choice is Shut Down The Computer. This is what you'll usually want to do, so to carry out the command simply click Yes or press Enter. (Right now, if you want to keep Windows 95 running, click No or press Esc to cancel the shutdown command.)

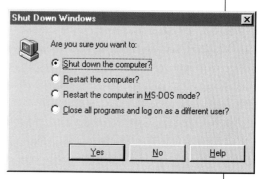

During shutdown, Windows 95 asks you to be patient while it prepares your computer for shutting down. During this time, Windows 95 is making sure that all data is safely stored, it's recording the status of your screen (so that it can show you the exact same thing next time), and it's recording any changes you've made to customize its behavior. All this is important work, so...

4. *Wait.*

5. When Windows 95 tells you it's safe, turn off the computer or press Ctrl+Alt+Del to restart the machine.

POWER PLAY

Choices, Choices

Are you wondering about those other choices in the Shut Down Windows dialog box? You would choose Restart The Computer if you wanted to restart Windows 95 from scratch—that is, go all the way back to the beeping and startup routines that normally occur when you turn the machine on.

The option Restart The Computer In MS-DOS Mode is a special-purpose command for use with MS-DOS programs, such as games, that cannot be run from Windows 95. When you restart in MS-DOS mode, Windows 95 turns off the visual "shell" that you normally see and sets up an environment in which your MS-DOS program should be happier. When you finish with the MS-DOS program, type *exit* or *win* to return to Windows 95.

The final option, Close All Programs And Log On As A Different User, is for people who use a network or share a computer and who want to shut down active programs and either log off or log on again under the same or a different user name. This option closes open programs and prompts you to log on, but without actually restarting either Windows 95 or your computer.

Chapter 4

My Computer

I *Know* It's My Computer

You don't have to be a rocket scientist to figure out that "it" is, indeed, *your* computer. But don't forget there's your computer, and there's My Computer—the icon that's been sitting in the upper left corner of your screen waiting for you to get around to it.

In the preceding chapter, you spent some time with the taskbar and the Start button. In this chapter, you'll dig into My Computer, the ever-present little onscreen symbol that represents the machine and resources—mostly files—that you can use. As you explore My Computer, you'll also see how easily you can customize some aspects of Microsoft Windows 95's behavior. Along the way, you'll also lay the groundwork for dealing with folders and files—knowledge you'll find essential when you advance to the Windows Explorer later on. To set off on your voyage of discovery:

1. Turn on your computer, and if necessary, log on to Windows 95.

2. Double-click My Computer to open its window.

This window shows how Windows 95 sees your computer—not as a nice, expensive piece of hardware, as a brand-name item, as a clone, or even as a label declaring that the machine has *intel inside.* To Windows 95, your com-

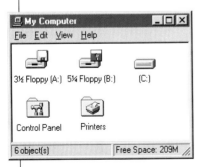

puter is a collection of parts including, at a minimum, disk drives on which you store programs and data; a Printers folder containing icons for the printer(s) through which you produce output; and a Control Panel folder through which you introduce Windows 95 to new hardware, software, and different ways of working. If you have a CD-ROM drive, you no doubt see an icon—decorated with a shiny compact disc—for it as well.

The icons in My Computer are of two types: "mechanical" icons, which represent the hardware on which information is stored, and "graphical" folders, which represent your collections of disk-based information. My Computer's primary goal is to help you visually browse these resources to find and manage your program and document files.

Another Window, Another View

When you open My Computer, you are taking the broad view of your computer and its contents. You are, in a sense, gazing at an entire landscape. Of course, a landscape is made of different objects, but then so is My Computer. Not surprisingly, just as you can narrow your focus in a landscape to concentrate on a clump of bushes or even on a particular shrub, so, too, can you focus on specific resources in My Computer. How? Step right up...or down, as is actually the case.

Right now, you're viewing the objects in My Computer. You can't see the names of any actual files, but you know they exist. How, then, do you focus on one file in particular—one that you know is there but haven't a clue as to where? *That* question has stumped so many new (and not-so-new) computer users that you could use it as a test for separating those who are truly comfortable with computers from those who are not. You're about to join the comfortable group by using My Computer to browse for a file "hidden" in a folder on your hard disk:

1. Open the icon representing the disk identified as (C:). Immediately, a new window opens, and you can see the contents of your hard disk, including a few or many folders containing programs and documents.

2. Now that you can see what your hard disk contains, open the icon for your Windows 95 folder. (The folder is probably named Windows, Windows 95, or something similar, as you can see in the illustration at the right.)

The Windows 95 folder on the computer used in writing this book

FILE

The smallest block of information Windows 95 handles for you. A file can be as short as one character or as long as a book. But whatever its length, a file always has a name. Whenever you create and want to save a file, be sure to assign it a *filename*.

FILENAME

The name by which you refer to a particular file. Under MS-DOS, which allows filenames no longer than eight characters, a descriptive filename can require... creativity. Under Windows 95, which allows *long filenames* (see Chapter 6, "Oh, Those Files and Folders"), you have a lot more flexibility. For example, your research paper with the MS-DOS filename TOADWART could easily be named TOADS AND WARTS under Windows 95.

If you open the wrong folder, just click the Close button in the upper right corner and try again. You'll know you've opened the right one when a list of folders named Command, Config, Help, and so on, appears in a new window.

3. You could continue opening folders for more practice, but really...if you can open one folder, you can open any other. You don't have to practice too much with a new can opener, do you? In your Windows 95 folder, find the System folder and open it. This folder contains the object of your search, a file you can have some fun with. Scan the list, and click (once) to highlight the file named Flying Windows.

POWER PLAY

Sometimes the Keyboard Is Faster

Even though the mouse is your boon companion, the keyboard offers some especially useful—and quick—shortcuts.

When you're scrolling through a list, try the following. As when you use the mouse, the slider's position on the scroll bar reflects your relative position in the list.

- Press Ctrl+Home to move directly to the first item in the list without changing the currently highlighted item.

- Press Ctrl+End to move to the last item in the last column of the list, again without changing the highlight.

- Type an item's name to move the highlight directly to that item.

- Press a letter key to move the highlight to the first item beginning with that letter.

- Press the same letter key repeatedly to move the highlight sequentially through only those items beginning with that letter.

- Press a direction key to move the highlight sequentially up (Z to A) or down (A to Z) through list items beginning with different letters.

The Flying Windows File

My Computer is especially useful for managing files and folders—it's designed for that purpose. But as you've been told several times now, Windows 95 often gives you more than one way to skin a furry feline. The window you're looking at now can show you a new way to start a program:

1. Double-click Flying Windows, and keep your mouse very still. The screen on the next page is what you'll see in a few seconds.

GETTING USED TO WINDOWS 95

It's easy: right-click everything in sight to see what Windows 95 allows you to do. You'll begin to see patterns and relationships, and that's what Windows 95 is all about.

FILE TYPES

Files come in two basic types, program files and data files. *Program* files contain the instructions and associated information that make up a program. *Data* files, such as letters and graphics images, contain information.

FOLDER

A "container," like a manila paper folder, that you use to hold a collection of related files. You can create and name a folder, just as you can create and name a file. A folder is a data file of sorts, but one that contains only the names of files, other folders, or both. (If you know MS-DOS, you know a folder by another name, *directory*.)

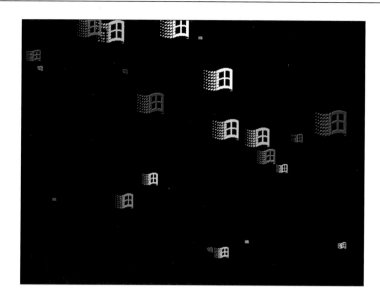

"MIND" SCAN

When you look at the contents of a window, do you ever think about what, exactly, you're looking at? What you see in each window represents information that's currently sitting in your computer's RAM. In a way, when you look into a Windows 95 window, you're seeing your computer's "thoughts"—arranged and displayed, of course, in a form that makes sense to people.

Flying Windows is one of several screen savers shipped with Windows 95. Others include Curves and Colors, which is pretty, and Scrolling Marquee, which rolls a message across the screen. Although Flying Windows is the only screen saver installed by default, you can install the others, too, as described in Chapter 12. For now, however, send your Flying Windows back to disk. To end this or any other Windows 95 screen saver:

2. Twitch the mouse a little bit. You've finished with your System folder, so clean up your screen. If you're using the default view, which opens a new window each time you open a folder, here's a nice way to close not only the current window but each "parent" window—that is, each window you opened to get to the current window.

3. Hold down the Shift key and click the Close button in the upper right corner of the System folder window.

Everything piles back into the My Computer icon. Too bad cleaning the house or the garage isn't as easy.

What You Did Earlier and Why It's Important

When you opened My Computer, the icon for your hard disk, and then your Windows 95 folder, what you did was work your way down (or into) the organizational structure of your hard disk. And by opening these icons one after the other, you were able to see, in successively more detail, what each contained, as shown on the next page.

JUST ONE WINDOW?

If Windows 95 replaces the contents of a single window instead of opening a new window for each object, don't think you've done something wrong. Someone set up Windows 95 on your machine to browse with a single window. It's a nice option, and you'll see how to do it yourself (and switch between single-window and multiple-window browsing) later in this chapter.

There are two important points to carry away from this practice session:

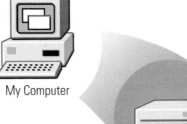

My Computer

- Files are usually arranged in folders.

- If you don't see the file you want in the window you've opened, you might have to *look* for it. This is the part that often trips up new computer users, so remember: if at first you don't succeed, open another folder and try, try again.

C:

Act purposefully, and you won't panic or throw your hands up in frustration when a file proves elusive. You'll have passed the "I understand what's going on" test, and you'll be in control of the situation. That's a nice way to feel.

Windows

So remember that the real purpose of working your way down to Flying Windows was to develop a feel for the way files and folders fit logically one into the other, like the measuring cups in your kitchen drawer. Even though starting a screen saver provided you with an entertaining "reward" to mark the end of your search for a file, the search itself was the important thing. Windows 95, like any other operating system, helps you prevent reams of stored information from turning into piles of confetti. All you need to understand is how Windows 95 goes about doing so.

System

If you'd like to take a break, now's a good time. When you come back, reopen My Computer and the window to your hard disk.

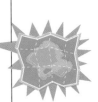

Flying Windows

Creating Folders

Now that you know a little about folders, it's time to create some of your own and see how they can help organize your work on disk. You should be looking at the window to your hard disk. Now:

1. Choose New from the File menu. As you can see from the submenu that appears, Windows 95 is smart enough to be able to create certain types of documents. You'll get to that, but first you need a folder to put a document in, so...

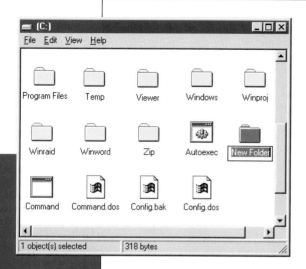

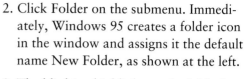

2. Click Folder on the submenu. Immediately, Windows 95 creates a folder icon in the window and assigns it the default name New Folder, as shown at the left.

3. The blinking highlight on the folder's name tells you that Windows 95 is pretty certain you want to assign a name of your own. Anything you type will replace the default name, so type *Alpha* and press Enter.

4. Double-click the Alpha folder to open it.

Notice that the window's title bar tells you that Windows 95's attention is now concentrated on this folder. (Sounds obvious, but there's a point to this.) Now use the File New Folder command to create another folder. Name it Beta, and then close the window to the Alpha folder. You're back looking at your hard disk.

5. So what *was* the point in the previous step? Try this. Highlight the Alpha folder, if necessary, and use the File New Folder command to create a third folder, named WrongWay. Do you see? Even though you highlighted Alpha, Windows 95 created WrongWay *directly on drive C*—not, as you might have expected, inside Alpha.

Keep the proper sequence in mind when you create your own folders:

1. Open the folder in which you want to create the new folder.

2. Create the new folder.

Do this, and you'll never go wrong like WrongWay (which, incidentally, you'll get rid of later).

Filling Folders

Folders aren't a whole lot of use if you don't put things in them. When you install new software or hardware, more often than not you'll find that the installation program creates and populates a folder for you, to keep the

WHY BOTHER?

Windows 95 *does* include a Find command that can help enormously when you're searching for a particular file. But using Find isn't always the same as understanding what it does, so read the accompanying text anyway. Once you know how files can be organized on disk, you'll be surprised at how efficient you become, how well-organized your documents can be, how easily you can work with whole sets of documents, and how simple file management really can be.

program's or device's files neatly bundled and easy to find. But most of your work with a computer involves creating files of your own, and you'll want to be able to "file" them away neatly too. You can do so either from within an application or with the help of Windows 95. You've already created and saved a WordPad document. This time, try another Windows 95 accessory named Notepad—along with an interesting way to use the File New command to create and open certain types of documents from within Windows 95:

1. Open the Alpha and Beta folders.

2. In the Beta window, choose File New and click Text Document. A document icon appears, bearing the suggested default name New Text Document, after which you might or might not see the letters *txt* (don't worry about them either way). *New Text Document* isn't exactly scintillating, but press Enter to accept the default name. This is just a sample file, and in the next chapter, you'll see how easy it is to rename a file.

3. Double-click the document icon. Because Windows 95 "knows" that text documents are created by Notepad, the Notepad window opens.

4. Put some text in your document by typing something. If you don't feel like thinking, try the following:

   I prefer brown, but you like red better,
   So I've got a collie, and you've got a setter.

   Choose File Save, close the Notepad window, and there you have it: a text-filled document in your Beta folder.

Well, now what? Remember that sample document you created in Chapter 3? It should still be hanging around on your desktop. Move it into your Beta folder, and at the same time, begin to sample the joys of drag-and-drop file management:

1. Arrange your windows so that you can see both the Beta window and the icon for the sample file on your desktop.

2. Drag the file from the desktop to the Beta window.

3. If you're the type who needs proof, close the window to the Beta folder and reopen it. The file will still be there.

That's basically all there is to it. Find what you want, drag it, and drop it where you want. You'll see a lot more of the drag-and-drop feature later on, but now your (relatively) quick hands-on tour suggests you move on to something new. To prepare for it, clean up the screen a little by closing all but the My Computer window. If you'd like a break, this is a good place to stop.

ABOUT NOTEPAD
Notepad, if you haven't already met it in an earlier version of Windows, is similar to WordPad but not as capable. It does not, for instance, allow the kind of character formatting that WordPad does. Notepad is, however, a great little program for creating quick, plain-text documents like the one you create in the example on this page.

Customizing a Window

You've noticed that every window has a border. The top part of the border includes the title bar and the menu bar, both labeled in the following illustration.

Title bar
Menu bar

What you haven't yet seen is that the top border of any window can also include a clever and useful set of buttons called the *toolbar*. The toolbar buttons let you use the mouse instead of menus for many often-used commands. Here's what the toolbar looks like.

Toolbar

The toolbar, like the message-bearing status bar that forms the bottom border of every window, is an option you can toggle off and on in any window. My Computer should be open right now, so use it for a little experimenting:

1. Open the View menu. The check mark at the left of the Status Bar command tells you that the status bar is toggled on—a fact you can easily verify by sliding the mouse (without clicking) down the View menu options. As you highlight different commands, notice that the status bar gives you a thumbnail description of what each command does. Now for the toolbar.

Now You See It, Now You Don't

Toolbars are useful and easy to use, but remember this: when you turn on the toolbar (or the status bar), Windows 95 remembers what you did and keeps that change in effect forever after…or until you make another change, which it then remembers instead. Here's another point: your preferences stick like glue, but they apply *only to the window you customized.* For example, turning on the toolbar in the My Computer window means you'll see the toolbar whenever you reopen My Computer. However, the turned-on toolbar applies only to the My Computer window. So, if you open a window to your hard disk, Windows 95 will not display the toolbar in the new window unless (or until) you turn the toolbar on with the View menu. This selectivity is a slick and sophisticated feature of Windows 95, but if you turn on the toolbar (or the status bar) in some windows but not in others, it's easy to end up feeling a little disoriented when different windows take on different "looks." Just remember that each window is a world unto itself. Just as you might hang drapes in one window of your home and not in another, you can turn on the toolbar in one Windows 95 window and leave it off in another.

2. Click Toolbar. The View menu disappears, and a toolbar appears at the top of the window. If you open the View menu again, you'll see that a check mark now sits at the left of the Toolbar command.

3. You're going to try out some of the toolbar buttons now, so if you can't see the entire bar, drag a side border to widen the window. (You should see about a dozen toolbar buttons.)

About Icons

By default, Windows 95 shows you what are known as large icons in My Computer. They're easy to absorb and friendly looking, but they do take up space. As you become more experienced with Windows 95, you might find that you prefer a little less personality and a little more information. That's why Windows 95 offers you a choice of different types of icons—a choice that experienced Windows users will particularly like. And not only can you display different types of icons, you can also change and arrange icons to match your preferences or the need of the moment.

Changing Icons   Altogether, Windows 95 supports four types of window displays: *large icons, small icons, list,* and what it calls *details.* You can use the toolbar (or the View menu) to try out all four. The window below shows the buttons you use.

First, try small icons.

- Click the Small Icons button.

Immediately, the display changes to show miniature versions of the large icons, along with their drive and folder names. Small icons take up much less space than large icons, so they are particularly useful in a crowded window.

Large Icons
Small Icons
List
Details

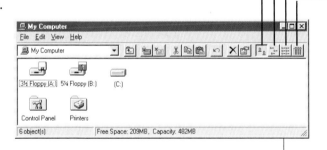

List view does not seem much different from small-icons view, but there *is* a distinction that can come in handy when you're reviewing long lists. First, switch to list view:

- Click the List button.

Here's the difference. In list view, Windows 95 arranges icons alphabetically *down* the window. In small-icons view, Windows 95 arranges icons alphabetically *across* the window. Your first reaction is probably "So what?" To see what it all means, switch to your Windows 95 folder. Before you do, however, take the following steps.

1. Restore your original My Computer view by clicking the Large Icons button and using the View menu to turn off the toolbar.

2. Open a window to your hard disk and your Windows 95 folder. Turn on the toolbar, and maximize the folder window for a good view.

As you can see, Windows 95 defaults to list view in your Windows 95 folder. Now, about that difference between lists and small icons:

1. Scan the list for the file named Tiles.

2. Click the Small Icons button, and scan for the file named Setver.

Which did you find easier to scan quickly? Whichever option suits....

And now to see what that last button, Details, does for you. In this view, you can also see how to arrange icons in different orders:

• Click the Details button.

This view is for when you want the real nitty-gritty—something you'll find useful when you need information about the size, type, or modification date of a particular document.

Arranging Icons Yourself   Details view is particularly appropriate for helping you see the benefit of a set of options on the View menu that allow you to arrange icons not only alphabetically (which is the default) but also by type, size, or date:

1. Open the View menu, and highlight Arrange Icons. Out pops a submenu, from which you can choose how you want the icons sorted.

2. Click By Size. Instantly, Windows 95 arranges the icons in the folder according to size, as you can see if you scroll down through the filenames.

3. Open the View menu again, and arrange the icons By Type. This time, you see all applications grouped together—and in alphabetic order—as well as all bitmap (graphics) images, Help files, system files, and so on. For simplicity, this option is better than easy-listening radio. (Just think, for example, of scanning a folder full of dozens of documents, all of them beginning *Letter To,* for the one you wrote to Bill on June 27.)

You're through with details view and, in fact, with your Windows 95 folder. To restore the default view and finish up:

1. Click the column header labeled Name, or open the View menu and arrange the icons By Name.

2. Click the List button, and then turn off the toolbar.

3. Restore the original window size by clicking the Restore button (the middle one of the three controls in the upper right corner).

4. Close the window.

LET WINDOWS 95 DO IT

When you're working in details view, there's an easier way to arrange icons than by using the View menu: click the column header for the type of arrangement you want. For example, click the header labeled Size to arrange files by size, from smallest to largest. Click it a second time to arrange files by size, but in the opposite order. Click the header labeled Type to arrange files by type (application, bitmap, document, and so on). And, of course, click the header labeled Name to return to the default alphabetic listing of filenames.

Letting Windows 95 Arrange Icons for You   When you were arranging icons by type and size, you might have noticed a grayed out (unavailable) option called Auto Arrange at the bottom of the Arrange Icons submenu. This option might be familiar to you if you've used Windows 3. Available when you view either large icons or small icons, Auto Arrange tells Windows 95 to redistribute icons for you when you change the size of a window (which often cuts down on the need to scroll). Like the toolbar and the status bar, Auto Arrange is an option you toggle on or off, so once turned on for a particular window, it remains on until you turn it off. To try out Auto Arrange:

1. Close your hard-disk window so that My Computer is the active window.

2. Open the View menu, and choose Auto Arrange from the Arrange Icons submenu. Windows 95 is now on "icon alert." Suppose, for example, that your My Computer window currently looks like the one shown at the right.

3. Drag the right window border to the left so that the window is no longer wide enough to display all your My Computer icons. Release the border, and the result is something like this.

   Each time you change the size of the window, Windows 95 will rearrange icons for the best possible fit.

To see how Auto Arrange differs from a "normal" icon arrangement, try this:

1. Turn off Auto Arrange, and make the window wide enough (roughly) to display all the icons in a single row across. Note that there's no change in the icon arrangement because you turned off Auto Arrange.

2. Now use the View menu to arrange the icons (by type) so that they're spread across the width of the window.

3. Narrow the window by dragging, as you did before. Again, the icons remain where they are, and Windows 95 provides a scroll bar to help you display the out-of-view icons.

4. Turn Auto Arrange back on if you like it; leave it off if you prefer the default.

THERE *ARE* LIMITS

If you turn on Auto Arrange, don't expect scroll bars to become extinct just because Windows 95 always arranges your icons for you. Sometimes, even with Auto Arrange, you'll still need to scroll or resize a window. After all, even the most groveling operating system in the world (which Windows 95 isn't) could not display 300 icons in a window the size of a postage stamp.

Same Window, Different Views

Before you leave My Computer, check out one more option you might like quite a lot, especially if you're the minimalist type who believes that "less is more." If all these windows opening and overlaying one another are not quite your cup of tea, try the following:

1. Hold down the Ctrl key as you double-click the icon for your hard disk. No new window.

2. Press the Backspace key. Back you go to viewing My Computer.

All right, what happened? Well, when you're browsing through different disks and folders, holding down Ctrl as you double-click tells Windows 95 to replace the contents of the current window instead of opening a new window for the disk or folder you want to see. Is there a way to make this standard practice without holding down Ctrl each time? Sure:

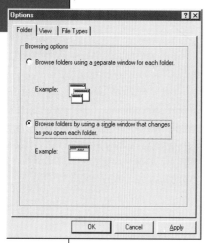

1. Choose Options from the View menu. The window at the left—the properties sheet that governs window characteristics—appears.

2. Click to put a dark dot in the circle (called a *radio button*) at the left of the Browse Folders By Using A Single Window…option, and click OK.

From now on, or until you reopen this properties sheet and reclick the option for browsing with separate windows, Windows 95 will use a single onscreen window to display the contents of the disks and folders you open. As you did in the preceding two-step maneuver with the Ctrl key, you can back up to a preceding disk or folder by pressing the Backspace key one or more times.

Ah, and can you use Ctrl here too? What happens if you hold down Ctrl after turning on single-window browsing? The result is rather clever: Windows 95 temporarily switches back to multiple-window browsing. Check it out:

1. Try out single-window browsing by double-clicking the icon for your hard disk. As you would expect, the contents of your hard disk replace the contents of My Computer.

2. Hold down Ctrl as you double-click your Windows 95 folder. This time, Windows 95 opens a new window to show you the folder contents. It could be that the Windows 95 window appeared on top of your hard-disk window. If so, it can be hard to tell that it's a new window, but it *is* new. If you're not a believer, point to the title bar of the Windows 95 window and drag to a new location on screen.

That's all there is to choosing between viewing one window or many. Use Ctrl+double-click if you want to switch on a case-by-case basis; use the View Options properties sheet when you want to make single-window or multiple-window browsing the default. However you work, enjoy.

Whenever you've worked your way down through one or more windows, press the Backspace key to move back up. Each press of the key takes you one window closer to the beginning. This works, remember, whether you've chosen to browse with one window (as here) or with many (the Windows 95 default).

To restore your original, multiwindow view:

1. Choose Options from the View menu again.

2. Click at the left of the Browse Folders By Using A Separate Window… option, and click OK.

Time for another break if you want. When you come back, reopen My Computer.

Tip!

FAST-FORWARD AND REVERSE

When you want to move from window to window, remember Alt+Tab and the Backspace key. Alt+Tab cycles you from one open window to the next. Backspace climbs up the window hierarchy heading for the light of My Computer—beyond which is the desktop, which you reach by minimizing all open windows.

The Control Panel

You've spent some time digging into your hard disk, and you've seen several ways to customize a window view. Now you'll take a look at one of the folders displayed in My Computer—the one labeled Control Panel.

The Control Panel is a collection of tools that help you maintain and customize Windows 95 and the way it works for you. See for yourself:

• Open the Control Panel folder. (Resize the window or turn on Auto Arrange if you can't see all of the window's contents.)

As you can see from the titles, Windows 95 gives you control over numerous aspects of your computer. To start any of these tools, simply double-click the one you want. Some, such as Add New Hardware, take you to specially designed programs called *wizards*, which considerably ease processes that might otherwise be confusing to people who prefer not to become computer scientists. If you installed Windows 95 yourself, you undoubtedly saw one wizard at the end of the setup procedure, when Windows 95 asked you to install a printer. Whether or not you've seen a wizard, however, just remember that wizards are automated and that they step you through procedures as

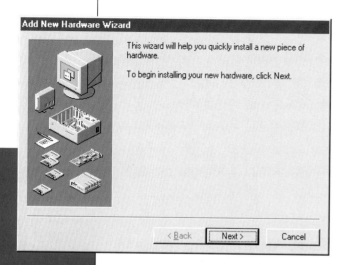

painlessly as possible. At the left, for instance, is the first screen of the wizard that helps you install a new piece of hardware, such as a new display adapter.

Not all Control Panel tools are wizards, of course. Many—in fact most—are designed to help you with tasks such as controlling the double-click speed of your mouse (the Mouse tool), changing your computer's idea of the date and time (the Date/Time tool), or helping Windows 95 be more responsive to special needs (the Accessibility Options tool). For your maiden voyage into the Control Panel, you're going to try out a tool that's especially fun to use. To do that, it'll help to see at least part of your desktop, so:

1. Double-click the tool labeled Display. Doing so brings up the Windows 95 Display Properties sheet shown below.

2. Close all other open windows.

The Display Properties sheet governs both the characteristics of your display and the way Windows 95 sets up your screen. Click the following tabs if you want to see for yourself:

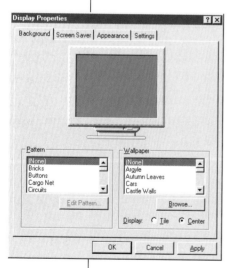

- The Background tab controls the look of your desktop. From this tab, as you'll see, you can choose an allover design (pattern), a particular "picture" (wallpaper), or both.

- The Screen Saver tab lets you choose whether, and how often, you want to use a screen saver to help keep the phosphor-coated glass of your screen from being "burned" by an unchanging image. In addition, this tab lets you control how much electricity your monitor consumes (if it is an energy saver unit, which not all are).

- The Appearance tab lets you control the colors, fonts, and font sizes that Windows 95 uses for displaying your desktop and window elements.

POWER PLAY

They're Not All That Easy

Lest you get the wrong impression: a few of the Control Panel tools are, admittedly, not for the fainthearted. The one below, for example, is what you use to go about modifying or installing network support.

Hmmm. Other than the File And Print Sharing button, which you can easily handle, most of this stuff is *technical*. But then, anyone who has

to become involved in something like this should either (a) know what to do or (b) know whom to call for help. Truly. Networks are fascinating, but they are also complex and best left to experts.

Computers on networks speak their own languages; check each other out; send, receive, and route messages; and even manage *handshakes* that keep them from babbling when another device isn't ready to listen. All this timing and cooperation rest on an elaborate *architecture* that helps both hardware and software send and receive on the same "wavelength." If you're a network user, especially on a large network, yours is not to reason why. If you're told to make a change, ask for specific instructions. If your network connection is not working properly, call your network administrator. Most of all, if you don't know what you're doing, *don't* muck around.

PROPERTIES SHEETS ARE...

Windows that show you, graphically, the characteristics associated with a particular object. The Windows 95 answer to confusing and often complex sets of configuration settings and information files, properties sheets let you click here and there to see and change the way hardware and software serve your needs. In the pantheon of Windows 95 features, properties sheets are a definite Wow.

- The Settings tab lets you control screen resolution and color. To change the number of colors displayed, Windows 95 must restart (changing colors is a heavy proposition). But choose a different resolution, and Windows 95 can do it on the fly. With this tab, for example, you can go from a 640 by 480 screen display (large and OK) to 800 by 600 (tighter and clearer) with a couple of mouse clicks. This capability is an absolute knockout.

But take a look for yourself. This is going to be fun.

Papering the Desktop

The Display Properties sheet gives you access to a number of interesting (and, of course, useful) ways to customize what you see on screen. You'll take a look at one of them here. Try changing the look of your desktop:

1. If necessary, click the Background tab to bring it to the fore. See that monitor at the top of the tab? It's kind of an "instant preplay" that shows what your selections will look like if you choose to keep them. What selections? Well…

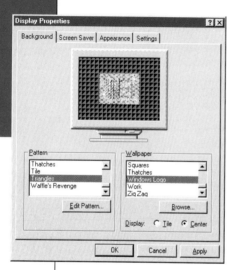

2. Click an item in the Pattern list box—any one will do. If you don't like the choices you see, scroll down the list until you find one you want.

3. Make a mental note of the item highlighted in the list under Wallpaper so that you can return to it later (if you want). Click a different item in the list. Most of the wallpaper designs are pretty small, so you probably see little more than a square blob in the center of the preview monitor, but don't let that bother you.

   Notice that as soon as you click a wallpaper the preview monitor shows both the pattern and the wallpaper you chose.

4. Combining a pattern with a wallpaper makes the screen a little busy, so go back to the top of the Pattern list and click None. That should look better.

5. By default, Windows 95 displays *centered* wallpaper, meaning that it displays the image you choose in the center of the screen. You can also *tile* the image, just as you can tile windows. To try this, click the radio button at the left of the Tile option. Again, the preview monitor shows the result. But what will it look like on your actual screen?

6. Click the Apply button.

7. Return your desktop to its normal self by clicking the Center option and the name of the wallpaper you had before. Click Apply again, and close the window.

MIND YOUR MONITOR

Some monitors can't handle every possible combination of color and resolution settings. If the color setting changes as you change the resolution setting, or vice versa, that's just Windows 95's way of telling you what your monitor can and can't handle.

And Speaking of the Desktop

Most, if not all, of the documents you create will eventually go to your printer, and most will end up there via the Print command in your applications. Windows 95, however, can help you out a great deal—not only with printing but also with managing the printer and the print *queue*, which is the set of documents waiting to be printed. Before you leave your tour of the desktop, take a quick look at the joy of printing.

First step: keep your printer handy. The real thing is on or near your real desktop, so why not place the electronic version on your electronic desktop? Doing so is a cinch:

1. Open My Computer, and then open the Printers folder. If you have a printer installed, you should see both an Add Printer icon (which is how you start the Add Printer wizard) and an icon for your printer, as shown at the right.

2. Point to your printer icon, right-click, and drag the icon to your desktop. Release the mouse button, and when the popup menu appears, choose Create Shortcut(s) Here. A printer icon labeled Shortcut To and the name of your printer now sit on the desktop.

So what? Well, turn on the printer and try this:

1. Double-click the shortcut icon on the desktop, and you see a window in which you manage both the printer and the documents you send to it.

2. Open the Printer menu. There are two important commands here: Pause Printing, which temporarily stops the printer, and Purge Print Jobs, which empties the queue (cancels all current printing). Now open the Document menu, and note the two commands here, which you can use to pause and cancel printing of a single document. Before you can use these commands, you must select the document to pause or cancel in the open area of the window, as you'll see next.

3. Open your Windows 95 folder, and move the windows around so that you can see the printer shortcut, the printer window, and a file shown as either Readme or Readme.txt. Got it?

4. Drag Readme to the printer shortcut icon, and watch what happens in the printer window. There's your document. Now, if your printer is directly connected to your computer (that is, it's a nonnetwork printer), quickly...

5. Select Readme in the printer window, open the Document menu, and choose Cancel Printing. In a second or two, the document stops printing. Although your printer might run on for a while, you've stopped the job.

NO PRINTER YET?

This section assumes that you have a printer hooked up and ready to work with Windows 95. If you just bought a computer with Windows 95 preinstalled on the hard disk, you might have to step through the process of identifying your printer to Windows 95 before you can print anything. Thanks to Windows 95, all you need is the Add Printer wizard. For details, including a step-by-step walkthrough, refer either to "Using a Network Printer" in Chapter 10 or to "Printers" in Chapter 12.

The Printer Menu

In normal work, the Printer commands you're likely to need are the two that pause the printer and get rid of print jobs you don't want. (Yes, it happens sometimes.) But what of the other commands in the Printer menu? Choose Work Offline when you want to tell Windows 95 to store all print jobs for printing at a later time. (This is a particularly great option if you're using a por-table computer and you don't have access to a printer at the moment.) Choose Set As Default if you're using more than one printer and you want to tell Windows 95 which one to use. If you have only one printer, that one is, of course, the default. Choose Properties to set such printer-specific options as paper size, paper orientation, and graphics resolution.

Cleanup Time and a Look at the Recycle Bin

You've covered a fair amount of ground in this chapter. Before you move on, take a few minutes to clean up your sample folders and files and quickly meet the Recycle Bin, a feature you'll investigate in more detail in Chapter 6, "Oh, Those Files and Folders." (Yes, there's a lot more than meets the eye in Windows 95, even in so mundane an object as a recycling container.)

If you've worked through the examples in this and the previous chapter, you should have one folder named WrongWay on your hard disk, and your document samples should all be tucked neatly into a set of folders, with a single folder named Alpha at the highest level. To get rid of them:

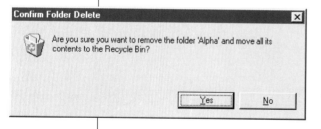

1. Open a window to your hard disk.

2. Highlight the Alpha folder, and press the Del (Delete) key. Windows 95 displays a request for confirmation.

3. You're sure (in this case), so click Yes. It's gone.

4. Highlight the WrongWay folder, press Del, and click Yes.

All done. Notice, however, that deletions are so simple it would be easy indeed to accidentally click on and delete a file or folder you meant to keep. A word of warning, at least until you reach Chapter 6: don't go gleefully trashing files and folders of your own until you understand how to get them back if you have to.

Chapter 5

Taking Care of Business

All That Stuff

If you worked through the last two chapters, you've done a fair amount of playing around with Microsoft Windows 95, so you should no longer feel like a drop-in visitor. Now that you're familiar with your surroundings, you can start getting a little down and dirty with some of the "stuff" that supports the

active, creative work you do with your computer. This is the "stuff" that applications usually assume you know—the stuff that's so simple when you know what to do, but so hopeless when you're clueless. It's the kind of stuff that can make the difference between enjoying your computer and wishing you'd spent the money on a new TV and a freezer full of pizza.

In this chapter, you'll concentrate on working with files. You won't cover glamour topics, such as portable computing and going on line, but the work will go quickly, and you won't even have to whistle while you're at it—unless you want to. Unlike people who never veer from the one way they learn to get something done, you've been building a reasonably broad foundation in the preceding chapters. You've put in time getting a feel for Windows 95, and you've gotten used to the idea, the reality, and the management of windows themselves. Now you can put what you know to work. If you're ready:

1. Start Windows 95 and log on, if necessary.

2. Open My Computer, and open a window to your hard disk.

Managing Files and Folders

COPY

To duplicate a file on another disk or in another folder. When you copy a file, the original remains at the *source* and a "carbon copy" appears at the *destination*. (MS-DOS users, note: with Windows 95, you can duplicate a file in the same folder. Windows 95 identifies the duplicate as Copy of *[filename]*, where *[filename]* is the name of the original file.)

DELETE

Under Windows 95, to send a file to the Recycle Bin. You delete files you no longer want or need.

RESTORE

Under Windows 95, to retrieve a deleted file from the Recycle Bin and return it to full and glorious health on disk or in a folder. The Recycle Bin is actually a storage location on disk—a temporary way station for files consigned to oblivion. While they are in the bin, you can fetch them back. Once you empty the bin, the files are not merely dead—they are really most sincerely dead.

As mentioned at the beginning of the preceding chapter, the real difference (as far as you're concerned) between a file and a folder is that:

- A file contains "workable" information, such as your thesis on the effect of sunshine on smiles.

- A folder contains files, other folders, or both.

As far as Windows 95 is concerned, files and folders are practically the same thing, at least when it comes to copying them, moving them, deleting them, and changing their names—all of which you'll do in this chapter.

Making Some Files to Work With

Before you can copy, move, delete, or rename anything, you need something to copy, move, delete, or rename. You could, of course, create a sample folder and then copy some files from your Windows 95 folder to it. But as a general rule, you should consider your Windows 95 files strictly off-limits, especially if you and your computer are still becoming acquainted. Because damaging or deleting one of your Windows 95 files could have serious—indeed, disastrous—consequences, you won't even work with *copies* of those files here. After all, once you start nibbling at a rule, it becomes less of a rule each time you take a bite. Besides, there's another way.

The steps outlined below easily create all the sample files you need. First, you'll create a new folder for the samples, and then you'll create the files:

1. Verify that the window to your hard disk is the active window.

2. Use the File New command to create a new folder named Expendable.

Now to create a set of files to play with. They'll all end up with the same contents, but that's all right. For these examples, you're interested in quantity, not quality. Although the following steps are somewhat tedious, they get you where you need to go. If you know MS-DOS or if you're in an adventurous frame of mind, you can use the procedure outlined in the shaded box on page 70, headed "A Faster Way to Create Those Files," instead. It's your choice.

Here's the easier way:

1. Open the Start menu, open the Programs and Accessories submenus, and click Notepad. Notepad, remember, is a text editor. It's not as fancy as WordPad, but it's small and quick to use—the equivalent of a tablet you would tuck into a pocket for notes and reminders.

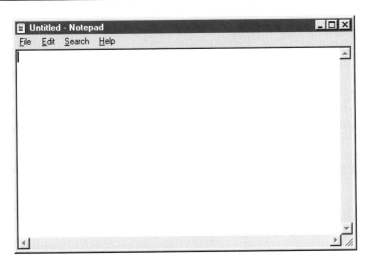

2. To create the file itself, type the following colored text, pressing Enter where you see *[Enter]*.

> This is a file I can throw away[Enter]
> when I finish this chapter.[Enter]

Now, save the file by choosing Save As from the File menu. When you see the window shown below, find your hard drive (C:) in the Save In drop-down list and click to open it.

Find your hard drive here and click.

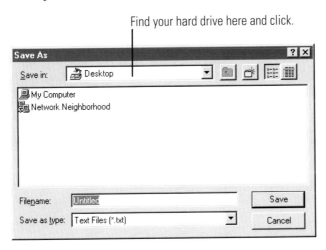

3. Double-click the Expendable folder.

4. Highlight *Untitled* in the Filename box, and then type *Sample1*. When you're done, click Save.

5. Choose the File Save As command again. This time, save the file as Sample2. (Don't worry if Notepad adds *.txt* to your filename.)

MOVE

To transfer a file from one disk or folder to another. Unlike a copy, a move does not duplicate a file. It takes the file from the source disk or folder and places it on the destination disk or in the destination folder.

THE SAVE AS COMMAND

Using the Save As command to create a set of files here is akin to using a dime to turn a screw: it works, but that's not quite what was intended. The Save As command is *supposed* to be used when you revise a file and want to keep both the original and the new version. Load a file into whatever program you used to create it, make your changes, use Save As (rather than Save), and assign a new name to the file. Your original will remain untouched under the original name, and the revised version will be saved under the new name you assign.

6. Save the file four more times, each time boosting the number by 1 to create Sample3, Sample4, Sample5, and Sample6.

To make the procedure as fast and effortless as possible, try the following:

- Press and release Alt, then F, and then A to choose the File Save As command.

- Press Home to move the blinking insertion point to the beginning of the filename. Press the Right direction key until the insertion point is just to the left of the number in the filename, and then press the Del key.

- Type the next number in line, and press Enter to carry out the command.

7. That's it, so close Notepad. You're ready to get to work.

POWER PLAY

A Faster Way to Create Those Files

Using Notepad and the Save As command multiple times works just fine, but it's repetitive. The following steps give you a faster way to create a set of six sample files. If you want to try this but you don't know MS-DOS, type the text shown in color *exactly*, and you'll be fine:

1. Open the Start menu and the Programs submenu, and click MS-DOS Prompt.

2. When the dark window titled COMMAND opens, type the following, pressing Enter where you see *[Enter]*.

```
cd c:\Expendable[Enter]
copy con c:\Expendable\Sample1.txt[Enter]
```

3. Now type the text that will be saved in the file. Again, press Enter where you see *[Enter]*, and press the F6 key, which will be represented on the screen as ^Z, where you see *[F6]*.

```
This is a file I can throw away[Enter]
when I finish this chapter.[F6][Enter]
```

4. To create Sample2 through Sample6, type the following. Be sure to match the spacing exactly.

```
for %f in (2 3 4 5 6) do copy Sample1.txt Sample%f.txt
```

(In case you're not sure what happened here, you used a command named *For* to duplicate, or copy, Sample1.txt five times, each time replacing *%f* with the next number in the set from 2 through 6. And yes, if you suspect you just had a close encounter of the programming kind, you did…sort of.)

5. Type *exit* and press Enter to leave the COMMAND window and return to Windows 95.

Whether you used Notepad or the MS-DOS Prompt to create the files, if you open the Expendable folder you should see what's shown at the right when you're done.

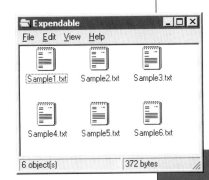

Take a break if you want. When you come back, restart Windows 95 and return to your Expendable window.

Selecting Files

To do something to a file (such as copy it from one place to another), you select the file and tell Windows 95 what you want to do to the file. You can select a single file simply by clicking it. To select multiple files, you can choose from several alternatives. Verify that Expendable is active. Now:

1. Press Ctrl+A. As simply as that, you can select every file in the active window. What does Ctrl+A stand for?

2. Open the Edit menu. Notice that the *keyboard shortcut* for the Select All command is Ctrl+A. Suppose, however, you didn't mean to select all.

3. Click Invert Selection. Like a film negative, this command reverses your selection—in this case, by deselecting all your sample files.

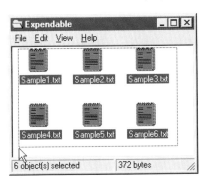

4. Now try the mouse. Point to the upper right corner of an imaginary rectangle surrounding all the sample files. Hold down the left mouse button and drag to the lower left, as shown at the left.

When the dotted outline surrounds all the sample files, release the mouse button, and all the files are selected. If you're a prior Windows user, this ability to corral a set of files with the mouse should have you standing up and cheering—especially because you can do this not only in a window but on the desktop too.

5. Finally, if you want to select a scattered group of files, say, samples 1, 2, and 5, you can use the Ctrl key:

- First, deselect all files by clicking anywhere in the blank part of the window.

- Now, hold down the Ctrl key and click the icons for samples 1, 2, and 5.

WHEN YOU SELECT FILES

Make sure you don't start your rectangle too close to an icon. You could end up inadvertently trying to move or copy a file instead. When you're using list view or details view, dragging to select a group of files can be difficult if you try to start at the upper or lower left of an imaginary rectangle. When you don't have much clearance along the left edge of a window, start dragging at the *right* of the filename. Doing so can make a world of difference.

THE SHIFT KEY WORKS TOO

When you want to select a continuous set of files arranged one next to the other either across or down a window, dragging is the easiest method when the window is displaying large or small icons. When you're viewing a list, however, the Shift key works nicely in combination with the mouse. All you do is click the *first* file you want, and then hold down the Shift key and click the *last* file you want. Because you're using the Shift key, Windows 95 selects the first file, the last file, and every file in between.

Because you used the Ctrl key, Windows 95 skipped around, selecting only the files you clicked. Remember this key when you're working with documents of your own. A little Ctrl can save a lot of time.

Copying Files

Now that you know how to tell Windows 95 which files interest you, you can breeze through some examples that let you work your will on them. First, make some copies.

Earlier, you used Save As or the MS-DOS For command to make duplicates, but that was kind of a special case. When you're working with Windows 95, you'll often find yourself turning copying into a three-step procedure:

1. Select.

2. Press Ctrl and drag.

3. Drop.

Your drop target will generally be a different disk or folder, but it can be the same folder. Duplicating a file in the same folder can be useful when you want to keep both a pristine original and an editable copy in the same place with (nearly) the same name. To give copying a try:

1. Use the File New command to create a folder named Expendabletoo in your Expendable window.

2. Open the Expendabletoo folder, and move it, if necessary, so that you can also see the sample files in the Expendable window.

3. Click in a blank part of the Expendable window to deselect the new folder.

4. Hold down the Ctrl key (active little thing, isn't it?) and reselect samples 1, 2, and 5; still holding down the Ctrl key, drag the files—actually, their ghostly outlines—to the Expendabletoo window.

5. Release the mouse button, and there you are. Three copies.

But what about copying to the same folder? No problem:

1. If necessary, make your Expendable window bigger so that you have plenty of working room.

2. If necessary, reselect samples 1, 2, and 5 in the Expendable window. Still pressing the Ctrl key, drag the file outlines to a blank part of the window. Release the key and the mouse button, and Windows 95 immediately duplicates the files, thoughtfully labeling each of them Copy Of *[filename]* so that you can tell the original from the clone.

As you can see, whether you copy to a different folder or to the same one, the procedure is the same. In fact, you can press Ctrl and drag icons to place copies of needed files on the desktop. Furthermore, because Windows 95 lets

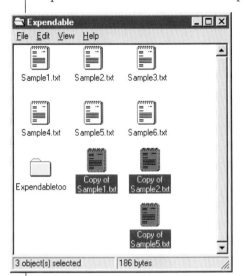

you drag and drop copies onto floppy disks and even into shared folders on other computers in a network, you can easily repeat a copy once, twice, three times, or more to distribute the same document to a number of people by dragging each person's copy to a suitable folder.

Before you go replicating documents all over the place, however, remember that changes you make to a duplicate are precisely that—changes to the *duplicate*. And if you create multiple copies of a file, you can easily lose track of which changes you've made to which copy. To avoid singing the "I know I made those

changes, but I'm not sure where I made them" blues, organize your work neatly—perhaps by moving all finished revisions to one folder and leaving only the originals and work in progress in the folder you work from. And speaking of moving files...

Making a Transfer

Instead of copying, you can choose to move files or folders from place to place—to other disks, folders, network computers, and (a particularly handy spot) your own desktop, where your current projects can remain as close at hand as the paper-and-ink files on your real desk. As a matter of fact, moving is even easier than copying:

1. To clear some space, close all but your Expendable window. Move the window to the left or right to make plenty of room on the desktop.

2. Select the copies of samples 1, 2, and 5, and drag the file outlines to an empty part of the desktop. Drop them there. The copies disappear from Expendable because you moved the files instead of copying them.

Select, drag, and drop. That's all it takes to move files or folders, at least when you haul them from one place to another on the same disk. If you move them to a different disk—for example, from drive C to a floppy in drive A—press Shift as you drag. Or, as mentioned in the tip to the right, use the right mouse button to be sure you move instead of copy, and vice versa.

WHAT KEY WAS THAT AGAIN?

Windows 95 supports a lot of mouse/ key combinations. Sometimes it's easy to forget which key you're supposed to use: is it Ctrl or Shift that lets you copy when you drag and drop? When in doubt, turn to the right...mouse button, that is. Drag with the right button, and when you drop selected files at their intended destination, Windows 95 displays a popup menu that lets you choose whether to move, copy, or create a shortcut (more about shortcuts later). When in doubt, let Windows 95 do some of the thinking for you. After all, that's what it's there for.

And now that you have those copies on your desktop, you can see just how handy that desktop can be:

1. Close the Expendable window.

2. Double-click the icon for the copy of Sample2. Windows 95 opens Notepad and displays the file's contents. Once a document is sitting on your desktop, a quick double-click is all you need to open both the document and the program you used to create it.

3. You're going to move on now, so close Notepad.

If you're ready for a break, this is a good stopping point. When you come back, restart Windows 95.

Renaming Files and Folders

The steps at the beginning of this chapter showed you how to use the Save As command to rename your sample file. Each time, Save As stored the newly named file as a separate document on disk. Normally, however, you don't want to save a bunch of files under a bunch of different names; you're more likely to want to save one file under a new name. With Windows 95, you can change the name of any folder or any file with ease. All you do is click to select the folder or file, wait just a hair, click the folder name or filename, and type in the new name. Here, try it:

1. Open your Expendable folder.

2. Click the Expendabletoo folder to select it.

3. Click the folder name. You'll know that Windows 95 is prepared to rename the folder when it highlights the name and surrounds it with a solid box, as shown below.

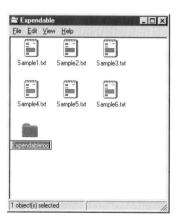

Notice, by the way, that even though you click twice to indicate that you want to rename a folder or a file, it is *not* the same as double-clicking. A double-click on the folder name would have opened Expendabletoo instead of merely highlighting its name. Remember to pause briefly between clicks when renaming.

4. Because the highlight covers the entire folder name, all you have to do now is type a new name. Type *Gotcha* and press Enter. All done.

Now this book is going to take a break for a little while. It's about time for you to try things on your own, so why not spend a few minutes getting comfortable with copying, moving, and renaming files? To be sure you can follow the remaining examples in this chapter, confine your experiments to Gotcha and the sample files in it. Have fun. When you come back, restart Windows 95 and reopen your Expendable folder, if necessary.

Shortcuts and Scraps

Copying and moving, valuable as they are, aren't the only ways Windows 95 can help you get things done. Windows 95 includes two new and special features known as *shortcuts* and *scraps*. As you saw in the last chapter when you created a shortcut to your printer, shortcuts can help make your desktop as personal as the one on which your computer sits. So can scraps. Start with the easier of the two, shortcuts.

Shortcuts

Windows 95 shortcuts, like any physical shortcut you might take to a friend's house, are ways for you to get where you want with the least amount of fuss and bother. For example, if you wanted to open a document, say, Sample4, you could select it from the Document list on the Start menu (assuming you'd used the file before); or you could start Notepad and choose the document using the File Open command; or you could open My Computer, your hard disk, and your Expendable folder and then double-click Sample4.

Regardless of the method you chose, opening the document would normally involve several steps—simple ones, but still steps, plural. A Windows 95 shortcut can reduce those steps to a single double-click. To add to their appeal, shortcuts work not only with documents but also with programs, folders, disks (even your hard disk), network drives, and any other resource available to your computer. Try creating another shortcut, and then you can spend a few minutes learning more about what you did:

1. Open a window to your Expendable folder. Close any other open windows, and then click to select Sample4.

2. Hold down the *right* mouse button and drag Sample4 to a blank part of the desktop.

3. Release the mouse button, and choose Create Shortcut(s) Here from the popup menu, as you can see in the illustration on the next page.

REMEMBER...

To create a shortcut, select the icon for the resource you want a shortcut to. Right-click, drag, drop, and choose Create Shortcut from the popup menu. It's easy, and over time, you'll probably find yourself relying on shortcuts as much as, or more than, the Start menu.

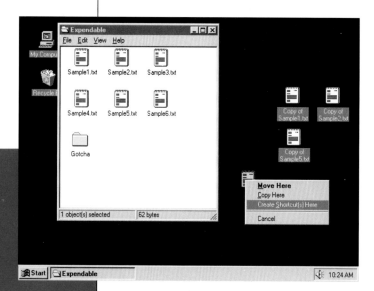

Windows 95 displays the file's icon on the desktop, just as it would with a move or a copy. Notice, however, that a small square that contains an arrow pointing northeast appears in the lower left corner of the icon. That arrow appears in every shortcut you create, as a reminder of what the icon represents. Notice, too, that the icon for Sample4, the original, remains in the Expendable folder.

The remainder of this example assumes that you created a desktop shortcut to your printer in the last chapter. If you did not, open My Computer and your Printers folder, and then:

- Select the icon for the printer you normally use. Again, hold down the right mouse button while you drag and drop the printer icon onto the desktop, and then choose Create Shortcut(s) Here from the popup menu.

Now you can see what shortcuts are all about:

1. Double-click the Sample4 shortcut. No slipping, no sliding, no searching. As quickly as that, you open the document in Notepad.

2. Add the following text to the file. Anywhere will do, but if you want to be neat about it, press Ctrl+End to move the cursor to the end of the document. Here's the text:

   I'm making this change to a document shortcut.[Enter]

   Use the File Save command to save the changed file.

3. Close the Notepad window. To see where your change was saved, double-click Sample4 in the Expendable window. Nice, isn't it? Even though you opened the file with a shortcut, Windows 95 was smart enough to save your change in the original document. Now, close Notepad again, and take a final look (in this chapter, that is) at what a shortcut can do.

4. Turn on your printer. When it's ready, drag and then drop the Sample4 shortcut onto your printer shortcut. Quick and easy. If that's your style, remember shortcuts and use them well.

Now, as for what a shortcut is all about. Basically, a shortcut is nothing more than a "note" that Windows 95 makes to tell itself where the original object represented by a shortcut resides. If you are or have ever been a Macintosh user, you know shortcuts by another name: *alias*. In terms of usability, a Windows 95 shortcut simply means that no matter where an object is stored or located, you can drag that object's icon to the desktop—or to another window or folder—and, by doing so, keep that object's icon in whatever place is most convenient for you. And because Windows 95 remembers shortcuts from one session to another, you don't have to worry about re-creating your shortcuts each time you start up.

POWER PLAY

Network Shortcuts

If you work with network resources a great deal, shortcuts to often-used files, folders, or shared printers or programs can make the distinction between your computer and the network resource virtually disappear. Once on your desktop, a network shortcut works like any other. To create a shortcut to a network resource, do the following:

1. Right-click the Network Neighborhood icon on your desktop, and choose Find Computer. (You could double-click to open the icon, but if you're on a large network with many available computers, that can take longer than specifying the particular computer you want to use. If you're new to networks, look for more information about your Network Neighborhood in Chapter 10, "Networks and *The* Network.")

2. Type the name of the shared resource you need in the Find window that appears. You can

see an example for a hypothetical computer named Hotdog in the following illustration.

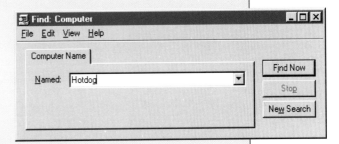

3. Click the Find Now button.

4. When Windows 95 finds the computer you need, double-click its name in the list that appears at the bottom of the Find window.

5. Locate the name of the resource you need, right-click, drag the icon to your desktop, and choose Create Shortcut from the popup menu. From that point on, as long as the network resource remains shared, all you need to do is double-click the shortcut to use the resource.

On a somewhat more conceptual level, shortcuts are Windows 95's means of letting you reorganize the way you *see* disks, files, and folders to your heart's content without ever disturbing the way your programs and documents are stored and neatly organized on disk. In a sense, shortcuts let you create your own "virtual reality," at least in terms of never having to worry about where something is actually stored.

Scraps

Going from the virtual to the sublime, move on now to the concept of creating and using scraps. A scrap is, simply, a piece of text, a graphic, a sound, or

any other object that you copy from one document for use in the same or another document. Sound a lot like scissors and glue or, if you're already familiar with software, like the Cut, Copy, and Paste commands? Scraps *are* like these, but with a drag-and-drop difference. (Drag-and-drop will appear often, both in this book and in your life.)

Like shortcuts, scraps are best seen to be appreciated, so go ahead and create one:

- Open WordPad (*not* Notepad), and type the following two lines:

  This is a line in a new document.[Enter]
  This is some more sample text.[Enter]

To add a little spice to this example and to see some of the ways Windows 95 and WordPad can support everyday tasks, take a short detour and add a graphics image to your sample document. (There's more about inserting objects in Chapter 9, "OLE!," so don't feel you have to master the steps here; this is mostly for fun.)

1. Choose Object from WordPad's Insert menu. You see a request for more specific information similar to the one shown at the right.

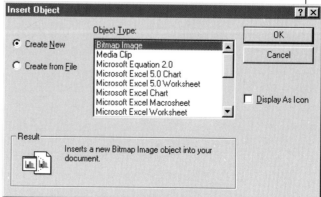

2. Click Bitmap Image, if it's not already highlighted, to tell WordPad the type of graphic you want. (A bitmap image is a "drawing" created as a bunch of dots through a program such as Paint.)

3. Windows 95 comes with an assortment of bitmap images—the cars and other patterns that Windows 95 uses as desktop wallpaper. Since those images all exist on your hard disk as files, click the radio button at the left of Create From File in the Insert Object window. The window changes to let you find the file you want.

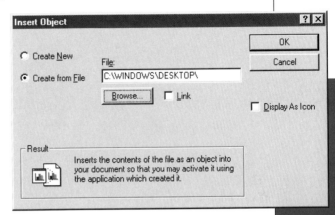

4. Click the Browse button. Windows 95 displays the Browse window shown at the left.

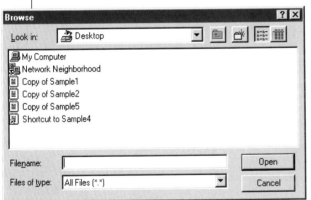

Open the drop-down list at the top, click your C drive, double-click the name of your Windows 95 folder, and then click one of the files, such as Cars, identified by a "bitmap" icon like the one shown below. Click Open.

5. Now you're almost done. Click OK in the Insert Object window, and in a short time, Windows 95 displays your image inside your WordPad document. Click to the right of the inserted object, and press Enter to move the insertion point to a new line.

There's your document: two lines of text and a graphics image. Now, suppose the document were much longer and you wanted to reorganize it. That's where scraps can come in handy:

1. Place the mouse pointer in the narrow "margin" to the left of the first line of your sample document. (The cursor will change into a pointer pointing northeast when you're at the right spot.) Click to select the entire line.

SCRAPS AND WORDPAD

Although the text here closely associates scraps with WordPad, that's simply because WordPad was the best means of working with scraps while this book was being prepared. In actuality, any program that is described as "OLE aware"—meaning that it will work with Windows 95's drag-and-drop capabilities— should also be able to cut, copy, and paste scraps to and from documents and the desktop.

2. Point to any part of the highlighted line, and using the left mouse button, drag and drop the "scrap" of document onto your desktop. Windows 95 displays the notation shown at the right.

There's your scrap. You can do the same with your inserted graphic:

1. Make sure WordPad is the active window.

2. Use the left "margin" to select the bitmap image.

3. Drag the image to the desktop and drop it.

Oh, wait. You wanted to *move* that first line of text? Well, that's easy:

1. Click anywhere in the WordPad window to activate it.

2. Select the first line again.

3. Press the left mouse button, press Alt and drag, and then drop the line at the bottom of the document.

Happy now? Good. Back to scraps.

Scraps can come in handy if you want to copy sections from one document to another. They're also better than pots of glue if you're working on a document and you want to keep bits and pieces close at hand for rearranging or, perhaps, to reuse if the original turns out to be better than a revised version. If you work on a network, you can also share scraps with other interested parties. If the scrap happens to be a graphic or other nontext file, you can even work your way from the scrap to the original application.

Try some of these applications. First, to insert a scrap into a different part of your document:

1. Select the text scrap you just created.

2. Drag it, and drop it at the bottom of the document. Piece of cake.

To place the scrap in a different document:

1. Choose the New command from WordPad's File menu. Click OK to accept the default (Microsoft Word 6 Document) when WordPad displays a window asking what type of document you want.

2. Click No when WordPad asks if you want to save the changes to your sample document. (You don't; you've finished with it.)

3. Drag your scrap of text from the desktop to the new document.

4. Click anywhere in the WordPad window to activate it.

5. Press Enter to create a new line.

TOO MUCH TOO FAST?

If the examples in this chapter seem to be showing you a lot of Windows 95, don't be discouraged. There *is* a lot to Windows 95, but you don't have to master everything at once. These first few chapters, remember, are here to help you get your feet wet. Later chapters, beginning with Chapter 6, "Oh, Those Files and Folders," will cover in more detail some of the features you encounter here. Scraps and drag-and-drop, for instance, are explained in Chapter 9, "OLE!" Right now, just try to get a feel for how much Windows 95 can help you do. As you learn more and, especially, as you become more comfortable with Windows 95, the rest will come. Really. It just takes time.

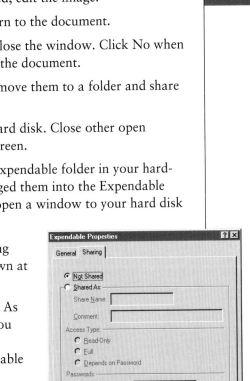

6. For color, drag your graphics image in as well. There you have it, just as shown at the right.

And suppose you wanted to touch up the graphics image or share your scraps on a network. Easy. To edit the graphic:

1. Activate the WordPad window again, if necessary.

2. Double-click the graphics image in your document. Windows 95 immediately changes the window to display the tools and menus for Paint, the accessory you use to create and modify bitmap graphics.

3. Click the Eraser tool (second button on the left, just below the star-shaped button). Move the cursor onto the image, and drag to create a clean spot on the image just to prove you can, indeed, edit the image.

4. Click a blank spot in the window to return to the document.

5. You're finished with WordPad now, so close the window. Click No when asked if you want to save the changes to the document.

To make the scraps available to others, you move them to a folder and share the folder as follows:

1. Open or return to the window to your hard disk. Close other open windows to reduce the clutter on your screen.

2. Drag the scraps, and drop them on the Expendable folder in your hard-disk window. (Yes, you could have dragged them into the Expendable window instead, but you'd still have to open a window to your hard disk in the next step.)

3. Right-click the folder, and choose Sharing from the popup menu. The window shown at the right appears.

4. Click the button at the left of the Shared As option. Windows 95 fills in the rest. If you were to click OK, the files and scraps in Expendable would become publicly readable by anyone with network access to your computer.

5. You don't really want to share this folder, especially because you'll be deleting it soon, so click Cancel to cancel the Sharing command.

Where They Go

If you're familiar with Windows 3, scraps probably remind you of items you used to cut or copy to the Clipboard. In some respects, they are similar. In one important way, however, they are not. Remember that the Clipboard was designed for temporary storage of reusable information. Although you were able to save Clipboard contents with the help of the Clipbook Viewer, an item you placed on the Clipboard normally remained in memory only until it was replaced by new information.

When you create a scrap, Windows 95 creates a file for it. If you're familiar with Windows 3 and MS-DOS filenames, you'll notice that the extension for these files is SHS. Although Windows 95 doesn't ask when, whether, or where you want to save a scrap, a scrap file is as real as any file you create with an application program. If the scrap is sitting on your desktop, Windows 95 places the SHS file in a folder named Desktop, which is stored within your Windows 95 folder. If the scrap is sitting in a folder, such as the Expendable folder, Windows 95 creates and saves the scrap file in that folder.

If you'd like to take a break, this is another good stopping point. When you return, restart Windows 95, and if you want to save yourself a click or two later, open My Computer and a window to your hard disk.

Cleaning Up

Barring disaster, extreme misfortune, or disk failure (which is rare, despite the horror stories that sometimes circulate), every file and folder and shortcut and scrap you create and save remains on disk in perpetuity, at least as far as Windows 95 is concerned. If there is any rule that a good operating system must follow, it's that every single character of every single piece of work you do must be remembered accurately, safely, and for as long as you want to keep it around. Such concern is admirable, and computers certainly could not have become as valuable as they are if data storage were more of a hit-and-miss affair.

What this unswerving devotion to the well-being of each and every file cannot cope with, however, is human productivity and, face it, human foible. People who use computers at some point find to their surprise that they've created tons of files. Some are indispensable. Others, well…the computer made it *so* easy to dash off that "haven't seen you in ages" note to Uncle Ferdinand, and, gee, it was so short, you didn't see any harm in saving it too. Sooner or later, the 520-MB hard disk that once seemed endless becomes as jam-packed as the hallway closet.

Because Windows 95 cannot—and should not—be allowed to delete even the oldest, most useless of files, housekeeping falls to you. Cleanup is a chore you must shoulder periodically, and Windows 95 gives you two related tools for sweeping away the clutter that inevitably builds up on your hard disk.

- To remove unwanted files, you Delete them to the Recycle Bin.

- To *really* remove those files, you empty the Recycle Bin.

Deleting

Windows 95 lets you delete documents, shortcuts, folders, and scraps. Although deletions from your hard disk move to the Recycle Bin by default, it pays to remember that not all deletions are necessarily equal. In particular, note that:

- Deletions move safely to the Recycle Bin if you delete by selecting one or more files and then either press the Del key or right-click and choose Delete from the popup menu. But…

- If you hold down Shift and press the Del key to delete, Windows 95 *permanently* removes the file(s) you're deleting. This happens whether you're deleting from a floppy or from your hard disk. And…

- If you modify the default settings, as described later in this chapter, you can tell Windows 95 to delete permanently without ever moving files to the Recycle Bin. This option can save storage space on your hard disk, but it can also be dangerous. Why? Because the Recycle Bin lets you fish around in the trash to find and recover accidental deletions. If you choose not to use the Recycle Bin, you'd best be accurate, well-organized, experienced, and practically infallible. Deleting an irreplaceable file and not being able to recover it is a hard lesson to learn. Very hard.

If you stick with the Recycle Bin for your hard disk, then, you'll be safe and secure. But what, exactly, is the Recycle Bin? It obviously isn't a Rubbermaid container sitting on your motherboard (that's the big circuit board in the bottom of your computer). What the Recycle Bin *is* is a portion of hard-disk storage that Windows 95 automatically sets aside for holding deleted material. When you use the Recycle Bin, you effectively give Windows 95 up to 10 percent of the disk to use for temporarily storing deletions. Because your deletions are in this electronic container, you can pick through them at will in the event that cleanup drudgery sends your mind temporarily out to lunch and you accidentally just say Yes to a deletion when you should have just said No.

NOTE, NOTE, NOTE
As you read this section of the chapter, note that it talks about folders, files, and shortcuts on your *hard* disk. Windows 95 can, obviously, help you delete files on floppies too, but those files are not saved in the Recycle Bin. When you delete from floppies, Windows 95 does prompt for confirmation, so you have a chance to back out. But if you give the go-ahead, Windows 95 removes the file permanently. At that point, the only way to recover the file is to use the MS-DOS Undelete command, which cannot always successfully recover a file.

ABOUT DELETING
If you create and delete shortcuts regularly, take a moment to actually read Windows 95's request for confirmation. The text in the popup request will verify that you are, in fact, deleting a shortcut and not the original. The message can be valuable information if the original happens to be an important file or an application.

You'll see the Recycle Bin itself in a moment, but to make your encounter memorable, first put something in it. At the moment, you should have two sample folders, a number of sample files, and miscellaneous shortcuts and scraps sitting on your desktop and on your hard disk. You've finished with them, so clean up as follows:

1. Select the copies of samples 1, 2, and 5 on the desktop.

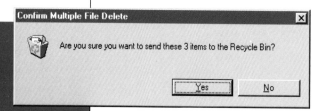

2. Right-click and choose Delete from the popup menu. Windows 95 displays the request for confirmation shown at the left.

   In this case, you're sure, so go ahead and press Enter or click Yes. You'll probably—though briefly— see an animated window showing your samples wafting into the Recycle Bin. When the window disappears, that's it. The samples are gone.

3. Select and delete the shortcut to Sample4. You might want to keep the printer shortcut handy, but if you don't, delete it too.

   Now for the rest.

4. If necessary, open a window to your hard disk.

5. Select and delete the Expendable folder—this time by dragging the folder to the Recycle Bin icon.

Yes, cleaning up was that simple. But also bear in mind that step 5 wiped out a number of files, a subfolder, and the files in the subfolder with a single mouse action—and didn't prompt for confirmation. When you delete your own material, double-check folders and even dubious files by opening them before deleting. Checking doesn't take that long, and you'll be sure you're not tossing one or more important files or folders into the trash along with the documents you know you don't want.

Using the Recycle Bin

As mentioned, whatever you delete normally goes into the Recycle Bin for temporary storage. Whenever you need to, you can easily take a look at the contents of the bin and retrieve one or many items:

1. Close all open windows, and then open the Recycle Bin icon on your desktop. Here you see all the objects you recently threw away.

2. If necessary, choose details view and maximize the window so you can see the complete entry for each deleted item. If any of the entries in the Original Location column ends in three dots, that column is too narrow. Widen it by placing the mouse pointer on the vertical bar between the Original Location and Date Deleted headers. When the mouse pointer

looks like the one circled in the illustration below, press the left mouse button and drag the border between the headers to the right.

Most of what you see in the Recycle Bin window should be self-explanatory. If you've never used MS-DOS or Windows, however, you might be some-what puzzled by the entries in the Original Location column. Don't be. They're easy to inter-pret. The entry C:\Expendable\ Gotcha, for example, tells you that the deleted file was located on your hard disk (C:), in the Expendable folder and the Gotcha subfolder. This way of showing the *path* to a particu-lar file dates back to MS-DOS conventions and is actually nothing more than a way of stringing the names of folders and subfolders together by separating them with a backslash (\). All you ever have to remem-ber is that such a path:

- Starts with the letter (always followed by a colon) of the drive on which a file is (or was) stored.

- Goes from highest (drive letter) to lowest (lowest-level subfolder) as you read from left to right.

- Sometimes ends with the name of an actual file. For example, while Sample1 was in the Gotcha folder, its full *pathname* would have been C:\Expendable\Gotcha\Sample1.

That said, you can try using the Recycle Bin itself. First of all, notice that deleted files are listed alphabetically by name. Often, however, date and time might prove to be more useful, so reorder the contents of the Recycle Bin by clicking column headers (which works, you'll recall, in any window showing its contents in details view):

1. Click the column header labeled Date Deleted. Windows 95 immediately reorders the files by date and time, oldest first.

2. Click the column header labeled Type. This time, Windows 95 orders the contents by type.

3. Click the header labeled Size.

Clicking the header you want is so easy and so convenient, this is a trick to remember.

As for recovering deleted files:

1. Select the copies of samples 1, 2, and 5. (Notice, by the way, that the path to those files, which were moved to the desktop, shows the hard disk, the Windows 95 folder, and the desktop.)

2. Choose Restore from the File menu. The files disappear from the Recycle Bin window.

3. Minimize the window so that you can see what happened. All three files should be back on your desktop.

4. You don't need these files anymore, so delete them again. Boring, but good practice.

That's all there is to recovering files: select and choose File Restore. Recovering an entire folder and its contents, including subfolders and *their* contents, is not much different:

1. Restore the Recycle Bin window.

2. Select every file that shows Expendable, Gotcha, or both in its path. (This can be tedious if the folders contain many documents, so you might want to sort the Recycle Bin by Original Location first.)

3. Choose File Restore.

And finally, here's yet another way to recover files—one that you'll particularly like if you've ever wanted both to recover a deleted file and to put it in a different folder or on a different disk:

1. Minimize the Recycle Bin window.

2. Open a window to your hard disk, and create a new folder named NewHome.

3. Restore and resize the Recycle Bin window so that you can see both its contents and the NewHome folder. (If the Recycle Bin window was maximized, click the Recycle Bin button on the taskbar to remaximize the window, and click the window's Restore button to restore the window's original size.)

4. Drag Copy Of Sample5 from the Recycle Bin to the new folder.

That's it now for the sample chapters, shortcuts, and scraps you created in this chapter. It's time to clean up for good and empty the Recycle Bin:

1. Delete the NewHome folder.

2. Delete the Expendable folder.

3. In the Recycle Bin window, choose Empty Recycle Bin from the File menu. Click Yes when Windows 95 asks for confirmation, as shown on the following page.

SELECTING FILES

When you work with the Recycle Bin (or any other window) in details view, it's natural to assume that you can put the mouse pointer on the file's path, size, type, or date and click to select the file. Not so. Point to the file's icon or name and click. Windows 95 is a little fussy that way. It has no problem, however, letting you place the mouse pointer anywhere in the window when you want to drag a rectangle to select a consecutive set of files. You will notice, though, that the files are not selected until the rectangle covers the filenames and icons. Quirky, perhaps, but that's the way it is.

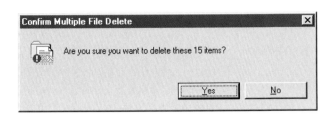

4. Close the Recycle Bin and hard-disk windows.

Finally, before you leave the subject (at least for a while), take a look at the Recycle Bin's properties sheet. That's what you use to customize the bin itself:

1. Right-click the Recycle Bin icon on your desktop.

2. Choose Properties from the popup menu.

(That's right, you get to the properties sheet from the *icon*, not from the bin window.) Requesting the properties sheet opens a window like the one shown at the right.

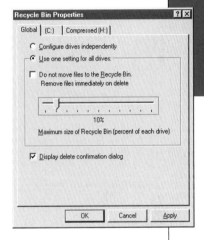

The tab titled Global lets you apply a single set of choices to all valid hard disks, compressed drives, and uncompressed drives on your system. (Compression is a means of making a disk hold more information by storing programs and data as compactly as possible; you'll meet it in Chapter 12, "Disks, Controls, and Other Delights.")

By default, Windows 95 sets your Recycle Bin's capacity to 10 percent of each drive and, as you can see, uses the same settings for all available drives. If you look at the bottom of the window, you also see the option that causes Windows 95 to prompt for confirmation before deleting a file. Ten percent of a large hard disk is generous, indeed, but all these settings are safe, and you should probably leave them as is until you're feeling confident with Windows 95. If you don't have a lot of room to spare for a Recycle Bin, however, you can reduce its size with the movable gauge in the middle of the window. Conversely, if you're planning to delete a large number of files, you can temporarily increase the size of the bin with the same gauge. No matter which way you want to go, all you do is drag the marker to the left or right. As you drag, Windows 95 changes the percentage displayed directly below to show you how much disk space the current position of the marker represents. If you want to give it a try:

1. Drag the marker on the gauge a little to the left.

2. To return to the default setting, drag the marker to the right until Windows 95 displays *10%*.

As for the rest of the options:

- Click Configure Drives Independently if you want to set the bin size for each drive. You might want to do this if you set aside a small *host* (uncompressed) portion of a compressed drive. To configure a particular drive, click the tab that Windows 95 displays for it on the properties sheet.

- Click Do Not Move Files To The Recycle Bin if you want deletions to be immediate *and* permanent. Be sure you want this, because the only way to recover from a mistake will be to use a separate file-recovery program (with no guarantee that the file can be recovered).

- Click to turn off Display Delete Confirmation Dialog if you don't want Windows 95 to prompt for confirmation. For safety's sake, Windows 95 will not allow you to both delete immediately and turn off confirmation. The two options combined would be dangerous indeed.

To finish up:

- Click Cancel to close the Recycle Bin properties sheet.

Restoring vs. Undoing

You use the Restore command to "undelete" files and folders, but immediately after a deletion you might notice an Undo Delete command on the Recycle Bin's Edit menu. What's the difference between Restore and Undo Delete? Undo is a general-purpose command that you see in many Edit menus in many windows. In all cases, Undo exists to allow you to reverse your latest action—not just a deletion but a copy or a move as well. The upshot is that whenever

you delete one or more files, Undo Delete becomes temporarily available on every visible Edit menu. If you *immediately* realize you've made a mistake, you can choose Undo Delete to reverse the deletion. The command is available, however, only until you do some other work with Windows 95. If Undo Delete is no longer available, select the file(s) you want to retrieve and use the Recycle Bin's Restore command instead.

③ Cruising

Windows 95

Chapter 6

Oh, Those Files and Folders

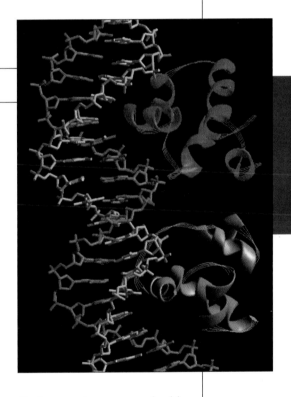

Building Blocks

"Sorry, boss. No can do."

That's what your computer would say if it could think and speak and you told it to add 2 plus 2 without using any files whatsoever. (Assuming, of course, that the ability to think and speak was not itself dependent on files, which it no doubt would be, even in such an intelligent machine.)

At any rate, why couldn't your computer do simple addition without using files? Because files are where computing, at least in this century, begins and ends. Although your computer's processor is the "brain" of the machine, files tell that brain not only what, but how, to think.

In the real world, paper files are commonplace, albeit sometimes very valuable, items. In the computer world, electronic files are equally commonplace and often equally valuable. Of course, "commonplace" doesn't mean "not worth noticing." Chromosomes and DNA are everyday things too, but you wouldn't get very far without them. Just as your DNA holds the key to you—the way you look, think, act, walk, and play the piano—files hold the key to your computer's "look and feel" and to its ability to solve problems, draw pictures, string words together, and—most important—interact with you.

Files are the building blocks of computer wisdom, both yours and the machine's.

About Files

You already know that all the work you do with your computer must be saved in files on disk if you ever want to use that work again. Disks are, in many ways, your computer's long-term memory, in contrast to RAM, which is fast and efficient but so volatile it goes blank as soon as you turn off the machine.

Creating a file is your business. Whether the file contains text, a drawing, a schedule, or a list of names and addresses, the content is entirely up to you. Although Microsoft Windows 95 is busily moving your input into memory and onto the screen as you work, its function, like that of your application program, is purely responsive at that point. You are in control. When you want to store your work on disk, however, Windows 95 needs you to play the game its way, by giving your file an acceptable filename and by telling Windows 95 where to save the file—that is, which disk or folder you want to use as a "file cabinet."

What's in a Name?

Naming a file is easy, especially in Windows 95. Why? Because Windows 95 is so relaxed about names that you can use just about anything you want. Before Windows 95, you had to follow (on MS-DOS–based computers, that is) what's known as the *8.3 rule* (pronounced "8 dot 3"). That means a filename could be no longer than eight characters, followed—optionally—by a period (dot) and a three-character *extension*. You could doll up an 8.3 filename with the characters $ % ' - _ @ ~ ` ! ( ) ^ # and &, but you weren't allowed to use certain other characters, such as commas, periods, spaces, square brackets, and plus signs.

Because of this 8.3 rule, people sometimes had to become, well, creative with filenames. A report to the company president, for instance, might be named PRESREPT.DOC, and a letter to the IRS admitting a mistake might be saved as TAXOOPS.DOC.

The Long and Short of It   Knowing what was, you can now really appreciate what is: Windows 95's ability to recognize *long filenames* (which you might someday see referred to as LFNs, since computer people like abbreviations as much as doctors do).

A long filename is, as far as you're concerned, any name you care to assign to a file. The name can:

• Contain up to 255 characters.

FILE EXTENSIONS
File extensions are commonly used to associate a particular type of file with a particular application, so that double-clicking the file opens both the document and the application. For example, Paint habitually tacks on the BMP extension; WordPad (and Microsoft Word) prefers DOC; Notepad likes TXT. Although you don't usually have to worry too much about extensions, do be aware that when you check a file's properties sheet, you'll often see an extension at the end of the file's MS-DOS name. And even though you don't see it, the same extension is also attached to the file's "Windows 95" name. Chapter 8, "Workout: Exploring Files," tells you more about extensions and how they affect your work. For now, just note that they exist.

- Be a mix of uppercase and lowercase, including letters, numbers, and special characters.

- Include spaces. You'll really need these if you're going to use all 255 characters.

- Include any of the following characters, some of which are also valid for 8.3 names: $ % ' - _ @ ~ ` ! ( ) ^ # & + , ; . = [ ].

Thanks to long filenames, then, you can easily save a file as Report To The Company President or as Dear IRS People, I Really Didn't Mean To Do That or even as @#$ That Cat! (assuming you expect to remember which symbols you used).

That's the long of it. But the heading of this section refers to the short of it too. Windows 95 recognizes short filenames as well as long ones. The relationship between long and short names is where the going can get a little sticky. It's nothing to break a sweat about, but it's nothing to ignore, either, so find a quiet spot and read on.

Long filenames are designed especially for the new generation of application software created to run with Windows 95 and its new 32-bit file system, known as VFAT. That makes sense, since Windows 95 is, itself, a new-generation operating system. You, as a computer user, however, are probably a little bit on the application cusp because you still might want to use some favorite programs designed for the older file systems supported by Windows 3 and MS-DOS through version 6.22.

Unfortunately, these older file systems and their applications do not understand or accept long filenames. To get around the generation gap, Windows 95 stores *two* filenames for each file with a long filename—the long name and a short, 8.3 name called an *alias* (which you can think of as kind of a nickname). Here's how it works:

- If you assign a long filename, Windows 95 automatically creates an alias for the file, for the benefit of older file systems.

- If you assign a filename that conforms to the 8.3 rule, Windows 95 uses that name as both the long filename and the alias.

- In creating an alias, Windows 95 takes the first six characters of the filename after removing any spaces, ignores uppercase/lowercase distinctions, and substitutes an underscore for each invalid character it finds (an alias cannot include any of the following characters: + , ; = [ ]). Then Windows 95 adds a tilde (~) followed by a sequence number. For the curious: the set of rules Windows 95 follows in creating an alias is called an *algorithm*. Because algorithms determine the way software behaves, they are, in a sense, the "human" part of the computer.

255 OR 256?

Technically, a long filename actually contains 256 characters. Windows 95 tacks a special character known as NULL onto the name, however, so the effective length for you is 255 characters. That's still *long*; this paragraph contains almost 255 characters. If you really need a name as long as the preceding paragraph, well…feel free.

ALGORITHM

A set of step-by-step instructions that describes how something is to be done. Although *algorithm* is a computer term, it represents a concept that's easy to understand if you put it in terms of everyday life. A recipe for brownies, for instance, is an algorithm that tells you how to make the dessert. Here's another example that might be more meaningful: if a person gives you directions to his or her house, those directions form an algorithm. When you use those directions to get to the house, you are doing what a computer would do in carrying out an algorithm.

At any rate, given all these algorithmic rules and regulations, what does an alias look like? Some examples are shown in the table below.

Long Filename	MS-DOS/Windows 3 Alias
Report To The Company President	REPORT~1.DOC
Report To Choc-o-Latte's	REPORT~2.DOC
Report.To.My.Boss	REPORT~3.DOC
Dear IRS People, I Really Didn't Mean To Do That	DEARIR~1.DOC
Two + Two = Four	TWO_TW~1.XLS

Aargh, you say? No. If all your applications are designed for use with Windows 95, assign all the long filenames you want and then proceed with gay abandon—you'll never need to worry about aliases. If some of your applications are designed for use with Windows 95 but others are meant for Windows 3 or MS-DOS, however, just follow a few simple rules to avoid some of the "mistakes" in the preceding examples, and you'll be fine:

- Most important, as the first three examples show, don't start long filenames with the same words. Windows 95 is smart, but you have to give it something to work with.

- As the IRS example shows, using spaces in long filenames is great, but when they're removed in an alias, the results can be…cryptic. Try hyphens or underscores instead.

Hands-On!

Seeing Long and Short Filenames

Windows 95 makes it easy for you to see both long filenames and aliases. Here's how to see some for yourself:

1. Use Notepad to create a sample file. Give the file a long filename, and save it—on the desktop is fine. (If you already have such a file lying around on the desktop or in an open window, you can use that instead.)

2. Right-click the file, and choose Properties from the popup menu. At the top of the properties sheet is the file's official Windows 95 long filename. Below, toward the middle of the sheet, you can also see the file's MS-DOS name, complete with extension.

That's all there is to it. Remember the file's properties sheet whenever you need to check on the file's name or alias. As you can see, the same sheet is also useful for checking the file's location, size, date and time of creation or modification, and even its attributes, such as whether the file has been hidden from casual view.

- Finally, as you can see by comparing Two + Two = Four with the alias TWO_TW~1, using characters that are invalid for aliases can, again, produce less than satisfactory results. Although invalid characters won't break Windows 95, you should probably avoid frequent use of such characters. Windows 95 won't get confused, but you might.

MS-DOS and Long Filenames

If you still like to work at the MS-DOS prompt, you'll save yourself time and trouble if you avoid starting long filenames with the same words and you avoid using spaces in long filenames. If your aliases all end up with the same first six letters, a Delete, Rename, or Copy command that includes the * or ? wildcard character could have unforeseen and possibly damaging consequences.

If you include spaces in long filenames, either you'll have to use aliases in your MS-DOS commands and batch files or you'll have to enclose all long filenames in quotation marks (" "). As you probably know, MS-DOS commands use spaces to separate command switches and parameters, so spaces in long filenames won't be interpreted correctly. So, for example, the Type command for a file named Dune Buggy would have to be either:

```
C:\>type "dune buggy"
```

or

```
C:\>type dunebu~1
```

On another, related, front, you should also consider the impact of long filenames on file storage. MS-DOS relied on a file-storage system known as the FAT (File Allocation Table). The way the FAT was organized, the root directory of a disk was limited to a set number of entries—512 on a

hard disk. What's so important about this? Nothing much, except that the root directory is the key to all file storage on a disk. Every single file and folder on the disk *must* trace back to an entry in the root directory.

Bear in mind that because of the way long filenames are stored, they require more than a single directory entry; thus, fewer long filenames than 8.3 names can fit in the root directory. If you're an experienced MS-DOS user, you probably know that the root directory of a hard disk is limited to 512 entries. And, of course, once you fill the root directory, it's bye-bye additional storage there, even if the disk isn't full. If you're going to use long filenames, do rely on subdirectories, which aren't limited in size. It's for your own good.

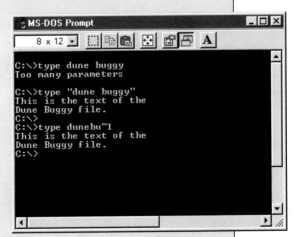

Close Relatives: Files and Folders

Definitions earlier in this book told you that files come in two basic types: program files and data files. Program files contain the instructions that make Windows 95 what it is. They also enable your word processor to process words and enable Paint to draw pictures. Data files contain the information you create, print, and save: the prizewinning poem you write with your word processor or the reproduction of the Sistine Chapel ceiling that you draw with Paint. (Such a picture would probably take you more time to create, by the way, than the original demanded of Michelangelo.)

Program files and data files are easy to understand. Folders are, too. Technically, they're files, but with a rather elegant twist to them. Instead of being full of information for you to use, they actually contain the names of other files. They're Windows 95 "data" files that enable Windows 95 to keep track of *groups* of other files. Why groups? That's obvious. You see the reason each time you open a window to a disk, especially your hard disk. Folders in Windows 95 serve the same purpose as the folders in your file cabinet: organization. With folders, you can:

- Organize information into categories in a way that makes sense to you—for example, all letters in a Letters folder, all payments in a Bills folder, all the kids' schoolwork in Kate, Mark, and Jerry folders. (True enough, the "organization" part of this depends on you. If your file cabinet is a mess, your disks probably won't be any better.)

- Keep closely related documents together, within categories, so that they're as easy to find as the papers in your file cabinet.

Visualizing Folders

If organization is the name of the game, then you need to know what type of organization Windows 95 works with. You already know that folders can contain subfolders, and those subfolders can contain still more subfolders. Often, the relationship between a "parent" folder and a "child" folder is described as a type of tree, in which branches divide into other "offspring" branches. That description is actually a holdover from the days of MS-DOS and even Windows 3.

A much easier way of visualizing folders and subfolders is to picture them as parts of an outline. You know the kind—you did tons of them in school and probably loved every one. Use the following diagram as an example. It shows a set of folders that work down from one folder named Birds. The Birds folder contains two subfolders, Eagles and Woodpeckers. The Woodpeckers subfolder is further divided into Sapsuckers and Red-Headed. And the Sapsuckers folder contains a document file named All I Know About Yellow-Bellied Sapsuckers.

If you were to outline the relationships of those folders, you'd end up with:

I. Birds

    A. Eagles

    B. Woodpeckers

        1. Sapsuckers

            All I Know About Yellow-Bellied Sapsuckers

        2. Red-Headed

Each level leads down to the next, until you reach the file All I Know About Yellow-Bellied Sapsuckers, which would be equivalent to the text under the heading "Sapsuckers." (True, the document isn't really part of the outline, but it does show how documents fit into the scheme of folder things.)

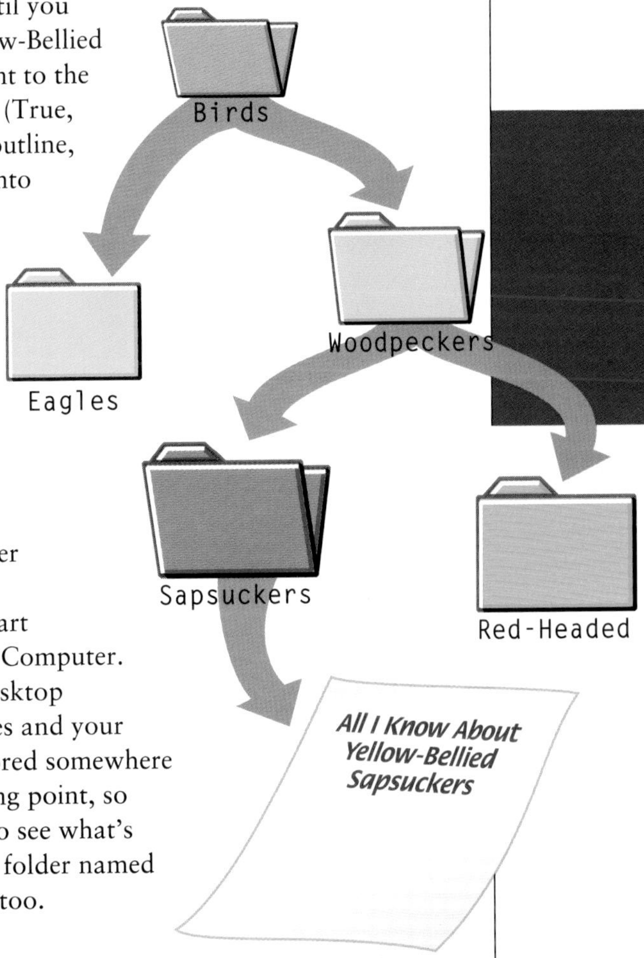

Now that you're able to visualize the relationships among folders, all you need to do is connect this structure (usually called a *hierarchy*) with what you see on screen. Suppose you have the folders illustrated at the right.

Your mission, similar to one in an earlier chapter, is to boot the computer and find your way unerringly to the Sapsuckers paper. All right, so you start Windows 95, and, say, you open My Computer. Its window is sitting there on your desktop displaying icons for your floppy drives and your hard disk. You know that Birds is stored somewhere on your hard disk. That's your starting point, so you double-click the hard-disk icon to see what's on it. Next step, find the icon for the folder named Birds. Got it? Good. Double-click it, too. Now you're getting there.

Birds

Eagles

Woodpeckers

Sapsuckers

Red-Headed

All I Know About Yellow-Bellied Sapsuckers

When you open the Birds folder, it blossoms into its own window, like the one shown below at the left.

When you open the Woodpeckers folder, you see the windows shown below at the right.

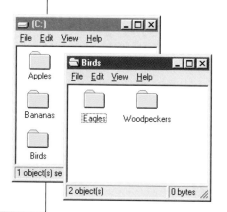
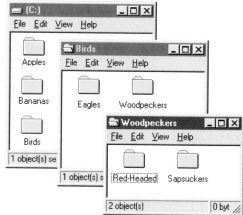

Each folder is in its own window. That's important, because whether you think of folders as belonging to trees or parents or outlines, you need to remember that Windows 95 considers each folder a separate object that merits its own window. In opening folders, you thus step through windows as you step up or down through one folder after the other. And because Windows 95 (by default) opens a new window for each folder, if you want to see and open a folder, you must first open the disk or folder that contains it.

Now, before you dig into these and many other facets of Windows 95, perhaps it's time for a short...

Pep Talk

As you work with Windows 95, one fact eventually forces its way into your understanding. It's been mentioned before in this book, but it deserves mention again: Windows 95 is a flexible operating system that usually gives you a lot of ways to accomplish the same task. This variety of options can confuse you when you're starting out, especially because those options sometimes apply not only to task A (right-click or double-click to open a file) but to task B (right-click or double-click to start a program). That's the case even if A and B are not—in your mind—clearly related. Sooner or later, you get to feeling, "Gee, now how did I do *that*? Did I drag? Did I choose from the menu? Why do I click that but double-click this?" And the confusion can deepen when well-meaning people who know the system better than you do offer advice or numerous alternatives.

But whether the realization is gradual or causes you to leap out of your bath and shout, "Eureka," you eventually *do* come to understand that Windows 95 isn't trying to measure your memory or your IQ and that people aren't trying to leave your mind in a whirl. Everyone's trying to give you the ability to use your system in the way that suits *you* best, and Windows 95 is trying to let you use the same approaches for a variety of tasks—copying, moving, printing, whatever.

So as you work, don't feel that you have to learn every possible way to copy or move or do anything else. By all means try different ways of working, but then trust yourself enough to discard what you don't like and settle on routines that suit you best. That's when everything will fall into place and you'll appreciate the fact that Windows' ways of working often apply across the board. (Oh, when the time comes, don't forget to smile and say, "thanks, but…" when "experts" admonish you for doing something the "wrong" way.)

Controlling the View

If you keep the Windows 95 default and open one folder after another, your screen eventually begins to resemble the popcorn machine at the movies: windows, windows, popping up everywhere. If you prefer less clutter, you can have Windows 95 use a single window to display one folder after another.

To apply a single-window view to a series of folders as you step down through them:

• Hold down Ctrl as you double-click the folders.

Ctrl+double-click temporarily toggles Windows 95 between *multiple-window browse* mode (the default) and *single-window browse* mode. This keystroke+mouse shortcut affects only the folder you're opening, so Windows 95 will continue to use multiple windows for everything else. In addition, it will revert to the default view the next time you open the same folder.

To make single-window browsing permanent, do the following:

1. From your My Computer window or from any open disk or folder (not document) window, choose View Options.

2. On the Folder tab, click the radio button at the left of the Browse Folders By Using A Single Window option.

3. Click OK to make the change.

Whether you choose Ctrl+double-click or View Options, you can easily move to a previous window. Either press the Backspace key or turn on the toolbar and use the Up One Level tool (which is marked with a file folder).

Creating Folders

Before you can save a file in a folder, you obviously have to create the folder. That's so easy it's a no-brainer. All you have to remember is to open the window (disk or folder) in which you want the folder to reside *before* you actually create the folder itself. Windows 95 creates a new folder in the active window, so:

- For a "top-level" folder—one that you see whenever you open a window to the disk—open a window to the disk and then choose File New Folder. Think of creating this type of folder as setting aside an entire file drawer for storage.

- For a subfolder, comparable to a section of a file drawer, open the folder in which you want to create the subfolder and then choose File New Folder.

In either case, when Windows 95 creates the new folder, it prompts for a name, as shown at the left.

If you simply press Enter, Windows 95 names the new folder New Folder, which is pretty yuck. To assign a name of your own, type any legal 8.3 or long filename and then press Enter.

Digging In

Whether you browse folders with a single window or with multiple windows, you'll often want to move from one folder to another. Windows 95 makes it easy. To move *down* through folders and subfolders:

- Double-click your way to the folder you want.

- Or right-click successive icons, each time choosing Open from the popup menu.

- Or choose File Open after selecting each icon.

If you start from the top, meaning the icon for the disk itself, you can always get where you want to go. You might, however, have to backtrack and try again if you're not sure of the route from, say, Folder 1 to Folder 7. Remembering that part is up to you.

CAN I KEEP CREATING SUBFOLDERS?

For all practical purposes, yes, you can. There are limits, however. If you are using long filenames, the maximum *path* to a folder—that is, the total combined length of the names of *all* folders leading to a particular sub-folder—cannot ex-ceed 259 characters. (All right, 260, if you include the NULL character Windows 95 attaches automa-tically.) If you are using 8.3 names, the maximum path is 80 characters. In either case, that's a lot. Unless you're really into *long* long file-names, you can safely figure that both the 259-character and 80-character limits allow you to create somewhere on the order of 6 to 10 subfolder levels. That should give you plenty of room for organizing, assuming that you even want to think or click your way that far down into a labyrinth of subfolders.

Other Ways to Go

Because Windows 95 is so flexible, you can not only move down through folders and subfolders, but you can also retrace your path, jump from one disk to another, or even leap up or down several levels in a single bound. The "how" of doing these things differs a little, depending on whether you're browsing with multiple windows or with just one. Multiple windows are easier, though less efficient in some ways, so start with them.

Moving Around in Many Windows   Retracing your steps once you've stepped down through several folder levels is obvious. You can:

- Click window buttons on the taskbar. (Move from right to left to step up through the levels in order.)

- Or click the close box in each window if you want to go back and clean up the screen at the same time.

TAKING THE EASY WAY ACROSS

If you often use files or folders on more than one disk, right-click the disk icon, drag it onto the desktop, and choose Create Shortcut(s) Here. With the disk on your desktop, you'll never have to bother opening My Computer to find it. (Creating shortcuts like this, by the way, also works for shared folders and disks on a network; more on this appears throughout the book.

Don't Go Hog-Wild

Although it's really easy to open a window to a disk and create one folder after another in the disk's window, you should practice some self-control. Creating folders in a disk window, although convenient because it makes the folders easy to find, actually puts those folders in what's called the disk's *root directory*. This is a super-special storage area that acts as the master catalog of every file, folder, and subfolder on the disk. Important as it is, however, the root directory cannot hold an unlimited number of filenames and folder names. Even on a large hard disk, the maximum number of entries the root can hold is 512. That sounds like a lot, right? Not.

At best—meaning when you use 8.3 names for files and folders—each file or folder requires one directory entry. When you use long filenames, each file or folder requires more than one entry. Files, more than folders, multiply like happy rabbits over time, and 512 can be used up before you know it. So when you create folders in the root directory, practice economy. Save the root for the broadest categories, and rely on subfolders for organizing files below that level. If you need inspiration, just look at the way all the files and subfolders in your Windows 95 folder are categorized. The groupings not only make sense, they require only one entry—for the main folder—in your root directory.

Hands-On!

Folders and Multiple Windows

The easiest way to get the hang of working with folders is to practice opening them and navigating from one to another. Here are some suggestions:

1. Open My Computer, and open a window to your hard disk.

2. Open your Windows 95 folder, and then work your way down through the following folders: Start Menu, Programs, and Accessories. As you go, notice that you can see and open a subfolder only after opening the folder that contains it.

3. Right-click the taskbar, and choose Minimize All Windows.

4. Now, click buttons on the taskbar to reopen one window or another, in any order you please.

5. Close all open windows.

To move *across* disks (for example, from drive C to drive A), you can open My Computer and either double-click or right-click as described above, or you can take a faster route:

1. From any disk or folder window, use View Toolbar to turn on the toolbar.

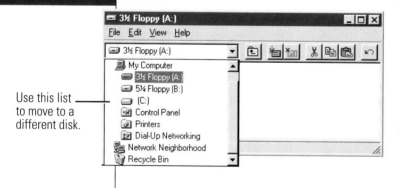

Use this list to move to a different disk.

2. Click the triangle at the right of the Go To A Different Folder list box at the left end of the toolbar (it's the miniature window at the left of the Up One Level button).

3. Click the disk you want, and then double-click or right-click your way down from there.

To jump up or down two, three, or more levels within a series of subfolders—for instance, from Sapsuckers back up to Birds in the earlier example—remember the taskbar:

- Click the button for the window you want. Any order, any time.

- Or use the Go To A Different Folder list box on the toolbar.

- Or organize the open windows by right-clicking a blank part of the taskbar and choosing Cascade, Tile Vertically, or Tile Horizontally. Don't forget that to work in a particular window, you must click in the window or on its title bar to make it the active window.

Moving Around in One Window   If you choose to browse in a single window, bear in mind that Windows 95 changes the window's button on the taskbar as you switch from one folder to another. That is, if you open Birds, the taskbar button says Birds. If you open Eagles, the label on the button changes to Eagles. Because of this, you can't simply click taskbar buttons to move up or down through subfolder levels. What you *can* do, however, is just as easy, and it works when you want to retrace your steps, jump up several subfolder levels, or skip across to a different disk:

1. Turn on the toolbar.

2. Open the list box at the left of the toolbar, and click the folder or disk you want. To move up successive levels, use the Up One Level button illustrated on the following page.

Hands-On!

Folders and a Single Window

To gain some practice working with folders in a single window, try the following. Don't forget to turn on both browsing with a single window *and* the toolbar.

1. Open a window to your hard disk, and work your way down from your Windows 95 folder, opening Start Menu, Programs, and Accessories. Pay attention to the label on the taskbar button as the window contents change.

2. Open the list box at the left of the toolbar. Notice that the current folder is highlighted and that the path to the current folder forms an indented "ladder" to help you see how the folders are related.

3. Use the list box to click your way, one step at a time, up to Start Menu. As you go, notice that the list changes and no longer displays the names of folders below the current level.

4. Use the folders in the window to move back down to Accessories.

5. From Accessories, use the list box to jump all the way back to the window to your hard disk.

6. Switch back to browsing with multiple windows if you prefer.

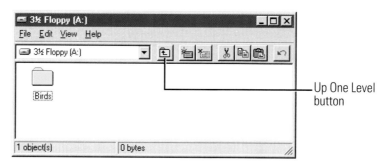

Up One Level
button

That's it. If you browse with a single window, make life especially easy for
yourself by turning on the toolbar.

Renaming Files and Folders

One of the practice sessions in an earlier chapter showed how easy it is to
change the name of a folder. The same tactic works for files:

1. Click to select the file or folder you want to rename. Wait a second, so
   that Windows 95 doesn't interpret the next action as the second half of
   a double-click, and then...

2. Click the *name* of the file or folder.

3. When Windows 95 highlights the name, type a new name. To edit the
   name, changing part but not all of it, use the following keys:

   • Home to move the blinking insertion point to the beginning of the
     name; End to move the insertion point to the end of the name.

   • Del to delete a character to the right; Backspace to delete a character
     to the left.

Although renaming is a simple matter for you, this is one area where you can
appreciate some of the behind-the-scenes work being done by Windows 95.
Remember that Windows 95 keeps track of two filenames—the long filename
and the alias. Even though you don't see it happen, Windows 95 changes *both*
names whenever you rename a file or a folder. For example, if you change Box
Turtle to Snapping Turtle, Windows 95 changes both the long filename and
the alias. The Box Turtle alias, BOXTUR~1, thus automatically becomes
SNAPPI~1. Nice, huh?

Name Changes and Shortcuts

There's one situation where you don't see a name change reflected on screen,
and it's one you'll have to watch for. When you've created a shortcut to a file
or a folder, the shortcut label doesn't change if you rename that file or folder,

but Windows 95 *does* maintain the shortcut connection to the proper file. For example, if you place a shortcut to Box Turtle on the desktop and then change the name of the original file to Snapping Turtle, the label below the shortcut icon remains Shortcut To Box Turtle but double-clicking the shortcut icon to open the file does, indeed, open Snapping Turtle. To keep from confusing yourself, keep shortcuts under control (don't scatter them everywhere) and rename affected shortcuts whenever you rename files or folders. To locate all your shortcuts, use the Find command described in the next section and type *shortcut* in Find's Named text box.

FINDING COMPUTERS

The Find command described here can also be used to find computers on a network. For more about this, refer to Chapter 10.

Finding Files and Folders

Because files eventually crowd your disk in multitudes and because subfolders can be nested several layers deep inside other folders, Windows 95 includes a most helpful command called Find. To find Find:

- Choose Find from the Start menu, and then choose Files Or Folders from the Find submenu.

- Or right-click My Computer, and choose Find from the popup menu.

Whichever way you go about it, the window at the right opens.

A Simple Search

By default, Find opens with the blinking insertion point in the Named text box, and it proposes to search all subfolders, so for a simple (but extensive) search, simply:

1. Type the name of the folder or file.

2. Press Enter or click Find Now.

When Find swings into action, it expands the window, as shown on the following page.

During the search, Find displays the name of the folder it is currently searching. (The *.* near the bottom of the illustration means that Find is checking "all files.")

The window along the bottom (labeled Results window in the illustration) is where Find lists all files and folders it locates that match the name you specified in the Named box. This is what the headings in the results window tell you:

- Name—the name of the file or the folder.

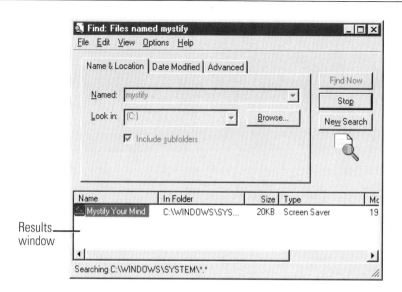

Results window

- In Folder—the path to the drive and the folder where the item is stored. (If you don't know how to read a path, refer to the shaded box headed "Following a Path.") If the path ends with an ellipsis (...), Find is telling you that it cannot display the complete path. To see it all, place the mouse pointer on the vertical bar between the In Folder and Size headings. When the pointer becomes a dark bar crossed east-west by a two-headed arrow, drag to the right and release the mouse button. If necessary, drag again until you can read the complete entry.

- Size—the size of the file. No size is listed for folders.

Hands-On!

Find It Simply

Windows 95 includes the screen saver named Flying Windows. Use it for practice with the Find command. First, perform a simple search:

1. Choose Find Files Or Folders from the Start menu.

2. Type *flying* in the Named text box.

3. Click Find Now.

   Notice that Flying Windows is in the Windows 95 System folder. If you can't see the entire path, widen the In Folder section: place the mouse pointer on the vertical bar at the right of the heading, and drag toward the right edge of the window.

4. To finish up, close the Find window.

- Type—whether the item is a file or a folder. If it is a file, Type also tells you what kind of file it is—a text document, a bitmap (Paint image), a screen saver, and so on. (The section "Controlling a Search," which begins on the next page, tells you how to limit searches to particular types of files.)

- Modified—the date and time the file or the folder was created or last modified.

Following a Path

Windows 95, like MS-DOS and Windows before it, uses paths to tell you where a particular file or folder is located. Although somewhat intimidating at first, paths are easy to read. Just interpret backslashes as separators between drive and folder names. Folders are always listed in descending order from left to right. For example, the path C:\LETTERS\MOM refers to the subfolder MOM in the LETTERS folder on drive C. If the path is shown as only a drive letter, a colon, and a backslash, Windows 95 is referring to the root directory of the drive—for example, C:\ refers to the root directory of drive C.

What to Do with It Now

Unless you're simply trying to find out where you stored a file or a folder, you'll probably want to look at it in some way. If more than one item was found, highlight the item you are interested in. To see what other files or folders the object of your search is stored with:

- Choose File Open Containing Folder to open a window to the folder or disk where the file or folder you searched for is stored.

To actually open a file or folder you've found:

- Choose File Open from the menu bar at the top of the window, or right-click the filename in the results window and choose Open. (This command might be different with certain files. The "open" command for a screen saver, for example, is Test. However it appears, the "open" command is always the one at the top of the File menu.)

- Or double-click the filename in the results window.

Note that Open, or an equivalent command, appears only if the file you are opening is already associated with an application, meaning that Windows 95 knows which application was used to create the file. Such associations don't exist for all files, especially those created by applications other than those that came with Windows 95. If an association does not yet exist, you'll see the command Open With instead. If that happens, you can open the file anyway by choosing Open With and then choosing from a list of applications that Windows 95 displays. For more on associations, refer to "Extensions, Open With, and the Registry" in Chapter 8.

Controlling a Search

Find gives you several ways to manipulate a search. Some are obvious, others are less so. Space unfortunately precludes covering them all, but the following list will set you on the road to discovery:

- You don't have to type the entire name of a file or a folder in the Named text box. Just type enough to be sure that (a) Find will recognize the file or folder you want and (b) Find will not locate a zillion other similarly named items. The characters you type don't even have to be at the beginning of the name—they can be anywhere in it. For example, if (as you were cautioned not to) you had a dozen files starting with *Report To* and you wanted to find the one named Report To Exterminator, typing *report* in the Named text box would cause Find to locate the entire dozen files. If, however, you typed *exterminator* in the Named text box, Find would locate only the report dealing with the exterminator—plus, of course, any other files with *exterminator* in their names.

- Find does not distinguish whole words (as in My *Term* Paper) from parts of words (as in Ex*termin*ator), even if you surround a word with spaces (as in [space]*term*[space]).

- To search a specific disk, click the downward-pointing triangle at the right of the Look In box and choose the disk you want from the drop-down list that appears. To choose from all the resources on your computer, including the desktop, your Network Neighborhood, and the Recycle Bin, click the Browse button and choose the resource you want. A window like the one at the left opens up.

To see a list of folders on a specific disk, click the plus sign at the left of the disk name, click the folder you want, and then click OK. (This type of display, by the way, forms the heart of Windows 95's "File Manager on Steroids"—real name, the Windows Explorer. More details are in Chapter 8, "Workout: Exploring Files.")

- To clear the last search and start a new one, click the New Search button and then click OK when Find prompts for confirmation. To save the results of your last search as an icon on the desktop, turn on Options Save Results before the search and choose File Save Search afterward if you're doing a lot of looking and you want to keep previous search results a mouse-click away for reference or reuse.

Hands-On!

Find It with Refinement

The previous Hands-On box suggested you use Find to locate Flying Windows. To try out some of Find's options, this time:

1. Choose Find Files Or Folders from the Start menu.

2. Type *win* in the Named box. (The folder you're going to search contains many files whose names include *win*, but only one of them is a screen saver.)

3. To limit the search to your Windows 95 System folder, click the Browse button. Click the plus sign at the left of your hard-disk icon. Scroll down, if necessary, until you can see your Windows 95 folder. Click the plus sign at the left of the folder. Scroll again, if necessary, click the System folder, and then click OK.

4. Click the Advanced tab.

5. Now limit the search to screen savers only. Click in the Of Type box. When the highlight appears, type *s, c, r,* and *e* in succession. (Don't pause too long between keystrokes, however.) As you type, notice that Find displays the first entry in the list that matches the letters you've pressed. That should do for now.

6. Click Find Now. Your search should be much faster than the earlier one that sent Find through every folder and file on your hard disk.

7. Right-click the filename in Find's results window, choose Test, and hold the mouse very still. There's the screen saver, up and running. (If the file were a document, you'd see it in its application window.) Move the mouse to send the test display packing.

8. Choose File Save Search, and then close the Find window.

9. Double-click the saved-search icon on your desktop.

10. To clean up, click the saved-search icon and press the Del key. Click OK or press Enter when Windows 95 asks for confirmation.

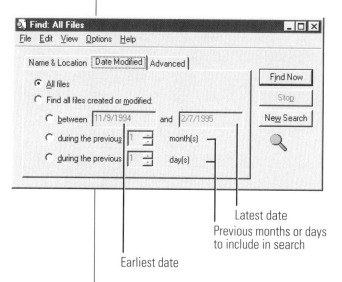

Latest date
Previous months or days
to include in search

Earliest date

- To search for files or folders you created or modified during a particular time period, click the Date Modified tab. Click the button at the left of the Find All Files Created Or Modified option, and then use the items labeled in the illustration at the left to specify the search period.

- By default, Find searches for all files and folders that match the name you specify. To limit the search to a specific type of file, including such exotics as sounds and shortcuts, click the Advanced tab and choose the type of file from the drop-down list in the box labeled Of Type. Once you're familiar with the file types listed, you can save some time by simply highlighting the default All Files And Folders and then pressing the first letter or two of the type you want. Find will automatically display the matching entry, so you won't have to scroll through the entire list. If the file type you want is not listed in this box, you'll have to use the default. You can, however, limit the number of files searched by specifying the disk or the folder, as described above.

- And last but far, far from least, you can search for specific text *inside* a document. To make matters better, Find distinguishes between whole words and parts of words during a text search, and if you turn on Options Case Sensitive, Find even distinguishes between uppercase and lowercase. Thus, you can search for *kipper* without also finding *skipper*, and you can search for *ET* but not *et*. (From extraterrestrials to Latin and French conjunctions, sure…. Well then, *you* come up with an example.) Closer to home, think of it this way: you can search for *Highway* without having to travel every *highway* on the disk.

Those are the highlights of Find, which, as you can see, is not so much a command as it is a digital bloodhound. The best way to become comfortable with it is to use it—simply, as described earlier, or by trying various combinations of options. Whichever way you put Find to work, you'll no doubt find (pun intended) it a valuable ally in sorting through your documents and folders.

Managing Files and Folders

All right. You've made them, named them, trotted through them, and even found them. What's left? Managing them. That's what this section is all about, and it's what you'll do a lot of, especially if you organize and periodically cull the contents of your hard disk. Management is mostly about copying, moving, and deleting, all of which are simple, as you saw for yourself if you worked through the first few chapters of this book.

Copying or Moving a File or a Folder

Copying and moving are closely related. The only way they really differ is that copying *duplicates* information, whereas moving *transfers* information from one place to another. Because these activities are so similar, Windows 95 uses pretty much the same approach to both. The basic and infallible methods are:

- Drag and drop

- Copy and paste (for copying) or cut and paste (for moving)

Drag-and-Drop   Early in this book, you were told that Windows 95 treats practically everything as an object—something you can "handle" much as you would handle a real, physical object. Drag-and-drop is the most visible and intuitive result of this object orientation. When you're working in a window or on the desktop, you can copy a folder or a file simply by dragging and dropping. Do remember, however, that Windows 95 responds to *both* the left and right mouse buttons:

- The easiest and most foolproof way to ensure success is to drag with the *right* mouse button so that you can choose from the popup menu shown at the right when you release the button.

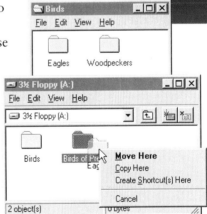

- If you prefer to drag with the *left* button, you might sometimes be surprised. Dragging and dropping on the same disk results in a move, but dragging and dropping from one disk to another produces a copy. To control what happens, however, you can hold down Ctrl as you drag to force a copy or hold down Shift as you drag to force a move.

Otherwise, using drag-and-drop is simple:

1. Open a window to the folder or file you want to copy.

2. Click to select the item. If you want to select more than one item, either drag or hold down Ctrl and click the items you want.

3. Drag the selected item(s) to their destination, which can be a disk, another folder, or the desktop.

SEEING DOUBLE

If you want to duplicate one or more files in the same folder, be sure you're viewing Large Icons or Small Icons. Windows 95 does not duplicate files in list view or details view.

When you copy, remember that Windows 95, unlike other operating systems, allows you to duplicate files in the same location. The original keeps its name, while duplicates are labeled Copy Of, Copy 1 Of, Copy 2 Of, and so on. Because of this, it's easy to keep both a pristine original and a working duplicate in the same folder or on the same disk. It's a capability that can come in handy, especially when you're revising a large or complex document.

(Windows 95 includes another method of copying called the Send To command. If you're duplicating information onto another disk or, perhaps, to a network resource, refer to the heading "You Send Me..." on the next page.)

Hands-On!

Copying and Moving with Drag-and-Drop

If you don't want to use the right mouse button to copy or move with drag-and-drop, you should practice a little with the left button until you can easily remember whether to press Ctrl or Shift as you drag.

Here's an easy way to do it:

1. Use Notepad to create a sample file for practice. Use the Save As default to save the file on the desktop.

2. Create a sample folder, either on your hard disk or on an expendable floppy. Because you're going to use Ctrl and Shift, it doesn't matter where the destination is.

3. First *copy* the file from the desktop to the sample folder by holding down Ctrl and dragging.

4. Select the copy in the folder window, press Ctrl, and drag within the window to make another copy. Repeat this copy once or twice if you want more practice.

5. Select all the files in your folder window, and drag them (no keys needed) to the Recycle Bin.

6. Now *move* the original file from the desktop by pressing Shift while dragging to the folder window.

7. Press Shift and drag to move the file back to the desktop.

8. To clean up, drag the sample file and folder to the Recycle Bin.

Copy and Paste Although drag-and-drop is faster and easier (and actually requires less of your computer's available memory), you can also copy files and even folders with the Edit Copy and Edit Paste commands. Copying and pasting is the electronic equivalent of photocopying and gluing, and it's easy. To copy a file or a folder:

1. Open a window to the file or the folder you want to copy.

2. Open a window to the destination folder or disk.

3. Select the file(s) or folder(s) you want to copy. Remember, you can select either by dragging around a group or by holding down Ctrl and clicking the items you want.

4. To copy, right-click and choose Copy; or choose Edit Copy from the menu bar; or press Ctrl+C.

5. Click in the destination window. Right-click and choose Paste; or choose Edit Paste from the menu bar; or press Ctrl+V.

That's copying with copy and paste. For moving, you use cut and paste.

Cut and Paste When you cut and paste, you use the equivalent of scissors and glue. Like copy and paste, this procedure is most often associated with reorganizing documents. It works perfectly well, however, with files and folders. To move a file or a folder:

1. Open windows to the source and destination as described above.

2. Select the file(s) or folder(s) you want to move, either by dragging or by holding down Ctrl and clicking.

3. Right-click and choose Cut; or choose Edit Cut from the menu bar; or press Ctrl+X.

4. Click in the destination window. Right-click and choose Paste; or choose Edit Paste from the menu bar; or press Ctrl+V.

That's it. Just remember to make the destination window active before choosing Edit Paste, and you're home free.

You Send Me... Although drag-and-drop makes it easy to copy or move files and folders to another disk, you can avoid the U-Haul and rely on Windows 95 shipping if you prefer. For this, you use the Send To command, which sounds as though it should *move* items but in actuality *copies* them. Copies them where? By default, Windows 95 lets you send to your floppy drives, and if you use Microsoft Exchange, to a Mail Recipient. (Exchange and e-mail are described in Chapter 10, "Networks and *The* Network.")

Because all Send To destinations are kept as shortcuts in a folder named Send To in your Windows 95 folder, you can also customize its contents by adding shortcuts of your own. So, for example, you can add shortcuts to your printer,

NOW YOU SEE IT, NOW YOU DON'T

Don't be dismayed if you open the File menu and don't see a Send To command. The command appears only after you've selected one or more files or folders. Stands to reason: you can't send nothing.

to a shared network folder, to a fax machine…practically anywhere you want, including any often-used folder on your own computer or a special container called My Briefcase, which lets you carry copies of documents on a disk or a portable computer and later synchronize updated versions of those documents with the originals on your main computer. (My Briefcase is described in Chapter 11, "Long-Distance Information.")

All right. To use Send To:

1. Select the file(s) or folder(s) you want to send. If you're sending to a floppy be sure to put a disk in the appropriate drive.

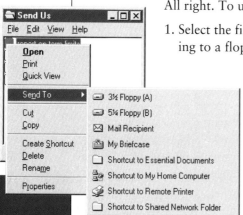

2. Right-click and choose Send To, or choose File Send To from the menu bar. Whichever way you do it, a submenu like the one at the left opens.

3. Choose the destination, and it's done.

To customize your Send To folder:

1. Open your Windows 95 folder, and scroll so that you can see the Send To folder.

2. Find the item you want to be able to send to. (If that item is a network resource, fax machine, or remote computer, you'll probably want to wait until you've found out about them in Part 4 of this book.)

3. Select the item, right-click, drag to the Send To folder, and then choose Create Shortcut(s) Here.

That's it. The next time you want to send a file or a folder, your new shortcut will appear on the Send To list.

Deleting a File or a Folder

Everybody has to delete files or folders now and then. Perhaps they're old and unneeded. Perhaps your hard disk is getting kind of crowded. Or perhaps you've backed up the files onto floppies and don't want to keep the originals hanging around. Whatever the reason, deleting has never been easier, thanks to the Recycle Bin, which sits on your desktop, ready for action whenever you are.

Although you can delete both files and folders, be cautious about deleting folders, especially if they contain subfolders. Windows 95 can recover everything for you, and it can even reconstruct a folder and its subfolders, but the process could be a lot more work than you care for. Windows 95 doesn't place entire folders in the Recycle Bin. It dumps the *files* into the bin. And that means *you* will have to pick through the rubbish to find and select every single file that originally belonged to the folder and subfolders you deleted. Once you find them all, of course, Windows 95 will restore them to their original locations. If you ever have to recover a folder and its subfolders and files, click the Original Location header in details view. That way, you'll be able to see and group the paths to all the deleted files, so picking out the ones you need to recover will be easier.

That said, here's how to delete:

1. Select the file(s) or the folder(s) you want to delete.

2. Drag them to the Recycle Bin. If you prefer, you can also either right-click and choose Delete, or choose File Delete from the menu bar. If you drag and drop, Windows 95 does not prompt for confirmation. If you choose either of the Delete commands, it does.

Wait: What Are You Deleting? Because Windows 95 allows you to create shortcuts and because Windows 95 saves documents by default on the desk-

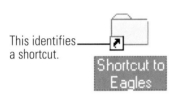

This identifies a shortcut.

top, you must pay attention, even if you are not deleting a folder. Are you deleting a short-cut, or are you deleting the actual document? Shortcuts, remember, are always identified by a small arrow in the lower left corner, like the one shown at the left.

It Doesn't Hurt to Be Sure

Before you delete, be sure that what you're getting rid of is, in fact, expendable. This is particularly true of folders containing files and subfolders. It's easy to overlook one valuable file in a welter of nonessentials, especially if all the files or folders you're deleting have similar names. If you don't want to waste time clicking your way through subfolders, there's an easy way to check on a folder and all its subfolders and files: choose MS-DOS Prompt from the Start menu. When an MS-DOS window appears, type the command shown below, substituting the drive letter for *[drive]* and the name of the folder you're deleting for *[folder]*. Enclose the folder name in quotation marks if it's a long filename, and don't forget the colon after the drive letter. Here's the command:

```
dir /og [drive]:\[folder] /s /p
```

For example, to check on all subfolders and files in a folder named My Unwanted Folder on drive C, the command would be:

```
dir /og c:\"my unwanted folder" /s /p
```

This command displays a list of subfolders, followed by subfolder names and the files they contain, with a pause after each screenful. To continue the display, just press a key, such as Enter.

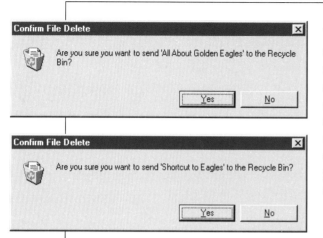

When you select files for deletion, especially if they are on the desktop, do check for the shortcut arrow. In this situation, you might also prefer to use the Delete command rather than drag-and-drop, because in its prompt for confirmation, Windows 95 tells you whether the item you're deleting is a file or a shortcut.

Removing Files and Folders from the Desktop   And speaking of files and folders on the desktop, bear in mind that Windows 95, by default, saves files on the desktop when you create them with Notepad, WordPad, or Windows 95's other accessory programs. Useful as this practice is in keeping files close at hand, how do you clean up the desktop?

• You *move* files and folders to a disk or to another folder.

Deleting their icons means you delete their contents. Remember that.

Recovering a Deletion

Well, after all those cautions to remember this and remember that, you know that no one is immune from error. Thankfully, although the Recycle Bin's main task is deleting, it also lets you *recover* files (and folders) when you make those occasional mistakes. Be grateful for this capability. Before file recovery became a computing staple, many a forlorn individual was known to gasp and shriek upon realizing that a valuable file had been deleted in a moment's thoughtlessness. At one time, in fact, you could even delete the entire contents of your hard disk. And in those days, *deleted* meant *gone*. Forever.

Now, before you start patting yourself on the back and chuckling about such stupidity, engrave this on your forehead: *It can happen to me.* Yes, it can, because you can fish deleted files and folders out of the Recycle Bin *as long as you don't empty the bin.* Once you empty it, those files and folders are gone, and the only way to get them back is by reconstructing them from scratch or, if you've been a good kid, by restoring them from archive (backup) disks or tape. Message received?

To recover deleted files, start by opening the Recycle Bin icon on your desktop. Windows 95 opens a window like the one shown on the next page.

To recover files:

1. Select the files you need to recover. Remember you can select multiple files either by dragging or by holding down Shift or Ctrl as you click.

Name	Original Location	Date Deleted	Type	Size
dragme	C:\WINDOWS\Desktop	5/31/95 2:54 PM	Text Document	1KB
longfilename	C:\WINDOWS\Desktop	5/31/95 2:51 PM	Text Document	1KB
My Sample WordP...	C:\WINDOWS\Desktop	5/31/95 2:51 PM	Microsoft Word Doc...	5KB
this is a long filena...	C:\WINDOWS\Desktop	5/31/95 2:51 PM	Text Document	1KB

Recycle Bin — 4 object(s), 4.50KB

2. Choose File Restore.

Hint: If you've opened a window to the disk or the folder to which you're restoring files but nothing appears in the window after you choose File Restore, don't worry. Either press F5 or choose Refresh from the window's Options menu. Sometimes Windows 95 needs a little nudge.

Emptying the Recycle Bin

This is a snap. You can either:

- Right-click the Recycle Bin icon and choose Empty Recycle Bin.

- Or open the Recycle Bin and choose File Empty Recycle Bin.

If the bin is full, opt for the second choice and scan the list of deleted files *before* you empty the bin. It's the only way you can be sure.

There's a lot more that could be said about working with files. There is, of course, the whole matter of creating and editing files, using drag-and-drop to modify them, inserting graphics and other objects in them, creating scraps, printing, and on and on. Some of this is covered in the next chapters, but many subjects belong in the realm of the actual applications you use and are therefore outside the scope of this book (which, after all, is about an operating system that deals more with files than with parts of files). You're not without aid and succor, however. If you're using Windows 95 accessories, remember that each accessory comes with its own Help and that Help is designed specifically to get you up and running. In addition, remember that Windows 95 itself offers Help on getting started, Help on files and folders, and (from the Help Contents tab) sets of How-To's and Tips And Tricks. Roam through these at your leisure, and most of all remember that the best way to learn is by trying.

CHANGING THE VIEW TO MEET YOUR NEEDS

If your Recycle Bin is full, you probably want to see the greatest number of files with the least amount of scrolling. Open the View menu, and choose the type of display you want. Small Icons and List show the same size entries, but because Small Icons arranges items across the window, whereas List arranges them down the window, list view will probably show you more. Details, the default, gives the most information, and because it shows the path to each deleted file, it is especially valuable if you're trying to recover a deleted folder.

Chapter 7

The Metaphorical Desktop

A metaphor is a way of describing one thing in terms of another. When you describe life as a bowl of cherries, you're using a metaphor. If you think life's more like a box of chocolates (never mind the implications of nutty centers), you're using another metaphor. The point of this flashback to freshman English class is that your Microsoft Windows 95 desktop is, as the chapter title states, a metaphor. Though you might not always view the desktop as being equivalent to a bowl of cherries or a sweet treat, the desktop is the digital metaphor that turns a batch of sophisticated programs into a visible operating system that's as natural and as easy to use and understand as the desk or table on which you work in the real world. That's why you have a desktop on your desktop and a computer in your computer.

Objects and Their Properties

Windows 95 places your computer and everything related to it on your computer screen—your digital desktop—just as you place files, documents, a printer, and a computer on your real desk. And just as you move and manipulate real-world desktop objects, you move and manipulate digital desktop objects.

Back in an early chapter, objects were described as things—like your mouse and modem, folders and files—that have certain *properties*. These properties not only describe such objects to Windows 95 and to your applications; they also determine how those objects behave and what you can do with (and to) them. Because objects and their properties have a lot to do with the way you control your Windows 95 desktop, Windows 95 gives you a way to:

- Find out what properties any particular object has.

- Manipulate those properties to bend Windows 95 to your will.

The way you go about all that is with *properties sheets.* These sheets are similar to, say, the sticker that tells you that the car of your dreams has a five-speed transmission, antilock brakes, and a sunroof. Just as you can customize—within limits—the car attached to the sticker, you can customize the object attached to a properties sheet. For instance, you can change the style of the hubcaps just as you can change the double-click speed of your mouse. In one case, the auto dealer makes the change for you; in the other, Windows 95, following your instructions, takes over the job.

Properties sheets are sophisticated, and they're brand-new with Windows 95, but there's really not much you need to understand about them other than:

- Every object has one.

- The contents of properties sheets can vary, sometimes considerably, from one type of object to another, but similar objects have similar properties sheets.

- Some properties sheets are multipage jobs whose pages you "turn" by clicking the labeled tab at the top of the page you want.

HARDWARE PROPERTIES

As mentioned in the text, all kinds of things in Windows 95 have properties. Files do, folders do, programs do…and so do the bits and pieces of hardware that make up your system. If you're a longtime PC user, you probably know that hardware sometimes requires exotic settings, such as IRQs (Interrupt Request lines), DMA (Direct Memory Access) channels, and I/O (Input/Output) ranges. If you've also read about Windows 95's support for Plug and Play (PNP), you know that one of the strongest features of this new operating system is its ability to detect and moni-tor these and other such hardware set-tings and to act as mediator if two or more devices have similar requirements. Although PNP is still in its infancy, look for Plug and Play–compatibility when you upgrade or add new hardware. As the technology be-comes more wide-spread, you can expect ease of hard-ware installation to follow.

That Term *Object*

This box contains an apology of sorts to software engineers, to whom objects are complex and delightful… objects. *Object* is used in this book to describe something that has certain properties and that behaves in ways related to those properties. Although that definition is true enough, it's really not a whole lot more descriptive than saying that cows are hairy, four-legged animals with tails. After all, so are horses and yaks and tigers and pigs. So let it be understood that this simple

definition of *object* doesn't even begin to address the intricacies of programming with objects. The term is used primarily because no better word came to mind (not even with the help of Microsoft Word's thesaurus); because *object* makes it easier to understand concepts like drag-and-drop; and because Win-dows 95 itself uses *object* in the status bar of a window whenever it tells you how many items are cur-rently visible or selected. Mea culpa.

Opening a Properties Sheet

To find out about or change the properties of an object, you open its properties sheet. There are two routes you can take, depending on the object you're interested in. If the object is an icon in a window or on the desktop:

- Either right-click the object's icon and choose Properties from the popup menu.

- Or click to select the icon and choose the File Properties command.

This approach works when you want information about any icon, from My Computer down to individual files and folders.

For information about both hardware and Windows 95 components, you take a different route to properties sheets—the Control Panel. To open the Control Panel window:

1. Double-click the Control Panel folder in your My Computer window, or click the Start button and choose Settings and then Control Panel. You'll see a window similar to the one shown at the right.

2. Choose the icon you want and double-click (or right-click and choose Open) to open the object's properties sheet.

   Note that not all the icons in the Control Panel lead to properties sheets. Those that do *not* lead to properties sheets have an X drawn through them in the preceding illustration. Note also that the System icon takes you to the same properties sheet you see when you choose Properties for the My Computer icon on your desktop.

Why Some But Not All?

The Control Panel is something like a master switchboard that allows you to manage your "controllable" pieces of hardware, such as the mouse and display, and to customize certain parts of Windows 95 through software installation and removal, network connections, password security, and so on. Some of these Control Panel tools rely on properties sheets. Others, because of the work they do, rely on special programs, including some called wizards, that help make relatively complex installations easy for beginners. Don't be thrown if you double-click a Control Panel icon and a wizard appears instead of a properties sheet. Just remember that the Control Panel is there to help you control Windows 95 and your computer, and take it one step at a time from there.

Using a Properties Sheet

The following two illustrations show vastly different properties sheets, but when you examine them, you can see that they do have a number of features in common.

This first properties sheet is a simple, one-tab job of the sort you're likely to consult every now and then when you want to check on the vital statistics of a file or a folder. (The same type of sheet opens when you want to find out about any folder except those in your My Computer window.)

And the properties sheet below gives information about a Hewlett-Packard LaserJet printer that is shared over a network. If you have a different printer, your Printer Properties sheet probably differs in some respects, but the basics should be similar. (To open a Printer Properties sheet, open the Printers folder in My Computer and request Properties for the printer you want to find out about.)

TABS

On any properties sheet, tabs are used to group related properties. For instance, the Paper tab on the Printer Properties sheet lets you set the paper size and orientation (portrait or landscape) of your printout. When you open an unfamiliar properties sheet with multiple tabs, take a minute and click through the different tabs to see how the object's features are grouped. It's a good way to get an idea of how Windows 95 "views" the object, and it can save hunting around later on.

Despite their differences, both properties sheets include:

- A ? button at the upper right for requesting information about options on the sheet.

- A close box for closing the properties sheet.

- Controls, such as check boxes, text boxes, and list boxes, for changing those properties that can be changed.

- Three buttons at the bottom for telling Windows 95 what to do next:

- OK, to make the changes you've indicated and close the properties sheet.

- Cancel, to discard your changes and close the properties sheet.

- Apply, to make your changes but keep the properties sheet open for further work. (To finish up, you can either click OK or the Close button at the top of the sheet.)

Asking for Advice   Properties sheets try to help you out with descriptions and drawings wherever possible, but if you need more help with any option, remember that you can request a short definition or explanation:

- Either by right-clicking an option and then clicking the What's This? box that appears.

- Or by clicking the ? button at the upper right of the window and then clicking the option that puzzles you.

And don't forget: there's always Help. If, for example, you want to customize your mouse but you've forgotten what to do, look up *mouse* in the Help index. Wherever possible, Windows 95's Help also includes "magic buttons," like the one in the Help window at the right, which take you directly to the program or properties sheet you need.

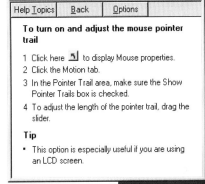

With guides like these, you should have few problems and most of those will undoubtedly be related to complex topics, such as network setups, that an expert really ought to advise you on anyway. (If *you've* been designated the expert, check out the *Windows 95 Resource Kit*, also from Microsoft Press. It's a set of books produced by Microsoft for those who need to know more than Windows 95 basics.)

Buttons and Boxes, but No Bows   You change object properties by dragging, clicking, typing, and selecting. The following list illustrates and briefly describes the types of controls you encounter:

- **Check box.** A check box appears at the left of any option you can turn on or off. A check mark in the box indicates that the option is turned on. Check boxes usually appear in sets, like those below. Options with check boxes are *not* mutually exclusive, meaning that you can turn on more than one if you choose.

- **Radio button.** A radio button, like a check box, lets you turn an option on or off. Like check boxes, radio buttons generally hang out in groups. The difference, however, is that radio buttons indicate options that *are* mutually exclusive. You can turn on only one option in the set.

- **Text box.** A text box, as you've seen many times, enables you to provide information that Windows 95 can't guess at—for example, the name you want to give a new file. You simply type the appropriate information in a text box. To edit an existing entry,

HERE, THERE, AND EVERYWHERE

Although this chapter describes various controls in terms of properties sheets, remember that properties sheets are just one form of window and that the controls you read about here work the same in other windows. A check box is a check box, no matter where you find it. So is a text box, a list box, a button, or a preview area. Learn a how-to in one window, and don't worry about whether the same approach will work in a not-quite-the-same situation. It will.

use the Home, End, and direction keys to move the insertion point. Use the Ins key to insert new text; use the Del key to delete existing characters. The illustration on the previous page shows a text box that can be used to display a comment—in this case, one that would be displayed for a network printer.

- **List box.** You've seen list boxes a million times by now. They contain lists of options you can choose from. Some, like the one shown at the left, are fully visible.

  Others, like the one at the right, drop down when you click the triangle at the right.

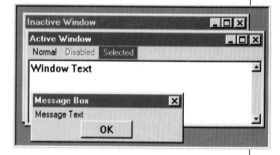

  In any case, you choose from the list simply by clicking the item you want.

- **Spinner.** A spinner appears next to an option with a range of possible values, as in the illustration at the left.

Click the upward-pointing triangle to increase the value; click the downward-pointing triangle to decrease the value. You can also select the value in the box and replace it by typing a new value.

- **Preview area.** A preview area appears only on certain properties sheets. It exists to show you the result of choosing a particular option, as on the Display Properties sheet shown at the right.

- **Slider.** A movable slider, like the volume control on your stereo, lets you adjust an option to whatever setting you prefer within a scale of potential values. Drag the movable marker left or right with the mouse to change the setting.

In a few cases, controls vary a little bit from the "classic" forms described above. The list of paper sizes on your Printer Properties sheet, for instance, consists of graphics rather than text. On the Mouse Properties sheet, an animated jack-in-the-box in a "preview area" allows you to test a new setting for double-click speed. All such variations are clear and easy to understand, however, so you shouldn't have any problems with them. If you have doubts, remember the ? button at the top of the window.

Hands-On!

Looking at Some Properties

You can easily familiarize yourself with several properties sheets by trying the following:

1. Right-click My Computer, and choose Properties from the popup menu. Click the tabs, one after the other, for a Windows 95's-eye view of your computer. Right-click, and then click What's This? for an explanation of interesting items that catch your eye. Only *look* at this properties sheet, please. As you can see, it is complex and controls a lot of things you're better off leaving alone. Click the Cancel button when you've finished looking.

2. For a less dazzling technological display, open My Computer and request the properties sheet for your hard disk. If you want, type a new name for the disk in the Label box (keep the name to 11 characters, including spaces). Click OK to keep the new name or Cancel to keep the old one.

3. Double-click the Printers folder in your My Computer window. Request the properties sheet for your printer. Click the various tabs to see details about the printer. To avoid problems, leave everything as is, but do remember this properties sheet if you ever need to make a change—for example, if you switch the printer to a different port (connector) on your computer.

4. Right-click a blank part of the taskbar, and choose Properties. You can use this properties sheet to customize the Start menu. Try clearing the document list if you've opened a lot of files you don't intend to use again for a while.

Customizing the Start Menu and the Taskbar

When you decide to make the desktop look and act more like you want, the obvious place to start is with the two parts of the desktop designed especially to help make Windows 95 easy to use. The Start menu, as you already know, is your one-stop shop for starting programs and documents. The taskbar is Windows 95's equivalent of the channel selector on your TV. Both are controlled by the Taskbar Properties sheet, which you get to from the Start menu or from the taskbar.

Tip!

ABOUT DOCUMENTS

Although the text describes working with programs on the Start menu, you should know that you can add documents to the menu too. This can be useful if you use the same document over and over. An easier approach, however, might be to create a shortcut to the document on the desktop as described later in this chapter.

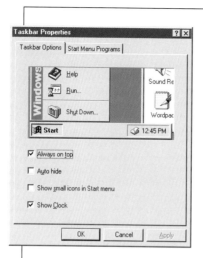

- Either click the Start button and choose Settings Taskbar.

- Or right-click a blank part of the taskbar and choose Properties.

Either way, the properties sheet shown at the left appears.

Adding to the Start Menu

It seems that the Start menu and its submenus provide access to every program and feature you can imagine, but there are still a few ways you might want to customize it. You can, for instance, modify the Start menu so that a favorite program appears on the main Start menu. You can have Windows 95 automatically start a program whenever you start your computer. If a program slips through the Start menu cracks because its installation software doesn't automatically add its name to the Start menu, you can add the program yourself. And, of course, if you stop using a program, you can also remove its name from the Start menu. All these things are possible.

By the way, if you do remove the name of a program from the Start menu or from one of its submenus, don't ever be concerned that you're removing the original. You're not. Menu entries are *shortcuts*. They are pointers to programs and documents; they don't represent the files themselves. And as you already know, when you delete a shortcut, you merely remove the pointer. The file remains intact on disk.

Customizing the Main Start Menu   As you've seen throughout this book, drag-and-drop can be as useful—indeed, as essential—as a wheelbarrow in the garden. It (drag-and-drop, that is) is all you need if you want to add to the main Start menu:

1. Open a window to the disk and folder in which the application is stored.

2. Locate the program's main application file. If you're not sure which this is, right-click some likely icons and choose Properties until you find a file whose properties sheet identifies it as an application file.

3. Finish up by dragging the icon to the Start button.

That's it. From now on, the program name will appear at the top of the main Start menu. If you later decide to remove the item, either open the Start Menu folder in your Windows 95 folder and delete the program shortcut, or use the Taskbar Properties sheet as described in "Removing an Entry from the Start Menu or from StartUp" later in this section.

EASY LIVING

If you're an experienced Windows user, you've probably already discovered the Windows Explorer, a feature that can—in conjunction with drag-and-drop —make your work with Windows 95 both fast and efficient. Although the Windows Explorer is mentioned only incidentally in this chapter, bear in mind that you can use it for many of the tasks described here. The Windows Explorer itself is described in more detail in the next chapter.

POWER PLAY

Command Line Aficionados

If there are certain MS-DOS commands you use often, drag their COM or EXE files to the Start button or create an MS-DOS submenu as described below. You might find this particularly useful with the MS-DOS Edit command, which gives you quick access to a small, fast text editor that, unlike Notepad, does not automatically attach a TXT extension to a new file.

Adding to and Organizing the Start Menu   Dragging an icon to the Start button lets you find and start a program without having to work your way through one or more submenus. You can also choose to organize additions to the Start menu by placing them on whichever submenus you prefer, including new submenus you create by yourself:

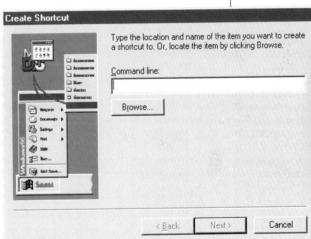

1. Open the Taskbar Properties sheet, and click the Start Menu Programs tab.

2. In the Customize Start Menu section, click the Add button. This button takes you to the Create Shortcut wizard, shown at the right, that handles most of the procedure for you.

3. Click the Browse button. If you're adding a program, double-click the folder containing the program and then click the name of the program to add. (If you're adding a document, open the Files Of Type list, choose All Files, and then locate the document you want to add.)

4. Click the Open button, and the wizard adds the correct startup command to the Command Line text box in the Create Shortcut window.

5. Click the Next button, and then select the folder (submenu) where you want the new entry to appear. If you want to create a new submenu, click the New Folder button and type the name of the new folder/submenu as you want the name to appear on the Start menu. Spaces and capital or lowercase letters are all fair game, just as in naming any other folders.

6. Click the Next button. If you want, name the shortcut-to-be, again including whatever spaces and capitalization you want. If you're prompted to select an icon, choose one from the "gallery" the wizard displays.

OPEN A DOCUMENT TOO

If you work with the same document for an extended period, you can place a shortcut to the document in the StartUp folder. To make life easier, be sure that an association exists between the document and the program you use to work with it. Such an association definitely exists if Windows 95 has had no trouble opening the document for you before. (For more on associations, refer to "Extensions, Open With, and the Registry" in the next chapter.)

7. Click the Finish button, click OK to close the Taskbar Properties sheet, and you're done. Open the Start menu, and you'll see your new entry exactly where you decided to put it.

Running a Program at StartUp   Windows 95, like Windows 3, includes a special folder named StartUp, which, as its name implies, starts any program it contains whenever you start or restart your computer. To run a favorite application at startup, all you have to do is put a shortcut to it in the StartUp folder. The "how" is easy:

1. Follow steps 1 through 4 in the preceding section.

2. In step 5, when the wizard asks you to choose a folder, choose StartUp.

3. Click Next, type a name if you want, click Finish, and then click OK to close the Taskbar Properties sheet.

Bear in mind that placing a program in the StartUp folder means that the program begins automatically at startup. You will not see its name on the Start menu, nor will you be prompted with a "Do you want to…" type of request. When Windows 95 starts, the program will too. The StartUp folder can be a tremendous help if you consistently start by running one particular program or if you are setting up a computer for someone who isn't as familiar with Windows 95 as you are. Automatic startup can also be a pain, however, if you use it unwisely and have to wait for a program to start, only to end up closing it right away. If you change your work habits or decide you made a mistake by putting something in StartUp, remove the entry as described in the next section.

Removing an Entry from the Start Menu or from StartUp   People change, and so do their responsibilities and their habits, at work and at play. Because you won't be the same you forever, you can "uncustomize" the Start menu and your StartUp folder as easily as you customized it. Just remove the entry you no longer want:

1. Open the Taskbar Properties sheet, and click the Start Menu Programs tab.

2. In the Customize Start Menu section, click the Remove button. The Remove Shortcuts/ Folders window opens, as shown at the left.

3. If the entry you want to remove is not visible, click the + sign at the left of the folder that contains the entry.

4. Click the entry to be removed, and then click the Remove button at the bottom of the window.

5. If you want to remove more entries, find each one and remove it the same way. When you've finished, click the Close button and then click the OK button to close the Taskbar Properties sheet.

Now if only troubles could be made to disappear as easily.

Tinkering with the Taskbar

You already know that the taskbar need not remain at the bottom of the screen. Nor does it have to remain the same size. The taskbar can *float*, which means you can drag, drop, and dock it along any of the four edges of the screen, and it is resizable, which means you can make it thicker or thinner. If you use the Taskbar Properties sheet, you can also control when and how the taskbar is displayed.

Moving and Sizing the Taskbar   Moving and sizing are simple matters. All you need is the mouse:

- To move the taskbar, point to a blank part of the bar. Press the *left* button and drag (the right button won't work). When you drag, a ghostly outline jumps to the nearest edge of the screen. Release the mouse button, and the taskbar follows its outline, parking itself along the edge you indicated.

- To resize the taskbar, which is one-button thick by default, point to its inner edge. When the mouse pointer becomes a two-headed arrow, press the left button (again, the right doesn't work) and drag in or out to make the bar thinner or thicker. Release the mouse button, and that's that.

Docking the taskbar along one edge or the other is wholly a personal choice. Making the bar thicker can be useful if you're working with a large number of open windows because, as you would expect, buttons become smaller as Windows 95 places more of them on the taskbar. And the smaller the buttons, the less information Windows 95 can display on them. Eventually, buttons can become a little difficult to read. If and when that happens, increase the thickness of the taskbar to increase the sizes of the buttons. (Admittedly, you have to have a *lot* of open windows to make this necessary.)

Hiding and Unhiding the Taskbar   As useful as it is, the taskbar *does* require about half an inch of onscreen real estate. That real estate is not extensive to begin with, and it can sometimes feel as cramped as new shoes, especially if you work in standard 640-by-480 (pixel) screen mode. One way to maximize available screen space is to switch your display, if possible, to a higher resolution, such as 800 by 600. (More about this later in the chapter.)

Another way to maximize working room is to change either or both of two taskbar properties, Always On Top and Auto Hide:

- Always On Top, which is turned on by default, tells Windows 95 to display the taskbar in front of—which is to say on top of—any other open window.

START MENU ICONS

By default, Windows 95 displays large icons on the Start menu and small icons on its sub-menus. If the size of the main Start menu seems a bit overwhelming, open the Taskbar Properties sheet and click to put a check mark at the left of the Show Small Icons In Start Menu option.

That means the taskbar has "dibs" on its screen space. Since no other window can use that parking spot, even a maximized window is reduced by the amount of space occupied by the taskbar. Turn off Always On Top to reverse the situation so that any other window can overlay and thus use the space otherwise occupied by the taskbar. Turning the option off, by the way, doesn't mean you lose use of the taskbar. Whenever you want to switch windows or programs, click any visible part of the taskbar to bring it to the forefront once again. If you can't see the taskbar at all, move, resize, or minimize windows until it becomes visible.

- Auto Hide, which is turned off by default, goes Always On Top one better by actually making the taskbar go away until you need it. Auto Hide obviously has the same advantages and benefits as Always On Top in terms of making the most of usable screen space, with the added benefit of reducing clutter on the desktop. Even though choosing Auto Hide makes the taskbar disappear, the game of hide-and-seek is only temporary. Move the mouse pointer to wherever you docked the taskbar, and it will return to view—on top of open windows if Always On Top is turned on, behind open windows if Always On Top is turned off.

In either case, the taskbar and its buttons remain as functional as ever, of course. To turn these options on or off:

1. Open the Taskbar Properties sheet.

2. Click the appropriate check box. Remember, a check mark means the option is turned on.

Hands-On!

For Maximum Effect

To make the taskbar as unobtrusive as possible:

1. Open the Taskbar Properties sheet.

2. Turn Always On Top *off,* and turn Auto Hide *on.*

Now the taskbar will remain out of sight, and even when you display it, it will appear behind other open windows. This combination of options is useful if you normally don't leave a lot of open windows on the desktop and if you generally work in a maximized application window. To use the taskbar, simply minimize the application window. On the other hand, if you have a lot of open windows and don't want to have to click the taskbar to bring it to the forefront:

1. Open the Taskbar Properties sheet.

2. Leave both Always On Top and Auto Hide turned on.

Organizing Windows   This section is going to be small, fast, and simple. It's just a refresher (from an earlier hands-on chapter) that reminds you of the two ways to organize windows on the desktop: cascading and tiling. Cascading, you'll recall, overlaps windows like playing cards spread on a table. Tiling sets windows either side by side or one above the other.

Cascading   Tiling

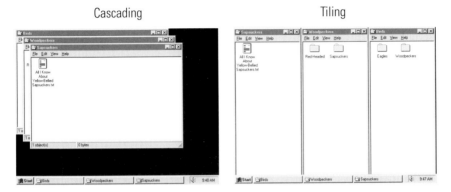

When it cascades windows, Windows 95 makes the windows similarly sized. When it tiles, Windows 95 makes windows whatever size is needed to fit the screen. To arrange windows:

1. Right-click a blank part of the taskbar.

2. Choose the option you want: Cascade, Tile Horizontally (windows stacked one above the other), or Tile Vertically (windows set next to one another).

To undo a cascade or a tile:

1. Right-click a blank part of the taskbar.

2. Choose Undo Cascade or Undo Tile.

Told you it would be short. Remember cascading and tiling, though, when you're working with multiple windows. If you want to see all title bars, cascade the windows. If you want to see at least some of the contents of each window, tile them. Of course, if all you want to do is see what's in a particular window, use the taskbar.

Setting the Clock   Your computer automatically keeps the time for you, courtesy of a small, battery-operated timekeeper that functions, among other things, as a clock. Because people measure their lives in hours and minutes rather than coffee spoons, Windows 95 helpfully displays the time at the right edge of the taskbar. If your computer's idea of the time isn't quite correct, or you move to a different time zone, or you have to adjust for daylight saving time, you can do so easily:

1. Point to the indented area on the taskbar where the time is displayed.

2. Right-click, and choose Adjust Date/Time from the popup menu. The properties sheet shown below appears.

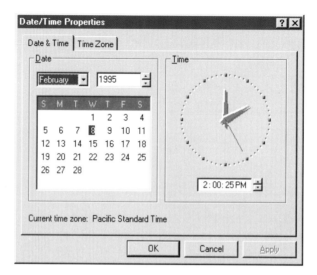

3. If you're off by a day, a month, or a year(!), adjust the date with the controls on the left side of the sheet. If you're off by hours or minutes, change the time with the spinner next to the digital time display under the clock.

4. If you need to change time zones, click the Time Zone tab to see the attractive sheet shown below.

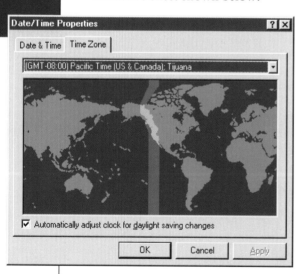

There's more here than meets the eye. To change to a different time zone, you can:

• Either choose the correct zone from the drop-down list at the top of the box.

• Or—more fun—*click* the zone you want directly on the map. If the time zone you choose observes daylight saving time, Windows 95 even automatically checks the daylight saving box for you. (You can uncheck the box, of course, if you want.)

5. As usual, click OK to make your changes and close the properties sheet.

Hands-On!

As the World Turns

It's always a pleasure to come across part of an operating system that is both elegantly designed and fun to use. The Time Zone tab is just such an animal, so give it a whirl:

1. Right-click the clock part of the taskbar, and choose Adjust Date/Time.

2. Click the Time Zone tab.

3. With the mouse, click your way through different time zones, but *without* clicking Apply or OK (unless you really need to switch from Pacific time to Bombay time).

4. East, west, whichever way you go, reset the map to your correct time zone.

5. To be on the safe side, click Cancel to close the properties sheet.

Customizing the Desktop Itself

Now it's time to move from the Start menu and the taskbar to the main part of your desktop. What can you do with it? A lot, and most of it is fun.

Shortcuts

A shortcut, sometimes known as a *link* or an *alias*, is a kind of shorthand note that enables Windows 95 to keep a program or document file in a single folder, yet make that program or document available to you in a variety of different locations—on the desktop, in a separate folder, on a separate disk—without your having to copy the item here, there, and everywhere. Sound confusing? It's not. Think about the way files are stored on disk. They're in folders, and in folders within folders. That's nice. That's logical. That's really organized. The trouble is, people don't necessarily work that way.

For example, you probably keep forks, plates, and napkins in different places. Do you want to run around fetching those items while you eat? Not likely. Windows 95 respects that, and so it lets you create shortcuts that help you "set the table" before you eat. When you create a shortcut, you tell Windows 95, "I want you to make this item available to me, and I don't want to have to go digging for it *there* while I'm working *here*."

You've already seen shortcuts, and you know they're always identified by a small arrow in the lower left corner. As a refresher, on the next page are the ways to create a shortcut.

1. If you're creating a shortcut on a disk or in a folder, open a window to the destination.

2. Select the object you want the shortcut *to*.

3. Do either of the following: right-click the object, drag it to where you want to create the shortcut, and choose Create Shortcut(s) Here from the popup menu; or press Ctrl+Shift as you drag the object to the shortcut location using the left mouse button.

After you've created a shortcut, you can even work with it to some degree:

1. Right-click the shortcut, and choose Properties.

2. Click the Shortcut tab.

   • Type a path in the Start In box if a program tells you that you need to specify the location of files related to using the shortcut's "target" file. (You probably won't have to do this.)

Tip!

WHY HERE?

Shortcuts are covered in this chapter because you're likely to find them really useful on the desktop. Do remember, however, that Windows 95 often lets you use the same techniques and tools in more than one way. That's true of shortcuts. You can create them in a folder or on a disk as easily as you can create them on the desktop. In fact, to keep your desktop uncluttered, try creating a new folder on the desktop and then placing your shortcuts *in* the folder. That way, you can group needed shortcuts together. If you create different shortcut folders for different projects, you can really get organized. And, of course, when the project's done, you can simply drag the shortcut folder to the Recycle Bin to clean up.

What, Exactly, Is a Shortcut?

A shortcut is actually a small disk file—on the order of a few hundred bytes—that tells Windows 95 the path to wherever the actual object is stored. This shortcut file is stored on the disk or in the folder where you create the shortcut, and the path in the file serves to link the shortcut location to the location of the object itself. So, whenever you use the shortcut, Windows 95 simply follows the path, finds the object, and swings into action. (Well, it's simple for you....) At any rate, that's why you can delete a shortcut without harming the original object: all you delete is the shortcut, which does nothing more than point the way to the original.

All shortcut files end with the extension LNK, as you can see if you open the properties sheet for a shortcut. If you'd like to see what a shortcut looks like, you can use the Type command from the MS-DOS prompt (you can't use File Open or a Windows 95 program like Notepad). For example, if you have a shortcut named SHORTCUT.LNK on the desktop, you could type:

```
C:\WINDOWS>cd desktop[Enter]
```

(The desktop is actually a folder in the Windows folder.) Then type:

```
C:\WINDOWS\DESKTOP>type shortcut.lnk[Enter]
```

You'll see some odd-looking characters that Windows 95 can interpret but that you can't, and somewhere in the display you'll also see the path to the object referenced by the shortcut.

- Click the Find Target button to open a window that shows the original item and other objects stored with it.

- Click the Change Icon button if you want to choose a spiffier icon for the shortcut.

As you work with them, you'll also notice that shortcuts don't remain needed forever. In fact, if you make use of them often, you'll find yourself using different shortcuts as you work with different files, folders, and programs.

Hands-On!

Some Handy Shortcuts to Try

Although most shortcuts are handy, some can be handier than others. Here are some you might like:

- Open My Computer, right-click the icon for your hard disk, drag it to the desktop, and create a shortcut. The next time you want to check your hard disk, just double-click the shortcut. No more having to open My Computer. If you don't mind some desktop clutter and you do use floppies a lot, you can also create shortcuts to your floppy drive(s).

- If you often use the same *program,* place a shortcut to it on the desktop. (If the program is on the Start menu and if you're not sure which of many files is the one that starts the program, open the Start Menu folder in your Windows 95 folder and work your way to Windows 95's own shortcut to the program. Right-click, drag the shortcut to the desktop, and create or copy the shortcut there.)

- If you often use the same *document,* place a shortcut to the document on the desktop. As long as an association exists between the document and a program, double-clicking the document will open both the program and the document.

- If you use network resources, open a window to the computer(s) and folder(s) you use most often and create shortcuts to them. Place the shortcuts on the desktop, and a simple double-click will save the time and effort of working through Network Neighborhood to find and use the shared resources you need.

To manage shortcuts, you can move, copy, delete, and even undelete them:

- To move a shortcut, simply drag it to its new location.

- To copy a shortcut, hold down Ctrl and drag to the new location.

- To delete a shortcut, either right-click the shortcut and choose Delete from the popup menu, or drag the shortcut to the Recycle Bin.

- To recover a deleted shortcut, open the Recycle Bin and drag the shortcut out. You can drag it to the shortcut's original location or to a different folder or disk if you want.

If you try shortcuts, you'll soon find them almost essential. They are, indeed, a very important part of what makes Windows 95 different from its predecessors.

What to Do with Those Icons

If you use your desktop a lot, it will probably become rather cluttered from time to time, especially if you create a lot of shortcuts. If you use the Windows 95 Paint, Notepad, and WordPad accessories and if you save new files to the desktop, your desktop could become downright messy after a while. When you feel the need to clean up a little:

- Delete unneeded shortcuts.

- Close unneeded windows, or switch to browsing with a single window. (Yes, this would seem to go without saying, but you *can* get so used to clutter that you don't realize how much there is.)

- Organize shortcuts in folders.

- Move Paint, Notepad, and WordPad documents to folders, rather than leaving them on the desktop. (*Don't* delete these icons unless you also want to delete the files.)

- Switch your display to a higher resolution if you can. (More about this in the next section.)

And, of course, take a moment to arrange the icons you have left. This alone can help a lot. Here's a refresher on what to do:

1. Point to a blank part of the desktop.

2. Right-click and choose:

   - Arrange Icons By Name, Type, Size, or Date to organize and align desktop icons by one of these categories.

   - Arrange Icons/Auto Arrange to tell Windows 95 to automatically arrange current and future desktop icons for you. (This is a good choice.)

   - Line Up Icons to arrange desktop icons in neat rows and columns.

Creating the Look You Like

And now you come to the best part of the desktop: color, pattern, pictures, and all those good things. If you worked through the first few chapters of the book, you tried some of this already. If you didn't, you're in for some fun. All you need is the Display Properties sheet, which you open by:

1. Pointing to a blank part of the desktop.

2. Right-clicking and choosing Properties from the popup menu.

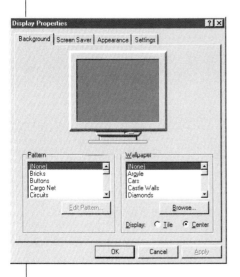

As you can see from the four tabs, the Display Properties sheet contains a sizable collection of options. Here they are, from the top.

Background The design of your Windows 95 desktop is made up of two possible parts: the pattern and the wallpaper. The pattern is basically the background of the screen—the color or design you choose for the overall desktop. The wallpaper is a design you can choose to place on the pattern. Unlike the stuff you hang in your house, however, Windows 95 wallpaper comes in two sizes: small (tiled) and large (centered). Tiled wallpaper acts something like a pattern in that its design is repeated "wall to wall." Centered wallpaper sits in the center of the screen.

Patterns are designs that overlay the background of your screen with bricks, buttons, fishnets, cobblestones, and such. Some of them, in combination with bright colors (which you can also set) can make you feel like a time-tripper to the sixties. Wallpapers, which tend to be a little more subdued, give you cars, castle walls, leaves, honeycombs, and the like. Between the two, you can choose to display:

• A pattern only.

• A pattern plus centered wallpaper.

• Wallpaper (tiled or centered) only.

• Or tiled wallpaper, which turns out looking much like the pattern-only option.

To work with patterns, wallpapers, or both, you use the Background tab of the Display Properties sheet.

If you simply want to change patterns, click the pattern you want in the pattern list. If you want to modify or remove a pattern:

1. Click the pattern you want to change or remove.

2. Click the Edit Pattern button to open the window shown at the right. (The pattern shown here, named Light Scales, is the result of removing the dark dots in the Scales pattern.)

3. If you've edited a pattern and want to save it under a new name, type the name in the Name box, as shown in the illustration.

4. Click the Add button to add an edited pattern to the pattern list. (If you prefer to save the edited pattern under the existing name, click Change instead.) Click Done to close the window.

Click the square "dots" here to switch colors.

Preview the results here.

5. If you're removing a pattern rather than editing one, select its name in the Name box, if necessary, and click Remove.

If you want to work with wallpaper:

1. Choose the design you want in the Wallpaper list. The list shows all bitmaps (equivalent to Paint files) in your Windows 95 folder. If you want to use a bitmap from a different folder, click the Browse button to find the image you want. (As described in the shaded box titled "Creating Your Own Wallpaper with Paint," you can have fun with bitmaps of your own.)

2. Click Tile or Center, whichever you prefer. (If you choose Tile, check that None is selected in the pattern list.)

Screen Savers   Screen savers, as even schoolchildren know, are pretty pictures or patterns you display on your monitor whenever the computer is on but inactive. You use screen savers because they're decorative and because—though it's less likely now than with older monitors—they prevent an unchanging image from "burning in" and damaging the coated inner surface of your screen.

SCREEN SAVERS

If your Display Properties sheet doesn't list much in the way of screen savers, it could be that the Flying Windows screen saver was the only screen saver installed at the time Windows 95 was set up on your computer. Windows 95 does come with additional screen savers, and if you want them, you can install them with the Add/Remove Programs utility in the Control Panel, as described in Chapter 12, "Disks, Controls, and Other Delights."

Hands-On!

Creating Your Own Wallpaper with Paint

You might enjoy creating an original wallpaper with Windows 95's Paint accessory. If you've never used Paint, however, be prepared to spend some time at this, because creating bitmap images—especially good ones—can take a while. To get started, experiment with the tools along the left edge of the Paint window. As you become more confident, refer freely to Help for instructions on techniques such as inserting text, editing parts of an image, and working with color. When your image is done, save the file. If you want to ensure that you don't include a lot of white "canvas" as part of your wallpaper:

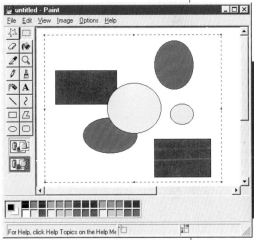

1. Open the file, if necessary, and then use the rectangular selection tool to select the part of your image you want to use, as shown at the right.

2. Choose Edit Copy To, and assign a filename. (This is the way to save part of an image as a file.) If you want the image to appear permanently in the list of wallpapers in the Display Properties sheet, save it in your Windows 95 folder.

3. Use File Open to open the file. Click No when Paint asks if you want to save changes to the original image.

4. Use File Set As Wallpaper, choosing either the Tiled or Centered option to tell Windows 95 to use your image as wallpaper. (Later, when you're not using Paint, use the Display Properties sheet to find and choose your Paint wallpaper.)

Windows has, for years, included several screen savers in the operating-system package. Windows 95 continues the tradition with several screen savers that run the gamut from merely blanking out the screen to displaying patterns, windows, and even a customizable "marquee" for you. By default, Windows 95 does not run a screen saver, but you can easily get one going. To do so, you need the Screen Saver tab on the Display Properties sheet:

- Choose the screen saver you want from the Screen Saver list. (Not exactly difficult, is it?) Whichever one you choose appears in the preview "screen" at the top of the window.

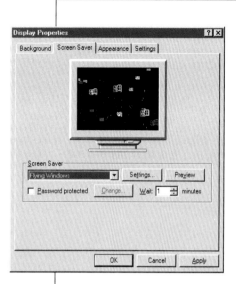

- By default, Windows 95 activates your screen saver if your computer remains inactive for one minute. If you want Windows 95 to wait a longer time, "dial" the spinner labeled Wait.

- You can't customize the Blank Screen screen saver, but the others offer various options, including speed and number of images. If you want to make any such adjustments, click the Settings button. The illustration below shows the settings window for the Flying Windows screen saver.

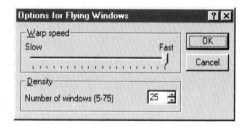

- To protect your computer from use while the screen saver is running, assign a password. First click the Password Protected check box, and then click the Change button. Type a password in the New Password box, press Tab, and then retype the password in the Confirm New Password box. (To remove password protection, simply uncheck the Password Protected check box.)

- For a full-screen preview showing what the screen saver will look like, click the Preview button and hold the mouse perfectly still.

- When you're satisfied, click OK. (Click Apply if you want to continue working with this screen saver, and when you're all done, click OK.)

Once you assign a screen saver, Windows 95 will run the one you chose whenever your keyboard and mouse remain inactive for the time you specified. To return to work, move the mouse and, if necessary, type the password you assigned when Windows 95 prompts for it.

Appearance and Colors   Your Windows 95 desktop and the windows you open on it include a large number of elements, many of which appear in different colors. There's the desktop surface itself, as well as title bars, scroll bars, icons, menus, and so on. The Windows 95 default color scheme is a pleasant mixture of blue-greens, blue, gray, and white. Your personality, however, might lean more toward browns, reds, pinks, yellows, or even plain black and white. Whatever your preference, Windows 95 allows you to customize the screen appearance, either wholly or in part, with the help of the Appearance tab on the Display Properties sheet.

ENERGY STAR?

Even though energy saving would seem to have little to do with screen savers, the lower section of the Screen Saver tab provides spinner controls that let you adjust the timing of energy-conservation features, including monitor shutoff.

If your monitor meets Energy Star standards but the energy-conservation section of the Screen Saver tab is inactive, click the Settings tab on the Display Properties sheet, click the Change Display Type button, and click the check box labeled Monitor Is Energy Star Compliant.

If you want to change the entire color scheme:

1. Pick a scheme you like from the list of "decorator" names in the Scheme list.

2. To see what the colors will look like on your real desktop rather than in the preview window at the top of the properties sheet, click Apply. If the effect isn't what you expected, choose another scheme.

3. When you're satisfied, click OK, and Windows 95 immediately changes to the new scheme.

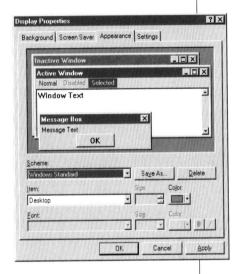

If you're content with most of your color scheme but you'd like to change the color or font (typeface) used in certain elements, use the Item and Font sections at the bottom of the Appearance tab. Note that the available options, such as size and color, become active or inactive depending on the item you want to change. You can't, for example, change the font of a scroll bar because there is no font in a scroll bar. Stands to reason. At any rate, choose the item you want to change from the list in the Item box. Then:

- To change the size (in pixels) of the item, click the spinner in the Size box.

- To change the color of the item, open the drop-down Color list. If you want, click the Other button to open the palette shown below.

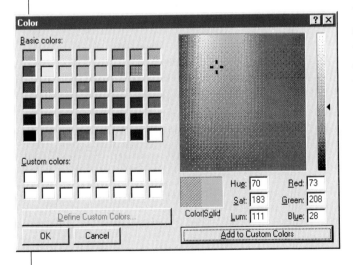

To define your own color, click a color in the Basic Colors section of the palette, and then use either the color "canvas" or the color values in the right side of the box to produce the color you want. When you're satisfied, click the Add To Custom Colors button. To choose a custom color, click the square of the color you want in the Custom Colors section of the window and then click OK. The color you chose will be applied to whatever screen element (menu bar, scroll bar, and so on) is selected in the Item box on the Appearance tab.

SOME COLORS ARE BETTER THAN OTHERS

Many of Windows 95's color schemes, such as Marine, Lilac, Pumpkin, and Rose, either don't look very good or give you unexpected colors if you're running Windows 95 in 16-color mode. If your monitor and display adapter cannot support 256 colors, stick to Windows Standard or one of the color schemes identified as VGA—Stars And Stripes, Storm, and Teal. (If you don't know whether or not your monitor supports 256 colors or more, check the final section of this chapter.)

• To change the look of text, such as the text in the title bar, choose a font from the Font list and make any adjustments you want in the Size and Color lists at the right. If you want boldfaced text, click the B button. If you want italics, click the button with the slanted *I* on it. If you want both, click both. To turn off boldfacing or italics, click the button to "unpress" it.

When you're finished, click Apply to see the effects of the change. If you like your new color-and-text scheme and you want to save it for future use, click the Save As button at the right of the Scheme text box and assign a name. The name will appear in the list of color schemes from then on—or until you select it and click the Delete button. Click OK to finish up and close the properties sheet.

Settings The Settings tab on the Display Properties sheet provides the ultimate in screen control. This is where you can tell Windows 95 what type of monitor you have (which should have been done when Windows 95 was installed, but there's always the chance that it wasn't or that you'll change monitors sometime). It's also where you can change the number of colors used on screen and where you can customize the size of the characters used in the display. Last, but not least by a long shot, this is where you can see one of Windows 95's more impressive tricks: the ability to change screen resolutions on the fly. This is a fine thing—no more need to change settings and restart the computer to put the change into effect. Here's the tab.

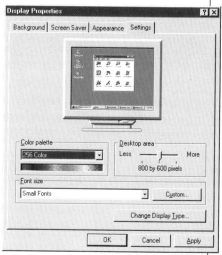

WOULDN'T IT BE NICE...

You might wonder why, if Windows 95 can change resolutions on the fly, it can't do the same with the number of colors used for your display. That would be nice, indeed, but unfortunately, changing the color palette requires Windows 95 to restart. There's nothing you can do about it. Of course, most people don't change palettes all that often, anyway....

• To change the color palette, choose the one you want from the Color Palette list. The palette you choose will be "previewed" in the colorful box below the list. Note here that the palettes available to you are dependent not on Windows 95 but on your monitor and your computer's display adapter.

When you change to a different color palette and click OK, Windows 95 displays a message telling you that you must restart the computer. When you see this message, click Yes—but only if all your applications are properly closed and all your files are safely stored on disk. If you have to do some cleanup work first, click No, tidy up, and then restart the computer.

• To change screen resolution, click or drag the movable marker in the Desktop Area slider. As with color palettes, possible resolutions are dependent on your monitor and display adapter. You might see only 640 by 480, or you might see a range of possibilities as high as 1024 by 768 or higher.

When you've chosen the resolution you want, click OK or Apply. Windows 95 will first display a message describing what will happen as it changes the resolution. Read the message, be reassured, and then click OK. Your screen might "jump" as the new resolution comes into play. Windows 95 will then display a second message asking whether you want to keep the new setting. If you do, click OK, and that will be that until the next time you want to play with this feature. This is smart and impressive.

- If your resolution is 800 by 600 or better, Windows 95 allows you to customize the size of the fonts displayed on screen. Choose Small Fonts or Large Fonts from the Font Size list. If you want to adjust the default size up or down, click the Custom button. Windows 95 displays the window shown at the right.

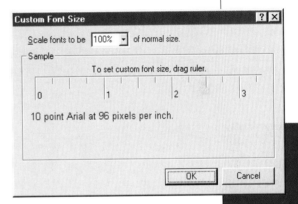

Now, either choose a percentage from the drop-down list at the top of the window or—for a more precise adjustment—drag any part of the ruler to the right or left. When you release the ruler, the sample text below it will change to show the actual size you've chosen. If you or someone you know has difficulty reading the screen, remember this option. It's a good one.

- Finally, if you change your monitor or your display adapter, use the Change Display Type button on this properties sheet to tell Windows 95 about the new hardware. When you click this button, Windows 95 displays the window shown below.

Click the appropriate Change button, and Windows 95 displays another window showing devices compatible with your hardware. To see a comprehensive list, click the Show All Devices radio button at the bottom of the window. The display will then change to something like the window shown on the following page (this one is for a new monitor).

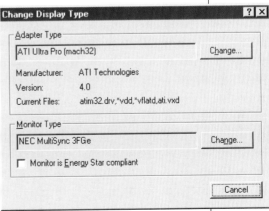

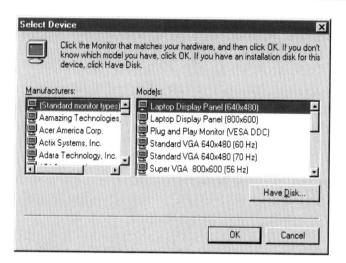

Choose the appropriate entry from the list of hardware manufacturers and models. If your particular make and model are not listed, choose Standard Monitor Types from the top of the list and select the "generic" description that matches your new hardware. (Refer to your hardware documentation for specifics, such as the frequency—Hz—of your monitor.)

Click the Have Disk button if your hardware came with an installation disk, and click OK to complete the operation.

That's it for desktop descriptions. The rest is up to you, so experiment and enjoy. Just be careful about changing hardware settings you don't understand. When in doubt, don't. That's the truth.

Chapter 8

Workout: Exploring Files

This chapter marks the end of the section on everyperson's uses of Microsoft Windows 95 for managing disks, files, folders, and the desktop. The next chapter marks the start of a new section that delves into options, such as networking and electronic mail, that take Windows 95 beyond the traditional definition of a file-and-disk-management operating system.

Before you move on, however, you'll benefit from a sort of valedictory look in this chapter at the following Windows 95 features: the Windows Explorer, Quick View, and file registration. As their names indicate, these features all have something to do with nosing around files. All three also make working with Windows 95 faster and more efficient than the tools you've learned to use so far. Give them a workout. You'll be glad you did.

FILE MANAGER FANS
The Windows Explorer is what you've been looking for. This piece of Windows 95, more than any other, will make you feel right at home. There's just one problem: as time goes by, you'll find you don't miss File Manager at all....

The Windows Explorer: Command Central

When you've had enough of clicking the Start button or opening one window after another to get where you want to go, turn to the Windows Explorer, which is something like the supermarket of Windows 95. With the Windows Explorer, you can view and work with the contents of any desktop icon, disk, or folder on your computer or on a network. The Windows Explorer is:

- *The* place to go whenever you want to see how files and folders are arranged on disk.

- Command central when you want access to everything from your desktop to your network resources.

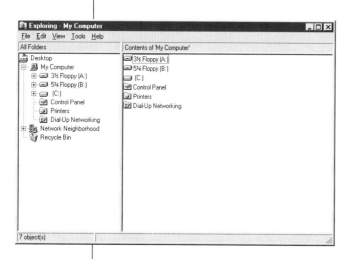

- A single window where you can drag and drop to duplicate and move disks, files, and folders.

- A fancy starting point from which you can run programs and open documents.

If you want quick and easy, the Explorer could turn out to be home base for you. It looks like the screen shown at the left.

At first glance, the Windows Explorer looks similar to and yet different from other windows. The big differences are the dual windowpanes and the "stepladder" list of resources in the left pane. The right pane more closely resembles other windows. There are, as usual, the old familiar title bar, borders, menu bar, and buttons, all of which work exactly as they do in any other window.

Starting the Windows Explorer

You can start the Windows Explorer in either of two ways. If you want to take a look at your hard disk, click the Start button and choose Windows Explorer from the Programs submenu. Alternatively:

1. Point to any icon, either on the desktop or in a window.

2. Right-click and choose Explore from the popup menu, or select the icon and then hold down Shift as you double-click.

What you first see in the Explorer window depends on which icon you chose. Exploring a folder, of course, shows you the contents of that folder. Exploring My Computer shows you the resources that are available on your computer. Exploring Network Neighborhood shows you all available network resources in the workgroup to which your computer has been assigned by your network administrator. Exploring the Recycle Bin shows you your "trash." And so on. Just think of the Explorer as a viewing tool, like the binoculars you can take anywhere, from football games to bird-watching walks.

Family Trees and Family Members

When you open an Explorer window, you see two panes. The left pane of the Windows Explorer contains a view of your system and its available resources. The right pane contains a view of whatever icon, disk, or folder you chose to explore:

THE TOOLBAR
Turn on the toolbar when you work with the Windows Explorer. The Delete and Properties buttons make it easy to find and cull files and folders. If you're a little too quick with the mouse, the Undo button comes in handy. And if you routinely connect to network resources, the Map Network Drive and Disconnect Net Drive buttons on the toolbar make using those resources a breeze. (You'll find out more about working on a network in Chapter 10, "Networks and *The* Network.")

- The left pane displays a "family tree" in which you can see how each "branch" is related to the desktop, which represents the ultimate object on your computer. Unlike the Windows File Manager of old, the Windows Explorer uses the left pane to display not only folders but the entire hierarchy of objects on the desktop. As you'll soon see, this difference is one of the "hot" features of the Windows Explorer when it comes to copying and moving files and folders.

- The right pane shows the individual members of the family. If you move the highlight in the left pane to a different disk or folder, the display in the right pane changes to show the contents of the new selection. And because the right pane shows the most specific view, it is where you'll usually do your selecting when you copy and move documents from one disk or folder to another.

The Left Pane By default, the Windows Explorer shows the desktop, My Computer, the object you're exploring, and the top layer of branches in (or on) that object. For example, if you're exploring your hard disk, the left pane does not display the name of every single folder and subfolder on the disk. Instead, you see the hard disk and the topmost tier of folders on it. The subfolders and sub-subfolders are hidden to keep the display from becoming too cluttered. To open and close lower levels of the hierarchy, you expand and collapse the branches of the tree in the left pane:

- To *expand* a branch, click the plus sign at the left of the branch.

- To *collapse* a branch, click the minus sign at its left.

The plus and minus signs work no matter what level you're exploring: desktop, hard disk, subfolder, or sub-sub-subfolder. Whenever you see a plus sign, the Windows Explorer is telling you there's more to see. Whenever you see a minus sign, the Windows Explorer is telling you that you can visually "prune" the branch to see less of it.

Bear in mind that no sign at all does *not* mean a branch is empty. A folder with no plus sign and no minus sign could well contain dozens or even hundreds of valuable files. The lack of a sign means only that the branch doesn't contain any subbranches. Remember this, and don't go deleting "signless" folders because you assume they're empty. Always check first by selecting the folder and seeing what the Windows Explorer displays in the right pane.

The Right Pane The right pane of the Explorer window must look mighty familiar by now. Like any other Windows 95 window, it shows the contents of whatever icon, disk, or folder you're viewing. And as in any other window, you can change the display to suit your needs. The easiest way to control your view is to turn on the toolbar (with the View Toolbar command).

Tip!

THE TREE
Even though the display in the left pane of the Explorer window doesn't look much like a tree, that's what it is. To longtime computer users it's known as a *hierarchical* tree because the branches form the hierarchy that shows how objects are related to one another. To read any hierarchical tree, just follow the path from one branch to the one above or below it. (And, yes, that's why the string of folders leading to a particular subfolder or file is called a *path*.)

Use the four buttons on the right end of the toolbar to select large icons, small icons, list view (the default), or display view, depending on how much you want to see.

Viewing Resources   As you work with the Windows Explorer, you'll notice that the left pane and the right pane each work a little bit differently. When

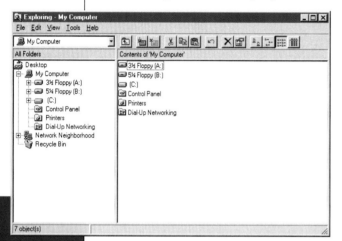

you click an object in the left pane, the object's contents immediately show up in the right pane. When you click an object in the right pane, however, all that happens is that you've selected that object. How, then, do you work with the display in the right pane? Easy: you *double-click*. What happens when you double-click, however, depends on the type of object you're working with:

- When you double-click a folder, you open the folder.

- When you double-click a program file, you start the program.

- When you double-click a document file, one of two things happens. If the document type is associated with a particular program, you open the document and start the program. If the document type is not associated with a program, you see the Open With window, which allows you to tell the Windows Explorer which program the file belongs to.

Information on document types comes at the end of this chapter, in the section "Extensions, Open With, and the Registry." If you're not comfortable with the idea of double-clicking documents and programs, confine your exploring to folders for a while. You won't go wrong.

What to Do Next

Well, there's the usual stuff. Managing disks and files with the Windows Explorer is no different from working in any other window:

1. Select the object(s) you want to work with.

2. Right-click and choose from a popup menu, use drag-and-drop, or choose from the menus (primarily the File and Edit menus) on the menu bar.

By either clicking or dragging, you can delete, create shortcuts, check properties, and so on, in both the left and right panes.

NEED TO SEE MORE? If you need to see more in either pane, simply drag the vertical bar separating the two panes to the left or right. That's it. That's the magic of a graphical user interface in which practically every part of the screen is sensitive to the mouse.

Scrolling to Move and Copy   Picture a lizard sitting quietly on a branch. One eye rolls forward to scan for dinner, the other eye swivels up and back to watch for hungry diners fond of lizard lunches. The Windows Explorer's two panes are similar to that lizard's eyes because the left and right panes can scroll independently to provide you with different but related views of your overall computing environment. Is this ability to see different views important? Probably not as important to you as it is to the lizard, but when it comes to moving and copying, being able to see different objects in each pane becomes a useful and welcome feature of the Windows Explorer:

- Because the left and right panes are independent of one another, you can display the contents of a disk or folder in the right pane and then scroll the left pane to some completely unrelated part of the tree. This is good.

- Combine this independent scrolling with drag-and-drop, and you find you can copy and move documents and folders, even from one disk to another, simply by dragging from one pane to the other. This is better.

You've learned about using drag-and-drop in numerous places already, so there aren't really any specifics you need to know about using it with the Windows Explorer. Until you're accustomed to the Windows Explorer, however, do use the right mouse button to avoid copying when you meant to move, or vice versa, and remember that you might have to expand or collapse the tree in the left pane to display the source or destination of a move or a copy. The following additional notes might also come in handy:

- Files are displayed only in the right pane, but you can copy or move them to another folder or to another disk by dragging them to the destination in the left pane.

- When you drag a folder to another folder, the folder you drag becomes a subfolder of the folder you drag to. (Obvious, but easy to forget when you drag from the left pane to the right pane.)

- You can select multiple folders in the right pane but not in the left pane. To select multiple files or folders, hold down the Shift or Ctrl key while clicking with the mouse or drag the mouse to create a box around the files or folders.

- You can also move or copy an entire folder by dragging it up or down in the left pane. If you can't see both the folder and its destination in the left pane, just select the folder and drag it up or down. As soon as the folder reaches the top or bottom edge of the pane, the Windows Explorer will scroll up or down to bring more of the tree into view. When you reach your destination, drop the folder and the move or copy will be complete.

- You can delete by simply selecting in the right pane the files or folders you want to delete and then dragging the selections to the Recycle Bin in the left pane—handy if the desktop Recycle Bin is temporarily covered by another window.

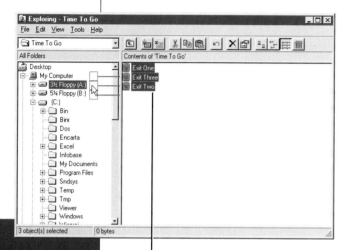

These files are being moved to the disk in drive A from the folder named Time To Go on drive C.

- Don't mess around with Windows 95 folders or with desktop icons other than shortcuts you (not Windows 95) have created. The Windows Explorer is a great tool, and it refuses to carry out mouse or keyboard commands that could harm your system, but *you* might not always be as careful.

- If you make a mistake, drag and drop in reverse or immediately use the Undo button on the Explorer's toolbar. Remember this option.

Getting There Fast   As you accumulate more programs and documents and you make good, solid use of folders for organizing your work, you'll sometimes want a really fast way to have the Windows Explorer fill the right pane with the contents of a particular disk or folder. (Computers, for some reason, make speed demons of everyone, and the faster you can do something, the faster you'll want to do it next time.)

To view a particular resource:

1. Display the toolbar in the Explorer window, if necessary.

2. Choose the resource you want from the drop-down list at the left of the toolbar as shown on the next page. If you just want to move up one level in the tree, click the Up One Level button at the right of the resource list.

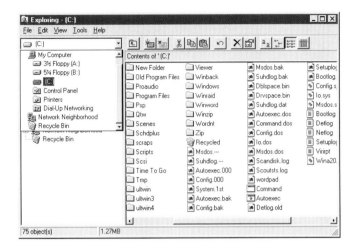

Swinging in the Tree

The best way to become thoroughly at home with (not in) a tree is to give it a workout. Try the following tasks:

1. To prepare, find a floppy disk you can experiment on and put it in drive A. Use Notepad to create a small sample file, and save it on the desktop. (Type the filename in ALL CAPITALS so it will be easy to find.) Close Notepad.

2. Right-click My Computer, and choose Explore.

3. To expand the tree, click the plus sign at the left of your hard disk; then expand your Windows 95 folder; then expand the Start Menu and System subfolders. That should give you a nice long display in the left pane.

4. Scroll back to the top of the left pane, and then click the Desktop icon to select it and display its contents in the right pane.

5. In the left pane, scroll back down through the tree until you reach the Recycle Bin. (The Recycled icon on your hard disk and the Recycle Bin icon one level below the Desktop icon will both work.)

6. In the *right* pane, select your sample file and drag it to the Recycle Bin in the left pane. As simply as that, the file is gone.

7. In the left pane, click the Recycle Bin to display its contents in the right pane.

8. Scroll up in the left pane until you reach the icon for drive A. Select the deleted sample in the right pane, and drag it to drive A in the left pane. That's all it takes for a move. Nice, isn't it?

When you want to go directly to a folder, there's yet another alternative, known as the Go To command:

1. In the left pane, select the *disk* containing the folder. Doing this first will help you avoid any "I can't find it" messages about folders you know exist.

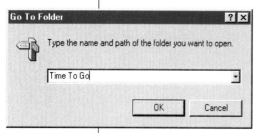

2. Choose Tools Go To (or press Alt+T, and then G). This opens the small window at the left.

3. Type the path to the folder whose contents you want to view in the right pane. If you didn't select a disk in step 1, precede the path with a backslash or (if the folder is on a different drive) with a drive letter followed by a colon. Separate all elements of the path with backslashes, as shown in the following examples:

```
\my letters\to mom\
```

or

```
b:\my letters\to mom
```

Notice that Tools Go To is handy, but you do have to know in advance where you're going. That is, you have to know both the full path and the correct spelling of each element in it. For instance, specifying *letters to\mommy* won't cut it with Windows 95, even though Mom would like your typing just fine. Furthermore, if the Windows Explorer is looking at a different disk, typing

Hands-On!

Moving Quickly

To see how useful the resource list is, try the following:

1. Right-click My Computer, and choose Explore.

2. Display the toolbar, if necessary.

3. Open the resource list on the toolbar, and choose the Recycle Bin. The contents of the bin appear immediately in the right pane.

Now try out the Go To command:

1. Choose Tools Go To from the menu bar.

2. In the Go To window, type *c:\windows\start menu*. (Replace *windows* with the name of your Windows 95 folder if it has a different name.) The display changes rapidly to the contents of the Start menu.

3. Finish up by experimenting with some Go To's on your own data folders.

the path correctly as *my letters**to mom* just doesn't work if the folder is on drive C and the Windows Explorer is currently concentrating on drive B.

Here are a few additional tips about using the Windows Explorer:

When you use the Go To command to view a folder on the desktop, you must type the path as Windows 95 follows it on disk. Even though the desktop is at the top of your Windows Explorer hierarchy, on disk it is a folder inside your Windows 95 folder. To open a desktop folder, therefore, you type the path as *[Windows 95 folder]**desktop**[folder name]*.

If you're a network user, you can use the Windows Explorer to view a folder on a shared network resource. Begin the path with two backslashes—that is, type *[network computer]**[folder name]*. If you're not used to this method of referring to network computers, Chapter 10, "Networks and *The* Network," will help you out.

Finally, one interesting point: Go To saves a list of the folders you've gone to, and you can see the list by clicking the triangle at the right of the Go To text box. You can also see the same list when you use the Run command on the Start menu.

Quick View, a Terrific Part of Windows 95

As you work with Windows 95, there will be times when you'd like to take just a quick look at a file to see what it contains. If you receive e-mail, for instance, you might want to scan a document someone attached to a message. If you're searching for one document among many on a network, being able to "thumb" through the pages of one document after another can be a tremendous help. And, of course, when you're working on your own, you'll almost

certainly one day find yourself searching disks and folders, one after the other, as you try to locate an elusive document.

Although it's easy enough to start an application and use it to view several files, the very act of finding, opening, and closing each file takes time. With Windows 95, you don't have to bother. Just select a file, right-click, choose Quick View, and a window opens to show you the contents of the file, as you can see at the left.

Quick View is the name applied to a collection of tools known as *file viewers*. These viewers are built into Windows 95 and were developed

ABOUT QUICK VIEW
Quick View is not installed by default, and it is not available on floppy disk–based Windows 95 packages. You'll know it's not installed if you select a common file type, such as a Notepad (txt) file, and you don't see a Quick View command on either the popup menu or (in a window) the File menu. Instructions for installing Quick View and other optional Windows 95 components are in "Add/Remove Programs" in Chapter 12, "Disks, Controls, and Other Delights."

by Microsoft and Systems Compatibility Corporation (SCC) to give you a way to look at documents without having to start the applications that created them. Although these viewers don't themselves allow you to edit anything within the Quick View window, they are fast and effective, and they support files stored in literally dozens of different formats ranging from plain text files to those created by applications as diverse as CorelDRAW, Lotus 1-2-3, WordPerfect, and Microsoft Word.

Viewing a File

Quick View will show you the contents of any document file for which it has a viewer. How do you know if a viewer exists? Windows 95 lets you know:

1. Select the file you'd like to view.

2. Either right-click or open the window's File menu. If you see a Quick View command, you're in. Click the command, and the document will open in a Quick View window. If you don't see the command, sorry—there's no viewer for that type of file.

No muss, no fuss, and best of all, no guessing.

Working in the Quick View Window

The Quick View window is elegant: simple to work with, yet impressive in what it can do. It lets you:

- View the document in a different font or font size.

- "Turn" pages to view a multiple-page document.

- Orient pages either vertically (portrait) or horizontally (landscape).

- Start the application that created a document.

- Choose to work in one Quick View window or open a different window for each document.

Changing the View Because the Quick View window is relatively small, you might have some difficulty reading the actual document contents. Not a problem. In fact, you can opt for either of two solutions:

- Switch to a close-up view.

- Increase or decrease the size of the text.

A command called Page View controls whether you see close-ups or entire pages. To change the view, turn the command on or off (the default):

1. Open the View menu.

2. Choose the Page View command. A check mark means that Page View is turned on; no check mark means Page View is turned off.

Turning Page View off is useful for short text documents and small graphics. It's also fine for viewing details, if you don't mind scrolling. Turn Page View on when you want to get a sense of a document's length or layout.

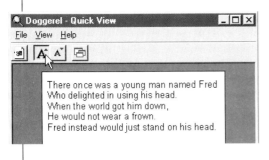

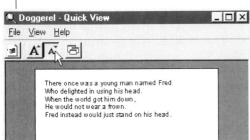

If you would like to see larger or smaller text, use the two buttons labeled with the letter A. You can click either of these buttons once, twice, or many times to incrementally change the size of the text displayed:

- Click the button with the large A to increase the size of the text.

- Click the button with the small A to decrease the size of the text.

You can even change the font (typeface) used to display documents if, for example, you hate the default (Arial) or you find the displayed font somewhat challenging to read. To change the Quick View font:

1. Choose View Font in the Quick View window. The window at the right appears.

2. Choose the typeface you want from the Font list. (The letters TT, which you can see in the Font list in the illustration, stand for *TrueType*, a class of fonts that show characters on screen exactly as they'll look in the printed document.)

3. If you want, choose a larger or smaller font size from the list under the Size box.

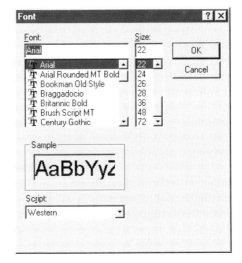

4. Preview your choice in the Sample box, and when you're satisfied, click OK. The new font (and size) will now become the default for all documents.

When you change fonts in the Quick View window, bear in mind that you change only the font that's used to *display* the document; you do not change

SCRIPT? WHAT'S THAT?
When you're working with fonts, Windows 95 will sometimes show you a list box titled Script. Script in this sense is neither the dialog for a play nor the flowing cursive penmanship you learned long ago. To Windows 95, script refers to language-specific characteristics of a particular font so that you can, for example, display Western, Greek, Baltic, or Cyrillic characters. This capability, however, requires multilingual support to be installed on your computer—support you probably don't have unless you routinely use more than one language in your documents. (To install multilingual support, use the Add/ Remove Programs option in the Control Panel, as described in Chapter 12, "Disks, Controls, and Other Delights.")

the font in the document itself. To do the latter, you must start the application used to create the file and make the change there.

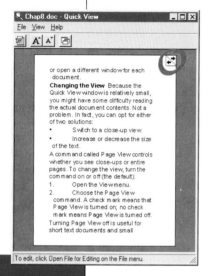

To edit, click Open File for Editing on the File menu.

Turning the Page   When you view a multiple-page document in Page View, you see arrows like the ones circled in the illustration at the left.

- Click the left-pointing arrow to move to the next page.

- Click the right-pointing arrow to return to the previous page.

(If it seems that it would be more logical to click the right-pointing arrow to move forward in a document and the left-pointing arrow to move backward, that's OK. Just change your point of view a little, and think of the arrows as pointing in the direction in which you "turn" the page. You'll no longer feel disoriented, and all will be well.)

Rotating the Page   Quick View also allows you to rotate pages by 90 degrees in Page View, essentially shifting from portrait to landscape orientation. Portrait orientation, which is what you normally get with most word-processed documents, means that the paper is longer than it is wide. Landscape orientation, which is particularly useful for wide spreadsheets, turns the page so that it is wider than it is long. The two orientations are shown in the drawing below.

TURN, TURN...
When you're viewing a picture with Page View turned off, Quick View enables the Rotate command, which appears just below Landscape on the View menu. You can use this command to rotate the image in the window by 90 degrees.

Portrait orientation

Landscape orientation

To switch from the default portrait orientation in Quick View:

1. Open the View menu.

2. Turn Page View on, if necessary, and then click to add a check mark to the left of the Landscape option.

Modifying the File   Quick View, as already mentioned, is strictly for looking at files. If you want to edit the file you're viewing, you must start the application in which the file was created. Doing this is simple:

- Choose Open File For Editing from the window's File menu.

- Or click the leftmost button (whose tooltip reads *Open File For Editing*) on the Quick View toolbar.

From here on, you work with the application and whatever commands it provides for editing the document. Quick View automatically closes.

Hands-On!

Using Viewers

Quick View is fast, fun, and friendly, and if you work with a lot of document files, you'll find it somewhere close to invaluable. You can check out Quick View easily:

1. Start the Windows Explorer.

2. Display the contents of your hard disk, find your Windows 95 folder, and select it to display its contents. (In the Explorer's right pane, you'll see a group of folders including Command, Config, and Start Menu, followed by files named Argyle, Autumn Leaves, Calc, Cars, and so on.)

3. Right-click a bitmap file, such as Autumn Leaves, and choose Quick View.

4. In the Quick View window, use the View menu to turn Page View on and off. Experiment with turning Landscape on and off while you're at it.

5. In the Explorer window, scroll to find a text file named Readme.txt.

6. Drag Readme to the Quick View window, and drop it. Fast, isn't it?

7. Now that you have a text file displayed, turn on Page View and then turn some pages with the arrows in the upper right corner of the document. Use the A buttons on the toolbar to increase and decrease the font size. Just for fun, change the font to Wingdings with the View Font command; then change the font back to Arial. (If you don't change back, Quick View will display all future documents in Wingdings. The font is fun the first time, but....)

8. Drag another bitmap to the Quick View window—Cars, maybe, or Castle Walls.

9. Click the Open File For Editing button on the Quick View toolbar. Easy, isn't it?

10. Close Paint to finish up.

How Many Windows?   When you work with Quick View, you can choose either to work in a single window or to open separate windows for each file you view. The easiest way to opt for a single window is simply to rely on drag-and-drop. Each time you drag a file's icon to an open Quick View window, the new file replaces whatever file was displayed in the window. If you want to be a little more procedural about the matter, however, you can also do this:

- Click the rightmost button (whose tooltip reads *Replace Window*) on the Quick View toolbar.

- Or turn on Replace Window on the View menu.

Replace Window, like Page View, is an option you toggle on and off. As usual, a check mark on the View menu means the option is turned on; no check mark means the option is turned off. The Replace Window button will also look pushed in when the option is turned on.

Extensions, Open With, and the Registry

Now that you know how to use the Windows Explorer and how to view files quickly with Quick View, it's time to turn to the Open With window and an associated topic, file registration. You might not need this information often, but when you do, a little knowledge can help you go a long way toward handling Windows 95 with assurance. Ready?

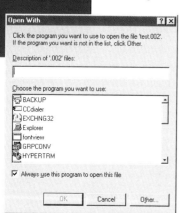

Remember that double-clicking a document file sometimes produces a window titled Open With, which looks like the one shown at the left.

Windows 95 displays this window whenever you double-click a document file that it cannot associate with a particular application. Why is Windows 95 at a loss here? Because it doesn't recognize the file's extension.

Filename Extensions

In many respects, filename extensions are relics of MS-DOS. An *extension* is the three characters that follow the final period in a filename. Here, for example, are some old-style and new-style filenames, with extensions shown in italics:

Old-Style 8.3 Filename	New-Style Long Filename
OUTLN3-3.*DOC*	Outline Heading Number 03.003.*Doc*
GOTIT.*YES*	Picked the Winning Lottery Number with This Spreadsheet.*Yes*

Extensions can be descriptive, especially in the space-limited 8.3 format, and you're certainly welcome to tack them on to your filenames whenever you want. But as mentioned earlier in the book, most applications, by default, search for certain extensions they identify as "their" files. WordPad and Microsoft Word, for example, assume that their document files have the extension DOC. Paint assumes its files end in BMP, and Notepad is partial to files ending in TXT.

Because applications favor certain extensions, Windows 95 does too. The problem is that it can't recognize every extension ever created (neither can

Now You See Them...

Extensions and their associations with particular programs are very important. That goes without saying. Even though Windows 95 can use a known (registered) extension to start a program and open a known document, it's often helpful to see filename extensions when you're browsing through lists of files. Extensions can help you distinguish between different types of program files and can, like icons, help you tell at a glance which program a document belongs to. But it's also true that a windowful of filenames plus extensions is a little busier than the same display *minus* extensions. Furthermore, because Windows 95 always displays unrecognized extensions, viewing the extensions of programs and documents that Windows 95 can handle on its own tends to blur the distinction between those that need your intervention and those that do not.

Whether you choose to view both known and unknown extensions is, of course, entirely up to you. To view or not to view known extensions:

1. Choose View Options from the menu bar in the Explorer window

or in any open window to a disk or a folder. A small secondary window will open.

2. Click the View tab to display the window shown at the right. (You see the last option, Include Description Bar..., only if you choose View Options from the Explorer window.)

3. Click to uncheck or check the Hide MS-DOS File Extensions For File Types That Are Registered option.

4. If you want to see the names of all files on your system, you can also click the Show All Files option at the top of the View tab. You probably don't want to do this, though. As you can see from the list of file types that Windows 95 hides, the only files you don't see are program files, which you shouldn't do anything to anyway.

5. Click OK when you're done.

humans). As a result, whenever you double-click a document with an unrecognized extension, Windows 95 asks for a little help by displaying the Open With window. You use this window not only to tell Windows 95 which programs you want to use but to make the association between extension and program permanent, if that's your pleasure.

Open With

Here's another look at the Open With window, this time with some choices made.

Telling Windows 95 which program to use is easy:

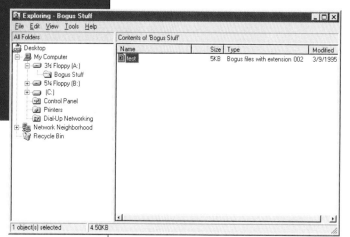

1. In the text box at the top of the Open With window, enter a description of the file type. This description is optional, but it's useful if you plan to use the same application to open many files with the same extension.

   The description will appear for files with that extension, both on the file properties sheet and in any window listing that you display in details view, as shown below.

2. From the list box, choose the program you want Windows 95 to open for this extension.

   The list box shows registered programs (those that either Windows 95's setup or your program-installation software entered in a special database called the registry, which is described later in more detail). If the program you want is not listed, click the Other button. You'll see the familiar window shown on the following page.

Type the name of the program or use the Look In list box to find the program on another disk or in a different folder. When you've found the program, click Open.

3. If you *don't* want Windows 95 to use the program you specified whenever you double-click a file of this type, uncheck the Always Use This Program… option. Otherwise, leave the box checked so that you don't have to go through the Open With scenario next time.

4. Click OK, and Windows 95 starts the program you specified and opens the file.

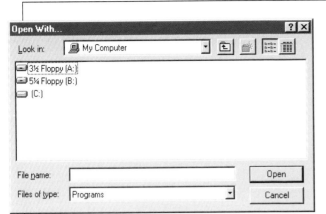

That's all it takes. If you want to understand a little more about how Windows 95 connects an extension with a program, continue on. If you're content just knowing how to use Open With, this chapter's done. See you in Part 4.

Hands-On!

Using Open With

The following steps show you an easy way to familiarize yourself with the Open With command. You'll use Notepad to create a sample file and then use the Windows Explorer to rename the file and give it an "unknown" extension. Here's what to do:

1. Start Notepad and type something. Save the file as *sample.txt.* You can save it in any location you want, but remember where you put it. Close Notepad.

2. Select your My Computer icon, and then Shift+double-click to start the Windows Explorer.

3. Find the folder containing your sample file, and click to display its contents in the right pane. (Remember, if you saved the file on the desktop, the file is in the Desktop subfolder of your Windows 95 folder.)

4. Select your sample file in the right pane, pause a second, and then click the name of your sample file and rename the file as *sample.zzz.* When Windows 95 warns against an extension and asks if you're sure, click Yes. (This time, you are. Most times, you won't want to do this.)

5. Double-click your newly renamed file. When the Open With window appears, choose Notepad from the list of registered programs.

6. So that Windows 95 won't take you seriously, uncheck the Use This Program... option. (If you left the box checked, you'd end up adding clutter to Windows 95's registry, which isn't what you want.)

7. Click OK, and there's your file, in Notepad. What could be simpler?

8. To finish up, close Notepad and drag your sample file to the Recycle Bin.

FOR WINDOWS 3 EXPERTS...
The portion of the registry described here might seem very familiar to you. Although the Windows 95 registry, as a whole, is new to Windows 95, the portion of the registry that deals with file associations is very similar to the registration database (REG.DAT) that you add to and modify with Windows 3's Regedit program. If you're familiar with the older registration database, you should feel right at home with the application-related part of the new registry and the File Types tab.

The Registry

To understand what the Open With command does for you and for Windows 95, back up for a moment and think about what happens when you double-click a document that *is* associated with an application—a text document, for instance, that Windows 95 knows should be opened in Notepad. How does Windows 95 know about the connection? It relies on the file's extension to guide it to specific information in the *registry*. The registry sounds rather bridal, and actually the name isn't entirely inappropriate because the registry is a database where hardware and software items are "married" to configuration settings that define these items to Windows 95. The registry is where, for

Don't Do It Yourself

The registry is a database filled with settings assigned by programs and by Windows 95 itself. Most of these settings are crucial to enabling Windows 95 to work correctly with your hardware and software, and many of them are entered in formats—such as binary values—that are meaningless to most people. Although the registry is discussed here only in terms of associating applications with file-name extensions, be aware that this database is a far more complex place than simply a home for such relatively noncritical information.

Although Windows 95 includes a program called the Registry Editor that allows people to view and modify the registry, the Registry Editor is really for use only by people who understand—technically understand—a lot about Windows 95 and how it works. Below left, for instance, is one small part of the registry—a part that is probably meaningless to you but essential for Windows 95's well-being.

As you can see, the registry is complex. And it contains many values that only software experts can interpret. As you come to understand more about Windows 95, by all means continue to admire the registry as an information warehouse. But unless you're given *specific* and *detailed* instructions, don't make any changes to it. Remember that fools rush in, and then convince yourself that you're no fool. Any time Windows 95 must change the registry to satisfy your preferences, it does so on its own, with the help of a properties sheet, a wizard, an application's setup program, or some other mechanism. Rely on them.

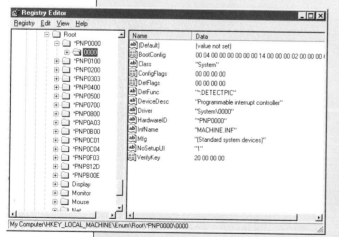

example, Windows 95 stores your current screen settings, including resolution and number of colors (as the number of bits per pixel).

More to the current point, the registry is where some application-related information is stored, including the path Windows 95 must follow to find the program file. The registry also stores any link that exists between the application and a particular file type (defined by the extension). The registry is thus where Windows 95 stores the association between DOC files and WordPad, BMP files and Paint. Because this information is readily accessible to Windows 95, it can check the registry, find out which application "owns" that file type, and then open both the application and the file for you.

Deeper into the Registry

If you're an experienced Windows user, you can try a more sophisticated way to define file types than using Open With. It's the File Types tab in the Explorer's View Options window.

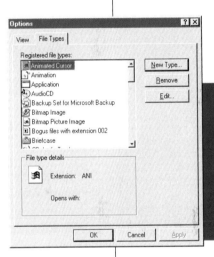

In this window and a series of secondary windows, you can either create a new file type or edit an existing type. You can assign the file type an icon and decide whether to use Quick View to display the document, and instead of simply associating the file type with a program, you can include commands that Windows 95 will display on the File menu and on a popup menu whenever you select a file of the type you're defining. If all this sounds a bit obscure, the following examples, which use the extension 003, should make things a little clearer.

Help with File Types

When you use the File Types tab, there are two ways to get help in figuring out some of the options. First, of course, use the ? button in the upper right corner of the window. Second, before you start defining your own file type, find a similar one in the list of registered file types. Click the existing type to select it, and then click the Edit button. When the Edit File Type window opens, select a command in the Actions list and click Edit to see how the existing file type has been defined to Windows 95. When you're satisfied, click Cancel to close the window without harming the existing definition. If you browse various file types and commands, you should begin seeing the pattern used by Windows 95 in defining file types. If all this makes you dizzy, stick to the Open With window, at least for a while. It's easier and accomplishes almost as much.

Creating a New File Type   When you create a new file type, you register the extension in much the same way as when you associate a program and a file type in the Open With window. With the File Types tab, there's just more you can do. To create a new file type:

1. Choose View Options, and click the File Types tab in the window that appears.

2. Click the New Type button. The following window opens.

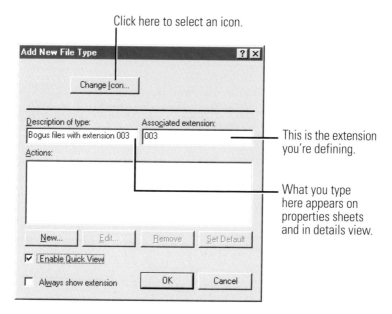

Click here to select an icon.

This is the extension you're defining.

What you type here appears on properties sheets and in details view.

As you can see from the entries in the illustration, this is where you start to tell Windows 95 about the extension. Use the Enable Quick View and Always Show Extension check boxes if you want either of these options.

3. When you're ready to tell Windows 95 what to do with the extension, click the New button to open the window shown below.

In the Action box, type the name of the command you want Windows 95 to display on the File menu and on the popup menu whenever you select a file with the extension you're defining.

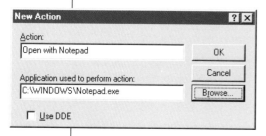

To specify the program to use, take the easy way out: click the Browse button, and cruise folders until you find the application you want. Click the application, and then click Open. When the New Action window reappears, the Application box will be correctly filled in, path and all.

4. If you want to add more commands, click the New button and run through step 3 again.

5. As you work, your decisions aren't yet chiseled in stone—or in the registry—so:

   - If you make a mistake, click the action you want to correct, click the Edit button, and fix the problem.

   - If you decide you don't want an action, select it, click Remove, and click Yes when Windows 95 prompts for confirmation.

   - Finally, if you have created more than one action, select the one you want to perform when you double-click a file and choose the Set Default button.

6. When you're finished, click OK (or Close—sometimes the button label changes) and then click Close again to close the File Types tab window.

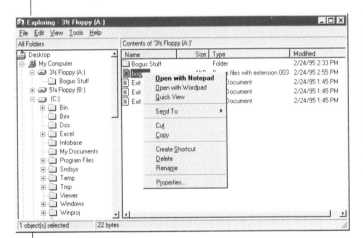

You're all set. The illustration at the left shows the menu results of defining a file type with two actions, Open With Notepad and Open With WordPad, and with Quick View enabled.

Modifying or Removing a File Type   Changing a defined file type is a lot like creating a new one. The differences are minimal:

1. Open the File Types tab.

2. Click in the Registered File Types list to select the file type you want to remodel.

3. Click the Edit button. This opens a window so similar to the New File Type window that you should have no trouble working in it. The options are the same as those outlined in step 5 above.

4. Click Close, and close the File Types window to register your changes.

Removing a file type is easy too. Just be sure you want to remove it, and then:

1. Open the File Types tab.

2. Click to select the file type you want to remove.

3. Click the Remove button, and click Yes when Windows 95 prompts for confirmation.

4. Click OK to finish up.

That's pretty much it, at least for the basics. This book doesn't have room for more, so you'll probably have to experiment with more complex commands. Also, enabling support for programs that use pre-OLE Direct Data Exchange (DDE) might prove challenging. But if you run into trouble, remember Microsoft's Windows 95 product-support people. They're very helpful.

A Look at What You Create

When you use either Open With or the File Types tab to tell Windows 95 which program to open whenever you double-click a file with a particular extension, Windows 95 creates and defines several entries and subentries for the extension in the registry. Suppose you add the extension XYZ to many of the text files you create, and you use Open With to tell Windows 95 that you want it to open Notepad whenever you double-click an XYZ file. The first entry (called a key) that Windows 95 creates in the registry looks like this:

Key:	Value:
.xyz	"xyz_auto_file"

The *"xyz_auto_file"* value, in turn, leads to this:

Key:	Value:
xyz_auto_file	"bogus XYZ files"

where *"bogus XYZ files"* is the text of the description entered in the Open With text box. Under this entry, you then find:

Key:	Value:
command	"C:\WINDOWS\NOTEPAD.EXE %1"

where *"C:\WINDOWS\NOTEPAD.EXE %1"* is the command that Windows 95 actually carries out to start Notepad when a file with the XYZ extension is double-clicked. In carrying out the command, Windows 95 replaces *%1* with the actual name of the file you want to open.

There's more than what's shown here, but this is basically the trail that Windows 95 follows whenever you double-click an XYZ file. You see much the same type of registry entries when you use the File Types tab instead of Open With. Whichever method you use, once a file type appears in the registry, Windows 95 lists it as a registered file type both in the Open With window and on the File Types tab. Interesting, isn't it, to see a little of the intricacy that creates a working operating system?

4 Life in the Fast Lane

Chapter 9

OLE!

OLE. No one's going to get mad if you pronounce it "oh-ell-ee," and no one's going to harrumph if you think it should sound like the name of Uncle Ole in Norway. But most people pronounce OLE as "olay."

Now that you've disposed of *that* burning question, what *is* OLE and why should you care? OLE is something like a "subconsciousness" that runs beneath the surface of Microsoft Windows 95. Where and how OLE affects you is what this chapter is all about. Even though OLE (the term, that is) looks and sounds kind of technical, this chapter's going to be short. It's also going to provide the basis for a lot of fun you can have on your own.

You're in the "fast lane" section of this book now. That means you'll be moving at a quicker pace. You should be comfortable enough with Windows 95 by now that you won't be left behind, and you won't need any coddling. This chapter and those that follow cover some interesting parts of Windows 95, but from here on they'll leave a lot of the experimenting up to you. You're ready.

What OLE Is

Technically, OLE is kind of a specification and kind of an environment. It runs throughout Windows 95 and in many respects forms the foundation on which a lot of Windows 95's functionality rests. Specification, environment, or foundation—however you choose to view it, OLE is definitely one part of Windows 95 that makes good things happen. Why? Because OLE is the part that enables Windows 95 to manipulate objects. Oh, yes, there's that "O" word again....

Originally, OLE was an acronym for a process known as *Object Linking and Embedding* (described in more detail later in the chapter). As an OL&E tool, OLE entered the world as a means of enabling you to create documents containing different types of elements (objects). With OLE, you could thus create a letter containing a spreadsheet chart, for example, or a database record enlivened by a bitmap image.

Right from the start, the benefits of OLE were obvious. You were no longer bound by the limits of an application. If you needed an element that an application couldn't create, you could tell that application to "consult" with an application that *could* produce the element you wanted. That was partnership, and it was the beginning of a style of working called *document-centric*, which let you think in terms of whole documents rather than in terms of which application you should use to do this or that task. Applications that supported OLE essentially became tools that you could call on as circumstances dictated, and document-centric thus became a more natural way of using your computer. That was good.

In the several years since OLE was developed, it has grown to support far more than simple(!) mix-and-match documents containing a piece of this and a piece of that. Now, in Windows 95, OLE is no longer simply a means of dropping a graphic into a report or a sound annotation into a spreadsheet. Sure, you can still do that. But OLE has evolved to the point that "object linking and embedding" covers only a part of what OLE is all about, and so today OLE is no longer short for "object linking and embedding" or for anything else. It is simply OLE. In addition to linking and embedding, OLE is also drag-and-drop. It is properties sheets. It is scraps. And most important for you, Windows 95 supports OLE far better than earlier versions of Windows did.

Neat Little Bundles, and They Ain't Kindling

At heart, OLE works by manipulating self-contained objects. But where you might think of a file or an application as a "self-contained object," OLE sees things differently. To OLE, and thus to Windows 95, an object is a package that includes both data and the instructions needed to work with that data. An OLE object is thus an independent little bundle. In everyday terms, you might think of such an object as a "child"—but a child that arrives with manners and the ability to balance your checkbook. (And wouldn't everybody like one of those.)

Independence aside, however, OLE objects do not rule themselves. They must be managed by *OLE-compliant* applications, which are applications designed to recognize and work with OLE objects. Once created by you via an OLE-compliant application, an OLE object kind of sits there in your computer, saying, "Here I am—use me if you can." It doesn't turn its back on all but the application that created it. It says to all comers, "If you can see me, go ahead and use me." It has a sharing personality, this object. And precisely because Windows 95 has built-in support for such objects, you can create a graphic with Paint, drag the graphic to your desktop, drop it into a WordPad document, and even plop the whole shebang onto a desktop shortcut to your printer. OLE support is there for you when you need it. Anything in the system can use an OLE object, as long as that anything has the ability to handle that type of object. (Objects do, of course, come in different types. After all, a graphic isn't the same as your printer, which isn't the same as a sound clip. They're different types of objects, with which you can do different things.)

Well, that's a pretty cursory overview of OLE. Not exactly what you need to get started in programming, but it should be enough to help you see files, devices, and other objects from Windows 95's point of view. Now, it's on to putting OLE to work. That's the fun part.

OLE on the Desktop

If you've tried even a few of the examples and procedures in this book, you've already done a great deal with OLE. You've no doubt worked out with drag-and-drop, and you might have created shortcuts, scraps, or some of the sample documents that contained both text and graphics. To help bring these features into focus as part of the OLE whole, here's a quick summary of the major ways you use OLE on the desktop:

- **Drag-and-Drop.** Of all the features of Windows 95, drag-and-drop is probably the most likely to be used by the most people. It's just so easy: click, drag, and drop. Once you're hooked, you'll probably never use Copy or Cut and Paste again. Drag-and-drop, as you know, permeates Windows 95. You can drag and drop just about anything, anywhere. Just remember the difference between the left and right mouse buttons. Windows 95 usually defaults to a move when you drag and drop with the left mouse button, but in some situations it performs a copy instead. To be sure you get what you want, drag and drop with the right button and choose Move from the popup menu.

- **Shortcuts.** To people who like to do things their way, shortcuts are one of the hottest features in Windows 95. Tired of going through the Start menu to get to Calculator? Stick a shortcut to Calculator wherever you want it. Need the same document file every day? Put a shortcut to the document on the desktop. Wish you could put Microsoft Office, a bunch of documents, and assorted graphics in the same folder? Create the folder, and populate it with shortcuts to whatever you want.

This short, dry list no doubt makes both drag-and-drop and shortcuts seem less than spectacular, but by now you surely don't believe that. In both cases, a few words say it all yet are inadequate to explain just how great these features are. Both are easy to describe yet almost limitless in the ways you can use them. Turn your imagination loose, and drag-and-drop will soon become a fact of your computing life. And shortcuts? They're your escape from the classic, but rigid, hierarchical file system that makes order out of potential chaos on your hard disk but pays little attention to the ways you actually work in real life. Oh, almost forgot. There's also:

- **Cut/Copy and Paste.** These actions, longtime staples of the Windows (and the Macintosh) way of working, use a reserved portion of memory called the Clipboard to temporarily store anything from segments of text to bitmaps to entire files so that you can copy or move these elements from one place to another. Cut/Copy and Paste are basically older versions of the more enticing drag-and-drop. You can, however, rely on these commands when you want to arrange and rearrange disks, folders, and documents or when the window you want to paste into is not currently visible. You can

USING THE LEFT BUTTON Remember that when you drag and drop with the left mouse button you can use the keyboard to control which actions you perform. In cases where Move is not the default, request a move by holding down the Shift key while you drag and drop. If you want to copy rather than move, hold down the Ctrl key as you drag and drop. And if you want to create a shortcut, hold down the Ctrl and Shift keys, select the file you want a shortcut to, drag, drop, and then release the Ctrl and Shift keys. (If you see a popup menu when you drop the item and release the keys, just choose Create Shortcut.)

also use Cut/Copy and Paste to transfer different types of data between documents as either *linked* or *embedded* objects (more about these later in this chapter).

OLE in Applications

Although applications are sort of incidental when you're thinking about Windows 95 as an operating system, OLE can play a big part in making applications fun and easy to use. When you use OLE in applications, what you do is create a *compound document,* which, as the boxed definition tells you, is a fancy name for a document that contains elements created by more than one application. The following illustration shows a compound document composed of a picture and a spreadsheet chart in a small bed of word-processed text.

When you create a compound document, each object you insert belongs to a different owner: text, for example, belongs to your word processor, but the

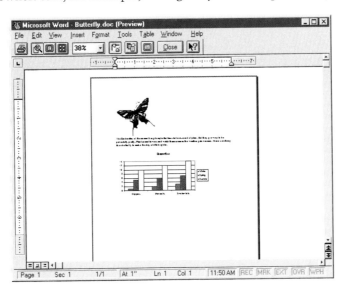

Keeping Things Straight

So that you don't become confused as you work with compound documents, bear in mind that even though Windows 95 *supports* OLE it does not automatically give applications the ability to *use* OLE. That capability must be built into the application itself. In a sense, Windows 95 is the conductor and your applications are orchestra members. If one member of the orchestra doesn't have a horn to play, it's not the conductor's fault.

chart you add belongs to your spreadsheet program, and the company logo might come from your drawing or painting program. The application handling the document in which you mix all these elements is known as the *container* application; the application from which you take an object is called the *server* or *object* application. (See why "object" is such a handy way to refer to these items? It's just so easy to think of taking an object and popping it into a container.)

As already mentioned, the beauty of a compound document is that it frees you from the limitations of a single application so that you can concentrate on whole *documents* rather than on "what I can make this application do if I really, really try." If you want a graphic, insert one. If you don't, don't. With the help of OLE, you can do whatever you want to do—as long as your application understands OLE, of course. Several of Windows 95's most frequently-used accessories—Notepad, WordPad, and Paint—have this kind of understanding and so are particularly nice subjects for experimenting with different ways to use OLE.

To create a compound document, you can insert objects in one of three ways:

- By dragging and dropping an existing object. This is OLE at its finest. Scraps, which are text or graphics you drag onto the desktop as you work, are special "file-type" objects in this category.

- By cutting or copying an existing object from one document and then pasting it into the container document.

- By creating a new object in the container document. This option requires the help of the server application and the application you're working with, so it's available only if your applications are able to let you insert objects.

Here's a look at what compound documents are all about. For specific commands and procedures, consult the online Help in the application you're working with.

Linking vs. Embedding Objects

When you insert all or part of one document into another without relying on scraps, there are two ways you can insert that "borrowed" information: you can *link* it, or you can *embed* it. The difference:

- A linked object remains connected to the original so that any changes you make to the original are reflected in the linked version. Linking is the option people choose when, for example, they want to be sure that copies of spreadsheet charts always reflect any changes to the original charts. The illustration on the following page shows an original bitmap, after editing, in Paint and a linked version of the bitmap in a WordPad document. Notice that the original and the linked object are identical.

COMPOUND DOCUMENT

That's a document that contains elements (objects) from different types of applications—a letter with a graphic in it, for instance, or a database that contains sounds or animation. Compound documents are kind of like mosaics made up of a piece of this and a piece of that. Compound documents *need* OLE.

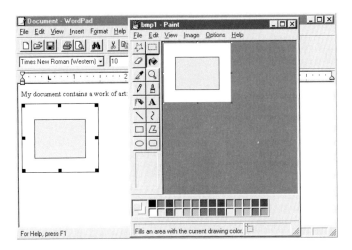

- An embedded object is like a clone of the original it came from: identical but completely separate. When you embed an object, it becomes, in essence, a different thing, so any changes you make to the original do not affect the embedded version at all. The following shows the same bitmap illustrated above, but with the WordPad document containing an embedded version of the original. Notice that the change to the original does not show up in the embedded version.

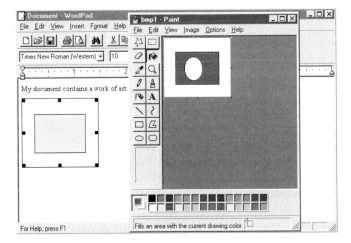

So what kinds of objects can you link or embed and into what kinds of documents? It all depends. As mentioned earlier, support for OLE must be built into your applications. In addition, your computer must have the appropriate equipment (such as a sound board) to handle the specific type of object. Given these "givens," however, the possibilities cover a range of objects.

MOVING OBJECTS AROUND
If you move an object-laden document from one computer to another, note that you might be prompted for information, such as a folder name, when you try to activate an object on the second computer. Assuming that the object file does, indeed, exist on the second machine, just go ahead and tell your application where to find it. If the object isn't available, of course, you'll either have to provide the file or do without the OLE object.

- Animation
- Bitmaps
- Video clips
- Sound "bytes" in the form of WAV files
- Microsoft Word documents
- Musical Instrument Digital Interface (MIDI) sequences

And so on.

Doing It   And how do you go about linking or embedding objects? Again, you have a choice of possibilities. (Remember, Windows 95 typically gives you several alternatives for just about anything you want to do.) You can:

- **Drag and drop.**   When you do this, you automatically create a link to the original object. You cannot drag from one application window to another, but you can easily drag from an open folder or an Explorer window to a document, so drag-and-drop is an excellent choice for file-type objects such as sounds.

- **Copy and paste.**   When you copy and paste an existing object, you can link it by choosing the Paste Special command and then clicking the Paste Link option, as shown in the illustration below, or you can embed it by choosing the Paste command.

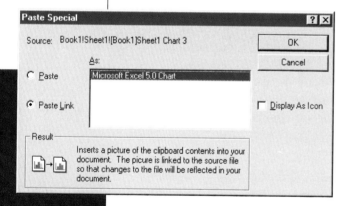

When you use Copy and Paste, you can work with part of a document, such as a paragraph of text or a piece of a Paint picture, or you can copy and paste entire files. To link the imported object to the original, however, bear in mind that the server and container applications must be able to support Paste Link. Not all applications can do this. Experiment, and if you run into difficulty, try…

- Your application's version of an Insert Object command. For details on this, alas, you must consult the application's documentation or online Help; this is a Windows 95 book. However…

Trying It Out   If you've installed WordPad, you can experiment to your heart's content with linking and embedding objects. The practice will even prove worthwhile because the principles you apply in WordPad transfer pretty nicely to other programs. To practice, all you need is WordPad's Insert Object command, which you were introduced to earlier in the book, in Chapter 5, "Taking Care of Business."

More than Cut and Paste or drag-and-drop, the Insert Object command is the guaranteed foolproof, user-friendly method for inserting either a new or an existing object into a text document. When you use Insert Object, you can choose to link or embed the incoming object and you can choose whether to display the object in all its glory or as a simple—and less memory-hungry—icon. Here's how it works:

1. In WordPad, place the insertion point where you want the object to appear.

2. Choose Insert Object, and the small window at the right appears.

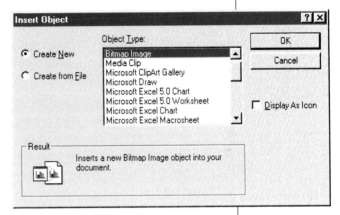

What you do now depends on whether you want to create a new object or use an existing one. If you want to create a *new* object, follow the steps at the top of the next page. If you want to insert an object from an existing file, skip to the next set of numbered steps.

Don't Have WordPad?

You can still install it, just as you can install any other Windows 95 component. Find your original Windows 95 CD-ROM or floppy disk, open Control Panel, double-click Add/Remove Programs, and click the Windows Setup tab. For WordPad, be sure the highlight is on Accessories and then click the Details button.

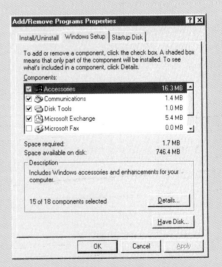

When the Accessories window opens, scroll down and click to check the box next to WordPad and then click OK. Click the Have Disk button. Next, either insert the floppy disk Windows 95 requests or choose your CD-ROM drive from the drop-down list in the Copy Manufacturer's Files From box. Click OK, and Windows 95's Setup program will do the rest.

(For more information on installing and uninstalling Windows 95 components and other software, refer to Appendix B, "Setting Up.")

To create a new object:

1. Go with the default option, Create New.

2. Select the type of object you want to create.

3. If you want to display the object as an icon instead of as itself, click the Display As Icon check box.

4. Click OK.

At this point, Windows 95 typically inserts a "placeholder" for the object-to-be into your document and also displays the tools you need to create the type of object you specified. For example, if you decided to create a new bitmap

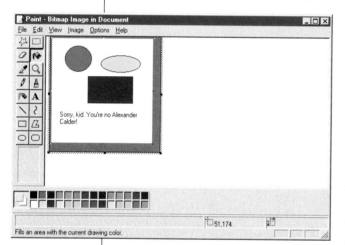

object in your WordPad document, you would work in the space shown at the left.

To insert the finished object and get back to the WordPad document from Paint, all you have to do is click anywhere outside the graphic's boundaries. With another paint program, however, remember that you might have to close the object's application window and, if prompted, click Yes or OK (whatever the prompt is) to update the object in your WordPad document. The actual steps involved depend on the application you use.

But back to WordPad. To insert an existing object:

1. In the Insert Object window, click the radio button at the left of Create From File. The window changes to the one shown below.

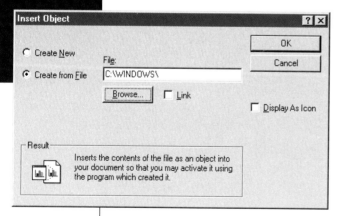

2. If you know the object's filename, including the complete path, type the whole thing in the File text box. (Drag over existing text to select it, and replace it with your typing.)

If you don't know the full path or the exact filename—or you'd just as soon let Windows 95 do the work—click the Browse button below the File text box and use the Browse window to find the file you want. Click the filename, and then click Insert (or double-click the file-name). Either returns you to the "main" Insert Object window.

3. If you want to link the object to the original, click the Link check box. If you want to display the object as an icon, click the Display As Icon check box. (The latter is recommended for large files inserted into large docu-ments, especially if your computer is not a high-performance model with a lot of RAM.)

4. Click OK, and the object you selected will appear in your document.

In the Real World

Although OLE can help you out in many ways, bear in mind that Windows 95 is a new operating system that incorporates support for the latest and greatest form of OLE. Although you can work with older applications that support earlier versions of OLE, be aware that those applications probably won't under-stand some things—for example, visual editing, which enables an OLE object to display its own menus and toolbars whenever you activate the object. Don't become confused if, for example, double-clicking one OLE object causes your window menus and toolbars to change, while double-clicking another OLE object causes the object's application win-dow to open. You're not seeing things…or at least not imaginary things. Visual editing is supported by some, but not all, applications. Just accept what happens.

Working with It   Windows 95 and its applications support a variety of objects: sound, animation, video clips…and even some mundane objects like text and bar charts. Given such a range of objects, are there any easy rules for opening or "playing" them? Sure. Linked or embedded, all you have to do is:

- Double-click.

- Or right-click and choose the appropriate action from a popup menu like the one shown at the right.

What happens next, of course, depends on the type of object. A bitmap will appear along with its application's menus and toolbars for editing, as will a spreadsheet chart. A video clip, how-ever, might begin to run, and a sound clip might send sweet music through your speakers.

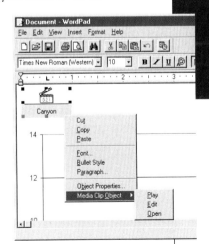

Scraps

Scraps are special drag-and-drop objects in that they are pieces of a document that you create by selecting part of a document and dragging it onto the desktop as you're working. What do you do with a scrap next? You can, of course, reinsert it into your original document. Each time you insert a scrap, however, you insert a copy of the text or graphic, and since people generally don't want to duplicate information in a document, chances are you'll probably want to put a scrap somewhere else or save it as a file in its own right.

To insert a scrap, you simply drag it into another document. If the scrap is made up of the same type of data as the document, the incoming information simply becomes part of the document—for example, a WordPad scrap dragged into a WordPad document becomes indistinguishable from the rest of the document. If the scrap is made of a different type of data (for example, a bitmap image dragged into a WordPad document), the incoming object is either linked or embedded.

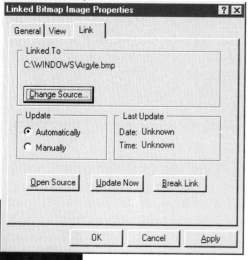

If a scrap is inserted into the document as a separate object rather than as "native" data, you can work with the object by:

- Right-clicking the inserted object and, if it is a linked object, choosing Object Properties from the popup menu and then clicking the Link tab. Do this if you want to work with the original version of a linked object or if you want to edit or break the connection. (Making and breaking links boils down to changing or disconnecting the path that Windows 95 follows to find the original, as you can see in the illustration at the left.)

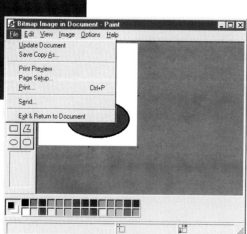

- Right-clicking the inserted object and choosing Open from the object type submenu on the popup menu. This opens the object in the application it came from. At that point, you can make changes to the object and then use File commands like the ones shown in the illustration at the left to update the original scrap object, to save the edited object as a file in its own right, or to update the original and close the application.

- If the scrap is still on the desktop, you can also right-click the object, choose Send To, and transfer a copy of the scrap object to any recipient listed in the Send To subfolder in your Windows 95 folder. (If you need a refresher on this, Send To was described in Chapter 6, "Oh, Those Files and Folders," under the heading "You Send Me.")

Behind the Scenes

Windows 95 sees scraps as small files with the extension SHS. Even though you create a scrap by selecting and dragging a document "clipping" to the desktop, the scrap itself consists of more than simply the text or graphic you selected. Windows 95 also tacks on a bit of cryptic information that tells about the text or graphic that makes up the scrap. If you try to insert a scrap into a document created by an application that can't handle data of the type you're inserting, you could see something like the illustration shown below.

The illustration shows what happens when you insert a scrap of text created by WordPad into a document created by Notepad. Notepad does not support drag-and-drop to the extent that WordPad does, so every bit of the scrap, background information and all, is inserted into the receiving document. Not what you want. As a commercial might say, for best results use with compatible software.

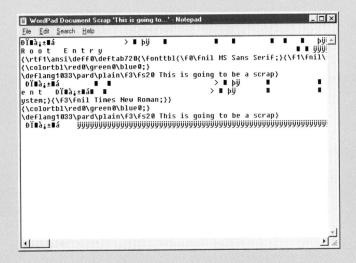

Hands-On!

OLE Tryouts

If you have installed WordPad, you can use it for some interesting trial runs with objects. Open WordPad, and try some or all of the following:

1. Type some text into WordPad. Move the mouse pointer to the left "margin" between the window border and the text you typed. When the pointer turns into a right-pointing arrow, click to select the text. Drag the text onto the desktop to create a scrap object, which Windows 95 automatically names for you.

2. Right-click the scrap object, and choose Open. The scrap text will appear in a WordPad window, identified as *WordPad Document In Scrap [scrap name]*. Make a change to the text, and then try the Update Scrap and Save Copy As commands. When you've finished, exit the scrap window.

3. In a new WordPad window, choose Insert Object. Use the Create From File option to insert various types of objects into your WordPad "document." Try inserting a bitmap from your Windows 95 folder, and then double-click the bitmap to activate it.

4. If your computer is equipped with a sound card, check the Media subfolder of your Windows 95 folder for a file named Canyon. If the file's there, choose WordPad's Insert Object command. Choose Create From File. In the Browse window that opens, find the Media folder and insert Canyon as the new object. When the new object appears in your WordPad document, give it a double-click. Neat, huh?

Try inserting some other objects on your own, and then investigate your applications to see what they can do.

Chapter 10

Networks and *The* Network

One of the great things about Microsoft Windows 95 is that it makes using resources on a network as easy as using your hard disk. Well, all right. Not quite that easy, since you have to *find* the resource you want. But it *is* true that Windows 95 blurs the distinction between hardware that's hardwired to your computer and hardware that's sitting in another room or even in another building. All you have to know is how to connect to those remote machines. That's what this chapter is about, but as you can see from the title, it's also about two very different kinds of networks: one that links computers primarily via cabling and another that lets you tap into the so-called information superhighway via telephone and The Microsoft Network.

A Network Is...

A computer network is a group of computers that all contain special cards with circuits called *network adapters*. These computers are cabled together, and they run special software that enables them to communicate and share resources. There are two basic types of networks, client-server and peer-to-peer.

A *client-server* network is one in which computers of the desktop variety cluster around a (usually) more powerful machine like puppies around a food dish. The small computers are the clients and the large one, which provides the resources needed by the clients, is the server. Client-server networks can be quite large, with hundreds or even thousands of clients busily connecting to, disconnecting from, using resources on, or communicating through many servers at any given time. The technology, timing, and support for all this is really impressive, but thanks to Windows 95, you don't have to understand it to appreciate it.

A TRIP BY ANY OTHER NAME

You've probably seen and heard enough about the information superhighway that the term already makes you gag. You're not alone. For the sake of your stomach, this book will simply refer to The Microsoft Network or to online services. (If you need a few generic alternatives to *superhighway*, open your heart to *I-way*, *infobahn*, or the ever-popular *cyberspace* coined by science-fiction author William Gibson.)

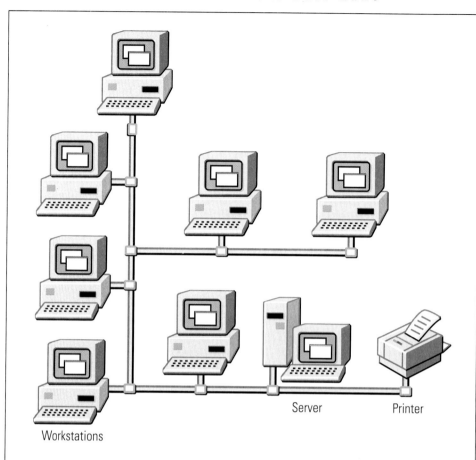

Workstations   Server   Printer

A *peer-to-peer* network, by contrast, is a smaller conglomeration that operates along the more democratic principle that each participant is a peer among equals. There is no server acting as overlord. When computers on such a network communicate, they do so like kids in a game of pass the beanbag—the beanbag being whatever information is being routed from one computer to another. Peer-to-peer networks are cheaper and less sophisticated than client-server networks, although just as impressive from a technical point of view. They are outstanding in situations where a few (two to half a dozen or so) computers need to share information.

Unless you plan to set up a network of your own, network setup and maintenance can remain an art form (and it is that) practiced by your network administrator. As a network user and a commander of Windows 95, you should know that, on Microsoft networks and Novell NetWare (version 2.15 and later, version 3.*x*, and version 4.*x*) networks:

- Windows 95 has built-in support for the client side of a client-server network. You can easily cruise and browse your "Network Neighborhood," and you can connect to and use resources on one or more servers.

- Windows 95 has built-in support for *peer* resource sharing as well, so you can use files and printers on Windows for Workgroups, Windows 95, and Windows NT computers in addition to network servers.

Thus, it's quite possible to have your cake and eat it too. Through the magic of Windows 95 network support, you can connect to your office network (Novell NetWare, Microsoft NT, or even both); to network peers sharing files and printers; and, via phone, to *the* network, as described later, and even to the fabled Internet. All at the same time. And if you need more connections than that, you probably belong in Washington (D.C., that is) or maybe Hollywood.

Network Diversity

As you probably know, networking software is designed, built, and delivered by many vendors. Each type of networking software has its own requirements and personality, including its own favored methods of enabling a client to connect to servers. As mentioned elsewhere in this chapter, Windows 95 includes both client-side and peer-sharing capabilities for Microsoft networks and Novell NetWare networks. But what about networks from other vendors? Windows 95 includes built-in support for a number of other networks, including Banyan, Digital Equipment, IBM, and SunSoft. But there's a "but," of sorts. The browsing and sharing capabilities described here are designed into Windows 95 as 32-bit protected-mode services (which, as you might recall from an early chapter, means that Windows 95 unleashes the full power of your computer's processor). Software that takes advantage of 32-bit protected mode is, as of mid-1995, still relatively new. If your networking software has not yet been fully adapted to Windows 95, you'll find that:

- Even though Windows 95 supports and can work quite nicely with older, 16-bit networking software, you do not have the full networking capabilities available to the Microsoft and Novell 32-bit protected-mode clients. That means some of Windows 95's features might not be available to you— among them the ability to use long filenames, to view servers through Network Neighborhood, to "open" a resource on a server without first mapping the network drive, and so on.

Depending on the type of network you use, you might be able to run both your 16-bit version and the 32-bit protected-mode client for Microsoft networks described here. The variables are many, however, and the only person who can truly tell you what you can do (as well as exactly how) and what you cannot do is your network administrator. If you have any questions about *your* network, turn first to *your* administrator. It's common sense, and it's the only way to be sure.

Logging On

To use network resources, you have to log on and be validated as a legitimate member of the electronic community. Logon details, such as your user name and password, are initially the responsibility of your network administrator, as are setting up your computer to connect in the first place and adding you to the list of users. Once you're set up to use the network, however, logging on simply involves using the familiar opening logon prompt.

Microsoft or Novell?

To avoid confusing everyone with "on Microsoft networks it looks like this" and "on NetWare networks it looks like that," the descriptions and illustrations from here to the beginning of the section called "Introducing *The* Network: MSN" reflect what happens with a computer connected to a Microsoft network—simply because that was the type of network available to the computer on which this book was written. If you belong to a Novell NetWare network, you might see and do things a little differently, even though the Windows 95 Client for Novell NetWare offers much the same functionality. Microsoft or Novell, whichever—this chapter should help you become comfortable with your Network Neighborhood. Tips in the margins will clue you in to some NetWare differences, but just remember that if you don't understand something, your network administrator is the person to help you out.

VARIATIONS
Networks are not implemented the same way in all organizations. Although the sections that follow all describe features built into Windows 95, it's possible that your network administrator has disabled some of them for the sake of security or to keep your network running smoothly. If, for example, you can't change your password or can't control file and printer sharing, those capabilities might be restricted on your computer.

What Do You Have?

If Windows 95 is installed on a computer connected to either a Microsoft or Novell network, the Setup program automatically detects the type of network and configures itself to work with that network. On Microsoft networks, Setup also selects the 32-bit Client for Microsoft Networks as your primary (first) logon. On Novell Networks, as long as Setup does not detect incompatible components, it sets the 32-bit Client for NetWare Networks as the primary logon. To see or change the primary logon:

• Open the Control Panel, and double-click the Network icon.

Your primary network logon is shown on the Configuration tab. If you log on to Microsoft networks and a Windows NT domain, you can also see the name of the domain you log on to:

• Double-click Client For Microsoft Networks in the list box at the top of the Configuration tab.

Look but don't touch—unless you are told to do so by your network administrator. If you make changes and suddenly can't log on to the proper domain, your ability to use network resources will evaporate.

Standardizing Your Passwords

If you belong to a Microsoft network, you're asked to provide both a network password and a Windows logon password when you start Windows 95 for the first time. If you type different passwords, you'll be prompted for both each time you start or restart Windows 95. Two different passwords can be hard to remember and irritating to type each time you start Windows 95. The solution is to use the same password for both. If you're stuck with two passwords, you can easily simplify matters:

Tip!

CHANGING A NETWARE PASSWORD

To change a password on a NetWare network, you connect to the server(s) on which you want to make the change. Make the Public directory on the server the current directory, and then type **SETPASS** at the MS-DOS prompt. Just as when you change passwords on a Microsoft network, you'll be asked to type your old password as well as the new one, and you'll be asked to confirm the new password. You'll be prompted to change your password on each server to which you are connected.

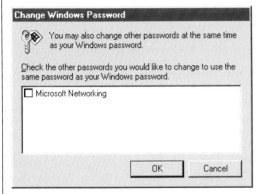

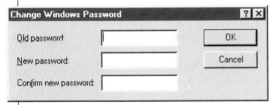

1. Open the Control Panel, and double-click the Passwords icon.

2. On the Passwords Properties sheet, click the Change Windows Password button. You'll see the window shown at the left.

   To change other passwords, such as your network password, at the same time, put a check mark next to each password you want to change in the Check The Other Passwords... list.

3. Click OK, and you'll see the Change Windows Password dialog box shown at the left.

4. Type your old Windows 95 password, press Tab, type your

Keeping in Sync

To maintain security, network administrators commonly rely on something called *aging*, which keeps track of how long you've used the same logon password. When your password reaches a certain age, you must change it. (You'll be told when to do this—with plenty of time to spare.)

To retire a geriatric password, you can use the Change Other Passwords button on the Passwords Properties sheet to change only your network

password. If you do, however, your network and Windows passwords will no longer be the same and the next time you log on you'll be prompted for both. To change your network password *and* your Windows 95 password, click the Change Windows Password button and then click your networking option in the Change Windows Password window. This changes both old passwords to the same new one, simultaneously.

new password, press Tab again, and retype your new password to confirm it. Click OK, and Windows 95 will respond with *The Windows password has been successfully changed.* And that's all there is to that.

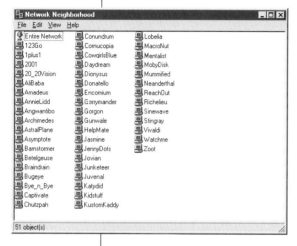

Once You're Connected...

How do you see your friends and neighbors?

• Open Network Neighborhood.

Is there anything else you have to do? Nope. Use Network Neighborhood and the resources you find there just as you use My Computer. On Microsoft networks, for example, Network Neighborhood looks like the illustration shown at the left. (This is not a real workgroup; names have been changed to protect the innocent.)

Double-clicking an icon or right-clicking it and choosing Open produces a window like the one shown at the left.

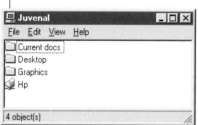

In this case, the sample computer (named Juvenal) contains four shared resources: a folder named *Current docs,* the computer's desktop and its contents, a folder named *Graphics,* and a shared Hewlett-Packard (*Hp*) printer. To use these resources, the "sharee" would open a folder or drag and drop to the printer and would otherwise treat the shared resources as if they were part of the local scenery.

The only real differences you're likely to find are that some resources might be password-protected (in which case, you can't use them unless you know the magic word), access to others might be restricted as read-only to keep documents from being changed, and a shared network printer might be busy or offline (in which case your print job will be placed in a queue). Other than that, everything you know about using resources on your local machine applies to using resources on the network. Well, except for one tip that might come in handy on a computer connected to a very large network via Microsoft networks:

• Avoid double-clicking Entire Network. You could be in for a wait, though not an extremely long one, as your computer looks for *everyone* it can find. Besides, if you have to take a look at the entire network to find the resource you need, you can learn to work faster and smarter, as described next.

Finding the Computer You Need

Cruising a network to see what's out there can be fun, but it's not the most effective way to get things done. Easier by far is to know what you want and where to find it. In Windows 95, you can locate specific resources in either of two ways: with your old friend the Find command or with the Run command on the Start menu.

Using Find Computer There's only one requirement you have to meet to use Find Computer: you have to know the name of the computer to find. As you probably know, each computer on a network has a name, just as yours does. (If you don't know the name of the computer you want, you'll have to ask someone. It's a low-tech approach, but it works.) To use Find Computer:

1. Right-click Network Neighborhood and choose Find Computer, or choose the Find Computer command from the Start menu.

2. When the Find window opens, type the name of the computer. If the computer is one you've searched for before, click the downward-pointing triangle at the right of the Named box and choose from the drop-down list.

3. Click Find Now. Shortly thereafter, assuming that the computer is available to you, its name will appear in the Find window.

4. Open the computer's icon, and off you go.

Find Computer is as quick and easy as a desktop shortcut for locating and opening a computer that you often use. There are, however, faster ways. Try the Run command, described on the next page, as well as *mapping* the resource to a drive letter and automatically reconnecting at startup, as described in the section immediately following "Using the Run Command." Both Run and drive mapping are easy to use, but to make them work right, you first need to know about UNC.

UNC UNC is short for *Universal Naming Convention*, and it's the form in which Windows 95 (and, by extension, you) refers to network pathnames. An earlier chapter explained that a pathname on a *local* disk, such as your C drive, starts with a drive letter, a colon, and a backslash, followed by a string of folder names, each separated from the one before by another backslash, like this:

```
C:\Folder1\Folder2\...FolderN\Filename.ext
```

UNC follows the same format but begins with a double backslash, followed by the name of the computer, followed by the name of the folder you want to use. In other respects, UNC names look a lot like pathnames; all you have to do is remember the \\ at the beginning:

```
\\Computer\Folder1\Folder2\...FolderN\Filename.ext
```

Now, with UNC under your belt, it's time to Run.

NAMELESS IN NETWORKLAND?

If you don't know the name of your computer, open the Control Panel, right-click the Network icon, and click the Identification tab.

NETWARE PATHS

If you're a NetWare user, you can map to a network drive by using either the UNC format or the NetWare pathname, which takes the form Server\Volume:Directory\Subdirectory. If this naming convention is not familiar to you, see your network administrator or refer to your network user's guide. If you map to a drive, you'll see that the Windows 95 Map Network Drive window also lets you connect to a directory as if it were the root directory of a drive. Doing this is comparable to using the NetWare MAP ROOT command. Again, refer to your documentation for specifics.

Using the Run Command   The Run command, which you can use for starting programs and for opening folders and files, is fast and slick when it comes to finding a shared computer. It's faster than Find Computer, it's just as easy, and it has the added advantage of being able to take you directly to the folder or file you want, as long as access to the resource is not restricted by password protection. In fact, if you end the UNC pathname with a filename followed by a registered extension, Run even opens the appropriate application and displays the file for you. To use the Run command:

1. Open the Start menu and choose Run. You'll see the window shown at the right.

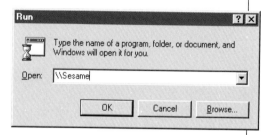

   Type the name of the computer you want to find. Be sure to start with the UNC double backslash. If you don't, Windows 95 will assume you're looking for a file and will come up dry. (If you want to go directly to a folder or a document, type the complete UNC pathname that will lead Windows 95 to the exact destination.)

2. Press Enter, and in a few seconds, a window opens. If you specified the name of a computer, the window will show the shared resources, including printers, on the computer you specified. If you specified a computer and a folder, you'll see the contents of the folder. And if you specified a document with a registered file type, you'll see the document.

From that point on, it's business as usual.

"Mapping" a Drive to a Network Resource   And now, what about "mapping" drives? Mapping a drive means telling Windows 95 to treat a network disk or folder as if it were a drive on your computer. For example, suppose you use a folder named Docs on a computer named Current. If you want to, you can map a drive letter—say, G—to \\Current\Docs. Thereafter, until you disconnect, all you have to do is send Windows 95 or your applications to drive G in order to use the shared files on \\Current\Docs. (By the way, all you specify when you map to a drive letter is the computer and the name of the shared folder you want. You don't specify subfolders, and you don't specify filenames, because files can't be shared individually on a network.)

To map to a network drive (on Microsoft networks):

1. Right-click Network Neighborhood, and choose Map Network Drive. Alternatively, if you have an open window to My Computer or a disk drive and if the toolbar is displayed, you can click the Map Network Drive icon. (It's just at the right of the Up One Level icon and looks a little like

a hard disk with a fizzy bubble coming out of the upper left corner.) However you choose this command, Windows 95 presents you with the Map Network Drive window shown at the right.

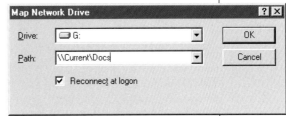

2. In the Drive box, Windows 95 displays the next available drive letter (A, B, C, and so on). If you want to use a specific drive letter or if a program insists on using one, either type the letter or choose it from the drop-down list.

3. In the Path box, type the path (in UNC format) to the computer and resource you want. If the path is one you've used recently, you can simply choose it from the drop-down list in the Path box.

4. If you want Windows 95 to reconnect to this resource every time you log on, be sure there's a check mark in the Reconnect At Logon box.

5. Click OK. If Windows 95 prompts for a password before it allows you to connect, type the password and press Enter.

Once you've gone through the drill, the resource you've mapped to a drive letter becomes a "virtual" part of your hardware until you disconnect or shut down, which you do by…

Disconnecting a Network Drive   When you no longer want to treat a network drive or a folder as if it were bonded to your computer, you:

1. Right-click Network Neighborhood, and choose Disconnect Network Drive. Or if you have an open window to My Computer or a disk drive and if the toolbar is displayed, click the Disconnect Network Drive icon (which is at the right of the Map Network Drive icon and looks just like it, but with the bubble replaced by a red *X*). The window at the right opens.

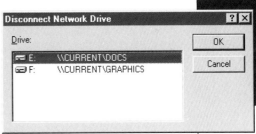

2. Select the drive to disconnect and click OK. If you want to disconnect from more than one drive, remember that you can either hold down Ctrl as you click to select assorted drives or hold down Shift as you click to select consecutive drives in the list.

When to Open, When to Map   Windows 95 supports a new feature called *common dialog boxes*, like the ones you see with the Open and Save As commands. Unlike dialog boxes in earlier versions of Windows, these common dialog boxes open up network resources which you can browse and use

DISCONNECTING OFTEN?

If you find yourself disconnecting from network resources every time you start Windows 95, remember that you might have enabled Reconnect At Logon when you mapped a network drive. Disconnect before shutting down or turn this option off the next time you map a network drive, and your problems are fewer.

without first mapping them. Browsing is the newfangled way of accessing network resources; mapping is the "old-fashioned" method. However, each has its own strengths, and if you're wondering when, or whether, to find and open shared resources as opposed to mapping a drive letter to them, here are a few tips that might help you decide:

- If you're installing a program that expects to install its files from one specified drive to another, map the drive.

- If you prefer referring to drive letters and seeing your network connections as part of My Computer, map the drive.

- If you're using a program that doesn't support common dialog boxes and you want to work with shared files, map the network resource to a drive letter. That way, when you want to open or save a file, you can specify the "drive" to work with. (There is an alternative you might prefer, and it's described below.)

However, you can save yourself the bother of mapping a drive:

- If you're using programs that understand common dialog boxes.

- Or if you don't mind typing a UNC specification.

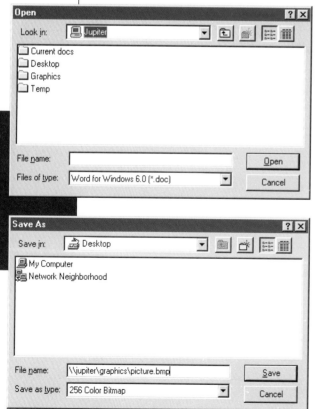

You can browse the network *directly* from within a common Open or Save As dialog box. This feature means that your network is virtually *inside* your desktop computer. For example, the illustration at the left shows a File Open window in WordPad with the shared folders on a network computer named Jupiter.

As you can see in the illustration of a File Save As dialog box in Paint at the left, you can just type a UNC pathname in the File Name text box instead of browsing. As long as the computer and the folder you specify are shared and you have both read access and write access to them, your application will be able to deal with the file as if it were on your own machine.

Specifying a UNC pathname, by the way, might work for you even if your program doesn't use common dialog boxes. If the application can work with UNC pathnames, you might be able to avoid mapping a drive and, instead, open and save files by specifying their UNC pathnames. Give it a try.

Using a Network Printer   Using a network printer is a lot like using the printer on your desktop, with a few differences. On the plus side, you can often depend on someone else to refill the paper tray. On the minus side, you might send a print job at a time when the printer is busy. And, of course, you probably have to walk down the hall to pick up your printout.

Nevertheless, using a network printer is a simple matter with Windows 95. Before you can use the printer, however, you have to install it, to tell Windows 95 what type of printer you're using and where it is. To do this, you can run the Add Printer wizard described in Chapter 12, "Disks, Controls, and Other Delights," but for a network printer there's a faster way, thanks to a feature called Point And Print, which shows off OLE at its finest and makes Windows 95 do most of the work for you.

To use Point And Print, you need the printer's location, meaning a UNC-type address consisting of the name of the server that collects and queues print jobs, followed by the name assigned to the printer itself—for example, \\Slow\Pig, where Slow is the server name and Pig is the printer name. If the printer is one you've never used before, you also need its make and model so that Windows 95 can install the appropriate driver software (the software that helps Windows 95 use the printer).

Armed with this information, you can then install a printer in a couple of different ways. Here's an easy one:

1. Use Network Neighborhood, Find Computer, or the Run command to open a window to the server and printer you want.

2. Double-click the printer's icon. Windows 95 will display a message telling you that the printer must be set up on your computer. This is what you want, so press Enter or click Yes. As soon as you do, Windows 95 swings into an abbreviated version of the Add Printer wizard and displays the screen at the right.

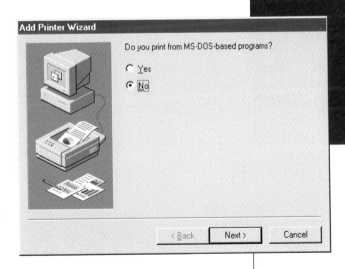

Leave the default setting of No and click Next, even if you do print from MS-DOS programs and you want to "capture" a printer port for their sake. As described in the shaded box titled "Gotcha," you can capture the port later.

3. Now...

- If Point And Print detects an appropriate printer driver on your system, it asks if you want to *Keep existing driver*. This is the recommended course of action, and you probably do want to keep it, so click Next.

- If Point And Print does not detect an appropriate driver, it displays a window in which you specify the make and model of printer. Make the appropriate choices and click Next.

Gotcha

A printer port has a name like LPT1 or LPT2. Because many MS-DOS programs need to have output specifically mapped to the location of a network printer, you probably have to "capture" your printer port in terms those programs understand. That is, you have to tell them that whenever they want to use LPT1, they are actually sending output to a network location, such as \\Slow\Pig.

As mentioned in text, you can capture your printer port while you're installing a network printer. If you don't do it at that time, you can find the appropriate command "behind" the Capture Printer Port button on the Details tab on the printer's properties sheet (which you display by right-clicking the printer's icon in your Printers folder).

The Capture Printer Port button opens the window shown below left.

In the Device box, choose the port you're going to print to—probably LPT1. In the Path box, type the path to your network printer. If you want to reconnect each time you log on, leave the Reconnect At Logon box checked. Click OK, and from then on, the MS-DOS programs that need the information will "know" where to send their output. To end capture—that is, to break the connection between your printer port and the network path—return to the Details tab on the printer's properties sheet, click the End Capture button, select the port/pathname combination you want to delete, and click OK.

4. In the next step, Windows 95 asks what name you'd like to assign to the printer. As with your computer, give it a descriptive name. On the same screen, specify whether you want Windows 95 to use the new printer as your default. Click Next.

5. Finally, Windows 95 asks if you want to print a test page. If you've used the printer with an earlier version of Windows, you can probably skip this step. Otherwise, choose the recommended default, Yes.

6. Click the Finish button, and in a short time, Windows 95 adds the printer to your Printers folder. From there, you can drag a shortcut to the desktop if you'd like to keep the printer handy.

Checking the Status of Your Print Jobs   When you send your print job to a network printer, you can always tell what's going on. If the printer is offline or otherwise unavailable, the printer icon appears on the taskbar next to the time display.

To see what's pending, place the mouse pointer over the icon on the taskbar. A short "tip" will appear telling you *X document(s) pending for*, followed by your user name. The icon will remain on your taskbar until you shut down. Oh, and don't worry that shutting down will mean losing your print job. The information has been safely *spooled* (sent, queued, and saved) on the server connected to the printer. In fact, even if the server is shut down, Windows 95 automatically saves all pending print jobs and reminds the next person who starts the server that there's unfinished business waiting for the printer.

Most of the time, however, your network printer will be up, online, and busy working. If you have one or more jobs pending (as indicated by the printer icon on the taskbar), you can check the status of the queue:

- By double-clicking the printer icon. (In addition to being able to drag and drop a document onto the printer, this is another good reason for keeping a shortcut handy on your desktop.)

- Or by double-clicking the printer icon next to the time display on the taskbar.

Whichever way you choose, you'll see a window like the one shown at the right.

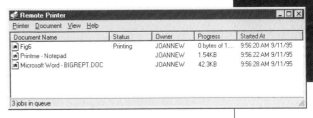

On a network printer, you don't have as much control over the print queue as you would on a printer attached to your own computer. You can right-click or use the Document menu to delete a document from the network printer's queue, as long as the document is not yet printing, but you can't change the order of the jobs in the queue nor can you delete anyone else's job or pause the printer. (If there's a printer problem, Windows 95 will tell you so with an error report in the Status column. In which case, of course, let the network administrator know.)

Allowing File and Printer Sharing

Now that you have the basics of using shared resources, it's time to find out a little about doing unto others.

Before anyone can use files on another computer, the folder(s) containing the files must be shared. On a Windows 95 computer, when you want to make files or printers available to others, you enable file and printer sharing. This option should be turned on by default, but if you right-click a folder and don't see a Sharing command, here's how to turn on and control sharing:

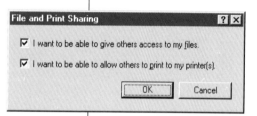

1. Open the Control Panel, and double-click the Network icon.

2. On the Configuration tab on the properties sheet that appears, click the File And Print Sharing button. The small window at the left opens.

To enable sharing, put a check mark in the appropriate box; to disable sharing of files or printers, remove the check mark from the appropriate box.

3. Click OK in the File And Print Sharing window, and then click OK in the main Network window to make the change.

When you change the status of file and printer sharing, you have to restart your computer for the change to take effect. Do so, and the sharing you enabled (or disabled) will be in place.

Making Files and Printers Available

Because shared files and printers are, theoretically, available to anyone who cares to find and use them, Windows 95 supports two types of security that allow you to limit access to shared resources on a computer running as a Client for Microsoft Networks:

NETWARE ACCESS

If you are on a Net-Ware network, Windows 95 provides user-level security only. Share-level access is available only on Microsoft networks.

• Share-level access, the default, lets you assign read-only or full-access rights, and it lets you protect each shared resource (disk, folder, or printer) with a password so that only those "in the know" can gain access. Read-only access, of course, means that someone can view but not change a shared document. Full access, which you might assume means the ability to both read and change a document, actually means more, so be careful about allowing this. With full access, a person can also add to a shared disk or folder, create new folders, delete folders and documents, and even change file attributes—for example, changing a document to read-only or hidden. If you're responsible for the documents in a shared folder, be judicious about allowing full access.

- User-level access lets you avoid bothering with passwords and instead specify which people are allowed to use each shared resource. As with share-level access, you can allow read-only and full-access rights. Unlike share-level access, however, you can also choose a Custom option that lets you determine exactly what any individual is allowed to do with a shared resource. At its most liberal, custom permission can give a person as much control over a shared disk or folder as you have. Because you can decide what to allow, however, custom permission is also the way to go if you want to provide both read and write access, but nothing else—no ability to create, delete, or change attributes.

To specify which type of access (share-level or user-level) you want to provide:

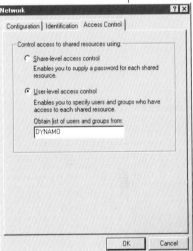

1. Open the Control Panel, and double-click the Network icon.

2. Click the Access Control tab to view the properties sheet at the right.

3. Click the type of access control you prefer. Although it would be nice, you can't have both at the same time.

Switching from one type of access control to another requires that you reboot the computer for the change to take effect, so when you're ready, shut down and then restart the machine. When Windows 95 restarts, you'll be ready for network show-and-tell. You can share a disk—including your entire hard disk—or any folder you choose. You cannot, however, share files individually. (To do that, create a shortcut to a shared folder on the recipient's computer and then drag the file to the shortcut. Or attach the file to an e-mail message as described a little later.)

Share-Level Access Once sharing is enabled, the act of sharing is simple. If you're using share-level access:

1. Right-click the disk or folder that you want to share, and choose either Sharing or Properties from the popup menu. If you choose Properties, click the Sharing tab.

2. Click the Shared As option. By default, Windows 95 displays the disk or folder name in the Share Name box. You can change the share name if you want to. Optionally, you can also type a comment in the Comment box. Whatever you type will be displayed in the Comment column for anyone

HALFWAY PERMISSION

Remember, read-only permission simply allows people to view and open the documents in a shared resource. To allow more than that (but *not* the ability to create folders, delete files, and change file attributes), opt for user-level access, choose Custom access rights, and check off only Read Files and Write To Files.

who uses details view in the Windows Explorer to check out the shared resources on your computer.

3. In the Access Type section, choose the option you want. If you choose Depends On Password, users will have either read-only or full access, depending on the password they type.

4. In the Passwords section, assign one or two passwords corresponding to the access type you chose. If you chose Depends On Password, type one read-only password and one full-access password. Read-only, full access, or both, Windows 95 will then prompt for confirmation with a window like the one shown at the right.

5. Type the password(s), click OK to close the confirmation window, and you're done.

From this point on, anyone wanting to use your shared resource will have to type a password in a window like the one at the left to gain access. You, of course, will have to provide the correct password(s) to your selected "subscribers."

Halt, Who Goes There?

Whether you opt for share-level or user-level access, the names of your shared resources will be visible to anyone with access to your Network Neighborhood. Don't worry, though. Only the approved few will be able to open them. Anyone just nosing around will either be prompted for a password (share-level protection) or be told in no uncertain terms that "access [is] denied" (user-level protection). If you go

with passwords, make sure that people don't leave them lying around. One way to do this is to tell people, when prompted for the password for the first time, to select the Remember Password option so that Windows 95 does the remembering for them. If you later need to change the list of people with access, you can always change the password and distribute the new one to the approved group.

User-Level Access   With user-level access, you use Windows 95 to control the list of people who can open a shared resource. You can also control what type of access people receive: read-only, full, or custom (which can potentially give the person as much control over the resource as you have). Providing user-level access is simple:

1. Right-click the disk or folder that you want to share, and choose either Sharing or Properties from the popup menu. If you choose Properties, click the Sharing tab.

2. Click the Shared As option, and—for a folder named Potluck—the window will look like the one shown at the right.

As with share-level access, Windows 95 displays the disk or folder name as the Share Name, but you can change it if you want to. You can also type a comment in the Comment box.

To control the list of users, you use the Add, Remove, and Edit buttons in the lower half of the Shared Properties window. The Add button opens the window shown at the right.

This is easy enough to use:

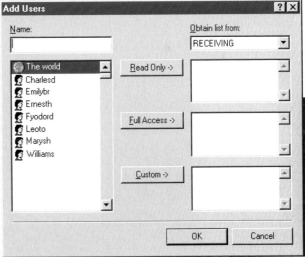

1. If you have access to more than one group of computers, use the Obtain List From box to choose the group to which the person you're adding belongs.

2. In the Name box, type enough letters to move the highlight to the name of the individual.

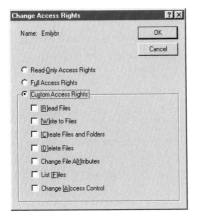

3. When the right person is selected, click Read Only, Full Access, or Custom to assign the permission level, and then click OK. If you choose Read Only or Full Access, that's all there is to it. If you choose Custom, you see the window shown at the left.

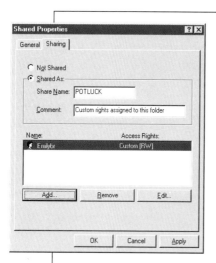

4. Click to put a check mark next to each option you want to allow, and then click OK.

Read-only, full, or custom access, the Sharing tab looks like the one at the left when you're done.

Later on, you can modify your list of users as follows:

- To delete a person's name, select the name and click the Remove button.

- To change a person's access rights, select the name, click Edit, and make the changes on the Custom option list that opens.

Microsoft Exchange

Now you come to one of the truly enjoyable parts of Windows 95. (Not that there are any other kinds, of course.) But this one is usable, useful, and very people-oriented. Everyone knows it as e-mail; in Windows 95, it is called Microsoft Exchange. With Exchange as your servant, you can send messages, faxes, and even files across a network, across the country, or around the world. You and your computer will never have to practice lives of solitary contemplation. This is what Exchange looks like.

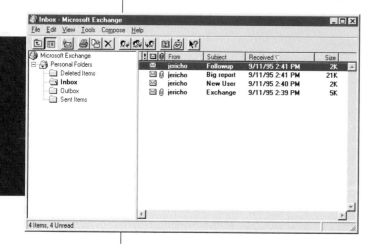

Exchange works with a number of information services, including the Internet, CompuServe, The Microsoft Network, Microsoft Fax, and a Microsoft Mail post-office—which you or the network administrator in your group can set up from within Windows 95. (For information on setting up a postoffice and specifying its users, refer to the section "Creating and Administering a Postoffice," later in this chapter.)

When you install Windows 95, Exchange is not installed by default, but it's easy to install and configure. You can do so either by double-clicking the Inbox icon on your desktop (if one is there) or by using the Control Panel's Add/Remove Programs utility as described in Chapter 12. Before you can successfully set up Exchange, however, you must have access to a postoffice, so contact your network administrator for the correct location and any additional information you need. The remainder of this section assumes that Exchange is up and running on your computer.

Your Inbox

The Inbox is where Exchange collects all the messages sent to you—e-mail, faxes, and messages with attached documents. Everything is in one place to make using your computer feel as natural as possible. In the real world, you probably don't maintain separate inboxes for mail, faxes, and documents, so Windows 95 sees no reason why you should do so on your computer.

When you want to see what's in your Inbox, you can do one of the following:

• Choose Microsoft Exchange from the Start Programs menu.

• Double-click the Inbox icon.

When the logon prompt appears, log on with your e-mail name and password.

Unlike other parts of Windows 95, Exchange allows you to choose the type of window you want to work in: a single-paned window like My Computer (in details view) or a double-paned window like the one you work with in the Windows Explorer. The Explorer-type window shows folders in the left pane and Inbox messages in the right. The two panes make it easy to manage messages, so once you're used to Exchange, the Windows Explorer, or both, you'll probably prefer the dual panes—perhaps even by a margin of two to one. To try out or switch between the two options:

• In the Exchange window, open the View menu and put a check mark next to the Folders option.

• Click the Show/Hide Folder List button (labeled below) on the toolbar.

You'll get around to customizing more of Exchange shortly, but first the most basic activity of all: how to send e-mail.

E-Mail

Everybody likes e-mail. It's fast, it's easy, it saves trees and postage, and it puts an end to telephone tag—sometimes, anyway. With Exchange, all you need in order to send a message is the New Message button on the toolbar at the top of the Exchange window.

New Message
Show/Hide Folder List

MAKING IT EASIER

When you start Exchange for the first time, you can tell it to skip the logon prompt in subsequent sessions by clicking the Remember Password button.

**E-MAIL
CLOSE TO HOME**

This chapter describes e-mail as you find it on a Microsoft network or on *The* Microsoft Network. If you're a traveler, the next chapter looks at ways to communicate when you're on the road.

WORD WINDOW?

If your e-mail window looks like a composite of the Microsoft Word window and the window shown at the right, Exchange is using Word as its default editor. If you prefer not to use Word, click in the Exchange window, open the Compose menu, choose WordMail Options, and remove the check in the box labeled Enable Word As Email Editor.

When you click the New Message button, Exchange opens the window at the right.

This is where you address and compose your message.

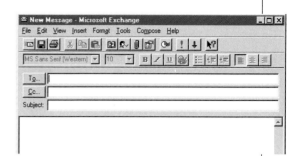

Your Address Books

When Exchange sets up an e-mail account for you in a Microsoft Mail post-office, it creates two address books. One, called the Postoffice Address List, contains the names of all authorized members of each postoffice you can access (some networks contain more than one) and is maintained by your network or postoffice administrator. The second is a Personal Address Book, which you can treat as your own e-mail "little black book."

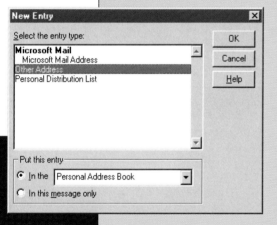

You choose which address book to use from the drop-down list that opens at the top of the Address Book window when you click the To or CC button in a new Message window.

To add a name from the Postoffice Address List to your Personal Address Book, select the name in the Address Book window, click Properties, and choose Personal Address Book.

To add a new name to your Personal Address Book, type the person's name at the top of the Address Book window and click the New button. When you do, the New Entry window opens. Depending on your setup, different types of entries might be available.

- Choose the type of entry you want. If you don't know, select Other Address. Click OK, and another window will open, this one asking for information about the person.

The contents of this window will vary, depending on which type of entry you chose. Fill in the blanks, and Exchange will add the person to the appropriate list. (Note that you must ferret out the actual information required, including the person's authorized e-mail name and address.)

- The To and CC lines are, of course, where you identify the recipient(s) of your message. Type e-mail names, and if you address more than one person, separate the names with semi-colons. If you don't know the e-mail name of the person you're addressing (on the To line) or copying (on the CC line), you can look it up by clicking either the To or CC button and choosing from a list like the one shown at the right.

Highlight the name you want, and click To or CC, as appropriate. If the person you want to send to is not on the currently displayed list, you can choose a different group from the drop-down list at the right of the Show Names From The section. If you're addressing someone new, you can add the person's name by clicking the New button. (For details on address lists, refer to the shaded box titled "Your Address Books.")

- The Subject line is, of course, where you type a header for your message. Try to make your header descriptive and relatively short; what you type here will be displayed in your recipient's Inbox.

- The remainder of the window is where you type your message, as described in the next section.

Rich but Guilt Free   You've probably read about or seen e-mail messages "customized" with symbols like :) or <grin> that add a little personality. That's because text-based e-mail systems don't allow much in the way of formatting. No longer. With Exchange it's not only your language that can be colorful. As you can see at the left, Exchange supports a great deal of formatting.

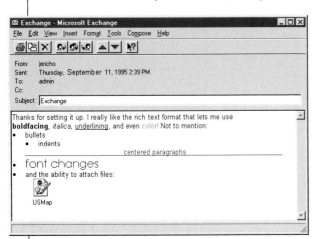

What you see in the illustration at the left is called *rich text format*, and it's a pleasure to use. To apply

FINDING A NAME
If you belong to a large postoffice, the list of possible recipients can be very long. To shorten your search for the correct person, type at least part of the person's name in the Type Name... box in the Address Book window and click the Find button. The highlight will jump to the first name that matches the characters you typed.

formatting, all you need are the buttons on the New Message window's toolbar.

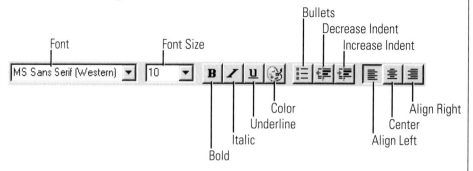

As you can see from the labels in the illustration, these toolbar buttons are self-explanatory. The only things you need to remember are:

- Click to depress the button to turn on a formatting feature; click again to "unpush" the button and turn it off.

- For character formatting, such as boldface or color, click the button before you type, or drag to select the text you want to format and then click the button.

- For paragraph formatting, such as centered or right alignment, place the vertical insertion point anywhere in the paragraph and click the button you want.

- To change fonts or font sizes, open the appropriate drop-down list and make your choice. If you haven't selected any text, the change will apply to whatever you type at the current insertion point. If you have selected text, the change will affect the selected portion only.

In composing and editing your message, it will also help to bear in mind that:

- Exchange will automatically break lines when they reach the right edge of the window. If one of your recipients informs you that the mail service you're sending to is character-based, however, and needs to find a carriage return or carriage return/linefeed character at the end of each line, end your lines by pressing Enter to keep them from breaking oddly on the recipient's screen.

- Ctrl+Home moves the insertion point to the beginning of your message.

- Ctrl+End moves the insertion point to the end of the message.

- Double-clicking a word selects the word. Triple-clicking selects a paragraph.

Inclusions and Attachments   If you want to include part or all of an existing document in an Exchange message, you can always use Cut or Copy and Paste, but there are a couple of other nifty ways to do this, too.

Use the Insert File paper clip on the New Message window's toolbar.

- Click the button, find the file in the Insert File window that opens, and either double-click the file or select it and click OK.

But remember OLE, too:

- If you want to send part of a document, open the document and open a New Message window (if it isn't already open). Arrange the windows on the screen, and then place the insertion point where you want the information inserted into your message. Now, select the information in the document, and then simply drag and drop into the message window. If you are using an OLE application, Exchange can even carry along formatting such as bullets and italics.

- If you want to send an entire file, open a window to the file or place the file on your desktop, and then drag and drop into the message.

Sending   When your message is all done and looking like perfection, what do you do to send it?

- Click the Send button on the toolbar, and your message is on its way.

End of story.

Checking for Mail   Sending e-mail is only half the story. Presumably, you get lots of it in return. By default, Exchange notifies you of new mail with a sound and a brief change in the look of the mouse pointer and then displays the subject of the new message in boldface within your Inbox. To open a new message:

- Double-click it.

By default, Exchange checks for new mail in your Microsoft Mail postoffice every 10 minutes. If you're expecting an important message and want to see if it has arrived or if you want to check a different information service, such as The Microsoft Network:

- Open the submenu for Deliver Now Using on the Tools menu, and choose the type of service you want to check. (If only one service is available, the menu command will be called simply Deliver Now.) If checking involves connecting to a service via modem, Exchange will handle that part of it for you too.

Viewing Other Messages   From within a message window, you can choose to view the previous or next message by clicking the buttons on the toolbar shown at the right.

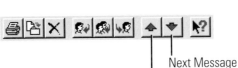

Next Message
Previous Message

NOT TOO BIG, PLEASE

Large files embedded in messages take up lots of room on a hard disk, which is where messages are stored. If you want to send a large file, such as a bitmap, and especially if you want to send it to a lot of people, take pity on the network and the machines on it. Instead of sending the file as an attachment, share the folder containing the document and use the Link Attachment To Original File option in the Insert File window. When you do that, the message will contain a pointer to the location of the file and the recipient will be able to open the version on *your* hard disk. Networks and postoffices, like freeways, can get clogged.

After you've read a message, Exchange continues to display it in your Inbox window but automatically changes the entry from boldfaced to normal characters.

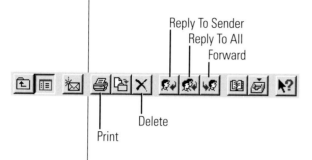

Reply To Sender
Reply To All
Forward

Delete

Print

Responding to Mail   Handling messages is almost as easy as reading them, thanks to these buttons on the toolbar in the Inbox window.

- Print obviously prints the message.

- Delete moves the message to the Deleted Items folder (which you can see in the left pane when you turn on View Folders). You don't get a warning about deleting here, because the message is really just being transferred to another location. If you delete from the Deleted Items folder, however, Exchange by default displays a warning asking if you're sure you want to delete. Deleting in Exchange is a lot like using the Recycle Bin on your desktop.

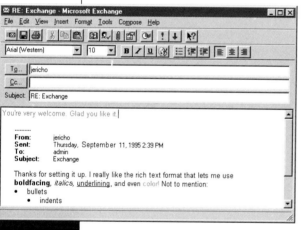

- Reply To Sender sends your response to the person on the From line of the message. Just click the button, and type your reply, as shown at the left.

  As you can see, you don't even have to worry about distinguishing your reply from the original message.

- Reply To All sends your response to everyone on the From, To, *and* CC lines of the message. If the original message was sent to a global *alias* (a nickname for a large group of people), use Reply To All only if such a response is warranted, as in "rumors of my demise have been greatly exaggerated." Many busy people do not want to be bothered by irrelevant responses along the lines of "ha, ha, very funny message." Nor do network administrators appreciate such junk mail clogging servers and network lines.

- Forward sends a copy of the message to the person whose e-mail name you enter on the To line of the message form that appears after you click the Forward button.

Personalizing Exchange

There are many ways to make Exchange truly your own—more than can really be covered here, but this section can at least hit some of the high spots. Browsing the Exchange menus and Exchange Help will clue you in to others that might be useful.

Creating Personal Folders   The left pane of the Exchange window, as you've seen, displays a "tree" of folders. At the top level is one labeled Personal Folders, which holds all the others. You can add to any part of the folder tree to set up an efficient filing system for your mail messages. All you need to do is:

1. Select the folder under which you want the new folder to appear.

2. Choose New Folder from the File menu.

3. Name the new folder.

Finding and Sorting Messages   One of the most frustrating things about e-mail, other than waiting for a message that doesn't come, is trying to find one or more messages you need to refer to. Perhaps it's a message you *know* you sent or received but about which you can remember very little. Or perhaps you want to see the set of messages about a certain subject. Exchange can help you out in two ways. First, the fast one:

- Click the header above the column you want to sort by, and Exchange will arrange your messages according to that criterion.

If that's not enough, Exchange also includes a Find command, which looks like the illustration at the right.

THE TOOLBAR

Exchange does not display a toolbar in the Find window by default, but there is one available. Open the View menu, and choose Toolbar to display it.

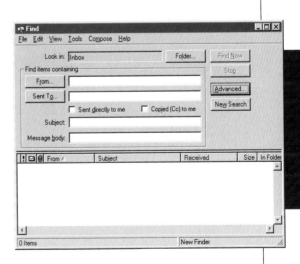

Most of these items are self-explanatory. You can search by location (folder), sender, subject, and so on. About the only entry that might give you pause is the one labeled Message Body. That's for filling in some unique string of text within the message that will help Find locate just the piece of e-mail you need—for example, the name of a company or an individual. If you want to narrow the search even further, click the Advanced button to specify only messages that fall within a range of sizes (in KB) or dates, only messages with attached files, only unread messages, and so on.

Whatever criteria you choose to search by, the rest is simple. Click the Find Now button, and Find will display the messages it found that match those criteria. If you're unsuccessful the first time or if Find locates too many files, click New Search to try again.

Customizing the Toolbar   As you've seen, the toolbars in Exchange are really useful. One nice feature you'll like is the ability to add additional tools for commands you often rely on. You can customize the toolbar in the main (Viewer) window and in the Send, Read, and Find windows. It's really easy too.

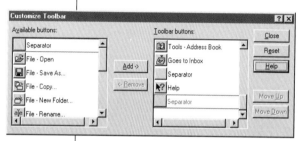

- In the window you want to customize, choose Tools Customize Toolbar. A window like the one at the left will open.

  The left list box shows buttons you can add; the right list box shows tools already on the toolbar.

When you add a tool, it appears on the toolbar at the left of whatever tool you select in the right list box, so:

1. In the *right* list box, click the tool that the new tool will precede.

2. In the *left* list box, click the tool you want to add.

3. Click the Add button.

If you want to separate a new group of tools from the others on the toolbar, add a Separator before and, if necessary, after the new group. If you want to rearrange the order of your tools, select the one you want to move and click the Move Up or Move Down button in the lower right corner of the window. (Move Up moves the button to the left on the toolbar; Move Down moves the button to the right.)

This is fun, so give it a try.

Creating and Administering a Postoffice

Windows 95 includes a workgroup version of the Microsoft Mail Server. If you are in charge of setting up a postoffice for your workgroup, this server is what you use to set up and administer a postoffice. Creating a postoffice involves a number of steps that are not difficult in and of themselves, but they do require you to create the postoffice, add authorized users, and set up (or help set up) the Exchange client on each user's computer. The following information summarizes the procedure to give you an idea of how to go about setting up a functional e-mail system for a (small) group of networked computers. The best source of step-by-step information, however, is the online

version of the *Microsoft Windows 95 Resource Kit,* which should be on your
Windows 95 CD-ROM and which you should review before starting.

1. The first step in setting up e-mail is to create a postoffice. To do this,
   open the Control Panel and double-click the Microsoft Mail Postoffice
   icon. This opens a Microsoft
   Workgroup Postoffice Admin
   wizard. Click the Create A New
   Workgroup Postoffice option,
   and fill in the information requested on the screens that follow.
   Enter the postoffice location,
   probably C:\, and then note the
   complete path to the postoffice,
   which will be something like
   C:\Wgpo0000 as shown at the
   right. Next, you'll be asked for
   some account details. At this
   point, you're creating an adminis-
   trative account, so you might
   want to name it something like
   "Admin" as a reminder.

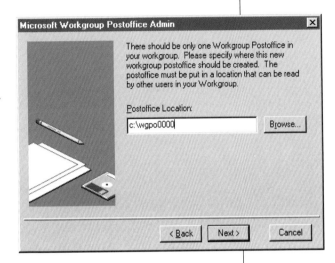

2. When you've created the postoffice, open My Computer, find your Postoffice folder, right-click, choose Sharing, and allow full access to the postoffice. You *must* do this, and you must provide *full* access so that people
   working at other machines can send and receive mail through the postoffice on your machine.

3. Return to the Control Panel, start the Microsoft Workgroup Postoffice
   Admin wizard again, and this time choose the Administer An Existing
   Workgroup Postoffice option. Enter the complete path to the postoffice,
   and then enter your administrator's account and password.

4. Now, add accounts for the people who will be sending e-mail through the
   postoffice—one account per person. (Only the administrator can do this,
   by the way.)

5. You must now set up Exchange on each user's computer. If Exchange is
   not yet installed on someone's computer, open the Control Panel and use
   the Windows Setup tab in the Add/Remove Programs window to install
   Exchange. On the desktop, double-click the icon and run the Microsoft
   Exchange Setup wizard, specifying the location of the postoffice, the user's
   name and password, and the names of additional information services
   (such as The Microsoft Network) that the person uses. Although you don't
   see any reference to it, this wizard is creating an Exchange *profile* for the

both a *Personal Information Store* (a database on disk that will be used to hold messages) and a Personal Address Book (for the individual's own list of e-mail recipients).

Satellite

Those are the basic steps involved. Later on, you can double-click the Microsoft Mail Postoffice icon in the Control Panel to add and remove users, change misremembered passwords, or back up the post-office. If you need to add or modify a profile on someone's computer, you can do so:

• By opening the Control Panel, double-clicking the Mail And Fax icon, and clicking the Show Profiles button.

• Or by choosing Options from the Tools menu in the Exchange window and then selecting the Services tab. (This lets you modify an existing profile only.)

Once you and other members of your workgroup have used Exchange for simple sending and receiving of messages, you'll find there's a lot more under the hood than can be described here. Exchange is intuitive and easy to navigate, however, so you shouldn't find yourself at a loss. Explore the commands on the Exchange menus, and swap discoveries with other people. Remember that you can always back out of a properties sheet or a set of configuration options by clicking the Cancel button. And remember, too, that Exchange includes its own detailed online Help, which you access not from the Start menu but from within the Exchange window. Enjoy your ability to communicate.

Introducing *The* Network: MSN

You may have read about it. Here it is: The Microsoft Network.

The Microsoft Network, or MSN, is the online information and e-mail service that you can join through Windows 95. MSN is a network, to be sure, but it's unlike those described so far in this chapter: it's subscription-based and accessible only by modem and telephone. In those respects, MSN more closely resembles CompuServe, America Online, or GEnie than it does a cabled-together corporate network.

Telecommunications

Modem

Microsoft Network

This final section of this chapter will take you on a quick tour of MSN. Bear in mind, however, that at the time this book was being written, MSN itself was also under development. What's the problem with that? Nothing. You'll see the basics here. But if you sign up and try it for yourself, what *you* see on The Microsoft Network will undoubtedly be richer and more satisfying than what this chapter can lead you to expect. More categories, more sources of information and entertainment…more of everything, including people with interests like yours.

Signing Up

To use The Microsoft Network you must sign up and become a member. This means you must have a functioning modem, you must install MSN (which is not installed by default), and, alas, you must have a credit card handy for billing purposes. Aside from this, joining MSN is a lot easier than joining the Army.

When Windows 95 is installed, its Setup program puts the icon at the right on your desktop. This icon enables Windows 95 to install the software that lets you set up, and later use, The Microsoft Network. If you decide to join, start the ball rolling by digging out your Windows 95 floppy disks or CD-ROM and then:

Set Up The Microsoft Network

- Double-click the "setup" icon.

From this point on, just follow the instructions on the screen.

When the needed software is installed and Windows 95 has been updated to reflect the installation, you'll be given the option of signing up for The Microsoft Network. If you choose to do so, Windows 95 walks you gently through the remainder of the process, even to the point of helping you set up a modem if you haven't already done so. (If you don't want to continue or if you're not sure you want to join, click Cancel; you can always change your mind later and sign up by clicking the Start button and choosing The Microsoft Network from the Programs submenu.)

During signup, Windows 95 connects you to MSN and displays a series of screens asking for your signup information. The only notable part of the first screen, other than the OK button, is the small check box in the lower left corner. If you've already joined MSN and are simply setting it up on a different computer, do not go through the signup process again. Click the box, and then click OK. MSN will set itself up with your existing account information.

INSTALLATION

The installation and signup procedure described here was accurate for The Microsoft Network at the time this book was written. Bear in mind, however, that MSN was still undergoing development, and it is possible that the signup procedure you go through will differ in some details. Information such as a member ID and a password, however, should be the same.

Telecommunications

Modem

Personal computer

Before you sign up, however, there are a couple of things you might want to think about:

- You'll be asked to provide a member ID. This can be any name you choose for yourself, but note that your ID will be your "moniker" on The Microsoft Network—the name people know you by. Think about how you want to be perceived, and then if you want, by all means go with BigDaddy, ProudMama, Cat_Hater, Dark_Vader, or whatever you choose.

- You'll also be asked for a password. Think this through too. If you don't want your kids to be able to connect whenever they want, make the password easy to remember but hard to guess, and don't click the Remember Password option when you connect for the first time.

- For your primary and backup access numbers, if possible, opt for the ones that are not only closest to you geographically but that match the speed of your modem. That is, if you have a 14.4 modem, don't choose a 2400 bps connection just because that's the first one you see in the list.

Security

The Microsoft Network, like any online service, is security conscious. At its most visible, this security is apparent each time you double-click to connect: MSN will not log you on until it has validated your member ID and your password. Although you can't see it, there's deeper security involved, too. The network:

- Protects the confidentiality of data—including your credit card number—and any monetary transactions that take place.

- Meets government standards for export to other countries.

- Requires member IDs that are unique within MSN.

- Does not reuse a member's ID for 12 months after someone terminates membership. (This is to avoid cases of mistaken identity.)

- Maintains a list of people who have been denied access to MSN and refuses to allow them to log on.

Connecting

Once you've joined MSN, all you do to connect is double-click the network's desktop icon. Starting up might take a minute or two because MSN always verifies your account and password before actually connecting you to the network. The first time you connect, you'll see a small modem icon and an MSN icon on the taskbar, as well as two MSN windows. One, titled Welcome, looks like the illustration on the following page.

The second window, known as MSN Central, is more functional. MSN Central looks like the illustration at the right.

And it's where you start your journey into the various bulletin boards(BBSs), chat sessions, and other services available on MSN.

You can simply close this window if you want to. The next time you connect to MSN, this window will be replaced by the MSN Today window, described below.

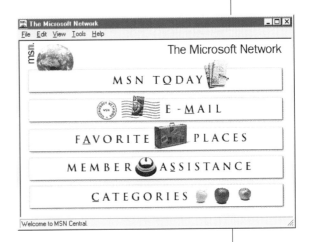

Looking Around

To actually go somewhere, click one of the labeled buttons in the MSN Central window. MSN Today provides a calendar of events and information on obtaining member assistance. As you would expect, clicking E-Mail takes you to the familiar Exchange Inbox window, from which you can exchange e-mail messages with any member of The Microsoft Network, as well as with individuals on other online services, including the Internet. The Favorite Places button, as you'll see a little later, opens a customizable window in which you can collect—and thus easily return to—your favorite spots on MSN.

Member Assistance, which you might want to check out when you first join, takes you to a window that looks (looked) something like the one at the right.

The Kiosk (like those in other areas) downloads a file of information about the Member Assistance area. The other folder icons take you further into

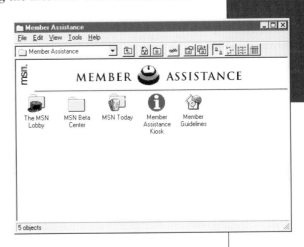

Member Assistance. Use them in the same way you open any folders to see the subfolders and files they contain.

The most interesting button in the MSN Central window, however, has got to be Categories. Click it, and you enter the core of MSN—the place where you can find forums (topics) on everything from pets to pop culture. In these forums, you'll have access to:

- Bulletin boards (BBSs) on which people exchange messages about topics that interest them.

- Chat rooms, where people send messages to one another live and in real time.

Depending on the forum and what it contains, you might also find file libraries, related Internet newsgroups (text-based Internet BBSs on the same subject), and of course, kiosks telling you about the forum and how to move around in it.

So what does a forum look like? Here's one, as it existed in June 1995.

What you see will undoubtedly be much richer.

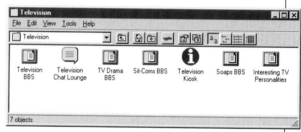

Navigating MSN

MSN is built around a "tree" structure that closely resembles the folder/subfolder trees you create on your own disks. The only difference is that in MSN each forum represented by a folder is controlled by a *provider* who is responsible for organizing and maintaining that portion of the network.

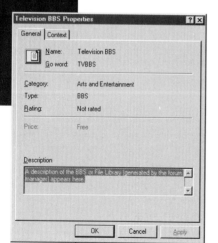

Going To The easiest way of exploring the MSN tree is, obviously, to continue double-clicking icons until you reach a BBS, chat, or other feature you want to poke around in for awhile. Once you've found a forum you like, here are some ways to help you revisit the same place quickly:

- Right-click the icon, and choose Properties. Make note of the Go Word shown at the top of the properties sheet, like the one at the left.

When you want to return to the same place, right-click the MSN icon on the taskbar, choose Go To, and type the Go Word for the service you want.

- Or right-click the icon, and choose Create Shortcut. In just a few seconds, MSN will create a shortcut to that location and place it on your desktop. When you want to return to the location, double-click the desktop icon. Windows 95 will start MSN and, when you're logged on, take you to the service you requested.

- Or right-click the icon, and choose Add To Favorite Places. When you do this, MSN adds the icon to your Favorite Places window. To return to the location, either click the Favorite Places button in the MSN Central window or right-click the MSN icon on the taskbar and choose Favorite Places. Either way, the Favorite Places window will open, and you can then double-click the icon for the place you want to go to.

Going Back   Because it's just as easy to click your way deep into MSN as it is to click down through multiple subfolder levels on your hard disk, the first thing to learn is how to get back to MSN Central. You can do it any time by:

- Placing the mouse pointer on the MSN icon on the taskbar, right-clicking, and choosing Go To MSN Central.

A better way to travel, however, is to turn on the MSN toolbar by choosing View Toolbar. When you do so, you can pinpoint your location in the network tree, as shown at the right.

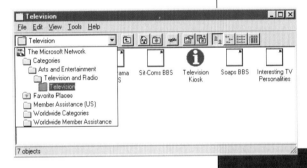

You can use the list to jump to another part of the network, and you can use the toolbar buttons to go to MSN Central or to work with your favorite places.

Leaving MSN

When you want to leave The Microsoft Network, you must disconnect. This is easy to do:

- From any window except MSN Today, choose Sign Out from the File menu.

- Right-click the MSN icon on the taskbar, and choose Sign Out.

- Close every open MSN window, or click the Sign Out button on the toolbar.

However you decide to sign off, the window at the right appears.

Click Yes, and MSN will neatly disconnect you. And speaking of disconnecting, this is where the chapter must leave you to your own exploration of The Microsoft Network.

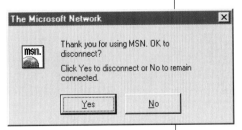

Long-Distance Information

In the beginning, personal computers sat on desktops, crunching numbers and clicking to themselves. They were pretty isolated. Modems were high-tech and not all that common. They were not all that fast, either—the average early-eighties modem sent and received information at a rate of about 40 characters per second, compared with 1800 or more today. Well, that's all history. These days, practically everyone has a modem, and the desktop computer or its portable counterpart that

sits in isolated splendor will eventually be a thing of the past. As indicated in the previous chapter, a great many people have already met the I-way and have found that it is them. And more are taking to the digital high road every month.

The upshot of these changes is that computing is becoming virtually virtual. The distinction between local and remote is blurring, and as you've seen from Network Neighborhood connections, it often doesn't matter whether a file or even a program is here on "My Computer" or there on "Your Computer." Software like Microsoft Windows 95 makes the difference negligible, if not immaterial.

This same virtuosity is softening the impact of larger geographic separations too. Given a modem and a phone line (and a receptive machine at the other end, of course), people are finding that making a computer-to-computer connection is no more stressful than calling Aunt Minnie in Mineola. And many, many people these days routinely send faxes or take their computers traveling with them, whether around the world or to and from the workplace. Regardless of the message sent, the road traveled, or the distance called, Windows 95 both recognizes and supports a long-distance lifestyle. Whether you call—or travel—for work, school, or pleasure, Windows 95 has a lot to offer in the way of helping you compute, transfer information, and communicate with anyone, anywhere.

Ready, Set, Connect

When you connect two computers so they can share information, you must, of course, have some physical way to move data between them. Somewhat nostalgic but still quite usable is the good old eighties sneakernet, in which people passed computer files on floppies hand-to-hand. (Of course, being a careful and ethical individual, you would copy only data files and shareware—no bootlegged software. And you'd check for viruses on a regular basis, especially if you were introducing your innocent hard disk to a gregarious floppy that's been known to get around.)

As the preceding chapter described, a much more "nineties" way of transferring information is via a network connection. Both the connections you can make with the Find command and the resource-equals-disk variety you can create by mapping a network drive make sharing information on a network particularly easy. No need to go into that anymore here though.

In addition to floppies and networks, you can also rely on either or both of two other features: Direct Cable Connection and Dial-Up Networking. With a *direct cable connection,* you use a serial or parallel computer cable to create a cheap but effective mini-network of two computers. Direct cable connection requires the computers to be pretty close physically, but it's really handy when you use more than one computer, and it's especially useful when the two computers are your primary desktop machine and your portable computer. (If you're familiar with MS-DOS version 6 and you think direct cable connection sounds like Interlnk, you're right; it *is* Interlnk, fancied up for Windows 95.)

Dial-up networking means that you use your modem and the phone system to tap into a remote computer and any shared resources it holds. Dial-up networking is the legal version of what "hackers" do when they invade remote systems, but in your case, dialing in to a remote computer is a convenience. In the hacker's case, it's…well, sneaky. And illegal.

Both direct cable connection and dial-up networking are covered in this chapter—direct cable connection immediately following because you might need it to use Windows 95's eminently luggable Briefcase, and dial-up networking in a later section titled "Calling Home."

Hardwiring a Host

Windows 95's direct cable connection lets you siphon files from one computer to another by "hardwiring" the two together with either a serial or parallel cable (similar to your printer cable). When you connect two computers in this way, the machine providing files is called the *host*; the one taking advantage of the largesse is the *guest*. To make direct cable connection work properly, it's important to understand the difference between host and guest because you have to decide, in advance, which role each computer is to play. Just remember that the connection is like a one-way street, and you'll always send your files in the right direction. In the case of a desktop machine and a portable, that might be from the desktop (host) to the portable (guest).

After you decide which computer is the host and which the guest, there are three things you should do before you actually set up direct cable connection:

- Get a cable. (If you don't know a null modem from a hole in the ground, check the information in the shaded box headed "First, Cable Me.")

- Check which *protocols* are installed on both computers. This is not as hard as it sounds. To provide you with direct cable connection, Windows 95 also installs dial-up networking, a special "device" called a Dial-Up Adapter, and certain protocols that help computers communicate. To work correctly, direct cable connection requires either or both of two protocols: IPX/SPX-compatible, which enables you to transfer files from the host to the guest, and NetBEUI, which enables the host computer to gain access to a network. If either or both of these protocols are already installed on the host and guest computers and if they are *bound* (linked) to the Dial-Up Adapter, you're home free. To check:

  1. Open the Control Panel, and double-click the Network icon. If possible, do this on both the host and the guest at the same time so that you can compare what you see next.

  2. When the Network window opens on each, check the list at the top of the Configuration tab—the list under *The following network components are installed.* Look for IPX/SPX-compatible and, if necessary, NetBEUI. If the protocols are correctly installed, click Cancel to close the Network window. If you need to add a protocol, click the Add button, click Protocol in the Component Type window, click Add again, choose your network type, click the protocol you need, and click OK. Windows 95 should automatically handle binding for you, but if you want to double-check, click Dial-Up Adapter, click Properties, click the Bindings tab, and verify that the protocol you need is checked in the list box.

- Share a folder or two on the host so that the guest will have something to look at when you establish the connection. (How to share folders was covered in the preceding chapter under "Making Files Available.")

INSTALLING VS. USING

Setting up a direct cable connection is not the same as installing the feature. You *install* the ability to use direct cable connection either during setup or by using the Add/Remove Programs tool in the Control Panel, as described in Chapter 12. You *set up* and *use* a direct cable connection as described here, with the help of a wizard that you launch by opening the Start menu and working your way through the Programs submenu to the Direct Cable Connection command on the Accessories submenu. This section of the chapter assumes that direct cable connection is already installed on your desktop computer and your portable. If it is not, refer to Chapter 12.

First, Cable Me

What you want for a direct cable connection is either a serial null-modem cable or one of the following types of parallel cables: Standard or Basic 4-bit cable; Extended Capabilities Port (ECP) cable, which requires an ECP-enabled parallel port, which, in turn, must be provided for in your computer's BIOS chip (and which you should be able to check on in your computer's documentation); or a Universal Cable Module (UCM) cable, which allows you to connect different types of parallel ports. Serial cables are slower than parallel cables but can carry signals over longer distances. If your computers are around 6 feet apart or less, either type of cable will do. If the machines are more than 6 feet apart, opt for the serial variety.

If you don't know about different types of cables—and not many people do—the easiest way out of this acronymic thicket is to see if you have an available serial port on each computer you want to connect. If you do, you can go to your local computer store and ask for a null-modem cable, which is inexpensive (in the $10 range), relatively easy to find, and simple to plug in.

The type of cable you choose will, of course, require matching ports on both computers—serial and serial or parallel and parallel. There's no foolproof advice that describes what to do with every possible type of computer, but a fairly close look at the back of the machine will often help you figure out what you've got:

- Most computers come with a single parallel port, which is commonly identified by an embossed icon representing a printer or, possibly, the label LPTx (where x is a number, probably 1). If your printer is plugged into such a connection, you obviously have a parallel port and equally obviously it is in use. If the port is free, a parallel cable will do fine.

- Serial ports generally come in twos and are identified by icons labeled either 1010 or COMx (where x is a number, usually 1 or 2). If you have one or more free serial ports, a null-modem cable will work for you.

If you're comfortable with hardware and with Windows 95, you can, instead, try the following: right-click My Computer, choose Properties, click the Device Manager tab, and click the View Devices By Connection option. You'll see your COM and LPT ports listed, as well as all devices connected to your computer. Unfortunately, however, it's up to you to know which devices are serial, which are parallel, and which are plugged into dedicated ports, such as a mouse port. Because computers and their attached devices vary widely, this book can't help you further except to say that (1) you probably have two serial ports on each machine and (2) if you run into trouble, the best place to turn will be either someone you know or your hardware dealer.

PROTOCOLS

When computers communicate with one another, they follow certain rules called *protocols*. These protocols, like those used by diplomats, describe appropriate behavior that enables the machines to get along without getting confused, losing information, or trying to transmit at the same time. Protocols are complex and have high-tech names like TCP/IP, NetBEUI (pronounced "net booey" or "net byooey"), and IPX/SPX. You don't have to know the details of any protocols to use them, but as mentioned in the text here and in online Help's troubleshooting, you might have to install a protocol or two to get some communication going. Don't be scared. Just follow instructions carefully, and avoid experimenting with settings you don't understand or are not told to alter.

Running the Wiz

To set up a direct cable connection, you run a little wizard on each machine. There's really nothing to it, as long as you've established which is the host and which is the guest. Here's all you do:

1. Cable the computers together.

2. On the *host* computer, open the Start menu and the Programs submenu, and choose Direct Cable Connection from the Accessories submenu. You'll see the wizard shown below.

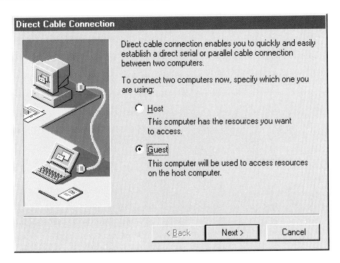

   Click the Host option button, and then click Next.

3. When the following screen appears, click the port you're using.

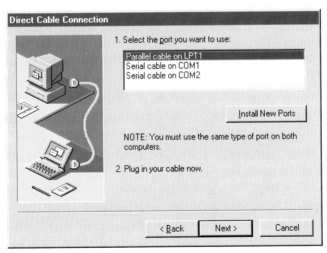

(Even though step 2 on this screen tells you to plug in your cable, it's OK to have done it already.) Click Next.

4. The screen shown below appears.

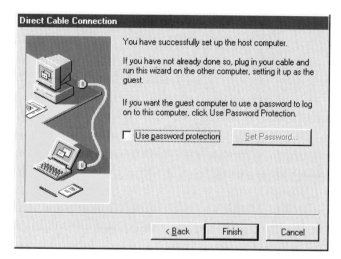

Click the check box, and type a password if you want. Click Finish when you're ready, and you'll soon be rewarded with the following message.

(During setup, to avoid a message telling you the guest hasn't arrived, click the Close button to shut down direct cable connection on the host while you set up the guest.)

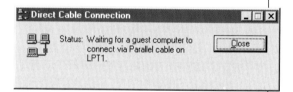

ROLE REVERSAL
Just because you set up one computer as host and the other as guest doesn't mean they're forever restricted to those roles. Any time you want to change the configuration, all you have to do is choose Direct Cable Connection and click the Change button on the opening screen. Doing so will take you back into the setup wizard described in this chapter. Mix and match whenever you want. Just be sure not to set up both computers as host or guest. They'll never start a relationship that way.

Setting up direct cable connection on the guest computer is almost exactly like the procedure outlined above, except that you specify *guest* on the opening screen of the wizard and you aren't prompted to assign an optional password. To make life easy, before you click the Finish button on the guest:

1. On the host computer, choose Direct Cable Connection from the Accessories submenu, and then click Listen on the opening screen. That's all you ever have to do to enable the host to share its files.

2. On the guest computer, click Finish.

In the future, when you want to connect the guest to the host, choose Direct Cable Connection from the Accessories submenu and then click the Connect button on the opening screen.

As soon as a connection is established between the two computers, you'll see a window showing all shared folders on the host. Use them just as if they were folders on the guest. If for some reason you close the window to the host, you can open the window again simply by clicking the View Host button in the Direct Cable Connection window on the guest computer.

Troubleshooting

If you walk through the direct cable connection setup flawlessly but the connection doesn't work, it could be that your cable is damaged, or the computers are not being nice about sharing files, or they aren't using the same protocol. Windows 95 can't determine exactly what's wrong, but it does offer aid and succor for the most common situations. Yell for Help:

1. Open Windows 95 Help, click the Index tab, and type *direct*.

2. When Help jumps to the index topics on direct cable connection, double-click *troubleshooting*.

3. Answer the questions that appear in the Help window. They look like the ones in the window at the right.

Some of the instructions, such as adding a network protocol, cover topics that aren't among the easiest to understand, but don't worry about having to know everything. The instructions are very clear and should help you get your direct cable connection going. If you still don't succeed, remember that telephone assistance is available from Microsoft if you're a registered Windows 95 user. If you use the Microsoft Network, you might also find help there.

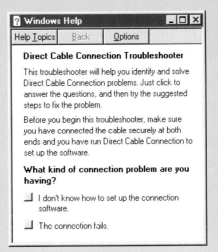

The Windows 95 Briefcase

If you're an experienced computer user, you've probably been in a situation where you copied a valuable file onto a floppy and took the file to another computer, where you modified said file and saved the edited version under the same name as that of the original you copied. Then came a time, perhaps a week or a month later, when you had to figure out which version of the document was the one you needed. It probably wasn't much fun.

Windows 95 eliminates such minor (or major) headaches in several ways. You can, if you remember to do so, use a long filename to identify the changed version of the document. Or you can check the file's properties sheet to find out when it was created, last modified, and last accessed. If you think ahead, you can create a copy of the original on the same disk or in the same folder and depend on Windows 95 to identify the copy for you. Or...you can use the Windows 95 Briefcase, which makes life really easy when you transport files from place to place.

What It Is

In essence, Windows 95's Briefcase makes the most of the difference between "home base" and "home away from home." Briefcase bridges the gap between the two. With it, you can keep a primary set of documents on your main computer and a working set on the other. When you alter the copy in either the primary set *or* the working set, all you need is a single mouse click to *synchronize* the two so that the unmodified version is updated to reflect all changes in the modified copy of the file. Briefcase is a really nice feature of Windows 95. If you move files from one computer to another, use it. It beats the heck out of transferring document revisions by hand.

If You Want (or Need) More than One

Once you've installed Briefcase, you need never install it again, even if you decide you need more than one Briefcase—say, if you want to pack My Briefcase with papers for Client A and you want a separate Briefcase for Client B. Whenever you want to, you can create another Briefcase on the desktop, in any folder you choose, or on a floppy disk (a particularly handy choice if you don't have a portable and you want to take work home with you).

To create a Briefcase on the desktop:

1. Right-click any blank part of the desktop.

2. Choose New from the popup menu, and then click Briefcase on the submenu.

To create a Briefcase in a folder or on a floppy disk:

1. Open a window to the disk or folder where you want to store the new Briefcase.

2. Either choose File New Briefcase on the menu bar or right-click any blank part of the window and choose New Briefcase from the popup menu.

No matter where you create a Briefcase and no matter how many Briefcases you create, you don't have to worry about keeping them straight. The one and only Briefcase named *My* Briefcase is the one Windows 95 creates when it installs the Briefcase accessory. When you create a second Briefcase, Windows 95 names it *New* Briefcase. If you create additional Briefcases in the same location, Windows 95 numbers the newcomers New Briefcase (2), New Briefcase (3), and so on, as you can see in the window at the left.

Oh, and don't forget that you can personalize your desktop objects by renaming them. My Briefcase is OK, as are My Computer and Network Neighborhood. But,

HAVE YOU GOT IT?

In order to use Briefcase, you have to install it. Installation happens automatically during Setup (the program that sets up Windows 95 on your computer) if you choose the Portable Setup option or if you choose a Custom Setup and specify (under Accessories) that you want to install Briefcase. You can easily tell if you've got Briefcase: if it's there, it's sitting right on your desktop as an icon labeled My Briefcase. If you don't have it and you think you want it, refer to Chapter 12 for help on installing Windows 95 options.

as described in Chapter 5, "Taking Care of Business," you can easily rename any of these icons by clicking the name and typing a new one. Or you can use the Home, End, Del, Insert, and direction keys to edit the old name. So go ahead. There's no reason My Briefcase can't become Gucci, Pucci, or Duffel Bag. Have some fun. You'll enjoy Windows 95 all the more for it.

Using Floppy Disks

Floppy disks provide a neat and easily transportable means of carrying a Briefcase between two computers. Floppies, however, do have a limited amount of storage—1.44 MB, for example, on a high-density 3.5-inch floppy. One way to develop a more capacious Briefcase is to use Windows 95's DriveSpace compression feature, which uses some digital wizardry to pack more data into the same physical amount of storage space.

If you're familiar with version 6.0 or later of MS-DOS, you might already be familiar with DriveSpace (or an earlier version called DoubleSpace). Drive-Space works under Windows 95 much as it did under MS-DOS, but it is prettier and easier to use and does not require you to compress your hard disk before you attempt to compress floppies. DriveSpace is installed by default during a Typical setup, so chances are good that it's on your Accessories sub-menu under System Tools.

To use DriveSpace to compress a floppy, here's what to do:

1. Open the Start menu, and work through Programs, Accessories, and System Tools. Click DriveSpace.

2. When the DriveSpace window opens, click the floppy drive containing the disk you want to compress.

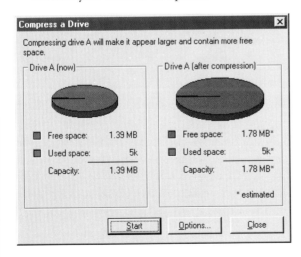

3. Open the Drive menu. Choose Compress, and you'll see the window shown at the left.

4. Click Start, and click Compress Now when Windows 95 asks if you're sure about this. From that point, sit back and let DriveSpace do the rest (which will take a few minutes).

HOW USABLE IS IT?

Once a disk is compressed, the compression becomes invisible to you. Windows 95 treats the disk just as it would treat any other disk. It's important to note, however, that the disk can only be used on another computer that understands DriveSpace. If you're considering using compression, read up on it in Chapter 12, "Disks, Controls, and Other Delights." In addition, bear in mind that compressing a disk that contains files linked to a Briefcase will break the connections. You won't damage or lose the files, but you will have to reestablish the connections by repacking the Briefcase.

Packing Up

Once you have a Briefcase available, all you have to do is pack up by dragging the files into the Briefcase. The only point of confusion you're likely to encounter here is remembering that the Briefcase you drag *to* should be the one you're going to take with you. Such a warning sounds so obvious as to be silly, but there's a good reason for it. Suppose you have one Briefcase on your primary computer and another on the portable you want to take with you. When you're packing, your tendency will probably be to pack the Briefcase on your primary computer, won't it? No—wrong Briefcase. The one you pack is the one on the portable.

Dragging Folders

If you're putting folders in a Briefcase, using the *right* mouse button to drag allows you to be more selective than simply dragging with the left button. Suppose, for example, you want to take along a folder that contains subfolders you won't need. Or suppose you want only files of certain types—for example, those with the extensions DOC, XLS, and BMP but not those with the extensions EXE, BAS, or BAT. No problem.

Select the folder you want, and drag with the right mouse button. You'll see a popup menu offering you two choices: Make Sync Copy and Make

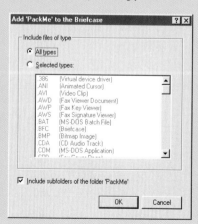

Sync Copy Of Type. Make Sync Copy automatically copies everything in the folder, including all subfolders and their contents. But here's the good part: Make Sync Copy Of Type lets you sort through the folder and take along only what you need. When you choose this command, the window below opens.

- To take all the files in the folder but leave the subfolders at home, leave the All Types radio button selected and click to remove the check mark in the Include Subfolders... check box.

- To take files of certain types, click the Selected Types radio button and then click the extensions you want in the list box. (Yes, you can select more than one extension.) Use the Include Subfolders... check box as described above to specify whether you want to include all subfolders.

This is an admirable feature of Windows 95—one to make you smile.

But start with the easiest packing job. Suppose you have a Briefcase on your Windows 95 desktop and you want to fill it with files and carry them off on a floppy disk. Simple. All you do is:

1. Place a floppy—regular or compressed—in the floppy drive.

2. Drag whatever files you want to take with you into the Briefcase on your desktop.

3. Drag the Briefcase to the floppy disk.

4. Pop out the floppy, put it in your (real) briefcase, and off you go.

If you already have a Briefcase on a floppy, you can pack additional files into it simply by dragging them to the existing Briefcase on the floppy.

If you're dragging to the Briefcase on a portable, the process of moving files from your primary machine to that Briefcase requires a little more logistical support in the form of either a network connection or a direct cable connection. Cruising a network was described in the preceding chapter; Windows 95's direct cable connection is in the earlier section headed "Hardwiring a Host."

Once you've got the connection, however, moving files to the Briefcase on a portable is a piece of cake:

1. On the host computer, share the folder or folders containing the files you want to pack into your Briefcase.

2. On the guest computer, open a window to the shared folders.

3. Drag the files or folders you want to the Briefcase on the portable.

4. Pack up the portable and go. (Well, disconnect from the host first.)

Changing and Synchronizing Files

When you put files in a Briefcase, you leave them there. Only if you leave a file in a Briefcase can Windows 95 keep track of whether the file has changed and, at your request, update the original to match. To work with files in a Briefcase, you:

1. Open the Briefcase.

2. Open the file and make your changes.

3. Save the file back to the Briefcase.

4. Synchronize the changed version with the original as described below.

When you're ready to update the original to match the version in the Briefcase, first check to be sure the disk or folder on a host or network computer containing the original is shared. If it is not, Windows 95 will not be able to find and synchronize the copy with the original. (If you don't leave disks or

ONE WAY TO TELL IF YOU DID IT RIGHT

If you're using direct cable connection between a desktop and a laptop, there's an easy way to tell if you made the correct decision about which machine should be the host and which the guest. Start direct cable connection on both machines, open the Briefcase on the guest, and drag a shared file into it from the host. If guest and host are correctly set up, you'll see the words *Up-to-date* in the status column in the Briefcase window. If your guest and host should be reversed, you'll see the word *Orphan* in the Briefcase window. In that case, restart the direct cable connection wizard, click the Change button on the Settings screen, and swap host and guest.

folders permanently shared, enabling sharing is easy to forget before you try to synchronize files.) Next:

1. Depending on how you originally made the Briefcase available, either establish the appropriate network connection, cable the machines, and start direct cable connection, or place the floppy containing the Briefcase in the computer's drive.

2. Double-click the Briefcase to open it and see its contents. The resulting window will look something like the one shown below.

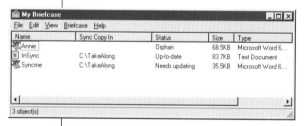

The Status column tells you which files are up-to-date and which need updating. (Files identified as *orphans* are new files in the Brief-case that are not yet associated with an original on another disk or computer.)

- To update all files that need updating, choose Update All from the Briefcase menu.

- To update only certain files, select them and choose Update Selection from the Briefcase menu. Remember, you can select either by dragging a "lasso" around the filenames or by holding down Ctrl or Shift as you click filenames.

Whichever command you choose, Windows 95 displays a window like the one shown below to let you know what needs to be done.

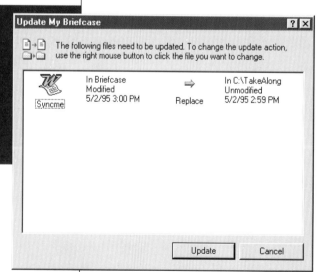

Most of the time, you'll probably just click the Update button to tell Windows 95 to go ahead. But Briefcase is more flexible than it first appears, as you can tell by reading the fine print at the top of the window, which tells you to use the right mouse button if you want to change the update action—for example, if you want to throw away the changes in the Briefcase version of a file and revert to the original. The window on the following page is what Briefcase offers when you right-click a file in the Update window.

Nice, isn't it?

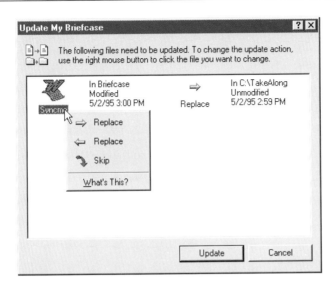

Want More Copies?

You can keep copies of the same file in more than one Briefcase. Synchronizing one copy, however, does not automatically synchronize them all. Windows 95 follows only the path to the location the Briefcase copy came from. It does not search for all existing Briefcase copies of the same file. So synchronizing copies in several Briefcases and eventually synchronizing all those versions with the original file is like working back

through a chain of dominoes: tip the last into the one that preceded it, and keep going until you get to the original file. For example, synchronize Briefcase 4 with Briefcase 3; synchronize Briefcase 3 with Briefcase 2; synchronize Briefcase 2 with Briefcase 1; and, finally, synchronize Briefcase 1 with the original version of the file. Or just keep things simple, and carry only a single traveling copy of the file.

Cutting the Tie that Binds

If you want to dissolve the union between the original version of a file and the copy in a Briefcase, it's easy:

1. Select the file or folder you want to be independent of the original.

2. In the Briefcase window, choose Split From Original from the Briefcase menu. Windows 95 will prompt with a message like the one at the right.

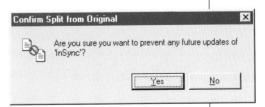

Click Yes to confirm the split, but be sure you want to do this. Unlike most other editing actions, a split cannot be undone by choosing Undo from the Edit menu. If you confirm the split, the file or folder is listed in the Briefcase window as an orphan.

Keeping Your Briefcase Organized

Working with files in a Briefcase can quickly become second nature because Windows 95 makes the difference between Briefcase and any other resource on your computer so transparent. You should remember, though, that the role of Briefcase is not only to make your computing more portable but to help you synchronize copies of files. Because of synchronization, you have to be a little more careful about how you work with files. The following list offers a few tips:

- If you rename a file in a Briefcase, the file becomes an orphan. A better way to go about renaming a file is to rename the original, drag it into the Briefcase again, and then delete the (Briefcase) version with the old name. Be sure to synchronize files before doing this to avoid losing any changes.

- If you recycle a file from a Briefcase and then realize you want it back, dragging from the Recycle Bin to the Briefcase doesn't work. Choose the Restore command from the Recycle Bin's File menu. (And remember: you can recover deleted files from a hard disk only. Be careful about deleting from a Briefcase on a floppy.)

- If you create a file in a Briefcase, it is created as an orphan and will not be updated when you synchronize the files in the Briefcase. You can, however, remove the orphan status and add the file to the traveling crew as follows:

  1. Drag the orphan file from the Briefcase to the disk or folder where you want it permanently stored.

  2. Drag the file from the disk or folder *back* to the Briefcase.

  3. Choose Yes when Windows 95 asks you if you want to replace the file in the Briefcase.

Or you can take another approach:

- The trick here is to keep at least one folder in the Briefcase. Then you can skip all the preceding steps but still guarantee that any new file you create will be added to the host and can be synchronized whenever you want, just like any others you place in the Briefcase. Here's what to do:

  1. If possible, drag a shared folder to the Briefcase you want to use—if necessary, create a new folder on your host computer, share it, and drag it to the Briefcase. (Remember that any new files you create will have to remain in the folder you save them to, so try to plan ahead.)

2. When you create a new file, save it inside this folder in the Briefcase (or inside any other folder in the Briefcase).

3. To add the new file to the host computer, select the file and choose Update Selection from the Briefcase menu.

   As simply as that, Windows 95 will transfer the new file to the folder on your host computer.

You will no doubt find many more ways to work with Briefcase, but you have enough to get comfortably started. Now, it's on to keeping in touch.

Calling Home

Dial-up networking is the way you reach out across the miles and touch an electronic pal from your desktop at work or at home. Where direct cable connection gives you an instant network via a hardware umbilical cord, dial-up networking provides the same type of connectivity with the help of a modem and a telephone line. Dial-up networking, though very complex internally, is simple to use:

1. Define the connection you want to make—that is, tell Windows 95 what number to call.

2. Make the call.

3. Use Network Neighborhood to find, look at, and use shared resources on the computer you called.

The only trick is to be sure the computer you're calling is turned on, able to answer the phone, and able to act as a server (about which there's information in the shaded box titled "Service, Please").

Defining a Connection

If you've ever had to define a modem connection prior to Windows 95, you'll really appreciate the ease with which you can do the same thing with Windows 95's Dial-Up Networking wizard. Gone are the old days of having to specify start bits, stop bits, transmission speed, and so on.

These days, you simply choose Dial-Up Networking from the Accessories submenu. Then:

1. Double-click the Make New Connection icon. Doing this starts one of the Windows wizards.

2. On the next screen (shown at the top of the following page), type a name— any name you like—for the connection you want to define. In the illustration, the connection is being named *JetStream*.

ANYONE CAN DO IT

Defining a dial-up connection is so easy that a child... or even an adult... can do it. Windows 95 doesn't even care if you haven't yet told it about your modem. When you choose Dial-Up Networking, if Windows 95 doesn't find a modem, it automatically opens the Install Modem wizard for you. And since Windows 95 does most of the work of finding out about and installing a modem, your role in joining the tele-commuting tele-computing community entails little more than clicking the mouse on request. It's great.

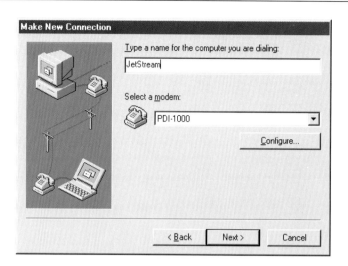

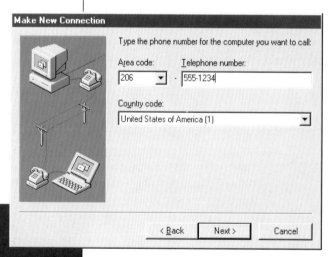

3. On the next screen (shown at the left), type the area code and the phone number you want to call. If necessary, select the country code for the country you're calling.

4. Click Next, click Finish on the final wizard screen, and you're off to the races.

And after you've defined a connection, Windows 95 puts an icon for it in a Dial-Up Networking folder. (If you've joined The Microsoft Network, you'll notice icons for the primary and backup connections. If you want, you can use these to connect to MSN.)

To open a window to the folder:

- Choose Dial-Up Networking from the Accessories submenu.

- Or open My Computer and double-click the Dial-Up Networking folder.

Either way, you see a window like the one shown at the right.

- To call a number, double-click the icon for its connection.

- To define a new connection, double-click the Make New Connection icon and step through the same procedure outlined above.

If you do a lot of connecting, remember that you can keep Dial-Up Networking at your fingertips by dragging the Dial-Up Networking folder either to the desktop (to create a shortcut) or to the Start button (to add dial-up networking to the top of the Start menu).

If You Can't Connect

Although dial-up networking, like installing a modem and using many other parts of Windows 95, is as easy to use as has ever been the case with operating systems and computers, it's also true that hardware, software, and Mother Nature can combine to make the process somewhat less than breezy. Sometimes cables come loose. Sometimes the calling and receiving modems aren't in sync. Sometimes people try to use the wrong communications ports, or they mistakenly set up incorrect communications protocols. If you run into problems communicating, there is a place to turn: Windows 95 Help. Specifically, start Help, choose the Index tab, and go to the Troubleshooting section listed under *dialing another computer*. As with problems that arise with direct cable connection, this troubleshooting guide provides a question-and-answer session to help you through common problems. If that doesn't succeed, remember Microsoft's Product Support Services. They can usually help you out, even with tough hardware or software puzzles.

TALK ABOUT SMART

After you've connected to a remote resource, Windows 95 is so clever that if you try to reconnect to that resource without first activating dial-up networking, Windows 95 automatically asks if you want to make the connection. This prompt also appears when you try to connect to a remote resource while working in an application. If you want, you can turn off the prompt by opening the Dial-Up Networking window, choosing Settings from the Connections menu, and then clicking the Don't Prompt To Use Dial-Up Networking option in the window that appears. Not much point in doing so, though, unless you really want to be the independent type.

Once You've Dialed Up...

All you do is pretend that the remote computer is really part of your own computer. You can, of course, access only shared resources on the remote machine, but assuming you've got all the necessary permissions, simply head toward your Network Neighborhood:

- If you don't want to treat the shared resource as if it were a separate drive on your local machine, right-click Network Neighborhood and use Find Computer to locate the computer. (Or choose Find Computer from the Start menu.)

- If you want to treat the shared resource as if it were a drive on your computer, right-click Network Neighborhood and use the Map Network Drive command, specifying the name of the computer and the name of the shared folder you want to use—for example, *jetstream**pilot*.

Dial-Up or HyperTerminal?

When you call up another computer, you might sometimes wonder whether you should use dial-up networking or HyperTerminal, which also lets you connect to remote computers. Dial-up networking, like direct cable connection, is something like your own personal version of networking software. Use it when you want to connect to another machine, such as your desktop computer, to access shared files and printers. HyperTerminal, which is closer to (if less pretty than) the Microsoft Network interface, is for transferring files and making online-service types of connections, such as those that let you browse information on electronic bulletin boards and download posted files. Both types of connection, like The Microsoft Network itself, have their uses. You just have to know which is more appropriate for a given situation.

E-Mail...Can't Live Without It?

Accessing shared resources via dial-up networking is one of Windows 95's better features. Dial-up networking also contributes to something that lots of people get hooked on: e-mail. Given a dial-up connection and the name of your e-mail postoffice, Windows 95 can tie you in to news and gossip whenever you long for that human connection.

The actual steps involved in enabling remote e-mail vary, depending on the mail program you use. They vary somewhat with different mail services, so you'll probably need some instructions from your network or postoffice administrator. In addition, you'll need to provide some information that generally isn't part of an "average" Windows 95 user's fount of basic knowledge:

A WORD OF ADVICE
The accompanying description of remote mail access was based on a pre-release version of Windows 95. What you see might differ in some respects, but the underlying concepts should still apply.

- For example, you need to ensure that the computer you're calling belongs to the same workgroup as the computer you're calling from.

- Microsoft Exchange needs to recognize who you are, and it must have the appropriate mail service, protocols, and assorted goodies listed in your profile.

- Before you can connect to your postoffice, Microsoft Exchange must know where to find the postoffice—its name and which server it's on.

- Microsoft Exchange must also know the name of your mailbox and your mailbox password.

Complex as all these things sound—and in some cases are—Windows 95 actually makes the process of arranging for remote mail a lot easier than it used to be. But, as already mentioned, this book can't help you with the details because it's not familiar with your mail system. For that, rely on your resident mail expert, who will no doubt be able to walk you through setup or might even do it for you.

POWER PLAY

Service, Please

If you use your portable (or any other computer for that matter) to call a work computer, your network administrator or resident computer expert has probably set up the receiving machine to respond to dial-up networking so that it can share files and printers.

If you're setting up such sharing on a computer of your own, however, you'll have to equip the computer you'll be calling with the ability to act as a server. The process isn't difficult, but you do need a file named RNASERV.DLL. This file is not part of Windows 95, but you can get it in an add-on package called Microsoft Plus! for Windows 95.

When the file is in the System subfolder of your Windows 95 directory:

1. Choose Dial-Up Networking from the Accessories submenu.

2. Choose Connections.

3. Choose Dial-Up Server. You'll see the window below.

4. Click Allow Caller Access, and optionally, click the Change Password button to require all callers to provide a password before being allowed to connect to the computer. (Password protection is a good thing, so do it if you've enabled share-level rather than user-level access. If you've enabled user-level access, select the users who can connect, rather than assigning a password.)

5. Click OK.

From now on, whenever your computer is turned on, it will be able to answer incoming calls and allow your selected guests to connect to shared resources through their Network Neighborhood icon and the Find Computer and Map Network Drive commands.

Oh, yes. You can turn off access to the computer whenever you want simply by clicking the No Caller Access option shown in the illustration below.

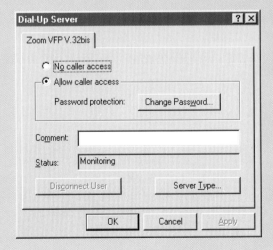

Setting Up for Yourself

If you're trying to set up a postoffice on your own computer and you want to enable remote mail on another machine, you can find detailed information in the *Microsoft Windows 95 Resource Kit*, an extremely useful technical guide to Windows 95 put together by Windows 95 experts at Microsoft and published by Microsoft Press.

If you're going to give this a try, here's a summary of the basic requirements and an overview, with some guidelines:

1. On the server, set up a postoffice. If Microsoft Mail is installed and you're going to use it, this part is straightforward because you can simply double-click the Microsoft Mail Postoffice icon in the Control Panel to start a Postoffice wizard that walks you through the entire process. When you finish, right-click the folder representing the postoffice, choose Sharing, and enable sharing with *full* access. Also, assign a password for security.

2. Next, set up Microsoft Exchange. If it hasn't been installed, add it through the Add/Remove Programs tool in the Control Panel, as described in Chapter 12.

3. Create an e-mail account for each user. To do this, start the Postoffice wizard again, but this time choose to administer an existing postoffice rather than create a new one.

4. Set up Microsoft Exchange on the computer that will be calling in to the postoffice.

5. Also on the calling machine, create a dial-up networking connection to the modem serving your e-mail postoffice. This part can be a little complex because you have to make sure that a description of all related information is added to your Microsoft Exchange Settings Properties sheet.

This sheet is the part of Microsoft Exchange that keeps track of where and how Exchange interacts with the world. To see it:

1. Double-click the Mail And Fax icon in the Control Panel. You'll see the properties sheet below.

2. Click your mail information service in the window at the top of the sheet (Microsoft Mail in this illustration), and then click Properties.

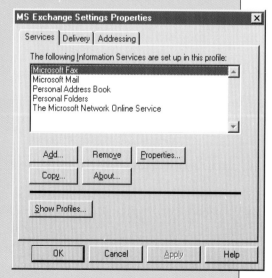

3. Click your way through the tabs (of which there are many), verifying or filling in any required information. For remote e-mail access, click the Remote Using A Modem And Dial-Up Networking option on the Connection tab. For most situations, the other default settings should work fine.

When you're done, you should be able to double-click the Inbox icon on the remote computer's desktop, choose Remote Mail from the Tools menu, and select the type of connection you want, as described in the text. Getting everything to work might take a little tinkering, but once you're set up, you're set up until you delete your mail service, your dial-up connection to the postoffice, or both.

One other word of advice, however: if you're installing remote mail on a shared computer or traveling laptop, think about security as well as server accessibility. There are ways to protect multiple users and prevent casual access by other people. Also, you might need to transfer documents, addresses, or Microsoft Exchange files to the traveling machine. For help with all this, read through Microsoft Exchange Help, which is on the Help menu that appears in the Microsoft Exchange window.

Once remote mail is set up, the hard part is done and connecting to e-mail is straightforward. Mail options and commands differ, however, so to avoid confusion the following descriptions outline what happens when you use remote access with Microsoft Mail. If you use a different mail service, remember that the procedures you follow might differ.

To connect to Microsoft Mail:

1. Double-click the Inbox icon on your desktop, choose Remote Mail from the Tools menu, and then choose your mail service from the submenu that appears. The window at the right appears (and should be familiar from the description of Microsoft Exchange in the preceding chapter).

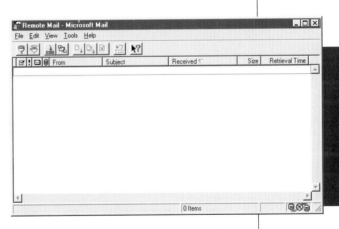

2. Choose a Connect command from the Tools menu in the Remote Mail window. Microsoft Mail offers the following options:

   • Connect dials your mail server and logs you on to mail.

   • Connect And Update Headers dials in, logs you on, and updates the list in the Remote Mail window so that you can see new mail.

CUTTING YOUR PHONE BILL

If you use Microsoft Mail, you can set up a remote session so that you automatically disconnect after updating headers. To do this, choose Services from the Microsoft Exchange Tools menu and then click the Remote Session tab in the window that appears. In the section headed Automatically End A Dial-Up Networking Session, click the check box at the left of the After Retrieving Mail Headers option. When you choose this tab, note also that you can click a Schedule Mail Delivery button. Use this button if you want to specify a particular date or time for connecting and sending mail.

• Connect And Transfer Items, which can save time on line, sends mail you've composed, retrieves mail you've chosen from the updated list of headers, and disconnects from your mail server when all is done.

So what about this business of updating and transferring items?

When you open the Remote Mail window, Microsoft Exchange shows the headers (From, Subject, Received, and Size) of mail you've already received. The Connect And Update Headers option in Microsoft Mail allows you to connect to your postoffice and collect headers for new mail. This alone is a nifty feature, but once you've retrieved these headers, you can also sort and dispose of your messages. Highlight each new message in turn, and use the commands on the Edit menu to:

• Mark To Retrieve, meaning that you want to see the message.

• Mark To Retrieve A Copy, meaning that you want to see and copy the message to your Inbox.

• Mark To Delete, meaning that you don't want to see the message.

What then? Well, when you use Microsoft Mail remotely, you don't have to waste connection time while you sit and think about what you want to do. By default, Microsoft Mail not only lets you mark messages for retrieval but also lets you compose and reply to mail in the Microsoft Exchange Inbox window. If the mail is being sent to a remote postoffice, Microsoft Mail holds it in the Outbox to await delivery. Later, when you connect to your remote postoffice, Microsoft Mail can zap everything across the miles in one fell swoop. That's the purpose of the Connect And Transfer Items command on the Tools menu in the Remote Mail window.

The Fax of Life

In addition to dial-up networking and remote e-mail, Windows 95 supports some pretty fancy faxing ability. You can send:

• A regulation fax, such as a letter or other document, that's printed out on a fax machine at the receiving end. (Windows 95 calls this a *rendered* fax.)

• An editable file (called a *binary* file), which you can attach to a mail message. If sent to another computer with Windows 95 Fax installed, such a "fax" can be opened, modified, saved, and otherwise treated like any other file by the person who receives it. This is excellent.

Windows 95 is even smart enough to determine whether an attachment can be sent as a file or whether it must be rendered into printed characters. It all depends on the type of fax recipient you're sending to: if the fax is going to a regular (Group 3) fax machine, Windows 95 converts the attachment to a printed image; if the fax is going to a fax modem, Windows 95 sends the attachment as an editable file. Clever.

Setting Up for Faxing   To use Microsoft Fax, you have to install it. Which means either choosing to install when Windows 95 is set up on your computer or doing it later, with the help of the Add/Remove Programs tool in the Control Panel (described in Chapter 12). Once Microsoft Fax is installed, you then configure it. Yup, more setup, but don't worry. It's easy:

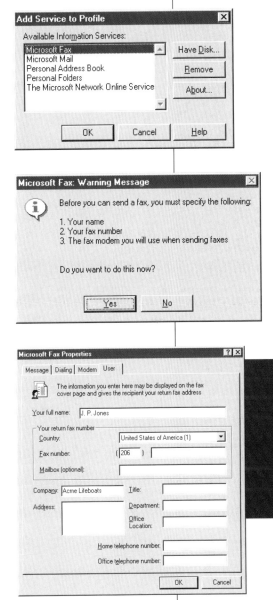

1. Double-click the Mail And Fax icon in the Control Panel. When the Microsoft Exchange Settings Properties sheet opens up, click the Add button to open the window shown at the right.

   (If you have more than one profile set up on your computer, you can click Show Profiles to create or select the profile to which you want to add Microsoft Fax capabilities, but do so *before* you click the Add button.)

2. Click Microsoft Fax, and then click OK. At this point, Windows 95 displays the message shown in the window at the right, telling you it needs your name, fax number, and modem identification.

   You might as well do it now, so click Yes.

3. You'll see the Microsoft Fax Properties sheet shown below.

   Fill in the appropriate spaces. Don't forget to check all the tabs. The default settings will probably be fine for you, but note that on the Message tab you can specify, among other things, the type of cover page you want to include by default. (You can choose a different type for individual faxes, too, as you'll see shortly.)

4. When you're finished, click OK to add the information to Microsoft Exchange.

5. If the wizard prompts you to specify which modem you will use to send faxes, do so.

You're now ready to fax.

Sending a Fax As usual, Windows 95 gives you a host of ways to reach your goal, all of them easy. The only part of this you might need to understand is that Microsoft Fax is the *sending* part of faxing. If you want to attach a document, the *creating* part belongs to you and to your usual Windows 95 applications. For the content, then:

- Use any of your Windows 95 applications to create and save the document you want to attach.

To actually transmit the beastie, you generally start the New Fax wizard, which is really simple to use. To get to the wizard, do one of the following:

- Open a window, select the file you want to send, right-click, choose Send To, and then choose Fax Recipient.

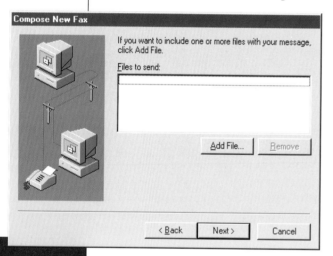

- If you want to send the document as an editable file, choose Compose New Fax in your Microsoft Exchange window and attach the file using the Add File button when the New Fax wizard displays the screen shown at the left.

(Note that for this to work, the recipient must have a fax modem; otherwise, Windows 95 will send the fax as a regular rendered document.)

- Choose Compose New Fax from the Start/Programs/Accessories/Fax submenu. (This allows you to attach a file, but the file is rendered rather than sent as an editable document.)

If you prefer, you can also choose to:

- Send a fax from within an application (such as Microsoft Word) that possesses fax capabilities. Doing this automatically starts Microsoft Exchange and attaches the open document to a new message.

- Or—and this is neat—drag the Microsoft Fax "printer" icon from your Printers folder and create a shortcut to it on the desktop. To send a rendered fax, you can then start the New Fax wizard simply by dragging and dropping a document onto the shortcut.

However you send your fax, the illustrations that follow show the most significant parts of the New Fax wizard. When you're asked about the recipient, the screen looks like the one shown at the top of the following page.

The fill-in-the-blanks part is pretty obvious here. If you want to send to multiple recipients, type their names or choose them from the address book and then add them to the recipient list.

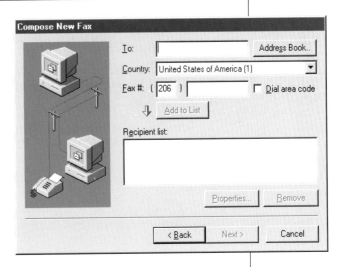

After you fill out the recipient information, the New Fax wizard asks about a cover page. If you want one, you can choose from the four built-in types: Confidential, For Your Information, Generic (the default), and Urgent. If you want to send the fax at a certain time or if you want to specify other options such as whether the message should be editable or rendered, click the Options button on the same screen.

When you get to the substance of your fax, the screen looks like the one shown below.

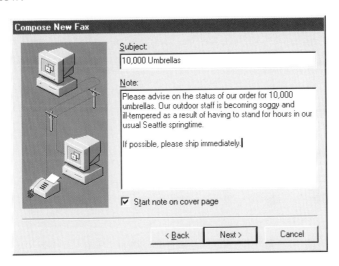

The subject, as you would expect, is printed on the cover page. The note is also printed on the cover page by default, but you can uncheck the check box to begin the note on the first page of the fax itself. When you finish here, click Next and you'll reach the end of the New Fax wizard—the Add File screen shown earlier. Use this, as mentioned, to attach a file to your fax if you want. When all is done, click Finish, and your fax is on its way, either immediately or at the time you scheduled.

Holding Print Jobs

You've seen all these fancy ways to transfer information. Is there anything special about that old standby, printing? You bet. In Windows 95, you can defer printing on a portable or to a network printer by choosing to work *off line* until such time as:

- Your portable is back at home and connected to your desktop or network printer.

- The network printer you normally use gets over its snit and becomes available for use again.

- You can break into your frenzied work schedule and take the time to print the documents you've been generating all morning.

Deferred printing works whether you're at home or on the road. Whenever you want to send jobs to the printer but can't or don't want to print right then and there, all you have to do is:

1. Find your default printer—either the real thing or a shortcut to it.

2. Right-click. If there is no check mark at the left of the Work Offline command, click the command to turn it on.

Work Offline is a toggle command; Windows 95 puts a check mark at the left when the command is turned on and clears the check mark when the command is turned off.

So what happens when you work off line? Nothing much. You continue working as usual. The only difference is that when you print a document—whether you do so by dragging and dropping or by using a Print command—Windows 95 adds the document to a *queue* waiting to be printed. When one or more documents are in the print queue, Windows 95 tells you so in two places:

- On the taskbar, where Windows 95 displays a small printer icon, as shown at the left.

If you point to this icon, Windows 95 even tells you the status of the queue with a message such as *2 document(s) pending for jericho.*

- In the queue window, which you open by double-clicking the icon on the taskbar or the printer icon (or shortcut) on the desktop or by right-clicking and choosing Open. However you open it, the print queue looks like this.

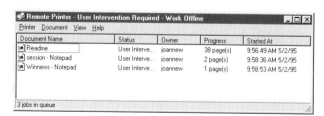

OFFLINE?

You can easily tell when Work Offline is turned on. Right-clicking the printer to check the Work Offline status is, of course, one easy way. Another way is to check the printer icon: when you work off line, the icon is dimmed. Because the icon changes like this, you can check off-line status at a glance.

Once a document is in the queue, Windows 95 takes responsibility for it. You can close the program that created the document, and you can even shut down Windows 95 and restart the computer. Regardless, the document will remain safely in the queue, waiting for you to go back on line so that it can be printed.

When you're ready to print:

1. Right-click the printer icon.

2. Turn on (or connect to) your printer.

3. Choose Work Offline to toggle the command to "off."

4. Go to lunch. Windows 95 will take care of the rest.

Conserving Power on the Road

Windows 95 pays special attention to portable computers in several different areas. First of all, Windows 95 Setup includes a laptop installation that sets up the most important components needed for mobile computing, among them the Windows 95 Briefcase, Dial-Up Networking, Quick View, and PCMCIA support, which lets you plug credit card–size modems, hard disks, and other such equipment into special slots on the computer. In addition to this laptop-centric installation option, Windows 95 also includes a feature called Advanced Power Management, designed with portables in mind.

Power management, which is automatically installed on a laptop, allows you to:

- See how much power remains in your battery.

- Conserve energy (if you have an Energy Star monitor).

- Use a Suspend command to put your computer "to sleep" temporarily and so save energy without having to turn off the machine.

Even though current batteries (no pun intended) manage to keep power flowing to a portable computer for hours, a battery isn't a real replacement for a wall socket. Mechanical bunnies can keep going and going, but computers can't. If you have a battery-powered laptop, it's thus important to know how much power remains in your battery. With Windows 95, it's easy:

1. Glance at the right end of the taskbar, next to the clock. Windows 95's power-management feature displays a battery icon there.

2. To see how much power remains, double-click the battery icon.

In addition to helping you watch your power consumption, Windows 95 can also help you conserve what you've got. If you have an Energy Star monitor,

DON'T PUSH IT

In addition to telling you how your battery is doing, Windows 95 also warns you when the battery power is running low. Do *not* ignore the warning. To avoid loss of information, clean up, shut down, and replenish the battery. Don't keep thinking, "Oh, I can get away with just another few minutes' work." You might at first, but eventually, you'll lose.

you can set it on "standby" or have it shut down automatically after a specified period of time. If your computer includes Advanced Power Management Support (which comes from the manufacturer, not from Windows 95), you can also use the Suspend command when you're not actively using the computer.

To check on, or change, Energy Star settings:

1. Open the Display Properties sheet by right-clicking the desktop and choosing Properties.

2. Click the Screen Saver tab. If your monitor is an Energy Star, you see the settings described in the next two steps. If your monitor is not Energy Star–compliant, these settings do not appear. (If you *know* the monitor is an Energy Star but you do not see standby and shutdown settings on the Screen Saver tab, check out the shaded box titled "Enabling Power Management.")

3. To enable your monitor to go into standby mode, in which it reduces power consumption but does not shut down, check the Low-Power Standby box on the Screen Saver tab.

4. To enable your monitor to shut down, check the Shut Off Monitor check box.

5. To specify a time period before energy conservation goes into effect, choose the number of minutes in the Minutes box.

To view the Suspend command:

1. Open the Power Properties sheet in the Control Panel.

2. Use the Suspend Command Options portion of the sheet to specify when you want to see the command.

3. To suspend your computer, lowering its power consumption without having to turn off the machine, choose Suspend from the Start menu.

Enabling Power Management

If your portable computer does not seem to support power management, right-click My Computer, choose Properties, and click the Device Manager tab. Open the System Devices list by clicking the plus sign at the left of the item. If you don't see an entry titled Advanced Power Management Support, your computer can't take advantage of Windows 95's power-management features. If you do see such an entry, double-click it, double-click the Settings tab, and check to be sure support for power management is turned on.

Hot Docking

Windows 95, unlike earlier versions of Windows, includes a feature called *hot docking*, which is specially designed for portable computers that can be used either as laptops or, when "plugged" into a docking station, as desktop machines. The intriguing part of hot docking is that Windows 95 is designed to automatically detect when the laptop is unplugged and working on its own and when the same machine is docked and using "desktop" equipment, including a full-size keyboard and a different monitor.

When you undock a freshly configured dockable laptop, Windows 95 detects the undocked condition and makes all necessary adjustments to work with the laptop's built-in display, its trackball, and other laptop-only hardware. Although Windows 95 leaves you little to do as it takes care of figuring out whether the laptop is docked or not, just watching the process is intriguing and can certainly make you appreciate the thought and complexity behind the friendly face of this operating system.

The first time Windows 95 reconfigures itself for running on the undocked laptop, the adjustments it makes can take a while—possibly 4 to 5 minutes or more. When Windows 95 is finished, you'll have to restart the computer, undocked, so that the changes can take effect. After that, however, Windows 95 will automatically detect whether the laptop is in or out of the dock and will set itself up accordingly.

Chapter 12

Disks, Controls, and Other Delights

You've reached the "ultimate" chapter of this "ultimate" book. Much remains for you to discover, but by now you should be comfortable and conversant enough with Microsoft Windows 95 to keep yourself afloat in most situations. To give you an idea of how much more awaits you, this chapter takes you on a quick tour of some of the many features that help define Windows 95 but that could not justify complete chapters in their own right. First stop: disks.

What You Can Do with Disks

All the programs and information you entrust to your computer you actually entrust to disks. Without disks, your computer remembers very little. Because disks are so important, Windows 95 gives you a number of ways of working with them and, through them, with your data. With the tools built into Windows 95, you can format, copy, scan, compress, defragment (clean up), and back up your floppy disks and hard disks.

Disk Anatomy

If you're not familiar with the recording medium inside either the plastic jacket of a floppy disk or the sealed box of your hard disk, the accompanying illustrations show what the innards of a floppy disk and a hard disk look like.

Floppy disks and hard disks are covered or enclosed because the data-holding portion is limited to a thin surface coat of magnetic material. This coating records the millions, possibly even billions, of bytes that make up your computer's information warehouse. Floppy disks are usually quite safe in their plastic jackets as long as you don't use them as substitute Frisbees for your dog. Although they are not as sensitive as hard disks, floppy disks belong either in your disk drive or in a storage container.

Sectors

Tracks

Two sides
(top and bottom)

Floppy disk

Even though hard disks are usually built into the computer and are protected by surrounding hardware, they are more delicate than floppy disks, so try not to move the machine or turn it off while the disk drive is in operation (while the drive light is on). Machined to extremely fine tolerances, hard disks contain read/write heads that float over the disk surfaces, which typically spin at a rate of 3600 RPM. The less bumping and shoving your hard disk is subjected to, the better off it will be.

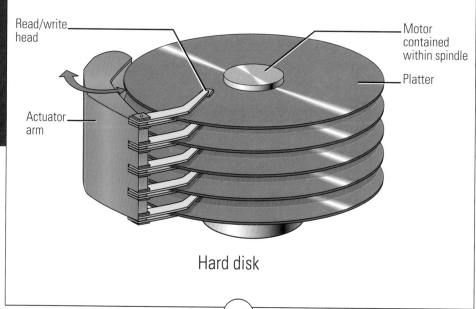

Read/write head

Motor contained within spindle

Platter

Actuator arm

Hard disk

Formatting and Copying

Probably the two most common disk operations are formatting and copying. Formatting prepares a new floppy or hard disk for use by Windows 95, but because it wipes out existing information, it can also be used to recycle a used disk. Formatting is simple:

1. Open My Computer, and select the drive you want to format.

2. Either right-click and choose Format, or choose Format from the window's File menu. The window at the right opens.

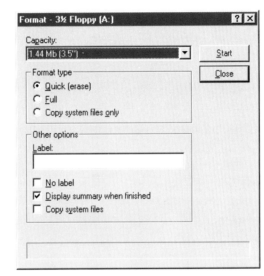

If you're formatting the disk for less than the normal capacity of the drive, choose the capacity you want from the drop-down list in the Capacity box. If you want to label the disk with a name that identifies its contents, type the name in the Label box. The only other question you might have is about format type:

- Choose Quick when all you want to do is clean off a used disk.

- Choose Full when you are formatting a new disk or trying to clean a used one as thoroughly as possible.

- Choose the third type, Copy System Files Only, when you *don't* want to format but *do* want to make a bootable disk. (If you want to format *and* make a bootable disk, choose Quick or Full, plus Copy System Files in the Other Options section.)

To copy a disk—that is, to make a mirror-image duplicate of the original—do this:

1. Open My Computer, and select the drive to copy.

2. Either right-click and choose Copy Disk, or choose Copy Disk from the File menu. The small window shown at the right opens.

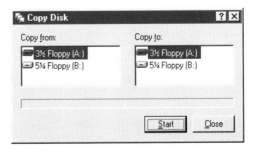

FORMATTING YOUR HARD DISK

Don't. Actually, Windows 95 is too smart to let you "kill" it by formatting your primary hard disk (drive C), but if you're ever told—by an expert— to reformat your hard disk, make sure that you back up all the data files you need and that you have installation disks for Windows 95 *and* for the programs you'll want to reinstall. You might also need a bootable floppy disk with the Format command on it (which you can create by formatting a floppy disk as described in text and then copying Format.com to the floppy disk).

Reformatting and then rebuilding a hard disk, especially a large one, can be a pain. Be very sure that you need to do so, and then be very careful.

Select the drive to copy from and the drive to copy to. Just remember that the source and destination disks must be of the same type and must have the same capacity. You cannot, therefore, copy from a 3.5-inch, 1.44-MB disk to a 5.25-inch, 1.2-MB disk, or vice versa. You can, however, copy from and to the same drive; Windows 95 will tell you when to insert the source disk and when to insert the destination disk.

Increasing Disk Capacity

When is a disk not a disk? When it's twice as big as it was before. Before what? Before DriveSpace. Windows 95's DriveSpace, which you might recognize from version 6.2 of MS-DOS, is a disk-compression utility that's installed by default when you install Windows 95. Using DriveSpace to increase the carrying capacity of a Briefcase on a floppy was described in Chapter 11, "Long-Distance Information." Here's a little more information about using DriveSpace.

DriveSpace works by squeezing as much "air" as possible out of files being stored on disk. And, yes, most files do contain a little to a lot of such air— white space (such as tabs and paragraph indents), repeated characters or character strings, and so on. Bitmaps, for instance, are made up of line after line of tiny dots, many of which do not differ in color from the dots above, below, and to each side. Instead of storing each dot of every line, compression shrinks such a file by using its own "shorthand" to describe how many identical dots need to be sequentially displayed or printed when the file is uncompressed.

To compress files, DriveSpace essentially creates a drive within a drive. That is, it uses your *physical* drive as a *host* for a compressed drive that, in turn, is used to hold your compressed files. Do you need to know a lot more? Not really, because DriveSpace acts on its own, compressing and uncompressing files "on the fly" so that the whole process is invisible to you. You should know the following, however, about the way DriveSpace works:

- It *needs* a special file named DRVSPACE.BIN, which you can see if you turn on Show All Files with the View Options command. Don't touch any file with this name.

- The compressed drive, known as a *compressed volume file*, or CVF, is an actual file with a name like Drvspace.000. Do not delete any CVF files. Doing so also deletes all the information stored on a compressed drive.

- When you compress a drive, DriveSpace creates an uncompressed host that it refers to by a different drive letter, such as G or H, as you can see in the illustration at the top of the next page. The host is where your compressed-volume file is located. Try not to copy files to it. In fact, unless you understand compression a lot better than you can from this short discussion, try to pretend it's not there, even if Windows 95 displays an icon for it. Instead, when working with files on a compressed disk, simply use your disk drive as if it were a normal drive. The only difference you will notice is that you will have about twice as much room on a compressed disk.

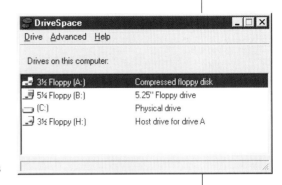

To use system tools with compressed drives, you must always use the DriveSpace utility as mediator:

• Open the Start menu, and work your way through Programs, Accessories, and System Tools to DriveSpace.

When DriveSpace starts, you see a window like the one illustrated above, which shows and identifies the floppy and hard disks on your system. The following list outlines the basic maneuvers. For more details, use the window's Help menu, which opens up a small but detailed online library of information about DriveSpace.

• To compress a disk, making it hold more than "normal," select the drive and then choose Compress from the Drive menu. Compression is a sophisticated undertaking and sometimes needs a substantial amount of time, depending on the size of the disk you're compressing. Be patient, however, and follow the onscreen instructions. If you are uncertain about anything, accept the default.

• To uncompress a disk, returning it to "normal," select the compressed drive and choose Uncompress from the Drive menu. Uncompressing can also take a fair amount of time, especially if the compressed disk (or volume) contains a lot of files, so it's a good idea to clean out unwanted files before uncompressing. If there is not much free space remaining on the compressed disk, DriveSpace might ask you to clean out files anyway, so save time and effort by deleting junk ahead of time.

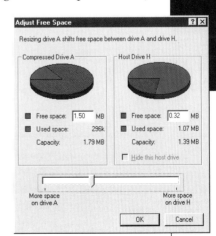

• Sizewise, the compressed and uncompressed portions of a single physical drive are directly related. The larger you make one, the smaller the other becomes. If a program tells you it needs more free space on either drive, select the compressed or uncompressed portion in the DriveSpace window and choose Adjust Free Space from the Drive menu. In the window that opens, use the slider shown at the right to alter the compressed-to-uncompressed ratio.

Keeping Disks Healthy

Windows 95 provides two tools that help you maintain your disks: ScanDisk, which lets you give a disk a "checkup," and Disk Defragmenter, which can tune up disk storage for speedier access. Both are installed by default when you install Windows 95.

ScanDisk   ScanDisk has two functions. It can examine and correct problems in the way files are stored on disk, and it can examine the surface of the disk itself:

- When it checks file storage, ScanDisk actually examines the "indexes" that Windows 95 uses for keeping track of the files you save on the disk. These indexes are known as the FAT (File Allocation Table) and the VFAT (Virtual FAT), and they contain critical information that Windows 95 needs to correctly store and retrieve every byte of every file you save on disk. This information is particularly important because Windows 95 breaks files into pieces for efficient storage, and on a much-used disk these pieces can be tucked into physically separated locations.

- When it checks the disk surface, ScanDisk looks for bad spots on the disk itself—spots that are unreliable or failing and that should not be used for data storage. If it finds a problem area (which it calls a *cluster*), ScanDisk notifies you of the problem and asks if you want it to mark the cluster as bad so that Windows 95 will avoid it in the future. (You do, by the way.)

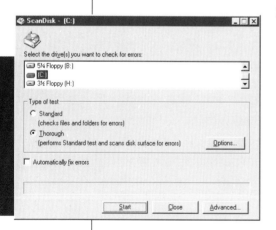

Running ScanDisk is easy:

1. Open the Start menu, and work your way through Programs, Accessories, and System Tools to ScanDisk. When ScanDisk starts, it displays the window shown at the left.

2. When you want to check file storage only, choose Standard. When you want to give the disk a complete physical, choose Thorough. (Note that a Thorough scan of a hard disk can take quite a while; if this is what you want, choose a time when you won't need to use your computer for half an hour or more.)

3. As explained in the shaded box titled "Disk Errors," some of the problems ScanDisk finds are kind of arcane. If you don't feel up to deciding what to do if ScanDisk detects a problem, check the Automatically Fix Errors option. That'll tell ScanDisk to rely on the (conservative) defaults you can see when you click the Advanced button.

4. When you're ready, click Start, and away you go.

Disk Errors

As you can see by clicking the Advanced button in the ScanDisk window, ScanDisk can find and fix several types of storage errors. The two most common, and what to do about them, are described below:

- *Cross-linked files* are files in which a single storage location (cluster, remember) has somehow become shared by two different files. The information at this location belongs to one of the files, but ScanDisk doesn't know which one. More important, the file that *doesn't* own the information cannot be linked to any of its pieces beyond this point. The easiest way to visualize cross-linking is to think genetics. At the point where the two files cross, they initially form an X, as in a female chromosome. Because one of the files loses its tail end, however, the female X effectively becomes a male Y (sorry, fellows). By default, when ScanDisk fixes cross-linked files, it tells you which files are affected and then

makes copies of both. Open both files afterward to see which one is complete. If the broken file belongs to a program, you'll have to reinstall the program.

- *Lost clusters,* pitiful as they sound, are bits of files that have become disconnected and can no longer be associated with the program or document they came from. Lost clusters can happen during an abnormal shutdown or when you must terminate a badly behaved program before it can save and close its open files. Usually, lost clusters are nothing to worry about, and rarely do they contain any salvageable information. By default, ScanDisk saves lost clusters as numbered files in the form *File0000.chk.* After the scan, you can use a program like Notepad to open and view the contents of these files. If they're not usable, delete them—they take up valuable space in your root directory.

Disk Defragmenter Disk defragmenting, affectionately known as "defragging," is a housekeeping procedure that optimizes disk storage. Defragging sometimes becomes necessary because files are not always stored byte after consecutive byte in a single disk location. To make the most efficient use of your disk's storage space, Windows 95 treats your disk as if it were made up of hundreds or thousands of equal-size compartments. When you save a file, Windows 95 breaks the file into pieces and stores the pieces in as many of these compartments as are needed. This is all well and good, but remember that not only do you save files, you delete them too. When you delete files, their storage compartments become available for reuse, and the next time you save a file, Windows 95 might well recycle one or more of these vacated storage compartments.

Tip!

WHICH TO CHOOSE
Disk scans are very much like your own physical exams. Thorough scans, like the ones that check everything from your brain to your toenails, are lengthy and, well, thorough. Standard checks, like your routine heart-and-blood-pressure checkups, are faster, but they're just fine for verifying that you remain in good shape. Where your disks are concerned, run a Thorough check when you're scanning a disk for the first time, when your software has problems reading from or writing to a disk, and whenever you feel the need to give the disk a good going over. Between these times, occasionally do a quick Standard scan to ensure that file storage is everything you need it to be.

This system works efficiently and well. Windows 95 keeps track of every single storage compartment it uses for every piece of every file you save, and it does so with perfect accuracy. Over time, however, the files on a busy disk become more and more *fragmented* as Windows 95 recycles more and more storage compartments. This fragmentation is not dangerous, nor is it even a nuisance. It can, however, cause your disk drive to work harder, because the read/write heads must travel longer and farther to find all the pieces of a large file.

To check on fragmentation and, if necessary, clean up disk storage, you use the Disk Defragmenter:

SCANDISK FIRST

By default, Disk Defragmenter checks for storage errors on the drive you're defragmenting. If it finds errors, it refuses to continue. To save time (and ensure that your disk is in top shape), run ScanDisk before you defragment a drive.

1. Open the Start menu, and work your way through Programs, Accessories, and System Tools to Disk Defragmenter. When you arrive, the window at the right opens.

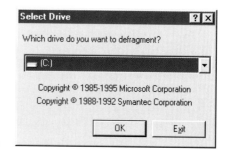

2. Open the list box, select the drive to defragment, and then click OK.

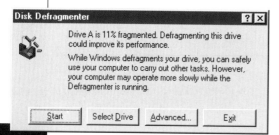

This simple procedure is about all that you need to do. Disk Defragmenter then checks the disk that you specified and tells you whether and how much it is fragmented, with a message like the one shown at the left.

3. If you want to choose the type of defragmentation, click the Advanced button. By default, Disk Defragmenter performs a full defragmentation, which can take quite a bit of time because it (1) rearranges storage so that all the pieces of each file occupy consecutive storage locations and (2) rearranges free—unused—space so that there are no gaps in storage. If you prefer, choose the Defragment Files Only or Consolidate Free Space Only option.

Stars on the Control Panel

Here and there throughout this book, you've seen notes telling you that the feature being described is not installed by default when you install Windows 95. You've also been told that's not a problem. Here's the solution.

Add/Remove Programs

Windows 95 is a big operating system with lots of nifty features. Everyone gets the basics, meaning the core of the operating system and standard features such as WordPad, Paint, and the Flying Windows screen saver. Many other features are optional and can be installed either during setup or at any time later. All you need is your original Windows 95 package—either the CD-ROM or floppies—and the Add/Remove Programs utility:

- If you have Windows 95 on CD-ROM, insert the disc in your CD-ROM drive. When the Windows 95 CD-ROM window opens, click the icon at the right of Add/Remove Software.

- Or, open the Control Panel, double-click the Add/Remove Programs icon, and click the Windows Setup tab. The window at the right is displayed.

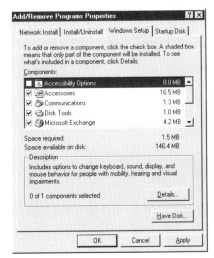

As you can see, the various Windows 95 features are grouped into categories. Those that are checked and unshaded are already completely installed on your computer; those that are checked and shaded include multiple options, not all of which are installed by default. You can see all the components in a category by clicking the Details button. The illustration below shows the Details window for the Accessories group.

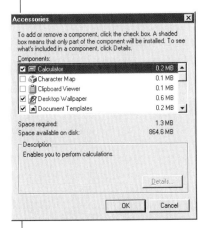

If you're browsing, notice that the lower half of the Windows Setup tab, as shown in the illustration above, gives you a considerable amount of valuable information: the amount of disk space required by the highlighted option, the amount of space available on your hard disk, and a short description of the feature itself.

You can use the Add/Remove Programs icon to (surprise) add or remove a Windows 95 feature. To add a component:

1. Open Add/Remove Programs.

2. Check the feature you want to add. If the item is shaded, you can either click the Details button to select what you want or you can clear and then recheck the box to add everything.

IF YOU HAVE FLOPPIES

Windows 95 is distributed on both CD-ROM and floppy disks. Because floppies do not hold anywhere near as much information as do CD-ROMs, less of Windows 95 is included in the floppy-disk package. You have the basics plus the most desirable options, including The Microsoft Network, Exchange, Microsoft Mail, Briefcase, disk tools, and so on. You do not, however, have certain additional features, such as extra wallpaper, some games, Quick View, the Windows 95 Tour, and more icons. To get the "full" package, unfortunately, you must add a CD-ROM drive to your system. There's simply too much of Windows 95 for floppies only.

3. Click OK on the Details tab (if you are viewing details). Click OK on the Windows Setup tab.

4. Insert the appropriate disk (CD-ROM or floppy) if Windows 95 prompts for it.

5. If Windows 95 displays a message telling you that you must restart your computer for the new settings to take effect, click Yes to restart and finish up or click No to continue working and leave the finishing up until your next restart.

To remove a Windows 95 component, perhaps because you no longer need it or because you're running low on disk space:

1. Open Add/Remove Programs.

2. Uncheck the item you want to remove, and click OK.

All gone.

Add New Hardware

In addition to adding new software, Windows 95 can help you add new hardware. This is a really fine feature because it uses a hardware installation wizard that does much of the work for you and makes the remainder quite easy to handle.

Adding new hardware is usually a two-step process. First, you physically connect the new device to your computer. This is your responsibility, but you should find adequately detailed instructions in the package with the device. (If you're inheriting a used mouse, modem, or whatever from someone else, ask for instructions from the device's donor.) Second, after the device is connected, you install the software, called a *driver*, that helps Windows 95 use the item correctly. This is where Windows 95 steps in with the Add New Hardware Wizard.

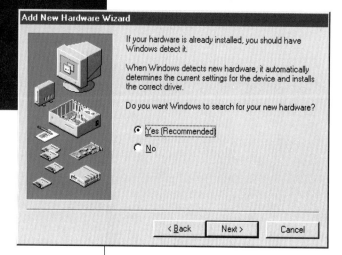

The following steps describe the general-purpose hardware wizard. Printers and modems rate a slight variation on this, so if you're installing either, you might want to read this section and then refer to the sections that follow. To install new hardware:

1. Open the Control Panel, and double-click the Add New Hardware icon. When you do, you'll see the first screen of the wizard. Click Next, and you'll see a screen like the one at the left.

2. If you accept the default, Yes, which lets Windows 95 find and figure out the new hardware, the wizard swings into a detection routine that can take several minutes. If you choose No, the wizard asks you to specify the type of hardware with a screen like the one shown above right.

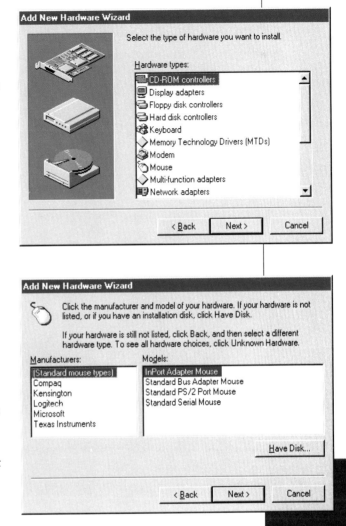

3. Specify the type of device you have, and click Next. At this point, the wizard will proceed according to the type of hardware you're installing. Except in a few cases (including modems and printers), the next stop will be a screen asking you to choose your device from a list like the one shown below right.

Choose the manufacturer and the model. If your hardware is not listed, click Have Disk to tell the wizard to get its setup instructions from the disk that came with your hardware, or choose one of the standard drivers shown at the top of the list.

4. From this point on, read the screens, follow the instructions, and let the wizard be your guide.

Printers Windows 95 automatically sets up your printer if it detects one during installation, but it's also easy to install a printer at a later time. Because the Add Printer Wizard differs somewhat from its Add New Hardware cousin and because printers in general are frequently added pieces of hardware, this section will point out some of the specifics.

To add a printer, start by opening the Printers folder:

1. Double-click the Printers folder in either the Control Panel or the My Computer window.

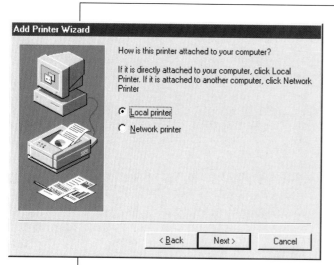

2. Double-click the Add Printer icon, click Next in the first screen of the wizard, and you'll see the screen at the left.

   Choose the Local Printer option if you're setting up a printer that will be located on or near your desktop. Choose the Network Printer option if you're connecting to a network printer.

What happens next depends on the type of printer you choose. In either case, you'll choose the printer from a list of supported manufacturers and models, like the one shown at the right.

If you have a setup disk, click Have Disk and insert the disk into the drive. If your printer is not listed, follow the instructions at the top of the screen.

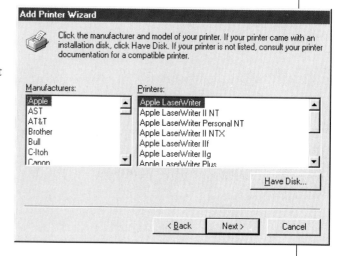

CHECK YOUR PORT

Network printers need to be identified only by their network addresses, but if you're installing a printer connected to your computer, do yourself a favor and find out which *port* you're using. Most computers these days label the ports. The printer port is often identified by an embossed printer symbol or by the letters LPT1 or LPT2. If you have a serial printer, the port is probably labeled COM*x* or, possibly, 1010.

In addition to asking for the printer make and model, the wizard will also ask for the following if you're installing a local printer:

- The printer port. If you have a parallel printer, it's probably LPT1. If you have a serial printer, it's probably either COM1 or COM2. (Unfortunately, you have to know what type of printer you've got; check your printer manual if you're not sure.)

- A printer name. By default, Windows 95 will refer to the printer by make and model, but you can provide a different name to use instead. The name is purely descriptive, so, for example, Old Reliable, Bubbles, or Laser Brain would all be acceptable.

- Whether you want to print a test page. If you've never used the printer, accept the default, Yes, to verify that the printer is set up and working properly.

The wizard will ask for the following if you're connecting to a network printer:

- The printer address, which is a UNC path in the form *server**printer* like the one shown below.

  If you don't know the path, either ask your network administrator which one to use or click the Browse button to choose from available printers. If you type the path, don't forget the double backslash at the beginning.

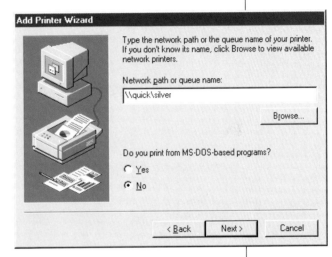

- Whether you print from MS-DOS programs. You can leave this set to No, if you want, even if you do print from MS-DOS programs. As described in the section headed "Using a Network Printer" in Chapter 10, this part of setup has to do with telling MS-DOS programs where to find the printer, and you can handle it later from the printer's properties sheet.

- A printer name. As mentioned above, this can be any descriptive name you choose. You can't use a UNC path because backslashes are invalid, but if you want to refer to the printer by its address, you can always turn something like \\quick\silver into quicksilver.

- Whether you want to print a test page. Again, this is not a bad idea if you haven't used this printer, or one of this type, before.

Local printer or remote, when you click the Finish button to complete the installation, the Add Printer Wizard might ask you to insert a Windows 95 disk so that it can copy the appropriate software to your computer. After this is done, the wizard adds an icon for the printer to your Printers folder, which will allow you to open a properties sheet that describes the printer's capabilities, along with the settings and name you provided.

That's all you have to do. While the Printers folder is open, however, you might want to drag a shortcut to the printer onto your desktop. Because you must double-click the printer to open and work with the print queue, the desktop is a good place to keep the icon close at hand.

Modems As with most good Windows 95 features, you add a modem with a wizard, the Install New Modem Wizard. What becomes intriguing, once you've worked with Windows 95 for a while, is just how many ways there are to start the Install New Modem Wizard. You can start it:

- By double-clicking the Modems icon in the Control Panel and then choosing Add from the Modems Properties sheet that appears.

- By double-clicking the Add New Hardware icon in the Control Panel and choosing to add a new modem.

- Or—and this is the fun part—by trying to use any Windows 95 feature that involves a modem when you haven't yet set up a modem. So sign up with MSN, and the wizard might pop up. Or start Dial-Up Networking for the first time; if it needs a modem, here comes the wiz.

Adding a modem is simple, indeed, because all you have to do is let the wizard find it, query it, and set it up. This is what the main screen looks like, at the right.

Click Next, and the wizard begins checking your communications (COM) ports. When it finds your modem, it determines what type it is and lets you know with a screen like the one below.

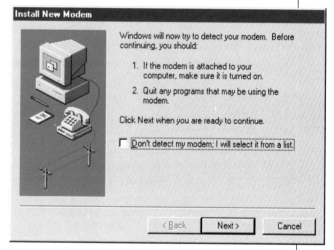

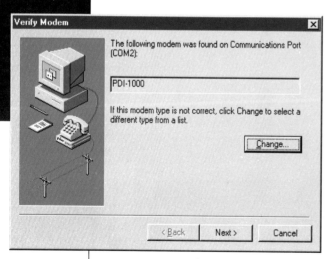

MAKING CHANGES
After you set up your modem, you can change its properties (transmission settings such as databits and parity), if you have to, with the Properties button on the Modems Properties sheet, and you can change the way the modem dials calls with the Dialing Properties button on the properties sheet.

If the wizard made a mistake, click the Change button to select the correct modem make and model from a list. (If your modem is not shown, choose one of the standard types at the top of the list.) Provide a setup disk or the appropriate Windows 95 disk if the wizard asks for it. Finish up, and the device will be set up for any Windows 95–based program that requires a modem.

The Fun Stuff: Multimedia

Multimedia, as any kid can tell you, is technology that combines—or can combine—text, sound, graphics images, animation, and video. It's the stuff of future everything from computer-based encyclopedias to really hot games. It's also supported well by Windows 95, and it's fun. To finish up this last chapter of the book, here's a quick look at one of the most entertaining parts of Windows 95. To get to your built-in Windows 95 multimedia support staff:

- Open the Start menu, and work your way through Programs and Accessories to Multimedia.

If on the Multimedia menu you don't see the items discussed in the remainder of the chapter, open the Add/Remove Programs icon in the Control Panel, click the Windows Setup tab, click the Multimedia category, and then click the Details button. Choose the multimedia components you want from there.

Sounds of Music

When you want to listen to some soothing (or not-so-soothing) audio as you work, turn to CD Player. On the screen, it looks like the window shown at the right.

To use CD Player:

1. Insert an audio CD in your CD-ROM drive.

2. Use the Start menu to open CD Player.

3. Click the Play button (the big one labeled with a large right-pointing triangle).

If you're a music fan, you can probably figure out what the other buttons do, but if you can't, rest the mouse pointer on a button you're not sure about and wait a second or two for a tooltip to appear and tell you what the button does.

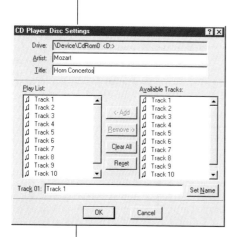

Naturally, CD Player lets you keep track of who and what you're listening to. To edit the Artist, Title, and Track text boxes:

1. Choose Edit Play List from the Disc menu. When the Disc Settings window appears, enter the artist and title, as shown at the left.

2. To select specific tracks, click the Clear All button, select the tracks you want in the Available Tracks list, and then click the Add button.

3. To name a track, select it in the Available Tracks list, type a name, and click the Set Name button.

4. And if you like to adjust the volume as you listen, open the View menu and choose Volume Control.

Which brings you to another multimedia option.

Volume Control

Although Volume Control appears at the end of the Multimedia submenu, this program is probably one you'll use often. You can open it either from CD Player's View menu, as described above, or from the Multimedia submenu. Volume Control looks just like the sound controls on your home music system, as shown at the right.

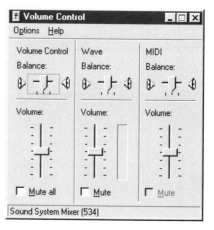

To use Volume Control:

1. Drag the Volume slider up or down to increase or decrease sound.

2. If you want to turn sound off completely, check the Mute All option in the Volume Control Balance section of the window. This can be handy if you work in a busy office and don't want to disturb your neighbors with the assorted beeps and chimes that Windows 95 normally plays when you start up, shut down, and perform other actions. (To list and change assigned sounds, double-click the Sounds icon in the Control Panel.)

3. To tell Windows 95 which volume controls you want to see, choose Properties from the Options menu. Check the controls you want in the list at the bottom.

Tip!

CAN'T HEAR?

Depending on your sound card and speaker setup, it's possible that you will have to disconnect your speaker cord from the output jack on your sound card and plug it into the output jack on your CD-ROM drive before you can hear an audio CD. Consult your hardware documentation on this, because you might be able to add an extra cord so that audio CD sound will be able to travel from the CD-ROM drive to the sound card and thence to the speakers. That will enable you to avoid switching your speaker cord between the sound card and the CD-ROM drive each time you switch from using a CD-ROM to listening to an audio CD.

Media Player

Windows 95's Media Player lets you open and play video (AVI), MIDI, and sound (WAV) files. This is an enjoyable program, even if you're not a media whiz, because Windows 95 comes with a number of sample sounds, including portions of Bach's "Third Brandenburg Concerto" and Mozart's "Jupiter Symphony," as well as collections of other classy sounds with names like Jungle and Utopia. To install these built-in aural delights, view the details for the Multimedia category of Windows Setup in Add/Remove Programs.

Media Player looks like this.

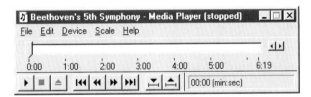

To play sounds (as well as MIDI and video clips, remember):

1. Use the Start menu to open Media Player, choose Open from the File menu, and then choose the file you want to play.

2. Click the Play button (the leftmost button at the bottom). Remember, if you leave the mouse pointer on any button, a tooltip will appear to tell you what the button does.

Sound Recorder

And finally, there's Sound Recorder for recording and saving your own sounds via microphone or another audio input device. This is what Sound Recorder looks like, at the right.

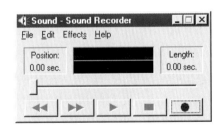

To record a sound:

1. Use the Start menu to open Sound Recorder. Open the File menu, and choose New.

2. Click the button with the red dot on it, and start making noise. When you're through recording, click the button with the rectangle on it.

3. Choose Save As from the File menu, and name the new file.

To play back a sound:

1. Open the File menu, and choose Open.

2. Find and open the sound file you want to play.

3. Click the Play button (the one with the single right-pointing triangle on it).

AutoPlay

Windows 95, unlike any earlier version of Windows, includes a multimedia feature called AutoPlay.

You see an example of AutoPlay when you insert your Windows 95 CD-ROM disc and the CD-ROM window opens up automatically. (If you haven't tried the buttons in this window, by the way, give them a shot. If you like Doom, you'll also enjoy Hover—and you'll see some pretty slick graphics to boot.)

Because AutoPlay has to be designed into a CD-ROM title, you might not see a lot of it for a while, but when you're exposed to it, you'll certainly like it. Here's what it's about.

Windows 95 can detect when you insert a disc into your CD-ROM drive. AutoPlay takes this detection one step further by enabling Windows 95 to automatically start whatever program is on that disc.

You still have to install the program, but once you've done that, you don't (or won't) have to choose the program from the Start menu or open a window to the CD-ROM drive and double-click the program icon. Instead, when you insert an AutoPlay disc into the CD-ROM drive, Windows 95 will automatically open and load the program into memory. The benefits to you: no hunting for the program, and a shorter wait while the program loads and prepares to run.

Oh, by the way, the "secret" to Windows 95's ability to detect and automatically run a CD-ROM program is a small file named Autorun.inf on the disc. This file must be set up and added by the program's developer, so you can't turn your old CD-ROM software into AutoPlay versions, much as you might like to.

Well, this is where the book must end, so that's your introduction to Windows 95. It's to be hoped that you enjoyed and learned from your journey. As you work with Windows 95, remember there's a lot more to discover. Relax and enjoy it all. And if you join The Microsoft Network, feel free to send e-mail.

Bye.

⑤ Road Signs

Roadblocks and Detours

This special chapter was written by Kyle Martin, who is both a technical writer and a member of Microsoft's Product Support Services (PSS) group. Presented in a question-and-answer format, the chapter covers frequently asked questions and topics. Do you need this chapter? Perhaps not, since Microsoft Windows 95 runs perfectly well for most people. But even if Windows 95 is problem-free on your computer, the information here is worth reading because it can help you understand a little more about Windows 95. And isn't a little more always better than a little less, except for the simple, sinful pleasures of life?

About Windows 95

Question: What resources do I have available for help with Windows 95?

Answer: There are many places you can go for help with Windows 95: this book; the *Windows 95 User's Guide;* Windows 95's Online Help; various TXT and WRI files that ship with Windows 95 (for example, the file named README.TXT in your Windows 95 folder); the *Microsoft Windows 95 Resource Kit* (for advanced technical information); and if you have a modem, WinNews via The Microsoft Network and most other major online services and networks. For more information on these resources and Microsoft Product Support Services, see the SUPPORT.TXT file located in your Windows 95 folder or on your Windows 95 disks or CD-ROM.

Question: I thought Windows 95 was a 32-bit operating system, but I've heard it still contains some 16-bit instructions (code). Is this true?

Answer: While Windows 95 is a 32-bit, preemptive multitasking operating system, it retains some 16-bit code to provide backward compatibility with your existing applications. Wherever possible, 16-bit code was replaced with faster, more reliable 32-bit code.

Upgrading to Windows 95

Question: Should I run the Windows 95 Setup program from MS-DOS or from an existing version of Windows?

Answer: Windows 95 Setup runs from MS-DOS or from Windows 3.1 and later or from Windows For Workgroups 3.1 and later. If you are running one of these versions of Windows or Windows For Workgroups, we recommend that you run Windows 95 Setup from within Windows.

Question: When I run Setup from within Windows 3.0, Setup tells me that this program requires a newer version of Windows. How do I upgrade Windows 3.0?

Answer: To upgrade Windows 3.0 to Windows 95, you must run Setup from MS-DOS and choose to install Windows 95 in the same directory (folder) as Windows 3.0.

Question: When I upgrade, if I do not install Windows 95 in my current Windows directory, will my Windows-based applications still run?

Answer: If you install Windows 95 in a new directory (folder), you must reinstall all your Windows-based applications in order for them to run properly. If you upgrade your current version of Windows to Windows 95, you do not need to reinstall any applications because Windows 95 retains your settings.

Question: What do I do if Setup stops responding (or *hangs*) while it is detecting my hardware?

Answer: Windows 95 Setup includes a feature called Safe Recovery. If your computer hangs while Setup is detecting your hardware, simply turn the computer off and then back on, run Setup again, and choose Safe Recovery when prompted. Setup picks up immediately after the point where it hung earlier.

Question: Why does Setup tell me I am running virus-protection software when I cannot find that software on my computer?

Answer: Some computers have built-in virus protection. If virus protection is enabled in your computer's BIOS, Setup cannot continue. Please contact your hardware vendor for information about temporarily disabling this feature. (Your computer's BIOS is a set of instructions on a special chip inside the machine. Because the BIOS is essential in order for your computer to run properly, it is normally protected from casual access. You usually have to press a special key or key combination to work with the BIOS. If you do this, be careful.)

Question: Do I have to reinstall Windows 95 to create a startup disk if I did not create one when I set up Windows 95?

Answer: No. To create a startup disk in Windows 95, do the following:

1. Open the Start menu and the Settings submenu, and click Control Panel.

2. Double-click the Add/Remove Programs icon, and click the Startup Disk tab.

3. Click the Create Disk button to create a startup disk.

Question: I've installed Windows NT in the same directory as Windows 3.1 so that I can run either version of Windows. How do I upgrade this version of Windows to Windows 95, and how do I start Windows 95 afterward?

Answer: First, you cannot upgrade this version of Windows to Windows 95 because of the Windows NT files. To install Windows 95 in addition to Windows NT, install Windows 95 in a new directory. Once Windows 95 is installed, when you start your computer, you'll be given a choice of running Windows NT or MS-DOS. Choose MS-DOS to load Windows 95.

Question: Since I upgraded to Windows 95, my fonts no longer appear in the WIN.INI file but I can still access them from my applications. Where did they go?

Answer: Windows 95 moves many of the items in INI (initialization) files, such as the fonts section, to the registry—which, as you've learned, is a "private" Windows 95 database of information about your computer, its attached devices, and your software.

Question: What files make up the registry that I keep hearing about?

Answer: The SYSTEM.DAT file is your system registry. This file stores all the information about your computer and software. Most of the information in the various INI files for previous versions of Windows now resides in this one file. You also have two other registry-related files:

- The SYSTEM.DA0 file is a backup copy of SYSTEM.DAT. If Windows 95 finds that your registry is damaged, it attempts to use SYSTEM.DA0 as its replacement.

- The SYSTEM.1ST file is a copy of SYSTEM.DAT from the first time your computer booted successfully under Windows 95.

These files are important for troubleshooting purposes, so we recommend that you do not delete them.

Setup

Question: Windows 95 Setup stops and gives me an error message. Where can I find more information regarding the error?

Answer: Windows 95 Setup generally provides useful information in the body of the error message. It also records the Setup progress in a file called SETUPLOG.TXT in the root directory of your startup drive. The file is hidden, but you can open it with a text editor to view its contents. If you are running MS-DOS 5.0 or later, type the following commands, in the order shown, at an MS-DOS prompt, pressing Enter where you see *[Enter]*:

```
C:\>attrib -h c:\setuplog.txt [Enter]

C:\>edit c:\setuplog.txt [Enter]
```

Question: How do I prevent the General Protection Fault message I receive after I insert a floppy disk to create the startup disk?

Answer: This error is generally caused by a virtual device driver (VxD) from Norton Utilities. You can work around this problem in either of the following ways:

- By restarting Setup. When Setup asks you if you want to create a startup disk, choose No.

- Or by removing the symevnt.386 line from the [386Enh] section of the SYSTEM.INI file before you run Windows 95 Setup. To do this:

    1. If you are running MS-DOS 5.0 or later, type the following, pressing Enter where you see *[Enter]*:

        ```
        C:\>edit <path>system.ini [Enter]
        ```

        where *<path>* is the drive and directory of your Windows installation. For example:

        ```
        C:\>edit c:\windows\system.ini
        ```

    2. Remove the device=symevnt.386 line, and then save and close the file.

Question: What does the error message *Incorrect MS-DOS version. MS-DOS 3.1 or greater required* mean? I'm using MS-DOS 6.22.

Answer: This error message might appear when you start Windows 95 Setup if you are using 386MAX software. You can work around this error by temporarily disabling any references to 386MAX in your CONFIG.SYS and AUTOEXEC.BAT files. If you are running MS-DOS 5.0 or later, type the following at an MS-DOS prompt, pressing Enter where you see *[Enter]*:

```
C:\>edit c:\config.sys [Enter]
```

Place a REM statement at the beginning of each line that references 386MAX. For example:

```
REM device=<path>386MAX.SYS
```

where *<path>* is the drive and directory for your 386MAX installation.

Question: I just finished running Setup, and now my computer hangs while Windows 95 is loading. Why?

Answer: A number of things can cause Windows 95 to hang while loading. It could be a device driver that loads from the CONFIG.SYS file or the SYSTEM.INI file, a TSR that loads from the AUTOEXEC.BAT file, or your video driver. Use the following to help you determine the cause:

First, press the F8 key when you see the *Starting Windows 95* message, and then choose Safe Mode from the list of startup options.

- If your computer does *not* boot in Safe Mode:

  - If your computer did not work with earlier versions of Windows or Windows for Workgroups, contact your hardware vendor about a possible BIOS upgrade.

  - If your computer supports ROM BIOS shadowing or has built-in virus checking, disable them. For instructions on how to do this, consult your owner's manual or contact the hardware manufacturer.

  - Reboot, press F8 when you see the *Starting Windows 95* message, choose the command prompt option, and run ScanDisk from an MS-DOS prompt by entering *scandisk* at the C:\> prompt.

  - Check for viruses.

- If your computer *does* boot in Safe Mode:

  - Reboot your computer as you normally would, and press Esc when you see the Windows 95 logo. This will allow you to watch the results as startup commands are executed.

  - Change your video driver to Standard VGA as follows:

    1. Open the Start menu and the Settings submenu, and click Control Panel.

    2. Double-click the Display icon.

    3. Click the Settings tab, click the Change Display Type button, and then click the Change button at the right of Adapter Type.

4. Click Show All Devices, and then find and click the (Standard Display Types) option in the Manufacturers list.

5. Double-click the Standard Display Adapter (VGA) option.

- If you are running on a network, remove the network components:

  1. Right-click the Network Neighborhood icon, and click Properties on the popup menu.

  2. For each client you have installed (listed under *The Following Network Components Are Installed*), select it and then click the Remove button.

  3. Restart your computer when prompted.

If you are still unable to boot Windows 95, try the following procedure:

1. Reboot, press F8 when you see the *Starting Windows 95* message, choose the command prompt option, and then rename your current SYSTEM.DAT file as SYSTEM.OLD. Before you do this you must remove its read-only, hidden, and system attributes. To do so, type the following, pressing Enter where you see *[Enter]*:

   ```
   C:\>cd\<path> [Enter]
   ```

   where *<path>* is your Windows 95 folder. For example if Windows 95 is installed in a folder called Windows, type *C:\>cd\windows [Enter]*. Next, type:

   ```
   C:\>attrib system.dat -r -s -h [Enter]

   C:\>ren system.dat system.old [Enter]
   ```

2. Now, rename the file SYSTEM.DA0 (the last character is a zero) to SYSTEM.DAT, and give it the read-only, system, and hidden attributes with the following commands:

   ```
   C:\>attrib system.da0 -r -s -h [Enter]

   C:\>ren system.da0 system.dat [Enter]

   C:\>attrib system.dat +r +s +h [Enter]
   ```

3. Restart your computer.

Startup

Question: After I install Windows 95, can I boot to (start with) my previous version of MS-DOS?

Answer: If you install Windows 95 in a clean new directory (rather than your old Windows directory), the ability to *dual-boot* to your previous operating system is enabled by default. However, if you upgrade your previous version of Windows to Windows 95 by installing in the *same* directory, and you want to boot to your previous operating system (MS-DOS), you must add the line "BootMulti=1" to the [Options] section of the MSDOS.SYS file. Make sure that the Show All Files option is turned on in your My Computer window or in the Windows Explorer, and then follow this procedure:

1. Open the Start menu and the Find submenu, and click Files Or Folders.

2. In the Named box, type *msdos.sys*. In the Look In box, click your boot drive (usually drive C). Click the Find Now button.

3. Right-click the Msdos.sys file, and click Properties on the popup menu.

4. Click the Read-Only and Hidden check boxes to remove these attributes from the Msdos.sys file, and click OK.

5. Right-click the Msdos.sys file, and click Open With on the popup menu.

6. In the Choose The Program You Want To Use box, click WORDPAD and click OK.

7. In the [Options] section of the file, add the following line:

```
BootMulti=1
```

8. Save the file and quit WordPad.

9. Right-click the Msdos.sys file, and click Properties on the popup menu.

10. Click the Read-Only and Hidden check boxes to turn these attributes back on for the file, and click OK. Close the Find window.

11. Quit and then restart Windows 95.

12. When you see the *Starting Windows 95* message press the F4 key to boot to your previous operating system.

Question: I added the BootMulti=1 line to the MSDOS.SYS file, but I still cannot start my previous operating system. Why?

Answer: Windows 95 supports dual-booting on computers with version 5.0 or later of MS-DOS, OEM-DOS, or IBM PC-DOS. If you have an earlier version of DOS or if you use Novell or DR DOS, you cannot boot to your previous operating system. Also, if you use disk compression, make sure you edit the copy of MSDOS.SYS on the *host* (not the compressed) drive.

Windows 95, Your Applications, and MS-DOS

Question: Will all the Windows-based applications that I currently run still work in Windows 95?

Answer: Most applications that you use should continue to run in Windows 95. Applications that might not work in Windows 95 are those that incorrectly check the Windows version number and those that conform to the old Windows 2.0 specification. These types of applications might need updating to work properly in Windows 95. The GENERAL.TXT file that ships with Windows 95 provides more details on certain applications in the "MS-DOS & Windows Programs" section. (GENERAL.TXT is in your Windows 95 folder. To open the file, double-click the file named General.)

Question: Will all the MS-DOS–based applications that I currently run work in Windows 95?

Answer: Windows 95 supports running MS-DOS–based applications in many different ways. For example, you can run an MS-DOS–based application in a window or a full screen. If you have a problem running a particular MS-DOS–based application, you can try to run it in MS-DOS mode. This feature lets you specify CONFIG.SYS files and AUTOEXEC.BAT files for this one application. It is available through the application's properties sheet, as follows:

1. Locate the executable (EXE file) for the application you need to modify. You can use the Windows Explorer, My Computer, or the Find command on the Start menu to locate the file.

2. Right-click the filename, and click Properties on the popup menu.

3. Click the Program tab, and click the Advanced button.

4. Click the MS-DOS Mode check box.

5. If you want to use a specific CONFIG.SYS, AUTOEXEC.BAT, or both, click the Specify A New MS-DOS Configuration button, and then either edit the files in the appropriate text boxes on the properties sheet or click the Configuration button to select from a set of options. Note that if you

set up a special configuration, you might need settings given in your application's manual. Also, it doesn't hurt to understand MS-DOS commands pretty well.

6. When the configuration is as you want it, click OK. Click OK again to close the properties sheet.

The GENERAL.TXT file that ships with Windows 95 provides more details on certain applications in the "MS-DOS & Windows Programs" section.

Question: My MS-DOS–based application will not load and tells me that Windows 95 is running. How can I run this program in Windows 95?

Answer: Some MS-DOS–based applications do not load if they detect that Windows 95 is running. To run such an application in Windows 95, click the Prevent MS-DOS–Based Programs From Detecting Windows check box on the Advanced properties sheet for this program. This feature returns a code to these applications that says, "Windows is not running."

1. Locate the executable file for the application you need to modify. You can use the Windows Explorer, My Computer, or the Find command on the Start menu to locate the file.

2. Right-click the filename, and click Properties on the popup menu.

3. Click the Program tab, and click the Advanced button.

4. Click the Prevent MS-DOS–Based Programs From Detecting Windows check box, and click OK.

Question: Is it true that I do not need a CONFIG.SYS or AUTOEXEC.BAT file to start Windows 95?

Answer: You need these files only if you want to load a third-party device driver or a terminate-and-stay-resident (TSR) program because Windows 95 automatically loads the files you need to boot your computer successfully. For example, Windows 95 automatically loads the following six files and settings:

```
HIMEM.SYS

IFSHLP.SYS

SETVER.EXE

FILES=60

BUFFERS=30

STACKS=9,256
```

If you specify a setting in CONFIG.SYS or AUTOEXEC.BAT for one of the files that Windows 95 normally loads, your setting overrides the Windows 95 default behavior. If you do not want Windows 95 to load any of the files or settings listed above, add DOS=NOAUTO to the CONFIG.SYS file, and Windows 95 will load only what is specified in your CONFIG.SYS and AUTOEXEC.BAT files.

Disks and Files

Question: When I delete a file at an MS-DOS prompt or in Windows 3.1 File Manager, the filename does not appear in the Recycle Bin. Why?

Answer: Windows 95 supports placing deleted files in the Recycle Bin from Windows 95 shell (GUI) components only, such as My Computer or the Windows Explorer.

Question: How do applications handle long filenames in Windows 95?

Answer: Even though Windows 95 provides long-filename support, your application must be long-filename–aware to take advantage of this feature. Applications that do not support long filenames use short filenames. Once such an application manipulates (saves, copies, and so on) a file using the short filename, the long filename is lost.

Question: Why do I see strange characters on the screen when I try to read my SCSI hard disk?

Answer: Some SCSI hard disks require double-buffering support to work properly in Windows 95. In most cases Windows 95 recognizes these drives and inserts the double-buffer command for you; however, you might need to do this manually:

1. Open the Start menu and the Find submenu, and click Files Or Folders.

2. In the Named box, type *msdos.sys.* In the Look In box, click your boot drive (usually drive C). Click the Find Now button.

3. Right-click the Msdos.sys file, and click Properties on the popup menu.

4. Click the Read-Only and Hidden check boxes to remove these attributes from the Msdos.sys file, and click OK.

5. Right-click the Msdos.sys file, and click Open With on the popup menu.

6. In the Choose The Program You Want To Use box, click WORDPAD and then click OK.

7. In the [Options] section, add the following line:

```
DoubleBuffer=1
```

If DoubleBuffer=1 is already present, change this line to:

```
DoubleBuffer=2
```

8. Save the file and quit WordPad.

9. Right-click the Msdos.sys file, and click Properties on the popup menu.

10. Click the Read-Only and Hidden check boxes to turn these attributes back on for the file, and click OK. Close the Find window.

11. Quit and then restart Windows 95.

Networks, Including Novell NetWare

Question: I've heard that a Windows 95 computer can act as a Novell NetWare server. Is this true?

Answer: Windows 95 includes a virtual device driver (NWSERVER.VXD) that allows Windows 95 computers to process NCP-based requests for file and printer input/output. Since NetWare servers process NCP-based requests, a Windows 95 computer can be used as a NetWare file and print server. To install this virtual device driver, you must have a NetWare server on your network and you must install the Microsoft "File And Printer Sharing For NetWare Networks" service:

1. Right-click Network Neighborhood, and click Properties on the popup menu.

2. Click Add, and double-click Service.

3. Click Microsoft, and double-click the File And Printer Sharing For NetWare Networks option.

4. Restart Windows when prompted.

Question: Can a Windows 95 computer act as a Novell NetWare server and a Microsoft Network server at the same time?

Answer: A Windows 95 computer can act as only one type of server at a time.

Question: Once I set up my Windows 95 computer to be a Novell NetWare server, can NetWare clients connect to it?

Answer: Any NetWare client running Novell's real-mode drivers or Microsoft's protected-mode drivers can use your computer as a NetWare file and print server.

Question: After I install Windows 95, what should I do if I have trouble connecting to my Novell NetWare server?

Answer: Either right-click your Network Neighborhood icon and choose Properties or double-click the Network icon in the Control Panel. On the properties sheet, make sure you have the IPX/SPX-compatible protocol installed. If you don't, click the Add button, choose Protocol, click Add, and select IPX/SPX.

If the protocol is installed, be sure that its frame type is set to AUTO. To do this, select IPX/SPX, click the Properties button, click the Advanced tab, click Frame Type, and check the setting. If you have problems connecting to your NetWare server, change the frame type from AUTO to the specific frame type your server is using. Novell NetWare version 3.11 servers default to a frame type of Ethernet 802.3. NetWare version 3.12 and 4.0 servers default to a frame type of Ethernet 802.2.

Question: After I installed Windows 95 I noticed that Setup remarked out (REM'ed out) the Novell NetWare drivers in my startup files so that they're not used. Why?

Answer: Windows 95 provides protected-mode versions of Novell's real-mode network drivers. When you use the Windows 95 protected-mode drivers, you do not need to load Novell's real-mode drivers. Protected-mode drivers provide many benefits over real-mode drivers. For example, the Windows 95 protected-mode drivers do not use conventional memory and are faster than their real-mode counterparts.

Question: I know Windows 95 supports long filenames, but can I store long filenames on a Novell NetWare server?

Answer: Windows 95 supports long filenames on a NetWare server if you load OS/2 name space on the NetWare server.

Question: What do I need to use user-level access control in Windows 95?

Answer: Windows 95 supports user-level security (access by individuals) only if you have a Windows NT server or a Novell NetWare server on your network. One of these servers is necessary so that Windows 95 can obtain the list of users and groups for your network. If you do not have a Windows NT or NetWare server, you can use share-level access control (access to shared resources) only.

Modems

Question: How do I install a modem in Windows 95?

Answer: There are several ways to install a modem in Windows 95. The recommended procedure is to double-click the Modems icon in the Control Panel and follow the instructions. If Windows 95 has trouble detecting your modem, manually select the appropriate type from the list of modems.

Question: What can I do if my modem isn't listed as an option in the Install New Modem wizard?

Answer: Windows 95 supports many modems. If your modem is not listed, select a similar modem model or similar modem from the same manufacturer.

If these do not work, try a Hayes-compatible modem or a Standard Modem Type modem. If you continue to have problems, contact your modem manufacturer for additional information.

Printing

Question: How do I go about troubleshooting printing problems in Windows 95?

Answer: Windows 95 provides a couple of different ways for you to access online print troubleshooting help: the Print Troubleshooter tool and online Help.

To access the Print Troubleshooter tool:

1. Open the Start menu, and click Help.

2. On the Contents tab, double-click the Troubleshooting topic.

3. Double-click the If You Have Trouble Printing topic.

4. Answer the questions you are asked, and you might solve your printing problem.

To access online Help, right-click a printer option field and then click *What's This?* on the menu that appears to see detailed information about that option.

Question: Why can't I get Windows 95 to print to my local printer?

Answer: If you cannot print to your local printer, try the following:

- Make sure that the printer is turned on and is online, that the printer is not jammed, and that there is paper in the tray.

- Try to print a test page:

  1. Open the Start menu and the Settings submenu, and click Printers.

  2. Right-click the printer icon for your local printer, and click Properties on the popup menu.

  3. Click the General tab, and click the Print Test Page button.

- Turn the printer off, wait a few seconds, and then turn the printer back on. This clears the printer's buffer.

- Try to print to a file:

  1. Open the Start menu and the Settings submenu, and click Printers.

  2. Right-click the printer icon for your local printer, and click Properties on the popup menu.

  3. Click the Details tab, and click FILE: in the Print To The Following Port drop-down list.

- If printing to a file was successful, try to copy that file to the port your printer is on:

  - Type the following line at an MS-DOS prompt, pressing Enter where you see *[Enter]*:

    ```
    C:\>copy c:\<filename> <printer port> [Enter]
    ```

    where *<filename>* is the path and name of the file you just created, and *<printer port>* is the port your local printer is on. For example, if you created a file called TEST1.TXT in your Windows folder and your printer is on LPT1, type the following:

    ```
    C:\>copy c:\windows\test1.txt lpt1 [Enter]
    ```

    If you have a PostScript printer, you can use the built-in test file. To do so, type:

    ```
    C:\>copy c:<path>testps.txt <printer port> [Enter]
    ```

    where *<path>* is the location of your Windows 95 System folder. For example, if your Windows 95 folder is named Windows and your printer is on LPT1, type the following:

    ```
    C:\>copy c:\windows\system\testps.txt lpt1
    ```

- If the previous step works, there is a problem with communications between Windows 95 and your printer. Try a different printer cable, try this printer on a different computer, or try a different printer on this computer.

- Try to print using the Generic/Text Only printer driver. To do so, follow these steps:

  1. Open the Start menu and the Settings submenu, and click Printers.

  2. Double-click the Add Printer icon, and follow the instructions in the Add Printer Wizard to install the Generic/Text Only printer driver.

  3. Try to print from your application with this driver.

- Try to use an emulation mode for your printer. Many printers have emulation modes that allow you to print with a different printer driver. Refer to the printer documentation, or ask the manufacturer about using emulation modes on your printer. (NOTE: most printers require that you change a setting on the printer itself to use emulation modes.)

  1. Open the Start menu and the Settings submenu, and click Printers.

  2. Double-click the Add Printer icon, and follow the instructions in the Add Printer Wizard to install the printer driver for the printer that your printer emulates.

For PostScript printers, try installing the Apple LaserWriter driver (a PostScript driver that works with most PostScript printers).

Question: What do the spool settings for printers do?

Answer: If you have a printing problem, changing the spool settings may resolve it.

1. Open the Start menu and the Settings submenu, and click Printers.

2. Right-click the printer you are trying to print to, and click Properties on the popup menu.

3. Click the Details tab, click the Spool Settings button, and click the Print Directly To The Printer option.

4. If your printer supports bidirectional communication, click the Disable Bi-Directional Support For This Printer option. (Bidirectional printing relies on the 1284 IEEE specification. If your printer cable does not conform to this specification and is not of reasonable length, bidirectional printing does not work in Windows 95.)

5. Click the OK button.

6. Try to print from Notepad or WordPad.

7. If you cannot print from Notepad or WordPad, try different combinations of spool settings and bidirectional support until you find a combination that works. For example, try disabling bidirectional support with RAW and EMF spool data format settings. Also, try bidirectional support with the RAW spool data format. (RAW is the only spool data format supported for PostScript printers.)

Question: I've heard that removing and reinstalling the printer driver might solve printing problems. How do I do this in Windows 95?

Answer: Follow these steps to remove and reinstall your printer driver:

1. Open the Start menu and the Settings submenu, and click Printers.

2. Right-click the printer you want to remove, and click Delete on the popup menu.

3. If you are prompted to remove all the files associated with the printer, click Yes.

4. Open the Start menu and the Settings submenu, and click Printers on the popup menu.

5. Double-click the Add Printer icon, and follow the instructions in the Add Printer Wizard to reinstall the Windows 95 printer driver.

Question: Why is printing slower than normal?

Answer: Printing speed in Windows 95 is measured in one of two ways:

- Return to application (RTA) speed. This is defined as the time elapsed from when you click Print to when you regain control of the system.

- Printer page drop speed. This is defined as the time elapsed from when you click Print to when the print job is complete.

You can affect each of these elapsed times by changing spool settings. To change spool settings, follow these steps:

1. Open the Start menu and the Settings submenu, and click Printers.

2. Right-click the printer you want to use, and click Properties on the popup menu.

3. Click the Details tab, and click the Spool Settings button.

   - For faster RTA speed, click the Start Printing After First Page Is Spooled option. In most cases you should also choose EMF as the spool data format. Note, however, that PostScript printers support only the RAW spool data format.

     For faster printer page drop speed, click either the Print Directly To The Printer option or the Start Printing After Last Page Is Spooled option. (Note that this is how the Windows 3.1 spooler works.) In some cases this option prevents laser-printer engines from turning on and off during a print job.

Question: When I print a Help topic, the font size is too small. Can I change it?

Answer: Windows 95 does not support changing the size of printed Help topics. However, you can copy the information from Help, paste it into another application (such as WordPad), and print it.

1. Highlight the text you want to print, right-click it, and click Copy.

2. Open the Start menu, open the Programs and Accessories submenus, and click WordPad.

3. On the Edit menu, click Paste.

4. On the File menu, click Print.

Video

Question: What do I do if my video adapter is not available in the list of video cards in Windows 95?

Answer: If Windows 95 does not have an option for your particular video adapter, it might have one for the chip set your card is based on. To determine the chip set, run the Microsoft Diagnostics (MSD) utility, which is available with earlier versions of MS-DOS and Microsoft Windows. If you do not have a copy of MSD, consult your video-adapter documentation or contact the manufacturer. If your video card's chip set is not compatible with one that Windows 95 supports, you can use the Standard Display Adapter (VGA) or Super VGA (SVGA) driver. The standard VGA and SVGA drivers do not, however, support acceleration. Using these drivers may hinder system performance.

Question: **Why does Windows 95 always start with the VGA driver even if I install the Windows 95 driver for my video card?**

Answer: Windows 95 provides a feature called VGA fallback mode. If Windows 95 detects a problem with your video card or driver, it starts itself with the VGA driver. You might be able to resolve this problem by reinstalling your video driver:

1. Open the Start menu and the Settings submenu, click Control Panel, and double-click the System icon. Or right-click My Computer, and click Properties on the popup menu.

2. Click the Device Manager tab, and double-click Display Adapters.

3. Click the display adapter you have installed, and click the Remove button.

4. Restart Windows when prompted.

After Windows 95 restarts, the Add New Hardware Wizard should start automatically. Run through the wizard so that Windows 95 can redetect your display adapter. If the wizard does not start, either rerun the Add New Hardware utility in the Control Panel and let Windows redetect your display adapter or do the following:

1. Right-click the desktop, and choose Properties from the popup menu.

2. Click the Settings tab, and click the Change Display Type button.

3. Click the Change button in the Adapter Type section, and then install the Windows 95 driver for your display adapter.

Question: **How do I keep my screen from flickering while I run Windows 95?**

Answer: Make sure that the frequency (*hertz* or *Hz*) of your monitor matches the frequency for your video card. If these settings do not match, you can cause *permanent* damage to your monitor. You might need to run a utility from your video-card manufacturer to set the frequency. Consult your video-adapter documentation or contact the manufacturer to determine if you need to do this.

Question: I've installed Windows 95. Why don't the animated cursors work?

Answer: If you use a Windows 3.1 display driver in Windows 95, you cannot take advantage of the new features of Windows 95's GDI (graphic-device interface), which include:

- Animated cursors.

- Dynamic resolution changes—the ability to change your video resolution without restarting Windows. (If you change the color depth or the actual video driver that is used, however, you must restart Windows.)

- VGA fallback mode, whereby Windows 95 restarts itself with the VGA driver if it detects an error or a problem with your video card or video driver.

A note for the technically adept: Windows 3.1 video drivers do not take advantage of the Windows 95 virtual flat-frame buffer device (VFLATD.VXD). VFLATD.VXD provides a frame buffer with a capacity of up to 1 MB. Windows 3.1 video drivers are limited to a 64-KB frame buffer. (The larger the frame buffer, the faster the video should be because there's more information in memory.)

Question: What can I do if my mouse cursor doesn't behave correctly?

Answer: If you have an S3-compatible or Western Digital-compatible (WD) video driver, set the Advanced Graphics Setting to Most:

1. Open the Start menu and the Settings submenu, click Control Panel, and double-click the System icon. Or right-click My Computer and click Properties on the popup menu.

2. Click the Performance tab, and click the Graphics button in the Advanced Settings section.

   Note that the Hardware acceleration slide bar has four settings, as shown in the illustration below.

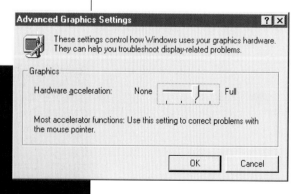

The first notch is for None, the second is for Basic, the third is for Most, and the fourth is for Full. The Most setting should fix your problem by adding the SWCursor=1 line to the [Display] section of the WIN.INI file, which will disable the hardware cursor. (This is similar to the /Y switch that can be used with some versions of the MS-DOS–level Microsoft Mouse driver.)

Question: What can I do if my machine randomly hangs?

Answer: If you have an S3-compatible video driver, set the Advanced Graphics Setting to Basic. If that doesn't solve the problem, try setting this bar to None:

- Follow steps 1 and 2 under the preceding question-and-answer topic, and set the bar to Basic or None. (For more about these settings, refer to the shaded box titled "The Basic and None Settings.")

The Basic and None Settings

If you're familiar with hardware and Windows, you might be interested in the following information about the hardware acceleration slide bar:

The None setting does the following:

- Adds *SafeMode=2* to the [Windows] section of the WIN.INI file. A setting of 2 disables all video-card acceleration; for example, the graphical device interface (GDI) calls the device-independent bitmap (DIB) engine directly for screen drawing rather than going through the display driver.

- Adds *MMIO=0* to the [Display] section of the SYSTEM.INI file. A setting of MMIO=0 disables memory-mapped I/O for S3-compatible drivers.

- Adds *SWCursor=1* to the [Display] section of the WIN.INI file. A setting of 1 disables the hardware cursor.

The Basic setting does the following:

- Adds *SafeMode=1* to the [Windows] section of the WIN.INI file. A setting of =1 allows for "basic acceleration" only (for example, pattern bit-block transfer, or bitblt ["bit-blit"], and screen-to-screen bitblt).

- Adds *MMIO=0* to the [Display] section of the SYSTEM.INI file. A setting of MMIO=0 disables memory-mapped I/O for S3-compatible drivers.

- Adds *SWCursor=1* to the [Display] section of the WIN.INI file. A setting of 1 disables the hardware cursor.

Question: I'm still having problems with my video card. What else can I do?

Answer: If you continue to have problems with your video card, remove and reinstall the video driver. The step-by-step procedure is described on page 283 under "Why does Windows 95 always start with the VGA driver even if I install the Windows 95 driver for my video card?"

Setting Up

If Microsoft Windows 95 is not yet installed on your computer, you'll be pleasantly surprised at how simple setup is. It involves little more than sticking the Windows 95 CD-ROM or the first of your Windows 95 floppies into the appropriate drive and answering a few questions. The actual installation *can* take a while, especially if you're installing from floppy disks, because Windows 95 does everything from checking out your hard disk to examining your hardware to rebooting the computer. But thanks to the sophistication of the Setup program, the process is typically painless and is even enjoyable to watch.

This appendix walks you through installation and helps you with some of the decisions you'll be asked to make as Windows 95 sets itself up to run on your computer. Before you get started, however, it behooves you to know what you've got and what you can expect from the type of installation (yes, there are several options) that you choose.

CD-ROM vs. Floppy Disks

Windows 95 is distributed on both CD-ROM and floppy disks for an obvious reason: not everyone has a CD-ROM drive...yet. But is there a difference between a CD-ROM installation and a floppy installation? Well, yes, there is. A CD-ROM holds far, far more than even a *box* of floppies can, so the Windows 95 that you receive on floppy disks is "lighter" than the CD-ROM version. You get the same basic operating system, with such hot features as Exchange, The Microsoft Network, WordPad and Paint, ScanDisk, Sound Recorder, Media Player, Direct Cable Connection, and Remote Access. You do not, however, get certain other features, such as:

- The Windows 95 Tour
- Quick View
- Games (Hearts, Solitaire, Freecell, Minesweeper, Reversi)
- Wallpapers
- CD Player

As you can see, these features are not integral parts of Windows 95. They are, however, useful and, in most cases, enjoyable features. The only way to get them, though, is on CD-ROM, which means you must have a CD-ROM drive (or, in the business world, access to a network server from which you can install Windows 95). Wherever possible, this book points out such differences between CD-ROM and floppy installations.

The remainder of this appendix concentrates mostly on setting up from a CD-ROM. If you are installing from floppies, the setup procedure is very similar. You will, however, be prompted to insert floppies periodically as Windows 95 Setup calls for them.

Starting Setup

To begin installation:

1. Start your computer (if necessary). If you already have a version of Windows, start Windows too.

2. Insert your CD-ROM or Setup Disk 1 into the appropriate drive.

3. If you're installing from Windows, open a window to the drive and double-click Setup.exe. If you're installing from MS-DOS, type a command in the form [*drive:*]*setup*, where *drive:* is the letter of the drive containing the disk—for example, *a:setup* if the disk is in drive A.

SETUP TIPS

If you make a choice during Setup and then change your mind, click the Back button at the bottom of the Setup window. If some part of Setup seems to be taking a while, wait—even as long as a minute or two. Certain parts of Setup take time, and even if your computer goes quiet the process might not be stalled. (Of course, if day becomes night while you're waiting, you probably should turn your computer off and then back on, restart Setup, and choose Safe Recovery when prompted.)

Memory-Resident Software

If Windows 95 Setup detects a memory-resident program (such as an antivirus program or an extended/expanded memory manager), it might display a message telling you that it can't continue while the program is running. To temporarily disable the program:

1. Go to the MS-DOS prompt, and edit the startup file (either AUTOEXEC.BAT or CONFIG.SYS) that starts the program by typing the command *edit c:\autoexec.bat* or *edit c:\config.sys.*

2. Scroll to the line that starts the program, and insert *rem* (short for *remark*) in front of it. Doing this identifies the command as a comment rather than an instruction. Your computer will ignore the command at startup, but because you'll still have the command in the startup file you will be able to restore the program easily (by removing the *rem*) after you set up Windows 95.

3. Save the file, and restart your computer.

The first step in installation is what Setup calls "a routine check on your system"; it's actually a check of your disk drives (of which the hard disk is the most important) performed by the ScanDisk utility. Setup does this to ensure that your hard disk is healthy and that it doesn't contain any file-storage problems that could cause trouble for both you and Windows 95. The scan is quick; if ScanDisk finds problems, refer to the shaded box below.

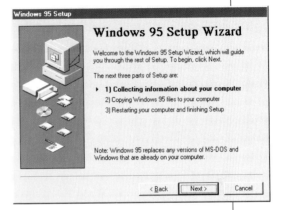

After the disk scan, Setup swings into action by loading a special program called the Windows 95 Setup Wizard, which opens with the screen illustrated at the right and which will guide you through the remainder of the installation process.

Disk Errors

During the disk check, you might receive a message telling you that your hard disk contains errors that you must correct before Setup can continue. If this happens, quit Windows (if necessary) and run ScanDisk separately. To do so, type a command in the form [*drive:*] *scandisk.exe /all* where *drive:* is the letter of the drive containing your Windows 95 floppy or CD-ROM. (Leave out the brackets [and].) If ScanDisk tells you that it found *lost clusters*, check your root directory with the command *dir c:*.chk*. If a lot of files there end in CHK, you can check the contents of each with the command *type c:\fileXXXX.chk | more* where *XXXX* is a number, such as 0001, that ScanDisk assigned to the file. If the contents are unusable (as most are), you can delete the file with the command *del c:\fileXXXX.chk* (again substituting the file number for *XXXX*).

Making Choices

As you can see from the opening screen, Setup starts out with a little information collecting. To get going:

1. Click the Next button.

2. Setup then displays a screen headed Choose Directory, which asks where you want to install Windows 95. The default (and the preferable option in most cases) is to install to a directory (folder) named Windows. Note, however, that doing so installs Windows 95 *over* any existing version of

Windows in that directory. If you do not want to do this, click the Other Directory option, but bear in mind that this choice requires you to reinstall *all* your programs after Windows 95 is installed. If you choose a different directory, give it a name when Setup prompts for one. If the other directory does not exist, Setup will create it. To avoid later confusion, do not install to a directory that contains other programs or data files.

Once you've made your choice, Setup prepares the directory, checks installed components, and checks to be sure there's enough space for Windows 95 on your hard disk. At this point, it asks what type of installation you want, as shown in the illustration at the left.

Typical, the default, is a reasonable choice for most systems, especially because it offers the best part of a custom installation by giving you the option of choosing which components (such as Games and Wallpapers) you want to install. Choose Portable if you have a portable computer, Compact if you're short on hard-disk space, and Custom if you want to control all aspects of setup (you probably don't).

Onward

After you've chosen your directory and type of installation, Setup tells you that it's going to check your hardware to determine what devices are attached and how they are set up. If Setup asks whether you have specific hardware, such as a CD-ROM drive, click the check box if you do. The actual hardware check, which occurs next, can take a fair amount of time, but be patient. If Setup stalls partway through, follow the instructions displayed by the wizard: turn your computer off and then back on, and choose Safe Recovery.

When the hardware check is finished, Setup will ask if you want to "get connected" by installing the software that enables you to connect to The Microsoft Network and to exchange mail and faxes. Check the boxes you want; skip them all if you prefer.

Going Shopping

Whether you chose a custom installation or a typical installation, Setup moves on to let you choose which components you want to install (other than MSN, Microsoft Mail, and Microsoft Fax). If you chose a custom installation, the list of choices appears automatically. If you chose a typical installation, you can see the list by clicking the Show Me The List Of Components... option when Setup reaches the screen headed Windows Components.

DON'T AGONIZE

If you're choosing options and you can't decide whether to install a particular component, don't worry. As described in Chapter 12, under the heading "Add/ Remove Programs," you can always install (or remove) a component later. All you'll need will be your Windows 95 installation CD-ROM or floppy disks.

If you choose to view and select from the list, Windows 95 displays the screen at the right.

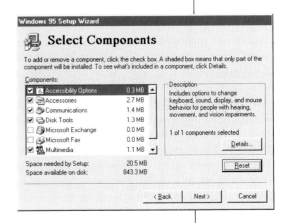

1. To select a component, click to put a check mark in the box at the left of the item.

2. If the check box is shaded, the component includes several options, only some of which will be installed. To see—and choose from—these options, click the Details button. When you've made your choices, click OK and continue through the components list.

Almost There

To finish up, Setup will show you your computer settings and will ask if you want to create a startup disk. Making the disk adds time to the setup process, but you *will* need such a disk if Windows 95 cannot start at all. On the other hand, Windows 95 starts reliably under most circumstances and can start in what's called Safe Mode if it detects problems at startup. For safety's sake, the default and recommended course is to make the disk. The final choice, however, is yours: safe or, possibly, sorry.

After all the questions, answers, and choices, you're just about done. At this point, you reach a screen headed Start Copying Files. This is it. This is where Setup actually installs Windows 95 onto your hard drive. Depending on the setup you chose and the components you're installing, this part of the procedure could take a while—especially if you're installing from floppies. Be patient; Setup has a lot of work to do here.

When everything has been copied and put in its proper place, Setup finishes with a bang instead of a whimper. Remove any floppy disks from their drives, and click Finish on the wizard's final screen.

1. Setup reboots your computer. If your computer doesn't restart, turn it off and then back on; it works…really. This initial restart, by the way, can be lengthy and can make your hard disk sound as if it's having quite a party. That's all as it should be. Here, too, Setup has a lot of work to do, so just let it "do its thing."

2. When Windows 95 appears for the first time, you'll see a message telling you that it's setting up your hardware. Its attention then turns to your Start menu, Windows 95 Help, and other matters, including your time zone. Along the way, Setup might also run wizards to set up other options, such as your printer, modem, or Microsoft Exchange. Follow the instructions

PROGRAM MANAGER

If you're installing over Windows 3 and you really want to keep Program Manager, choose a custom installation and scroll to the User Interface item when Setup displays the window headed Computer Settings. Click User Interface, click Change, and choose Windows 3.1 (Program Manager). The Windows 95 interface is a lot better, though….

TIME ZONE

The easiest way to choose the correct zone is to click your location on the world map that Windows 95 displays. When the correct zone appears in the box at the top of the window, click Close.

these wizards display. If you run into trouble, don't worry. You can cancel these wizards and return to them later, when you understand Windows 95 a little better.

When all is done, the final step is to restart your computer once again. Do it, and when the startup process ends, Windows 95 will be up and running.

Windows Then, Windows Now

As mentioned several times in this book, the changeover from using Microsoft Windows 3 to Windows 95 won't always be a simple one, especially if you're in the "thoroughly comfortable" to "power user" Windows 3 category. Windows 95 is different in many ways—not least of them its graphical interface and how you use it.

The simplest and, probably, fastest way to push yourself into high gear with Windows 95 is, frankly, to try to avoid drawing comparisons. If you work with Windows 95 *as it is*, you and your mouse will soon be happily cruising into a bright future. If, on the other hand, you keep trying to pretend that Windows 95 is nothing more than a simple enhancement of Windows 3, you won't learn valuable new skills (such as using drag-and-drop and clicking the right mouse button) and you'll become frustrated when something doesn't happen as you think it should—for example, when you can't pause the printer because you can't find Print Manager because Windows 95 doesn't have a Main window.

To help you get (and keep) your bearings, the following table lists common tasks and the ways you carry them out in Windows 3 and in Windows 95.

Task	Windows 3	Windows 95
Do things easily:		
	Learn how.	Right-click, and choose from the popup menu.
Get Help:		
	Press F1.	Same.
Manage objects:		
Open an object	Double-click.	Double-click, or right-click and choose Open from the popup menu.
Open an object with Windows Explorer	N/A	Shift+double-click, or right-click and choose Explore from the popup menu.
View a properties sheet	In Program Manager, choose File Properties (but bear in mind that properties sheets are more sophisticated in Windows 95).	Right-click, and choose Properties.
Manage windows:		
Cascade or tile windows	Choose Window Cascade or press Shift+F5; choose Window Tile or press Shift+F6.	Right-click a blank part of the taskbar, and choose Cascade or Tile.
Update window contents	Press F5 or choose Window Refresh.	Press F5 or choose View Refresh.
Close a window and all its parent windows	N/A	Hold down Shift and click the window's Close button.
Switch to a different window	Press Alt+Tab to cycle through open windows.	Click the application's button on the taskbar, or use Alt+Tab as in Windows 3.
Toggle between single-window browsing and multiple-window browsing	N/A	Ctrl+double-click in the parent window to affect individual windows; use View Options and choose single-window or multiple-window browsing to affect all windows.
Manage files and folders:		
Select files or folders	Click to select one; Shift+click to select a block; Ctrl+click to select discontinuous items.	Same, or drag to select a block.
Copy	Drag if copying to a different disk; Ctrl+drag if copying on the same disk.	Same; or right-click, drag, and choose Copy from the popup menu.
Move	Drag if moving to a different disk; Shift+drag if moving on the same disk.	Same; or right-click, drag, and choose Move from the popup menu.
Create a shortcut	N/A	Ctrl+Shift+drag; or right-click, drag, and choose Create Shortcut(s) Here from the popup menu.

Task	Windows 3	Windows 95
Up one level to parent folder	Press Backspace (File Manager only).	Press Backspace (any view, including Windows Explorer).
Permanent delete (bypass Recycle Bin)	N/A	Shift+Delete.
Print:		
Print a document	Use your application's Print command.	Drag to the printer icon or to the printer window.
View the print queue or manage the printer	Open Print Manager (in the Main window).	Double-click the printer icon on the desktop or in a window, or double-click the small printer icon at the left of the time display on the taskbar.
Use the keyboard:		
Cut	Press Ctrl+X.	Same.
Copy	Press Ctrl+C.	Same.
Paste	Press Ctrl+V.	Same.
Undo	Press Ctrl+Z.	Same.
Move between panes in the Windows Explorer (or the equivalent File Manager in Windows 3)	Press Tab or F6.	Same.
Open or collapse a "tree" branch in the Windows Explorer (File Manager in Windows 3)	Press plus (+) to open, minus (-) to close.	Same.
Move up or down one level in the tree in the Windows Explorer (File Manager in Windows 3)	Press the left direction key to move up; press the right direction key to move down.	Same.

Index

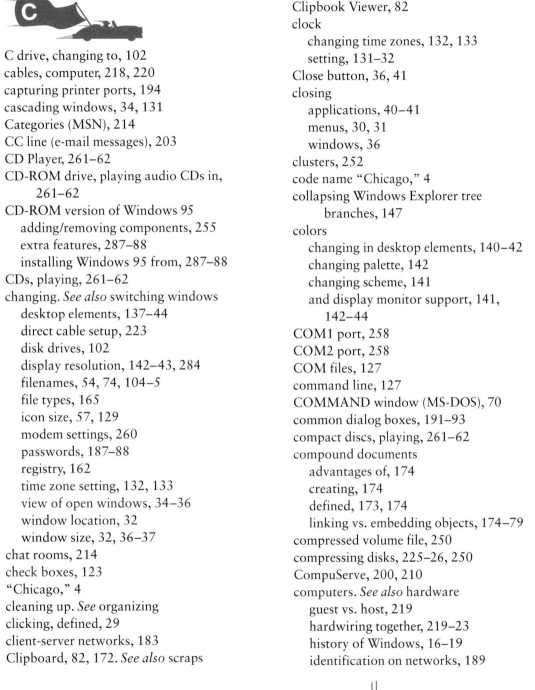

C drive, changing to, 102
cables, computer, 218, 220
capturing printer ports, 194
cascading windows, 34, 131
Categories (MSN), 214
CC line (e-mail messages), 203
CD Player, 261–62
CD-ROM drive, playing audio CDs in, 261–62
CD-ROM version of Windows 95
 adding/removing components, 255
 extra features, 287–88
 installing Windows 95 from, 287–88
CDs, playing, 261–62
changing. *See also* switching windows
 desktop elements, 137–44
 direct cable setup, 223
 disk drives, 102
 display resolution, 142–43, 284
 filenames, 54, 74, 104–5
 file types, 165
 icon size, 57, 129
 modem settings, 260
 passwords, 187–88
 registry, 162
 time zone setting, 132, 133
 view of open windows, 34–36
 window location, 32
 window size, 32, 36–37
chat rooms, 214
check boxes, 123
"Chicago," 4
cleaning up. *See* organizing
clicking, defined, 29
client-server networks, 183
Clipboard, 82, 172. *See also* scraps

Clipbook Viewer, 82
clock
 changing time zones, 132, 133
 setting, 131–32
Close button, 36, 41
closing
 applications, 40–41
 menus, 30, 31
 windows, 36
clusters, 252
code name "Chicago," 4
collapsing Windows Explorer tree
  branches, 147
colors
 changing in desktop elements, 140–42
 changing palette, 142
 changing scheme, 141
 and display monitor support, 141, 142–44
COM1 port, 258
COM2 port, 258
COM files, 127
command line, 127
COMMAND window (MS-DOS), 70
common dialog boxes, 191–93
compact discs, playing, 261–62
compound documents
 advantages of, 174
 creating, 174
 defined, 173, 174
 linking vs. embedding objects, 174–79
compressed volume file, 250
compressing disks, 225–26, 250
CompuServe, 200, 210
computers. *See also* hardware
 guest vs. host, 219
 hardwiring together, 219–23
 history of Windows, 16–19
 identification on networks, 189

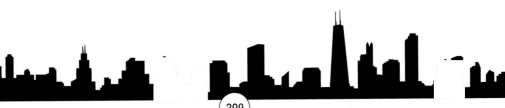

JoAnne Woodcock

JoAnne Woodcock, currently a master writer for Microsoft Press, is author of *The Ultimate MS-DOS Book* as well as the *MS-DOS 6 Companion*, *Running Microsoft Works 3 for Windows*, the *Concise Guide to MS-DOS 5*, and the *Concise Guide to Microsoft Works for Windows*—all published by Microsoft Press. She is also coauthor of *Running XENIX* and *Microsoft Word Style Sheets* and a contributor to the *Microsoft Press Computer Dictionary*.

The manuscript for this book was prepared and submitted to Microsoft Press in electronic form. Text files were prepared using Microsoft Word 6.0 for Windows. Pages were composed by Microsoft Press using Aldus PageMaker 5.0 for Windows, with text in Sabon and display type in Univers Condensed.

Cover Graphic Designer
Rebecca Geisler

Cover Illustrator
Henk Dawson

Interior Graphic Designers
Hansen Design Company
Kim Eggleston

Interior Illustrators
David Holter
Michael Victor

Principal Compositor
Peggy Herman

Principal Proofreader/Copy Editor
Deborah Long

Indexer
Julie Kawabata

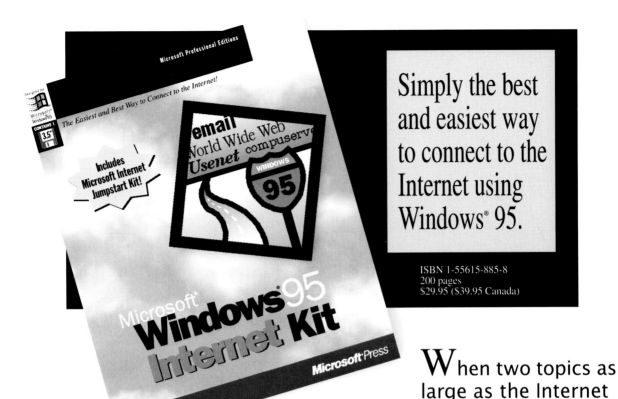

WHO KNOWS MORE
ABOUT WINDOWS® 95
THAN
MICROSOFT® PRESS?

ISBN 1-55615-816-5
224 pages
$19.95 ($26.95 Canada)

ISBN 1-55615-683-9
320 pages
$29.95 ($39.95 Canada)

These books are essential if you are a newcomer to Microsoft® Windows® or an upgrader wanting to capitalize on your knowledge of Windows 3.1. Both are written in a straightforward, no-nonsense way, with well-illustrated step-by-step examples, and both include practice files on disk. Learn to use Microsoft's newest operating system quickly and easily with MICROSOFT WINDOWS 95 STEP BY STEP and UPGRADING TO MICROSOFT WINDOWS 95 STEP BY STEP, both from Microsoft Press.